Stu Slayen
Magazine Editor
Page 206

Kelly Milner-Halls
Writer
Page 176

Floyd Cooper
Illustrator/Author
Page 120

1997
CHILDREN'S
WRITER'S &
ILLUSTRATOR'S
MARKET

Managing Editor, Market Books Department: Constance J. Achabal;
Supervising Editor: Michael Willins;
Production Editor: Anne Bowling.

International Standard Serial Number 0897-9790
International Standard Book Number 0-89879-765-9

Cover illustration: Brenda Grannan
Portraits: Ann Barrow

Attention Booksellers: This is an annual directory of F&W Publications.
Return deadline for this edition is April 30, 1998.

1997
CHILDREN'S WRITER'S & ILLUSTRATOR'S MARKET

WHERE & HOW TO SELL YOUR FICTION, NONFICTION, ILLUSTRATIONS AND PHOTOS FOR EVERY AGE GROUP—FROM TODDLERS TO TEENS

EDITED BY
ALICE P. BUENING

WRITER'S DIGEST BOOKS
CINCINNATI, OHIO

Contents

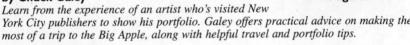

Page 31

The Markets

Page 244

From the Editor

When I was young, my mom and big sister read several story books to me over and over (on my insistence). One was Ludwig Bemelmans's *Madeline*. I knew the story of the little French girl by heart: *In an old house in Paris that was covered with vines, lived twelve little girls in two straight lines . . . . They left the house at half past nine in two straight lines in rain or shine—the smallest one was Madeline . . . .*

Several decades later, I've experienced Madeline in a way I (and Ludwig) would never have dreamed—on CD-ROM. And what fun it was! I clicked my way through *Madeline and the Magnificent Puppet Show* until my wrist tingled and my eyes were red, delighting in Madeline's darling French accent, and the enchanting surprises I found clicking on the hotspots and traveling from room to room helping Madeline gather items for a puppet show to raise money for poor Monsieur Benet.

While Madeline (who first appeared in a book in 1939) has made the leap into new technology, *Children's Writer's & Illustrator's Market* is on its way there. For our 1997 edition, we've put together a brand new Multimedia section, listing companies that produce CD-ROMs and software for kids. You'll find an Insider Report with **Annie Fox**, co-designer of the above mentioned CD-ROM, on page 214 of the section—read it for a lesson in CD-ROM design.

If all the talk of new technology makes you a little dizzy, Kelly Quiroz put together a great article entitled Get Plugged In! Opportunities in the Children's Multimedia Market (page 19) to help you get a grip on multimedia—and to decide if it's right for you.

Also note the additions of computer- and CD-ROM-related terminology to our Glossary (page 338), the addition of e-mail addresses and websites to many of the listings, and the list of websites in the Helpful Resources section on page 335.

To complement our multimedia pieces, we offer a wealth of articles on good, old-fashioned writing and illustrating, like Patrick G. Souhan's piece, **Virginia Hamilton**'s Work: Blending the Known, the Remembered and the Imagined (page 37). Read how Hamilton's childhood in rural Ohio with a large, extended family shapes her work even today, and get advice from this wonderful, award-winning author.

Insider Reports tackle an array of topics. Author/illustrator **William Joyce** shares views on where new media is taking children's publishing (page 76). Read about opportunities in nonfiction from Raintree Steck-Vaughn editor **Frank Sloan** (page 130). And writer **Kelly Milner-Halls** shares some great strategies for getting the most mileage from every magazine assignment (page 176). (Turn to the inside covers of the book for quick Insider Report page numbers accompanying **Ann Barrow**'s beautiful portraits.)

We've also continued our popular and inspirational feature, First Books, on page 28. Anne Bowling talked to Ukrainian-born illustrator **Katya Krenina**—whose first picture book is *The Magic Dreidels* (Holiday House), by Eric Kimmel—as well as a young adult novelist, a picture book author and a photographer. (We found Katya, by the way, because she sent me an e-mail message.)

Of course, we've gathered up-to-date information for more than 800 listings. And to keep you abreast of changes throughout the year, look for our quarterly column of updates in *Children's Book Insider*. (See Helpful Resources on page 335 for more information on this newsletter.)

Whatever vein of children's writing or illustration interests you—be it picture books or the world of multimedia—I hope you give it your best shot. (After all, it couldn't be any worse than getting your appendix out!) We've tried our best to give you the tools to get started. And along the way feel free to call, write, or (better yet) drop me an e-mail message—I'd love to hear from you. Until then . . . . *"Good night little girls! Thank the Lord you are well! And now go to sleep!" said Miss Clavel. And she turned out the light—and closed the door—and that's all there is—there isn't anymore.*

Alice P. Buening
wdigest@aol.com

How to Use This Book to Sell Your Work

As a writer, illustrator or photographer first picking up *Children's Writer's & Illustrator's Market*, you may not know quite how to start using the book. Your impulse may be to flip through the book and quickly make a mailing list, then submit to everyone in hopes that someone will take interest in your work. Well, there's more to it. Finding the right market takes time and research. The more you know about a company that interests you, the better chance you have of getting work accepted.

We've made your job a little easier by putting a wealth of information at your fingertips. Besides providing listings, this directory includes a number of tools to help you determine which markets are the best ones for your work. By using these tools, as well as researching on your own, you raise your odds of being published.

USING THE INDEXES

This book has more than 675 potential buyers of freelance material. To learn which companies want the type of material you're interested in submitting, start with the indexes.

The Age-level Index

Age-groups are broken down into these categories in the Age-level Index:
- Picture books or **picture-oriented material** are written and illustrated for preschoolers to 8-year-olds.
- **Young readers** are for 5- to 8-year-olds.
- **Middle readers** are for 9- to 11-year-olds.
- **Young adults** are for ages 12 and up.

These age breakdowns may vary slightly from publisher to publisher, but using them as guidelines will help you target appropriate markets. For example, if you've written an article about the latest teen fashions, check the Magazines Age-level Index under the Young Adult subheading. Using this list, you'll quickly find the listings for young adult magazines.

The Subject Index

But let's narrow the search further. Take your list of young adult magazines, turn to the Subject Index, and find the Fashion subheading. Then highlight the names that appear on both lists (Young Adult and Fashion). Now you have a smaller list of all the magazines that would be interested in your teen fashion article. Read through those listings and decide which ones sound best for your work.

Illustrators and photographers can use the Subject Index as well. If you specialize in painting animals, for instance, consider sending samples to book and magazine publishers listed under Animals and, perhaps, Nature/Environment. Illustrators, however, can simply send general examples of their style (in the form of tearsheets or postcards) to art directors to keep on file. The indexes may be more helpful to artists sending manuscripts/illustration packages. Always read the listings for the potential markets to see the type of work art directors prefer and what type of samples they'll keep on file.

The Photography Index

You'll find lists of book and magazine publishers, as well as greeting card, puzzle and game manufacturers, that buy photos from freelancers in the Photography Index. Copy the lists and read the listings for specific needs.

USING THE LISTINGS

Many listings begin with one or more symbols. Here's what each stands for:

(*) symbol indicates a listing is new to this edition.

(□) symbol indicates a listing is a book packager or producer.

(✤) symbol indicates a listing is Canadian.

(‡) symbol indicates a contest or organization is open to students.

The subheadings under each listing contain specific information about what a company needs. In Book Publishers and Magazines, for example, you'll find such things as age-levels and subjects needed under the Fiction and Nonfiction subheads. Here's an example from a listing in the Book Publishers section:

Fiction: Picture books: adventure, animal, contemporary, fantasy, humor. Young readers: animal, contemporary, humor, sports, suspense/mystery. Middle readers: adventure, humor, sports. Young adults: humor, problem novels.

Also check the listings for information on how to submit your work and response time. In Book Publishers and Magazines, writers will find this information under the How to Contact/Writers subhead:

How to Contact/Writers: Query; submit outline/synopsis and 2 sample chapters. Reports on queries on 6 weeks; mss in 3 months.

For information on submission procedures and formats, turn to Guide to Submitting Your Work on page 6.

Also look for information regarding payment and rights purchased. Some markets pay on acceptance, others on publication. Some pay a flat rate for manuscripts and artwork, others pay advances and royalties. Knowing how a market operates will keep you from being shocked when you discover your paycheck won't arrive until your manuscript is published— a year after it was accepted. This information is found under Terms in Book Publishers, Magazines and Play Publishers. Here's an example from the Magazines section:

Terms: Pays on acceptance. Buys first North American serial rights or reprint rights. Pays $50-100 for stories/articles. Pays illustrators $75-125 for b&w or color inside; $150-200 for color cover.

Under Tips you'll find special advice straight from an editor or art director about what their company wants or doesn't want, or other helpful advice:

Tips: "We are looking for picture books centered on a strong, fully-developed protaganist who grows or changes during the course of the story."

Additional information about specific markets in the form of comments from the editor of this book is set off by bullets (●) within listings:

● This publisher accepts only queries and manuscripts submitted by agents.

Many listings indicate whether submission guidelines are available. If a publisher you're interested in offers guidelines, send for them and read them. The same is true with catalogs. Sending for catalogs and seeing and reading about the books a publisher produces gives you a better idea whether your work would fit in. (You may even want to look at a few of the books in the catalog at a library or bookstore.)

Especially for artists and photographers

Along with information for writers, listings provide information for photographers and illustrators. Illustrators will find numerous markets that maintain files of samples for possible future assignments. If you're both a writer and illustrator, look for markets that accept manuscript/illustration packages.

If you're a photographer, after consulting the Photography Index, read the information under the Photography subhead within listings to see what format buyers prefer. For example, some want 35mm color transparencies, others want b&w prints. Note the type of photos a buyer wants to purchase and the procedures for submitting. It's not uncommon for a market to want a résumé and promotional literature, as well as tearsheets from previous work. Listings also note whether model releases and/or captions are required.

Especially for young writers

If you're a parent, teacher or student, you may be interested in Young Writer's & Illustrator's Markets. The markets in this section encourage submissions from young writers and artists. Some markets require a written statement from a teacher or parent, noting the work is original. Also watch for age limits.

Young people should also check Contests & Awards for contests that accept work by young writers and artists. Some of the contests listed are especially for students; others accept both student and adult work. These are marked with a double dagger (‡). Some listings in Clubs & Organizations may also be of interest to students. Organizations which accept or are especially for students are also marked with a double dagger.

COMMON ABBREVIATIONS

Throughout the listings, the following abbreviations are used:
- **ms** or **mss** stands for manuscript or manuscripts.
- **SASE** refers to a self-addressed, stamped envelope.
- **SAE** refers to a self-addressed envelope.
- **IRC** stands for International Reply Coupon. These are required with SAEs sent to markets in countries other than your own.

Guide to Submitting Your Work

Good research of publishers is a basic element of submitting your work successfully. Editors and art directors hate to receive inappropriate submissions—handling them wastes a lot of their time, not to mention your time and money. By randomly sending out material without knowing a company's needs, you're sure to meet with rejection.

If you're interested in submitting to a particular magazine, write to request a sample copy, or see if it's available in your local library or bookstore. For a book publisher, obtain a book catalog and check a library or bookstore for titles produced by that publisher. Studying such materials carefully will better acquaint you with a publisher's or magazine's writing, illustration, and photography styles and formats.

Most of the book publishers and magazines listed in this book (as well as many companies such as greeting card and paper product producers) offer some sort of writer's, artist's or photographer's guidelines for a SASE. Some publishers and magazines even have websites that include submission guidelines. It's important to read and study guidelines before submitting work. You'll get a better understanding of what a particular publisher wants. You may even decide, after reading the submission guidelines, that your work isn't right for a company you considered.

IMPORTANT SUBMISSION ELEMENTS

Throughout the listings you'll read requests for particular elements to include when contacting markets. Here are explanations of some of these important submission components. Note: For good advice and examples of queries, cover letters and other correspondence, consult *How to Write Attention-Grabbing Query & Cover Letters*, by John Wood (Writer's Digest Books).

- **Query letters for nonfiction.** A query letter is a no-more-than-one-page, well-written piece to arouse an editor's or art director's interest in your work. Queries are usually required when submitting nonfiction material to a publisher, in which case, your goal is to convince the editor your idea is perfect for her readership and that you're qualified to do the job. Note any previous writing experience and include published samples to prove your credentials, especially samples related to the subject matter you're querying about.

Many query letters start with leads similar to those of actual manuscripts. In the rest of the letter, briefly outline the work you're proposing and include facts, anecdotes, interviews or other pertinent information that give the editor a feel for the manuscript's premise—entice her to want to know more. End your letter with a straightforward request to write (or submit) the work, and include information on its approximate length, date it could be completed, and whether accompanying photos or artwork are available.

- **Query letters for fiction.** More and more, queries are being requested for fiction manuscripts. For a fiction query, explain the story's plot, main characters, conflict and resolution. Just as in nonfiction queries, make the editor eager to see more.

- **Cover letters for writers.** Some editors prefer to review complete manuscripts, especially for fiction. In such cases, the cover letter (which should be no longer than one page) serves as your introduction, establishes your credentials as a writer, and gives the editor an overview of the manuscript.

If an editor asked for a manuscript because of a query, note this in your cover letter.

Also, if an earlier rejection letter included an invitation to submit other work, mention that as well. Editors should know the work was solicited.

• **Cover letters for illustrators and photographers.** For an illustrator or photographer, the cover letter serves as an introduction to the art director and establishes credentials as a professional. Explain what services you can provide as well as what type of follow-up contact you plan to make, if any.

When sending samples of your work, indicate whether they should be returned or filed. Never send original work. If you wish to have the samples returned, include a SASE.

• **Résumés.** Often writers, illustrators and photographers are asked to submit résumés with cover letters and samples. They can be created in a variety of formats, from a single page listing information, to color brochures featuring your work. Keep your résumé brief, and focus on your achievements, including your clients and the work you've done for them, as well as your educational background and any awards you've received. Do not use the same résumé you'd use for a typical job application.

• **Book proposals.** Throughout the listings in the Book Publishers section, publishers refer to submitting a synopsis, outline and sample chapters. Depending on an editor's preference, some or all of these components, along with a cover letter, make up a book proposal.

A *synopsis* summarizes the book, covering the basic plot (including the ending). It should be easy to read and flow well.

An *outline* covers your book chapter by chapter and provides highlights of each. If you're developing an outline for fiction include major characters, plots and subplots, and book length.

Sample chapters give a more comprehensive idea of your writing skill. Some editors may request the first two or three chapters to see how your material is set up. Find out what the editor wants before writing or revising sample chapters.

FORMATS FOR MANUSCRIPTS

When submitting a complete manuscript, follow some basic guidelines. In the upper-left corner of your title page, type your legal name (not pseudonym), address, phone number and Social Security number (publishers need this to file payment records with the government). In the upper-right corner, type the approximate word length. All material in the upper corners should be typed single-spaced. Then type the title (centered) almost halfway down the page with the word "by" two spaces under that and your name or pseudonym two spaces under "by."

The first page should also include the title (centered) one-third of the way down. Two spaces under that type "by" and your name or pseudonym. To begin the body of your manuscript, drop down two double spaces and indent five spaces for each new paragraph. There should be 1-inch margins around all sides of a full typewritten page. (Manuscripts with wide margins are more readable and easier to edit.)

Set your computer or typewriter on double-space for the manuscript body. From page two to the end of your manuscript include your last name followed by a comma and the title (or key words of the title) in the upper-left corner. The page number should go in the top right corner. Drop down two double spaces to begin the body of each page. If you're submitting a novel, type each chapter title one-third of the way down the page. For more information on manuscript formats read *Writer's Digest Guide to Manuscript Formats*, by Dian Dincin Buchman and Seli Groves, or *Manuscript Submission*, by Scott Edelstein (both Writer's Digest Books). SCBWI offers submission guidelines to members. Send a SASE and request "From Typewriter to Printed Page . . . Facts You Need to Know."

PICTURE BOOKS FORMATS

The majority of editors prefer to see complete manuscripts for picture books. When typing the text of a picture book, do not include page breaks or supply art. Editors will find their own illustrators for picture books. Most of the time, a writer and an illustrator who work on the same book never meet. The editor acts as a go-between in case either the writer or illustrator has any problems. *How to Write and Sell Children's Picture Books*, by Jean E. Karl (Writer's Digest Books), offers advice on preparing text and marketing your work.

If you're an illustrator who has written your own book, create a dummy or storyboard containing both art and text. Then submit it along with your complete manuscript and sample pieces of final art (color photocopies or slides—never originals). Publishers interested in picture books specify in their listings what should be submitted. For a step-by-step guide on creating a good dummy, refer to *How to Write and Illustrate Children's Books and Get Them Published*, edited by Treld Pelkey Bicknell and Felicity Trotman (North Light Books), or Frieda Gates's book, *How to Write, Illustrate, and Design Children's Books* (Lloyd-Simone Publishing Company).

MAILING SUBMISSIONS

Your main concern when packaging material is to be sure it arrives undamaged. If your manuscript is less than six pages, simply fold it in thirds and send it in a #10 (business-size) envelope. For a SASE, either fold another #10 envelope in thirds or insert a #9 (reply) envelope which fits in a #10 neatly without folding.

Another option is folding your manuscript in half in a 6×9 envelope, with a #9 or #10 SASE enclosed. For larger manuscripts use a 9×12 envelope both for mailing the submission and as a SASE (which can be folded in half). Book manuscripts require a sturdy box for mailing. Include a self-addressed mailing label and return postage.

If asked to send artwork and photographs, remember they require a bit more care in packaging to guarantee they arrive in good condition. Sandwich illustrations and photos between heavy cardboard that is slightly larger than the work. The cardboard can be secured by rubber bands or with tape. If you tape the cardboard together, be sure the artwork does not stick to the tape. Write your name and address on the back of each piece of art or each photo in case the inside material becomes separated. For the packaging use either a manila envelope, foam-padded envelope, brown paper or a mailer lined with plastic air bubbles. Bind non-joined edges with reinforced mailing tape and affix a typed mailing label or clearly write your address.

Mailing material first class ensures quick delivery. Also, first-class mail is forwarded for one year if the addressee has moved, and can be returned if undeliverable. If you're concerned about your original material safely reaching its destination, consider other mailing options, such as UPS or certified mail. If material needs to reach your editor or art director quickly, you can elect to use overnight delivery services.

Remember, companies outside your own country can't use your country's postage when returning a manuscript to you. When mailing a submission to another country, include a self-addressed envelope and International Reply Coupons or IRCs. (You'll see this term in many Canadian listings.) Your post office can help you determine, based on a package's weight, the correct number of IRCs to include to ensure its return.

If it's not necessary for an editor to return your work (such as with photocopies) don't include return postage. You may want to track the status of your submission by enclosing a postage-paid reply postcard with options for the editor to check, such as "Yes, I am interested," "I'll keep the material on file," or "No, the material is not appropriate for my needs at this time."

Some writers, illustrators and photographers simply include a deadline date. If you don't hear from the editor or art director by the specified date, your manuscript, artwork or photos are automatically withdrawn from consideration. Because many publishing houses and companies are overstocked with material, a minimum deadline should be at least three months.

Unless requested, it's never a good idea to use a company's fax number or e-mail address to send manuscript submissions. This can disrupt a company's internal business.

KEEPING SUBMISSION RECORDS

It's important to keep track of the material you submit. When recording each submission, include the date it was sent, the business and contact name, and any enclosures (such as samples of writing, artwork or photography). You can create a record keeping system of your own or look for record keeping software in your area computer store. The 1997 *Writer's Market: the Electronic Edition* CD-ROM features a submission tracker that can be copied to your hard drive.

Keep copies of articles or manuscripts you send together with related correspondence to make follow-up easier. When you sell rights to a manuscript, artwork or photos you can "close" your file on a particular submission by noting the date the material was accepted, what rights were purchased, the publication date and payment.

Often writers, illustrators and photographers fail to follow up on overdue responses. If you don't hear from a market within its stated response time, wait another month and follow up with a note inquiring about the status of your submission. Include the title or description, date sent, and a SASE for response. Ask the contact person when she anticipates making a decision. You may refresh the memory of a buyer who temporarily forgot about your submission. At the very least you'll receive a definite "no," and free yourself to send the material to another publisher.

SIMULTANEOUS SUBMISSIONS

If you opt for simultaneous (also called "multiple") submissions—sending the same material to several editors at the same time—be sure to inform each editor your work is being considered elsewhere. Many editors are reluctant to receive simultaneous submissions but understand that for hopeful freelancers, waiting several months for a response can be frustrating. In some cases, an editor may actually be more inclined to read your manuscript sooner if she knows it's being considered by another publisher.

The Society of Children's Book Writers and Illustrators cautions writers against simultaneous submissions. The official recommendation of SCBWI is to submit to one publisher at a time, but wait only three months (note you'll do so in your cover letter). If no response is received, then send a note withdrawing your manuscript from consideration. SCBWI considers simultaneous submissions acceptable only if you have a manuscript dealing with a timely issue.

It's especially important to keep track of simultaneous submissions, so if you get an offer on a manuscript sent to more than one publisher, you can instruct other publishers to withdraw your work from consideration.

Tips on Contracts & Negotiation

Before you see your work in print or begin working with an editor or art director on a project, there is negotiation. And whether negotiating a book contract, a magazine article assignment, or an illustration or photo assignment there are a few things to keep in mind. First, if you find any clauses vague or confusing in a contract, get legal advice. The time and money invested in counseling up front could protect you from problems later. If you have an agent or rep, she will review any contract.

A contract is an agreement between two or more parties that specifies the fees to be paid, services rendered, deadlines, rights purchased and, for artists and photographers, whether original work is returned. Most companies have standard contracts for writers, illustrators and photographers. The specifics (such as royalty rates, advances, delivery dates, etc.) are typed in after negotiations.

Though it's okay to conduct negotiations over the phone, get a written contract once both parties have agreed on terms. Never depend on oral stipulations; written contracts protect both parties from misunderstandings. Watch for clauses that may not be in your best interest, such as "work-for-hire." When you do work-for-hire, you give up all rights to your creations.

Some reputable children's magazines, such as *Highlights for Children*, buy all rights, and many writers and illustrators believe it's worth the concession in order to break into the field. However, once you become more established in the field, it's in your best interest to keep rights to your work.

When negotiating a book deal, find out whether your contract contains an option clause. This clause requires the author to give the publisher a first look at her next work before offering it to other publishers. Though it's editorial etiquette to give the publisher the first chance at publishing your next work, be wary of statements in the contract that could trap you. Don't allow the publisher to consider the next project for more than 30 days and be specific about what type of work should actually be considered "next work." (For example, if the book under contract is a young adult novel, specify that the publisher will receive an exclusive look at only your next young adult novel.)

BOOK PUBLISHERS' PAYMENT METHODS

Book publishers pay authors and artists in royalties, a percentage of either the wholesale or retail price of each book sold. From large publishing houses, the author usually receives an advance issued against future royalties before the book is published. Half of the advance amount is issued upon signing the book contract; the other half is issued when the book is finished. For illustrations, one-third of the advance should be collected upon signing the contract; one-third upon delivery of sketches; and one-third upon delivery of finished art.

After your book has sold enough copies to earn back your advance, you'll start to get royalty checks. Some publishers hold a reserve against returns, which means a percentage of royalties is held back in case books are returned from bookstores. If you have a reserve clause in your contract, find out the exact percentage of total sales that will be withheld and the time period the publisher will hold this money. You should be reimbursed this amount after a reasonable time period, such as a year. Royalty percentages vary with each publisher, but there are standard ranges.

BOOK PUBLISHERS' RATES

According to the latest figures from the Society of Children's Book Writers and Illustrators, picture book writers can expect advances of $3,500-5,000; picture book illustrators' advances range from $7,000-10,000; text and illustration packages can score $8,000-10,000. Royalties for picture books are generally about 5 percent (split between the author and illustrator), but can go as high as 10 percent. Those who both write and illustrate a book, of course, receive the full royalty.

Advances for chapter books and middle-grade novels vary slightly from picture books. Hardcover titles can fetch authors advances of $4,000-6,000 and 10 percent royalties; paperbacks bring in slightly lower advances of $3,000-5,000 and royalties of 6-8 percent. Fees for young adult novels are generally the same, but additional length may increase fees and royalties.

As you might expect, advance and royalty figures vary from house to house and are affected by the time of year, the state of the economy and other factors. Some smaller houses may not even pay royalties, just flat fees. First-time writers and illustrators generally start on the low end of the scale, while established and high-profile writers are paid more.

REMAINDERING

When a book goes out of print, a publisher will sell any existing copies to a wholesaler who, in turn, sells the copies to stores at a discount. When the books are "remaindered" to a wholesaler, they are usually sold at a price just above the cost of printing. When negotiating a contract with a publisher you may want to discuss the possibility of purchasing the remaindered copies before they are sold to a wholesaler. Then you can market the copies you purchased and still make a profit.

PAY RATES FOR MAGAZINES

For writers, price structures for magazines are based on a per-word rate or range for a specific article length. Artists and photographers have a few more variables to contend with before contracting their services.

Payment for illustrations and photos can be set by such factors as whether the piece(s) will be black and white or four-color, how many are to be purchased, where the work appears (cover or inside), circulation, and the artist's or photographer's prior experience.

You can determine an hourly rate by using the annual salary of a staff artist or photographer doing similar work in an economically similar geographic area (try to find an artist or photographer willing to share this information), then dividing that salary by 52 (the number of weeks in a year) and again by 40 (the number of hours in a work week). To figure in overhead expenses such as rent, utilities, supplies, etc., multiply the hourly rate you came up with by 2.5. Research again to be sure your rate is competitive.

THE FACTS ABOUT AGENTS AND REPS

Many children's writers, illustrators or photographers, especially those just beginning, are confused about whether to enlist the services of an agent or representative. The decision is strictly one that each writer, illustrator or photographer must make for herself. Some are confident with their own negotiation skills and believe acquiring an agent or rep is not in their best interest. Others feel uncomfortable in the business arena or are not willing to sacrifice valuable creative time for marketing.

It's estimated that about half of children's publishers accept unagented work, so it is possible to break into children's publishing without an agent. Some agents avoid working with children's books because traditionally low advances and trickling royalty payments over long periods of time make children's books less lucrative. Writers targeting magazine markets do not need the services of an agent. In fact, it's practically impossible to find an agent interested in marketing articles and short stories—there simply isn't enough financial incentive.

One benefit of having an agent, though, is it may speed up the process of getting your work reviewed, especially by publishers who don't accept unagented submissions (a policy becoming more and more common in children's publishing). If an agent has a good reputation and submits your manuscript to an editor, that manuscript may actually bypass the first-read stage (which is done by editorial assistants and junior editors) and end up on the editor's desk sooner.

When agreeing to have a reputable agent represent you, remember that she should be familiar with the needs of the current market and evaluate your manuscript/artwork/photos accordingly. She should also determine the quality of your piece and whether it is saleable. When your manuscript sells, your agent should negotiate a favorable contract and clear up any questions you have about monetary payments.

Keep in mind that however reputable the agent or rep, she has limitations. Representation does not guarantee sale of your work. It just means an agent or rep sees potential in your writing, art or photos. Though an agent or rep may offer criticism or advice on how to improve your work, she cannot make you a better writer, artist or photographer or give you fame.

Literary agents typically charge a 15 percent commission from the sale of writing; art and photo representatives usually charge a 25 to 30 percent commission. Such fees are taken from advances and royalty earnings. If your agent sells foreign rights to your work, she will deduct a higher percentage because she will most likely be dealing with an overseas agent with whom she must split the fee.

Be advised that not every agent is open to representing a writer, artist or photographer who lacks an established track record. Just as when approaching a publisher, the manuscript, artwork or photos, and query or cover letter you submit to a potential agent must be attractive and professional looking. Your first impression must be that of an organized, articulate person.

For a detailed directory of literary agents, refer to *Guide to Literary Agents*; for listings of art reps, consult *Artist's & Graphic Designer's Market*; and for photo reps, see *Photographer's Market* (all Writer's Digest Books).

Know Your Rights

A copyright is a form of protection provided to creators of original works, published or unpublished. In general, copyright protection ensures the writer, illustrator or photographer the power to decide how her work is used and allows her to receive payment for each use.

Essentially, copyright also encourages the creation of new works by guaranteeing the creator power to sell rights to the work in the marketplace. The copyright holder can print, reprint or copy her work; sell or distribute copies of her work; or prepare derivative works such as plays, collages or recordings. The Copyright Law is designed to protect work (created on or after January 1, 1978) for her lifetime plus 50 years.

If you collaborate with someone else on a written or artistic project, the copyright will last for the lifetime of the last survivor plus 50 years. The creators' heirs may hold a copyright for an additional 50 years. After that, the work becomes public domain. Works created anonymously or under a pseudonym are protected for 100 years, or 75 years after publication. Under work-for-hire agreements, you relinquish your copyright to your "employer."

THE COPYRIGHT NOTICE

Some feel a copyright notice should be included on all work, registered or not. Others feel it is not necessary and a copyright notice will only confuse publishers about whether the material is registered (acquiring rights to previously registered material is a more complicated process).

Although it is not necessary to include a copyright notice on unregistered work, if you don't feel your work is safe without the notice, it is your right to include one. Including a copyright notice—© (year of work, your name)—should help safeguard against plagiarism.

LAWSUITS AND REGISTRATION

Registration is a legal formality intended to make copyright public record. Registration can help you win more money in a court case. By registering work within three months of publication or before an infringement occurs, you are eligible to collect statutory damages and attorney's fees. If you register later than three months after publication, you will qualify only for actual damages and profits.

Ideas and concepts are not copyrightable, only expressions of those ideas and concepts. A character type or basic plot outline, for example, is not subject to a copyright infringement lawsuit. Also, titles, names, short phrases or slogans, and lists of contents are not subject to copyright protection, though titles and names may be protected through the Trademark Office.

You can register a group of articles, illustrations or photos if it meets these criteria:
- the group is assembled in order, such as in a notebook;
- the works bear a single title, such as "Works by (your name)";
- it is the work of one writer, artist or photographer;
- the material is the subject of a single claim to copyright.

It is a publisher's responsibility to register your book for copyright. If you have previously registered the same material, you must inform your editor and supply the previous copyright information, otherwise, the publisher can't register the book in its published form.

GETTING THE FACTS AND FORMS

For more information about the proper procedure to register works, contact the Copyright Office, Library of Congress, Washington DC 20359. The forms available are TX for writing (books, articles, etc.); VA for pictures (photographs, illustrations); and PA for plays and music. (To order copyright forms by phone, call (202)707-9100.) For information about how to use the copyright forms, request a copy of Circular I on Copyright Basics. All of the forms and circulars are free. Send the completed registration form along with the stated fee and a copy of the work to the Copyright Office.

For specific answers to questions about copyright (but not legal advice), call the Copyright Public Information Office at (202)707-3000 weekdays between 8:30 a.m. and 5 p.m. EST. Copyright information is also available over the Internet. Call the Information Services Referral Desk at (800)444-4345 for a list of providers.

For members of SCBWI, information about copyrights and the law is available. Send a SASE to the Society of Children's Book Writers and Illustrators, 22736 Vanowen St., Suite 106, West Hills CA 91307. Request "Copyright Facts for Writers."

THE RIGHTS PUBLISHERS BUY

The copyright law specifies that a writer, illustrator or photographer generally sells one-time rights to her work unless she and the buyer agree otherwise in writing. Many publications will want more exclusive rights to your work than just one-time usage; some will even require you to sell all rights. Be sure you are monetarily compensated for the additional rights you relinquish. If you must give up all rights to a work, carefully consider the price you're being offered to determine whether you'll be compensated for the loss of other potential sales.

Writers who only give up limited rights to their work can then sell reprint rights to other publications, foreign rights to international publications, or even movie rights, should the opportunity arise. Artists and photographers can sell their work to other markets such as paper product companies who may use an image on a calendar, greeting card or mug. Illustrators and photographers may even sell original work after it has been published. And there are now galleries throughout the U.S. that display the work of children's illustrators.

Rights acquired through the sale of a book manuscript are explained in each publisher's contract. Take time to read relevant clauses to be sure you understand what rights each contract is specifying before signing. Be sure your contract contains a clause allowing all rights to revert back to you in the event the publisher goes out of business. (You may even want to have the contract reviewed by an agent or an attorney specializing in publishing law.)

The following are the rights you'll most often sell to publishers, periodicals and producers in the marketplace:

• **First rights.** The buyer purchases the rights to use the work for the first time in any medium. All other rights remain with the creator. When material is excerpted from a soon-to-be-published book for use in a newspaper or periodical, first serial rights are also purchased.

• **One-time rights.** The buyer has no guarantee that she is the first to use a piece. One-time permission to run written work, illustrations or photos is acquired, then the rights revert back to the creator.

• **First North American serial rights.** This is similar to first rights, except that companies who distribute both in the U.S. and Canada will stipulate these rights to ensure that a company in the other country won't come out with simultaneous usage of the same work.

• **Second serial (reprint) rights.** In this case newspapers and magazines are granted the right to reproduce a work that has already appeared in another publication. These rights are also purchased by a newspaper or magazine editor who wants to publish part of a book after the book has been published. The proceeds from reprint rights for a book are often split 50/50 between the author and his publishing company.

• **Simultaneous rights.** More than one publication buys one-time rights to the same work at the same time. Use of such rights occurs among magazines with circulations that don't overlap, such as many religious publications.

• **All rights.** Just as it sounds, the writer, illustrator or photographer relinquishes all rights to a piece—she no longer has any say in who acquires rights to use it. All rights are purchased by publishers who pay premium usage fees, have an exclusive format, or have other book or magazine interests from which the purchased work can generate more mileage. If a company insists on acquiring all rights to your work, see if you can negotiate for the rights to revert back to you after a reasonable period of time. If they agree to such a proposal, get it in writing.

Note: Writers, illustrators and photographers should be wary of "work-for-hire" arrangements. If you sign an agreement stipulating that your work will be done as work for hire, you will not control the copyrights of the completed work—the company who hired you will be the copyright owner.

• **Foreign serial rights.** Be sure before you market to foreign publications that you have sold only North American—not worldwide—serial rights to previous markets. If so, you are free to market to publications that may be interested in material that's appeared in a North American-based periodical.

• **Syndication rights.** This is a division of serial rights. For example, if a syndicate prints portions of a book in installments in its newspapers, it would be syndicating second serial rights. The syndicate would receive a commission and leave the remainder to be split between the author and publisher.

• **Subsidiary rights.** These include serial rights, dramatic rights, book club rights or translation rights. The contract should specify what percentage of profits from sales of these rights go to the author and publisher.

• **Dramatic, television and motion picture rights.** During a specified time the interested party tries to sell a story to a producer or director. Many times options are renewed because the selling process can be lengthy.

• **Display rights or electronic publishing rights.** They're also known as "Data, Storage and Retrieval." Usually listed under subsidiary rights, the marketing of electronic rights in this era of rapidly expanding capabilities and markets for electronic material can be tricky. Display rights can cover text or images to be used in a CD-ROM or online, or may cover use of material in formats not even fully developed yet. If a display rights clause is listed in your contract, try to negotiate its elimination. Otherwise, be sure to pin down *which* electronic rights are being purchased. Demand the clause be restricted to things designed to be read only. By doing this, you maintain your rights to use your work for things such as games and interactive software.

Business Basics

An important part of being a freelance writer, illustrator or photographer is running your freelance business. It's imperative you maintain accurate business records to determine if you're making a profit as a freelancer. Keeping correct, organized records will also make your life easier as you approach tax time.

When setting up your system, begin by keeping a bank account and ledger for your business finances apart from your personal finances. Also, if writing, illustration or photography is secondary to another freelance career, keep separate business records for each.

You will likely accumulate some business expenses before showing any profit when you start out as a freelancer. To substantiate your income and expenses to the IRS, keep all invoices, cash receipts, sales slips, bank statements, canceled checks and receipts related to travel expenses and entertaining clients. For entertainment expenditures, record the date, place and purpose of the business meeting as well as gas mileage. Keep records for all purchases, big and small—don't take the small purchases for granted; they can add up to a substantial amount.

File all receipts in chronological order. Maintaining a separate file for each month simplifies retrieving records at the end of the year.

RECORD KEEPING

When setting up a single-entry bookkeeping system, record income and expenses separately. Use some of the subheads that appear on Schedule C (the form used for recording income from a business) of the 1040 tax form so you can easily transfer information onto the tax form when filing your return. In your ledger include a description of each transaction—the date, source of income (or debts from business purchases), description of what was purchased or sold, the amount of the transaction, and whether payment was by cash, check or credit card.

Don't wait until January 1 to start keeping records. The moment you first make a business-related purchase or sell an article, book manuscript, illustration or photo, begin tracking your profits and losses. If you keep records from January 1 to December 31, you're using a calendar-year accounting period. Any other accounting period is called a fiscal year.

There are two types of accounting methods you can choose from—the cash method and the accrual method. The cash method is used more often: You record income when it is received and expenses when they're disbursed.

Using the accrual method, you report income at the time you earn it rather than when it's actually received. Similarly, expenses are recorded at the time they're incurred rather than when you actually pay them. If you choose this method, keep separate records for "accounts receivable" and "accounts payable."

SATISFYING THE IRS

To successfully—and legally—work as a freelancer, you must know what income you should report and what deductions you can claim. But before you can do that, you must prove to the IRS you're in business to make a profit, that your writing, illustration or photography is not merely a hobby.

The Tax Reform Act of 1986 says you should show a profit for three years out of a five-year period to attain professional status. The IRS considers these factors as proof of your professionalism:

- accurate financial records;
- a business bank account separate from your personal account;
- proven time devoted to your profession;
- whether it's your main or secondary source of income;
- your history of profits and losses;
- the amount of training you have invested in your field;
- your expertise.

If your business is unincorporated, you'll fill out tax information on Schedule C of Form 1040. If you're unsure of what deductions you can take, request the IRS publication containing this information. Under the Tax Reform Act, only 30 percent of business meals, entertainment and related tips, and parking charges are deductible. Other deductible expenses allowed on Schedule C include: car expenses for business-related trips; professional courses and seminars; depreciation of office equipment, such as a computer; dues and publications; and miscellaneous expenses, such as postage used for business needs.

If you're working out of a home office, a portion of your mortgage interest (or rent), related utilities, property taxes, repair costs and depreciation may be deducted as business expenses—under special circumstances. To learn more about the possibility of home office deductions, consult IRS Publication 387, Business Use of Your Home.

The method of paying taxes on income not subject to withholding is called "estimated tax" for individuals. If you expect to owe more than $500 at year's end and if the total amount of income tax that will be withheld during the year will be less than 90% of the tax shown on the current year's return, you'll generally make estimated tax payments. Estimated tax payments are made in four equal installments due on April 15, June 15, September 15 and January 15 (assuming you're a calendar-year taxpayer). For more information, request Publication 505, Self-Employment Tax.

SOCIAL SECURITY TAX

Depending on your net income as a freelancer, you may be liable for a Social Security tax. This is a tax designed for those who don't have Social Security withheld from their paychecks. You're liable if your net income is $400 or more per year. Net income is the difference between your income and allowable business deductions. Request Schedule SE, Computation of Social Security Self-Employment Tax, if you qualify.

If completing your income tax return proves to be too complex, consider hiring an accountant (the fee is a deductible business expense) or contact the IRS for assistance (look in the White Pages under U.S. Government—Internal Revenue Service). In addition to numerous publications to instruct you in various facets of preparing a tax return, the IRS also has walk-in centers in some cities.

INSURANCE CONCERNS

As a self-employed professional be aware of what health and business insurance coverage is available to you. Unless you're a Canadian who is covered by national health insurance or a fulltime freelancer covered by your spouse's policy, health insurance will no doubt be one of your biggest expenses. Under the terms of a 1985 government act (COBRA), if you leave a job with health benefits, you're entitled to continue that coverage for up to 18 months—you pay 100 percent of the premium and sometimes a small administration fee.

Eventually, you must search for your own health plan. You may also need disability and life insurance. Disability insurance is offered through many private insurance companies and state governments. This insurance pays a monthly fee that covers living and business expenses during periods of long-term recuperation from a health problem. The amount of money paid is based on the recipient's annual earnings.

Before contacting any insurance representative, talk to other writers, illustrators or photographers to find which insurance companies they recommend. If you belong to a writers' or artists' organization, ask the organization if it offers insurance coverage for professionals. (SCBWI has a plan available. Look through the Clubs & Organizations section for other groups that may offer coverage.) Group coverage may be more affordable and provide more comprehensive coverage than an individual policy.

Get Plugged In! Opportunities in the Children's Multimedia Market

BY KELLY QUIROZ

Let's play a game. Close your eyes and try to picture a billion dollars. That's how much some analysts think the children's multimedia industry will be worth by the year 2000. A billion dollars. Like you, I have trouble comprehending a gigantic number like that; but I have no trouble at all seeing the enormous potential that a billion-dollar industry offers to writers and illustrators like us whose business it is to create works for children.

Now close your eyes again. This time, imagine yourself as a writer or illustrator on a children's multimedia project. Is the picture kind of fuzzy? Is the software world as foreign to you as the concept of a billion dollars? Then you're in good company. Even those of us who have long experience in the computer industry are often confused, mystified and intimidated by our ever-changing field. So in the interest of de-mystification, let me share with you what I know about writing and illustrating for children's multimedia—and help you snap into focus that picture of yourself in a billion-dollar business.

WHAT IS MULTIMEDIA?

Literally, the word "multimedia" means "many ways of communicating." In the computer world, a multimedia product is one that uses a combination of sound, graphics and/or video to communicate with the user. This broad definition can be applied to many products, such as video tapes or television programming. But when people in the computer industry talk about the multimedia market, they are referring specifically to software (both floppy disks and CD-ROMs); sites on the Internet and the World Wide Web; and commercial online services like America Online and CompuServe. That's the list for right now. But as the industry grows and matures, there's no telling how many other exciting new markets will emerge in the world of multimedia.

OPPORTUNITIES FOR WRITERS & ILLUSTRATORS

Okay, now that you've got the background, let's start talking specifics. Exactly what opportunities exist for writers and illustrators in children's multimedia? Well, if you're a published writer, there's always the chance that you could get your book turned into an interactive storybook, like Mercer Mayer's Little Monster series or Marc Brown's *Arthur's Teacher Trouble*. Both of these titles were published by Living Books, a joint venture of Broderbund software and Random House books. Talk to your agent or publisher about the possibility of turning your book into an interactive storybook, but don't

KELLY QUIROZ (kelly@simply.com) has been a writer and editor on several CD-ROM projects, including "Reading SEARCH" by Great Wave Software, and "Kids' Web Kit" by Peach Pit Press. She is also a former editor of Club KidSoft, a computer and technology magazine for kids. Currently, she is a writer and Web Site Project Manager at Simply Interactive, an educational software company (http://www.simply.com). She and her computer programmer husband live a very wired life in Cupertino, Silicon Valley, California.

get your hopes up—multimedia titles are expensive to produce, and although there are exceptions, most publishers won't be interested in your book unless it's already a tried-and-true bestseller.

Although the interactive storybook market is difficult to crack, there are many other roles a writer can play in the development of a children's software title. Like movies, all software titles need scriptwriters. Some types of software need more scripting than others. A math game, for instance, requires very little scriptwriting, while an interactive storybook or a language arts title will require much more.

Writers can also be game designers. A game designer takes an idea for a software title, develops characters, plots out a story line, and decides what kinds of activities or games will be included. Sometimes, the game designer writes the dialogue scripts as well.

If a title is strongly targeted at the educational market, the project will need a curriculum designer. Writers who are also teachers will find many opportunities in this area.

After you get past the design and scripting stage, each software title has its own set of unique written elements. Most software titles need documentation to help the buyer understand how to use the product. Some require songwriting. Others need reference materials, like dictionary or encyclopedia entries. And some, especially language arts titles, need short stories. Recently, I was the editor on a children's reading title that required 63 retold folktales. Needless to say, we were able to keep a team of seven freelance writers very busy for several months.

There are lots of opportunities in children's multimedia for illustrators, too. During the design phase, most publishers need storyboard artists to sketch out the basic flow of the program. During development, they need artists to do computer illustrations, animation, 3-D modeling, backgrounds and textures. Then, of course, the product must be packaged in a bright, alluring box that will cause consumers to go on a buying frenzy. With all the competition for retail shelf space these days, some people argue that box design is the most important graphic element that goes into software production.

But, you must remember that children's multimedia is no longer limited to the software industry. The online world is booming, and the opportunities for both writers and illustrators are booming right along with it. Online services like America Online and Compuserve have children's areas sponsored by companies like Nickelodeon and Scholastic. While most of these companies use staff writers and illustrators, some supplement their content with freelance material.

Other opportunities exist on the World Wide Web. Right now, the Web is in its infancy, and opportunities for freelancers are limited . . . and often not very lucrative. Few companies have figured out how to make money on the Internet—and if they're not making money, they can't afford to pay you very much. But the march of technology is fast bringing us sound, animation and video over the Internet and as companies find new ways to profit from these new market opportunities, the industry will continue to grow . . . and the need for compelling online content will grow right along with it.

LANDING THOSE FREELANCING JOBS

As you can see, there are lots of opportunities for freelancers in children's multimedia. But how do you break in? Does the software industry, like the book publishing world, have certain rules and standard procedures for submission? Not hardly. As Matt Costello, author of the bestselling game *The 7th Guest*, said recently, "Oh, there are lots of rules in multimedia production; but no one's using the same rules." But despite the chaos characteristic of any new industry, there are a few steps you can follow to get you going in the right direction:

1. Decide if you really want to do this. Although there are some similarities, the computer industry is very different from print publishing. When you work for a software company, you deal with producers and project managers, not editors. Often, these folks don't know what they want, but they need it done yesterday. There's a lot of stress and often impossible deadlines. You must be patient and *very* flexible.

There are also other less dramatic differences between the two industries. More than likely, you will be required to work in a team environment, where you may have lots of input, but little creative control over the product. You may also be required to work at least part time on site at the publisher's building. This can be inconvenient, and even expensive if you don't live nearby.

There are also differences in the creative process. Few multimedia titles unfold like a traditional story with a linear beginning, middle and end. Even interactive story-books—the most linear kind of multimedia title—have lots of activities that are ancillary to the story: clickable objects, related puzzles, creativity games. To develop good multimedia titles, you must think, write and illustrate in a non-linear way.

If all of this sounds discouraging, it's meant to. This market is not for everyone, and you should be absolutely sure you want to work in this industry before you spend the time and money required to be successful.

If, on the other hand, my description of working in the software industry sounds a little intimidating, but also kind of challenging or fun, you should definitely consider taking a crack at the market by going on to Step 2 . . .

2. Get wired. If you plan to work in the software industry, you absolutely must have the tools of the trade. Get a computer; preferably one with a CD-ROM drive, a modem, and a printer. Then get an account with an online service (like America Online) or Internet service provider (like Netcom) so you can have access to the Internet and to electronic mail. In the computer world, e-mail is the preferred form of communication. When I was an editor at a children's computer magazine, I wouldn't even consider a freelancer if she didn't have an e-mail address. Now, as a project manager, I feel the same way. Seeing an e-mail address on an unsolicited submission also reassures me that a freelancer feels at home with technology.

Once you're all wired in, become familiar with the market. (Now there's advice you've never heard before, right?) Order catalogs from the major software companies to check out their product lines. Most software companies will send you a catalog for free if you call their sales number. Then, look at the actual children's software products and online areas for content and graphic design. You don't have to buy tons of products for this. Lots of schools, and some libraries and children's science museums, have computer labs where children's software titles are in use. Arrange a visit, or better yet, volunteer to spend some time working with kids in those labs. Besides giving you valuable insights, being with kids around computers can be a magical experience in and of itself.

And finally, subscribe to a couple computer magazines, like *Multimedia World* and *Family PC*. Becoming familiar with these publications will not only help you keep up on the industry, but since they often carry stories and reviews of children's software, these magazines could be another market for your skills.

3. Get credits. When a software producer hires a writer or an artist for the first time, they want some kind of assurance that she knows her stuff. From writers, they look for published credits. Although most companies prefer to work with writers who are already experienced in multimedia, they are more concerned that you can write well. Books, magazine articles, and newspaper pieces are all good evidence that you can write—and they show a software producer who might be uncertain in her own ability to judge writing talent that someone else thought your stuff was good enough to put into print.

For illustrators, it's a different story. For you, it's not necessary to have published work; but it is absolutely essential to have the skills to create great computer art. No matter how good your pen and ink skills are, or how talented you are with oils, software publishers will not consider using you unless you can create on the computer. If your portfolio consists solely of pieces in the print medium, and you want to move into software, I'd strongly suggest that you take a few courses at your local community college, or just start playing with computer graphics tools. And then you'll be ready for Step 4 . . .

4. Prepare a portfolio. Last year at the first annual SCBWI Children's Multimedia Conference in Los Angeles, a writer friend of mine showed me the portfolio she had prepared to give out at the conference. In it, she had printed out her resume, and copies of some stories she had written for a CD-ROM. She also had a color copy of the CD-ROM box, plus all the documents saved in text format on a floppy disk. All of this was neatly packaged in a vinyl folder that had a special flap for storing the disk. When my friend presented her portfolio to a producer from Broderbund, the producer's eyes widened and she said, "Wow! I wish everyone did this!"

Whether you're a writer or an illustrator, if you want to catch the attention of a busy software producer or project manager, make yourself a portfolio that shows off your work. Writers, make sure to include a resume and only published writing samples. Unpublished manuscripts hold no meaning to a software publisher, and they're likely to get trashed. Illustrators, include only samples of your electronic work; no oils or pastels. Color printouts are fine; but electronic files are even better.

In packaging your portfolio, you can follow the example of my friend, or get even fancier by adding a few more bells and whistles to your presentation. Consider creating a slide show of your work using Microsoft Powerpoint or other presentation software. Most of these products have "viewers," which allow others to view your presentation, even if they don't have a full copy of the software. Or, build yourself a website where you can showcase your best work. If you have worked on other online projects, this also gives you a chance to link to those sites. Unlike the more conservative book publishing industry, software publishers work in a world where glitz and snazziness are highly valued; so if you want to impress them, make it pretty, make it slick, make it WOW!

5. Get connected. Producers and project managers at software companies are usually extremely busy people who are trying to get a tough job done under impossible deadlines. When they need a quick script written, or some animation done, they go to someone they know, or to someone who comes highly recommended from a colleague. They don't have time to waste on strangers. The trick is to make yourself familiar to them; to get your name in front of their faces as often as possible so they think of you whenever they have a need. There are many ways to do this:

• **Send out targeted mailings of your portfolio.** Select several companies for which you would like to work. You'll find names and addresses here in the new Multimedia section of the *Children's Writer's & Illustrator's Market*. Another very good resource is *The Multimedia Directory,* published by The Carronade Group (800-529-3501). Writers, send your portfolio to everyone with "writer," "producer," "project manager" or "development" in their title. Illustrators, send your portfolio to everyone with "art," "graphics" or "creative" in their title. Unlike the book industry, it is a good idea to send your portfolio to multiple people at the same company, giving you wider exposure and a better chance of getting your material in front of the right person. There is no need to include a self-addressed stamped envelope because, if your contact is interested, they will call or e-mail you. Also, never send anything you expect to get back. Whatever you send, they'll keep.

• **Attend conferences, trade shows, and workshops**. These are great places to network with industry insiders. Introduce yourself, tell them what you do, and give them a copy of your portfolio.

• **Join e-mail mailing lists and online newsgroups**. By networking with other "wired" writers, you can often get good market information and referrals.

• **Join organizations that can refer people to you as a multimedia writer**. Good choices are SCBWI, the Children's Multimedia Development Group (check the Web for their site which was being developed at press time), and the Writer's Guild. I found all seven writers for the folktale project through organizations.

• **Work with an agent**. There are a few agents who specialize in multimedia products. You don't have to have an agent to work in multimedia, but they are especially helpful in wading through complicated software contracts. If you already have an agent, let her know that you are interested in doing multimedia work. If she knows nothing about the market, ask if there's someone else in her firm who does.

• **Affiliate yourself with a temporary agency**. Agencies such as the Computer Resources Group specialize in matching freelance writers and artists with companies who are looking to fill short-term writing or design contracts. They are particularly popular in areas with a high concentration of high-tech companies, like San Francisco, Seattle, Los Angeles and New York. If you live in one of these areas, signing up with a temp agency is a great way to get some experience. Keep in mind, though, that the probability of landing an immediate contract with one of the relatively few children's software publishers is slim. More than likely, you'll be asked to write or design for a whole range of companies, from Hewlett-Packard to Mom and Pop's Software Design and Pizza Shoppe. But word of good work travels fast in high-tech communities. If you're willing to do a little work outside of the children's market in return for experience and good exposure, this is a good way to go.

• **Get a full-time job in the industry**. That's what I decided to do two years ago, and since then I've worked on five CD-ROMs, three websites, two sets of product documentation, and one area on America Online. I've also had a chance to meet, work and "do lunch" with colleagues from many other companies. I'm networking like crazy, and my goal is that by the year 2000, I'll know enough people in the industry that I can start freelancing fulltime.

Okay, close your eyes one last time. How's that picture of yourself in the children's multimedia market? If it's still fuzzy and dark—and perhaps even a little more uninviting than before—it's okay. As I said earlier, multimedia is not for everyone.

If, however, that picture has started to pop into focus—hooray! I welcome you to a small but ever-increasing band of professional children's writers and illustrators who are destined to make a difference in children's multimedia. The field is new and there are few established rules. But that's the exciting part, because it means that we can step in here at the beginning as leaders, as visionaries, as experienced professionals in children's publishing, and we can help make this industry into what it will become.

Showing Your Portfolio in Person: An Artist's Trip to New York City

BY CHUCK GALEY

After months of manuscript and art sample submissions and declines, I decided that as an illustrator, I would have to take an extra step to try to get published in children's picture books. I'd read that if you're serious about illustrating picture books, you must go to New York City to meet personally with art directors and get direct feedback. Through personal meetings, you're attaching a name and a face to the art—thus beginning professional relationships.

If you've been thinking about making a special trip to the Big Apple to visit art directors, or even if you'll be in New York for another reason and could extend your trip for portfolio showing, there's a lot to be done first. Here I'll share my experience and tips for getting ready for the trip and making the most of it.

PREPARING YOURSELF AND YOUR PORTFOLIO

Before planning my trip, I sought out the opinions of others with more experience in the children's book market. I found a writers' club and a chat group on America Online where I met published authors who live and work in New York as well as those who live elsewhere, but had visited New York City publishers, so I got several viewpoints on how to approach art directors.

My first step in learning how to get my portfolio in shape was attending a seminar called "Two Perspectives" presented by Berthe Amoss and Erice Suben, authors of *Writing and Illustrating Children's Books for Publication, Two Perspectives* (Writer's Digest Books). This taught me the basics. Attending a seminar or workshop may also give you the opportunity to find mentors who have been in the business for a while and pick their brains for information. (Check the Conferences & Workshops section for events in your area.)

There are a number of books available to help with portfolio preparation. In addition to Amoss's and Suben's book, I found *Writing With Pictures*, by Uri Shulevitz (Watson-Guptill Publications), to be a great resource. And one of my favorites is Martha Metzdorf's *The Ultimate Portfolio* (North Light Books). Metzdorf explains how to create a portfolio that keeps art directors interested from the first dynamic illustration to the last.

I also found helpful information in newsletters such as those published by the Society

CHUCK GALEY *has been in the business of freelance illustration for more than a dozen years. His client list includes magazines like* Ladies Home Journal, R-A-D-A-R *and* Discoveries *and a long list of advertising and corporate clients. Galey, who has a degree in graphic design from Mississippi State University and previously worked as an advertising art director, lives in Jackson, Mississippi, with his wife, son and two cats.*

This portfolio piece was created by illustrator Chuck Galey in response to art directors' comments he received during a trip to New York City to show his portfolio. "I created this scene as part of a dream sequence the little boy in the picture had," says Galey. "I like this illustration because it shows a different perspective as well as an overwhelming feeling of how big the sunflowers have grown."

© Chuck Galey

of Children's Book Writers and Illustrators and the Institute of Children's Literature (*Children's Writer*), and magazines like *The Horn Book*.

It took me about nine months to carefully craft my portfolio to make the most impact. I created 12 new pieces of art, rounding the number up to 15 with three illustrations I'd done for clients. From my research, I found that art directors like to see children in various situations; animals; characters in a story scene; and a variety of different-aged figures such a mothers, fathers, brothers and sisters. I consulted some of my favorite picture books to see how the main characters were presented, then created my own main characters and put them in scenes of my own composition as samples for my portfolio.

I also compared different publishers' styles by perusing their books. As I discovered the style of art each publishes, I could then focus on those publishers that use a style similar to my own. Those publishers would probably respond best to my work.

Once I determined which publishers were the best ones for me to pursue, I researched each one to find the correct addresses, art directors' and editors' names, and phone numbers. Sources for such information are books like *Children's Writer's & Illustrator's Market* and *Literary Market Place*. You can also write to the Children's Book Council (568 Broadway, Suite 404, New York NY 10012), a nonprofit organization made up of publishers of children's literature or check their website, *CBC*Online, (http://www.cbcboo ks.org/index.html) for a list of their members including contact names and addresses. It never hurts to make a phone call to check the information you find, as books on the ever-changing publishing industry can become outdated.

CONTACTING PROSPECTIVE PUBLISHERS

I sent the publishers I wanted to visit a few color copies of artwork with a letter describing my plans to visit the city, and requested an interview. I included a self-addressed, stamped postcard with my letters to encourage art directors and editors to respond quickly. On the postcard I created boxes the art directors could mark: "Yes, please call for an appointment," or "Yes, I would like to see your portfolio." I'd advise sending these query letters at least six weeks before your scheduled trip to New York. I began to get responses about a week-and-a-half after sending my queries.

An important part of my research was studying a map of Manhattan and becoming familiar with the grid patterns of the streets. Some travel books I found even had subway maps included with the street map section. For me, the subway was the easiest and most economical way around the city.

About a month before I left, I called each of the publishers I'd queried to ask if they'd received the samples, and asked to set up an appointment with them, courteously asking for their building's cross street and address so I'd know where they were located in Manhattan. Then I checked my map.

I discovered that many publishers have specific days they review portfolios in person or drop-off portfolios, so I prepared both a drop-off portfolio, made up of laminated copies of my illustrations, and a portfolio of matted originals. In some cases, I doubled the number of meetings in one day because of the drop-off portfolio. I was able to get appointments with 14 different publishers (including Scholastic; Crown; Simon & Schuster; Farrar, Straus & Giroux; Morrow Jr.; Greenwillow; Henry Holt; and Houghton Mifflin) in the five days that I was in the city.

As I made my appointments, I created a week-long day grid with one-hour increments in daily columns. This was a handy visual reminder of how my day was shaping up and allowed me to judge whether I was including too much in one day. I suggest you schedule at least three to four appointments each day with at least an hour in between each. If you don't know the city, as I didn't, this will give you plenty of time between appointments.

PRE-TRAVEL TIPS

As I prepared for my trip, I also considered my physical conditioning. I knew I'd be doing a lot of walking in the city and I didn't want to become fatigued by noon. My portfolio weighed 20 pounds with my matted samples inside. I realized that I'd be really exhausted by the end of the day for the late afternoon appointments that were inevitable, so I undertook a strength and aerobic training regimen. As it turned out, I was in great shape and with each night's rest, I was ready for the next day without any soreness from the day before.

To help save money for meals, I shipped myself a care package from home including my favorite snacks and a small travel coffeemaker. I shipped the package UPS 2nd Day Air the week before my trip and had the hotel hold it for me. My plan was to eat at least one good meal a day with the rest of my meals to be snacks, sandwiches, etc. I got to eat at a nice restaurant at least once a day as a reward. (I saved enough money to afford lunch at the ice rink restaurant in Rockefeller Center!)

About a month before I left for New York, to help myself visualize my success in each appointment, I began thinking about how I'd like to feel before, during and after each meeting. I imagined myself being open and receptive to the advice I'd receive. When I was actually in each appointment, it was like I'd been there before and I was very relaxed and accepting. Remember art directors *want* to see your work, and if you have something they like you've made their jobs easier.

Most of my appointments lasted about 15 minutes—visiting illustrators are only a small portion of an art director's day. I made a note if an art director commented more than once on a particular piece in my portfolio, a clue that a piece may have hit home with him. It's wise to make notes on everything art directors tell you. You can use these suggestions and comments later as you create new pieces for your portfolio in response to their critiques. Since I'd been freelancing advertising and editorial illustrations most of my career, I got comments that suggested more action in the composition and more

© Chuck Galey

"This illustration is pure magic," says illustrator Chuck Galey, of the scene he conjured. "The insects decided to fight back after the little boy and girl have caught several of their kind for their bug collections." The action in this scene of angry airborne insects races towards the right "which prompts the reader to turn the page." The piece is part of the portfolio Galey showed during his second trip to the Big Apple to visit art directors in person.

expressions on the children as they were engaged in their activities. I found the comments and suggestions from art directors were direct and honest—take their suggestions, make the necessary adjustments in your work and keep sending samples.

After each appointment, I sat down, drew a funny picture on some stationery and thanked the editor or art director for the time they spent with me. I mailed these thank-you notes a few days after the appointments. You'd be surprised how many art directors post such drawings on their bulletin boards, thus creating a constant reminder of your work. Now, once a month, I draw something and photocopy it several times, jot a sentence or two, and mail them to the art directors I met—it's an easy way to keep in touch.

So far no picture book illustration work has come out of my first trip to New York City, but I believe the personal contact was needed to build relationships with art directors—if they know me and see my work every once in a while, either in person or through the mail, eventually they'll think of me when projects come up.

I've even been planning a second trip. This time, I've thinned the meetings out, and am visiting only publishers I feel will most likely use my art because of subject matter, style, etc. I'm trying to get more efficient in my efforts. I've created smaller pieces of art which will mat smaller, thus fitting into a smaller—and lighter—portfolio.

Editor's note: At press time Galey had just returned from an encouraging second trip to New York—two publishers expressed interest in a manuscript/illustration package he prepared. "I can't tell you how much the research, contacts and revisions are beginning to pay off!" says the illustrator.

First Books

BY ANNE BOWLING

Writing or illustrating books for children is deceptively difficult. Those who have never tried can be quick to assume that it's a simple art form—concoct a little story, draft a few cute animals, and ship it off to a publisher. How complicated can that be?

But those who are trying to break into children's publishing may appreciate better than anyone just how complex a process it is. In many ways the art is like poetry: it requires sharp observation, keen intuitions, and the ability to communicate complicated ideas in incredibly tight spaces. Even writers for young adults—who have the leisure of a little more space in which to get their ideas across—are working from the disadvantage of being a decade or two removed in age from the audience for whom they are writing.

While there is no formula available that will guarantee you publication, a little advice can go a long way. Here four newcomers to the field of children's publishing—a picture book author, an illustrator, a young adult novelist and a photographer—share their first publication experiences. They say that, by fine-tuning your craft and approaching the business professionally, you may get the break you're working so hard for.

KATYA KRENINA
The Magic Dreidels: A Hanukkah Story (Holiday House, 1996)

To Katya Krenina, being an illustrator is not just a profession but a way of seeing the world and translating life's experiences.

"I constantly carry a sketchbook with me and I constantly draw," says Krenina. "I learn new things, and I don't just mean in the field of illustration. The beauty of being an illustrator is that nothing you learn through your experience is ever irrelevant. You can put it all together and use it in your work."

A native of Lvov, Ukraine ("close to Poland," she adds helpfully), Krenina has spent a lifetime pulling her disparate interests into a single, sharp focus. Her career path preceding publication of *The Magic Dreidels* included designing color graphics for computer games, working in the Russian clothing industry and serving as a translator.

"I have many loves, and it all comes together being a book illustrator," she says. "I worked as a translator and interpreter, and I'm interested in textile design. Book illustration combines my interest in languages with my passion for illustration, because it's like I'm translating the written word into art. Studying textiles taught me how to research costumes and those kinds of things, and that's really helpful, too."

Although she was not raised in an artistic family, "I knew I wanted to be a professional artist very early on, even when I was a kid, really," Krenina says. As a young girl she would spend hours drawing with pencil, "the ground and chalk, whatever was available."

THE MAGIC DREIDELS
A Hanakkah Story
Eric A. Kimmel
illustrated by Katya Krenina

In *The Magic Dreidels*, Katya Krenina used dark, angled images and exaggerated proportions to illustrate the more fantastic elements of the Jewish folktale. "The goblin
was interesting to work on," she says. "There was a lot of potential for fantasy
there." Her break with Holiday House was the first step in a series of projects for
publishers which has helped the Ukraine native to become a full-time children's book
illustrator.

During the 1980s, Krenina attended two Ukrainian art institutes where she studied
anatomy, perspective, drawing, painting, typography and color theory—the framework
for her profession—and majored in textile and tapestry design. "I did want to be a
book illustrator while I was in Ukraine, but I really couldn't afford it," Krenina says.
"It was really complicated because you had to have connections to go to an institution
to study illustration. I knew that was not available to me, so I didn't even try."

Krenina was able to pursue her interest in illustration in the U.S., and in 1994 she
graduated from Syracuse University in New York with a degree in illustration. It was
then that she got her first break with Holiday House for *The Magic Dreidels,* a Hanukkah
story retold by Eric Kimmel about a young boy who outsmarts a neighborhood busy-
body in a seasonal tale of honesty and generosity.

Krenina's dark, angled paintings underscore the tale's folkloric roots. Her work has
been compared to that of Russian painter Marc Chagall, although she calls it "an

unconscious influence. What's similar is this intuitive, dreamlike quality. I do like his work, and when people started pointing out the similarities to me I started seeing it myself."

Krenina had spent a month putting together her portfolio and sending out samples before hearing from Holiday House. While she was in New York City reaching a contract agreement for *The Magic Dreidels*, she was also contacted by Dutton Children's Books, Charlesbridge Publishing and *Ladybug* magazine.

"It pretty much happened all at once," Krenina says. "I've been lucky." But luck wasn't the whole of it—before sending her work out, Krenina carefully researched the publishing companies she targeted to receive her samples, and once contacted, personally walked her work through the interested art departments.

"I took a very good class at Syracuse called the business of freelance illustration, and it gave me a lot of good ideas," Krenina says. "Before I even sent out the samples I did a lot of research about the publishers. I went to the bookstores and saw books that I liked and looked up their publishers, and I also used *Children's Writer's & Illustrator's Market* for information about what would be appropriate, because I didn't want to waste my time sending out samples that would not be appropriate."

Krenina opted not to look for an agent "because I wanted to see how the process really works, and I wanted to get feedback about my work," she says. While she concedes seeking an agent is a personal decision, "I'm a believer that nobody can really represent your work as well as you can yourself."

With publication of *How Yussel Caught the Gefilte Fish* (Dutton Children's Books) scheduled for this year and an as yet untitled project for Charlesbridge Publishing scheduled for 1998, Krenina says she is happy to focus fulltime on her illustration.

"I would encourage people who really want to do this to pursue their dream. All the hard work will eventually pay off," she says. "Also, it's important to trust yourself and your intuition about your work. Be tough on yourself and put the love and passion into your work, and other people will see it, too."

ROB THOMAS
Rats Saw God (Simon & Schuster Books for Young Readers, 1996)

"Getting published for the first time opens a lot of doors. I think the first deal is the toughest," says Rob Thomas, author of the young adult novel *Rats Saw God*. "Once you've got a book out there, you're in better shape—it's just a lot easier to get publishers to read your work."

With *Rats Saw God*, Thomas had his work more than cut out for him. Not only was he pitching a first-time novel, but his included substance abuse and explicit sexuality—not the usual territory for the more routine, *Sweet Valley High*-style, young adult fare.

"My book is edgy in terms of drug use, and language, and sexual content, and I think it really kind of pushes what can be done in young adult fiction," Thomas says. "Yeah, I was worried about it. Four or five publishing houses said, 'We like this, but it's a little too far out there for us.' " Thomas says he considered following the path of contemporary Trey Ellis (*Platitudes*, *Home Repairs*) by marketing the novel as fiction for an older age group.

© Stanley W. Hensley

"I was really considering trying to market the novel as adult fiction," Thomas says. "In bookstores, if you've got *Rats Saw God* next to *The Babysitters' Club* and *Sweet Valley High* books, what self-respecting 18-year-old is going to walk into that section and pull out my book, unless they know specifically what they want? The other option is to stock books like mine in the young adult and adult sections."

Finding a readership for this first novel may not be an issue if early reviews are any indicator. "A high-energy debut" is how *Kirkus Reviews* describes the novel, the story of Steve York, an underachieving National Merit Scholar assigned to write a 100-page essay for failing English. *Rats Saw God* follows York through his sophomore to his senior year in high school, including the highs and lows of love and navigating relationships with his parents. "Layers of cynical wit and careful character development accumulate achingly in this beautifully crafted, emotionally charged story," wrote a critic for *School Library Journal*.

Despite its raw, direct approach to such difficult topics as sexuality and substance abuse, Rob Thomas's *Rats Saw God* manuscript was snapped up by the fourth agent he contacted. And it was a brief ten weeks from the time Thomas landed an agent to his receiving multiple offers from major publishers. This success came despite the author's admission that the edgy quality of his book had him concerned about whether publishers would market his novel to young adults. Thomas is working a second two-book contract for Simon & Schuster Books for Young Readers.

Illustration by Chris Raschka. © 1996 Simon & Schuster

Thomas did not have to look hard to find the voice that would speak so clearly and credibly to teenagers. A graduate of the University of Texas at Austin, Thomas taught high school journalism for five years, advised for the University of Texas student magazine, and worked for Channel One in Los Angeles, which he calls "sort of like a CNN for teenagers." Of the young people he has taught and written about, Thomas says, "I genuinely like teenagers—I think they're interesting people. Everything in their lives is sort of automatically dramatic, whether it's their hair or their complexion on a given day."

It was during his year at Channel One that he wrote *Rats Saw God*. To take the job, Thomas left behind his teaching and rock band, "two things that kind of drained me of any excess creativity," he says. "So while I was in Los Angeles I had more left over than I knew what to do with."

Finding an agent to handle the completed manuscript was step two. "I'm not a read-the-directions kind of guy, but on this I actually read the books, took notes, and followed the how-to explicitly," Thomas says. Using industry periodicals such as *Writer's Market* and *Insider's Guide to Publishing*, he targeted the agencies that were looking for young adult fiction, and the names of their agents who handled those manuscripts. If more than one agent handled young adult fiction, Thomas says, he tried to pinpoint which agent would be most receptive to his manuscript. He created a priority list of contacts, and put the final polish on his query package by laser printing the letters with matching resumes, envelopes and SASEs.

It was writing his query letter which took the most time and care. "You've got to do two things in the body of it—you've got to show that you can write, and make sure it's as well-written as the novel. The second thing you've got to do is grab their attention in the same way that book flap copy makes you want to read the book. I figured I wasn't going to write a book every month, and that package was my shot at getting it published." The effort paid off—the fourth agent Thomas queried agreed to represent the manuscript.

It took about ten weeks for Thomas's agent to secure an offer from Simon & Schuster, in a contract which included a second novel (titled *Slave Day*, Thomas's second book will be published in the spring of 1997). Now a fulltime writer, Thomas has completed the first book on a second two-book contract for Simon & Schuster (as yet untitled), and is working on a collection of short stories.

"I keep getting this question, 'Do you want to write a serious novel or an adult novel?' I am kind of interested in writing about people my age; I think I could handle adults," Thomas says. "I may someday write adult novels, but it won't be because I think teenagers are less serious or less important to write about."

To young novelists, Thomas says focus on the product and write the best book you're able to write. "The best I felt about (the process) was when I was writing, and not thinking about getting published, or about the audience, or about what was selling or not selling," he says. "People who talk to me about publishing seem to be putting the publishing cart before the writing horse. So many writers who talk to me about publishing haven't written. Or they've started writing, and they already want to know who to talk to to sell the book. I think your first effort needs to be write a really good book. And then selling it will take care of itself."

SUSAN MIDDLETON ELYA
Say Hola to Spanish (Lee & Low Books, 1996)

Author Susan Middleton Elya is a staunch believer that in the competitive world of children's book publishing, different is better. Experience has taught her so.

"I think the reason *Say Hola to Spanish* sold was because it was something unusual, and it hadn't been done before," says Middleton. "I had written several charming little stories, but there were other stories a lot like them. Publishers kept saying 'Charming little story, but we don't want it.' I still have all my 'charming little story' letters."

Raised in Iowa and living in Danville, California, with her family, Elya has a degree in Spanish and elementary education, and taught Spanish for 10 years to junior high school students. Despite her background, she says, it took

Olan Mills Studio

awhile to land on the idea of a Spanish-English primer in a picture book format.

"I had been writing for years and hadn't sold a thing, and my mother said 'Why don't you write something in Spanish?,' which had never occurred to me," Elya says. "My daughter was asking me to teach her Spanish, and I was just thinking of some fun way to do it."

Elya began writing and submitting children's manuscripts in 1988, completing a young adult novel ("It was ridiculous," she says), and several picture books. While her submissions didn't get the results she was looking for, "I got enough to keep me going, personal notes from editors that were just enough to keep me so I wouldn't quit, but I never could make that sale."

Say Hola was started during this time. Elya began the manuscript but soon tucked it away in a file, because it wasn't going anywhere, she says. It stayed in the file drawer for two years, "until right before my third child was born," Elya says. "I was thinking, 'I'll never write again after I have three kids.' I was going through the file looking for something to work on and I thought, 'Hmmm, maybe I can fix this.' And I did."

Elya credits her writers' group—of which she is an eight-year veteran—with helping her refine the manuscript before she shipped it off to prospective publishers. "They're real honest," she says. "If something's not working, they'll tell me. I'd rather find out from them than an editor. I had a whole big geographical introduction—about where in the world people speak Spanish—and they said get rid of that. It didn't work. Start with this couplet here."

After patiently persisting through six years of re-jection letters, author Susan Middleton Elya was more than happy to receive an acceptance notice from Lee & Low Books for *Say Hola to Spanish*. This particular manuscript sat in a drawer for two years because it was "going nowhere," says the author. Elya revised it just before the birth of her third child, convinced she would never have time to write again. ¡Sorpresa!—she has since com-pleted a second version of the Spanish-English primer, and has a handful of other projects on standby.

Elya credits her research with helping her match her manuscript with the New York-based Lee & Low Books, which publishes only multicultural fiction and nonfiction. She joined the Society of Children's Book Writers and Illustrators, and using their literature targeted publishers looking for the key elements in *Say Hola*—rhyme, multi-cultural themes, nonfiction picture books.

Eight publishers rejected the manuscript before Elya hit on Lee & Low Books. And once Lee & Low editors accepted the manuscript, they continued modifications, editing out more references to specific Spanish-speaking countries. The end result became a Children's Book of the Month Club selection—a tight, bouncy, rhyming introduction to Spanish about which *Kirkus Reviews* wrote: "Outwardly, this book . . . looks like a language lesson from Looney Tunes. Then—*¡sorpresa!*—it turns out to be innovative, useful, and fun."

Much of the fun in the book is provided by the gouache and colored pencil illustrations from first-timer Loretta Lopez. About midway through the book, what were fairly straightforward drawings begin to give way to snatches of wit—a boy sleeping at his desk in school depicts 'siesta'—until by the end silliness reigns with dancing chickens, singing cats and cows in pink lipstick and blue eyeshadow.

"When they bought my manuscript, they called me and said 'we want to make this into a funny book'," Elya says. "I'd never thought about it like that." But in many ways *Say Hola* echoes what Elya calls one of her favorite children's books, *The Cat in the Hat Comes Back*, with lines like "You bite with dientes/Don't bite the dentista/Just wait for your check-up/and read a revista."

With the success of her first book to propel her, Elya is ready to continue writing around her children's schedules and working toward subsequent sales. "I have a second *Say Hola* ready to go, and I'm working on a third," she says. "I also have several other projects waiting in the wings," among them chapter books and other nonfiction projects.

To other writers seeking publication, she offers some very specific advice: send a straightforward, professional submission package free of attention-getting gimmicks and fancy fonts. "I had somebody suggest to me that I get a stamp and put little doggie pictures all over my envelope. No, no, no." She adds, "You need to have an editor's name. A lot of industry newsletters list the names of editors that wouldn't be listed elsewhere because they're not editors-in-chief or senior editors. I looked for names like that, because I figured they would be more apt to look at my work than an editor-in-chief would."

LISA MAIZLISH
The Ring (Greenwillow Books, 1996)

Unearthing dinosaur bones as a paleontologist's assistant in Montana was not enough to hold the imagination of picture book photographer Lisa Maizlish for long.

"I loved doing the field work—there were a lot of dinosaur bones out there," says Maizlish, who has a bachelor's degree in geology. "It was once we got home and started cataloging and research and office stuff that it got a little boring. I was sort of feeling like I needed to do something a little more creative."

© 1996 Hugh Hales-Tooke

The result of Maizlish's creative impulse is *The Ring*, the story of a boy who finds he can take flight for a bird's eye view of New York City by picking up an innocuous-looking yellow ring in the park. In a wordless tale reminiscent of *The Red Balloon*, black and white backgrounds give way to color, winter clothes fall away for t-shirts in the warm sun, and flying over the Statue of Liberty never looked like so much fun. The digitally-enhanced photos inspired one *Publishers Weekly* critic to write: "Maizlish's first book attests to her sparkling creativity, first-rate photographic skills and impressive technological acumen."

This was fairly lavish praise for a relative newcomer to photography—Maizlish had not purchased her first camera until after she graduated college. She had worked as a freelance photographer in New York City, doing promotional work for theater compa-

THE RING

BY LISA MAIZLISH

© Lisa Maizlish

To find a publisher for *The Ring*, photographer Lisa Maizlish approached Greenwillow Books with a full storyboard and one completed sample of a photo image digitally composed with Adobe Photoshop. The story—in which a boy learns he can fly with the help of a yellow ring he finds in the park—appeals most to four- and five-year-olds, Maizlish says. "They are just the perfect age, because they are old enough to know they can't actually fly, but not quite old enough to know there might not be magic rings out there."

nies and a local school, for a little more than three years. "In part because I didn't start photography until after I had finished college, I felt like I needed to do something a little bit different to accelerate my learning process, so I was sort of searching around for some idea for a project with photography," she says.

Digital technology was equally new to Maizlish, who taught herself to use Adobe Photoshop to create the photo images in *The Ring*. "More and more photographers are starting to get interested in what can be done to photographs on the computer," she says. "So when I had the idea for the book, I decided I would try to do it on the computer. I asked everybody I could who knew anything about it for awhile, and I got some books, and a computer, and just started trying it."

The area of children's books was more familiar territory to Maizlish, who names a range of authors from Maurice Sendak to Louise Fitzhugh (*Harriet the Spy*) to Norman Juster (*Phantom Tollbooth*) as early favorites. She has also always loved comic books, she says, "and how those stories are told with pictures. Without words, you're much more deliberate in the illustration. And I also liked the idea of this being a book for kids who are just getting interested in books, who can't necessarily read yet. They're just learning how to follow a story sequentially."

Because of the complexity of the project, Maizlish needed to get a publisher committed before she devoted the hours necessary to create her photo story. "I didn't want to do the whole thing first without running it by an editor," she says. To prepare a submission package, Maizlish sketched a storyboard and set to work on one illustration—a photo of a boy flying through the air past the Empire State Building, with an onlooker pointing, amazed—to show her abilities.

To do this, Maizlish had to shoot background and subject photos which could be merged into one image, taking care to have the same light source from the same angle shot at the same time of day, "or else it would look like it was pasted on, even if there was no visible seam between them," Maizlish says. "In putting them together on the computer it's kind of like doing a collage."

It was a lucky coincidence that brought Maizlish, unagented, to Greenwillow Books. At a children's book convention in New York, Maizlish met an industry contact through a friend who would help her through the process. "She liked the idea, but thought I needed to do a little bit more with it, so she kind of coached me through my first draft," Maizlish says. Her contact also connected her with an editor at Greenwillow Books.

"It took a little time before they gave me the go-ahead," Maizlish says. "But when I look back now I can't believe the foresight they had to publish this book. Part of what I was pitching was that this was going to be the first book of its kind, but I went in and pitched an idea that was still pretty rough, and I can't believe they entrusted me with this."

Maizlish's advice to children's publishing newcomers? Make personal contacts in the field through professional organizations, writer's groups and informal meetings. "Bookstores are a great place to meet people. In children's bookstores, particularly since I started this book, I've met so many people who've published books," says Maizlish, who had an extensive list of credits published in the back of *The Ring*. "I think if you have people you trust, or whose taste you like, you can show them your work and get a lot of good advice."

Virginia Hamilton's Work: Blending the Known, the Remembered & the Imagined

BY PATRICK G. SOUHAN

"Watch out what you say around Virginia, or you'll end up in a book!" So laughs the family of celebrated children's author Virginia Hamilton. They ought to know. For more than 30 children's books, Hamilton has drawn upon her extraordinarily rich childhood, growing up African-American in rural southwest Ohio.

"I come from a large, extended family as many people already know, I've talked about them enough," says Hamilton. "I grew up on a farm. My cousins lived on adjacent farms. And we'd roam all day on family land. We could run in and out of people's houses—they were relatives and they always had something good for us. It was very protective, very nice.

"I think you'll find that most children's authors have wonderfully vivid memories of their childhood. Maybe that's why we write about it—because it was such pleasure being a child."

These comfortable, rural family experiences inform much of Hamilton's work. While books like *Zeely* (Simon & Schuster, 1968) and *Cousins* (Philomel, 1990) may have nothing to do with Hamilton in the sense that she "created" the stories, they have everything to do with the fact that she knows how relatives and friends relate and interact within a close community. "I grew up in that kind of environment," says Hamilton. "I know it very well. I can move large numbers of people across the page and have them really live because I lived with them and still do today."

This closeness of family, however, was not enough to keep Hamilton from leaving home to seek her fortune as a writer in the sixties. Coming from a family of storytellers, she had always known that she wanted to write. One of the first tales she remembers related the true story of her grandfather's escape from slavery as a small boy. That tale and the many others she heard at family gatherings inspired her. "I attended Antioch (a small liberal arts school in Yellow Springs, Ohio) and then went to New York City and posed as a writer," recalls Hamilton. "It was all very romantic. I wore a beret and had a long cigarette holder and velvet slacks—I did the whole (Greenwich) Village thing."

But clothes alone do not the writer make. "When I got to New York, I didn't have a clue," says Hamilton. "I really didn't know how you did it—how you became 'pub-

---

PATRICK G. SOUHAN, *a production editor in the trade book division of F&W Publications and resident of Dayton, Ohio, is practically Virginia Hamilton's neighbor. Souhan is former managing editor of* Dayton Monthly *magazine.*

lished.' " And for awhile she didn't. To pay the rent, Hamilton worked a variety of jobs, including a stint as a cost accountant and some time on the night club singing circuit. But perhaps most importantly she kept on writing. "I submitted frequently to *The New Yorker* and other publications. They just kept sending me these nice encouraging letters. That was it."

A chance meeting with an old college friend, who just happened to work in the marketing department of Macmillan Publishing, changed all that. Hamilton refers to the encounter as a "happy accident—the kind that hits you if you hang around New York long enough.

"She remembered some of the stories I had written and wanted to know what happened to them," recalls Hamilton. "She thought they'd make great children's books. I asked, 'What's a children's book?' Because I didn't think of writing in those terms, I had never made such a distinction. I just read whatever—whether it was *David Copperfield* or something by Faulkner. So before then, I never really envisioned myself a children's writer."

After speaking with her friend, Hamilton went back home and dusted off a 20-page manuscript she had written while at Antioch. It was to become her first novel, *Zeely*, published in 1968. It relates the tale of a young girl, Geeder, who spends her summer on an uncle's farm. While there she befriends an older girl named Zeely, whom she likens to a Watusi princess because of a picture she once saw in a magazine.

Not only did the novel create the standard for contemporary African-American children's fiction, but it also established Hamilton as one of America's foremost authors of children's literature, period. She had not set out to be a children's author, but upon the publication of *Zeely*, there would be little thought of anything else.

Hamilton followed up *Zeely* with the Edgar Allan Poe Award-winning mystery *The House of Dies Drear* (Macmillan, 1968). And shortly thereafter came the Newbery Medal, Boston Globe-Horn Book Award and the National Book Award-winner, *M.C. Higgins, the Great* (Dell, 1974). She was the first African-American to receive the John Newbery Medal, and the only author to receive all three distinctions for a single book.

Since then, Hamilton has received practically every honor the field of children's literature has to offer—and then some. One of her most recent accomplishments was being awarded the prestigious MacArthur Fellowship. The grant honors "hard working experts who often push the boundaries of their field in ways that others will follow." She is the first and only children's fiction author to receive the award.

After 15 years of the writer's life in New York, Hamilton returned to her family home in bucolic southern Ohio, along with her husband, poet Arnold Adoff, whom she met in New York. She had "followed her bliss" and made it as a writer; she could come home. Still today, the beautiful countryside, her memories of it and its history, continue to feed her work.

"I think I work differently than most writers," says Hamilton. "I don't make outlines, and I never know until the end exactly how a story is going to come out. Oh, I do have some idea of where a story is going, but I'm not really sure what's inside that shape of the story."

When Hamilton writes, she says it is the synthesis of three elements: the known, the remembered and the imagined. "The known is the facts that you have to have in order to write. The remembered is all the stuff you pull out of your past that assists you and allows you to write in the present. It is all the things you know about living and people interacting and emotions. Then you have the imagined which puts it all together into the story. This is how I write. I've been doing it for a long time."

In her fiction, Hamilton strives to present human stories, rather than any sort of social agenda or political stance. "I just write stories about people," says Hamilton.

Virginia Hamilton's *Her Stories: African American Folktales, Fairy Tales* and *True Tales* (Blue Sky Press, 1996) is a collection of traditional and true stories of African-American women retold by the award-winning author in an impressive illustrated volume. "The book will be well used by storytellers and others interested in traditional literature and 'her stories,' " says a review in *The Horn Book*. Hamilton includes informal observations following each tale she retold in this Coretta Scott King Award-winning volume.

"Only they're about people who, for the most part, happen to be of a different race and whose experiences are different from many of the readers."

Besides her ability to spin a great tale with memorable characters and evocative imagery, Hamilton is recognized for her unflinching belief that children can handle difficult ideas, which is evidenced in many of her novels. *Cousins*, one of her most popular books, tackles death, guilt and redemption. *Plain City* (Scholastic, 1993) deals with the mental illness of a family member. *A White Romance* (Philomel, 1987) examines drug addiction and the tensions in a recently integrated magnet high school. Each subject is handled deftly and elegantly. Moralizing and preachiness are thrown over for frankness and honesty. "I can't believe it when people say something should not be written about because 'they are only children.' Children are often in the midst of trouble when there's trouble anyway.

"I don't think you can take kids out of the real world. All the time things happen. They see their friends get hurt or worse. Whole families break up. Kids are abandoned. Kids see everything. An innocent childhood? I don't know where it exists. The more

Retold in plantation-era colloquial speech, the collection of fables in Hamilton's *When Birds Could Talk and Bats Could Sing* (Blue Sky Press, 1996) contains humorous tales about small creatures—birds, bats, deer and little children. These trickster-type stories with origins in African-American folklore, first popularized in the 1880s by a journalist named Martha Young, each end with a moral or small truth. "I try to do a kind of speech that is literally folk-telling. Though you feel it is casual, it is studied," says Hamilton. "It makes everything orderly . . . and tells a good story."

children understand—the more that can be explained to them about the world, the better they are able to handle themselves. The more knowledge you have, the safer you are."

While her novels are what she's best known for, Hamilton has also received much acclaim for her beautifully illustrated compilations of traditional African-American folklore. Resurrecting fantastic age-old stories, Hamilton recasts the tales in her own elegant prose without losing their sense of being folk-told. Two of her most recent collections are *Her Stories: African American Folktales, Fairy Tales and True Tales*, and *When Birds Could Talk and Bats Could Sing*. The former presents stories of strong African-American women—real and imagined—from the legendary Annie Christmas, the seven-foot-tall riverboat captain, to clever little Malindy who sold her sole (from her shoe) to the devil. The latter relates humorous trickster tales from a hidden animal kingdom in Uncle Remus fashion.

However, it is still the children's novels that Hamilton enjoys the most. "Children are on their way to becoming," says Hamilton. "I like the idea of taking these little beings who become adults and posing all the conflicts of growing and changing. This provides story."

This is also the fundamental distinction between adult fiction and children's fiction, says Hamilton. Adult fiction is driven by a different set of questions. Adults are already there, and so they're asking the questions "How did this come to pass?" "How did I get here?" or "What do I do with this?" It's a different way of thinking.

In her 30-plus years of writing children's literature, Hamilton has seen much change. Most of it good. "People are learning to sell vast numbers of books. Look at R.L. Stine. It's a phenomenon. And there is room for all kinds of books. The whole idea of children's books is so broad—you've got books with no words, just pictures, and young adult novels at the other end. There is popular fiction, and there is the more thoughtful or literary fiction. Something like 5,000 new titles come out every year. Of course, you've got a lot of mediocre stuff, but you've got some really good titles as well."

Children are reading and reading with some diversity. About this Hamilton is enthusiastic. "You know what else is great about it? Kids don't just read one kind of book. They may pick up a R.L. Stine, a Babysitters' Club and one of my books. There are all these different kinds of books and all these different kinds of writers and illustrators and all these different kinds of kids who want to read all these different kinds of things." The fact we can get kids to read at all with all the other choices out there—sports, computers—is pretty amazing, she adds.

Hamilton is also pleased with the growing cultural diversity in the field of children's literature. "More and more groups outside the so-called 'mainstream' are being represented—Japanese, Chinese, Mexican-Americans, African-Americans. Many different voices are being heard and many more cultures are being represented. There is a very broad painting that's being made across America and it's quite a beautiful thing. It should be interesting to see how it continues."

In this seemingly burgeoning children's market, how can a new writer make it? On this, Hamilton is adamant. There is no other way than hard work, a lot of research and maybe even a little luck. "You've got to know the field," advises Hamilton. "You have to know who reads what. Who's accepting unsolicited manuscripts. Talk to editors and agents. Get out of where you are; go to New York if you have to. If this is really what you want to do, you have to take it seriously. And you've got to be good, this is an incredibly competitive field. Take classes. Hone your skills and write, write and write."

Editor's note: To learn more about Virginia Hamilton and her work, visit her website (http://www.cris.com/~bonfire2) which includes a complete library of her books, a photo gallery, lists of her awards, and a schedule of her personal appearances.

KEY TO SYMBOLS & ABBREVIATIONS

* Symbol indicating a listing new in this edition

✤ Symbol indicating a Canadian listing

☐ Symbol indicating a book packager/producer

‡ Symbol indicating a contest, organization or conference is open to students

● Symbol indicating a comment from the editor of *Children's Writer's & Illustrator's Market*

ms or **mss** stands for manuscript or manuscripts.

SASE refers to a self-addressed stamped envelope.

SAE refers to a self-addressed envelope.

IRC stands for International Reply Coupon. These are required with SAEs sent to markets in countries other than your own.

IMPORTANT LISTING INFORMATION

● Listings are based on questionnaires, phone calls and updated copy. They are not advertisements nor are markets reported here necessarily endorsed by the editor of this book.

● Information in the listings comes directly from the companies and is as accurate as possible, but situations may change and needs may fluctuate between the publication of this directory and the time you use it.

● *Children's Writer's & Illustrator's Market* reserves the right to exclude any listing that does not meet its requirements.

The Markets

Book Publishers

It's important that writers and illustrators pay attention to trends in the marketplace. That said, keep in mind that what you're seeing in the bookstores may be a year or two behind what publishers are working on right now. Don't base your writing decisions solely on the trend of the day, and don't try to tailor your work to a certain house—find the house that fits your material.

In the past few years, nonfiction picture books have grown in popularity. Nonfiction accounts for half of all children's books published. Both institutional (intended for libraries and schools) and retail nonfiction publishers are looking for books with strong graphic appeal as more and more nonfiction picture books are being published. For more on this facet of the industry, see the Insider Report with Frank Sloan of Raintree Steck-Vaughn on page 130.

The awareness of the need for multicultural offerings is still alive in the children's book market. Books dealing with the African-American, Hispanic, and Asian-American experiences are being published in increasing numbers. Publishers like Lee & Low are specializing in this area of the market. See First Books for an interview with Lee & Low author Susan Middleton Elya as she talks about getting her first book, *Say Hola to Spanish*, published.

Paperbacks are still enjoying blockbuster sales, which have risen steadily since 1990. Horror series like genre leader R.L. Stine's *Goosebumps*, whose sales have surpased the 100 million mark, still dominate the bestseller lists. *Goosebumps* has even made the leap to TV in a top-rated series. Deborah Forte, head of Scholastic Productions, talks about the risks of moving from paperback to television in an Insider Report on page 220 in our brand new Multimedia section.

A number of paperback series are produced by book packagers for large publishers like Bantam/Doubleday/Dell. Writing for packagers usually involves a work-for-hire arrangement, and often the books in a series are written by several authors under a single pseudonym—but packagers can provide regular income and good experience. There are several packagers among our listings, all marked with an open box (□).

FINDING THE RIGHT PUBLISHER

As always, the key to marketing children's writing, illustration and photography is to match your interests with those of the publisher. To help you locate publishers seeking your type of work, we've included several indexes at the back of this book.

The Subject Index lists book and magazine publishers according to their fiction and nonfiction needs or interests. The Age-Level Index indicates which age-groups publishers cater to. And we've compiled a Photography Index, indicating which markets buy photography for children's publications.

Use the indexes to hone your list of markets. For instance, if you specialize in contemporary fiction for young adults and you're trying to place a book manuscript, go first to the Subject Index. Locate the fiction categories under Book Publishers, find

Contemporary, and copy the list. Now go to the Age-Level Index and find all the publishers on the Contemporary list that are included under the Young Adults heading and highlight them. Read the listings for the highlighted publishers and see if your work matches their needs.

Photographers can also use the indexes to narrow their list of possible publishers. If you're interested in selling nature photos to kids' magazine, for example, first copy the Magazine list in the Photography Index. Next check the Subject Index under Nature/Environment (you could check fiction, nonfiction or both). Highlight those markets on the Magazine list and the Nature/Environment list. Again, read the highlighted listings to determine which magazines are most appropriate for your work.

A WORD ON SUBSIDY PUBLISHING

Some writers who are really determined to get their work into print, but who receive rejections from royalty publishers, may look to subsidy and co-op publishers as an option. These publishers ask writers to pay all or part of the costs of producing a book. We strongly advise writers and illustrators to work only with publishers who pay them. For this reason, we've adopted a policy not to include any subsidy or co-op publishers in *Children's Writer's & Illustrator's Market* (or any other Writer's Digest Books market book).

If you're interested in publishing your book just to share it with friends and relatives, self-publishing is a viable option, but it involves a lot of time and energy. You oversee all of the book production details. A local printer may be able to help you, or you may want to arrange some type of desktop computer publishing.

Remember that the road to publication is not easy. The business is competitive, and everyone gets her share of rejections. Every writer, illustrator and photographer must find the path that works best for her.

*ABC, ALL BOOKS FOR CHILDREN, The All Children's Co., Ltd., 33 Museum St., London WC1A 1LD United Kingdom. (171)436-6300. Fax: (171)240-6923. Imprints: softbABCks (paperback); factbABCks (nonfiction). Book publisher. Unsolicited Manuscripts: Carol Mackenzie. Publisher: Sue Tarsky. Publishes 40 picture books/year. 50% of books by first-time authors.
Fiction: Picture books: adventure, animal, concept, contemporary, multicultural, nature/environment. Average word length: picture books—under 1,000. Recently published *Angelina Ice Skates*, by Katharine Holabird, illustrated by Helen Craig; *Three Bags Full*, by Ragnhild Scamell, illustrated by Sally Hobson; and *My Map Book*, by Sara Fanelli.
Nonfiction: Picture books, young readers, middle readers: concept, history nature/environment.
How to Contact/Writers: Picture books: Submit complete manuscript. Nonfiction: Query. Reports on queries in 1 month; ms in 2-3 months. Publishes a book 12-18 months after acceptance. Will consider simultaneous submissions.
Illustration: Works with 15 illustrators/year. Uses color artwork only. Reviews ms/illustration packages from artists. Submit ms with 2 color photocopies. Illustrations only: Reports in 1 month. Samples returned with SASE (IRC); samples filed.
Terms: "Payment decided on individual basis." Sends galleys to authors; color proofs to illustrators. Original artwork returned at job's completion. Book catalog available for SAE.

*ABINGDON PRESS, The United Methodist Publishing House, 201 Eighth Ave. S., Nashville TN 37203. (615)749-6384. Fax: (615)749-6512. Children's Book Editor: Peg Augustine.
Nonfiction: Picture books: religion. Does not want to see animal stories.
How to Contact/Writers: Query; submit outline/synopsis and 1 sample chapter. Reports on queries in 4-6 weeks; mss in 3 months.
Illustration: Uses color artwork only. Reviews ms/illustration packages from artists. Query with photocopies only. Contact: Peg Augustine, children's book editor. Samples returned with SASE; samples not filed.
Photography: Buys stock images. Contact: Peg Augustine, children's book editor. Wants scenics, landscape, still life and multiracial photos. Model/property release required. Uses color prints. Submit stock photo list.

ADVOCACY PRESS, P.O. Box 236, Santa Barbara CA 93102. (805)962-2728. Fax: (805)963-3580. Division of The Girls Incorporated of Greater Santa Barbara. Book publisher. Editorial Contact: Bill Sheehan. Publishes 2-4 children's books/year.
Fiction: Picture books, young readers, middle readers: adventure, animal, concepts in self-esteem, contemporary, fantasy, folktales, gender equity, multicultural, nature/environment, poetry. "Illustrated children's stories incorporate self-esteem, gender equity, self-awareness concepts." Published *Nature's Wonderful World in Rhyme* (birth-age 12, collection of poems); *Shadow and the Ready Time* (32-page picture book). "Most publications are 32-48 page picture stories for readers 4-11 years. Most feature adventures of animals in interesting/educational locales."
Nonfiction: Middle readers, young adults: careers, multicultural, self-help, social issues, textbooks.
How to Contact/Writers: "Because of the required focus of our publications, most have been written inhouse." Reports on queries/mss in 1-2 months. Include SASE.
Illustration: "Require intimate integration of art with story. Therefore, almost always use local illustrators." Average about 30 illustrations per story. Reviews ms/illustration packages from artists. Submit ms with dummy. Contact: William Sheehan. Reports in 1-2 months. Samples returned with SASE.
Terms: Authors paid by royalty or outright purchase. Pays illustrators by project or royalty. Book catalog and ms guidelines for SASE.
Tips: "We are not presently looking for new titles."

AFRICA WORLD PRESS, P.O. Box 1892, Trenton NJ 08607. (609)844-9583. Fax: (609)844-0198. Book publisher. Editor: Kassahun Checole. Publishes 5 picture books/year; 15 young reader and young adult titles/year; 8 middle readers/year. Books concentrate on African-American life.
Fiction: Picture books, young readers: adventure, concept, contemporary, folktales, history, multicultural. Middle readers, young adults: adventure, contemporary, folktales, history, multicultural.
Nonfiction: Picture books, young readers, middle readers, young adults: concept, history, multicultural. Does not want to see self-help, gender or health books.
How to Contact/Writers: Query; submit outline/synopsis and 2 sample chapters. Reports on queries in 30-45 days; mss in 3 months. Will consider previously published work.
Illustration: Works with 10-20 illustrators/year. Reviews ms/illustration packages from artists. Query. Contact: Kassahun Checole, editor. Illustrations only: Query with samples. Reports in 3 months.
Terms: Pays authors royalty based on retail price. Pays illustrators by the project or royalty based on retail price. Book catalog available for SAE; ms and art guidelines available for SASE.

AFRICAN AMERICAN IMAGES, 1909 W. 95th St., Chicago IL 60643. (312)445-0322. Fax: (312)445-9844. Book publisher. Editor: Jawanza Kunjufu. Publishes 2 picture books/year; 1 young reader title/year; 1 middle reader title/year. 90% of books by first-time authors.
Fiction: Picture books, young readers, middle readers: multicultural. "We publish books from an Africentric frame of reference that promote self-esteem, collective values, liberation and skill development." Does not want to see poetry, essays, novels, autobiographies, biographies, religious materials or mss exclusively addressing the continent of Africa.
Nonfiction: Picture books, young readers, middle readers: multicultural.
How to Contact/Writers: Fiction/Nonfiction: Query or submit complete ms. Reports on queries in 2 weeks; mss in 6 weeks. Publishes a book 9 months after acceptance. Will consider simultaneous submissions. Include SASE for return of ms.
Illustration: Works with 4 children's illustrators/year. Illustrations only: Submit tearsheets. Reports on art samples in 2 weeks. Samples returned with SASE; samples filed.
Terms: Pays 10% royalty based on wholesale price. Illustrators paid by the project ($500-$1,000 range). Original artwork returned at job's completion. Book catalog, ms guidelines free on request.

*AFTER MIDNIGHT PRESS, P.O. Box 1755, Simi Valley CA 93062. (805)558-2234. E-mail: yrjg92a@prodigy.com. Book publisher. Editor: Dawn Royer. Publishes 1 middle reader/year; 1 young reader/year. 50% of books by first-time authors. Books are primarily educational.
Fiction: All levels: special needs. Middle readers, young adult/teens: health, history, multicultural, problem novels, special needs. "We don't publish a great deal of fiction!" Average word length: picture books—300-500.
Nonfiction: Picture books: how-to, textbooks. "We are open to considering all types of nonfiction!" Does not want to see nonfiction that has not been well researched or talks down to children.

Average word length: picture books—300-500. Recently published *Creative Kids Writer-Handbook for Parents/Teachers*, by Christina D. Carpenter (educational text for ages 9-12); *Creative Kids Write—20 Way Cool Ways to Practice Writing*, by Christina D. Carpenter (activity book for ages 9-12); and *Mountain View Young Authors Book*, compilation, written for and by kids 9-12 years.

How to Contact/Writers: Fiction/nonfiction: Query. Reports on queries in 1-2 months; ms in 2-6 months. Publishes a book 1 year after acceptance.

Illustration: Works with less than 5 illustrators/year. Uses b&w artwork only. Illustrations only: Query with samples. Contact: Dawn Royer, editor. Reports in 1-2 months or only if interested. Samples returned with SASE.

Photography: Buys stock. Contact: Dawn Royer, editor. Model/property releases required. Uses b&w, 3×5 prints. Submit cover letter, résumé.

Terms: Payment varies. Send galleys to authors; dummies to illustrators. All imprints included in a single catalog. Ms guidelines available for SASE.

Tips: "We publish very few manuscripts per year. Querying us with your ideas for a project is encouraged before submitting your manuscript. We are looking for well-written, innovative works. I would suggest researching the children's literature industry and taking writing classes to help a new author."

ALADDIN PAPERBACKS, 1230 Avenue of the Americas, 4th Floor, New York NY 10020. Paperback imprint of Simon & Schuster Children's Publishing Division.

● Aladdin publishes primarily reprints of successful hardcovers from other Simon & Schuster imprints. They publish very little original material and are unable to consider unsolicited manuscripts; accepting query letters only. Send SASE for writer's and artist's guidelines.

ALYSON PUBLICATIONS, INC., P.O. 4371, Los Angeles CA 90078. (213)871-1788. Fax: (213)467-6805. Book publisher. Editorial Contact: Julie K. Trevelyan. Publishes 4 (projected) picture books/year; 3 (projected) young adult titles/year. "Alyson Wonderland is the line of children's books. We are looking for diverse depictions of family life for children of gay and lesbian parents."

● Alyson has recently been purchased and moved from Boston to L.A. There may be more changes in store.

Fiction: All levels: adventure, animal, contemporary, fantasy, history, humor, multicultural, nature environment, science fiction. Young readers and middle readers: suspense, mystery. Teens: anthology.

Nonfiction: Teens: concept, social issues. "We like books that incorporate all racial, religious and body types, as well as dealing with children with gay and lesbian parents—which all our books must deal with. Our YA books should deal with issues faced by kids growing up gay or lesbian." Published *Heather Has Two Mommies*, by Lesléa Newman; and *Daddy's Wedding*, by Michael Willhoite.

How to Contact/Writers: Submit outline/synopsis and sample chapters (young adults); submit complete manuscript (picture books/young readers). Reports on queries/mss within 3 months. Include SASE.

Illustration: Works with 4 illustrators/year. Reviews mss/illustration packages from artists. Illustrations only: Submit "representative art that can be *kept on file*. Good quality photocopies are OK." Reports only if interested. Samples returned with SASE; samples kept on file.

Terms: Pays authors royalty of 8-12% based on retail price. "We *do* offer advances." Pays illustrators by the project (range: $25-500). Pays photographers per photo (range: $50-300). Book catalog and/or ms guidelines free for SASE.

Tips: "We only publish kids' books aimed at the children of gay or lesbian parents."

AMERICAN BIBLE SOCIETY, 1865 Broadway, New York NY 10023. (212)408-1200. Fax: (212)408-1435. Book publisher. Estab. 1816. Product Design: Christina Murphy. Publishes 2

✱ **THE ASTERISK** before a listing indicates the listing is new in this edition.

picture books/year; 1 young reader/year; 1 young adult/year. Publishes books with spiritual/ religious themes based on the Bible. "Please do not telephone. Submit all samples, résumés, etc. for review via mail."
Nonfiction: All levels: activity books, multicultural, religion, self-help, nature/environment, reference, social issues and special needs. Multicultural needs include intercity lifestyle; African-American, Hispanic/Latino, Native American, Asian; mixed groups (such as choirs, classrooms, church events). "Unsolicited manuscripts will be returned unread! We prefer published writing samples with résumés so that we can contact copywriters when an appropriate project comes up." Recently published *Teach Me, Jesus* children's activity booklet (ages 7-10, full color cover and 16 b&w interior illustrations and activities).
How to Contact/Writers: All mss developed inhouse. Query with résumé and writing samples. Contact: Barbara Bernstengel. Unsolicited mss rejected. No credit lines given.
Illustration: Works with 1 illustrator/year. "Would be more interested in artwork for children and teens which is influenced by the visual 'vocabulary' of videos." Reviews ms/illustration packages from artists. Contact: Christina Murphy. Illustrations only: Query with samples; arrange a personal interview to show portfolio; send "résumés, tearsheets and promotional literature to keep; slides will be returned promptly." Reports on queries within 1 month. Samples returned; samples sometimes filed. Book catalog free on written request.
Photography: Contact: Christina Murphy. Buys stock and assigns work. Looking for "nature, scenic, multicultural, intergenerational people shots particularly interested in seeing photographs from the country of Israel, i.e. natural settings such as the Dead Sea as well as the Christian Easter Procession." Model/property releases required. Uses any size b&w prints; 35mm, 2¼×2¼ and 4×5 transparencies. Photographers should query with samples first before trying to arrange for a personal interview to show portfolio; provide résumé, promotional literature or tearsheets.
Terms: Photographers paid by the project (range: $800-5,000); per photo (range $100-400). Credit line given on most projects. Most photos purchased for all rights basis. Factors used to determine payment for ms/illustration package include "nature and scope of project; complexity of illustration and continuity of work; number of illustrations." Pays illustrators $200-30,000; based on fair market value. Sends 2 complimentary copies of published work to illustrators. ABS owns all publication rights to illustrations and mss.
Tips: Illustrators: "Submit in a form that we can keep on file if we like such as tearsheets, postcards, photocopies, etc."

AMERICAN EDUCATION PUBLISHING, An Imprint of Landoll, Inc., 425 Orange St., Ashland OH 44805. (419)281-5333. Book publisher. Publishes 6-8 picture books/year. 20% of books by first-time authors; 80% of books developed inhouse.
Fiction: Picture books: adventure, animal, concept, contemporary. Young readers: adventure, animal, concept, contemporary, fantasy, folktales, humor. Does not want to see dinosaurs, talking animals and environment.
Nonfiction: Picture books: activity books, animal, concept and science. Young readers: activity books, animal, concept, hobbies and science. Does not want to see dinosaurs, environment.
How to Contact/Writers: Fiction/Nonfiction: Submit outline/synopsis and 3 sample chapters. Reports on queries in 2 months; mss in 3-4 months. Publishes a book 6-8 months after acceptance. Will consider simultaneous submissions and previously published work.
Illustration: Works with 5 illustrators/year. Reviews ms/illustration packages from artists. Submit ms with 2 pieces of final art. Illustrations only: Query with samples, résumé, tearsheets. Reports in 2 months. Samples returned with SASE; samples kept on file. Original artwork returned at job's completion.
Terms: Pays authors royalty of 5-10% based on wholesale price or work purchased outright. Pays illustrators by the project or royalty of 5-10% based on wholesale price. Sends galleys to authors.

ARCHWAY/MINSTREL BOOKS, 1230 Avenue of the Americas, New York NY 10020. (212)698-7000. Fax: (212)698-7337. Imprint of Pocket Books. Book publisher—Minstrel Books (ages 7-11) and Archway Paperbacks (ages 12-16). Vice President/Editorial Director: Patricia MacDonald. Publishes originals and reprints.
Fiction: Middle readers: animal stories, adventures, fantasy, funny school stories, science fiction, thrillers. Young adults: adventure, romance, romantic suspense, contemporary stories, horror, suspense. Recently published (Archway) *The Last Vampire* series, by Christopher Pike and *Fear Street* series, by R.L. Stine; *Summer* series (Minstrel), by Katherine Applegate; *Aliens Are My Homework*, by Bruce Coville; *French Fries Up My Nose*, by M.M. Ragz; and *Dragonling*, by Jackie French Koelle.

Nonfiction: Middle readers: environment, sports. Young adults: sports, popular media figures.
How to Contact/Writers: Fiction/Nonfiction: Query; submit outline/synopsis and sample chapters. SASE mandatory.
Terms: Pays authors in royalties.

*☐ARROYO PROJECTS STUDIO**, 1413 Second St., Santa Fe NM 87501. (505)988-2331. Fax: (505)988-2164. Independent book producer/packager. Editorial Director: Marcy Heller. Creative Director: Sally Blakemore. Publishes 20-40 novelty books/year.
Fiction: Picture books: adventure, animal, concept, contemporary, fantasy, folktales, humor, nature/environment, special needs, sports, suspense/mystery. Young readers: adventure, animal, concept, multicultural, nature/environment, special needs, sports. Middle readers: adventure, animal, multicultural, nature/environment, special needs, sports. Young adult/teens: adventure, animal, multicultural, nature/environment, science fiction, special needs, sports. "Novelty books have minimal text—look at any pop-up books as a guide."
Nonfiction: All levels: activity books, animal, arts/crafts, biography, careers, concept, cooking, geography, health, hi-lo, history, hobbies, how-to, multicultural, music/dance, nature/environment, reference, religion, science, self help, social issues, special needs, sports. Multicultural material must "show real relationships between diverse peoples—no preachy 'how it should be' stuff." Special needs include "human strengths in the face of challenge." Does not want to see fairy or elf stories. Average word length: picture books—300-360; young readers—9,000-10,000; middle readers—9,000.
How to Contact/Writers: Fiction/nonfiction: Query or submit complete ms. Reports on queries/ms in 3 months. Publishes a book 18-24 months after acceptance. Will consider simultaneous submissions and previously published work.
Illustration: Works with 20 illustrators/year. Uses color artwork only. Reviews ms/illustration packages from artists. Query. Send ms with dummy and 3 pieces of final art. Contact: Sally Blakemore, creative director. Illustrations only: Query with samples; send promo sheet, tearsheets, any format. Reports in 3 months. Samples returned with SASE.
Photography: Buys stock. Contact: Edy Keller. Uses photos only relevent to children's novelty books. Model/property releases required; captions required. Uses color prints and 2¼×2¼, 4×5 transparencies. Submit promo piece.
Terms: Authors' payments negotiated per project. Offers advances. Pays illustrators by the project (range: $150-8,000). For photographers and illustrators, "each project is negotiated." Ms and art guidelines available for SASE.
Tips: "Have an original style—no art styles copying latest trends—work from your heart and talent; send only the best five pieces; include complete concepts—submit finished stories or artwork; submit original concepts. We are a start-up company—all projects are in process for spring and fall 1997—Toddler Books, Young Readers, Activity Books."

ATHENEUM BOOKS FOR YOUNG READERS, 1230 Avenue of the Americas, New York NY 10020. (212)698-7200. Simon & Schuster Children's Publishing Division. Book publisher. Vice President/Associate Publisher and Editorial Director: Jonathan Lanman. Editorial Contacts: Anne Schwartz, editorial director of Anne Schwartz books; Marcia Marshall, executive editor; Ana Cerro, associate editor. Publishes 15-20 picture books/year; 4-5 young readers/year; 20-25 middle readers/year; 10-15 young adults/year. 10% of books by first-time authors; 50% of books from agented writers.
Fiction: Picture books and middle readers: animal, contemporary, fantasy. Young readers and young adults: contemporary, fantasy.
Nonfiction: All levels: animal, biography, education, history.
How to Contact/Writers: Fiction/Nonfiction: Query only for all projects. Reports on queries in 6-8 weeks. Publishes a book 18-24 months after acceptance. Will consider simultaneous submissions from previously unpublished authors; "we request that the author let us know it is a simultaneous submission."

☐ **THE OPEN BLOCK** before a listing indicates that the listing is a book packager/producer.

Illustration: Editorial reviews ms/illustration packages from artists. Query first. Illustrations only: Submit résumé, tearsheets. Reports on art samples only if interested.
Terms: Pays authors in royalties of 8-10% based on retail price. Illustrators paid royalty or flat fee depending on the project. Sends galleys to authors; proofs to illustrators. Original artwork returned at job's completion. Ms guidelines for #10 SAE and 1 first-class stamp.

AUGSBURG FORTRESS, PUBLISHERS, 426 S. Fifth St., Box 1209, Minneapolis MN 55440. (612)330-3300. Fax: (612)330-3455. Acquisition Editor: Alice Peppler. Managing Editor: Pam McClanahan. Publishes 3-4 Christian picture books/year; 2 Bible information books/year; 3-4 devotionals/year. 5% of books by first-time authors.
• Augsburg Fortress does not accept unsolicited children's or picture book manuscripts. Writers must query.
Fiction: Looking for picture books of Christian children from American multicultural homes and single parent homes. Also interested in Christmas and Easter picture books.
Nonfiction: Looking for Christian devotions for children; Christian information books on the Bible, people in the Bible, etc.
How to Contact/Writers: Query. Reports in 3 weeks. Publishes a book 1½ years after acceptance. Will consider simultaneous and previously published submissions.
Illustration: Works with 6 illustrators/year. Reviews ms/illustration packages from artists. Contact: Pam McClanahan. Illustrations only: Query with samples, résumé, promo sheet and client list. Reports back in 3 months only if interested. Samples are not returned; samples filed.
Terms: Pays authors royalty. Pays illustrators by the project (range: varies). Originals not returned. Book catalog, ms and artist's guidelines available for SASE.
Tips: "Devotion authors must be familiar with Lutheran and other mainline church denominations. Bible information book authors must have educational or comparable criteria for writing this genre. Be sure to get our ms guidelines before mailing a proposal."

A/V CONCEPTS CORP., 30 Montauk Blvd., Oakdale NY 11769. (516)567-7227. Fax: (516)567-8745. Educational book publisher. Editor: Laura Solimene. President: Phil Solimene. Publishes 6 young readers/year; 6 middle readers/year; 6 young adult titles/year. 20% of books by first-time authors. Primary theme of books and multimedia is classic literature 1 math, science, language arts, self esteem.
Fiction: Middle readers: hi-lo. Young adults: hi-lo, multicultural, special needs. "We hire writers to adapt classic literature."
Nonfiction: All levels: activity books. Young adults: hi-lo, multicultural, science, self help, textbooks. Average word length: middle readers—300-400; young adults—500-950.
How to Contact/Writers: Fiction: Submit outline/synopsis and 1 sample chapter. Reports on queries in 1 month.
Illustration: Works with 4-6 illustrators/year. Reviews ms/illustration packages from artists. Submit ms with 3-4 pieces of final art. Contact: Phil Solimene, president. Illustrations only: Query with samples. Contact: Phil Solimene, president. Reports in 1 month. Samples returned with SASE; samples filed.
Photography: Submit samples.
Terms: Work purchased outright from authors (range $50-1,000). Pays illustrators by the project (range: $50-1,000). Pays photographers per photo (range: $25-250). Ms and art guidelines available for 9×12 SASE.

AVON BOOKS/BOOKS FOR YOUNG READERS (Avon Flare, Avon Camelot, Avon Young Camelot and Avon hard cover), 1350 Avenue of the Americas, New York NY 10019. (212)261-6817. Division of The Hearst Corporation. Book publisher. Executive Editorial Director: Elise Howard. Senior Editor: Gwen Montgomery. Assistant Editor: Stephanie Siegel. Editorial Assistant: Ana Schwartzman. Publishes 12 hard covers, 25-30 middle readers/year; 20-25 young adults/year. 10% of books by first-time authors; 60% of books from agented writers.
Fiction: Middle readers: comedy, contemporary, problem novels, sports, spy/mystery/adventure. Young adults: contemporary, problem novels, romance. Average length: middle readers—100-150 pages; young adults—150-250 pages. Avon does not publish preschool picture books.
Nonfiction: Middle readers: hobbies, music/dance, sports. Young adults: "growing up." Average length: middle readers—100-150 pages; young adults—150-250 pages.
How to Contact/Writers: "Please send for guidelines before submitting." Fiction/nonfiction: Submit outline/synopsis and 3 sample chapters. Reports on mss in 1-2 months. Publishes a book 18-24 months after acceptance. Will consider simultaneous submissions.

Illustration: Very rarely will review ms/illustration packages. Illustrations only: "Send samples we can keep. Need line art."

Terms: Pays authors in royalties of 6% based on retail price. Average advance payment is "very open." Book catalog available for 9×12 SAE and 4 first-class stamps; ms guidelines for #10 SASE.

Tips: "We have three young readers imprints: Young Camelot, books for beginner readers; Avon Camelot, books for the middle grades; Avon Flare, young adults; and Avon hardcover. Our list includes both individual titles and series, with the emphasis in our paperback originals on high quality recreational reading—a fresh and original writing style; identifiable, three-dimensional characters; a strong, well-paced story that pulls readers in and keeps them interested." Writers: "Make sure that you really know what a company's list looks like before you submit work. Is your work in line with what they usually do? Is your work appropriate for the age group that this company publishes for? Keep aware of what's in your bookstore (but not what's in there for too long!)" Illustrators: "Submit work to art directors and people who are in charge of illustration at publishers. This is usually not handled entirely by the editorial department."

B&B PUBLISHING, INC., 820 Wisconsin St., P.O. Box 96, Wallworth WI 53184. (414)275-9474. Fax: (414)275-9530. Book publisher, independent book producer/packager. Managing Director: Katy O'Shea. Publishes 4 young adult titles/year. All titles are nonfiction, educational, usually curriculum related. "Especially interested in geography-based material."

Nonfiction: Middle readers, young adults: biography, careers, concept, geography, history, multicultural, nature/environment, reference, science, social issues. Multicultural needs include smaller ethnic groups, sociological perspective, true stories; no folktales. "Please no personal war experiences, most such material is unsuitable for younger readers." Average word length: middle readers—15,000; young adults—20,000. Recently published *Awesome Almanac™ Ohio*, by Margie Benson and *Awesome Almanac Texas™*, by Suzanne Martin.

How to Contact/Writers: Nonfiction: Query. Submit outline/synopsis and 1 sample chapter. Reports in 3 months. Usually publishes a book 1 year after acceptance. Will consider simultaneous and previously published submissions. "Send SASE or submission will not be acknowledged."

Illustration: Works with 3-4 illustrators/year. Reviews ms/illustration packages from artists. Query. Submit sample chapter with illustration. Contact: Katy O'Shea, managing director. Reports back in 3 months. Illustrations only: Query with samples, resume, promo sheet and tearsheets. Reports only if interested on non-manuscript sample submissions. Samples returned with SASE; samples filed. Original artwork returned at job's completion.

Photography: Buys photos from freelancers. Contact: photo editor. Buys stock and assigns work. Photos used vary by project—wonders of the world, nature/environment, etc. Uses color or b&w prints and 35mm, 2¼×2¼, 4×4 or 8×10 transparencies. Submit cover letter, resume, published samples, stock photo list and promo piece.

Terms: Usually uses work-for-hire contracts for authors. Offers advances (up to $2,000). Pays illustrators by the project. Pays photographers by the project or per photo. Sends galleys to authors; dummies to illustrators. Ms guidelines available for SASE.

BANTAM DOUBLEDAY DELL, Books for Young Readers, 1540 Broadway, New York NY 10036. (212)354-6500. Book publisher Vice President/Publisher: Craig Virden. Deputy Publisher/Editor-in-Chief: Beverly Horowitz. Publishes 16 picture books/year; new line of first choice chapter yearling; 60 middle reader books/year; 60 young adult titles/year. 10% of books by first-time authors; 70% of books from agented writers.

Fiction: Picture books: adventure, animal, contemporary, easy-to-read, fantasy, humor. Young readers: animal, contemporary, humor, easy-to-read, fantasy, sports, suspense/mystery. Middle readers: adventure, animal, contemporary, humor, easy-to-read, fantasy, sports, suspense/mystery. Young adults: adventure, contemporary issues, humor, coming-of-age, suspense/mystery. Published *Brian's Winter*, by Gary Paulsen; *Expecting The Unexpected*, by Mavis Jukes; and *Shadowmaker*, by Joan Lowery Nixon.

Nonfiction: "Bantam Doubleday Dell Books for Young Readers publishes a very limited number of nonfiction titles."

How to Contact/Writers: Submit through the agent only. "All unsolicited manuscripts returned unopened with the following exceptions: Unsolicited manuscripts are accepted for the Delacorte Press Prize for a First Young Adult Novel contest (see Contests and Awards section) and the Marguerite de Angeli Prize for a First Middle Grade Novel contest (see Contests and Awards section)." Reports on queries in 6-8 weeks; mss in 3 months.

Illustration: Number of illustrations used per fiction title varies considerably. Reviews ms/ illustration packages from artists. Query first. Do not send originals. "If you submit a dummy, please submit the text separately." Reports on ms/art samples only if interested. Cannot return samples; samples filed. Illustrations only: Submit tearsheets, résumé, samples that do not need to be returned. Original artwork returned at job's completion.

Terms: Pays authors advance and royalty. Pays illustrators advance and royalty or flat fee.

BARRONS EDUCATIONAL SERIES, 250 Wireless Blvd., Hauppauge NY 11788. (516)434-3311. Fax: (516)434-3723. Book publisher. Estab. 1945. Managing/Acquisitions Editor: Grace Freedson. Publishes 20 picture books/year; 20 young readers/year; 20 middle reader titles/year; 10 young adult titles/year. 25% of books by first-time authors; 25% of books from agented writers.

Fiction: Picture books: animal, concept, multicultural, nature/environment. Young readers: Adventure, multicultural, nature/environment, suspense/mystery. Middle readers: adventure, horror, multicultural, nature/environment, problem novels, suspense/mystery. Young adults: horror, problem novels. Recently published *Red Lace & Yellow Lace*, by Mike Casey, adapted by Judith Herbst, illustrated by Jenny Stanley; and *What in the World is a Homophone?*, by Leslie Presson, illustrated by Jo-Ellen Bosson.

Nonfiction: Picture books: concept, reference. Young readers: how-to, reference, self help, social issues. Middle readers: hi-lo, how-to, reference, self help, social issues. Young adults: how-to, self help, social issues.

How to Contact/Writers: Fiction: Query. Nonfiction: Submit outline/synopsis and sample chapters. "Submissions must be accompanied by SASE for response." Reports on queries in 1 month; mss in 6-8 months. Publishes a book 1 year after acceptance. Will consider simultaneous submissions.

Illustration: Works with 10 illustrators/year. Reviews ms/illustration packages from artists. Query first; 3 chapters of ms with 1 piece of final art, remainder roughs. Contact: Grace Freedson. Illustrations only: Submit tearsheets or slides plus résumé. Reports in 3-8 weeks.

Terms: Pays authors in royalties of 10-16% based on wholesale price or buys ms outright for $2,000 minimum. Pays illustrators by the project based on retail price. Sends galleys to authors; dummies to illustrators. Book catalog, ms/artist's guidelines for 9 × 12 SAE.

Tips: Writers: "We are predominately on the lookout for preschool storybooks and concept books. No YA fiction/romance or novels." Illustrators: "We are happy to receive a sample illustration to keep on file for future consideration. Periodic notes reminding us of your work are acceptable." Children's book themes "are becoming much more contemporary and relevant to a child's day-to-day activities."

✱❀BEACH HOLME PUBLISHERS, 2040 W. 12th Ave., Suite 226, Vancouver, British Columbia V6J 2G2 Canada. (604)733-4868. E-mail: bhp@softwords.bc.ca. Book publisher. Managing Editor: Antonia Banyard. Publishes 1 middle reader/year; 4 young adult titles/year. 20% of books by first-time authors. "We publish primarily regional historical fiction (Northwest region).
   • Beach Holme only accepts work from Canadian writers.

Fiction: Middle readers: contemporary, history, multicultural, nature/environment, poetry. Young adult/teens: contemporary, history, multicultural, nature/environment. Multicultural needs include themes reflecting cultural heritage of the Pacific Northwest, i.e., first nations, Asian, East Indian, etc. Does not want to see generic adventure or mystery with no sense of place. Average word length: middle readers—15-20,000; young adults/teens—30,000-40,000. Recently published *Shabash!*, by Ann Walsh (ages 8-12, young adult fiction); *White Jade Tiger*, by Julie Lawson (ages 10+, young adult fiction); and *Finders Keepers*, by Andrea Spalding (ages 8-12, young adult fiction).

How to Contact/Writers: Fiction: Submit outline/synopsis and 3 sample chapters. Reports on queries in 8-10 weeks; mss in 4-6 months. Publishes a book 18 months-2 years after acceptance. Will consider simultaneous submissions (if specified) and previously published work.

Terms: Pays authors 8-12% royalty based on retail price. Offers advances (average amount: $500). Sends galleys to authors. Book catalog available for 9 × 12 SAE and 3 first-class stamps; ms guidelines available for SASE.

Tips: "Research what we have previously published to familiarize yourself with what we are looking for. Please, be informed."

BEHRMAN HOUSE INC., 235 Watchung Ave., West Orange NJ 07052. (201)669-0447. Fax: (201)669-9769. Book publisher. Project Editor: Adam Siegel. Publishes 3 young reader titles/year; 3 middle reader titles/year; 3 young adult titles/year. 12% of books by first-time authors; 2% of books from agented writers. Publishes books on all aspects of Judaism: history, cultural, textbooks, holidays.

Fiction: All levels: Judaism.

Nonfiction: All levels: Judaism, Jewish educational textbooks. Average word length: young reader—1,200; middle reader—2,000; young adult—4,000. Published *My Jewish Year*, by Adam Fisher (ages 8-9); and *It's a Mitzvah!*, by Bradley Artson (adult).

How to Contact/Writers: Fiction/Nonfiction: Submit outline/synopsis and sample chapters. Reports on queries in 1 month; mss in 2 months. Publishes a book 2½ years after acceptance. Will consider simultaneous submissions.

Illustration: Works with 6 children's illustrators/year. Reviews ms/illustration packages from artists. "Query first." Illustrations only: Query with samples; send unsolicited art samples by mail. Reports on queries in 1 month; mss in 2 months.

Photography: Purchases photos from freelancers. Contact: Adam Siegel. Buys stock and assigns work. Uses photos of families involved in Jewish activities. Uses color and b&w prints. Photographers should query with samples. Send unsolicited photos by mail. Submit portfolio for review.

Terms: Pays authors in royalties of 3-10% based on retail price or buys ms outright for $1,000-5,000. Offers advance. Pays illustrators by the project (range: $500-5,000). Sends galleys to authors; dummies to illustrators. Book catalog free on request.

Tips: Looking for "religious school texts" with Judaic themes.

BESS PRESS, P.O. Box 22388, Honolulu HI 96823. (808)734-7159. Fax: (808)732-3627. E-mail: besspr@aloha.net. Editor: Revé Shapard. Publishes 1-2 picture books/year; 1-2 young readers/year; 0-1 middle readers/year. 60% of books by first-time authors. "Books must be about Hawaii, Asia or the Pacific."

Fiction: Picture books, young readers, middle readers: adventure, animal, anthology, concept, contemporary, folktales, hi-lo, history, humor, multicultural, nature/environment, sports, suspense/mystery. Multicultural material must be specific to Hawaii. Published *The Little Makana*, by Helen M. Dano, illustrated by Wren (ages 3-8); *Too Many Curls*, by Marilyn Kahalewai (ages 3-8, picture book); *Let's Call Him Lau-wili-wili-humuhumu-nukunuku-nukunuku-apuaa-oioi*, by Tim Myers, illustrated by Daryl Arakaki (ages 3-8, picture book).

Nonfiction: Picture books: activity books, concept, multicultural. Young readers: activity books, concept, multicultural, textbooks. Middle readers: activity books, multicultural, textbooks. Published *Filipino Word Book*, by Teresita V. Ramos and Josie Clausen, illustrated by Jerri Asuncion and Boboy Betco (ages 5-11, introductory language book); *Flowers of Hawaii Coloring Book*, by Wren (ages 3-8, coloring book); Keiki's First Books, by Maile and Wren (toddlers, concept books).

How to Contact/Writers: Fiction/Nonfiction: Submit complete ms. Reports on queries in 2 weeks; on mss in 3-4 weeks. Publishes a book 6-12 months after acceptance. Will consider simultaneous submissions and previously published work.

Illustration: Works with 3 illustrators/year. Reviews ms/illustration packages from artists. Submit ms with dummy. Contact: Revé Shapard, editor. Illustrations only: Query with samples. Reports only if interested. Samples returned with SASE; samples filed.

Terms: Pays authors royalty of 2½-10% based on wholesale price or work purchased outright. Pays illustrators by the project, royalty of 2½-5% based on wholesale price. Sends galleys to authors; dummies to illustrators. Original artwork returned at job's completion. Book catalog available for SASE; ms and art guidelines available for SASE.

Tips: Looks for "books with commercial or educational appeal in our primary markets—Hawaii, Asia, the Western United States and libraries."

BETHANY HOUSE PUBLISHERS, 11300 Hampshire Ave. S., Minneapolis MN 55438. (612)829-2500. Book publisher. Children's Book Editor: Rochelle Glöege. Publishes 10 early readers/year; 16 young readers/year; 16 young adults/year. Publishes books with spiritual and religious themes.

MARKET CONDITIONS are constantly changing! If you're still using this book and it is 1998 or later, buy the newest edition of *Children's Writer's & Illustrator's Market* at your favorite bookstore or order directly from Writer's Digest Books.

Fiction: Early readers, middle readers, young adults: adventure, contemporary, problem novels, romance, suspense/mystery. Does not want to see poetry or science fiction. Average word length: early readers—10,000; young readers—20,000; young adults—35,000. Published *Too Many Secrets*, by Patricia H. Rushford (young adult/teens, mystery-adventure series); *Becky's Brainstorm*, by Elaine L. Schulte (young readers, adventure series with strong Christian values theme); *The Double Dabble Surprise*, by Beverly Lewis (early readers, adventure series).

Nonfiction: Middle readers, young adults: religion, self-help, social issues. Published *Can I Be a Christian Without Being Weird?*, by Kevin Johnson (early teens, devotional book); *Dear Judy, Did You Ever Like a Boy (who didn't like you?)*, by Judy Baer (young adult/teen, advice book on social issues).

How to Contact/Writers: Fiction/Nonfiction: Query. Reports on queries in 2 months; mss in 3 months. Publishes a book 12-18 months after acceptance. Will consider simultaneous submissions and previously published work.

Illustration: Works with 8 illustrators/year. Reviews ms/illustration packages from artists. Query. Illustrations only: Query with samples. Reports in 6 weeks. Samples returned with SASE.

Terms: Pays authors royalty based on retail price. Pays illustrators by the project. Sends galleys to authors. Book catalog available for 11 × 14 SAE and 5 first-class stamps.

Tips: "Research the market, know what is already out there. Study our catalog before submitting material. We look for an evangelical message woven delicately into a strong plot and topics that seek to broaden the reader's experience and perspective."

BETHEL PUBLISHING, 1819 S. Main, Elkhart IN 46516. (219)293-8585. Book publisher. Contact: Senior Editor. Publishes 1-2 young readers/year; 1-2 middle readers/year.

Fiction: Young readers: animal, religion. Middle readers and young adults: adventure, religion. Does not want to see "New-Age—Dungeon & Dragons type." Published *Janette Oke Classic Collection*, by Janette Oke (ages 7-12, religion); *Rebecca of Sunnybrook Farm Series*, by Eric Wiggin (juvenile); *Who's New at the Zoo*, by Janette Oke (ages 7-12, religion). Does not want to see workbooks, cookbooks, coloring books, books on theological studies, poetry or preschool/elementary age stories. Average word length: 30,000-50,000.

Nonfiction: Young readers, middle readers and young adults: religion.

How to Contact/Writers: Fiction/Nonfiction: Query. Submit complete ms. Reports on queries in 3 weeks; mss in 3 months. Publishes a book 1 year after acceptance. Will consider simultaneous submissions and previously published work.

Illustration: Works with 2 illustrators/year. Reviews ms/illustration packages from artists. Ms/illustration packages and illustrations only: Query. Reports in 1 month. Samples returned with SASE.

Photography: Purchases photos from freelancers. Contact: Senior Editor. Buys stock. Model/property releases required. Uses color and b&w glossy prints; 35mm and 2¼ × 2¼ transparencies. Photographers should send cover letter.

Terms: Pays authors royalty of 5-10% on wholesale price. Pays illustrators by the project. Photographers paid by the project. Sends galleys to authors. Originals not returned. Book catalog available for 9 × 12 SAE and 3 first-class stamps. Ms guidelines available for SASE. Artist's guidelines not available.

BLACKBIRCH PRESS, INC./BLACKBIRCH GRAPHICS, INC., 260 Amity Rd., Woodbridge CT 06525. Fax: (203)389-1596. Book publisher, independent book producer/packager. Editorial Director: Bruce Glassman. Art Director: Sonja Kalter. Publishes 20 middle readers; 70 young adult titles. 15% of books by first-time authors.

Nonfiction: Picture books: animal, concept, geography, history, nature/environment, science. Young readers: animal, biography, geography, multicultural, nature/environment, special needs. Middle readers and young adults: geography, nature/environment, reference, special needs. Does not want to see dogs, spiritual, medical themes. Average word length: young adult readers—8,000-10,000; middle readers—5,000-7,000. Recently published *Mount Rushmore*, *Marine Biologist* (ages 8-10); and *Lennon & McCartney* (ages 11-15).

How to Contact/Writers: Nonfiction: Query. SASE "if material needs to be returned." Reports on queries in 2 months. Publishes a book 1 year after acceptance. Will consider simultaneous submissions.

Illustration: Works with 10 illustrators/year. Uses color artwork only. Reviews ms/illustration packages from artists. Submit query. Contact: senior editor. Illustrations only: Query with samples; send résumé, promo sheet. Reports in 1 month. Samples not returned; samples filed.

Photography: Buys photos from freelancers. Contact: Sonja Kalter, art director. Buys stock and assigns work. Uses animal, human culture, geography. Captions required. Uses 35mm,

2¼×2¼, 4×5 transparencies. Submit cover letter, published samples and promo piece.

Terms: Pays authors royalty or work purchased outright from author. Offers advances. Pays illustrators by the project or royalty. Pays photographers by the project, per photo or royalty. Original artwork returned at job's completion. Book catalog available for 8×10 SAE and 2 first-class stamps. Ms guidelines available for SASE.

✤**BLIZZARD PUBLISHING**, 73 Furby St., Winnipeg, Manitoba R3L 2A2 Canada. (204)775-2923. Fax: (204)775-2947. E-mail: atwood@blizzard.mb.ca. Website: http://www.blizzard.mb.ca/catalog/. Book publisher. Acquisitions Assistant: Todd Scarth. Publishes 2-3 picture books/year; 1-2 young readers/year; 1-2 middle readers/year; 1-2 young adult titles/year. 20% of books by first-time authors.

Fiction: Picture books: folktales, humor. Young readers: fantasy, folktales, humor, nature/environment, science fiction. Middle readers, young adult/teens: contemporary, fantasy, folktales, humor, nature/environment, science fiction.

Nonfiction: Young readers, middle readers, young adult: biography, cooking, history, nature/environment.

How to Contact/Writers: Query; submit outline/synopsis. Reports on queries in 2-3 months; mss in 4-5 months. Publishes a book 1 year after acceptance. Will consider electronic submissions via disk or modem.

Illustration: Works with 2-3 illustrators/year. Reviews ms/illustration packages from artists. Send ms with dummy. Contact: Todd Scarth, acquisitions editor. Illustrations only: Query with samples. Reports only if interested. Samples returned with SASE; samples filed.

Terms: Pays authors 10% royalty based on retail price. Offers advances. Pays illustrators 10% royalty based on retail price. Sends galleys to authors. Original artwork returned at job's completion. Book catalog free for legal-size SAE and 2 Canadian stamps (or IRC); ms guidelines available for SASE.

Tips: "Secondary materials (reviews, etc.) are important to us. The more we know about you, the better. Submit *only* nonfiction in age-appropriate subjects."

BLUE SKY PRESS, 555 Broadway, New York NY 10012. (212)343-6100. Book publisher. Imprint of Scholastic Inc. Contact: Editorial Submissions. Publishes 8 picture books/year; 2 young adult titles/year. 1% of books by first-time authors. Publishes various categories.

   • Blue Sky's title *Her Stories*, by Virginia Hamilton, received the 1996 Coretta Scott King author award. For more on the renowned writer see Virginia Hamilton's Work: Blending the Known, the Remembered and the Imagined on page 37.

Fiction: Picture books: adventure, animal, concept, contemporary, fantasy, folktales, history, humor, multicultural, nature/environment, poetry. Young readers: adventure, anthology, contemporary, fantasy, folktales, history, humor, multicultural, nature/environment, poetry. Young adults: adventure, anthology, contemporary, fantasy, history, humor, multicultural, poetry. Multicultural needs include "strong fictional or nonfictional themes featuring non-white characters and cultures." Does not want to see mainstream religious, bibliotherapeutic, adult. Average length : picture books—varies; young adults—150 pages. Recently published *The Sorcerer's Apprentice*, by Nancy Willard, illustrated by Leo and Diane Dillon (ages 7 and up, picture book); *Freak the Mighty*, by Rodman Philbrick (ages 8 and up, young adult, middle readers); and *How Georgie Radbourn Saved Baseball*, by David Shannon (ages 5 and up, picture book).

Nonfiction: Picture books: animal, biography, concept, history, multicultural, nature/environment. Young readers: biography, history, multicultural, nature/environment. Young adults: biography, history, multicultural. Nonfiction multicultural themes "usually best handled in biography format." Average length: picture books—varies; young adults 150 pages. "Often there is a nonfiction element to Blue Sky Press fiction picture books; otherwise we have not yet published nonfiction."

How to Contact/Writers: "Due to large numbers of submissions, we are discouraging unsolicited submissions—send query (don't call!) only if you feel certain we publish the type of book you have written." Fiction: Query (novels), submit complete ms (picture books). Reports on

✤ **THE MAPLE LEAF** before a listing indicates that the market is Canadian.

queries/mss in 6 months. Publishes a book 1-3 years after acceptance; depending on chosen illustrator's schedule. Will not consider simultantous submissions.

Illustration: Works with 10 illustrators/year. Uses both b&w and color artwork. Reviews ms/illustration packages "only if illustrator is the author." Submit ms with dummy. Contact: Editorial Submissions. Illustrations only: Query with samples, tearsheets. Reports only if interested. Samples returned with SASE. Original artwork returned at job's completion.

Photography: Buys photos from freelancers. Contact: Photo Research Department. Buys stock and assigns work. Uses photos to accompany nonfiction. Model/property releases required. Captions required. Submit cover letter, résumé, client list, stock photo list.

Terms: Author's royalty varies by project—usually standard trade rates. Offers variable advance. Pays illustrators by the project or standard royalty based on retail price. Pays photographers by the project or royalty.

Tips: "Read currently published children's books. Revise—never send a first draft. Find your own voice, style, and subject. With material from new people we look for a theme or style strong enough to overcome the fact that the author/illustrator is unknown in the market. Children's book publishers are becoming more selective, looking for irresistible talent and fairly broad appeal; yet most are still willing to take risks, just to keep the game interesting."

☐**BOINGO BOOKS, INC.**, 339 Park Ave., Park Ridge NJ 07656. Also, 3857 Coral Tree Circle, Suite 208, Coconut Creek FL 33073. (305)979-1085. Fax: (305)979-1354. Book producer. Creative Director: Lisa McCourt. Submissions Editor: Aimee Foster. Produces mostly trade picture books for major children's book publishers. Averages 30 titles/year. 10% by first-time authors.

Fiction/Nonfiction: "Our specific needs change frequently. Before submitting, please obtain current guidelines by sending a #10 SASE to Aimee Foster at the New Jersey address listed above.

How to Contact/Writers: Fiction and Nonfiction: Send entire ms to Aimee Foster, Submissions Editor, 339 Park Ave., Park Ridge NJ 07656. Reports within 3 months. All submissions must include SASE. Guidelines available for #10 SASE.

Illustration: Works with 30 illustrators/year. Uses color artwork only. "We use a wide variety of styles." Reviews mss/illustration packages from artists. Submit with dummy or submit ms with copies of some final art. Illustrations only: Send samples, résumé, promo sheet, client list to the Florida address above. Samples are filed unless illustrator has included a SASE and "requested the return of the materials." Contact: Lisa McCourt.

Photography: Buys photos from freelancers. Contact: Lisa McCourt. Works on assignment only. Submit résumé, client list, samples or promo pieces.

Terms: All contracts negotiated separately; offers variable advance.

Tips: "Please do not submit until you have obtained our most current guidelines, as our needs tend to be specific and change frequently."

BOYDS MILLS PRESS, 815 Church St., Honesdale PA 18431. (800)490-5111. Fax: (717)253-0179. Imprint: Wordsong (poetry). Book publisher. Manuscript Coordinator: Beth Troop. Art Director: Tim Gillner. 5% of books from agented writers.

Fiction: All levels: adventure, contemporary, history, humor. Picture books, young readers, middle readers: animal. Young readers, middle readers, young adult: poetry. Middle readers, young adults: problem novels. Multicultural themes include any story showing a child as an integral part of a culture and which provides children with insight into a culture they otherwise might be unfamiliar with. "Please query us on the appropriateness of suggested topics for middle grade and young adult. For all other submissions send entire manuscript." Does not want to see talking animals, coming-of-age novels, romance and fantasy/science fiction. Recently published *Imitate the Tiger*, by Jan Cheripko (ages 12-up, problem novel); and *The Jade Horse*, by Ann Tompert (ages 6-9, multicultural, picture book).

Nonfiction: All levels: nature/environment. Does not want to see reference/curricular text. Recently published *Harvest Year*, by Cris Peterson (ages 3-7, nature/environment).

How to Contact/Writers: Fiction/Nonfiction: Submit complete manuscript or submit through agent. Query on middle reader, young adult and nonfiction. Reports on queries/mss in 1 month.

Illustration: Works with 25 illustrators/year. Reviews ms/illustration packages from artists. Submit complete ms with 1 or 2 pieces of art. Illustrations only: Query with samples; send résumé and slides.

Photography: Assigns work. Contact: Tim Gillner, art director.

Terms: Authors paid royalty or work purchased outright. Offers advances. Illustrators paid by the project or royalties; varies. Photographers paid by the project per photo, or royalties; varies. Mss/artist's guidelines available for #10 SASE.

Tips: "Picture books—with fresh approaches, not work themes—are our strongest need at this time. Check to see what's already on the market before submitting your story. An increasing number of publishers seem to be closing their doors to unsolicited submissions, but at the same time, many new publishing houses are starting. Sometimes a new author can get a foot in the door with a new or small house, then develop credentials for approaching bigger houses. Authors should keep this in mind when looking for a publisher."

BRIGHT RING PUBLISHING, 1900 N. Shore Dr., Box 5768, Bellingham WA 98227-5768. (206)734-1601 or (800)480-4ART. Fax: (206)676-1271. Estab. 1985. Editor: MaryAnn Kohl. Publishes 1 young reader title/year. 50% of books by first-time authors. Uses only recipe format— "but no cookbooks unless woven into another subject like art, music, science."

Nonfiction: Young readers and middle readers: activity books involving art ideas, hobbies, cooking, how-to, multicultural, music/dance, nature/environment, science. "No picture books, no poetry, no stories of any kind and no crafts." Average length: "about 125 ideas/book." Multicultural needs include: arts of world cultures or relate to kids' literature. "We are moving into only recipe-style resource books in any variety of subject areas—useful with children 2-12. Interested in integrated art with other subjects." Recently published: SCRIBBLE ART: *Independent Creative Art Experiences for Children*; MUDWORKS: *Creative Clay, Dough, and Modeling Experiences*; and SCIENCE ARTS: *Discovering Science Through Art Experiences* (all by Mary Ann Kohl).

How to Contact/Writers: Nonfiction: submit complete ms. Reports on queries in 2 weeks; mss in 6 weeks. Publishes a book 1 year after acceptance. Will consider simultaneous submissions.

Illustration: Works with 2 illustrators/year. Prefers to review "black line (drawings) for text." Reviews ms/illustration packages from artists. "Query first." Illustrations only: Query with samples; send tearsheets and "sample of ideas I request after query." Reports in 6-8 weeks.

Terms: Pays authors in royalties of 3-10% based on net sales. Work purchased outright (range: $500-2,000). Pays illustrators $500-2,000. Also offers "free books and discounts for future books." Book catalog, ms/artist's guidelines for business-size SAE and 29¢ postage.

Tips: "Bright Ring Publishing is not looking for picture books, juvenile fiction, or poetry at this time. We are, however, highly interested in creative activity and resource books for children to use independently or for teachers and parents to use with children. Must work for pre-school through age 12." We cannot accept book ideas which require unusual packaging such as attached toys or unique binding or paper."

BROADMAN & HOLMAN PUBLISHERS, Baptist Sunday School Board, 127 Ninth Ave. N., Nashville TN 37234. Fax: (615)251-3752. Book publisher. Acquisitions & Development Editor: Janis M. Whipple. Publishes 4 middle readers/year; 4 young adult titles/year. 25% of books by first-time authors. "All books have Christian values/themes."

Fiction: Middle readers, young adult: adventure, concept, contemporary, humor, problem novels, religion, sports, suspense/mystery.

Nonfiction: Picture books: activity books, religion. Middle readers, young adults: biography, health, how-to, reference, self-help, social issues, sports. All levels: religion.

Special needs include books on parenting or friendship with special-needs children. Average word length: middle readers—30,000; young adults—45,000-60,000. Recently published *258 Great Dates While You Wait*, by Susie Shellenberger and Greg Johnson (dating book for teens); *First Days in High School* and *First Days of College*, both by Mary Sayler (devotional books for young adult/teens); *Real Kids, Real Adventures*, by Deborah Morris (real life adventure stories about kids for middle readers).

How to Contact/Writers: Nonfiction: Query, submit outline/synopsis and 2 sample chapters. Reports on queries in 4-6 weeks; mss in 2 months. Publishes a book 1 year after acceptance. Will consider simultaneous submissions.

Illustration: Works with 1-2 illustrators/year. Samples returned with SASE; samples filed.

Terms: Pays authors royalty 12-20% based on wholesale price. Offers variable advance. Sends galleys to authors. Original artwork returned at job's completion. Book catalog available for 9 × 12 SAE and 2 first-class stamps. Ms guidelines available for SASE.

Tips: "We're looking for fiction and nonfiction Christian issues/devotions for middle readers and teens. Write us asking for guidelines before submitting. We prefer a proposal to a full manuscript for middle readers and teens."

*CALLAWAY EDITIONS, INC., 70 Bedford St., New York NY 10014. (212)929-5212. Fax: (212)929-8087. Independent book producer/packager. Editor-in-Chief: Nicholas Callaway. Imprints: Callaway & Kirk Company (Editor-in-Chief: Nicholas Callaway). Publishes 5 picture books/year; 1 middle reader/year. 60% of books by first-time authors.
Fiction: Picture books: adventure, animal, fantasy, folktales, humor, nature/environment. Young readers: adventure, contemporary, fantasy, folktales, history, humor, nature/environment, suspense/mystery. Middle readers: adventure, contemporary, fantasy, folktales, history, nature/environment, problem novels, science fiction, suspense/mystery. Average word length: picture books—750 words; middle readers—20,000 words. Recently published *Miss Spider's Wedding*, written and illustrated by David Kirk (age 2-10, picture book with rhymes); and *Miss Spider's Tea Party*, written and illustrated by David Kirk (age 2-10, picture book with rhymes).
How to Contact/Writers: Submit complete ms. Reports on queries in 2-4 weeks; mss in 1-2 months. Publishes book 10 months after acceptance. Will consider simultaneous submissions.
Illustration: Works with 3 illustrators/year. Uses color artwork only. Reviews ms/illustration packages from artists. Send ms with dummy; submit ms with 5 pieces of final art. Contact: Nicholas Callaway, editor-in-chief. Illustration only: Query with samples. Contact: Nicholas Callaway, editor-in-chief. Reports back only if interested. Samples not returned; samples filed.
Tips: "The closer to a finished product, with text and illustrations (color photocopies, no originals), the better. Our projects are very high quality, and proposals to us should reflect that quality also. If you do not have your own illustrations, try to have an idea of whom you would like to get, or the style you would like to eventually use. Do not call us a thousand times—we will be in touch as soon as we can."

CANDLEWICK PRESS, 2067 Massachusetts Ave., Cambridge MA 02140. (617)661-3330. Fax: (617)661-0565. Children's book publisher. Senior Editor: Mary Lee Donovan; Editor: Susan Halperin; Art Director: Gill Willis; Senior Designer: Anne Moore. Publishes 120 picture books/year; 6 young readers/year; 10 middle readers/year; and 6 young adult titles/year. 5% of books by first-time authors.
● Candlewick's book, *In the Rain with Baby Duck*, by Amy Hest, illustrated by Jill Barton, received the 1996 Boston Globe-Horn Book Award for a picture book.
Fiction: Picture books, young readers: animal, concept, contemporary, fantasy, folktales, history, humor, multicultural, nature/environment, poetry. Middle readers, young adults: animal, anthology, contemporary, fantasy, history, humor, multicultural, poetry, science fiction, sports, suspense/mystery.
Nonfiction: Picture books: activity books, concept, biography, geography, nature/environment. Young readers: activity books, biography, geography, nature/environment.
How to Contact/Writers: Candlewick Press is not accepting queries or unsolicited mss at this time. Publishes a book 12-18 months after acceptance.
Illustration: Works with 10-20 illustrators/year. "We prefer to see a variety of the artist's style." Reviews ms/illustration packages from artists. "General samples only please." Illustrations only: Submit résumé and portfolio to the attention of Brandy Button. Reports on samples in 4-6 weeks. Samples returned with SASE; samples filed.
Terms: Pays authors royalty of 2.5-10% based on retail price. Offers advances. Pays illustrators 2.5-10% royalty based on retail price. Sends galleys to authors; dummies to illustrators. Photographers paid 2.5-10% royalty. Original artwork returned at job's completion.

*CAPSTONE PRESS INC., P.O. Box 669, Mankato MN 56002. (507)388-6650. Fax: (507)625-4662. Book publisher. Acquisitons: Helen Moore. Imprints: Capstone Press, Bridgestone Books (both Helen Moore, acquisitions). Publishes 36 picture books/year; 48 young readers/year; 48 middle readers/year; 48 young adult titles/year. 15% of books by first-time authors.
Nonfiction: All levels: activity books, animal, arts/crafts, biography, careers, concept, cooking, geography, health, hi-lo, history, hobbies, how-to, multicultural, music/dance, nature/environment, reference, science, self help, social issues, sports. Average word length: picture book—100-500 words; young readers—500-1,200 words; middle readers—2,500-3,500 words; young adults—2,500-3,500 words. Recently published *African-American Inventors*, by Fred Amram (ages 5-8); *The Quarter Horse*, by Gail B. Stewart (ages 5-8); and *Abraham Lincoln*, by T.M. Usel.

How to Contact/Writers: Query; submit outline/synopsis. Reports on queries in 3 weeks; mss in 6 weeks. Publishes a book 18 months after acceptance. Will consider simultaneous submissions, electronic submissions via disk or modem or previously published work.

Photographers: Buys stock and assigns work. Contact: Helen Moore, acquisitions. Model/property release required. Uses 4×5, 8×10 transparencies. Submit slides, stock photo list.

Terms: Work purchased outright for $500-1,000. Photographers paid by the project, per photo. Originals returned to artist at job's completion. Book catalog available for SAE; ms guidelines available for SASE.

Tips: "See catalog prior to submitting."

CAROLINA WREN PRESS/LOLLIPOP POWER BOOKS, 120 Morris St., Durham NC 27701. (919)560-2738. Book publisher. Carolina Wren, Estab. 1976; Lollipop Power, Estab. 1971. Both are nonprofit, small presses. Children's Editor: Ruth A. Smullin. Designer: Martha Scotford. Publishes an average of 1 picture book/year.

Fiction: Picture books: bilingual (English/Spanish), multicultural, multiracial, nonsexist. Average length: 30 pages.

How to Contact/Writers: "Query and request guidelines; enclose SASE with request. All manuscripts must be typed, double-spaced and accompanied by SASE of appropriate size with sufficient postage. If you do not wish your manuscript returned, you may simply enclose SASE for our response. Do not send illustrations." Reports on queries/ms in 3 months. Publishes a book 2-3 years after acceptance.

Illustration: Reviews ms/illustration packages from artists. Contact: Martha Scotford, designer. Illustration only: Query with tearsheets. Reports on art samples only if SASE enclosed.

Terms: Pays authors and illustrators in royalties of 5% of print-run based on retail price, or cash, if available. Original artwork returned at job's completion.

Tips: "Lollipop Power Books offer alternative points of view to prevailing stereotypes. Our books show children: girls and women who are self-sufficient, with responsibilities beyond those of home and family; boys and men who are emotional and nurturing and involved in domestic responsibilities; families that use day care or alternative child care; families that consist of one parent only, working parents, or extended families; realistic portrayals of children of all races and ethnic groups, who have in common certain universal feelings and experiences. We believe that children must be taken seriously. Our books present their problems honestly and without condescension. Lollipop Power Books must be well-written stories that will appeal to children. We are not interested in preachy tales where message overpowers plot and character. We are looking for good stories told from a child's point of view. Our current publishing priorities are: a) African-American, Hispanic or Native American characters; b) bilingual books (English/Spanish); c) books that show gay men or lesbian women as ordinary people who can raise children. To request a catalog, send a 9×12 envelope with postage sufficient for two ounces."

CAROLRHODA BOOKS, INC., 241 First Ave. N., Minneapolis MN 55401. (612)332-3344. Book publisher. Estab. 1969. Submissions Editor: Rebecca Poole. Publishes 5 picture books/year; 25 young reader titles/year; 30 middle reader titles/year. 20% of books by first-time authors; 10% of books from agented writers.

Fiction: Picture books: folktales, multicultural, nature/environment. Young readers, middle readers: historical, special needs. Average word length: picture books—1,000-1,500; young readers—2,000. Recently published *Everybody Bakes Bread*, by Norah Dooley and *A Place to Belong*, by Emily Crofford.

Nonfiction: Young readers, middle readers: animal, biography, history, hobbies, multicultural, nature/environment, science, social issues, special needs. Multicultural needs include biographies. Average word length: young readers— 2,000; middle readers—6,000. Recently published *The Road to Seneca Falls: A Story About Elizabeth Cady Stanton*; and *Grand Canyon*, by Patrick Cone.

How to Contact/Writers: Fiction/Nonfiction: Submit complete ms. Reports on queries in 3-4 weeks; mss in 3 months. Publishes a book 18 months after acceptance. Will consider simultaneous submissions. Must enclose SASE.

Illustration: "Do not send originals. We like illustrators to send samples we can keep on file." Reviews ms/illustration packages from artists. Submit at least 1 sample illustration (in form of photocopy, slide, duplicate photo) with full ms. Contact: Rebecca Poole, submissions editor. Illustrations only: Query with samples; send résumé/slides. Reports on art samples only if interested. Samples kept on file.

Photography: Purchases photos from freelancers. Buys stock and assigns work.
Terms: Buys ms outright for variable amount. Factors used to determine final payment for illustrations: color vs. b&w, number of illustrations, quality of work. Sends galleys to authors; dummies to illustrators. Book catalog available for 9×12 SAE and 3 first-class stamps; ms guidelines for #10 SAE and 1 first-class stamp.
Tips: Writers: "Research the publishing company to be sure it is in the market for the type of book you're interested in writing. Familiarize yourself with the company's list. We specialize in beginning readers, photo essays and books published in series. We do very few single-title picture books and no novels. For more detailed information about our publishing program, consult our catalog. We do not publish any of the following: textbooks, workbooks, songbooks, puzzles, plays and religious material. In general, we suggest that you steer clear of alphabet books; preachy stories with a moral to convey; stories featuring anthropomorphic protagonists ('Amanda the Amoeba,' 'Frankie the Fire Engine,' 'Tonie the Tornado'); and stories that revolve around trite, unoriginal plots. Be sure to avoid racial and sexual stereotypes in your writing, as well as sexist language." (See also Lerner Publications.)

CHARIOT BOOKS, 4050 Lee Vance View, Colorado Springs CO 80918. (719)536-3280. An imprint of Chariot Family Products and a division of David C. Cook Publishing Co. Book publisher. Managing Editor: Liz Duckworth. Publishes 20-30 picture books/year; 6-8 young readers/year; 10-15 middle readers/year; 4-6 young adult titles/year. Less than 5% of books by first-time authors; 15% of books from agented authors. "All books have overt Christian values, but there is no primary theme."
   • Chariot does not read unsolicited manuscripts. Writers must query.
Illustration: Works with 20 illustrators/year. "Send color material I can keep." Query with samples; send résumé, promo sheet, portfolio, tearsheets. Reports only if interested. Samples returned with SASE; samples filed.
Terms: Pays illustrators by the project, royalty or work purchased outright. Sends dummies to illustrators. Original artwork returned at job's completion. Ms guidelines available for SASE.

CHARLESBRIDGE, 85 Main St., Watertown MA 02172. (617)926-0329. Fax: (617)926-5720. Book publisher. Publishes educational programs and supplementary materials as well as trade picture books and board books. Managing Editor: Elena Dworkin Wright. Publishes nature or science picture books.
Nonfiction: Picture books: geography, language arts, math/counting, environment, science, school materials. "We look for a cognitive-based curricula that has been field-tested in more than the author's classroom." Average word length: picture books—1,500. Recently published: *The M&M Counting Book*, by Barbara McGrath (picture book); and *Insights: Reading as Thinking* (K-8 program).
How to Contact/Writers: Submit proposal. Reports on queries/mss in 6 months. Publishes a book 1-2 years after acceptance.
Illustration: Works with 2 illustrators/year. Uses color artwork only. Illustrations only: Query with samples; provide résumé, tearsheets to be kept on file. "Send no original artwork, please." Reports back only if interested.
Terms: Pays authors in royalties or work purchased outright. Pays illustrators by the project. Manuscript/art guidelines available for SASE.
Tips: Wants "books that have humor and are factually correct. Concerning educational material, we want to integrate the reading of good stories with instructional material."

CHICAGO REVIEW PRESS, 814 N. Franklin St., Chicago IL 60610. (312)337-0747. Book publisher. Editorial Director: Cynthia Sherry. Art Director: Joan Sommers. Publishes 1 middle reader/year; "about 4" young adult titles/year. 50% of books by first-time authors; 30% of books from agented authors. "We publish activity books for young children and project books in the arts and sciences for ages 10 and up (our Ziggurat Series). We do not publish fiction."

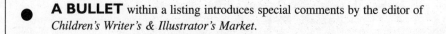

A BULLET within a listing introduces special comments by the editor of *Children's Writer's & Illustrator's Market*.

Nonfiction: Young readers, middle readers and young adults: activity books, arts/crafts. "We're interested in hands-on, educational books; anything else probably will be rejected." Average length: young readers and young adults—175 pages. Recently published *Westward Ho!*, by Laurie Carlson (ages 4-12); *Why Design? Activities & Projects From The National Building Museum*, by Anna Slafer and Kevin Cahill (ages 12 and up) and *Video Cinema: Techniques and Projects for Beginning Filmmakers*, by John Parris Frantz (ages 11 and up). Reports on queries/mss in 2 months. Publishes a book 1-2 years after acceptance. Will consider simultaneous submissions and previously published work.

How to Contact/Writers: Reports on queries/mss in 2 months.

Illustration: Works with 4 illustrators/year. Uses primarily b&w artwork. Reviews ms/illustration packages from artists. Submit 1-2 chapters of ms with corresponding pieces of final art. Illustrations only: Query with samples, résumé. Contact: Joan Sommers, art director. Reports back only if interested. Samples not returned; samples filed.

Photography: Buys photos from freelancers ("but not often"). Contact: Joan Summers, art director. Buys stock and assigns work. Wants "instructive photos. We consult our files when we know what we're looking for on a book-by-book basis." Uses b&w prints.

Terms: Pays authors royalty of 7½-12½% based on retail price. Offers advances ("but not always") of $500-1,500. Pays illustrators by the project (range varies considerably). Pays photographers by the project (range varies considerably). Sends galleys to authors. Original artwork "usually" returned at job's completion. Book catalog/ms guidelines available for $3.

Tips: "We're looking for original activity books for small children and the adults caring for them—new themes and enticing projects to occupy kids' imaginations and promote their sense of personal creativity. We like activity books that are as much fun as they are constructive. For older kids, age 10 and up, we publish Ziggurat Books—activity books geared to teach a discipline in the arts or sciences. Our Ziggurat books are intended to encourage children to pursue interests and talents inspired but not thoroughly covered by their schoolwork or other influences. When a kid becomes curious about say, videography or graphic design, we want to provide the challenging hands-on book that will cultivate enthusiasm while teaching him or her all about that intriguing subject. We are also providing teachers with a myriad of projects for various subjects taught in the classroom. Please write for guidelines so you'll know what we're looking for."

CHILDREN'S BOOK PRESS, 246 First St. #101, San Francisco CA 94105. (415)995-2200. Contact: Submissions Editor. Publishes 6-8 picture books/year. 50% of books by first-time authors. "Children's Book Press is a nonprofit publisher of multicultural and bilingual children's literature. We publish folktales and contemporary stories reflecting the traditions and culture of the emerging majority in the United States and from countries around the world. Our goal is to help broaden the base of children's literature in this country to include more stories from the African-American, Asian-American, Hispanic and Native American communities as well as the diverse Spanish-speaking communities throughout the Americas."

Fiction: Picture books, middle readers, young adults: contemporary, multicultural. Average word length: picture books—800-1,600.

How to Contact/Writers: Fiction: Submit complete ms to Submissions Editor. Reports on queries in 2-4 months, mss in 1-4 months. Publishes a book 1 year after acceptance. Will consider simultaneous submissions.

Illustration: Works with 4-8 illustrators/year. Uses color artwork only. Reviews ms/illustration packages from artists. Send ms with 3 or 4 color photocopies. Illustrations only: Send slides. Reports in 1-12 months. Samples returned with SASE.

Terms: Pays authors royalty. Pays illustrators by the project. Original artwork returned at job's completion. Book catalog available for SAE; ms guidelines available for SASE.

Tips: "Vocabulary level should be approximately third grade (eight years old) or below. Keep in mind, however, that many of the young people who read our books may be nine, ten, or eleven years old or older. Their life experiences are often more advanced than their reading level, so try to write a story that will appeal to a fairly wide age range. We are especially interested in humorous stories and original stories about contemporary life from the multicultural communities mentioned above by writers *from* those communities."

CHILDRENS PRESS, Sherman Turnpike, Danbury CT 06816. (203)797-3500. Book publisher. Creative Director: M. Fiddle. Publishes more than 100 titles/year. 5% of books by first-time authors. Publishes informational (nonfiction) for K-6; picture books for young readers K-3.

● Childrens Press is not accepting fiction or nonfiction submissions during 1997.

Fiction: Picture books, young readers: adventure, animal, concept, contemporary, folktales, multicultural. Middle readers: contemporary, hi-lo, humor, multicultural. Young adults: hi-lo.

Does not want to see young adult fiction, romance or science fiction. Average word length: picture book—300; middle readers—4,000.

Nonfiction: Picture books: arts/crafts, biography, concept, geography, hi-lo, history, hobbies, how-to, multicultural, nature/environment, science, special needs. Young readers: animal, arts/crafts, biography, careers, concept, geography, health, hi-lo, history, hobbies, multicultural, nature/environment, science, social issues, sports. Middle readers: hi-lo, history, multicultural, reference, science. Average word length: picture books—400; young readers—2,000; middle readers—8,000; young adult—12,000.

How to Contact/Writers: Fiction: Query; submit outline/synopsis or submit outline/synopsis and 1 sample chapter. Nonfiction: Query; submit outline/synopsis. SASE required for response. Reports in 2-3 months. Publishes book 18 months after acceptance. Will consider simultaneous submissions.

Illustration: Works with 14 illustrators/year. Uses color artwork only. Reviews ms/illustration packages from artists. Illustrations only: Query with samples or arrange personal portfolio review. Contact: V. Fischman, art director. Reports back only if interested. Samples returned with SASE. Samples filed. Originals not returned.

Photography: Purchases photos from freelancers. Contact: Photo Editor. Buys stock and assigns work. Model/property releases and captions required. Uses color and b&w prints; $2\frac{1}{4} \times 2\frac{1}{4}$, 35mm transparencies. Photographers should send cover letter and stock photo list.

Terms: Pays authors royalty of 5% based on net or work purchased outright (range: $500-1,000). Offers average advances of $1,000. Pays illustrators by the project (range: $1,800-3,500). Photographers paid per photo (range: $50-100). Sends galleys to authors; dummies to illustrators. Book catalog available for SAE; ms guidelines for SASE.

Tips: "Never write down to reader; keep language lively."

CHILDREN'S WRITER'S & ILLUSTRATOR'S MARKET, 1507 Dana Ave., Cincinnati OH 45207. (513)531-2690, ext. 546. E-mail: wdigest@aol.com. Publication of Writer's Digest Books. Editor: Alice P. Buening. Annual directory of freelance markets for children's writers, illustrators and photographers.

Illustration: Send samples—photographs, tearsheets or good quality photocopies of artwork. Continuous tone b&w artwork reproduces best. Since *Children's Writer's & Illustrator's Market* is published only once a year, submissions are kept on file for the upcoming edition until selections are made. Material is then returned by SASE.

Terms: Buys one-time rights to 8-12 illustrations/year. Pays $50 to holder of reproduction rights and free copy of *CWIM* when published.

Tips: "I need examples of art that have been sold to one of the listings in *CWIM*. Thumb through the book for examples. The art must have been freelanced; it cannot have been done as staff work. Include the name of the listing that purchased the work, what the art was used for and the payment you received."

CHRISTIAN ED. PUBLISHERS, P.O. Box 26639, San Diego CA 92196. (619)578-4700. Book publisher. Managing Editor: Carol Rogers. Publishes 64 curriculum titles/year.

Fiction: Picture books and young readers: contemporary. Middle readers: adventure, contemporary, suspense/mystery. "We publish fiction for Bible club take-home papers."

Nonfiction: Publishes Bible curriculum and take-home papers for all ages. Recently published *Jet Flight Take-Home Papers*, by Treena Herrington and Letitia Zook, illustrated by Beverly Warren (Bible club curriculum for grades 4-6); and *Honeybees Classroom Activity Sheets*, by Janet Miller and Wanda Pelfrey, illustrated by Aiko Gilson and Terry Walderhaug (Bible club curriculum for ages 2-3).

How to Contact/Writers: Fiction/Nonfiction: Query. Reports on queries in 3-4 weeks. Publishes a book 1 year after acceptance.

ALWAYS INCLUDE a self-addressed, stamped envelope (SASE) with submissions within your own country. When sending material to other countries, include a self-addressed envelope (SAE) and International Reply Coupons (IRCs).

Illustration: Works with 4-5 illustrators/year. Uses primarily b&w artwork. Query; include a SASE; we'll send an application form. Contact: Carol Rogers, managing editor. Reports in 3-4 weeks. Samples returned with SASE.

Terms: Work purchased outright from authors for 3¢/word. Pays illustrators by the project (range: $300-400/book). Book catalog available for 9×12 SAE and 5 first-class stamps; ms and art guidelines available for SASE.

Tips: "Read our guidelines carefully before sending us a manuscript or illustrations. All writing and illustrating is done on assignment only, and must be age-appropriate (preschool-6th grade)."

*CHRISTIAN PUBLICATIONS, INC., 3825 Hartzdale Dr., Camp Hill PA 17011. (717)761-7044. Fax: (717)761-7273. E-mail: editors@cpi~horizon.com. Website: cpi~horizon.com. Managing Editor: David Fessenden. Promotions Coordinator: Marilynne Foster. Imprints: Christian Publications, Horizon Books. Publishes 1-2 young readers/year; 1-2 young adult titles/year. 50% of books by first-time authors. The missions of this press are promoting participation in spreading the gospel worldwide and promoting Christian growth.

Fiction: All levels: religion. Average word length: young adults—25,000-40,000 words.

Nonfiction: All levels: religion. Does not want to see evangelistic/new Christian material. "Children and teens are too often assumed to have a shallow faith. We want to encourage a deeper walk with God." Average word length: young adults—25,000-40,000 words. Recently published *Grace and Guts to Live for God*, by Les Morgan (Bible study on Hebrews, 1 and 2 Peter); *Holy Moses! And Other Adventures in Vertical Living*, by Bob Hostetler. (Both are teen books which encourage a deeper commitment to God. Both illustrated by Ron Wheeler.)

How to Contact/Writers: Fiction/nonfiction: Submit outline/synopsis and 2 sample chapters (including chapter one). Reports on queries in 6 weeks; mss in 2 months. Publishes a book 8-16 months after acceptance. Will consider simultaneous submissions, electronic submissions via disk or modem ("one page, please").

Illustration: Works with 1-2 illustrators/year. Reviews ms/illustration packages from artists. Query. Contact: David Fessenden, managing editor. Query with samples. Contact: Marilynne Foster, promotions coordinator. Reports back only if interested. Samples returned with SASE; samples filed.

Terms: Pays authors royalty of 5-10% based on retail price. Offers advances. Pays illustrators by the project. Sends galleys to authors; dummies to illustrators (sometimes). Originals returned to artist at job's completion (if requested). Manuscript guidelines available for SASE.

Tips: "Writers: Best opportunity is in teen market, especially if you have experience working with and speaking to teens. Illustrators: Show us a few samples. Opportunities are limited, and on a work-for-hire basis."

CHRONICLE BOOKS, 275 Fifth St., San Francisco CA 94103. (415)777-7240. Fax: (415)495-2478. Book publisher. Associate Publisher, Children's Books: Victoria Rock. Assistant Editor: Erica Jacobs. Editorial Assistant: Amy Novesky. Publishes 25-50 (both fiction and nonfiction) picture books/year; 2-4 middle readers nonfiction titles/year; 2-4 beginning readers or middle readers fiction/year. 10-50% of books by first-time authors; 10-50% of books from agented writers.

Fiction: Picture books: animal, folktales, history, multicultural, nature/environment. Young readers: animal, folktales, history, multicultural, nature/environment, poetry. Middle readers: animal, history, multicultural, nature/environment, poetry, problem novels. Young adults: multicultural needs include "projects that feature diverse children in everyday situations." Recently published *I Love You the Purplest*, by Barbara M. Joasse; and *Hawk Hill*, by Sylvia Long.

Nonfiction: Picture books: animal, history, multicultural, nature/environment, science. Young readers: animal, arts/crafts, cooking, geography, history, multicultural and science. Middle readers: animal, arts/crafts, biography, cooking, geography, history, multicultural and nature/environment. Young adults: biography and multicultural. Recently published *A Rainbow at Night*, by Bruce Hucko; and *Artist in Overalls: The Life of Grant Wood*, by John Duggleby.

How to Contact/Writers: Fiction/Nonfiction: Submit complete ms (picture books); submit outline/synopsis and 3 sample chapters (for older readers). Reports on queries/mss in 2-18 weeks. Publishes a book 1-3 years after acceptance. Will consider simultaneous submissions, as long as they are marked "multiple submission." Will not consider submissions by fax. Must include SASE.

Illustration: Works with 15-20 illustrators/year. Wants "unusual art, graphically strong, something that will stand out on the shelves. Either bright and modern or very traditional. Fine art, not mass market." Reviews ms/illustration packages from artists. "Indicate if project *must* be considered jointly, or if editor may consider text and art separately." Illustrations only: Submit samples of artist's work (not necessarily from book, but in the envisioned style). Slides, tearsheets and color photocopies OK. (No original art.) Dummies helpful. Résumé helpful. "If samples sent for files, generally no response—unless samples are not suited to list, in which case samples are returned. Queries and project proposals responded to in same time frame as author query/ proposals."

Photography: Purchases photos from freelancers. Works on assignment only. Wants nature/ natural history photos.

Terms: Generally pays authors in royalties based on retail price "though we do occasionally work on a flat fee basis." Advance varies. Illustrators paid royalty based on retail price or flat fee. Sends proofs to authors and illustrators. Book catalog for 9 × 12 SAE and 8 first-class stamps; manuscript guidelines for #10 SASE.

Tips: "Chronicle Books publishes an eclectic mixture of traditional and innovative children's books. We are interested in taking on projects that have a unique bent to them—be it in subject matter, writing style, or illustrative technique. As a small list, we are looking for books that will lend our list a distinctive flavor. Primarily we are interested in fiction and nonfiction picture books for children ages infant-8 years, and nonfiction books for children ages 8-12 years. We are also interested in developing a middle grade/YA fiction program, and are looking for literary fiction that deals with relevant issues. Our sales reps are witnessing a resistance to alphabet books. And the market has become increasingly competitive. The '80s boom in children's publishing has passed, and the market is demanding high-quality books that work on many different levels."

CLARION BOOKS, 215 Park Ave. S., New York NY 10003. (212)420-5889. Houghton Mifflin Company. Book publisher.
- Clarion's book *The Midwife's Apprentice*, by Karen Cushman, received the Newbery Medal in 1996. The publisher is currently inundated with submissions.

CLEAR LIGHT PUBLISHERS, 823 Don Diego, Santa Fe NM 87501. (505)989-9590. Fax: (505)989-9519. Book publisher. Publisher: Harmon Houghton. Publishes 3 middle readers/year; 3 young adult titles/year.

Nonfiction: Middle readers and young adults: multicultural, American Indian only.

How to Contact/Writers: Fiction/Nonfiction: Submit complete ms. Will consider simultaneous submissions. Reports in 3 months.

Illustration: Reviews ms/illustration packages from artists. Submit ms with dummy. Contact: Harmon Houghton, publisher.

Terms: Pays authors royalty of 10% based on wholesale price. Offers advances (average amount: up to 50% of expected net sales). Sends galleys to authors.

Tips: Looking for "authentic American Indian art and folklore."

COBBLEHILL BOOKS, 375 Hudson St., New York NY 10014. (212)366-2628. Affiliate of Dutton Children's Books, a division of Penguin Books USA Inc. Book publisher. Editorial Director: Joe Ann Daly. Executive Editor: Rosanne Lauer.

Fiction: Picture books, young readers: adventure, animal, contemporary, easy-to-read, sports, suspense/mystery. Middle readers: adventure, contemporary, problem novels, sports, suspense/ mystery. Young adults: adventure, suspense/mystery.

Nonfiction: Picture books, young readers: animal, nature/environment, sports. Middle readers: nature/environment.

How to Contact/Writers: Fiction/Nonfiction: Query. Will consider simultaneous submissions "if we are informed about them."

Illustration: Illustrations only: Submit samples to keep on file, no original artwork.

Terms: Pays authors in royalties. Pays illustrators royalties or a flat fee. Original artwork returned at job's completion. Book catalog available for 8½ × 11 SAE and 2 first-class stamps; ms guidelines available for #10 SASE.

*COLONIAL WILLIAMSBURG FOUNDATION, Publications Department, P.O. Box 1776, Williamsburg VA 23187-1776. Website: http://www.history.org. Living history museum. Senior Editor/Writer: Donna C. Sheppard. Publishes 2-5 books/year. 50% of books by first-time authors. Focuses on eighteenth-century Williamsburg, Virginia, and colonial Virginia. Also the modern Colonial Williamsburg Foundation.

Fiction: All levels: adventure, animal, concept, history, multicultural, nature/environment, suspense/mystery. Average word length: young readers—1,000; middle readers—31,000. Recently published *The Nutmeg Adventure*, by Lisa A. Reinhard, illustrated by Barbara Leonard Gibson (young readers, picture book); and *Mystery of the Blue-Gowned Ghost*, by Linda Wirkner (middle reader, novel).

Nonfiction: All levels: activity books, animal, arts/crafts, biography, concept, history, how-to, multicultural, music/dance, nature/environment. Average word length: picture books—250; middle readers—6,500. Recently published *A Colonial Williamsburg ABC*, by Amy Zakrzewski Watson, illustrated by Louis S. Glanzman (preschool-8 years); and *Archaeology for Young Explorers: Uncovering the Past at Colonial Williamsburg*, by Patricia Samford and David A. Ribblett (middle readers, history).

How to Contact/Writers: Fiction/Nonfiction: Query. Submit outline/synopsis and 1-2 sample chapters. Reports on queries in 1 month; ms in 4 months. Publishes a book 2 years after acceptance. Will consider previously published work.

Illustration: Works with 2-3 illustrators/year. Reviews ms/illustration packages from artists. Query; send ms with dummy and 1-2 pieces of final art. Contact: Donna C. Sheppard, senior editor/writer. Illustrations only: Query with samples; send résumé, promo sheet, tearsheets. Contact: Donna C. Sheppard, senior editor/writer. Reports in 1 month. Samples not returned; samples filed.

Terms: Work purchased outright from authors. Pays illustrators by the project. Original artwork returned at job's completion. Book catalog available for 9×12 SAE and 3 first-class stamps.

Tips: "The best thing an author who is not familiar with Colonial Williamsburg can do is purchase a ticket and see what ideas suggest themselves as he/she tours the trade shops, buildings, and museums. The second best thing a potential author can do is read the *Official Guide to Colonial Williamsburg* and visit our website at http://www.history.org. Also, keep in mind that half of the population of 18th-century Williamsburg was African-American. Authors and illustrators should remember the need to represent colonial Williamsburg's African-American citizens."

CONCORDIA PUBLISHING HOUSE, 3558 S. Jefferson Ave., St. Louis MO 63118. (314)268-1000. Fax: (314)268-1329. Book publisher. Family and Children's Resources Editor: Dawn Weinstock. Art Director: Ed Luhmann. "Concordia Publishing House publishes a number of quality children's books each year. Most are fiction, with some nonfiction, based on a religious subject."

Fiction: All levels: contemporary, humor, religion. Young readers: adventure, suspense/mystery. Middle readers: adventure, romance, suspense/mystery. Young adults: adventure, romance, suspense/mystery. "All books must contain explicit Christian content." Published *Make a Christmas Memory*, by Julaine Kammath (family devotional book); *Hang Your Toes Over the Edge*, by Robert Ingram (ages 4-7); *The Secret Society of the Left Hand*, by Dandi Daley Mackall (grades 2-3, first chapter books); and *The Catnapping Caper*, by Vicki Berger Erwin (ages 8-12).

Nonfiction: Picture books: activity, arts/crafts, concept, religion. Young readers, middle readers: activity books, arts/crafts, religion. Young adults: religion.

How to Contact/Writers: Fiction: Query. Submit complete ms (picture books); submit outline/synopsis and sample chapters (novel-length). Reports on queries in 1 month; mss in 2 months. Publishes a book 1 year after acceptance. Will consider simultaneous submissions. "No phone queries."

Illustration: Illustrations only: Query with samples. Contact: Ed Luhmann, art director.

Terms: Pays authors in royalties based on retail price or outright purchase (minimum $500). Sends galleys to author. Ms guidelines for 1 first-class stamp and a #10 envelope.

Tips: "Do not send finished artwork with the manuscript. If sketches will help in the presentation of the manuscript, they may be sent. If stories are taken from the Bible, they should follow the Biblical account closely. Liberties should not be taken in fantasizing Biblical stories."

*COPPER BEECH BOOKS, Imprint of The Millbrook Press, 2 Old New Milford Rd., Brookfield CT 06804. (203)740-2220. Book publisher. Editor: Sheilah Holmes.

MARKET CONDITIONS are constantly changing! If you're still using this book and it is 1998 or later, buy the newest edition of *Children's Writer's & Illustrator's Market* at your favorite bookstore or order directly from Writer's Digest Books.

Nonfiction: Picture books, young readers: animal, arts/crafts, concept, cooking, geography, health, history, how-to, music/dance, nature/environment, religion, science, sports. Beginning readers, middle readers: animal, arts/crafts, biography, cooking, geography, history, how-to, music/dance, nature/environment, reference, science, sports.

How to Contact/Writers: Nonfiction: Submit complete ms. Reports on queries in 2 weeks; mss in 1 month. Will consider simultaneous submissions and previously published work.

Illustration: Reviews ms/illustration packages from artists. Query. Reports in 1 month. Samples returned with SASE; samples filed.

Photography: Uses color or b&w prints. Submit cover letter, résumé, published sample, promo piece.

Terms: Pays authors royalty of 4-6%. Manuscript guidelines available for SASE.

♣**COTEAU BOOKS LTD.**, 401-2206 Dewdney Ave., Regina, Sasketchewan S4R 1H3 Canada. (306)777-0170. Thunder Creek Publishing Co-op Ltd. Book publisher. Publisher: Geoffrey Ursell. Publishes 1-2 juvenile and/or young adult books/year, 12-14 books/year. 10% of books by first-time authors.

● Coteau Books publishes Canadian writers and illustrators only; manuscripts from the U.S. are returned unopened.

Fiction: Young readers, middle readers, young adults: adventure, contemporary, fantasy, history, humor, multicultural, nature/environment, science fiction, suspense/mystery. "No didactic, message pieces, nothing religious. No picture books. Material should reflect the diversity of culture, race, religion, creed of humankind—we're looking for fairness and balance." Recently published *Melanie Bluelake's Dream*, by Betty Fitzpatrick Dorion, cover painting by Sherry Farrell Racette (ages 8-10, novel); and *The Invisible Polly McDoodle*, by Mary Woodbury, cover painting by Janet Wilson (ages 9-11, mystery novel).

Nonfiction: Young readers, middle readers, young adult: biography, history, multicultural, nature/environment, social issues.

How to Contact/Writers: Fiction: Submit complete ms to acquisitions editor Barbara Sapergia. Reports on queries in 3-4 months; mss in 3-4 months. Publishes a book 1-2 years after acceptance.

Illustration: Works with 1-4 illustrators/year. Illustrations only: Submit nonreturnable samples. Contact: Production Coordinator. Reports only if interested. Samples returned with SASE; samples filed.

Photography: "Very occasionally buys photos from freelancers." Buys stock and assigns work.

Terms: Pays authors in royalties of 5-12½% based on retail price. Pays illustrators and photographers by the project. Sends galleys to authors; dummies to illustrators. Original artwork returned at job's completion. Book catalog free on request with 9×12 SASE.

Tips: "Truthfully, the work speaks for itself! Be bold. Be creative. Be persistent! There is room, at least in the Canadian market, for quality novels for children. Booksellers obviously like series like Goosebumps and Babysitters Club, but they indicate there is room for unique stories. Certainly at Coteau, this is a direction we will continue to take."

CRESTWOOD HOUSE, 250 James St., Morristown NJ 07960. Imprint of Silver Burdett Press, Simon & Schuster Education Group. Book publisher. Editor: Debby Biber. See listing for Silver Burdett Press.

CROCODILE BOOKS, 46 Crosby St., Northhampton MA 01060. (413)582-7054. Imprint of Interlink Publishing Group, Inc. Book publisher. Vice President: Ruth Moushabeck. Publishes 16 picture books/year. 25% of books by first-time authors.

● Crocodile does not accept unsolicited manuscripts.

Fiction: Picture books: animal, contemporary, history, spy/mystery/adventure.

Nonfiction: Picture book: history, nature/environment.

Terms: Pays authors in royalties. Sends galleys to author; dummies to illustrator.

*☐**CROSSPOINT INTERNATIONAL, INC.**, 30 Monument Square #150B-2, Concord MA 01742. (508)371-2300. Fax: (508)287-5325. Book publisher, independent book producer/packager. Product Developer: Noah Tier. Publishes 2 picture books/year; 2 young readers/year. 100% of books by first-time authors.

Fiction: Picture books: all categories. Average word length: picture books—30 pages. Recently published *John and Sara's First Book of Colors*; and *Tricky Ricky Goes to Nanel & Papas*.

Nonfiction: Picture books: all categories. Average word length: 30 pages.
How to Contact/Writers: Fiction/nonfiction: Submit complete ms. Reports on queries/mss in 3 months. Publishes a book 1 year after acceptance. Will consider previously published work.
Illustration: Works with 2 illustrators/year. Uses color artwork only. Reviews ms/illustration packages from artists. Submit ms with 5 pieces of final art. Illustrations only: Query with samples. Reports in 4 months. Samples not returned.
Terms: Payment negotiable.
Tips: "We specialize in books with a building self-esteem theme."

CROSSWAY BOOKS, Good News Publishers, 1300 Crescent, Wheaton IL 60187. (630)682-4300. Fax: (630)682-4785. Book Publisher. Editorial Director: Leonard Goss. Publishes 1-2 picture books/year; 1-2 middle readers/year; 2-4 young adult titles/year. "Crossway Books is committed to publishing books that bring Biblical reality to readers and that examine crucial issues through a Christian world view."
Fiction: Picture books: religion. Middle readers: adventure, contemporary, history, humor, religion, suspense/mystery, Christian realism. Young adults: contemporary, history, humor, religion, suspense/mystery, Christian realism. Does not want to see horror novels, romance or prophecy novels. Not looking for picture book submissions at present time. Published *Tell Me the Secrets*, by Max Lucado, illustrated by Ron DiCianni.
How to Contact/Writers: Fiction: Submit outline/synopsis. Reports on queries/mss in 4-6 weeks. Publishes a book 12-18 months after acceptance. Will consider simultaneous submissions.
Illustration: Works with 5 illustrators/year. Reviews ms/illustration packages from artists. Query. Illustrations only: Query with samples; provide résumé, promo sheet and client list.
Terms: Pays authors royalty based on net sales. Pays illustrators by the project. Sends galleys to authors; dummies to illustrators. Book catalog available; ms guidelines available for SASE.

CROWN PUBLISHERS (CROWN BOOKS FOR CHILDREN), 201 E. 50th St., New York NY 10022. (212)940-7742. Imprint of Random House, Inc. See Random House listing. Book publisher. Publisher: Simon Boughton. Publishes 20 picture books/year; 10 nonfiction titles/year. 5% of books by first-time authors; 70% of books from agented writers.
Fiction: Picture books: animal, humor, nature/environment. Young readers: history, nature/environment. Does not want to see fantasy, science fiction, poetry. Average word length: picture books—750. Recently published: *My Little Sister Ate One Hare*, by Bill Grossman; and *Me on the Map*, by Joan Sweeney.
Nonfiction: Picture books, young readers and middle readers: activity books, animal, biography, careers, health, history, hobbies, music/dance, nature/environment, religion, science, sports. Average word length: picture books—750-1,000; young readers—20,000; middle readers—50,000. Does not want to see ABCs. Recently published: *Rosie the Riviter*, by Penny Coleman (ages 9-14); and *Children of the Dust Bowl*, by Jerry Stanley (9-14 years, middle reader).
How to Contact/Writers: Fiction/nonfiction: Submit query letter. Reports on queries/mss in 3-4 months. Publishes book approximately 2 years after acceptance. Will consider simultaneous submissions.
Illustration: Works with 20 illustrators/year. Reviews ms/illustration packages from artists. "Submit double-spaced, continuous manuscripts; do not supply page-by-page breaks. One or two photocopies of art are fine. *Do not send original art*. Dummies are acceptable." Reports in 2 months. Illustrations only: Submit photocopies, portfolio or slides with SASE; provide business card and tearsheets. Contact: Isabel Warren-Lynch, Art Director. Original artwork returned at job's completion.
Terms: Pays authors royalty based on retail price. Advance "varies greatly." Pays illustrators by the project or royalty. Sends galleys to authors; proofs to illustrators. Book catalog for 9 × 12 SAE and 4 first-class stamps. Ms guidelines for 4½ × 9½ SASE; art guidelines not available.

CSS PUBLISHING, 517 S. Main St., P.O. Box 4503, Lima OH 45802-4503. (419)227-1818. Fax: (419)222-4647. E-mail: prpublish@aol.com. Book publisher. Editor: Terry Rhoads. Publishes books with religious themes.
Fiction: Picture books, young readers, middle readers, young adults: religion. Needs children's sermons (object lesson) for Sunday morning worship services; dramas for Advent, Christmas or Epiphany involving children for church services; activity and craft ideas for Sunday school or mid-week services for children (particularly pre-school and first and second grade). Does not want to see secular picture books. Published *That Seeing, They May Believe*, by Kenneth Mortonson (lessons for adults to present during worship services to pre-schoolers-third graders); *What*

Shall We Do With This Baby?, by Jan Spence (Christmas Eve worship service involving young-sters from newborn babies-high school youth); *Miracle in the Bethlehem Inn*, by Mary Lou Warstler (Advent or Christmas drama involving pre-schoolers-high school youth and adult.)

Nonfiction: Picture books, young readers, middle readers, young adults: religion. Needs chil-dren's sermons (object lesson) for Sunday morning workship services; dramas for Advent, Christ-mas or Epiphany involving children for church services; activity and craft ideas for Sunday school or mid-week services for children (particularly pre-school and first and second grade). Does not want to see secular picture books. Published *Mustard Seeds*, by Ellen Humbert (activity/bulletins for pre-schoolers-first graders to use during church); *This Is The King*, by Cynthia Cowen.

How to Contact/Writers: Reports on queries in 1 month; mss in 4-6 months. Publishes a book 9 months after acceptance. Will consider simultaneous submissions.

Terms: Work purchased outright from authors. Ms guidelines and book catalog available for SASE.

Tips: "We are seeking material for use by clergy, Christian education directors and Sunday school teachers for mainline Protestant churches. Our market is mainline Protestant clergy."

MAY DAVENPORT, PUBLISHERS, 26313 Purissima Rd., Los Altos Hills CA 94022. (415)948-6499. Independent book producer/packager. Estab. 1976. Editor: May Davenport. Pub-lishes 1-2 picture books/year; 2-3 young adult titles/year. 99% of books by first-time authors. Seeks books with literary merit. "We are overstocked with picture book/elementary reading material."

Fiction: Young adults: contemporary, humorous fictional literature. Average word length: 40,000-60,000. Recently published *The Newman Assignment*, by Kurt Haberl, illustrated by Keith Neely (ages 12 and up, novel with teachers' lesson plans to read/discuss/write); *When the Dancing Ends*, by Judy L. Hairfield; illustrated by Theresa Wanex (ages 12 and up), and *Drivers' Ed is Dead*, by Pat Delgado, illustrated by Keith Neely (ages 12 and up, novel with teachers' lesson plans to read/discuss/write).

Nonfiction: Young readers: special needs activity books to read alone or aloud, or to color. Special needs include dyslexia, tricks to develop for reading skills. Published *History of Papa Frog*, by William F. Meisburger (Spanish/English, grades 1-2, paper); *Sumo, The Wrestling Ele-phant*, by Esther Lee (Spanish/English, grades 1-2, paper).

How to Contact/Writers: Fiction: Query. Reports on queries/mss in 2-3 weeks. "We do not answer queries or manuscripts which do not have SASE attached." Publishes a book 6-12 months after acceptance.

Illustration: Works with 1-2 illustrators/year. Reviews ms/illustration packages from artists. Submit ms with 2-3 pieces of final art. Reports in 2 weeks. Samples returned with SASE. Illustra-tions only: "We have enough samples for our files for future reference."

Terms: Pays authors in royalties of 15% based on retail price. Pays "by mutual agreement, no advances." Pays illustrators by the project (range: $75-300). Book catalog, ms guidelines free on request with SASE.

Tips: "Create stories to enrich the non-reading 12-and-up readers. They might not appreciate your similies and metaphors and may find fault with your alliterations with the letters of the alphabet, but show them how you do it with memorable characters in today's society. Just project your humorous talent and entertain with more than two sentences in a paragraph."

DAVIS PUBLICATIONS, INC., 50 Portland St., Worcester MA 01608. (508)754-7201. Fax: (508)753-3834. E-mail: davispub@aol.com. Book publisher. Acquisitions Editors: Claire M. Gol-ding (grades K-8) and Helen Ronan (grades 9-12). Publishes 10 titles total/year. 30% of books by first-time authors. "We publish books for the art education market (elementary through high school), both technique-oriented and art appreciation resource books and textbooks."

Nonfiction: Middle readers, young adults: activity books about art and art-related textbooks; multicultural books detailing the arts of other cultures (Hispanic, Native American, African-American, Asian); textbooks. Recently published *Puppets and Masks: Stagecraft & Storytelling*, by Nan Rump; *African Arts and Cultures*, by Jacqueline Chanda; *Jacob Lawrence: American Scenes, American Struggles*, by Nancy Howard; *Pueblo*, by Nancy Howard; *3-D Wizardry Design in Papier-Mâché, Plaster and Form*, by George Wolfe.

How to Contact/Writers: Submit outline/synopsis and 1 sample chapter. Reports on queries in 3 months; mss in 6 months. Publishes a book 1 year after acceptance. Will consider simultaneous submissions and electronic submissions via disk.

Illustration: Works with 2 illustrators/year. We use a combination of photos and line drawings (200-300/nonfiction title). "We are not major purchasers of illustrations; we generally need clear, informative line art that can be used to explain, demonstrate and elucidate art procedures and materials." Reviews ms/illustration packages from artists. Ms/illustration packages and illustration only: Query with samples. Reports only if interested. Samples returned with SASE or kept on file. Originals returned at job's completion.

Photography: "Rarely" purchases photos from freelancers. Contact: Jane DeVore. "Usually need photos of particular artists, artworks or art forms." Model/property releases required; captions required. Publishes photo concept books. Uses 5×7 and 8×10 glossy, b&w prints and 4×5 and 8×10 transparencies.

Terms: Pays authors royalties of ½-12½% based on retail price or by outright purchase ($1,000-2,000). Pays illustrators by the project (range $50-300). Sends galleys to authors. Book catalog available for 8½×11 SASE; ms guidelines available for 6×9 SASE.

Tips: "Look at our catalog and get a feel for the kind of books we publish. The majority of our books are for *teachers* of children, but used as resources that children may peruse in the classroom. We do occasional resource books that are written *for* children (A Closer Look Series, *Pictures & Poetry*) plus textbooks that children use. Most of our textbooks are written by art teachers/professors, not freelance writers."

DAWN PUBLICATIONS, 14618 Tyler Foote, Nevada City CA 95959. (916)478-7540. Fax: (916)478-7541. Book publisher. Publisher: Bob Rinzler. Publishes works with holistic themes dealing with nature..

Fiction: Picture books: animal, nature/environment.

Nonfiction: Picture books: animal, nature/environment. Recently published *Discover the Seasons*, written and illustrated by Diane Iverson; and *Wonderful Nature, Wonderful You*, by Karen Ireland, illustrated by Christopher Canyon.

How to Contact/Writers: Fiction/Nonfiction: Query; submit complete ms; submit outline/synopsis and sample chapters. Reports on queries/mss in 2 months maximum. Publishes a book 1 year after acceptance. Will consider simultaneous submissions and previously published work.

Illustration: Works with 4 illustrators/year. Will reviews ms/illustration packages from artists. Query; send ms with dummy. Contact: Glenn Hovemann, editor. Illustrations only: Query with samples, résumé.

Terms: Pays authors royalty based on wholesale price. Offers advance. Pays illustrators by the project or royalties based on wholesale price. Sends galleys to authors; dummies to illustrators. Book catalog available for 8½×11 SASE; ms guidelines available for SASE.

Tips: Looking for "picture books expressing nature awareness with inspirational quality leading to enhanced self-awareness. Usually no animal dialogue."

T.S. DENISON CO. INC., 9601 Newton Ave. S., Minneapolis MN 55431. (612)888-6404. Fax: (612)888-6318. Editor: Danielle DeGregory. 25% of books by first-time authors. "We publish only teacher resource/activity books."

Nonfiction: Young readers, middle readers: activity books, animal, geography, health, history, multicultural, nature/environment, reference, social issues, textbooks, teacher resource. Average length: middle readers—150 pages. Published *Let's Meet Famous Composers*, by Harriet Kinghorn, illustrated by Margo De Paulis (grades 3-6, teacher resource); *Toddler Calendar*, by Elaine Cummins, illustrated by Anita Nelson (Pre-K, teacher resource); *FairyTale Mask*, by Gwen Rives Jones, illustrated by Darcy Myers (grades 1-3, teacher resource).

How to Contact/Writers: Query; submit complete ms; submit outline/synopsis and 2 sample chapters. Reports on queries/mss in 3 months. Publishes a book 12-18 months after acceptance. Will consider simultaneous submissions and electronic submissions via disk.

Illustration: Works with 15 illustrators/year. Illustrations only: Query with samples; arrange a personal interview to show portfolio. Reports back only if interested. Samples returned with SASE or kept on file. Original artwork not returned at job's completion.

Terms: Work purchased outright from authors. Pays illustrators by the project (range: $300-400 for covers; $20-25 for b&w interior). Book catalog available for 9×12 SAE and 3 first-class stamps; ms guidelines available for SASE.

DIAL BOOKS FOR YOUNG READERS, Imprint of Penguin Books USA Inc., 375 Hudson St., New York NY 10014. (212)366-2800. President/Publisher: Phyllis J. Fogelman. Publishes 70 picture books/year; 10 young reader titles/year; 5 middle reader titles/year; 10 young adult titles/year.

• Dial's book *The Middle Passage: White Ships Black Cargo*, by Tom Feelings, received the Coretta Scott King illustrator award. They no longer accept unsolicited manuscripts; only agented material will be read.

Fiction: Picture books: adventure, animal, contemporary, fantasy, folktales, history, nature/environment, poetry, religion, science fiction, sports, suspense/mystery. Young readers: animal, contemporary, easy-to-read, fantasy, folktales, history, nature/environment, poetry, science fiction, sports, mystery/adventure. Middle readers, young adults: animal, contemporary, fantasy, folktales, history, health-related, nature/environment, poetry, problem novels, religion, science fiction, sports, spy/mystery/adventure. Published *Brother Eagle, Sister Sky*, illustrated by Susan Jeffers (all ages, picture book); *Amazing Grace*, by Mary Hoffman (ages 4-8, picture book); and *Soul Looks Back in Wonder*, by Tom Feelings, Maya Angelou, et al (ages 7 and up, poetry picture book.)

Nonfiction: Uses very little nonfiction but will consider submissions of outstanding artistic and literary merit. Picture books: animal, biography, history, nature/environment, sports. Young readers: activity books, animal, biography, history, nature/environment, religion, sports. Middle readers: animal, biography, careers, health, history, nature/environment, religion, sports. Young adults: animal, biography, careers, health, history, hobbies, music/dance, nature/environment, religion, sports. Recently published *Big-Top Circus*, by Neal Porter (ages 4-8, picture book); *Hand, Heart, and Mind*, by Lou Ann Walker (middle readers).

How to Contact/Writers: Only interested in agented material.

Illustration: To arrange a personal interview to show portfolio, send samples and a letter requesting an interview.

Photography: Only interested in agented material.

Terms: Pays authors and illustrators in royalties based on retail price. Average advance payment "varies." Ms guidelines for SASE.

DILLON PRESS, INC., 299 Jefferson Rd., P.O. Box 480, Parsippany NJ 07054-0480. (201)236-7000. Imprint of Silver Burdett Press, Simon & Schuster Education Group. Book Publisher. Editor: Debbie Biber. See listing for Silver Burdett Press.

DISNEY PUBLISHING, Subsidiary of Walt Disney Co., 500 S. Buena Vista, Burbank CA 91521. Prefers not to share information.

DORLING KINDERSLEY, INC., 95 Madison Ave., New York NY 10016. (212)213-4800. Book publisher.
• This publisher is currently inundated with material.

*DOVE KIDS BOOKS, Imprint of Dove Entertainment, 8955 Beverly Blvd., Los Angeles CA 90048. (310)786-1600. Fax: (310)247-2924. Book publisher. Editorial Director: Brenda Pope-Ostrow. Publishes 25 picture books/year. 90% of books by first-time authors. "Books are based on fun and education and are written by celebrities. We accept few manuscript submissions."

Fiction: Picture books: adventure, animal, contemporary, folktales, history, humor. Does not want to see heavy themes, such as cancer (illness), death, adoption, loss; also no fantasy. Average word length: picture books—1,000. Recently published *The Adventures of Little Nettie Windship*, by Cheryl Ladd (ages 3-6, picture book); *The Adventures of Drippy the Runaway Raindrop*, by Sidney Sheldon (ages 3-6, picture book); and *Snow White and the Seven Dwarfs*, retold by Richard Hack (ages 4-7, picture book).

Nonfiction: Picture books: animal, biography, history, religion, sports. Average word length: picture books—100-1,000. Recently published *I'm Hiding! A Pop-Up Counting Book*, by Joy Cockle (ages 3-5, hardcover pop-up book).

How to Contact/Writers: Fiction/Nonfiction: Query. Reports on queries in 1 week; mss in 4 months. Publishes a book 1-2 years after acceptance. Will consider simultaneous and previously published submissions.

Illustration: Works with 30 illustrators/year. Uses mostly color artwork. Reviews ms/illustration packages from artists. Submit ms with 2 pieces of final art. Contact: Brenda Pope-Ostrow, editorial director. Illustrations only: Query with samples. Send résumé, promo sheet, client list, tearsheets. Contact: Brenda Pope-Ostrow, editorial director. Reports in 1 month. Samples filed.

Photography: Buys stock and assigns work. Contact: Rick Penn-Kraus, art director. Uses color or b&w prints and 35mm transparencies. Submit cover letter, résumé, published samples, client list, stock photo list, promo piece.

Tips: "We offer many free copies of the works and loads of national publicity for the projects, as they are written by celebrities or contain audios recorded by celebrities."

© 1996 The Russell and Tucker Partnership

The Adventures of Little Nettie Windship, by Cheryl Ladd, tells the story of a little boat who, with the help of new-found friends Ottie Otter and Perry Pelican, rescues a large steam tanker from disaster. Husband and wife team Ezra Tucker and Nancy Krause used acrylics to bring sweet Little Nettie Windship and her friends to life in this adventure published by Dove Kids Books.

DOWN EAST BOOKS, P.O. Box 679, Camden, ME 04843. (207)594-9544. Fax: (207)594-7215. Book publisher. Editor: Karin Womer. Publishes 1-2 young middle readers/year. 70% of books by first-time authors. All books pertain to Maine/New England region.

Fiction: Picture books, middle readers: adventure, animal, history, nature/environment. Published *Silas the Bookstore Cat*, by Karen Mather (young-middle readers, animal); and *A Penny for a Hundred*, by Ethel Pochocki, illustrated by Mary Beth Owens (picture book about 9-year-old girl who befriends a German POW boy during WWII).

Nonfiction: Picture books, young readers: animal, geography, nature/environment. Recently published *Island Alphabet, An ABC of Maine Islands*, written and illustrated by Kelly Paul Brigs (picture book of rhyming couplets introducing islands).

How to Contact/Writers: Fiction/Nonfiction: Query. Reports on queries in 2-4 weeks; mss in 2-8 weeks. Publishes a book 6-18 months after acceptance. Will consider simultaneous and previously published submissions.

Illustration: Works with 2-3 illustrators/year. Reviews ms/illustration packages from artists. Query. Contact: Karin Womer, editor. Illustrations only: Query with samples. Reports in 2 weeks to 2 months. Samples returned with SASE; samples filed sometimes.

Terms: Pays authors royalty (varies widely). Pays illustrators by the project or by royalty (varies widely). Sends galleys to authors; dummies to illustrators. Original artwork returned at job's completion. Book catalog available. Manuscript guidelines available for SASE.

DUTTON CHILDREN'S BOOKS, 375 Hudson St., New York NY 10014. (212)366-2600. Division of Penguin USA. Book publisher. Editor-in-Chief: Lucia Monfried. Art Director: Sara Reynolds. Art Associate: Julia Goodman. Publishes approximately 60 picture books/year; 4 young reader titles/year; 10 middle reader titles/year; 8 young adult titles/year. 10% of books by first-time authors.

Fiction: Picture books: adventure, animal, folktales, history, multicultural, nature/environment, poetry. Young readers: adventure, animal, contemporary, easy-to-read, fantasy, pop-up, suspense/mystery. Middle readers: adventure, animal, contemporary, fantasy, history, multicultural, nature/environment, suspense/mystery. Young adults: adventure, animal, anthology, contemporary, fantasy, history, multicultural, nature/environment, poetry, science fiction, suspense/mystery. Recently published *Isla*, by Arthur Dorrus, illustrated by Elisa Kleven (picture book); *The Bravest Thing*, by Donna Jo Napoli, (novel); and *The Eye of the Pharaoh*, by Iain Smith (pop-up mystery).

Nonfiction: Picture books: animal, history, multicultural, nature/environment. Young readers: animal, history, multicultural, nature/environment. Middle readers: animal, biography, history, multicultural, nature/environment. Young adults: animal, biography, history, multicultural, nature/environment, social issues. Recently published *Chile Fever: A Celebration of Peppers*, by Elizabeth King (ages 7-10, photo essay); *Part of Me Died, Too: Stories of Creative Survival Among Bereaved Children and Teenagers*, by Virginia Lynn Fry (ages 10 and up).

How to Contact/Writers: Query. Reports on queries in 1 month; mss in 3 months. Publishes a book 12-18 months after acceptance. Will consider simultaneous submissions.

Illustration: Works with 40-60 illustrators/year. Reviews ms/illustration packages from artists. Query first. Illustrations only: Query with samples; send résumé, portfolio, slides—no original art please. Reports on art samples in 2 months. Original artwork returned at job's completion.

Photography: Purchases photos from freelancers. Assigns work. Wants "nature photography."

Terms: Pays authors royalties of 4-10% based on retail price. Book catalog, ms guidelines for SAE. Pays illustrators royalties of 2-10% based on retail price unless jacket illustration—then pays by flat fee. Photographers paid royalty per photo.

Tips: Writers: "We publish high-quality trade books and are interested in well-written manuscripts with fresh ideas and child appeal. Avoid topics that appear frequently. We have a complete publishing program. Though we publish mostly picture books, we are very interested in acquiring more novels for middle and young adult readers. We are also expanding our list to include more books for preschool-aged children. In nonfiction, we are looking for history, general biography, science and photo essays for all age groups." Illustrators: "We would like to see samples and portfolios from potential illustrators of picture books (full color), young novels (b&w) and jacket artists (full color)." Foresee "even more multicultural publishing, plus more books published in both Spanish and English."

E.M. PRESS, INC., P.O. Box 4057, Manassas VA 20108. (540)439-0304. Book publisher. Publisher/Editor: Beth Miller. Publishes 2 middle readers/year; 2 young adult titles/year. 50% of books by first-time authors.

Fiction: All levels: contemporary, problem novels, religion. Picture books, young readers: nature/environment. Recently published *Santa's New Reindeer*, by Judie Schrecker; *The Search For Archerland*, by H.R. Coursen (adventure, 12 and up); and *Some Brief Cases of Inspector Alec Stuart of Scotland Yard*, by Archibald Wagner MD (mystery, 12 and up).

Nonfiction: Young adults: religion.

How to Contact/Writers: Fiction: Query. Submit outline/synopsis. Nonfiction: Query. Reports on ms/queries in 6 weeks. Publishes a book 18 months after acceptance. Will consider simultaneous submissions.

Illustration: Works with 3 children's illustrator/year. Illustration packages should be submitted to Beth Miller, Publisher. Reports back in 6 weeks. Samples returned with SASE; samples kept on file.

Terms: "We've used all means of payment from outright purchase to royalty." Offers varied advances. Sends galleys to authors. Original artwork returned at job's completion. Book catalog for SASE.

Tips: "Present the most professional package possible. The market is glutted, so you must find a new approach."

WM. B. EERDMANS PUBLISHING COMPANY, 255 Jefferson Ave. SE, Grand Rapids MI 49503. (616)459-4591. Book publisher. Children's Book Editor: Amy Eerdmans. Publishes 6 picture books/year; 4 young readers/year; 4 middle readers/year.

Fiction: All levels: parables, religion, retold Bible stories from a Christian perspective. Picture books: animal, poetry.

Nonfiction: All levels: biography, religion.

How to Contact/Writers: Fiction/Nonfiction: Query; submit complete ms. Reports on queries in 3-6 weeks; mss in 6 weeks.

Illustration: Works with 6-8 illustrators/year. Reviews ms/illustration packages from artists. Reports on ms/art samples in 1 month. Illustrations only: Submit résumé, slides or color photocopies. Contact: Willem Mineur, art director. Samples returned with SASE; samples filed.

Terms: Pays authors and illustrators royalties of 5-10% based on retail price. Sends galleys to authors; dummies to illustrators. Original artwork returned at job's completion. Book catalog free on request; ms and/or artist's guidelines free on request.

Tips: "We are looking for material that will help children explore their faith. Look at our list. We're interested in a Christian message in novels, picture books and biographies. We accept all genres."

ENSLOW PUBLISHERS INC., 44 Fadem Rd., Box 699, Springfield NJ 07081. Vice President: Brian D. Enslow. Estab. 1978. Publishes 30 middle reader titles/year; 30 young adult titles/year. 30% of books by first-time authors.

Nonfiction: Young readers, middle readers, young adults: activity books, animal, biography, careers, health, history, hobbies, nature/environment, sports. Average word length: middle readers-5,000; young adult-15,000. Published *Louis Armstrong*, by Patricia and Fredrick McKissack (grades 2-3, biography); *Lotteries: Who Wins, Who Loses?*, by Ann E. Weiss (grades 6-12, issues book).

How to Contact/Writers: Nonfiction: Query. Reports on queries/mss in 2 weeks. Publishes a book 18 months after acceptance. Will not consider simultaneous submissions.

Illustration: Submit résumé, business card or tearsheets to be kept on file.

Terms: Pays authors royalties or work purchased outright. Sends galleys to authors. Book catalog/ms guidelines available for $2.

EVAN-MOOR EDUCATIONAL PUBLISHERS, 18 Lower Ragsdale Dr., Monterey CA 93940-5746. (408)649-5901. Fax: (408)649-6256. Website: http://www.evan-moor.com. Book publisher. Acquisitions Editor: Marilyn Evans. Production Director: Joy Evans. Publishes 30-50 books/year. Less than 10% of books by first-time authors.

• Evan-Moor does not publish fiction.

Nonfiction: Picture books, young readers, middle readers: animal, geography, nature/environment, science. Young readers, middle readers: activity books. "We publish pre-K through 6th grade classroom activity books in all subjects. Thematic units, teaching resources and strategy books. Also books for home use by parents and their children: Average length 48, 64 or 80 pages." Recently published 40 activity books for science and social studies aimed at both school and home use (many full-color); *More Than a Report*, 3 titles: *Social Studies, Science, Celebrations* by Yvonne Despard, illustrated by Jo Supancich (step-by-step report writing projects for grades 3-6); 14 cross-curricular theme units, such as *My Neighborhood* (pre-K-1), *From Farm to Table* (grades 1-3), and *My State*, (grades 1-3).

How to Contact/Writers: Nonfiction: Submit complete ms. Reports on queries in 3 weeks; mss in 4 months. Publishes a book 12-18 months after acceptance. Will consider simultaneous submissions if so noted.

Illustration: Works with 7-10 illustrators/year. Uses b&w artwork primarily. Illustrations only: Query with samples; send résumé, tearsheets. Contact: Joy Evans, production director. Reports only if interested. Samples returned with SASE; samples filed.

Terms: Work purchased outright from authors, "dependent solely on size of project and 'track record' of author." Pays illustrators by the project (range: varies). Sends galleys to authors. Artwork is not returned. Book catalog available for 9×12 SAE; ms guidelines available for SASE.

Tips: "Writers—know the supplemental education or parent market. Tell us how your project is unique and what consumer needs it meets. Illustrators—you need to be able to produce quickly, and be able to render realistic and charming children and animals."

*FACTS ON FILE, 11 Penn Plaza, New York NY 10001. (212)967-8800. Book publisher. Editorial Director: Laurie Likoff. Editors: Nicole Bowen, Drew Silver and Hilary Poole. Publishes 35-40 young adult titles/year. 5% of books by first-time authors; 25% of books from agented writers; additional titles through book packagers, co-publishers and unagented writers.

Nonfiction: Middle readers, young adults: animal, biography, careers, geography, health, history, multicultural, nature/environment, reference, religion, science, social issues and sports. Recently published *Great Women Writers 1900-1950*, by Christina Gombar; *African American Explorers*, by Catherine Reef; and *Modern Mathematics*, by Harry Henderson.

How to Contact/Writers: Nonfiction: Submit outline/synopsis and sample chapters. Reports on queries in 6-8 weeks. Publishes a book 10 months after acceptance. Will consider simultaneous submissions. Sends galleys to authors. Book catalog free on request.

Tips: "Most projects have high reference value and fit into a series format."

*FAIRVIEW PRESS, Imprint of Growing and Reading with Bob Keeshan, 2450 Riverside Ave. S, Minneapolis MN 55454. (612)672-4180, (800)544-8207. Fax: (612)672-4980. Website: http://www.press.fairview.org. Book publisher. Contact: Children's Book Editor. Publishes 9-10 picture books/year. 75% of books by first-time authors.

Fiction: Picture Books: contemporary, health, family issues, special needs. Special needs include any titles specifically for or about physically or mentally challenged children. Average word length: picture books—1,000. Recently published *Clover's Secret*, written and illustrated by Christine M. Winn (ages 5-9, fiction about domestic violence); and *My Dad Has HIV*, by Alexander, Rudin, Sejkova, illustrated by Shipman (ages 4-8, girl deals with father's illness).

Nonfiction: Picture books, young readers: activity books, family issues, health, multicultural, self help, social issues, special needs. Average word length: picture books—1,000. "No children's nonfiction published yet—we're interested in expanding, though."

How to Contact/Writers: Fiction/Nonfiction: Submit complete ms. Reports on queries/ms in 8-10 weeks. Publishes a book 18 months after acceptance. Will consider simultaneous submissions and previously published work.

Illustration: Works with 3-5 illustrators/year. Uses color artwork only. Reviews ms/illustration packages from artists. Submit query. Contact: children's book editor. Illustrations only: Query with samples; arrange personal portfolio review. Contact: children's book editor. Reports back only if interested. Samples not returned; samples filed.

Terms: Pays authors fee negotiated by project. Offers advances (50% total). Pays illustrators fee negotiated by project. Originals returned at job's completion. Book catalog available; ms guidelines available for SASE.

Tips: "Fairview Press publishes children's books on family issues—virtues, values, coping skills, parental/familial relationships, etc. Submitted work must fit under that 'umbrella.' "

FARRAR, STRAUS & GIROUX, 19 Union Square W., New York NY 10003. (212)741-6934. Fax: (212)633-2427. E-mail: mmfergu@fsgee.com. Book publisher. Children's Books Editor-in-Chief: Margaret Ferguson. Estab. 1946. Publishes 21 picture books/year; 6 middle reader titles/year; 15 young adult titles/year. 50% of books by first-time authors; 5% of books from agented writers.

Fiction: All levels: all categories. "Original and well-written material for all ages." Published *Tell Me Everything*, by Carolyn Coman (ages 12 up).

Nonfiction: All levels: all categories.

How to Contact/Writers: Fiction/Nonfiction: Query; submit outline/synopsis and sample chapters. Reports on queries in 6-8 weeks; mss in 1-3 months. Publishes a book 18 months after acceptance. Will consider simultaneous submissions.

Illustration: Works with 30-60 illustrators/year. Reviews ms/illustration packages from artists. Submit ms with 1 example of final art, remainder roughs. Illustrations only: Query with tearsheets. Reports back in 1-2 months. Samples returned with SASE; samples sometimes filed.

Terms: "We offer an advance against royalties for both authors and illustrators." Sends galleys to authors; dummies to illustrators. Original artwork returned at job's completion. Book catalog available for 6½×9½ SAE and 64¢ postage; ms guidelines for 1 first-class stamp.

Tips: "Study our catalog before submitting. We will see illustrator's portfolios by appointment. Don't ask for criticism and/or advice—it's just not possible. Never send originals. Always enclose SASE."

FAWCETT JUNIPER, 201 E. 50 St., New York NY 10022. (212)751-2600. Imprint of Ballantine/DelRey/Fawcett Books. Book publisher. Editor-in-Chief/Vice President: Leona Nevler. Executive Administrative Assistant to the Editor-in-Chief: Louis Mendez. Publishes 36 young adult titles/year.

Fiction: Middle readers: contemporary, romance, science fiction. Young adults: contemporary, fantasy, romance.

How to Contact/Writers: Fiction: Query.

Terms: Pays authors in royalties.

Tips: "Do not send children's manuscripts—only manuscripts appropriate for young people ages 12 and up!"

THE FEMINIST PRESS AT THE CITY UNIVERSITY OF NEW YORK, 311 E. 94th St., New York NY 10128. (212)360-5790. Book publisher. Children's Books: Kim Mallett. Publishes 1-2 middle reader, young reader and young adult books/year.

Fiction: Picture books and young readers: adventure fantasy, folktales, history, humor, multicultural. Middle readers: adventure, fantasy, folktales, history, humor, multicultural, science fiction, suspense. Young adults: concept, contemporary, humor, multicultural, science fiction, sports, suspense/mystery.

Nonfiction: Picture books, young reader: history, multicultural. Middle reader: history multicultural, science. Young adult: multicultural, science.

How to Contact/Writers: Fiction/Nonfiction: Query. Reports on queries/mss in 4-6 weeks. Publishes a book 1-2 years after acceptance.

Illustration: Works with 1 illustrator/year. Uses primarily b&w artwork. Reviews ms/illustration packages from artist. Submit query or ms with final art. Contact: Kim Mallett, assistant to the publisher. Reports back in 1 month only if interested and only if SASE. Samples returned with SASE; samples kept on file.

Terms: Pays authors royalty. Offers advances (average amount: $100). Pays illustrators by the project or royalty; "depends on project." Sends galleys to authors. Original artwork returned at job's completion. Book catalog available; ms guidelines available.

❖FIFTH HOUSE PUBLISHERS, 201-165 3rd Ave. S., Saskatoon, Saskatchewan 57K 1L8 Canada. Book publisher. Managing Editor: Charlene Dobmeier.
 • This publisher no longer accepts unsolicited manuuscripts.
Illustration: Works with 1-2 illustrators/year. Illustration only: Query with samples. Reports in 2 months only if interested. Samples returned with SASE; samples filed.

*❖FIREFLY BOOKS LTD., 3680 Victoria Park, Willowdale, Ontario M2H 3K1 Canada. (416)499-8412. Fax: (416)499-8313. Book publisher.
 • Firefly Books Ltd. does not accept unsolicited manuscripts.

❖FITZHENRY & WHITESIDE LTD., 195 Allstate Pkwy., Markham, Ontario L3R 4T8 Canada. (905)477-9700. Fax: (905)477-9179. Book publisher. President: Sharon Fitzhenry. Vice President: Robert W. Read. Publishes 2 picture books/year; 5 young readers/year; 5 middle readers/year; 5 young adult titles/year. 15% of books by first-time authors. Publishes mostly nonfiction—social studies, visual arts, biography, environment. Prefers Canadian subject or perspective.

Fiction: Picture books: folktales, history, multicultural, nature/environment and sports. Young readers: contemporary, folktales, health, history, multicultural, nature/environment and sports. Young readers: contemporary, folktales, health, history, multicultural, nature/environment and sports. Middle readers: adventure, contemporary, folktales, history, humor, multicultural, nature/environment and sports. Young adults: adventure, contemporary, folktales, history, multicultural, nature/environment, sports and suspense/mystery. Average word length: young readers—less than 2,000; middle readers—2,000-5,000; young adults—10,000-20,000.

Nonfiction: Picture books: arts/crafts, biography, history, multicultural, nature/environment, reference and sports. Young readers: arts/crafts, biography, geography, history, hobbies, multicultural, nature/environment, reference, religion and sports. Middle readers: arts/crafts, biography, careers, geography, history, hobbies, multicultural, nature/environment, reference, social issues and sports. Young adults: arts/crafts, biography, careers, geography, health, hi-lo, history, multicultural, music/dance, nature/environment, reference, social issues and sports. Average word length: young readers—500-1,000; middle readers—2,000-5,000; young adults—10,000-20,000. Recently published *Inuit of the North*, by Stan Garrod (ages 8-12, nonfiction native studies); *Ladybug Garden*, by Celia Godkin (ages 5-10, environment/nature); and *Wayne Gretzky*, by Fred McFadden (ages 8-12, sports biography).

How to Contact/Writers: Fiction: Submit outline/synopsis and 1 sample chapter. Nonfiction: Submit outline/synopsis. Reports in 3 months. Publishes a book 1 year after acceptance. Will consider simultaneous submissions.

Illustration: Works with 5-10 illustrators/year. Reviews ms/illustration packages from artist. Submit outline and sample illustration (copy). Illustrations only: Query with samples and promo sheet. Reports in 3 months. Samples returned with SASE; samples filed if no SASE.

Photography: Buys photos from freelancers. Buys stock and assigns work. Captions required. Uses b&w 8×10 prints; 35mm and 4×5 transparencies. Submit stock photo list and promo piece.

Terms: Pays authors royalty of 10%. Offers "modest" advances. Pays illustrators by the project and royalty. Pays photographers per photo. Sends galleys to authors; dummies to illustrators.
Tips: "We respond to quality."

 THE MAPLE LEAF before a listing indicates that the market is Canadian.

FORWARD MOVEMENT PUBLICATIONS, 412 Sycamore St., Cincinnati OH 45202. (513)721-6659. Fax: (513)421-0315. E-mail: forward.movement@ecunet.org. Website: http://www.dfms.org/fmp.
Fiction: Religion.
Nonfiction: Religion.
How to Contact/Writers: Fiction/Nonfiction: Query. Reports in 1 month.
Illustration: Query with samples. Samples returned with SASE.
Terms: Pays authors honorarium. Pays illustrators by the project.
Tips: "Forward Movement is now exploring publishing books for children and does not know its niche. We are an agency of the Episcopal Church and most of our market is to mainstream Protestants."

FRANKLIN WATTS, Sherman Turnpike, Danbury CT 06816. (203)797-3500. Subsidiary of Grolier Inc. Book publisher. Director: E.R. Primm. 10% of books by first-time authors; 5% of books from agented writers.
 ● Franklin Watts is not accepting unsolicited submissions in 1997.
Nonfiction: Young readers: activity books. Middle readers: activity books, animal, arts/crafts, biography, concept, cooking, geography, health, hi-lo, history, multicultural, music/dance, nature/environment, reference, religion, science, social issues, special needs, sports. Young adults: arts/crafts, biography, careers, concepts, geography, health, history, multicultural, music/dance, nature/environment, reference, religion, science, social issues, special needs, sports. Does not want to see fiction or poetry. Average word length: middle readers—5,000; young adult/teens—16,000-35,000.
How to Contact/Writers: Query. No mss. Include SASE. Reports on queries in 6-8 weeks.
Illustration: Works with 10-15 illustrators/year. Reviews ms/illustration packages from artist. Query with samples, résumé, promo sheet, client list. Contact: Vicki Fischman, art director. Reports back only if interested. Samples returned with SASE or filed. Original artwork returned at job's completion.
Photography: Purchases photos from freelancers. Contact photo editor. Buys stock and assigns work.
Terms: Pays authors royalties or work purchased outright. Illustrators paid by the project. Photographers paid per photo. Book catalog for 10×13 SASE.
Tips: Looks for children's nonfiction grades 5-8 or 9-12.

FREE SPIRIT PUBLISHING, 400 First Ave. N., Suite 616, Dept. CWI, Minneapolis MN 55401-1730. (612)338-2068. Fax: (612)337-5050. Book publisher. Acquisitions Editor: Elizabeth Verdick. Publishes 15-20 titles/year for children and teens, teachers and parents.
 ● Free Spirit no longer accepts fiction or picture book submissions.
Nonfiction: "Free Spirit Publishing specializes in SELF-HELP FOR KIDS®, with an emphasis on self-esteem and self awareness, stress management, school success, creativity, friends and family, social action, and special needs (i.e., gifted and talented, children with learning differences). We prefer books written in a natural, friendly style, with little education/psychology jargon. Need books in our areas of emphasis, and prefer titles written by specialists such as teachers, counselors, and other professionals who work with youth." Recently published *The Kid's Guide to Social Action: How to Solve the Social Problems You Choose—and Turn Creative Thinking into Positive Action*, by Barbara A. Lewis; *Stick Up for Yourself! Every Kid's Guide to Personal Power and Positive Self-Esteem*, by Gershen Kaufman, Ph.D. and Lev Raphael, Ph.D.; and *Bringing Up Parents: The Teenager's Handbook*, by Alex J. Packer, Ph.D.
How to Contact/Writers: Send query letter, or outline with sample chapters. Reports on queries/mss in 2 months. "If you'd like materials returned, enclose a SASE with sufficient postage." Write or call for catalog and submission guidelines before sending submission.
Illustration: Submit samples to acquisitions editor for consideration. If appropriate, samples will be kept on file and artist will be contacted if a suitable project comes up. Enclose SASE if you'd like materials returned.
Photography: Submit samples to acquisitions editor for consideration. If appropriate, samples will be kept on file and photographer will be contacted if a suitable project comes up. Enclose SASE if you'd like materials returned.
Terms: Pays authors in royalties of 7-12% based on wholesale price. Offers advance. Pays illustrators by the project. Pays photographers by the project or per photo.
Tips: "Prefer books that help kids help themselves, or that help adults help kids help themselves; that complement our list without duplicating current titles; and that are written in a direct, straightforward manner."

INSIDER REPORT

As books become multimedia agent may be best ally

As more and more children's books are adapted for film and CD-ROM, an agent is an author's most important ally in negotiating the complex terrain of contracts, says writer/illustrator William Joyce.

Since Joyce's *George Shrinks* was published in 1985, doors opened by technology and a changing market have led that book to CD-ROM adaptation, and his later works *Santa Calls* and *A Day With Wilbur Robinson* to film.

William Joyce

"You need an agent more than ever these days," says Joyce, who admits that after having published 12 children's books, he too is looking for representation. When he signed his publishing contract with Harper & Row for *George Shrinks*, "ignorance was my ally," he says. No one then anticipated the market demand for children's films or advent of CD-ROM that would make the field of children's literature a ripe source for new material.

Joyce points to the successful film adaptations of the works of Chris Van Allsburg (*Jumanji*), Roald Dahl (*James and the Giant Peach, Matilda*) and Frances Hodgson Burnett (*Secret Garden*) as examples of the boom in demand for quality children's entertainment, and how filmmakers are mining children's literature for sources.

"They're all clamoring for it," he says. Joyce retained creative control over his work, and in the case of *George Shrinks* was able to work screen by screen with the animators who brought his story to life on computer.

Contracts must specify the artist's control over future use of his work, because "studio executives are for the most part not creative and are concerned more with what's going on with profits and whether something's going to sell. They base their decisions often on financial instincts rather than what's good for the production," he says.

Professionally, it has taken Joyce a while to reach the enviable position of worrying about creative control over adaptation of his books into film. And he may be justified in being protective of the quirky characters he's spent a lifetime developing. In many ways they reflect the temperament of the author, who "reinvents" his Shreveport, Louisiana, home for each major holiday—Halloween brings a living room bedecked with hundreds of candlelit skeletons; Christmas brings tall clusters of evergreens for each room in the house; and plans for one Fourth of July included backyard construction of a castle surrounded by a moat and armada in flames.

This innate sense of drama and grandeur comes through loud and clear in

INSIDER REPORT, *Joyce*

Joyce's books. In *Bentley & Egg* (Laura Geringer Books, 1992), the swashbuckling frog Bentley saves the egg of his best friend Kak Kak the duck from sure doom in the rough hands of a little boy. In *Santa Calls* (Laura Geringer Books, 1993), Art Atchison Aimesworth of Abilene, Texas, travels to the North Pole and saves sister Esther from the Dark Elves and their evil Queen. The Family Lazardo meets up with a brontosaurus while on safari in Africa, and transports him home to Pimlico Hills via an ocean liner in *Dinosaur Bob* (Harper & Row, 1988).

It is no coincidence that *Dinosaur Bob* was dedicated to *King Kong*—Joyce counts that movie among his early influences, the stories that inspired him to "sit and doodle all kinds of epics that weren't really in book form," he says. "Me being eaten by dinosaurs, my sister being eaten by dinosaurs, my teachers being eaten by dinosaurs. An assignment came along in the fourth grade that said 'make a book.' That's what I can legitimately say was the first book I wrote."

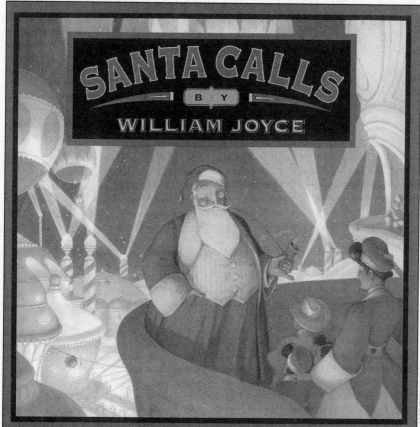

© 1993 William Joyce

In *Santa Calls*, author/illustrator William Joyce tells in his inimitable style the story of Art Atchison Aimesworth's trip to "the glittering city of Toyland, home of Santa and Mrs. Claus" on special invitation of Santa himself.

INSIDER REPORT, *continued*

The fact that this first book, *Billy's Booger*, got Joyce hauled to the principal's office didn't dampen his enthusiasm for crafting stories. By age 16, he had submitted the manuscript for *My Friend and Me* ("deliberately ungrammatical—it's a sweet story about two kids goofing around on a summer's day") to both Scribner's and Harper & Row. Joyce continued sending manuscripts and art samples to publishers throughout his stay at Southern Methodist University, where he studied film, learning to "tell stories with pictures, and color and composition."

With graduation approaching, Joyce faced two choices—head to California and start a career in film, or continue trying to break through in children's publishing. "I didn't want to go to Hollywood and try to get into the movie business, because I already had stories I wanted to tell. I could tell that if I went straight from college I wasn't going to get to tell my stories any time soon. I would be a gopher or a production assistant or something. And I was ready then.

"I was getting discouraged. I could go into the bookstore and see what was being published, and I said 'I really think mine is as good, if not better, than what I'm seeing, and what is the problem?' "

It took a personal contact "through a friend of a friend" at Harper & Row (which later became HarperCollins) to get Joyce's work noticed. "And sure enough, during the first interview, they said, 'We like your stuff. We'll find something for you to do.' " Joyce kept busy illustrating other writers' manuscripts until 1985, when he convinced Harper & Row to publish his manuscript/illustration package *George Shrinks*. Even at that stage, Joyce was still smoothing and developing his storytelling ability.

"My storytelling was pretty much of a mess at the beginning," he says. "I redid *George Shrinks* a couple of times. The first draft was pretty much the way you see it now. Then I got kind of crazed and had George actually get eaten by the cat, and then George grows back to regular size and the cat bursts and there were guts everywhere and somebody said, 'Bill, you've been watching too many *Tom & Jerry* cartoons.' I spent three months on that very detailed dummy and had to pitch about 90 percent of it."

Despite the fact that Joyce got his break illustrating for other writers, he thinks those who can both write and illustrate stand a better chance of getting published "because it involves one less decision that the publishers need to make," Joyce says.

A lot of times they'll say, 'We'll publish it when we find the right illustrator.' Well, years can tumble by and there have been many manuscripts I was offered three or four years ago that I'm finally seeing come out as books," Joyce says. "So you may have written a very nice little story, but until they find the illustrator you're not going to be published."

For writers and illustrators who opt not to find an agent, personal contacts in publishing are all-important, because "they're going to pay a lot more attention to you," Joyce says. "They'll put a face with what you're doing, and they may like you. It's not just how good your stuff is, it's luck and how you come across. If there's a rapport, you have a better chance of getting something going."

—Anne Bowling

FRIENDS UNITED PRESS, 101 Quaker Hill Dr., Richmond IN 47355. (317)962-7573. Fax: (317)966-1293. Book publisher. Editor: Ardith Talbot. Publishes 1 middle reader/year; 1 young adult title/year. 90% of books by first-time authors.

Fiction: Young readers, middle readers and young adults: history, religion. Recently published *Luke's Summer Secret*, by Randall Wisehart, Jr. (historical fiction); *Stories for Jason*, by Mary Cromer (historical fiction); and *Betsy Ross, Quaker Rebel*, by Ethlyn Walkington (historical fiction for young adults).

Nonfiction: Young readers, middle readers and young adults: history, religion.

How to Contact/Writers: Fiction/Nonfiction: Submit outline/synopsis and complete ms. Reports on queries in 1-12 months on queries/mss. Publishes a book 1 year after acceptance. Will consider simultaneous, previously published work.

Terms: Pays authors royalty of 7½% based on wholesale price. Book catalog and ms guidelines available for SASE.

Tips: "Write or call before submitting materials."

LAURA GERINGER BOOKS, 10 E. 53rd St., New York NY 10022. (212)207-7554. Fax: (212)207-7192. Imprint of HarperCollins Publishers. Editorial Director: Laura Geringer. Editor: Caitlun Dlouhy. Publishes 10-12 picture books/year; 2 middle readers/year; 2-4 young adult titles/year. 20% of books by first-time authors; 50% of books from agented authors.

Fiction: All levels: adventure, contemporary, folktales, hi-lo, humor, sports, suspense/mystery. Picture books: animal, concept. Young readers: animal, history, poetry, multicultural. Middle readers: animal, poetry, problem novels. Young adults: history, multicultural, problem novels. Average word length: picture books—250-1,200. Recently published *Buz*, by Richard Egielski (ages 3-7, picture book); *Zoe Rising*, by Pam Conrad (ages 10 and up, middle grade fiction); and *The Leaf Men*, by William Joyce (ages 4-8, picture book).

How to Contact/Writers: Submit complete ms. Reports on queries in 2-4 weeks; mss in 3-4 months. Publishes a book 1½-3 years after acceptance. Will consider simultaneous submissions.

Illustration: Works with 15-20 illustrators/year. Reviews ms/illustration packages from artists. Submit complete package. Illustrations only: Query with samples; submit portfolio for review; provide résumé, business card, promotional literature or tearsheets to be kept on file. Contact: Laura Geringer or Harriett Barton, art director. Reports in 2-3 months. SASE for return of samples; samples kept on file.

Terms: Pays authors royalties of 5-6¼% (picture book) or 10-12½% (novel) based on retail price. Offers advances. Pays illustrators royalties of 5-6¼% based on retail price. Sends galleys to authors; proofs to illustrators. Original artwork returned at job's completion. Book catalog available for 9 × 11 SASE; ms/artist's guidelines available for SASE.

Tips: "Write about what you *know*. Don't try to guess our needs. And don't forget that children are more clever than we give them credit for!" Wants "artwork that isn't overly 'cutesy' with a strong sense of style and expression."

GIBBS SMITH, PUBLISHER, P.O. Box 667, Layton UT 84041. (801)544-9800. Fax: (801)544-5582. Imprint: Peregrine Smith Books. Book publisher. Editorial Director: Madge Baird. Publishes 6-8 books/year. 10% of books by first-time authors. 50% of books from agented authors.

Fiction: Picture books: adventure, contemporary, humor, multicultural, nature/environment, suspense/mystery, western. Average word length: picture books—1,000. Recently published *Once There Was a Bull . . . Frog*, by Rick Walton, illustrated by Greg Hally (ages 4-8, picture book); and *I Know What You Do When I Go to School*, by Ann Edwards Cannon, illustrated by Jennifer Mazzucco (ages 4-8, picture book).

Nonfiction: Middle readers: activity, arts/crafts, cooking, how-to, nature/environment, science. Average word length: up to 10,000. Recently published *Cooking on a Stick*, by Linda White, illustrated by Fran Lee (ages 7-11, cookbook).

How to Contact/Writers: Fiction/Nonfiction: Submit several chapters or complete ms. Reports on queries and mss in 8-10 weeks. Publishes a book 1-2 years after acceptance. Will consider simultaneous submissions. Ms returned with SASE.

Illustration: Works with 6-8 illustrators/year. Reviews ms/illustration packages from artists. Query. Submit ms with 3-5 pieces of final art. Contact: Theresa Desmond, associate editor. Illustrations only: Query with samples; provide résumé, promo sheet, slides (duplicate slides, not originals). Reports back only if interested. Samples returned with SASE; samples filed.

Terms: Pays authors royalty of 4-7½% based on wholesale price or work purchased outright ($500 minimum). Offers advances (average amount: $2,000). Pays illustrators by the project or royalty of 4-5% based on wholesale price. Sends galleys to authors; color proofs to illustrators. Original artwork returned at job's completion. Book catalog available for 9 × 12 SAE and postage. Ms guidelines available.

Tips: "We target ages 5-11."

DAVID R. GODINE, PUBLISHER, P.O. Box 9103, Lincoln MA 01773. (617)259-0700. Fax: (617)259-9198. Book publisher. Estab. 1970. Contact: Editorial Department. Publishes 3-4 picture books/year; 2 young reader titles/year; 3-4 middle reader titles/year. 10% of books by first-time authors; 50% of books from agented writers.

● This publisher is no longer considering unsolicited manuscripts of any type.

Fiction: Picture books: adventure, animal, contemporary, folktales, nature/environment. Young readers: adventure, animal, contemporary, folk or fairy tales, history, nature/environment, poetry. Middle readers: adventure, animal, contemporary, folk or fairy tales, history, mystery, nature/environment, poetry. Young adults/teens: adventure, animal, contemporary, history, mystery, nature/environment, poetry. Recently published *The Empty Creel*, by Geraldine Pope (Paterson Prize winning book with vinyl-cut illustrations); and *An Animated Alphabet*, by Marie Angel.

Nonfiction: Picture books: alphabet, animal, nature/environment. Young readers: activity books, animal, history, music/dance, nature/environment. Middle readers: activity books, animal, biography, history, music/dance, nature/environment. Young adults: biography, history, music/dance, nature/environment.

How to Contact/Writers: Query. Reports on queries in 2 weeks. Reports on solicited ms in 2 weeks (if not agented) or 2 months (if agented). Publishes a book 2 years after acceptance.

Illustration: Only interested in agented material. Works with 4-6 illustrators/year. Reviews ms/illustration packages from artists. "Submit roughs and one piece of finished art plus either sample chapters for very long works or whole ms for short works." Illustrations only: "After query, submit slides, with one full-size blow-up of art." Reports on art samples in 2 weeks. Original artwork returned at job's completion. "Almost all of the children's books we accept for publication come to us with the author and illustrator already paired up. Therefore, we rarely use freelance illustrators." Samples returned with SASE; samples filed (if interested).

Terms: Pays authors in royalties based on retail price. Number of illustrations used determines final payment for illustrators. Pay for separate authors and illustrators "differs with each collaboration." Illustrators paid by the project. Sends galleys to authors; dummies to illustrators. Originals returned at job's completion. Book catalog available for SASE.

Tips: "Always enclose a SASE. Keep in mind that we do not accept unsolicited manuscripts and that we rarely use freelance illustrators."

GOLDEN BOOKS, 850 Third Ave., New York NY 10022. (212)583-6700. Fax: (212)371-1091. Imprint of Golden Books Family Entertainment Inc. Co-Editorial Directors: Marilyn Salomon and Kenn Goin. Book publisher. 100% of books from agented authors.

Fiction: Board books, novelty books, picture books: adventure, animal, concept, contemporary, folktales, humor, nature/environment, religion. Young readers: adventure, animal, contemporary, history. Middle readers: adventure, animal, nature/environment, suspense/mystery. Young adults: animal, history. "Our Essence line is written and illustrated by African-Americans; the books feature African-Americans." Recently published *The Easter Bunny's Wish*, by Justine Korman, illustrated by Maggie Swanson (Wishing Star book, 8 × 8 die-cut with cardstock, ages 2-5); *My First Church Book*, by Beth Hermann, art by Peggy Tagel (Golden Shaped Naptime Tale, 7½ × 8, die-cut board book, ages 1-3); and Sesame Street: *Elmo Can . . . Taste! Touch! Hear! Smell! See!*, by Michaela Muntean, illustrated by Maggie Swanson (Golden Little Look-Look, 5½ × 6, ages 3-5).

Nonfiction: All levels: animal, nature/environment, reference, science. Picture books: concept. Young readers: arts/crafts, cooking, geography, music/dance.

How to Contact/Writers: Only interested in agented material.

Illustration: Only interested in agented material. Sometimes reviews ms/illustration packages from artists. Query first. Illustrations only: Will review work for possible future assignments. Contact: Remo Cosentino and Sandra Forrest, art directors.

Terms: Work purchased outright from authors and illustrators; occasionally pays in royalties based on retail price. Book catalog available for SASE.

GRAPEVINE PUBLICATIONS, INC., P.O. Box 2449, Corvallis OR 97339-2449. (541)754-0583. Fax: (541)754-6508. E-mail: gpi@proaxis.com. Book publisher. Managing Editor: Chris Coffin. Publishes 5 picture books/year; 5 young readers/year. 50% of books by first-time authors.

Fiction: Picture books, young readers, middle readers: adventure, animal, concept, contemporary, fantasy, folktales, hi-lo, history, humor, nature/environment, poetry, suspense/mystery. Average length: picture books—16-32 pages; young readers—32 pages; middle readers—64 pages.
Nonfiction: Young adult: computers/electronics, how-to, mathematics.
How to Contact/Writers: Submit complete ms only. Reports in 3 months. Publishes a book 6-12 months after acceptance. Will consider simultaneous and previously published submissions.
Illustration: Works with 3-4 illustrators/year. Reviews ms illustration packages from artists. Submit ms with dummy. Contact: Chris Coffin. Illustrations only: Query with samples; provide tearsheets. Reports only if interested. Samples returned with SASE (please indicate if return is desired"); samples filed.
Terms: Pays authors royalty of 9% on wholesale price. Pays illustrators and photographers by the project. Sends galleys to authors; dummies to illustrators. Guidelines available for SASE with 2 oz. postage.
Tips: "Test books on kids other than those who know you. Match the 'look and feel' of text and illustrations to the subject and age level." Wants "early/middle reader fiction with polished writing and 'timeless' feel."

*GREENE BARK PRESS, P.O. Box 1108, Bridgeport CT 06601-1108. (203)372-4861. Fax: (203)371-5856. E-mail: greenebark@aol.com. Website: http://www.bookworld.com//greenebark. Book publisher. Associate Publisher: Michele Hofbauer. Publisher: Thomas J. Greene. Publishes 4 picture books/year; 1 young reader/year. 40% of books by first-time authors.
Fiction: Picture books, young readers: adventure, fantasy. Average word length: picture books—650; young readers—1,400. Recently published *Bug & Slug in the Rug*, by Steve Allen, illustrated by Michele Hofbauer (ages 5-9, young reader); *Cookie for the President*, by Anita Bott, illustrated by Pat Collins (ages 5-9, young reader); and *Queen of the Kisses Meets Sam Under A Soup Pot*, by Sherly Kayne, illustrated by Maribeth Blouski (ages 5-8, picture book).
How to Contact/Writers: Reports on queries in 1 month; ms in 2-4 months. Publishes a book 18 months after acceptance. Will consider simultaneous submissions.
Illustrations: Works with 2 illustrators/year. Uses color artwork only. Reviews ms/illustration packages from artists. Submit ms with 3 pieces of final art (copies only). Contact: Thomas J. Greene, publisher. Illustrations only: Query with samples. Contact: Thomas J. Greene, publisher. Reports in 2 months only if interested. Samples returned with SASE; samples filed.
Terms: Pays authors royalty of 10-15% based on wholesale price. Pays illustrators by the project (range: $1,500-3,000) or 5-7½% royalty based on wholesale price. Send galleys to authors; dummies to illustrators. Originals returned to artist at job's completion. Book catalog available for 8½×11 SAE. All imprints included in a single catalog. Ms and art guidelines available for SASE.
Tips: "As a guide for future publications do not look to our older backlist. Please no telephone queries."

GREENHAVEN PRESS, 10911 Technology Place, San Diego CA 92127. (619)485-7424. Book publisher. Estab. 1970. Senior Editor: Bonnie Szumski. Publishes 40-50 young adult titles/year. 35% of books by first-time authors.
Nonfiction: Middle readers: biography, controversial topics, history, issues. Young adults: biography, history, nature/environment. Other titles "to fit our specific series." Average word length: young adults—15,000-25,000.
How to Contact/Writers: Query only. "We accept no unsolicited manuscripts. All writing is done on a work-for-hire basis."
Terms: Buys ms outright for $1,500-3,000. Offers advances. Sends galleys to authors. Book catalog available for 9×12 SAE and 65¢ postage.
Tips: "Get our guidelines first before submitting anything."

GREENWILLOW BOOKS, 1350 Avenue of the Americas, New York NY 10019. (212)261-6500. Imprint of William Morrow & Co. Book publisher. Editor-in-Chief: Susan Hirschman. Art Director: Ava Weiss. Publishes 50 picture books/year; 10 middle readers books/year; 10 young adult books/year.
• See First Books, page 28, for an interview with Greenwillow's Lisa Maizlish, photographer of *The Ring*.
Fiction: Will consider all levels of fiction; various categories.
How to Contact/Writers: Submit complete ms to editorial department "not specific editor." Do not call. Reports on mss in 10-12 weeks. Publishes a book 18-24 months after acceptance. Will consider simultaneous submissions.

INSIDER REPORT

Drawing picture book ideas from real life

Illustrators and writers both can learn from artist/ author Judith Caseley. Illustrators can learn that it's possible to overcome fear and shyness and break into the picture book market. Writers can learn the rewards of pulling inspiration from real life.

Early in Caseley's career as an artist, she was so shy she had a hard time showing her work to anyone. "I'd get slides together, send them off to a gallery, and I'd be so afraid to make the phone call asking about my slides, I'd just leave them there forever. It was just terrible."

Despite her reticence, Caseley did get a few gallery shows, some work painting for greeting cards, and one book illustration job. "I'd gone to several publishers, but I'm talking two a year because I was so shy. They'd say 'no,' then I'd cry and not go to a publisher for another year."

Judith Caseley

Then Caseley took a course with picture book guru Uri Shulevitz in Greenwich Village and began to think about doing picture books herself. She even managed to find an agent. "I was working in a skin clinic and a woman came in who was a children's book agent, so I showed her my greeting cards and a couple of things I'd done at the workshop." The agent took Caseley on as a client, but didn't get any work for her. "I'll always remember, she said, 'There are apples and there are oranges. The apples are selling. You're the orange.'"

So Caseley timidly started doing the rounds again. "My heart would be hammering every time I'd pick up the telephone. And the truth is, it still does. It's all bravado. I guess it's like working into the phobia. I present myself as if I'm very confident and outgoing—sometimes if you act like that you start believing it. But still . . . it haunts me a little bit."

Caseley got her career break when she met Susan Hirschman at Greenwillow Books. "She told me that the cards [in my portfolio] were very nice, but they needed good stories for children." So Caseley began to write and illustrate picture books for Greenwillow. Not surprisingly, *Molly Pink*, the first book Caseley wrote and illustrated, is about a little girl with stage fright, a story based on an event from Caseley's childhood.

The original version of *Molly Pink* "was called *Lester Chester* and he had blue hair," Caseley says. "Susan set me straight, and said, 'Listen—let's forget about the blue hair. Let's make this a real child.' Then I started tapping into my own childhood and my children's childhoods, and then other children. If they'd tell me a story, I'd jot it down."

INSIDER REPORT, *Caseley*

This scene from author/illustrator Judith Caseley's *Slumber Party* shows a tense moment at young Zoe's birthday party, as her four guests argue over who gets to sleep next to the birthday girl. The problem is solved as they decide Zoe will sleep on the couch so each little girl will be sleeping next to part of her. *Slumber Party* is based on a real-life slumber party of Caseley's daughter Jenna.

Since *Molly Pink*, Caseley has written and illustrated about two dozen picture books, and written several middle grade and young adult novels. If you spend a few hours reading her books, you'll probably feel like you've gotten to know her. The stories she writes and illustrates are very real. She believes in writing what you know, and tackles real-life issues—from the death of a grandparent or a new baby in the family to noisy kids and slumber parties.

Despite the topics she deals with in her picture books, Caseley's illustrations are full of bright colors and feature clothing, decor and furniture in an array of fun, bold patterns. "When I handed *Priscilla Twice* in to the art director, I told her it was going to be somber because it was about divorce. But I had just bought a set of really beautiful watercolor inks and it was my brightest book yet."

Caseley got the idea for *Priscilla Twice* on a classroom visit. The children, in fact, asked her to do a book about divorce. "I was really naive. I remember thinking that if you live in a place like Ohio, you have fewer divorces than New York. Five or six children asked me to write a story about divorce."

On another school visit, Caseley found out just how real her stories seem. "I was proud because the librarian said, 'Are you divorced?' I said, 'No, I'm not.' She announced, 'We were wrong, class. We thought Judith Caseley was divorced because of *Priscilla Twice*.' I thought, 'Yes! The fiction worked!' "

For ideas, "sometimes I'll sit there and listen to [my daughter] Jenna and her friends. It's like fodder." But Caseley must be sensitive about what she usurps for books when it comes to her daughter and her friends. "They don't think in terms of fiction when they're involved. They think of it as exactly them.

"There's this one little girl who's been bugging Jenna, and Jenna had this other little girl over and they were discussing how Jenna could get rid of the little girl without hurting her feelings. It was just wonderful, but if I write that into a story, the little girl might recognize herself and get offended. And Jenna will certainly recognize herself."

Caseley jokes that she had her second child "for inspiration. So I could write about sibling rivalry and things like that." And although she has written a few books for older readers, she doesn't think she'll grow out of doing picture books, that her books will get older as her children do. "My great love is illustrating picture books. It feels to me like going home. I hope I can keep doing them. I'll keep asking children for ideas."

—Alice P. Buening

Illustration: Reviews ms/illustration packages from artists. Illustrations only: Query with samples, résumé.
Terms: Pays authors royalty. Offers advances. Pays illustrators royalty or by the project. Sends galleys to authors. Book catalog available for 9 × 12 SAE with $2 postage; ms guidelines available for SASE.

GROSSET & DUNLAP, INC., 200 Madison Ave., New York NY 10016. (212)951-8700. Imprint of The Putnam & Grosset Group.
• Grosset & Dunlap is no longer accepting unsolicited submissions.

GRYPHON HOUSE, P.O. Box 207, Beltsville MD 20704-0207. (301)595-9500. Fax: (301)595-0051. E-mail: kathyc@ghbooks.com. Book publisher. Editor-in-Chief: Kathy Charner.
Nonfiction: Parent and teacher resource books—activity books, textbooks. Recently published *500 Five Minute Games*, by Jackie Silberg; *MathArts*, by MaryAnn Kohl and Cindy Gainer; *Never, EVER, Serve Sugary Snacks on Rainy Days*, by Shirley Raines; and *The Complete Learning Center Book*, by Rebecca Isbell.
How to Contact/Writers: Query. Submit outline/synopsis and 2 sample chapters. Reports on queries/mss in 3 months. Publishes a book 18 months after acceptance. Will consider simultaneous submissions, electronic submissions via disk or modem.
Illustration: Works with 3-4 illustrators/year. Uses b&w artwork only. Reviews ms/illustration packages from artists. Submit query letter with table of contents, introduction and sample chapters. Illustrations only: Query with samples, promo sheet. Reports back in 2 months. Samples returned with SASE; samples filed.
Photography: Buys photos from freelancers. Contact: Kathy Charner, editor-in-chief. Buys stock and assigns work. Submit cover letter, published samples, stock photo list.
Terms: Pays authors royalty based on wholesale price. Offers advances. Pays illustrators by the project. Pay photographers by the project or per photo. Sends galleys to authors. Original artwork returned at job's completion. Book catalog and ms guidelines available for SASE.
Tips: "Send a SASE for our catalog and manuscript guidelines. Look at our books, then submit proposals that complement the books we already publish or supplement our existing books. We are looking for books of creative, participatory learning experiences that have a common conceptual theme to tie them together. The books should be on subjects that teachers want to do on a daily basis in the classroom. If a book caters to a particular market in addition to teachers, that would be a plus."

HACHAI PUBLISHING, 156 Chester Ave., Brooklyn NY 11218. (718)633-0100. Fax: (718)633-0103. Book publisher. Submissions Editor: Devorah Leah Rosenfeld. Publishes 3 picture books/year; 3 young readers/year; 1 middle reader/year. 75% of books published by first-time authors. "All books have spiritual/religious themes, specifically traditional Jewish content. We're seeking books about morals and values; the Jewish experience in current and Biblical times; and Jewish observance, Sabbath and holidays."
Fiction: Picture books and young readers: contemporary, history, religion. Middle readers: adventure, contemporary, problem novels, religion. Does not want to see animal stories, romance, problem novels depicting drug use or violence. Recently published *As Big As An Egg*, by Rachel Sandman, illustrated by Chana Zakashanskaya (ages 3-6, picture book); and *David the Little Shepherd*, by Dina Rosenfeld, illustrated by Ilene Winn-Lederer (ages 3-6, picture book).
Nonfiction: Published *My Jewish ABC's*, by Draizy Zelcer, illustrated by Patti Nemeroff (ages 3-6, picture book).
How to Contact/Wrtiers: Fiction/Nonfiction: Submit complete ms.
Illustration: Works with 4 illustrators/year. Uses color artwork only. Reviews ms/illustration packages from authors. Submit ms with 1 piece of final art. Contact: Devorah Leah Rosenfeld, submissions editor. Illustrations only: Query with samples; arrange personal portfolio review. Reports in 2 weeks. Samples returned with SASE.
Terms: Work purchased outright from authors for $1,000. Pays illustrators by the project (range: 2,000). Book catalog, ms/artist's guidelines available for SASE.
Tips: "Write a story that incorporates a moral . . . not a preachy morality tale. Originality is the key. We feel Hachai is going to appeal to a wider readership as parents become more interested in positive values for their children."

HARCOURT BRACE & CO., 525 B St., Suite 1900, San Diego CA 92101-4495. (619)231-6616. Children's Books Division includes: Harcourt Brace Children's Books, Gulliver Books,

Voyager Paperbacks, Odyssey Paperbacks, Jane Yolen Books, Browndeer Press, Silver Whistle Books, Red Wagon Books and Magic Carpet Books. Book publisher. Publishes 70-75 picture books/year; 15-20 middle reader titles/year; 8-12 young adult titles/year. 20% of books by first-time authors; 50% of books from agented writers.

● The staff of Harcourt Brace's children's book department is no longer accepting unsolicited manuscripts. Only query letters and manuscripts submitted by agents will be considered.

Fiction: Picture books, young readers: animal, contemporary, fantasy, history. Middle readers, young adults: animal, contemporary, fantasy, history, problem novels, romance, science fiction, sports, spy/mystery/adventure. Average word length: picture books—"varies greatly"; middle readers—20,000-50,000; young adults—35,000-65,000.

Nonfiction: Picture books, young readers: animal, biography, history, hobbies, music/dance, nature/environment, religion, sports. Middle readers, young adults: animal, biography, education, history, hobbies, music/dance, nature/environment, religion, sports. Average word length: picture books—"varies greatly"; middle readers—20,000-50,000; young adults—35,000-65,000.

How to Contact/Writers: Only interested in agented material.

Illustration: Reviews ms/illustration packages from artists. "For picture books ms—complete ms acceptable. Longer books—outline and 2-4 sample chapters." Send several samples of art; no original art. Illustrations only: Submit résumé, tearsheets, color photocopies, color stats all accepted. "Please DO NOT send original artwork or transparencies. Include SASE for return, please." Reports on art samples in 6-10 weeks.

Terms: Pays authors in royalties based on retail price. Pays illustrators either by the project or by royalties. Sends galleys to authors; dummies to illustrators. Original artwork returned at job's completion. Book catalog available for 9×12 SASE; ms/artist's guidelines for business-size SASE.

Tips: "Become acquainted with Harcourt Brace's books in particular if you are interested in submitting proposals to us."

*HARKEY MULTIMEDIA PUBLISHING, P.O. Box 20001, Seattle WA 98102. (206)213-1366. Fax: (206)329-9791. E-mail: harkeymp@aol.com. Book publisher. Editor: Charlotte Bosarge. Publishes 3 picture books/year; 3 young readers/year; 2 middle readers/year; 1 young adult/year. 90% of books by first-time authors.

Fiction: Picture books, young readers: fantasy, special needs. Middle readers; fantasy, folktales, history. Young adult/teens: fantasy, folktales, multicultural, religion, religious multicultural, science fiction, suspense/mystery. Sees too much of sports material. Average word length: picture books—1-1,000; young readers—5,000-10,000; middle readers—10,000; young adult/teens—10,000-20,000.

Nonfiction: Picture books, young readers, middle readers: activity books, special needs. Young adults/teens: activity books, biography, concept, religious multicultural, multicultural, religion, special needs. Does not want to see music/dance material.

How to Contact/Writers: Fiction/Nonfiction: Query. Submit outline/synopsis and 1 sample chapter. Reports on queries/mss in 2 weeks. Publishes a book 6-12 months after acceptance. Will consider simultaneous submissions and electronic submissions via disk or modem.

Illustration: Works with 15-20 illustrators/year. Reviews ms/illustration packages from artists. Query. Send ms with dummy and at least 3 pieces of final art. Samples returned with SASE; samples filed.

Photography: "We will be taking photography starting in 1998." Model/property releases required; captions required. Submit cover letter.

Terms: Pays authors royalty of 8-10% based on retail price. Pays illustrators by the project or royalty of 6-8% based on retail price. "If for picture book, 50% shared with author." Sends

---

 A BULLET within a listing introduces special comments by the editor of *Children's Writer's & Illustrator's Market.*

galleys to authors; dummies to illustrators. Originals returned to artist at job's completion. Ms/art guidelines available for SASE.

HARPERCOLLINS CHILDREN'S BOOKS, 10 E. 53rd St., New York NY 10022-5299. (212)207-7044. Fax: (212)207-7192. Website: http://www.harpercollins.com. Book publisher. Contact: Submissions Editor. Creative Director: Harriett Barton. Imprints: Laura Geringer Books, Michael diCapua Books, Joanna Cotler Books.
Fiction: Picture books: adventure, animal, anthology, concept, contemporary, fantasy, folktales, hi-lo, history, multicultural, nature/environment, poetry, religion. Middle readers: adventure, hi-lo, history, poetry, suspense/mystery. Young adults/teens: fantasy, science fiction, suspense/mystery. All levels: multicultural. "Artists with diverse backgrounds and settings shown in their work."
Nonfiction: Picture books: animal, arts/crafts, biography, geography, multicultrual, nature/environment. Middle readers: how-to.
Illustration: Works with 100 illustrators/year. Reports only if interested. Samples returned with SASE; samples filed only if interested.
Terms: Manuscript and art guidelines available for SASE.

HARVEST HOUSE PUBLISHERS, 1075 Arrowsmith, Eugene OR 97402. (503)343-0123. Book publisher. Manuscript Coordinator: Kristi Hirte. Publishes 1-2 picture books/year; 2 young reader titles/year; 2 young adult titles/year. 2-5% of books by first-time authors. Books follow a Christian theme.
 • Harvest House no longer accepts unsolicited children's manuscripts.
Illustration: Reviews ms/illustration packages from artists. Submit "3 chapters of ms with copies (do not send originals) of art and any approximate rough sketches. Illustrations only: Send résumé, tearsheets. Submit to color design coordinator. Reports on art samples in 2 months.
Terms: Pays authors in royalties of 10-15%. Average advance payment: "negotiable." Pays illustrator: "Sometimes by project." Sends galleys to authors; sometimes sends dummies to illustrators. SASE for book catalog, ms guidelines.

HAYES SCHOOL PUBLISHING CO. INC., 321 Pennwood Ave., Wilkinsburg PA 15221. (412)371-2373. Fax: (412)371-6408. Contact: Mr. Clair N. Hayes. Estab. 1940. Produces folders, workbooks, stickers, certificates. Wants to see supplementary teaching aids for grades K-12. Interested in all subject areas. Will consider simultaneous and electronic submissions.
How to Contact/Writers: Query with description or complete ms. Reports in 3-4 weeks. SASE for return of submissions.
Terms: Work purchased outright. Purchases all rights.

HENDRICK-LONG PUBLISHING COMPANY, P.O. Box 25123, Dallas TX 75225. Book publisher. Vice President: Joann Long. Publishes 1 picture book/year; 4 young reader titles/year; 4 middle reader titles/year. 20% of books by first-time authors.
Fiction: Middle readers: history books on Texas and the Southwest. No fantasy or poetry. Recently published *Baxter Badger's Home*, by Doris McClennan, illustrated by Vicki Diggs (young reader picture book); and *Race to Velasco*, by Paul Spellman (ages 9 and up).
Nonfiction: Middle, young adults: history books on Texas and the Southwest, biography, multicultural. Recently published *Camels for Uncle Sam*, by Diane Yancey (ages 9 and up); and *Race to Velasco*, by Paul Spellman (ages 9 and up).
How to Contact/Writers: Only interested in agented material. Fiction/Nonfiction: Query with outline/synopsis and sample chapter. Reports on queries in 2 weeks; mss in 2 months. Publishes a book 18 months after acceptance. No simultaneous submissions. Include SASE.
Illustration: Works with 3-4 illustrators/year. Uses primarily b&w interior artwork; color covers only. Illustrations only: Query first. Submit résumé or promotional literature or photocopies or tearsheets—no original work sent unsolicited. Contact: Joann Long. Material kept on file. No reply sent.
Terms: Pays authors in royalty based on selling price. Advances vary. Pays illustrators by the project or royalty. Sends galleys to authors; dummies to illustrators. Ms guidelines for 1 first-class stamp and #10 SAE.
Tips "Material **must** pertain to Texas or the Southwest. Check all facts about historical firgures and events in both fiction and nonfiction. Be accurate."

HERALD PRESS, 616 Walnut Ave., Scottdale PA 15683. (412)887-8500. Fax: (412)887-3111. Division of Mennonite Publishing House. Estab. 1908. Publishes 1 picture storybook/year; 1

Writing is a labor of love

Sharon Creech, 1995 Newbery Medalist for the young adult novel *Walk Two Moons*, has always felt an affinity for anything having to do with books or writing. As a child, she was intrigued by poetry and stories, and even liked pencils, pens, spelling tests and grammar. But it wasn't until her father's death in 1986 that she got serious about her own writing.

Sharon Creech

Six years previously, her father had suffered a stroke that left him paralyzed and unable to speak or understand words. "It affected me profoundly," says Creech. A month after his death, she started her first novel. "It was as if suddenly I was aware that I was mortal . . . that you can't just keep on saying, 'I'm going to do this.' If you want to do it, then just do it."

Without stopping, she completed one novel after another—a "flood" of words. Creech sometimes believes all the words that couldn't be communicated to her father just burst forth into her writing—as if she had an obligation to use the words he couldn't. Having since passed beyond this "emotional" impetus, she now writes for the sheer love of it. Her works include two adult novels, one play and four juvenile novels.

Creech finds that the hardest part of writing is reconciling her devotion to her work with everyday responsibilities. When she starts a book, her impulse is to immerse herself in it. "I would love to go hide in a cabin for a month, but that's not practical or possible."

For nine months of the year, Creech and her husband live in England where he works as headmaster of an international day/boarding school. When she started writing, her duties as the mother of two school-age children, a full-time English teacher, and the wife of a headmaster left her little time for personal projects. After finishing dinner, grading papers and completing lesson plans, she might grab an hour to write while her children were busy with their homework.

As she published more and more, she gradually reduced her teaching hours and increased her writing hours until she was writing full time. "I was worried for a while, though," she says. "Because, as with most writers, with your first few books, you don't earn any money—very small advances—and you're not selling enough in the first year to earn royalties. I felt very guilty, because we were also trying to put our kids through college." Writing seemed like a luxury and Creech thought after a couple of years she might return to full-time teaching. Then she won the Newbery and her writing career was sealed.

The more Creech writes, the more challenges she finds in exploring new forms and ways of saying things. Her first four novels alternated between adult and juvenile. "Each was feeding the next," she says. When she wrote about older

INSIDER REPORT, *Creech*

people, she'd become intrigued about what they were like when they were young. She has also worked with different narrative forms and levels of plot complexity. Her novel *Absolutely Normal Chaos*, presented as 13-year-old Mary Lou Finney's summer journal, gives a humorously breezy account of first romance and chaotic family give-and-take. *Walk Two Moons* retains the light touch of a 13-year-old's first-person narrative, but intertwines several storylines to explore intensely serious themes of love and loss. This richly layered tale earned her the reputation of a master plot-weaver.

Creech feels her job as a writer is to explore whatever idea prompted her to start writing and then to tell the story in the most interesting way she can. She observes that some fiction writers plan their stories before they write; others just begin and discover the stories as they write them. Creech is in the second group. She wrote three versions of *Walk Two Moons* before her editor felt it was right. The protagonist, Salamanca Hiddle, did not surface until the third version, and only about a quarter of the first and second versions ended up in the finished piece.

Each time her editor asked her to rework the manuscript, Creech's first thought was, "What's wrong with it? I think it's perfect." But about a week later, her mind was toying with things she might change. She'd become so interested in the possibilities, she didn't mind reworking her core idea. "That's my favorite part," says Creech. She jokes that she probably could have gone on rewriting *Walk Two Moons* for another ten years. "I'm glad somebody told me to stop."

Creech urges new writers to remember that they write because they want to write. Her optimistic viewpoint is that if you keep writing and sending things out, eventually you will get a match—"someone who wants what you write." She isn't one to pontificate, but when urged to give advice, she offers four suggestions: Read a lot, write a lot, educate yourself about publishing, and relax.

—*Holly Davis*

Newbery Medal winner Sharon Creech's latest offering, *Absolutely Normal Chaos*, is the journal of 13-year-old Mary Lou Finney, written as an over-the-summer school project. Mary Lou does a lot of growing up as the summer unfolds learning about romance, death and her cousin's search for his biological father.

Jacket art © 1996 Roger Motzkus. Jacket © 1996 HarperCollins Publishers

young reader title/year; 2-3 middle reader titles/year; 1-2 young adult titles/year. Editorial Contact: S. David Garber. Art Director: Jim Butti. 20% of books by first-time authors; 3% of books from agented writers.

Fiction: Young readers, middle readers, young adults: contemporary, history, problem novels, religious, self-help, social concerns. Recently published *April Bluebird*, by Esther Bender; *Whispering Brook Farm*, by Carrie Baker. Does not want stories on fantasy, science fiction, war, drugs, cops and robbers.

Nonfiction: Young readers, middle readers, young adults: how-to, religious, self-help, social concerns. Published *Storytime Jamboree*, by Peter Dyck; and *We Knew Jesus*, by Marian Hostetler (both fiction and nonfiction collections).

How to Contact/Writers: Fiction/Nonfiction: "Send to Book Editor, the following: (1) a one-page summary of your book, (2) a one- or two-sentence summary of each chapter, (3) the first chapter and one other, (4) your statement of the significance of the book, (5) a description of your target audience, (6) a brief biographical sketch of yourself, and (7) SASE for return of the material. You may expect a reply in about a month. If your proposal appears to have potential for Herald Press, a finished manuscript will be requested. Herald Press depends on capable and dedicated authors to continue publishing high-quality Christian literature." Reports on queries in 1 month; mss in 2 months. Publishes a book 12 months after acceptance. Will consider simultaneous submissions but prefers not to.

Illustration: Works with 3 illustrators/year. Reviews ms/illustration packages from artists. Illustrations only: Query with samples. Send résumé, tearsheets and slides. Contact: Jim Butti, art director.

Photography: Purchases photos from freelancers. Contact: Debbie Cameron. Buys stock and assigns work.

Terms: Pays authors in royalties of 10-12% based on retail price. Pays for illustrators by the project (range: $220-600). Sends galleys to authors. Book catalog for 3 first-class stamps; ms guidelines free on request.

Tips: "We invite book proposals from Christian authors in the area of juvenile fiction. Our purpose is to publish books which are consistent with Scripture as interpreted in the Anabaptist/Mennonite tradition. Books that are honest in presentation, clear in thought, stimulating in content, appropriate in appearance, superior in printing and binding, and conducive to the spiritual growth and welfare of the reader."

HIGHSMITH PRESS, P.O. Box 800, Ft. Atkinson WI 53538. (414)563-9571. (414)563-4801. E-mail: hpress@highsmith.com. Website: http://www.hpress.highsmith.com. Imprint: Alleyside Press, Book publisher. Publisher: Donald Sager.

Nonfiction: All levels: activity books, library skills, multicultural, reference, study skills. Multicultural needs include storytelling resources. Average length: 48-120 pages. Published *Research to Write*, by Maity Schrecengost (study skills for ages 8-11); *An Alphabet of Books, Literature Based Activities for Schools and Libraries*, by Robin Davis (activity book for ages 3-7); and *World Guide to Historical Fiction for Young Adults*, by Lee Gordon (reference for ages 11-17).

How to Contact/Writers: Query; submit complete ms; submit outline/synopsis. Reports on queries in 1 month; mss in 6-8 weeks. Publishes a book 6 months after acceptance. Will consider simultaneous submissions.

Terms: Pays authors royalty of 10-12% based on wholesale price. Offers advances. Sends galleys to authors. Book catalog available for 9×12 SAE and 2 first-class stamps; ms guidelines available for SASE.

Tips: "Review our catalog and ms guidelines to see what we publish. Our complete catalog and current guidelines can be found at our website on the Internet (address above), as well as a list of projects for which we are seeking authors. It's getting to be a tougher market, with more electronic versions, especially reference."

HODDER CHILDREN'S BOOKS, Hodder Headline PLC, 338 Euston Rd., London NW1 3BH England. (0171)873-6000. Fax: (0171)873-6229. Book publisher. Contact: Editorial Dept. Children's Art Dept. Publishes 12 picture books/year; 24 young readers/year; 50 middle readers; 6 young adult titles/year.

Fiction: Picture books, young readers and middle readers: adventure, animal, concept, contemporary, fantasy, humor, nature/environment and suspense/mystery. Young adults: adventure, contemporary, fantasy, humor, science fiction, suspense/mystery, horror. Average word length: picture books—1,000; read alones (6-8 years) 2,000-4,000; story books (7-9 years) 8,000-12,000; novels (8 and up) 20,000-50,000.

Nonfiction: Picture books: animal. Young readers: activity books, humor. Middle readers: activity books. Young adults: careers, health, self-help, social issues. Average word length: picture books—1,000; young readers—5,000; middle readers—15,000; young adults—20,000. Published *Just 17 Quiz Book*, by Anita Naik (ages 10-14, teen self help/fun); *Addition and Subtraction*, by R. Whiteford and J (ages 5-7, infant home-learning).

How to Contact/Writers: Fiction: Submit outline/synopsis and 3 sample chapters. Reports on queries in 1 month; mss in 1 month. Publishes a book 12-18 months after acceptance. Will consider simultaneous submissions.

Illustration: Uses both b&w and color artwork. Reviews ms/illustration packages from authors. Submit ms with dummy. Contact: Children's Editor. Illustrations only: query with photocopied samples. Reports in 1 month. Samples returned with SASE; samples filed.

Photography: Buys photos from freelancers. Contact: Children's Art Dept. Buys stock and assigns work. Submit cover letter.

Terms: Pays authors royalty or work purchased outright. Pays illustrators by the project or royalty. Pays photographers by the project. Original artwork returned at job's completion. Sends galleys to authors. Ms guidelines available.

Tips: "Write from the heart. Don't patronize your reader. Do your research—read the finest writers around, see where the market is. We're looking for something original with a clear sense of the first reader."

HOLIDAY HOUSE INC., 425 Madison Ave., New York NY 10017. (212)688-0085. Fax: (212)421-6134. Book publisher. Vice President/Editor-in-Chief: Regina Griffin. Associate Editor: Allison Cunningham. Publishes 30 picture books/year; 3 young reader titles/year; 10 middle reader titles/year; 3 young adult titles/year. 20% of books by first-time authors; 10% from agented writers.

• See First Books, page 28, for an interview with Holiday House artist Katya Krenina, illustrator of *The Magic Dreidels*, by Eric A. Kimmel.

Fiction: All levels: adventure, contemporary, history, humor, multicultural, nature/environment, sports. Picture books: animal. Middle readers, young adults: fantasy, suspense/mystery. Recently published *The Magic Dreidels*, by Eric A. Kimmel, illustrated by Katya Krenina; *The Golem*, by Barbara Rogasky, illustrated by Trina Schart Hyman; and *The Life and Death of Crazy Horse*, by Russell Freedman, photos by Amos Bad Heart Bull.

Nonfiction: All levels: animal, biography, concept, geography, math, nature/environment, science, sports. Picture books, young readers: religion.

How to Contact/Writers: Send queries and mss to Allison Cunningham. Reports on queries in 3 weeks; mss in 8-10 weeks. Manuscripts returned only with SASE.

Illustration: Works with 15 illustrators/year. Reviews ms illustration packages from artists. Send ms with dummy. Contact: Allison Cunningham, associate editor. Reports back only if interested. Samples returned with SASE or filed.

Terms: Pays authors and illustrators an advance against royalties. Originals returned at job's completion. Book catalog, ms/artist's guidelines available for a SASE.

Tips: "Fewer books are being published. It will get even harder for first timers to break in."

HENRY HOLT & CO., INC., 115 W. 18th St., New York NY 10011. (212)886-9200. Book publisher. Editor-in-Chief/Vice President/Associate Publisher: Margery Cuyler. Publishes 20-40 picture books/year; 4-6 young reader titles/year; 10-15 middle reader titles/year; 10-15 young adult titles/year. 5% of books by first-time authors; 40% of books from agented writers.

Fiction: Picture books: animal, concept, history, humor, multicultural, religion, sports. Middle readers: adventure, animal, contemporary, fantasy, history, humor, multicultural, religion, sports, suspense/mystery. Young adults: contemporary, fantasy, history, multicultural, nature/environment, problem novels, sports.

How to Contact/Writers: Fiction/Nonfiction: Submit complete ms. Reports on queries/mss in 3 months. Publishes a book 12-18 months after acceptance. Will consider simultaneous submissions.

Illustration: Works with 50 illustrators/year. Reviews ms/illustration packages from artists. Random samples OK. Illustrations only: Submit tearsheets, slides. Do *not* send originals. Reports on art samples in 1 month. Samples returned with SASE; samples filed. If accepted, original artwork returned at job's completion.

Terms: Pays authors/illustrators royalty based on retail price. Sends galleys to authors; dummies to illustrators.

HOUGHTON MIFFLIN CO., Children's Trade Books, 222 Berkeley St., Boston MA 02116 and 215 Park Ave. S., New York NY 10003. (617)351-5000. Fax: (617)351-1111. Website: http://www.hmco.com. Book publisher. Publisher: Norma Jean Sawicky. Editor: Matilda Welter. Editors: Audrey Bryant, Margaret Raymo. Assistant Editor: Amy Thrall. Art Director: Amy Bernstein. Averages 80 titles/year. Publishes hardcover originals and trade paperback reprints.
  • Ticknor & Fields has merged with Houghton Mifflin and kept its Boston address. Houghton's book *Orphan Train Rider: One Boy's True Story*, by Andrea Warren, received the 1996 Boston Globe-Horn Book Award for nonfiction. See the listing for Houghton Mifflin Interactive in the Multimedia section.
Fiction: All levels: all categories except religion. "We do not rule out any theme, though we do not publish specifically religious material." Published *The Giver*, by Lois Lowry (novel); *Owl in Love*, by Patrice Kindl (ages 10 and up, novel); and *The Sweetest Fig*, by Chris Van Allsburg (all ages, picture book).
Nonfiction: Published *Grandfather's Journey*, by Allen Say (all ages picture book); and *Amish Home*, by Raymond Bial (ages 7-14, photo essay).
How to Contact/Writers: Fiction: Submit complete ms. Nonfiction: Submit outline/synopsis and sample chapters. Reports on queries in 2 weeks; on mss in 6-8 weeks.
Illustration: Works with 60 illustrators/year. Reviews ms/illustration packages from artists. Ms/illustration packages or illustrations only: Query with samples (colored photocopies are fine); provide tearsheets. Reports in 6-8 weeks. Samples returned with SASE; samples filed if of interest.
Terms: Pays standard royalty; offers advance. Illustrators paid by the project and royalty. Ms and artist's guidelines available for SASE.

HUMANICS CHILDREN'S HOUSE, Humanics Limited, 1482 Mecaslin St. NW, Atlanta GA 30309. (404)874-2176. Fax: (404)874-1976. Book publisher. Acquisitions: W. Arthur Bligh. Publishes 6 picture books/year. 50% of books by first-time authors. "Primary themes include self-esteem, and building the child's awareness of self and others through a multicultural, non-ethnocentric approach."
Fiction: Picture books and young readers: animal, concept, contemporary, fantasy, folktales, multicultural, nature/environment. Multicultural needs include stories dealing with bridging cultural gaps. Average length: picture books—32 pages; young readers—32 pages. Published *The Adventure of Paz in the Land of Numbers*, by Miriam Bowden (English and Spanish counting, picture book); *Planet of the Dinosaurs*, by Dr. Barbara Carr (adventure, picture book); and *Cambio Chameleon*, by Mauro Magellan (self-esteem, picture book), all for ages pre-K to grade 3.
Nonfiction: Picture books: activity books, animal, arts/crafts, multicultural, music/dance, nature/environment, self help, social issues. Young readers: activity books, animal, multicultural, music/dance, nature/environment, self help, social issues. Average length: activity books—160 pages; young readers—160 pages.
How to Contact/Writers: Fiction: Query. Will consider simultaneous submissions.
Illustration: Samples returned with SASE. Original artwork returned at job's completion.
Terms: "All pay is negotiable." Sends galleys to authors; dummies to illustrators. Book catalog available for 9 × 12 SAE and 2 first-class stamps; ms and art guidelines available for SASE.
Tips: "Please send query letters which detail your writing experience and goals, plus a product that is innovative and memorable."

HUNTINGTON HOUSE PUBLISHERS, P.O. Box 53788, Lafayette LA 70505. (318)237-7049. Fax: (318)237-7060. Book publisher. Editor-in-Chief: Mark Anthony. Publishes 6 young readers/year. 30% of books by first-time authors. "All books have spiritual/religious themes."
Fiction: Picture books, young readers, middle readers, young adults: all subjects. Does not want to see romance, nature/environment, multicultural. Average word length: picture books—12-50; young readers—100-300; middle readers—4,000-15,000; young adults/teens—10,000-40,000.

"PICTURE BOOKS" are for preschoolers to 8-year-olds; "Young readers" are for 5- to 8-year-olds; "Middle readers" are for 9- to 11-year-olds; and "Young adults" are for those ages 12 and up.

Published *Greatest Star of All*, by Greg Gulley and David Watts (ages 9-11, adventure/religion). **Nonfiction:** Picture books: animal, religion. Young readers, middle readers, young adults/teens: biography, history, religion. No nature/environment, multicultural. Average word length: picture books—12-50; young readers—100-300; middle readers—4,000-15,000; young adult/teens— 10,000-40,000. Published *To Grow By Storybook Readers*, by Marie Le Doux and Janet Friend (preschool to age 8, textbook) *High on Adventure*, by Steve Arrington (young adult).
How to Contact/Writers: Fiction/Nonfiction: Query. Submit outline/synopsis, table of contents and proposal letter. One or two sample chapters are optional. Send SASE. Reports on queries/mss in 2-3 months. Publishes a book 8 months after acceptance. Will consider simultaneous submissions.
Illustration: Works with 2 illustrators/year. Reviews ms/illustration packages from artists. Query; submit ms with dummy. Contact: Mark Anthony, editor-in-chief. Reports in 1 month. Illustrations only: Query with samples; send résumé and client list. Reports in 2-3 months. Samples returned with SASE; samples filed. Original artwork returned at job's completion.
Photography: Buys photos from freelancers. Contact: Managing Editor. Buys stock images. Model/property releases required. Submit cover letter and résumé to be kept on file.
Terms: Contracts negotiable. Pays authors royalty of 10% based on wholesale price. Pays illustrators by the project (range: $50-250) or royalty of 10% based on wholesale price. Sends galleys to authors; dummies to illustrators. Book catalog available for #10 SAE and 2 first-class stamps; ms guidelines for SASE.

HYPERION BOOKS FOR CHILDREN, 114 Fifth Ave., New York NY 10011. (212)633-4400. Fax: (212)633-4833. An operating unit of Walt Disney Publishing Group, Inc. Book publisher. Vice President/Publisher: Lisa Holton. 30% of books by first-time authors. Publishes various categories.
Fiction: Picture books, young readers, middle readers, young adults: adventure, animal, anthology (short stories), contemporary, fantasy, folktales, history, humor, multicultural, poetry, science fiction, sports, suspense/mystery. Middle readers, young adults: problem novels, romance. Published *Countdown*, by Ben Mikaelsen (ages 10-14, adventure).
Nonfiction: All trade subjects for all levels.
How to Contact/Writers: Only interested in agented material.
Illustration: Works with 100 illustrators/year. "Picture books are fully illustrated throughout. All others depend on individual project." Reviews ms/illustration packages from artists. Submit complete package. Illustrations only: Submit résumé, business card, promotional literature or tearsheets to be kept on file. Contact: Ellen Friedman, art director. Reports back only if interested. Original artwork returned at job's completion.
Photography: Contact: Ellen Friedman, art director. Works on assignment only. Publishes photo essays and photo concept books. Provide résumé, business card, promotional literature or tearsheets to be kept on file.
Terms: Pays authors royalty based on retail price. Offers advances. Pays illustrators and photographers royalty based on retail price or a flat fee. Sends galleys to authors; dummies to illustrators. Book catalog available for 9×12 SAE and 3 first-class stamps; ms guidelines available for SASE.

✤HYPERION PRESS LIMITED, 300 Wales Ave., Winnipeg, Manitoba R2M 2S9 Canada. (204)256-9204. Fax: (204)255-7845. Book Publisher. Editor: Dr. M. Tutiah. Publishes authentic-based, retold folktales/legends for ages 4-12.
Fiction: Young readers, middle readers: folktales/legends. Published *The Wise Washerman*, by Deborah Froese, illustrated by Wang Kim; *Zarah's Magic Carpet*, written and illustrated by Stefan Czernecki; and *The Day Sun Was Stolen*, by Jamie Oliviero, illustrated by Sharon Hitchcock (all ages 5-9, picture books).
How to Contact/Writers: Fiction: Query. Reports on mss in 3 months.
Illustration: Reviews ms/illustration packages from artists. Ms/illustration packages and illustration only: Query. Samples returned with SASE.
Terms: Pays authors royalty. Pays illustrators by the project. Sends galleys to authors; dummies to illustrators. Book catalog available for 8 1/2×11 SAE and $1.40 postage (Canadian).

IDEALS CHILDREN'S BOOKS, an imprint of Hambleton-Hill Publishing, Inc., 1501 County Hospital Rd., Nashville TN 37218. Book publisher. Manuscript Contact: Suzanne Smith. Art Contact: Gary Bozeman. Publishes 30-35 picture books/year; 3-4 young reader titles/year. 10-15% of books by first-time authors; 5-10% of books from agented writers.

• Ideals only accepts manuscripts from members of the Society of Children's Book Writers and Illustrators (SCBWI), agented authors, and/or previously published book authors (submit with a list of writing credits).

Fiction: Picture books and young readers: adventure, animal, concept, contemporary, fantasy, folktales, history, humor, multicultural, nature/environment, religion, sports, suspense/mystery. Average word length: picture books—200-1,200. Published *See the Ocean*, by Estelle Condra, illustrated by Linda Crockett-Blassingame, (ages 5 to 8); *I Wish I Was the Baby*, by D.J. Long, illustrated by Gary Johnson (ages 3 to 7); and *Sea Maidens of Japan*, by Lili Bell, illustrated by Erin McGonigle Brammer (ages 5-9).

Nonfiction: Picture books and young readers: activity books, animal, arts and crafts, cooking, history, multicultural, nature/environment, science, sports. Does not want "ABC" and counting books of a general nature. "Only interested in them if they incorporate a unique approach or theme." Average word length: picture books—200-1,200; young readers—1,000-2,400. Recently published: *Why Did the Dinosaurs Disappear?* by Melvin and Gilda Berger, illustrated by Susan Harrison (ages 5-9, early reader); *Lunchbox Love Notes*, illustrated by Gary Johnson (ages 4-10, novelty); and *Five Minute Art Ideas: Draw* (ages 4-up, activity).

How to Contact/Writers: Fiction/Nonfiction: Prefers to see complete manuscript rather than queries. Reports in 3-6 months. Publishes a book 18-24 months after acceptance. Must include SASE for response.

Illustration: Works with 15-20 illustrators/year. Uses color artwork only. No cartoons—tight or loose, but realistic watercolors, acrylics. Editorial reviews ms/illustration packages from artists. Submit ms with 1 color photocopy of final art and remainder roughs. Illustrations only: Submit résumé and tearsheets showing variety of styles. Reports on art samples only if interested. "No original artwork, please." Samples returned with SASE, but prefers to keep them on file.

Terms: "All terms vary according to individual projects and authors/artists." Book catalog, ms guidelines, and artist guidelines for 9×12 SASE and 12 first-class stamps.

Tips: "Searching for strong storylines with realistic characters as well as 'fun for all kids' kinds of stories. We are not interested in young adult romances, and have little interest in anthropomorphism." Illustrators: "Be flexible in contract terms—and be able to show as much final artwork as possible. Work must have strong storyline with realistic characters."

INCENTIVE PUBLICATIONS, INC., 3835 Cleghorn Ave., Nashville TN 37215. (615)385-2934. Editor: Anna Quinn. Send mss to Catherine Aldy. Approximately 20% of books by first-time authors.

Nonfiction: Young reader, middle reader, young adult: education. "Any multicultural material or any manuscripts received about physical or mental challenges are reviewed for possible publication." Recently published *Integrating Instruction* series, by Imogene Forte and Sandra Schurr (grades 5-8, resource book for middle school teachers); and *Preparing Students to Raise Achievement Scores* series, by Leland Graham and Darrel Ledbetter (grades 1-6, general practice and specific concept development).

How to Contact/Writers: Nonfiction: Submit outline/synopsis, sample chapters and SASE. Usually reports on queries/mss in 1 month. Typically publishes a book 18 months after acceptance. Will consider simultaneous submissions.

Illustration: Works with 4-6 illustrators/year. Reports back in 4-6 weeks if reply requested. Samples returned with SASE; samples filed.

Terms: Pays authors in royalties or work purchased outright. Pays illustrators by the project (range: $200-1,500). Original artwork not returned. Book catalog and ms guidelines for SAE and $1.78 postage.

Tips: "We buy only teacher resource material. Please do not submit fiction!"

*IVORY TOWER, Imprint of Russ Berrie & Co., Inc., 111 Bauer Dr., Oakland NJ 07436. (201)339-7000. Book publisher. Director: Angelica Berrie. Publishes 10 picture books and young readers/year. 50% of books by first-time authors. Primary themes include stories with characters to be merchandised also as plush animals, soft dolls, etc.

Fiction: Picture books, young readers: animal, fantasy. Average word length: picture books—100-250; young readers—100-500. Recently published *I'm a Snowman*; *I'm a Duck* and *I'm Santa*.

Nonfiction: Picture books, young readers: animal. Average word length: picture books—100-250; young readers—100-500.

How to Contact/Writers: Fiction: Query or submit outline/synopsis and 1 sample chapter. Nonfiction: Query. Reports on queries/mss in 2 months. Publishes a book 6 months after acceptance. Will consider previously published work.

This colorful illustration by Melanie Hope Greenberg paints a picture of a Jewish family sitting Shivah when a loved one dies. "Children find her bright palette and whimsical figures particularly inviting," says Bruce Black, children's editor at The Jewish Publication Society. Greenberg's illustration, created using gouache and ink, appeared in her book *Blessings: Our Jewish Ceremonies*, which teaches young Jewish children about the traditions and ceremonies of their faith.

Illustration: Works with 20 illustrators/year. Reviews ms/illustration packages from artists. Send ms with dummy. Contact: Angelica Berrie, director. Illustrations only: Query with résumé, promo sheet, portfolio, tearsheets, color xerox—things to keep on file. Contact: Angelica Berrie, director. Reports back only if interested. Samples returned with SASE; samples filed.

Terms: Pays authors based on wholesale price (varies according to amount and type of work). Sometimes offers advances. Pays illustrators by the project; royalty based on wholesale price (varies as for author). Originals sometimes returned.

Tips: "Work must be presented professionally without too much left to our imagination. Our preference is to work with writers/illustrators (one person who does *both*) or with illustrators who are adept at producing camera-ready art. We also like cute, whimsical characters and folk-art styles."

JALMAR PRESS, 2675 Skypark Dr., #204, Torrance CA 90505. (310)784-0016. Fax: (310)784-1379. E-mail: blwjalmar@aol.com. Subsidiary of B.L. Winch and Associates. Book publisher. Estab. 1971. President: B.L. Winch. Publishing Assistant: Jeanne Iler. Publishes 3 picture books and young reader titles/year. 10% of books by first-time authors. Publishes self-esteem (curriculum content related), drug and alcohol abuse prevention, peaceful conflict resolution, stress management, whole brain learning and accelerated learning.

Fiction: All levels: concept, self-esteem. Does not want to see "children's fiction books that have to do with cognitive learning (as opposed to affective learning) and autobiographical work." Published *Hilde Knows: Someone Cries for the Children*, by Lisa Kent, illustrated by Mikki Macklen (child abuse); *Scooter's Tail of Terror: A Fable of Addiction and Hope*, by Larry Shles (ages 5-105). "All submissions must teach (by metaphor) in the areas listed above."

Nonfiction: All levels: activity books, social issues, self-help. Does not want to see autobiographical work. Published *Esteem Builders Program*, by Michele Borba, illustrated by Bob Brochett (for school use—6 books, tapes, posters).

How to Contact/Writers: Only interested in agented material. Fiction/Nonfiction: Submit complete ms. Reports on queries/mss in 6 months. Publishes a book 6-12 months after acceptance. Will consider simultaneous submissions.

Illustration: Works with 2 illustrators/year. Reports in 1 week. Samples returned with SASE; samples filed.

Terms: Pays authors 15% royalty based on net receipts. Average advance "varies." Illustrators and photographers paid by the project. Book catalog/ms guidelines free on request.

Tips: Wants "thoroughly researched, tested, practical, activity-oriented, curriculum content and grade/level correlated books on self-esteem, peaceful conflict resolution, stress management, drug and alcohol abuse prevention and whole brain learning and books bridging self-esteem to various 'trouble' areas, such as 'at risk,' 'dropout prevention,' etc. Illustrators—make artwork that can be reproduced."

JEWISH PUBLICATION SOCIETY, 1930 Chestnut St., Philadelphia PA 19103. (215)564-5925. Fax: (215)564-6640. Editor-in-Chief: Dr. Ellen Frankel. Children's Editor: Bruce Black. Book publisher. All work must have Jewish content.

Fiction: Picture books, young readers, middle readers and young adults: adventure, contemporary, folktales, history, mystery, problem novels, religion, romance, sports. Recently published *Of Heroes, Hooks and Heirlooms*, by Faye Siltoa (ages 9 and up, middle reader).

Nonfiction: Picture books: biography, history, religion. Young readers, middle readers, young adults: biography, history, religion, sports. Recently published *Moe Berg: The Spy Behind Home Plate*, by Vivian Grey (ages 10 and up, biography); *Elie Wiesel: A Voice for Humanity*, by Ellen Norman Sterla (10 and up, biography); and *The Kids' Catalog of Jewish Holidays*, by David A. Adler.

How to Contact/Writers: Fiction/Nonfiction: Query, submit outline/synopsis and sample chapters. Will consider simultaneous submissions (please advise). Reports on queries/mss in 6-8 weeks.

Illustration: Works with 3-4 illustrators/year. Will review ms/illustration packages. Query first or send 3 chapters of ms with 1 piece of final art, remainder roughs. Illustrations only: Query with photocopies; arrange a personal interview to show portfolio.

Terms: Pays authors and illustrators flat fees or royalties based on net. Reports back only if interested. Samples returned with SASE. Orginals returned at job's completion.

Tips: Writer/illustrator currently has best chance of selling picture books to this market.

BOB JONES UNIVERSITY PRESS/LIGHT LINE BOOKS, 1500 Wade Hampton Blvd. Greenville SC 29614. (803)242-5100, ext. 4316. E-mail: uunet!wpo.bju.edu!grepp. Website: http://www.bju.edu/press/freelnce.html. Book publisher. Editor: Mrs. Gloria Repp. Publishes 4 young reader titles/year; 4 middle reader titles/year; 4 young adult titles/year. 50% of books by first-time authors.

Fiction: Young readers, middle readers, young adults: adventure, animal, concept, contemporary, easy-to-read, fantasy, history, multicultural, nature/environment, sports, spy/mystery. Average word length: young readers—10,000; middle readers—30,000; young adult/teens—50,000. Published *The Treasure of Pelican Cove*, by Milly Howard (grades 2-4, adventure story); *Right Hand Man*, by Connie Williams (grades 5-8, contemporary).

Nonfiction: Young readers, middle readers: concept, history, multicultural. Young readers, middle readers, young adults: animal, biography, geography, nature/environment. Young adults/teens: biography, history, nature/environment. Average word length: young readers—10,000; middle readers—30,000; young adult/teens—50,000. Recently published *With Daring Faith*, by Becky Davis (grades 5-8, biography); *Someday You'll Write*, by Elizabeth Yates (how-to).

How to Contact/Writers: Fiction: "Send the complete manuscript or the first five chapters and synopsis for these genres: Christian biography, modern realism, historical realism, regional realism and mystery/adventure. Query with a synopsis and five sample chapters for these genres: fantasy and science fiction (no extra-terrestrials). Do not send stories with magical elements. We do not publish these genres: romance, poetry and drama." Nonfiction: Query, submit complete manuscript or submit outline/synopsis and sample chapters. Reports on queries in 3 weeks; mss in 2 months. Publishes book "approximately one year" after acceptance. Will consider simultaneous and electronic submissions via IBM-compatible disk or modem.

Illustration: Works with 4 illustrators/year. Reports back only if interested. Samples returned with SASE; samples filed.

Terms: Pays authors royalty of 7-10% based on wholesale price. Or work purchased outright ($800-1,000). Pays illustrators by the project. Originals returned to artist at job's completion. Book catalog and ms guidelines free on request. "Check our web page for guidelines" (address above) or send SASE for book catalog and mss guidelines.

Tips: "Writers—give us original, well-developed characters in a suspenseful plot that has good moral tone. Artists—be good with both color and black & white illustrations. Be willing to take suggestions and follow specific directions. Today's books for children offer a wide variety of well-done nonfiction and rather shallow fiction. With the growing trend toward increased TV viewing, parents may be less interested in good books and less able to distinguish what is worthwhile. We are determined to continue to produce high-quality books for children."

JUST US BOOKS, INC., 356 Glenwood Ave., East Orange NJ 07017. (201)676-4345. Fax: (201)677-7570. Imprint of Afro-Bets Series. Book publisher; "for selected titles" book packager. Estab. 1988. Vice President/Publisher: Cheryl Willis Hudson. Publishes 4-6 picture books/year; "projected 6" young reader/middle reader titles/year. 33% of books by first-time authors. Looking for "books that reflect a genuinely authentic African or African-American experience. We try to work with authors and illustrators who are from the culture itself." Also publishes *Harambee*, a news journal for young readers, 6 times during the school year. (Target age for *Harambee* is 10-13.)

• Just Us Books is not accepting new manuscripts until further notice.

Fiction: Middle readers: adventure, contemporary, easy-to-read, history, multicultural (African-American themes), romance, suspense/mystery. Average word length: "varies" per picture book; young reader—500-2,000; middle reader—5,000. Wants African-American themes. Gets too many traditional African folktales. Published *Land of the Four Winds*, by Veronica Freeman Ellis, illustrated by Sylvia Walker (ages 6-9, picture book).

Nonfiction: Middle readers, biography (African-American themes). Published *Book of Black Heroes Vol. 2: Great Women in the Struggle*, by Toyomi Igus.

How to Contact/Writers: Fiction/Nonfiction: Query or submit outline/synopsis for proposed title. Reports on queries/ms in 3-4 months "or as soon as possible." Publishes a book 12-18 months after acceptance. Will consider simultaneous submissions (with prior notice).

Illustration: Works with 10 illustrators/year. Reviews ms/illustration packages from artists ("but prefers to review them separately"). "Query first." Illustrations only: Query with samples; send résumé, promo sheet, slides, client list, tearsheets; arrange personal portfolio review. Reports in 2-3 weeks. Samples returned with SASE; samples filed. Original artwork returned at job's completion "depending on project."

Photography: Purchases photos from freelancers. Buys stock and assigns work. Wants "African-American themes—kids age 10-13 in school, home and social situations for *Harambee* (newspaper)."

Terms: Pays authors royalty based on retail price or work purchased outright. Royalties based on retail price. Pays illustrators by the project or royalty based on retail price. Sends galleys to authors; dummies to illustrators. Book catalog for business-size SAE and 65¢ postage; ms/artist's guidelines for business-size SAE and 65¢ postage.

Tips: "Multicultural books are tops as far as trends go. There is a great need for diversity and authenticity here. They will continue to be in the forefront of children's book publishing until there is more balanced treatment on these themes industry wide." Writers: "Keep the subject matter fresh and lively. Avoid 'preachy' stories with stereotyped characters. Rely more on authentic stories with sensitive three-dimensional characters." Illustrators: "Submit 5-10 good, neat samples. Be willing to work with an art director for the type of illustration desired by a specific house and grow into larger projects."

KAR-BEN COPIES, INC., 6800 Tildenwood Lane, Rockville MD 20852. (301)984-8733. Fax: (301)881-9195. Book publisher. Estab. 1975. Vice President: Madeline Wikler. Publishes 5-10 picture books/year; 20% of books by first-time authors.

Fiction: Picture books: folktales, multicultural, *Must be* on a Jewish theme. Average word length: picture books—2,000. Published *Kingdom of Singing Birds*, by Miriam Aroner; *Northern Lights*, by Diana Cohen Conway; *Sammy Spider's First Hanukkah*, by Sylvia Rouss; and *Matzah Ball, A Passover Story*, by Mindy Avra Portnoy.

Nonfiction: Picture books, young readers: religion—Jewish interest. Average word length: picture books—2,000. Published *Jewish Holiday Games for Little Hands*, by Ruth Brinn; *Tell Me a Mitzvah*, by Danny Siegel; *My First Jewish Word Book*, by Roz Schanzer.

How to Contact/Writers: Fiction/nonfiction: Submit complete ms. Reports on queries/ms in 6 weeks. Publishes a book 1 year after acceptance. Will consider simultaneous submissions.

Illustration: Works with 6-10 illustrators/year. Prefers "4-color art to any medium that is scannable." Reviews ms/illustration packages from artists. Submit whole ms and sample of art (no originals). Illustrations only: Submit tearsheets, photocopies, promo sheet or anything representative that does *not* need to be returned. Enclose SASE for response. Reports on art samples in 4 weeks.

Terms: Pays authors in royalties of 6-8% based on net sales or work purchased outright (range: $500-2,000). Offers advance (average amount: $1,000). Pays illustrators royalty of 6-8% based on net sales or by the project (range: $500-3,000). Sends galleys to authors. Book catalog free on request. Ms guidelines for 9×12 SAE and 2 first-class stamps.

Tips: Looks for "books for young children with Jewish interest and content, modern, non-sexist, not didactic. Fiction or nonfiction with a *Jewish* theme—can be serious or humorous, life cycle, Bible story, or holiday-related."

*KINGFISHER BOOKS, Imprint of Larousse Kingfisher Chabers, 95 Madison Ave., New York NY 10016. (212)686-1060. Fax: (212)686-1082.
• Kingfisher Books is not currently accepting unsolicited manuscripts.

KNOPF BOOKS FOR YOUNG READERS, 29th Floor, 201 E. 50th St., New York NY 10022. (212)751-2600. Random House, Inc. Book publisher. Estab. 1915. Publishing Director: Simon Boughton. Publisher, Apple Soup Books: Anne Schwartz. 90% of books published through agents.

Fiction: All levels: considers all categories.

Nonfiction: All levels: animal, arts/crafts, biography, history, how to, multicultural, music/dance, nature/environment, science, self help, sports.

How to Contact/Writers: Fiction/nonfiction: "We read agented material immediately. We will read queries from nonagented authors and then, possibly, request ms." Publishes a book 12-18 months after acceptance. Will consider simultaneous submissions.

Illustration: Reviews ms/illustration packages from artists through agent only. Illustration only: Contact: Art Director. Reports back only if interested. Samples returned with SASE; samples filed.

Terms: Pays authors in royalties. Pays illustrators and photographers by the project or royalties. Original artwork returned at job's completion. Book catalog and ms guidelines free on request with SASE.

LAREDO PUBLISHING CO. INC., 8907 Wilshire Blvd., Beverly Hills CA 90211. (310)358-5288. Fax: (310)358-5282. E-mail: laredo@online2000.com. Book publisher. Vice President: Raquel Benatar. Publishes 5 picture books/year; 15 young readers/year. 10% of books by first-time authors. Spanish language books only.

Fiction: Picture books: adventure, multicultural, suspense/mystery. Young readers: multicultural. Middle readers: multicultural, suspense/mystery. Published *Pregones*, by Alma Flor Ada (middle readers, personal experience in Spanish); *Pajaritos*, by Clarita Kohen (young readers, counting book in Spanish); *El Conejoyel Coyote*, by Clarita Kohen (young readers, folktale in Spanish).

Nonfiction: All levels: textbooks. Young adults: careers, health. Published *Los Aztecas*, by Robert Nicholson (middle readers, history, culture and traditions of the Aztecs in Spanish); *Los Sioux*, by Robert Nicholson (middle readers; history, culture and traditions of the Sioux in Span-

---

MARKET CONDITIONS are constantly changing! If you're still using this book and it is 1998 or later, buy the newest edition of *Children's Writer's & Illustrator's Market* at your favorite bookstore or order directly from Writer's Digest Books.

ish); *La Antigua China*, by Robert Nicholson (middle readers; history, culture and traditions of the Chinese in Spanish).
How to Contact/Writers: Fiction: Submit complete ms. Reports in 2 weeks. Publishes a book 1 year after acceptance. Will consider simultaneous submissions.
Illustration: Works with 20-30 illustrators/year. Uses color artwork only. Reviews ms/illustration packages from artists. Illustrations only: Query with samples, promo sheet. Reports in 2 weeks. Samples returned with SASE. Originals not returned.
Terms: Pays authors royalty of 5-7% based on wholesale price or work purchased outright (range: $1,000-2,000). Offers advances (varies). Pays illustrators by the project (range: $250-500). Sends galleys to authors; dummies to illustrators. Book catalog available for SASE.
Tips: "We specialize in multicultural materials—all languages."

LEADERSHIP PUBLISHERS, INC., Talented and Gifted Educ. P.O. Box 8358, Des Moines IA 50301. (515)278-4765. Fax: (515)270-8303. Book publisher.
Nonfiction: Publishes self help and textbooks. Wants to see material for enrichment programs for talented and gifted students and teacher reference. Published *What Do You Think: Opinions & Ideas*, by Sandy Achterberg (for ages 7-16); and *Readers' Theatre: Volume Three, Entrepreneurs* and *Incomplete Plays*, by Lois Roets.
How to Contact/Writers: Reports on queries in 1 month; mss in 3 months. Publishes a book 3-6 months after acceptance.
Terms: Pays authors royalty of 10% based on wholesale (dealer) or retail (school market) price. Pays illustrators by the project ($25 and up) or royalty of 2%. Book catalog available for $8½ × 11 SAE and 2 first-class stamps. Ms guidelines available for SASE.
Tips: "Leadership Publishers, Inc. publishes educational material for high-ability students. Study our catalog before submitting your manuscript or query and picture your book among our published titles. Will it fit?"

*LEARNING TRIANGLE PRESS, Imprint of McGraw-Hill, 11 West 19th St., New York NY 10010. (800)233-1128, ext. 233. Fax: (717)794-5433. Book publisher. Editor-in-Chief: Judith Terrill-Breuer. Publishes 20 young readers, middle readers/year. 10% of books by first-time authors.
Fiction: Picture books, young readers and middle readers: science and math/technology. Average word length: picture books—64; young readers and middle readers—96-122.
Nonfiction: Picture books, young readers and middle readers: nature/environment, science and math/technology.
How to Contact/Writers: Fiction/Nonfiction: Submit complete ms or outline/synopsis and 2 sample chapters. Publishes a book 1 year after acceptance.

*THE LEARNING WORKS, 5720 Thornwood Dr., Goleta CA 93117. (805)964-4220. Fax: (805)964-1466. Book publisher. President: Linda Schwartz. Publishes 16 young readers/year; 5 middle readers/year. 10% of books by first-time authors. "The majority of our books are activity oriented. Many are primarily educational in nature."
Nonfiction: Young readers, middle readers, young/adults: activity books, animal, arts/crafts, biography, careers, concept, cooking, geography, health, hi-lo, history, how-to, multicultural, nature/environment, reference, science, social issues, special needs. "We like to see books that expand awareness of other cultures whether the books are about cultures or as part of other subject areas. We do not publish materials that are limited to use in the special ed classroom, but welcome materials that can be used in mainstreamed classrooms." Does not want to see cookbooks. "Cooking is included as an activity to reinforce other learning such as math or science lessons." Recently published *Gobble Up Nature*, by Carol Johmann and Elizabeth Rieth, illustrated by Kelly Kennedy (young readers, nature/environment); *Kids With Special Needs*, by Veronica Getskow and Dee Konczal, illustrated by Bev Armstrong (special needs, young readers and middle readers); and *AIDS: What Teens Need to Know*, by Barbara Dever, illustrated by Marcy Ramsey (young adults/teens; health).
How to Contact/Writers: Query; submit outline/synopsis and 10 sample activities. Reports in 3 weeks. Publishes a book 1 year after acceptance. Will consider simultaneous submissions, electronic submissions via disk or modem or previously published work.
Illustration: Works with 4 illustrators/year. Uses primarily b&w artwork. Reviews ms/illustration packages from artists. "While we would look at manuscript/illustration packages, we would look at the material separately. We would not guarantee that we would accept both." Illustrations only: Query with samples. Contact: Linda Schwartz, president. Reports in 3 weeks. Samples returned with SASE; samples filed.

Photography: Buys stock and assigns work. Contact: Linda Schwartz, president. "We do not use many photos. We use photos primarily for covers. They are assigned according to the subject matter." Model/property releases required.

Terms: Author's payment varies. Pays illustrators by the project. Photographers paid by the project. Book catalog for 8½ × 11 and 2 first-class stamps; ms guidelines for SASE.

Tips: "We are looking for unique materials that involve children in active learning. We accept most curricular areas, arts, crafts, self-esteem, and teacher resource materials. We do not accept story or picture books, poetry books, or music. Our primary focus is children ages 5-14."

LEE & LOW BOOKS, INC., 95 Madison Ave., New York NY 10016-7801. (212)779-4400. Book publisher. Editor-in-Chief: Elizabeth Szabla. Publishes 8-10 picture books/year. 50% of books by first-time authors.

• Lee & Low publishes only books with multicultural themes. See First Books, page 28, for an interview with Lee & Low's Susan Middleton Elya, author of *Say Hola to Spanish.*

Fiction: Picture books: Concept. Picture books, young readers: anthology, contemporary, history, multicultural, poetry. "We are not considering folktales or animal stories." Average word length: picture books—1,000-1,500 words. Recently published *Sam and the Lucky Money,* by Karen Chinn, illustrated by Cornelius Van Wright and Ying'HwaHu (ages 3-9, picture book); and *The Palm of My Heart; Poetry by African American Children,* edited by Davida Adedjouna, illustrated by Gregory Christie (ages 4 and up, picture book).

Nonfiction: Picture books and young readers: biography, history and multicultural. Average word length: picture books—1,500. Recently published *Dia's Story Cloth: The Hmong People's Journey of Freedom,* by Dia Cha; illustrated by Chue and Nhia Thao Cha (ages 6 and up, picture book).

How to Contact/Writers: Fiction/Nonfiction: Submit complete ms. Reports in 1-3 months. Publishes a book 12-24 months after acceptance. Will consider simultaneous submissions.

Illustration: Works with 8-10 illustrators/year. Uses color artwork only. Reviews ms/illustration packages from artists. Submit ms with dummy. Contact: Elizabeth Szabla, editor-in-chief. Illustrations only: Query with samples, résumé, promo sheet and tearsheets. Reports in 1-3 months. Samples returned with SASE; samples filed. Original artwork returned at job's completion.

Photography: Buys photos from freelancers. Works on assignment only. Model/property releases required. Submit cover letter, résumé, promo piece and book dummy.

Terms: Pays authors royalty based on retail price. Offers advances. Pays illustrators royalty based on retail price plus advance against royalty. Photographers paid royalty based on retail price plus advance against royalty. Sends galleys to authors; dummies to illustrators. Book catalog available for 9 × 12 SAE and $1.01 postage; ms and art guidelines available for SASE.

Tips: "We strongly urge writers to familiarize themselves with our list before submitting."

LERNER PUBLICATIONS CO., 241 First Ave. N., Minneapolis MN 55401. (612)332-3344. Fax: (612)332-7615. Book publisher. Editor: Jennifer Martin. Publishes 10-15 young readers/year; 50-70 middle readers/year; 5 young adults/year. 20% of books by first-time authors; 5% of books from agented writers. "Most books are nonfiction for children, grades 3-9."

Fiction: Middle readers: adventure, contemporary, hi-lo, multicultural, nature/environment, sports, suspense/mystery. Young adults: hi-lo, multicultural, nature/environment, problem novels, sports, suspense/mystery. "Especially interested in books with ethnic characters." Published the Kerry Hill Casecrackers series, by Joan Warnor and Peggy Nicholson (grades 4-7, mystery).

Nonfiction: Middle readers, young adults: animal, arts/crafts, biography, careers, concept, cooking, geography, health, hi-lo, history, hobbies, how-to, multicultural, music/dance, nature/environment, sports, science/math, social issues, self-help, special needs. Multicultural material must contain authentic details. Does not want to see textbooks, workbooks, song books, audiotapes, puzzles, plays, religious material, books for teachers or parents, picture or alphabet books. Average word length: young readers—3,000; middle readers—7,000; young adults—12,000. Published *Frank Lloyd Wright: Maverick Architect,* by Brad Townsend (grades 5 and up, Lerner Biographies series); *Shaquille O'Neal: Center of Attention,* by Brad Townsend (grades 4-9, Sports Achievers series).

How to Contact/Writers: Fiction: Submit outline/synopsis and sample chapters. Nonfiction: Query; submit outline/synopsis and sample chapters. Reports on queries in 3-4 weeks; mss in 3 months. Publishes a book 12-18 months after acceptance. Will consider simultaneous submissions.

Illustration: Works with 1-2 illustrators/year. "We tend to work mostly with local talent." Reviews ms/illustration packages from artists. Ms/illustration packages and illustrations only:

Query with samples and résumé. Contact: Art Director. Samples kept on file.
Photography: Contact: Photo Research Department. Buys stock and assigns work. Model/property releases required. Publishes photo essays. Photographers should query with samples.
Terms: Pays authors royalty or work purchased outright. Pays illustrators by the project. Sends galleys to authors. Book catalog available for 9×12 SAE and $1.90 postage; ms guidelines for 4×9 SAE and 1 first-class stamp.
Tips: Wants "straightforward, well-written nonfiction for children in grades 3-9 backed by solid current research or scholarship. Before you send your manuscript to us, you might first take a look at the kinds of books that our company publishes. We specialize in publishing high-quality educational books for children from second grade through high school. Avoid sex stereotypes (e.g., strong, aggressive, unemotional males/weak, submissive, emotional females) in your writing, as well as sexist language." (See also Carolrhoda Books, Inc.)

LION BOOKS, PUBLISHER, Suite B, 210 Nelson, Scarsdale NY 10583. (914)725-2280. Imprint of Sayre Ross Co. Book publisher. Editorial contact: Harriet Ross. Publishes 5 middle readers/year; 10 young adults/year. 50-70% of books by first-time authors. Publishes books "with ethnic and minority accents for young adults, including a variety of craft titles dealing with African and Asian concepts."
Nonfiction: Activity, art/crafts, biography, history, hobbies, how-to, multicultural. Average word length: young adult—30,000-50,000.
How to Contact/Writers: Query, submit complete ms. Reports on queries in 3 weeks; ms in 2 months.
Illustration: Reports in 2 weeks.
Terms: Work purchased outright (range: $500-5,000). Average advance: $1,000-2,500. Illustrators paid $500-1,500. Sends galleys to author. Book catalog free on request.

LITTLE, BROWN AND COMPANY, 34 Beacon St., Boston MA 02108. (617)227-0730. Book publisher. Editor-in-Chief: Maria Modugno. Art Director: Bob Kosturko. Estab. 1837. Publishes 5% picture books/year; 50% young reader titles/year; 30% middle reader titles/year; 15% young adult titles/year.
  • Little, Brown accepts manuscripts only through agents or from writers with previous children's publishing credits (submit with list of credits).
Fiction: Picture books: adventure, animal, contemporary, fantasy, folktales, history, humor, multicultural, nature/environment. Young readers: adventure, animal, contemporary, fantasy, history, humor, multicultural, nature/environment, science fiction, suspense/mystery. Middle readers: adventure, contemporary, fantasy, history, humor, multicultural, nature/environment, science fiction, suspense/mystery. Young adults: contemporary, health, humor, multicultural, nature/environment, suspense/mystery. Multicultural needs include "any material by, for and about minorities." No "rhyming texts, anthropomorphic animals that learn a lesson, alphabet and counting books, and stories based on an event rather than a character." Average word length: picture books—1,000; young readers—6,000; middle readers—15,000-25,000; young adults—20,000-40,000. Recently published *Fairy Wings*, by Lauren Mills (ages 4-8, picture book); *People of Corn*, by Mary-Joan Gerson (ages 4-8, picture book); *All Star Fever*, by Matt Christopher (ages 7-9, first chapter book); *On Winter's Wind*, by Patricia Hermes (ages 8-12, middle reader).
Nonfiction: Picture books: animal, biography, concept, history, multicultural, nature/environment. Young readers: activity books, biography, multicultural. Middle readers: activity books, arts/crafts, biography, cooking, geography, history, multicultural. Young adults: multicultural, self-help, social issues. Average word length: picture books—2,000; young readers—4,000-6,000; middle readers—15,000-25,000; young adults—20,000-40,000. Recently published *Hearing Us Out*, by Roger Sutton (ages 12 and up, young adult); *The Great Midwest Flood*, by Carole G. Vogel (ages 8-12, picture book).
Illustration: Works with 40 illustrators/year. Illustrations only: Query art director with samples; provide résumé, promo sheet or tearsheets to be kept on file. Reports on art samples in 6-8 weeks. Original artwork returned at job's completion.
Photography: Works on assignment only. Model/property releases required; captions required. Publishes photo essays and photo concept books. Uses 35mm transparencies. Photographers should provide résumé, promo sheets or tearsheets to be kept on file.
Terms: Pays authors royalties of 3-10% based on retail price. Offers advance (average amount: $2,000-10,000). Pays illustrators and photographers by the project (range: $1,500-5,000) or royalty of 3-10% based on retail price. Sends galleys to authors; dummies to illustrators. Book catalog, manuscript/artist's guidelines for SASE.

Tips: "Publishers are cutting back their lists in response to a shrinking market and relying more on big names and known commodities. In order to break into the field these days, authors and illustrators research their competition and try to come up with something outstandingly different."

LODESTAR BOOKS, 375 Hudson St., New York NY 10014. (212)366-2627. Fax: (212)366-2011. E-mail: vbuckley@penguin.com. Affiliate of Dutton Children's Books, a division of Penguin Books, USA, Inc. Estab. 1980. Editorial Director: Virginia Buckley. Executive Editor: Rosemary Brosnan. Publishes 6 picture books/year; 6 middle readers/year; 7 young adults/year (20 books/year). 5-10% of books by first-time authors; 37% through agents.
   ● Lodestar is looking especially for material for new Penguin imprint of titles for translation into Spanish: Penguin Ediciones.
Fiction: Picture books: adventure, animal, contemporary, folktales, history, humor, multicultural, nature/environment. Young readers: adventure, animal, contemporary, family humor, multicultural, nature/environment. Middle reader: adventure, animal, contemporary, folktales, humor, multicultural, nature/environment, suspense/mystery. Young adult: adventure, contemporary, history, humor, multicultural, nature/environment. Multicultural needs include "well-written books with good characterization. Prefer books by authors of same ethnic background as subject, but not absolutely necessary." No commercial picture books, science fiction or genre novels. Published *Toads and Diamonds*, retold and illustrated by Robert Bender (ages 4-8, picture book); *A Midnight Clear: Stories for the Christmas Season*, by Katherine Paterson (all ages, short stories); and *Like Sisters on the Homefront*, by Rita Williams-Garcia (ages 12 up, YA fiction).
Nonfiction: Picture books: activity books, animal, concept, geography, history, multicultural, nature/environment, science, social issues. Young reader: animal, concept, geography, history, multicultural, nature/environment, science, social issues, sports. Middle reader: animal, biography, careers, geography, history, multicultural, music/dance, nature/environment, science, social issues, sports. Young adult: history, multicultural, music/dance, nature/environment, social issues, sports. Multicultural needs include authentic, well-written books about African-American, Native American, Hispanic and Asian-American experiences. Also, books on Jewish themes. Published *Fiesta U.S.A.*, written and phtographed by George Ancona, English and Spanish editions (ages 8-10, photographic essay); *One Nation, Many Tribes*, by Kathleen Krull, photographs by David Hautzig (ages 8-12, A World of My Own series); and *For Home and Country* by Norman Bolotin and Angela Herb, (Young Readers' History of the Civil War series).
How to Contact/Writers: Fiction: Submit synopsis and sample chapters or submit complete ms. Nonfiction: Query or submit synopsis and sample chapters. Reports on queries in 1 month; mss in 3 months. Publishes a book 7-8 months after acceptance. Will consider simultaneous submissions.
Illustration: Works with approximately 7-8 illustrators/year. Reviews ms/illustration packages from artists. Submit "manuscript and copies of art (no original art please)." Illustrations only: Query with samples; send portfolio or slides. Drop off portfolio for review. Reports back only if interested.
Photography: Buys photos from freelancers (infrequently).
Terms: Pays authors and illustrators royalties of 5-10% based on retail price. Pays illustrators by the project (range: $4,000-10,000—more for well-known artists) or royalty of 2-6% based on retail price. Pays photographers by the project (range: $800 for jacket-$6,000 for photo essay), per photo (range: $25-400 for jackets) or royalty of 5% (for photo essay). Sends galleys to author. Original art work returned at job's completion. Book catalog for SASE; manuscript guidelines for #10 SAE and 1 first-class stamp.
Tips: Wants "well-written books that show awareness of children's and young people's lives, feelings and problems; arouse imagination and are sensitive to children's needs. More books by African-American, Hispanic, Asian-American and Native American writers. More nonfiction early readers."

✤JAMES LORIMER & CO., 35 Britain St., Toronto, Ontario M5A 1R7 Canada. (416)362-4762. Book publisher. Publishing Assistant: Laura Ellis. Publishes 3 middle readers/year; 2 young adult titles/year. 20% of books by first-time authors. Uses Canadian authors only; wants realistic, contemporary material with Canadian settings.
Fiction: Middle readers: adventure, contemporary, hi-lo, multicultural, problem novels, sports and suspense/mystery. Young adults: contemporary, multicultural, problem novels and sports. Canadian settings featuring characters from ethnic/racial/cultural minorities—prefers author from same background. Does not want to see fantasy, science fiction, verse, drama and short stories. Average word length: middle readers—18,000; young adults—20,000. Recently published *The*

Great Pebble Creek Bike Race, by Kathy Stinson (ages 7-10, sport/adventure); *Gallop for Gold*, by Sharon Siamon (ages 7-10, adventure novel); *Curve Ball*, by John Danakas (ages 9-12, sport novel).

How to Contact/Writers: Submit outline/synopsis and 2 sample chapters. Reports on queries in 2 months; mss in 6 months. Publishes a book 8 months after acceptance.

Illustration: Works with 3 illustrators/year. Prefers realistic style.

Illustrations only: Submit promo sheet, photocopies OK. Reports only if interested. Samples returned with SASE; samples filed. Original artwork returned at job's completion.

Photography: Buys photos from freelancers. Contact: Laura Ellis, publishing assistant. Buys stock and assigns work. Uses color prints and 35mm transparencies. Submit letter.

Terms: Pays authors royalty of 6-10% based on retail price. Pays illustrators and photographers by the project. Sends galleys to authors. Ms and art guidelines available for SASE.

Tips: "Follow submission guidelines and research the market—read current kids' books, talk to kids." Wants realistic novels, set in Canada, dealing with social issues. Recent trends include hi-lo and multicultural.

LOTHROP, LEE & SHEPARD BOOKS, 1350 Avenue of the Americas, New York NY 10019. (212)261-6500. Division and imprint of William Morrow Co. Inc.
- Lothrop, Lee & Shepard is currently not accepting unsolicited manuscripts. They publish 30 total titles per year.

*□LOWELL HOUSE JUVENILE, 2020 Avenue of the Stars, Suite 300, Los Angeles CA 90067. (310)552-7555. Fax: (310)552-7573. Book publisher, independent book producer/packager. Fiction Editor: Barbara Schoichet. Nonfiction Editor: Amy Downing. Art Director: Lisa Lenthall. Publishes 1-2 picture books/year; 30 young readers/year; 60 middle readers/year; 5 young adult titles/year. 25% of books by first-time authors.
- Lowell House does not accept manuscripts. Instead they generate ideas inhouse then find writers to work on projects.

Fiction: Middle readers, young adults: adventure, anthology, contemporary, fantasy, humor, nature/environment, science fiction, sports, suspense/mystery. Recently published *Qwan: the Showdown*, by A.L. Kim, cover art by Richard Kirk (ages 13 and up, action novel); *Six-Minute Mysteries*, by Don Wulffson, illustrated by Laurel Long (ages 10-12, collection of short mystery stories); and *Classic Ghost Stories*, illustrated by Barbara Kiwak (ages 13 and up, collection of short scary stories).

Nonfiction: Picture books, young readers: activity books. Middle readers: activity books, arts/crafts, concept, cooking, geography, health, history, hobbies, reference, religion, science, self help, sports. Recently published *The 25 Strangest Mysteries in the World*, by Q.L. Pearce, illustrated by Brian W. Dow (ages 10-12, short, strange but true-type stories); *Super Nifty Origami Crafts*, by Andrea Urton and Charlene Olexiewicz, illustrated by Dianne O'Quinn Burke, photos by Ann Bogart (ages 10-12, step-by-step how-to); *Puzzles & Games for Reading and Math: Book Two Workbook for Ages 6-8*, by Martha Cheney, illustrated by Larry Nolte.

Illustration: Works with 75 illustrators/year. Send samples to give a feel for style. Include sample drawings with kids in them. Contact: Lisa Lenthall, art director. Illustrations only: arrange personal portfolio review; send promo sheet, portfolio, tearsheets. Contact: Lisa Lenthall, art director. Reports back only if interested. Samples returned with SASE; files samples.

Photography: Buys stock and assigns work. "We're not looking for more photographers at this time."

Terms: Payment decided on project-by-project basis.

Tips: "Art: Send lots of drawings of kids, samples to keep on file. Don't be afraid to send b&w art—never see enough junior-high aged kids! Editorial: We are interested in writing samples to lead to future jobs, but we do not accept manuscripts, preferring to generate ideas ourselves."

LUCAS/EVANS BOOKS INC., 407 Main St., Chatham NJ 07928. Executive Director: Barbara Lucas.
- Lucas/Evans is no longer accepting new clients. The company is downsizing, no longer doing book packaging, only agenting.

LUCENT BOOKS, P.O. Box 289011, San Diego CA 92128-9009. (619)485-7424. Sister Company to Greenhaven Press. Book publisher. Editor: Bonnie Szumski. 20% of books by first-time authors; 10% of books from agented writers.
- This publisher does not accept unsolicited manuscripts.

Nonfiction: Middle readers, young adults: education, health, topical history, nature/environment, sports, "any overviews of specific topics—i.e., political, social, cultural, economic, criminal, moral issues." No fiction. Average word length: 15,000-25,000. Published *The Persian Gulf War*, by Don Nardo (grades 6-12, history); *Photography*, by Brad Steffens (grades 5-8, history); and *Rainforests*, by Lois Warburton (grades 5-8, overview).

How to Contact/Writers: "Writers should query first; we do writing by assignment only. If you want to write for us, send SASE for guidelines."

Illustration: "We use photos, mostly." Uses primarily b&w artwork and prefers 7×9 format—4-color cover. Reviews ms/illustration packages from artists. Query first. Illustrations only: Query with samples; provide résumé, business card, promotional literature or tearsheets to be kept on file.

Terms: "Fee negotiated upon review of manuscript." Sends galleys to authors. Ms guidelines free on request.

Tips: "Books must be written at a 7th-8th-grade reading level. There's a growing market for quality nonfiction. Tentative topics: free speech, tobacco, alcohol, discrimination, immigration, poverty, the homeless in America, space weapons, drug abuse, terrorism, animal experimentation, endangered species, AIDS, pollution, gun control, etc. The above list is presented to give writers an example of the kinds of titles we are seeking. If you are interested in writing about a specific topic, please query us by mail before you begin writing to be sure we have not assigned a particular topic to another author. The author should strive for objectivity. There obviously will be many issues on which a position should be taken—e.g. discrimination, tobacco, alcoholism, etc. However, moralizing, self-righteous condemnations, maligning, lamenting, mocking, etc. should be avoided. Moreover, where a pro/con position is taken, contrasting viewpoints should be presented. Certain moral issues such as abortion and euthanasia, if dealt with at all, should be presented with strict objectivity."

McCLANAHAN BOOK COMPANY INC., 23 W. 26th St., New York NY 10010. (212)725-1515. Fax: (212)725-5911. Book publisher. CEO: Susan McClarahan. Editorial Director: Elise Donner. Rights Director: Meredith Hatch. Publishes 90 picture books/year. Publishes "affordable, high quality massmarket children's books, including activity books, workbooks and storybooks.

Fiction: Board and paperback story books (picture books): animal, concept. Recently published *Baby's World*, 4 title series, by Judy Nayer (ages 0-2); *At Your Fingertips—Horses & Ponies*, by Marc Gave (ages 2-7); and *My First Word Book*, by Carole Osterink (ages 4-8).

Nonfiction: Picture books: activity books, animal, concept, reference.

How to Contact/Writers: Submit complete ms. Reports in 2-4 months. Will consider simultaneous submissions.

Illustration: Works with 15-30 illustrators/year. Reports in 2-4 months. Samples returned with SASE; samples filed.

Terms: Pays authors on work-for-hire basis (flat fee $400-1,500/job). Pays illustrators/photographers by the project. Originals returned at job's completion. Ms guidelines available for SASE.

MARGARET K. McELDERRY BOOKS, 1230 Sixth Ave., New York NY 10020. (212)698-2761. Fax: (212)698-2796. Imprint of Simon & Schuster Children's Publishing Division. Publisher: Margaret K. McElderry. Art Director: Ann Bobco. Publishes 10-12 picture books/year; 2-4 young reader titles/year; 8-10 middle reader titles/year; 5-7 young adult titles/year. 10% of books by first-time authors; 33% of books from agented writers.

Fiction: Young readers: adventure, contemporary, fantasy, history. Middle readers: adventure, contemporary, fantasy, mystery. Young adult: contemporary, fantasy, mystery, poetry. "Always interested in publishing picture books and beginning reader stories by people of color about cultures and people other than Caucasian American. We see too many rhymed picture book manuscripts which are not terribly original or special." Average word length: picture books—500; young readers—2,000; middle readers—10,000-20,000; young adults—45,000-50,000. Recently published *Flowers on the Wall*, by Miriam Nerlove; *The Moorchild*, by Eloise McGraw; and *Eliza's Dog*, by Betsy Hearne.

Nonfiction: Young readers, young adult teens, biography, history. Average word length: picture books—500-1,000; young readers—1,500-3,000; middle readers—10,000-20,000; young adults—30,000-45,000. Recently published *Dreams and Wishes: Essays on Writing for Children*, by Susan Cooper; and *We Have Conquered Pain: The Discovery of Anesthesia*, by Dennis Fradin.

How to Contact/Writers: Fiction/nonfiction: Submit query only with SASE. Reports on queries in 2-3 weeks; mss in 3-4 months. Publishes a book 18 months after contract signing. Will consider simultaneous submissions (only if indicated as such).

Illustration: Works with 20-30 illustrators/year. Query with samples; provide, promo sheet or tearsheets; arrange personal portfolio review. Contact: Ann Bobco, art director. Reports on art samples in 2-3 months. Samples returned with SASE or samples filed.

Terms: Pays authors royalty based on retail price. Pay illustrators by the project or royalty based on retail price. Pays photographers by the project. Sends galleys to authors; dummies to illustrators. Original artwork returned at job's completion. Book catalog, ms guidelines free on request with 9 × 12 SASE.

Tips: "We're looking for strong, original fiction. We are always interested in picture books for the youngest age reader."

MAGE PUBLISHERS INC., 1032 29th St. NW, Washington DC 20007. (202)342-1642. Book publisher. Editorial contact: A. Sepehri. Publishes 2-3 picture books/year.

Fiction: Contemporary/myth, Persian heritage. Average word length: 5,000.

Nonfiction: Average word length: 5,000.

How to Contact/Writers: Fiction/Nonfiction: Query. Reports on queries/ms in 3 months. Will consider simultaneous submissions.

Illustration: Reviews ms/illustration packages from artists. Illustrations only: Submit résumé and slides. Reports in 3 months. Original artwork returned at job's completion.

Terms: Pays authors in royalties. Sends galleys to authors. Book catalog free on request.

MAGINATION PRESS, 19 Union Square West, New York NY 10003. (212)924-3344. Brunner/Mazel, Inc. Book publisher. Editor-in-Chief: Susan Kent Cakars. Publishes 4-8 picture books and young reader titles/year. Publishes "books dealing with the psycho/therapeutic treatment or resolution of children's serious problems—written by mental health professionals."

Fiction: Picture books, young readers: concept, mental health, multicultural, problem novels, special needs. Published *Gentle Willow: A Story for Children About Dying*, by Joyce C. Mills, Ph.D. (ages 4-8); *Sammy's Mommy Has Cancer*, by Sherry Kohlenberg (ages 4-8); *What About Me? When Brothers & Sisters Get Sick*, by Allan Peterkin, M.D. (ages 4-8).

Nonfiction: Picture books, young readers: concept, mental health, how-to, multicultural, psychotherapy, special needs. Published *Putting on the Brakes: Young People's Guide to Understanding Attention Deficit Hyperactivity Disorder (ADHD)*, by Patricia O. Quinn, M.D. and Judith M. Stern, M.A. (ages 8-13).

How to Contact/Writers: Fiction/nonfiction: Submit complete ms. Reports on queries/mss: "up to 3 months (may be only days)." Publishes a book 1 year after acceptance.

Illustration: Works with 4-8 illustrators/year. Reviews ms/illustration packages. Will review artwork for future assignments.

How to Contact/Illustrators: Illustrations only: Query with samples. Original artwork returned at job's completion.

Terms: Pays authors in royalties. Offers vary but low advance. Pays illustrators by the project, $2,000 maximum, or royalty of 2% maximum. Sends galleys to authors. Book catalog and ms guidelines on request with SASE.

MEADOWBROOK PRESS, 18318 Minnetonka Blvd., Deephaven MN 55391. (612)473-5400. Fax: (612)475-0736. Book publisher. Submissions Editor: Anita Newhead. Art Director: Amy Unger. Publishes 1-2 middle readers/year; 2-4 young readers/year. 20% of books by first-time authors; 10% of books from agented writers. Publishes children's activity books, gift books, humorous poetry anthologies and story anthologies.

Fiction: Young readers and middle readers: anthology, folktales, humor, multicultural, poetry). "Poems representing people of color encouraged." Published *The New Adventures of Mother Goose; Girls to the Rescue*, (fairytale-style short stories featuring strong girls, for ages 8-12); and *A Bad Case of the Giggles* (children's poetry anthology).

Nonfiction: Young readers, middle readers: activity books, arts/crafts, hobbies, how-to, multicultural, self help. Multicultural needs include activity books representing traditions/cultures from all over the world, and especially fairy tale/folk tale stories with strong, multicultural heroines and diverse settings. "Books which include multicultural activities are encouraged." Average word length: varies. Recently published: *Kids' Party Games and Activities*, by Penny Warner; *Free Stuff for Kids* (activity book); and *Kids' Holiday Fun* (activity book).

How to Contact/Writers: Fiction/Nonfiction: Query, submit outline/synopsis and sample chapters or submit complete ms with SASE. Reports on queries/mss in 2-3 months. Publishes a book 1-2 years after acceptance. Send a business-sized SAE and 2 first-class stamps for free writer's guidelines and book catalog before submitting ideas. Will consider simultaneous submissions.

Illustration: Only interested in agented material. Works with 2-3 illustrators/year. Reviews ms/illustration packages from artists. Submit ms with 2-3 pieces of final art. Contact: Submissions editor. Illustrations only: Submit résumé, promo sheet and tearsheets. Contact: Amy Unger, art director. Reports back only if interested. Samples not returned; samples filed.

Photography: Buys photos from freelancers. Buys stock and assigns work. Model/property releases required. Submit cover letter.

Terms: Pays authors in royalties of 5-7½% based on retail price. Offers average advance payment of $2,000-4,000. Pays for illustrators: $100-25,000; ¼-¾% of total royalties. Pays photographers per photo ($250). Originals returned at job's completion. Book catalog available for 5 × 11 SASE and 2 first-class stamps; ms guidelines and artists guidelines available for SASE.

Tips: "Illustrators and writers should send away for our free catalog and guidelines before submitting their work to us. Also, illustrators should take a look at the books we publish to determine whether their style is consistent with what we are looking for. Writers should also note the style and content patterns of our books. For instance, our children's poetry anthologies contain primarily humorous, rhyming poems with a strong rhythm; therefore, we would not likely publish a free-verse and/or serious poem. I also recommend that writers, especially poets, have their work read by a critical, objective person before they submit anywhere. Also, please correspond with us by mail before telephoning with questions about your submission. We work with the printed word and will respond more effectively to your questions if we have something in front of us."

MERIWETHER PUBLISHING LTD., 885 Elkton Dr., Colorado Springs CO 80907. Book publisher. Estab. 1969. Executive Editor: Arthur L. Zapel. Art Director: Tom Myers. "We do most of our artwork in-house; we do not publish for the children's elementary market." 75% of books by first-time authors; 5% of books from agented writers. Publishes primarily how-to activity books for teens. Most books are related to theater arts or activities for church youth.

Fiction: Middle readers, young adults: anthology, contemporary, humor, religion. "We publish plays, not prose-fiction."

Nonfiction: Middle readers: activity books, religion. Young adults: activity books, how-to church activities, religion, drama/theater arts. Average length: 250 pages. Recently published *Directing for the Stage*, by Terry John Converse; *Let's Play a Bible Game*, by Ed Dunlop; and *Acting Natural*, by Peg Kehret.

How to Contact/Writers: Nonfiction: Query or submit outline/synopsis and sample chapters. Reports on queries in 3 weeks; mss in 6 weeks. Publishes a book 6-12 months after acceptance. Will consider simultaneous submissions.

Illustration: Works with 3 illustrators/year. Reviews ms/illustration packages from artists. Query first. Illustrations only: Query with samples; send résumé, promo sheet or tearsheets. Reports on art samples in 4 weeks.

Terms: Pays authors in royalties of 10% based on retail or wholesale price. Pays for illustrators by the project (range: $150-3,000); royalties based on retail or wholesale price. Sends galleys to authors. Book catalog for SAE and $2 postage; ms guidelines for SAE and 1 first-class stamp.

Tips: "We are currently interested in finding unique treatments for theater arts subjects: scene books, how-to books, monologs and short plays for teens."

JULIAN MESSNER, 250 James St., Morristown NJ 07960. (201)739-8353. Imprint of Silver Burdett Press, Simon & Schuster Education Group. Book publishers. Editor: Adrianne Ruggiero. See listing for Silver Burdett Press.

MILKWEED EDITIONS, 430 First Ave. North, Suite 400, Minneapolis MN 55401-1743. (612)332-3192. Book Publisher. Writers Contact: Children's Reader. Illustrators Contact: Art Director. Publishes 2-3 middle readers/year. 25% of books by first-time authors. "Works must embody humane values and contribute to cultural understanding. There is no primary theme."

Fiction: Middle readers, young adults: adventure, animal, contemporary, fantasy, history, humor, multicultural, nature/environment. Does not want to see anthologies, folktales, health, hi-lo, poetry, religion, romance, sports. Average length: middle readers—90-200 pages. Recently published *Behind the Bedroom Wall*, by Laura E. Williams (history, middle readers); *Summer of the Bonfire Monster*, by Aileen Kilgore Henderson, illustrated by Kim Cooper (adventure/contemporary, middle reader); *Gildaen*, by Emilie Buchwald (middle reader, fantasy); *I Am Lavina Cumming*, by Susan Lowell (middle reader, contemporary).

How to Contact/Writers: Fiction: Query; submit complete manuscript. Reports on queries in 2 months, mss in 2-6 months. Publishes a book 1-12 months after acceptance. Will consider simultaneous submissions.

Illustration: Works with 3 illustrators/year. Reviews ms/illustration packages from artists. Query; submit manuscript with dummy. Illustrations only: Query with samples; provide resume, promo sheet, slides, tearsheets and client list. Samples filed or returned with SASE; samples filed. Originals returned at job's completion.

Terms: Pays authors royalty of 7½% based on retail price. Offers advance against royalties. Sends galleys to authors. Book catalog available for $1.50 to cover postage; ms guidelines available for SASE. Must include SASE with ms submission for its return.

© 1996 Sal Murdocca and reprinted with permission of The Millbrook Press, Inc.

Clearly distressed about something, this screaming banshee illustrated by Sal Murdocca for Brian J. Heniz's *The Monster's Test* is making her feelings known. "The artist imbues everyone and everything with personality and life," says Jean Reynolds, editor at the Millbrook Press, when describing the appeal of this scary yet humorous scene. "Look at each frog and bug—and even the tree. Without being overly cartoonish or anthropomorphic, each is reacting individually to the sound. The tree is just plain mad; the frog on the mushroom is disgusted; the one on the log is overwhelmed; and the timid fellow falling off the bullrushes is just plain scared!"

THE MILLBROOK PRESS, 2 Old New Milford Rd., Brookfield CT 06804. (203)740-2220. Fax: (203)775-5643. Website: http://www.neca.com/mall/millbrook. Book publisher. Manuscript Coordinator: Dottie Carlson. Art Director: Judie Mills. Publishes 20 picture books/year; 40 young readers/year; 50 middle readers/year; 10 young adult titles/year. 10% of books by first-time authors; 20% of books from agented authors. Publishes nonfiction, concept-oriented/educational books.

Fiction: Picture books: concept. Young adults: history.
Nonfiction: All levels: animal, arts/craft, biography, cooking, geography, how-to, multicultural, music/dance, nature/environment, reference, science. Picture books: activity books, concept, hi-lo. Middle readers: hi-lo, social issues, sports. Young adults: careers, social issues. No poetry. Average word length: picture books—minimal; young readers—5,000; middle readers—10,000; young adult/teens—20,000. Published *Frog Counts to Ten*, by John Liebler (grades K-3, picture book); *The Scopes Trial: Defending the Right to Teach*, by Arthur Blake (grades 4-6, history); *The U.S. Health Care Crisis*, by Victoria Sherrow (grades 7-up, contemporary issues).
How to Contact/Writers: Query. Submit outline/synopsis and 1 sample chapter. Reports on queries/mss in 1 month.
Illustration: Work with 75 illustrators/year. Reviews ms/illustration packages from artists. Query; submit 1 chapter of ms with 1 piece of final art. Illustrations only: Query with samples; provide résumé, business card, promotional literature or tearsheets to be kept on file. Samples returned with SASE; samples filed. Contact: Judie Mills, art director. Reports back only if interested.
Photography: Buys photos from freelancers. Buys stock and assigns work.
Terms: Pays author royalty of 5-7½% based on wholesale price or work purchased outright. Offers advances. Pays illustrators by the project, royalty of 3-7% based on wholesale price. Sends galleys to authors. Book catalog, ms and artist's guidelines for SASE.

*MITCHELL LANE PUBLISHERS, 17 Matthew Bathon Court, Elkton MD 21921. (410)392-5036. Fax: (410)392-4781. Book publisher. President: Barbara Mitchell. Publishes 4-5 young adult titles/year. Publishes multicultural, multiethnic authorized biographies.
Nonfiction: Middle readers, young adults: biography, multicultural. Average word length: 40,000 words. Recently published *Tommy Nuñez: NBA Referee/Taking My Best Shot*, by B. Marvis (ages 10-16, biography); *Famous People of Hispanic Heritage*, by Marvis and Swanson, illustrated by B. Tidman (ages 9-16, collection of biographies); and *Famous People of Asian Ancestry* (ages 9-15).
How to Contact/Writers: Nonfiction: Query; submit outline/synopsis and 3 sample chapters. Reports on queries/mss in 2 months. Publishes a book 18 months after acceptance.
Illustration: Works with 2-3 illustrators/year. Reviews ms/illustration packages from artists. Query; arrange portfolio review, including color copies of work. Contact: Barbara Mitchell, president. Illustration only: query with samples; arrange personal portfolio review; send résumé, portfolio, slides, tearsheets. Contact: Barbara Mitchell, president. Reports back only if interested. Samples not returned; filed.
Photography: Buys stock images. Contact: Barbara Mitchell, president. Needs photos of famous and prominent minority figures. Captions required. Uses b&w prints. Submit cover letter, résumé, published samples, stock photo list.
Terms: Pays authors 5-10% royalty based on wholesale price or purchased outright for $250-2,000. Pays illustrators by the project $40-250. Sends galleys to authors.
Tips: "Most of our assignments are work-for-hire. Submit résumé and samples of work to be considered for future assignments."

MONDO PUBLISHING, One Plaza Rd., Greenvale NY 11548. (516)484-7812. Fax: (516)484-7813. Book publisher. Publisher: Diane Snowball. Senior Editor: Louise May. Publishes 60 picture books/year. 20% of books by first-time authors. Publishes various categories.
Fiction: Picture books, young readers, middle readers: adventure, animal, contemporary, fantasy, folktales, history, humor, multicultural, nature/environment, poetry, sports. Multicultural needs include: stories about children in different cultures or about children of different backgrounds in a U.S. setting. Recently published *Zoo-looking*, by Mem Fox (3-7 year olds).
Nonfiction: Picture books, young readers, middle readers: animal, arts/crafts, biography, geography, history, how-to, multicultural, nature/environment, science, sports. Recently published *Beavers*, by Helen H. Moore (7-10 year-olds, animal).
How to Contact/Writers: Fiction/Nonfiction: Query, submit complete ms. Reports on queries in 1 month; mss in 3-4 months. Will consider simultaneous submissions and previously published work. Mss returned with SASE.
Illustration: Works with 40 illustrators/year. Reviews ms/illustration packages from illustrators. Contact: Louise May, senior editor. Illustration only: Query with samples, résumé, portfolio. Reports in 1 month. Samples returned with SASE; samples filed.
Photography: Uses freelance photographers. Contact: Diane Snowball, publisher. Buys stock images. Uses mostly nature photos. Uses color prints, transparencies.

Terms: Pays authors royalty of 2-5% based on wholesale/retail price. Offers advance based on project. Pays illustrators by the project (range: 3,000-8,000), royalty of 2-5% based on wholesale/retail price. Pays photographers by the project, per photo. Sends galleys to authors depending on project. Book catalog available for 9 × 12 SASE.

Tips: "Prefer illustrators with book experience or a good deal of experience in illustration projects requiring consistency of characters and/or setting over several illustrations. Prefer manuscripts targeted to trade market plus crossover to educational market."

MOREHOUSE PUBLISHING CO., 871 Ethan Allen Hwy., Ridgefield CT 06877. (203)431-3927. Fax: (203)431-3964. Book publisher. Estab. 1884. Editor: Deborah Grahame-Smith. Publishes 4 picture books/year. 25% of books by first-time authors.

Fiction: Picture books: folktales, multicultural, religion. Young readers: adventure, folktales, humor, multicultural. Middle readers: folk tales, history, multicultural, poetry, religion. Young adults: contemporary, multicultural, mystery. Multicultural themes include "working together for the betterment of God's world." Does not want to see "anything other than traditional Christian values."

Nonfiction: Picture books: nature/environment, religion. Young readers: biography, nature/environment, religion. Middle readers: biography, religion, social issues. Young adults: biography, social issues.

How to Contact/Writers: Fiction/nonfiction: Submit outline/synopsis and sample chapters to Deborah Grahame-Smith. Reports on queries in 4-6 weeks; mss in 3 months. Publishes a book 1 year after acceptance. "Agented ms are preferred."

Illustration: Works with 3 illustrators/year. Reviews ms/illustration packages from artists. Submit 3 chapters of ms with 1 piece of final art. Illustrations only: Submit résumé, tearsheets. Contact: Deborah Grahame-Smith, art director. Reports on art samples in 4-6 weeks.

Photography: Buys photos from freelancers. Buys stock images. Uses photos of children/youth in everyday life experiences.

Terms: Pays authors royalty of 6-15% based on retail price, and purchases more outright. Offers modest advance payment. Pay illustrators by the project. Sends galleys to authors. Original artwork returned at job's completion. Book catalog free on request if SASE ($1.25 postage) is supplied.

Tips: Writers: "Prefer authors who can do their own illustrations. Be fresh, be fun, not pedantic, but let your work have a message." Illustrators: "Work hard to develop an original style." Looks for ms/illustration packages "with a religious or moral value while remaining fun and entertaining."

A little bear pulls on his red rain boots while another checks his reflection in this watercolor illustration rendered by Mary Ellen King. Taken from King's first children's book, *A Good Day for Listening*, King's delicate colors and homespun charm caught the eye of Morehouse Publishing Editor Deborah Grahame-Smith, who received an unsolicited submission from King in the mail. "Her beautifully illustrated *outer* envelope created excitement from the day it arrived in the mail," she says. "It definitely stood out from the usual volume of mail we receive each day."

© 1995 Mary Ellen King

MORGAN REYNOLDS PUBLISHING, 620 S. Elm St., Suite 384, Greensboro NC 27406. (910)275-1311. Fax: (910)274-3705. Editor: John Riley. Book Publisher. Publishes 12 young adult titles/year. 50% of books by first-time authors.
Nonfiction: Middle readers, young adults/teens: biography, history, multicultural, social issues. Multicultural needs include Native American, African-American and Latino subjects. Average word length: 12,000-20,000. Recently published: *Nathaniel Hawthorne: American Storyteller*, by Nancy Whitelaw; *Smart Money: The Story of Bill Gates*, by Aaron Boyd; and *Boris Yeltsin: First President of Russia*, by Calvin Craig Miller.
How to Contact/Writers: Query; submit outline/synopsis with 3 sample chapters. Reports on queries in 1 month; mss in 2 months. Publishes a book 6 months after acceptance. Will consider simultaneous submissions or electronic submissions via disk (ASCII format).
Terms: Pays authors royalty of 8-12% based on wholesale price. Offers advances. Sends galleys to authors. Book catalog available for business-size SAE with 1 first-class stamp; ms guidelines available for SASE.
Tips: "We are open to suggestions—if you have an idea that excites you send it along. Recent trends suggest that the field is open for younger, smaller companies. Writers, especially ones starting out, should search us out."

JOSHUA MORRIS PUBLISHING, 221 Danbury Rd., Wilton CT 06897. (203)761-9999. Fax: (203)761-5655. Subsidiary of Reader's Digest, Inc. Contact: Acquisition Editor. Art Director: Julia Sabbagh. "We publish mostly early concept books and books for beginning readers. Most are in series and contain some kind of novelty element (i.e., lift the flap, die cut holes, book and soft toy, etc.). We publish approximately 200 books per year." 5% of books by first-time authors; 5% of books from agented authors; 90% of books published on commission (Book packaging).
Fiction: Picture books and young readers: activity books, adventure, animal, concept, nature/environment, reference, religion. Middle readers: animal, nature/environment, religion. Does not want to see poetry, short stories, science fiction. Average word length: picture books—300-400. Published *Whooo's There?*, by Lily Jones (ages 3-7, sound and light); *Ghostly Games*, by John Speirs, with additional text by Gill Speirs (ages 8-12, puzzle).
Nonfiction: Picture books, young readers and middle readers: activity books, animal, nature/environment, religion. Average word length: varies. Published *Alan Snow Complete Books (Dictionary, Atlas* and *Encyclopedia)*, by Alan Snow (ages 3-7, first reference); *Rain Forest Nature Search*, by Paul Sterry (ages 7-12, puzzle/activity).
How to Contact/Writers: Fiction/Nonfiction: Query. Nonfiction: Query. Reports on queries/mss in 3-4 months. Publishes a book 12-18 months after acceptance. Will consider simultaneous submissions and previously published work.
Illustration: Reviews ms/illustration packages from artists. Query. Illustrations only: Query with samples (nonreturnable). Provide résumé, promo sheet or tearsheets to be kept on file. Contact: Julia Sabbagh, art director and Ira Teichberg, creative director. Reports back only if interested. Original artwork returned (only if requested).
Photography: Buys stock and assigns work. Contact: Ira Teichberg, creative director. Uses photos of animals and children. Model/property releases required. Publishes photo concept books. Uses 4×6 glossy, color prints and 4×5 transparencies. Submit résumé, promo sheet or tearsheets to be kept on file.
Terms: Pays authors royalty or work purchased outright. Offers advances. Pays illustrators by the project or royalty. Photographers paid per photo.
Tips: Best bets with this market are "innovative concept and books that have a novelty element."

MORROW JUNIOR BOOKS, 1350 Avenue of the Americas, New York NY 10019. Division of the Hearst Corporation.
  • Morrow Junior does not accept unsolicited manuscripts.

JOHN MUIR PUBLICATIONS, INC., P.O. Box 613, Santa Fe NM 87504-0613. (505)982-4078. Book publisher. Editorial Contact: Steven Cary. Publishes 25 middle reader nonfiction picture books/year.
Nonfiction: Middle readers: animal, arts/crafts, biography, concept, hobbies, multicultural, nature/environment, science, social issues. Average word length: middle readers—12,000-15,000. Published *Kids' Explore* series (5 titles), by different authors (middle readers); *Extremely Weird* series, by Sarah Lovett (ages 8-12).
How to Contact/Writers: Query. Reports on queries/mss in 3-6 months. Publishes a book 8-12 months after acceptance. Will consider simultaneous submissions.

Illustration: Reviews ms/illustration packages. Query, outline and 1 chapter for illustration; 4 original finished pieces and roughs of ideas. Illustrations only: Submit résumé and samples of art that have been reproduced or samples of original art for style.

Photography: Purchases photos from freelancers. Buys stock images. Buys "travel, animal" photos.

Terms: Pays authors on work-for-hire basis, occasionally royalties. Some books are paid by flat fee for illustration or by the project. Book catalog free on request.

Tips: "We want nonfiction books for 8- to 12-year-old readers that can sell in bookstores as well as gift stores, libraries and classrooms."

NEW DISCOVERY BOOKS; 299 Jefferson Rd., P.O. Box 480, Parsippany NJ 07054-0480. (201)236-7000. Imprint of Silver Burdett Press, Simon & Schuster Education Group. Book publisher. Editor: Debbie Biber. See Silver Burdett Press listing.

NORTHLAND PUBLISHING, P.O. Box 1389, Flagstaff AZ 86002-1389. (520)774-5251. Fax: (520)774-0592. E-mail: info@northlandpub.com. Website: http://www.northlandpub.com. Book publisher. Editor-in-Chief: Erin Murphy. Senior Designer: Rudy Ramos. Publishes 6 picture books/year; 2 young readers/year. 75% of books by first-time authors. Primary theme is West and Southwest regionals, Native American stories.

Fiction: Picture books, young readers and middle readers: animal. Picture books, young readers: folktales, humor. Middle readers: adventure. Middle readers, young adults: suspense/mystery. All levels: history, nature/environment, multicultural. "Multicultural needs include stories with characters/plots that have to do with multicultural aspects of the Southwest; i.e. Hispanic and Native American. Our Native American folktales are enjoyed by readers of all ages, child through adult." No religion, science fiction, anthology. Average word length: picture books—800; young readers—1,500; middle readers—20,000. Published *Grandmother Spider Brings the Sun*, by Geri Keams, illustrated by James Bernardin (ages 5 and up); *Carlos and the Cornfield*, by Jan Romero Stevens, illustrated by Jeanne Arnold (ages 5 and up); *Less Than Half, More Than Whole*, by Kathleen and Michael Lacapa, illustrated by Michael Lacapa (ages 5 and up).

Nonfiction: Picture books, young readers and middle readers: animal, multicultural, historical. Average word length: picture books—800; young readers—1,500; middle readers—20,000.

How to Contact/Writers: Reports on queries in 4-6 weeks; mss in 10-12 weeks. "Acknowledgment sent immediately upon receipt." If ms and art are complete at time of acceptance, publication usually takes 18 months. Will consider simultaneous submissions if labelled as such.

Illustration: Works with 6-8 illustrators/year. Uses color artwork only. Reviews ms/illustration packages from artists. Submit ms with samples; slides or color photocopies. Illustrations only: Query art director with samples, promo sheet, slides, tearsheets. Reports only if interested. Samples returned with SASE; samples filed.

Terms: Pays authors/illustrators royalty of 4-7% based on wholesale price. Offers advances. "This depends so much on quality of work and quantity needed." Original artwork returned at job's completion. Book catalog, artists' and ms guidelines available for SASE.

Tips: Receptive to "Native American folktales (must be retold by a Native American author). Please research our company (look at our catalog) before submitting your work. No phone queries, please."

NORTHWORD PRESS, INC., P.O. Box 1360, Minocqua WI 54548. (715)356-7644. Fax: (715)356-7644. E-mail: nwpedit@newnorth.net. Managing Editor: Barbara Harold. Production Coordinator: Russ Kuepper. Publishes 10 picture books/year. 50% of books by first-time authors; 10% of books from agented authors. Publishes books pertaining to nature and wildlife. Also Native American topics.

Fiction: All levels: animal, nature. Teens: adventure. Does not want to see "anything without a strong nature/animal focus; no moralizing animal/nature stories (didactic). No anthropomorphism."

Nonfiction: All levels: animal, nature. Average word length: picture books—500-3,000; young readers—2,500-3,000. Published *Dolphins for Kids*, by Patricia Corrigan (ages 4-10, photo picture book); *Take Along Guides* (ages 8-12); *Secrets of the Forest*, by Muriel Steffy Lipp; and *My Little Book of Wood Ducks*, by Hope Irvin Marston, illustrated by Maria Magdalena Brown (ages 1-10).

How to Contact/Writers: Fiction: Query. Nonfiction: Query; submit outline/synopsis and 1 sample chapter. Reports on queries in 2 months; mss in 3 months (with SASE only). Publishes a book 12-24 months after acceptance. Will consider simultaneous submissions.

Illustration: Works with 1-3 illustrators/year. Reviews ms/illustration packages from artists. Query. Submit 1 chapter of ms with 3 pieces of final art. Illustrations only: Query with samples. Contact: Russ Kuepper, production coordinator. Reports back only if interested. Samples returned with SASE; samples filed.

Photography: Buys photos from freelancers. Contact: Larry Mishkar, photo editor. Uses nature and wildlife photos, full-color. Buys stock. Model releases required. Uses transparencies. Query with samples. "Not responsible for damage to, or loss of, unsolicited materials."

Terms: Pays authors royalty based on wholesale price or work purchased outright. Offers negotiable advances. Pays illustrators by the project. Pays photographer by the project or per photo. Sends galleys to authors. Original artwork returned at job's completion. Book catalog available for 9×12 SAE and 7 first-class stamps; ms and artist's guidelines available for SASE.

Tips: "The three key words are 'educational,' 'nature' and 'wildlife.' Beyond that, we're looking for fun, unusual and well-written manuscripts. We are expanding our children's line to include picture books that express a certain value or moral lesson related to nature."

THE OLIVER PRESS, INC., Charlotte Square, 5707 West 36th Street, Minneapolis MN 55416. Phone: (612)926-8981. Fax: (612)926-8965. Book publisher. Editor: Denise Sterling. Publishes 8 young adult titles/year. 10% of books by first-time authors. "We publish collective biographies of people who made an impact in one area of history, including science, government, archaeology, business and crime."

Nonfiction: Middle reader, young adults: biography, geography, history, science. "Authors should only suggest ideas that fit into one of our existing series. We would like to add to our list of biographies on African Americans and women." Average word length: young adult—20,000 words. Recently published *America's Third-Party Presidential Candidates*, by Nathan Aaseng (ages 10 and up, collective biography); *Women Business Leaders*, by Robert B. Pile (ages 10 and up, collective biography); and *Amazing Archaeologists and Their Finds*, by William Scheller (ages 10 and up, collective biography).

How to Contact/Writers: Nonfiction: Query. Submit outline/synopsis. Contact: Denise Sterling. Reports in 6 months. Publishes a book approximately 1 year after acceptance.

Photography: Buys photos from freelancers. Contact: Denise Sterling, editor. Buys stock images. Looks primarily for photos of people in the news. Captions required. Uses 8×10 b&w prints. Submit cover letter, résumé and stock photo list.

Terms: Work purchased outright from authors ($750 and up). Sends galleys to authors upon request. Book catalog and ms guidelines available for SASE.

Tips: "Authors should read some of the books we have already published before sending a query to The Oliver Press. Authors should propose collective biographies for one of our existing series."

OPEN HAND PUBLISHING INC., P.O. Box 22048, Seattle WA 98122. (206)447-0597. Book publisher. Acquisitions Editor: Pat Andrus. Publishes 1-3 children's books/year. 50% of books by first-time authors. Multicultural books: African-American theme or bilingual.

• Open Hand is not currently accepting manuscripts, only queries.

Fiction: Picture books: history and African-American. Young readers and middle readers: history and African-American. Young adult/teens: African-American. Average length: picture books— 32-64 pages; young readers—64 pages; middle readers—64 pages; young adult/teens—120 pages.

Nonfiction: All levels: history and African-American. Average length: picture books—32-64 pages; young readers—64 pages; middle readers—64 pages; young adult/teens: 64-120 pages.

How to Contact/Writers: Fiction/nonfiction: Query. Reports on queries in 3 weeks; reports on mss in 5 weeks. Publishes a book 12-18 months after acceptance. Will consider simultaneous submissions.

Illustration: Reviews ms/illustration packages from artists. Query. Contact: P. Anna Johnson, publisher. Illustrations only: Query with samples. Reports in 3 weeks. Original artwork returned "depending on the book."

Terms: Pays authors royalty of 5-10% based on wholesale price. Offers advances. Pays illustrators by the project; commission for the work. Sends galleys to authors. Book catalog available for SAE and 2 first-class stamps; ms guidelines available for SAE and 1 first-class stamp.

✿ORCA BOOK PUBLISHERS, P.O. Box 5626 Station B, Victoria, British Columbia V8R 6S4 Canada. (604)380-1229. Fax: (604)380-1892. Book publisher. Children's Books Editor: Ann Featherstone. Publishes 8 picture books/year; 1-2 middle readers/year; 2-3 young adult titles/year. 25% of books by first time authors. "We only consider authors and illustrators who are Canadian or who live in Canada."

Fiction: Picture books: animals, contemporary, fairy tales, folktales, nature/environment. Middle readers: adventure, contemporary, history, nature/environment, problem novels, suspense/mystery. Young adults: adventures, contemporary, history, multicultural, nature/environment, problem novels, suspense/mystery. Average word length: picture books—500-2,000; middle readers—20,000-35,000; young adult—25,000-45,000. Published *The Magic Ear*, by Laura Lanston, illustrated by Victor Bosson (picturebook, ages 5-8); and *The Moccasin Goalie*, written and illustrated by William Roy Brownridge (picturebook, ages 4-8).

Nonfiction: Young readers, middle readers: history, nature/environment. Young adult: history. "We have enough whale stories to hold us for a while." Average word length: picture books—300-500; middle readers—2,000-3,000. Recently published *In the Company of Whales*, by Alexandra Morton, photos by Alexandra Morton (ages 8-12).

How to Contact/Writers: Fiction: Submit complete ms if picture book; submit outline/synopsis and 3 sample chapters. Nonfiction: Query with SASE. "All queries or unsolicited submissions should be accompanied by a SASE." Reports on queries in 3-6 weeks; mss in 1-3 months. Publishes book 12-18 months after acceptance.

Illustration: Works with 6-8 illustrators/year. Reviews ms/illustration packages from artists. Submit ms with 3-4 pieces of final art. "Reproductions only, no original art please." Illustrations only: Query with samples; provide résumé, slides. Reports in 6-8 weeks. Samples returned with SASE; samples filed. Original artwork returned at job's completion if picture books.

Terms: Pays authors royalty of 5% for picture books, 10% for novels, based on retail price. Offers advances (average amount: $1,000). Pays illustrators royalty of 5% minimum based on retail price or advance on royalty of $1,000. Sends galleys to authors. Book catalog available for legal or 8½×11 manila SAE and $1.45 postage. Ms guidelines available for SASE. Art guidelines not available.

Tips: "American authors and illustrators should remember that the U.S. stamps on their reply envelopes cannot be posted in any country outside of the U.S."

ORCHARD BOOKS, 95 Madison Ave., New York NY 10016. (212)951-2600. Division and imprint of Grolier, Inc. Book publisher. President and Publisher: Neal Porter. "We publish between 60 and 70 books yearly including fiction, poetry, picture books, and some non-fiction." 10-25% of books by first-time authors.

● Orchard Books received several awards in 1996: the IRA Children's Book Award for *More Than Anything Else*, by Marie Bradby, illustrated by Chris K. Soentpiet; the 1996 ALA Pura Belpré Award for *An Island Like You*, by Judith Ortiz Cofer; and a Boston Globe-Horn Book Award for fiction for *Poppy* by Avi, illustrated by Brian Floca.

Fiction: All levels: animal, anthology, contemporary, fantasy, folktales, history, humor, multicultural, nature/environment, poetry, science fiction, sports, suspense/mystery.

Nonfiction: Picture books, young readers: animal, history, multicultural, nature/environment, science, social issues. "We publish nonfiction on a very selective basis."

How to Contact/Writers: Orchard Books was not accepting unsolicited ms at the time of publication. Query only with SASE. Submit to: Editor, Orchard Books.

Illustration: Works with 40 illustrators/year. Art director reviews ms/illustration portfolios. Submit "tearsheets or photocopies or photostats of the work." Contact: Art Director. Reports on art samples in 1 month. Samples returned with SASE. No disks or slides, please.

Terms: Most commonly an advance against list royalties. Sends galleys to authors; dummies to illustrators. Original artwork returned at job's completion. Book catalog free on request with 8½×11 SASE with 4 oz. postage.

Tips: "Read some of our books to determine first whether your manuscript is suited to our list."

OUR CHILD PRESS, 800 Maple Glen Lane, Wayne PA 19087-4797. (610)964-0606. Fax: (610)293-9038. Book publisher. President: Carol Hallenbeck. 90% of books by first-time authors.

Fiction/Nonfiction: All levels: adoption, multicultural, special needs. Published *Don't Call Me Marda*, written and illustrated by Sheila Kelly Welch; *Is That Your Sister?* by Catherine and Sherry Burin; and *Oliver: A Story About Adoption*, by Lois Wichstrom.

How to Contact/Writers: Fiction/Nonfiction: Query or submit complete ms. Reports on queries/mss in 6 months. Publishes a book 6-12 months after acceptance.

Illustration: Works with 1 illustrator/year. Uses primarily b&w artwork. Reviews ms/illustration packages from artists. Ms/illustration packages and illustration only: Query first. Submit résumé, tearsheets and photocopies. Contact: Carol Hallenbeck, president. Reports on art samples in 2 months. Samples returned with SASE; samples kept on file.

Terms: Pays authors in royalties of 5-10% based on wholesale price. Pays illustrators royalties of 5-10% based on wholesale price. Original artwork returned at job's completion. Book catalog for business-size SAE and 52¢ postage.
Tips: Won't consider anything not related to adoption.

OUR SUNDAY VISITOR, INC., 200 Noll Plaza, Huntington IN 46750. (219)356-8400. Fax: (219)356-8472. Book publisher. Acquisitions Editors: Jacquelyn M. Lindsey, James Manney. Publishes primarily religious, educational, parenting, reference and biographies.
• Our Sunday Visitor, Inc., is publishing only those children's books that tie in to sacramental preparation. Contact the acquisitions editor for manuscript guidelines and a book catalog.
How to Contact/Writers: Nonfiction: Query, submit complete ms, or submit outline/synopsis, and 2-3 sample chapters. Reports on queries in 2 months. Publishes a book 18-24 months after acceptance. Will consider simultaneous submissions, electronic submissions via disk or modem, previously published work.
Illustration: Reviews ms/illustration packages from artists. Contact: Jacquelyn Lindsey or James Manney, acquisitions editors. Illustration only: Query with samples. Contact: Aquisitions Editor. Reports in 2 weeks. Original artwork returned at job's completion.
Photography: Buys photos from freelancers. Contact: Jacquelyn M. Murphy, acquisitions editor.
Terms: Pays authors based on net receipts. Offers royalty. Sends galleys to authors; dummies to illustrators. Book catalog available for SAE; ms guidelines available for SASE.
Tips: "Stay in accordance with our guidelines."

RICHARD C. OWEN PUBLISHERS, INC., P.O. Box 585, Katonah NY 10536. (914)232-3903. Fax: (914)241-2873. Book publisher. Editor/Art Director: Janice Boland. Publishes 10-20 picture story books/year. 90% of books by first-time authors. Publishes "child focused, meaningful books about characters and situations with which five, six, and seven-year-old children can identify. We include multicultural stories that present minorities in a positive and natural way. Our stories show the diversity in America."
Fiction: Picture books for young readers: adventure, animal, contemporary, folktales, humor, multicultural, nature/environment, sports, suspense/mystery. Does not want to see holiday, religious themes, moral teaching stories. "No talking animals with personified human characteristics, jingles and rhymes, holiday stories, alphabet books, stories without plots, stories with nostalgic views of childhood, soft or sugar-coated tales. No stereotyping." Average word length: 40-100 words.
Nonfiction: Picture books for young readers: animals, careers, multicultural, science, sports. Multicultural needs include: "Good stories respectful of all heritages, races, cultural—African-American, Hispanic, American Indian." Wants lively stories. No "encyclopedic" type of information stories. Average word length: 40-100 words.
How to Contact/Writers: Fiction/nonfiction: Submit complete ms. "*Must* request guidelines first with #10 SASE." Reports on mss in 1-6 months. Publishes a book 2-3 years after acceptance. Will consider simultaneous submissions.
Illustration: Works with 12 illustrators/year. Uses color artwork only. Reviews ms/illustration packages from artists. Send ms with dummy. Illustration only: Send color copies/reproductions or photos of art or provide tearsheets. Must request guidelines first. Reports in 1-6 months only if interested. Samples filed.
Photography: Buys photos from freelancers. Contact: Janice Boland, art director. Wants photos that are child-oriented; candid shots; not interested in portraits. "Natural, bright, crisp and colorful—of children and of interesting subjects and compositions attractive to children. If photos are assigned, we buy outright—retain ownership and all rights to photos taken in the project." Sometimes interested in stock photos for special projects. Uses 35mm, 2¼ × 2¼, color transparencies.
Terms: Pays authors royalties of 5% based on retail price. Offers no advances. Work purchased outright from illustrators (range: $1,000-2,500). Work purchased outright from photographers ($800-2,000) or per photo ($100-150). Sends galleys to authors. Original artwork returned 12 months after job's completion. Book brochure, ms/artists guidelines available for SASE.
Tips: Seeking "stories (both fiction and nonfiction) that have charm, magic, impact and appeal; that children living in today's society will want to read and reread; books with strong storylines, child-appealing language, action and interesting, vivid characters. Write from your heart—for the ears and eyes and heart of your readers—use an economy of words. Frequent children's hour at public library."

*♣OWL BOOKS, Imprint of Grey de Pencier Books, 179 John St. Fifth Floor, Toronto, Ontario M5T 3G5 Canada. (416)971-5275. Fax: (416)971-5294. Book publisher. Contact: Submissions Editor or Art Director. Publishes 2 picture books/year; 3 young readers, middle readers/year. 10% of books by first-time authors. Publishes nature, science and children's crafts and hobbies. "We give preference to work by Canadian writers living in Canada or the U.S."

Fiction: Picture books, young readers: animal, concept, humor, nature/environment. Does not want to see "clichéd environmental stories." Average word length: picture books—1,000; young readers—2,000. Recently published *Wild in the City*, written and illustrated by Jan Thornhill (ages 5-10, picturebook/nature); and *Dragon in the Rocks*, written and illustrated by Marie Day (ages 5-10, picturebook/biography).

Nonfiction: Picture books, young readers, middle readers: animal, arts/crafts, concept, hobbies, how-to, nature/environment, science. Average word length: picture books—1,000-1,500; young readers—2,000-3,500; middle readers—7,500-10,000. Recently published *Cyber Surfer: The Owl Kid's Guide to the Internet*, by Nyla Ahmad (ages 8-12, science/tech); *Little Wonders: Animal Babies and their Families*, by Marilyn Baillie (ages 5 and up, nature); and *I Can Make Toys*, by Mary Wallace (ages 4 and up, crafts).

How to Contact/Writers: Fiction: Submit complete ms. Nonfiction: Submit outline/synopsis and 2 sample chapters. Reports on queries/mss in 3 months. Publishes a book 18 months after acceptance.

Illustration: Uses color artwork only. Reviews ms/illustration packages from artists. Send ms with dummy and 3 pieces of final art. Contact: Submissions Editor, Owl Books.

Photography: Buys stock images. Contact: Photo Editor, Owl Books. Uses photos of nature, science, children. Model/property release required; captions required. Uses 35mm, $2\frac{1}{4} \times 2\frac{1}{4}$, color transparencies. Submit cover letter, résumé, published samples, client list, stock photo list.

Terms: Pays authors royalties based on retail price, outright purchase. Offers advances. Pays illustrators royalty or by the project. Pays photographers by the project or per photo. Sends galleys to authors; dummies to illustrators. Book catalog available for SAE and 6 first-class stamps.

Tips: "We are affiliated with *Owl* and *Chickadee* magazines. We publish mainly nonfiction, and look for innovative ideas, top-notch research, and an understanding of what children want in an information or activity book. Read some Owl Books for an appreciation of our approach!"

♣PACIFIC EDUCATIONAL PRESS, Faculty of Education, UBC, Vancouver British Columbia V6T 1Z4 Canada. (604)822-5385. Fax: (604)822-6603. E-mail: cedwards@unixq.ubc.ca. Director: C.V. Edwards. Publishes 2 juvenile or young adult fiction books and 2 nonfiction books/year. 20% of books by first-time authors.

• Pacific Educational discourages picture book submissions. They only publish picture books on the subjects listed below.

Fiction: Picture books, young readers: folktales, multicultural. Middle readers: contemporary, folktales, history, multicultural. Young adults: contemporary, folktales, history, multicultural. Average word length: picture books—2,500; middle readers—25,000. Published *A Sea Lion Called Salena*, by Dayle Gaetz (ages 8-11, novel with environmental theme); *Trapped by Coal*, by Constance Horne (ages 8-11, novel with historical setting); and *The Reluctant Deckhand*, (ages 8-11, novel/video package focusing on coastal life).

Nonfiction: Picture books: history, multicultural, music/dance, nature/environment, science, social issues. Young readers and middle readers: biography, history, multicultural, music/dance, nature/environment, science, social issues. Young adults: biography, history, multicultural, music/ dance, nature/environment, science, social issues. Multicultural material must apply to Canadian multicultural mosaic—must be authentic voice. Average word length: picture books—5,000; middle readers—25,000; young adults—35,000. Published *Folk Rhymes from Around the World*, by Evelyn Neaman and Sally Davies (ages 7-9, collection of folk poems for children from 20 countries) and *It's Elementary! Investigating the Chemical World*, by Douglas Hayward and Gordon Bates, illustrated by Nyla Sunga (ages 11-15, collection of chemistry experiments and background information science).

How to Contact: Fiction/Nonfiction: Query or submit complete ms. Reports in 3 months. Publishes a book a year or so after acceptance, "depending on a large number of factors." Will consider electronic submissions via disk or modem.

Illustration: Works with 3-4 illustrators/year. Uses both b&w and color artwork. Contact: CV Edwards, director. Illustration only: Query with samples, résumé, tearsheets, color photocopies that we can keep on file. Reports in 4 months. Samples returned with SASE; samples filed, "but I'm not likely to even use an illustrator who won't send samples I can keep."

Photography: Buys photos from freelancers. Contact: C.V. Edwards, director. Sometimes buys stock and assigns work. Uses mostly photos of kids, West Coast flora and fauna. Submit cover letter, résumé, published samples, slides, client list, stock photo list.

Terms: Pays authors royalty of 10-12% based on wholesale price. Pays illustrators: by the project or royalty of 5% based on wholesale price. Pays photographers by the project or per photo. Sends galleys to authors. Book catalog available for 9 × 12 SAE and IRC.

*PACIFIC VIEW PRESS, P.O. Box 2657, Berkeley CA 94702. (510)849-4213. Fax: (510)843-5835. Book publisher. President: Pam Zumwalt. Publishes 1-2 picture books/year. 50% of books by first-time authors.

Fiction: Young readers: multicultural. Middle readers: history, multicultural.

Nonfiction: Young readers, middle readers: multicultural.

✒PACIFIC-RIM PUBLISHERS, RR1, Site 28C7, Gabriola, British Columbia V0R 1X0 Canada. (604)247-0014. Fax: (604)247-0015. Book publisher and distributor. Contact: Naomi Wakan. Publishes 2-4 middle readers/year.

 • Pacific-Rim Publishers will not be accepting any new submissions in 1997.

Fiction: Middle readers: folktales, multicutural. Multicultural needs include Pacific Rim and global subjects.

Nonfiction: Middle readers: activity books (with a link to social studies), multicultural (Pacific Rim countries), music/dance (Pacific Rim countries).

How to Contact/Writers: Fiction/Nonfiction: submit complete ms if under 50 pages. Reports on queries in 2 weeks; mss in 6 weeks. Publishes a book 1 year after acceptance.

Illustration: Uses primarily b&w artwork. Illustration only: b&w. "Send a few samples for our files. Nothing is returned. Don't send originals." Reports back only if interested.

Terms: Pays authors royalty based on retail price. Pays illustrators royalty based on retail price. Sends galleys to authors; dummies to illustrators. Book catalog available for $2, US; $3, Canadian.

Tips: "If you are not writing from the heart, please do not submit work."

PANDO PUBLICATIONS, 5396 Laurie Lane, Memphis, TN 38120. (901)682-8779. Book publisher. Estab. 1988. Owner: Andrew Bernstein. Publishes 2-6 middle readers/year; 2-6 young adults/year. 20% of books by first-time authors.

 • Because of the large number of manuscripts Pando Publications has recently received, the company will not accept unsolicited manuscripts in 1997.

Fiction: Animal, concept, folktales, history, nature/environment. No poetry, science fiction, religion.

Nonfiction: Middle readers, young adults: activity books, animal, arts/crafts, biography, concept, cooking, geography, history, hobbies, how-to, multicultural, nature/environment, reference, science, social issues, special needs, sports. Average length: middle readers—175 pages; young adults—200 pages.

How to Contact/Writers: Fiction/Nonfiction: Query only. "All unsolicited manuscripts are destroyed. Please, no phone calls." Reports on queries in 6 months; on mss in 7 months. Publishes a book 1 year after acceptance. Will consider simultaneous submissions. "Prefers" electronic submissions via disk.

Illustration: Works with 2 illustrators/year. Editorial reviews all illustration packages from artists, and illustration-only submissions. Ms/illustrations: Query first. Illustrations only: Query with samples. Reports on art samples in 3 months. Original artwork returned at job's completion.

Terms: Pays authors royalty of 7-10%. Offers average advance payment of "⅓ royalty due on first run." Sends galleys to authors; dummies to illustrators. "Book descriptions available on request."

Tips: Writers: "Find an untapped market then write to fill the need." Illustrators: "Find an author with a good idea and writing ability. Develop the book with the author. Join a professional

---

"PICTURE BOOKS" are for preschoolers to 8-year-olds; "Young readers" are for 5- to 8-year-olds; "Middle readers" are for 9- to 11-year-olds; and "Young adults" are for those ages 12 and up.

group to meet people—ABA, publishers' groups, as well as writers' groups and publishing auxiliary groups. Talk to printers." Looks for "how-to books, but will consider anything."

*PAPERSTAR BOOKS, Imprint of The Putnam & Grosset Group, 200 Madison Ave., New York NY 10016. Book publisher. Associate Editor: Susan Kochan. Art Director: Cecilia Yung. Publishes 50 picture books/year; 20 middle readers/year.
• PaperStar does not publish original fiction in paperback, only reprint picture books that were first hardcovers and middle grade novels from Putnam, Philomel and other publishers.
Fiction: Middle readers: adventure, contemporary, humor, multicultural, sports, suspense/mystery. Recently published *The Big Bazoohley*, by Peter Carey; *The War of Jenkins' Ear*, by Michael Morpurgo; and *Rimwalkers*, by Vicki Grove.
How to Contact/Writers: Only interested in agented material. Reports on mss in 6 weeks. Publishes a book 18 months after acceptance. Previously published work only.
Illustration: Works with 20 illustrators/year. Send samples of cover art (tearsheets). Reports back only if interested. Samples returned with SASE.
Terms: Pays authors royalty of 6%. Offers advances (Average amount: $4,000-5,000). Pays illustrators by the project. Originals returned to artist at job's completion. Book catalog available for 9×11 SAE and 2 first-class stamps.

PARENTING PRESS, INC., P.O. Box 75267, Seattle WA 98125. (206)364-2900. Fax: (206)364-0702. Website: http://www.parentbooks.com/. Book publisher. Estab. 1979. Associate Publisher: Carolyn Threadgill. Publishes 4-5 books/year for parents or/and children and those who work with them. 40% of books by first-time authors.
Fiction: Publishes social skills books, problem-solving books, safety books, dealing-with-feelings books that use a "fictional" vehicle for the information. "We rarely publish straight fiction." Recently published *I Can't Wait, I Want It, My Name Is Not Dummy*, by Elizabeth Crary, illustrations by Marina Megale (ages 3-8, social skill building); and *Telling Isn't Tattling*, by Kathryn Hammerseng, illustrations by Dave Garbot (ages 4-12, personal safety).
Nonfiction: Picture books: health, social skills building. Young readers: health, social skills building books. Middle readers: health, social skills building. No books on "new baby; coping with a new sibling; cookbooks; manners; books about disabilities (which we don't publish at present); animal characters in anything; books that tell children what they should do, instead of giving options." Average word length: picture books—500-800; young readers—1,000-2,000; middle readers—up to 10,000. Published *Kids to the Rescue*, by Maribeth and Darwin Boelts (ages 4-12).
How to Contact/Writers: Fiction: "We publish educational books for children in story format. *No straight fiction*." Nonfiction: Query. Reports on queries/mss in 3 months, "after requested." Publishes a book 18 months after acceptance. Will consider simultaneous submissions.
Illustrations: Works with 3 illustrators/year. Reviews ms/illustration packages from artists. "We do reserve the right to find our own illustrator, however." Query. Illustrations only: Submit "résumé, samples of art/drawings (no original art); photocopies or color photocopies okay." Reports in 3 weeks. Samples returned with SASE; samples filed.
Terms: Pays authors in royalties of 3-4% based on wholesale price. Outright purchase of ms, "negotiated on a case-by-case basis. Not common for us." Offers average advance of $150. Pays illustrators (for text) by the project; 3-4% royalty based on wholesale price. Pays illustrators (for covers) by the project ($300-800). Pays photographers royalty of 3-4%. Sends galleys to authors; dummies to illustrators. Book catalog/ms/artist's guidelines for #10 SAE and 1 first-class stamp.
Tips: "Make sure you are familiar with unique nature of our books. All are aimed at building certain 'people' skills in adults or children. Our publishing for children follows no trend that we find appropriate. Children need nonfiction social skill-building books that help them think through problems and make their own informed decisions."

PAULIST PRESS, 997 Macarthur Blvd., Mahwah NJ 07430. (201)825-7300. Fax: (201)825-8345. Book publisher. Estab. 1865. Editor: Karen Scialabba. Publishes 9-11 picture books/year; 6-7 young reader titles/year; 3-4 middle reader titles/year. 70% of books by first-time authors; 30% of books from agented writers.
Fiction/Nonfiction: Picture books, young readers, middle readers and young adults: interested mainly in values, morals, devotional, religious and Roman Catholic material. Recently published *Countdown to Christmas*, by Susan Heyboer O'Keefe, illustrated by Christopher Fay; *After the Funeral*, by Jane L. Winsch, illustrated by Pamela Keating; *I Hate Goodbye*, by Kathleen Szaj; and *Little Blessings*, by Sally Anne Conan.

How to Contact/Writers: Fiction/nonfiction: Submit complete ms. Reports on queries in 1-2 months; mss in 2-3 months. Publishes a book 12-16 months after acceptance.

Illustration: Works with 10-12 illustrators/year. Editorial reviews all varieties of ms/illustration packages from artists. Submit complete ms with 1 piece of final art, remainder roughs. Contact: Karen Scialabba, children's book editor. Illustrations only: Submit résumé, tearsheets. Reports on art samples in 6 weeks. Original artwork returned at job's completion, "if requested by illustrator."

Photography: Buys photos from freelancers. Contact: Karen Scialabba. Works on assignment only. Uses inspirational photos.

Terms: Pays authors royalty of 6-8% based on retail price. Offers average advance payment of $500. Pays illustrators by the project (range: $50-100) or royalty of 2-6% based on retail price. Factors used to determine final payment: color art, b&w, number of illustrations, complexity of work. Pay for separate authors and illustrators: Author paid by royalty rate; illustrator paid by flat fee, sometimes by royalty. Sends galleys to authors; dummies to illustrators.

Tips: "We cannot be responsible for unsolicited manuscripts. Please send copies, not originals. We try to respond to all manuscripts we receive—please understand if you have not received a response within six months the manuscript does not fit our current publishing plan. We look for authors who diligently promote their work."

*PAWS IV PUBLISHING, P.O. Box 2364, Homer AK 99603. (907)235-7697. Fax: (907)235-7698. E-mail: pawsiv@ptialaska.net. Book publisher. Marketing Director: Celeste Fenger. Publishes 1 young reader/year; 1 young adult/year. 20% of books by first-time authors.

Fiction: Picture books, young readers: adventure, animal, concept, contemporary. Middle readers, young adult/teens: adventure, animal, contemporary. Sees too much non-Alaskan material. Recently published *Swimmer*, by Gill/Cartwright (ages 9-11, journey of a salmon); *Thunderfeet*, by Gill/Cartwright (ages 5-8, verse and rhyme in prehistoric time); and *Alaska Mother Goose*, by Gill/Cartwright (ages preschool-8 years, nursery rhymes).

Nonfiction: All levels: activity books, animal, arts/crafts, biography, nature/environment. Sees too much non-Alaskan material. Recently published *Adventure at the Bottom of the World*, by Gill (ages young adult, mountain climbing); *Denali Curriculum*, by Palmer/Cartwright (ages 9 and up, mountain climbing); and *Iditarod Curriculum*, by Gill/Cartwright (ages 9 and up, Iditarod-related activities).

How to Contact/Writers: Fiction/Nonfiction: Submit outline/synopsis. Reports on queries/mss in 1 month. Publishes a book 6 months after acceptance.

Illustration: Works with 1-2 illustrators/year. Reviews ms/illustration packages from artists. Query. Contact: C. Fenger, marketing director. Illustrations only: Query with samples. Contact: C. Fenger, marketing director. Reports in 1 month. Samples returned with SASE; samples filed.

Photography: Buys stock and assigns work. Contact: C. Fenger, marketing director. "Subject matter depends on current project, i.e., mountaineering, rainforests, etc." Uses 35mm transparencies. Submit cover letter.

Terms: Pays authors royalty of 5% based on wholesale price. Illustrators and photographers paid by the project. Sends galleys to authors; dummies to illustrators. Originals returned to artist at job's completion. Book catalog for SASE. All imprints included in a single catalog.

Tips: "We are looking for Alaskan children's/young adult material."

PEACHTREE PUBLISHERS, LTD., 494 Armour Circle NE, Atlanta GA 30324. (404)876-8761. Fax: (404)875-2578. Book publisher. Editorial: Helen Harriss.

Fiction: Picture books: adventure, animal, concept, history, nature/environment. Young readers: adventure, animal, concept, history, nature/environment, poetry. Middle readers: adventure, animal, history, nature/environment, sports. Young adults: history, humor, nature/environment. Does not want to see science fiction, romance.

Nonfiction: Picture books: animal, history, nature/environment. Young readers, middle readers, young adults: animal, biography, history, nature/environment. Does not want to see sports, religion.

How to Contact/Writers: Fiction/Nonfiction: Submit complete manuscript. Reports on queries in 2-3 months; mss in 4 months. Publishes a book 1-1½ years after acceptance. Will consider simultaneous and previously published submissions.

Illustration: Works with 4 illustrators/year. Illustrations only: Query with samples, résumé, slides, color copies to keep on file. Reports back only if interested. Samples returned with SASE; samples filed.

Terms: Manuscript guidelines for SASE, or call for a recorded message.

PELICAN PUBLISHING CO. INC., 1101 Monroe St., Gretna LA 70053. (504)368-1175. Book publisher. Estab. 1926. Editor-in-Chief: Nina Kooij. Publishes 6 young readers/year; 2 middle reader titles/year. 10% of books from agented writers.

Fiction: Young readers: folktales, history, multicultural, religion. Middle readers: folktales, history, multicultural, religion. Multicultural needs include stories about Native Americans, African-Americans and Hispanics. Does not want animal stories, general Christmas stories, "day at school" or "accept yourself" stories. Average word length: "when printed" young readers—32 pages; middle readers—160 pages. Recently published *Mimi and Jean-Paul's Cajun Mardi Gras*, by Alice Couvillon and Elizabeth Moore (describes a Cajun Mardi Gras).

Nonfiction: Young readers: biography, history, multicultural, music/dance, nature/environment, religion, sports. Middle readers: biography, cooking, history, multicultural, music/dance, nature/environment, religion, sports. Published *Olympic Black Women*, by Martha Ward Plowden, illustrated by Ronald Jones (ages 8-12, short biographies in one book).

How to Contact/Writers: Fiction/Nonfiction: Query. Reports on queries in 1 month; mss in 3 months. Publishes a book 12-18 months after acceptance.

Illustration: Works with 6 illustrators/year. Reviews ms/illustration packages from artists. Query first. Reports only if interested. Illustrations only: Query with samples (no originals). Contact: Nina Kooij, editor-in-chief. Reports only if interested. Samples returned with SASE; samples kept on file.

Terms: Pays authors in royalties; buys ms outright "rarely." Sends galleys to authors. Illustrators paid by "various arrangements." Book catalog and ms guidelines available for SASE.

Tips: "No anthropomorphic stories, pet stories (fiction or nonfiction), fantasy, poetry, science fiction or romance. Writers: Be as original as possible. Develop characters that lend themselves to series and always be thinking of new and interesting situations for those series. Give your story a strong hook—something that will appeal to a well-defined audience. There is a lot of competition out there for general themes." Looks for: "writers whose stories have specific 'hooks' and audiences, and who actively promote their work."

PENGUIN USA, 375 Hudson St., New York NY 10014. (212)366-2000. See listings for Cobblehill, Dial Books for Young Readers, Dutton Children's Books and Puffin Books.

PERFECTION LEARNING CORPORATION, Cover to Cover, 10520 New York, Des Moines IA 50322. (515)278-0133. Fax: (515)278-2245. E-mail: perflern@netins.net. Book publisher, independent book producer/packager. Senior Editors: J. Cosson (K-6), M. James (6 and up). Art Director: Randy Messer. Publishes 10 middle readers/year; 10 young adult titles/year.

 ● Perfection Learning Corp. publishes all hi-lo children's books on a variety of subjects.

Fiction: Middle readers and young adults: adventure, folktales, sports. Picture books, middle readers, young readers: nature/environment. All levels: history. Average word length: middle readers—10,000-30,000; young adults: 10,000-30,000. Recently published *When a Hero Dies*; and *Kimo and the Secret Waves*.

Nonfiction: Middle readers and young adults: biography, geography, nature/environment, sports. Picture books, middle readers, young readers: science. All levels: history, multicultural. Multicultural needs include stories, legends and other oral tradition narratives by authors who are of the culture. Does not want to see ABC books. Average word length: middle readers—10,000; young adults—10,000.

How to Contact/Writers: Fiction/Nonfiction: Submit complete ms. Reports on queries in 2 weeks; mss in 3 months. Publishes a book 18 months after acceptance.

Illustration: Works with 10-15 illustrators/year. Illustration only: Query with samples; send résumé, promo sheet, client list, tearsheets. Contact: Randy Messer, art director. Reports only if interested. Samples returned with SASE; samples filed.

Photography: Buys photos from freelancers. Contact: Randy Messer, art director. Buys stock and assigns work. Uses children. Uses color or up to 8× b&w glossy prints; 2¼×2¼, 4×5 transparencies. Submit cover letter, client list, stock photo list, promo piece (color or b&w).

Terms: Pays authors "depending on going rate for industry." Offers advances, Pays illustrators by the project. Pays photographers by the project. Original artwork returned on a "case by case basis."

Tips: "Our materials are sold through schools for use in the classroom. Talk to a teacher about his/her needs."

PERSPECTIVES PRESS, P.O. Box 90318, Indianapolis IN 46290-0318. (317)872-3055. Book publisher. Estab. 1982. Publisher: Pat Johnston. Publishes 1-3 picture books/year; 1-3 young reader titles/year. 95% of books by first-time authors.

INSIDER REPORT

Seize every opportunity in the picture book market

In the competitive world of children's books, illustrator Floyd Cooper succeeded with a combination of savvy marketing, flexibility and, he admits with a chuckle, "a little bit of luck." Having illustrated 15 picture books, several poetry collections and a variety of related publications, he recently expanded his expertise by both writing and illustrating two picture book biographies.

Floyd Cooper

Cooper, like most freelance artists, began his career working in an established field. After a brief stint freelancing while a student at the University of Oklahoma, he secured a position at a large greeting card company. He eventually yearned for more freedom in his work, and receiving a boost of confidence from mentor and renowned illustrator Mark English, moved to the East Coast and began illustrating textbooks. Finally, he got the assignment that would jump-start his career in children's books. In 1988, Eloise Greenfield's *Grandpa's Face* was published and Cooper's illustrations captured national acclaim. *Mandela: From the Life of the South African Statesman*, which he wrote and illustrated was published in fall, 1996. His latest book, *Miz Berlin Walks*, will be out soon (both Philomel Books).

Describing his style, he says, "I work backwards. I erase the picture (done with oil paint on illustration board) using a kneaded eraser. The eraser has no hard, definable shape," so the result is a very soft, warm image. He then layers on color with acrylics, pastels, oils, colored pencils, etc. "I love it all," he says of his media choices. He uses this layering technique "to achieve a certain mood, to invoke a feeling. There's an infinite number of combinations."

Mark English introduced this technique to him. It's common in the advertising world because it's quick, Cooper notes. Why his success with this method? "No one had done it with picture books. I've taken it in a certain direction. It's something I claim. But I'm still looking over my shoulder. My technique is still evolving. I'm always trying to do something different." And with a sigh he adds, "The competition is fierce."

Although Cooper doesn't struggle to find work these days, his obstacles were once those of every fledgling freelancer. He first faced New York with little more than his portfolio and $3,000. He made some wise choices and took full advantage of every opportunity he recognized.

Wary to write a prescription for marketing in the picture book field, Cooper says, "There isn't one way to go about it." However, he claims one of his wisest

INSIDER REPORT, *Cooper*

© 1994 Floyd Cooper

Coming Home, author/illustrator Floyd Cooper's tale from the childhood of African-American poet Langston Hughes, features illustrations depicting heartwarming childhood scenes on every page. Cooper uses a unique technique in which he covers a page with paint, erases the shapes of images in the scenes and them fills them in with color. The technique produces soft illustrations with a warm, almost fuzzy, look to them.

decisions was obtaining an agent to do much of the legwork for him, an advantage particularly needed by artists far removed from publishing houses. New York provides great opportunity, but "there is Federal Express," he notes. "You can live in Jamaica" and be successful in this field.

Whether you're working with a rep or going it alone, always "keep a broad perspective," Cooper advises. "Be flexible and remember what sells" when soliciting and accepting work. "Appeal to the audience." Cooper eagerly accepted assignments of all sorts, and his willingness to tackle a variety of challenges paid off in the long run.

He has been able to switch gears and concentrate on the projects of his choice because of his experience. He completed several books with African-American themes (such as Coretta Scott King Honor Books *Brown Honey and Broomwheat Tea* and *Meet Danitra Brown*), yet noticed with dismay that he was being approached largely with similar proposals. Preferring to work with diverse subjects, he extended his range by illustrating such books as the 12th-century Japanese tale *The Girl Who Loved Caterpillars* and *One April Morning: Children Remember the Oklahoma City Bombing*.

To achieve this type of creative freedom, Cooper began early on by presenting only his best work to art directors and allowing them to choose what he was best suited for in their venue. "Consistency in style is preferred by some art directors," he says. But he asserts that if you present a portfolio containing no more than seven to 12 pieces of your finest work, regardless of the style, you'll have the best chance of attracting attention. And after you've completed work for a variety of projects and publishers, you'll "get a feel for each type of work," and discover where your talents lie.

Such creative growth is largely achieved through listening, particularly to art directors. "Everyone has an opinion. You'll get more stature as you get further on," so learn to get along with everyone. "I got more out of it by being a listener," he points out in his soft-spoken manner. He's often disagreed with an art director, but kept his thoughts to himself.

To further broaden your knowledge and make professional connections, Cooper advises every novice illustrator to take advantage of conferences, such as those sponsored by SCBWI and the Author's Guild. He also recommends the Rutgers Reading Council's annual roundtable discussion as a forum for those interested in books for children and young adults.

While you're researching and learning don't be discouraged, Cooper says. The road to publication can be a long one, and he states unequivocally that persistence is essential. "You have to weather rejection, believe in what you're doing. Keep your head above water long enough for someone to throw you a life preserver . . . Tough it out. You'll make it if you're meant to."

And if you do, don't rest on your laurels. Cooper scoffs at the notion that he is "established" in the world of picture book illustration. "I'm still not there yet. I'm always trying to do something better," he says. The market is changing quickly, due greatly to the influence of expanding technology and computers. "I'm at a crossroads. I may want to alter my direction," he says. "I may want to exploit [my technique] to its full potential" to stay abreast of the competition.

—*Jennifer Hogan-Redmond*

Fiction/Nonfiction: Picture books, young readers: adoption, foster care, donor insemination or surrogacy. Does not want young adult material. Published *Lucy's Feet*, by Stephanie Stein, illustrated by Kathryn A. Imler, *Two Birthdays for Beth*, by Gay Lynn Cronin, illustrated Joanne Bowring, *Let Me Explain: A Story about Donor Insemination*, by Jane Schnitter, illustrated by Joanne Bowring and *The Mulberry Bird* (revised), by Anne Brodzinsky, illustrated by Diana L. Stanley.

How to Contact/Writers: Fiction/nonfiction: Query or submit outline/synopsis and sample chapters. "No query necessary on subject appropriate picture books." SASE required for reply. Reports on queries in 2 weeks; mss in 6 weeks. Publishes a book 10-12 months after acceptance.

Illustration: Works with 1-2 illustrators/year. Illustrations only: Submit promo sheet and client list. Reports in 2-6 weeks. Samples returned with SASE.

Terms: Pays authors royalties on a sliding scale based on net sales or by work purchased outright. Pays illustrators royalty or by the project. Sends galleys to authors; dummies to illustrators. Book catalog, ms guidelines available for #10 SAE and 2 first-class stamps.

Tips: "Do your homework! I'm amazed at the number of authors who don't bother to check that we have a very limited interest area and subsequently submit unsolicited material that is completely inappropriate for us. For children, we focus *exclusively* on issues of adoption and interim (foster) care plus families built by donor insemination or surrogacy; for adults we also include infertility issues."

PHILOMEL BOOKS, 200 Madison Ave., New York NY 10016. (212)951-8700. Imprint of The Putnam & Grosset Group. Book publisher. Editorial Director: Patricia Gauch. Editor: Michael Green. Art Director: Cecilia Yung. Publishes 30 picture books/year; 5-10 young reader titles/year. 20% of books by first-time authors; 80% of books from agented writers.

Fiction: All levels: adventure, animal, fantasy, folktales, history, nature/environment, special needs, multicultural. Middle readers, young adults: problem novels. No concept picture books, mass-market "character" books, or series.

Nonfiction: All levels: arts/crafts, biography, history, multicultural, music/dance. "Creative nonfiction on any subject." Average length: "not to exceed 150 pages."

How to Contact/Writers: Fiction/Nonfiction: Query; submit outline/synopsis and first three chapters. Reports on queries in 4-6 weeks. Publishes a book 2 years after acceptance.

Illustration: Works with 20-25 illustrators/year. Reviews ms/illustration packages from artists. Query first. Illustrations only: Query with samples. Send resume, promo sheet, portfolio, slides, client list, tearsheets or arrange personal portfolio review. Contact: Cecilia Yung. Reports on art samples in 2 months. Original artwork returned at job's completion.

Terms: Pays authors in royalties. Average advance payment "varies." Illustrators paid by advance and in royalties. Sends galleys to authors; dummies to illustrators. Book catalog, ms/artist's guidelines free on request with SASE (9 × 12 envelope for catalog).

Tips: Wants "unique fiction or nonfiction with a strong voice and lasting quality. Discover your own voice and own story—and persevere." Looks for "something unusual, original, well-written. Fine art. The genre (fantasy, contemporary, or historical fiction) is not so important as the story itself, and the spirited life the story allows its main character. We are also interested in receiving adolescent novels, particularly novels that contain regional spirit, such as a story about a young boy or girl written from a Southern, Southwestern or Northwestern perspective."

*PHOENIX LEARNING RESOURCES, 12 W. 31st St., New York NY 10001. (212)629-3887. (212)629-5648. Book publisher. Executive Vice President: John A. Rothermich. Publishes 10 textbooks/year.

Nonfiction: All levels: textbooks. Recently published *New Practice Readers*, Third Edition.

How to Contact/Writers: Nonfiction: Submit outline/synopsis. Reports on queries in 2 weeks; mss in 1 month. Will consider simultaneous submissions and previously published work.

Photography: Buys stock. Contact: John A. Rothermich, executive vice president. Uses color prints and 35mm, 2¼ × 2¼, 4 × 5 transparencies. Submit cover letter.

Terms: Pays authors royalty based on wholesale price or work purchased outright. Pays illustrators and photographers by the project. Sends galleys to authors. Book catalog available for SASE.

Tips: "We look for classroom tested and proven materials."

*PIEPER PUBLISHING, P.O. Box 9136, Virginia Beach VA 23450. Fax: (757)554-0573. E-mail: pieperpub@aol.com. Publisher/Editor: Ron Pieper.

Fiction: Young readers: all categories except religion. Does not want to see violent or morally questionable subject matter. "Being a new company Pieper Publishing has only recently consid-

ered children books; however, manuscripts are presently being reviewed and considered."
Nonfiction: Picture books, young readers: considers all categories except religion.
How to Contact/Writers: Fiction/nonfiction: Query. Reports on queries in 1-2 weeks; mss in 1-2 months. Publishes a book 6-10 months after acceptance. Will consider simultaneous submissions, electronic submissions via disk or modem.
Illustration: Reviews ms/illustration packages from artists. Query. Contact: Ron Pieper, publisher/editor. Illustrations only: Query with samples. Contact: Ron Pieper, publisher/editor. Samples returned with SASE.
Photography: Buys stock and assigns work. Contact: Ron Pieper, publisher/editor. "At present, we have no specific need for photos; however, we are interested in establishing a file of photographers for future books." Model/property release required; captions required. Submit cover letter, portfolio.
Terms: Pays authors royalty of 8-12% based on wholesale price. Illustrators paid by the project or royalty based on wholesale price. Photographers paid by the project, per photo or royalty based on wholesale price. Sends galleys to authors. Originals returned to artist at job's completion if requested and agreed to before contract. Manuscript and art guidelines available for SASE.
Tips: "Pieper Publishing is a relatively new publishing company having concentrated in nonfiction and fiction for adults and now recently expanding our efforts in the children's market. We look forward to contributing to the entertainment and education of our younger counterparts, particularly the early years from preschool to grades 1-2. We are also interested in developing a file of available illustrators and photographers who may provide artwork for children's book manuscripts. Our policy is to not limit the types of queries and manuscripts we review. We believe this policy offers more opportunities to writers and other artists. The writing and publishing market is extremely competitive. Consider those that interest you and submit, submit, submit."

*PIÑATA BOOKS, Imprint of Arte Publico Press, University of Houston, Houston TX 77204-2090. (713)743-2841. (713)743-2847. Book publisher. Director: Nicolas Kanellos. Managing Editor: Rita Mills. Publishes 2-4 picture books, middle readers/year; 8-10 young adult/year. 60% of books by first-time authors. "Piñata Books specializes in publication of children's and young adult literature that authentically portray themes, characters and customs unique to U.S.-Hispanic culture."
Fiction: Picture books, young readers: adventure, contemporary, folktales, multicultural, poetry. Middle readers, young adult/teens: adventure, anthology, contemporary, folktales, multicultural, poetry, problem novels. Recently published *Walking Stars*, by Victor Villaseñor; *The Desert Is My Mother/El desierto es mi madre*, by Pat Mora; and *Pepita Talks Twice/Pepita habla dos veces*, by Ofelia Dumas Lachtman, illustrated by Alex Pardo DeLange.
Nonfiction: All levels: Biography, multicultural.
How to Contact/Writers: Fiction/Nonfiction: Query; submit complete ms; outline/synopsis and 2 sample chapters. Reports on queries in 2-4 weeks; ms in 3-6 months. Publishes a book 2 years after acceptance. Will consider electronic submissions via disk or modem and previously published work.
Illustration: Works with 2-4 illustrators/year. Reviews ms/illustration packages from artists. Query. Send ms with dummy; submit ms with 2-4 pieces of final art. Contact: Nicolas Kanellos, director. Illustrations only: Query with samples. Send resume, promo sheet, slides, client list, tearsheets or arrange personal portfolio review. Contact: Rita Mills, managing editor. Samples returned with SASE; samples filed.
Terms: Pays authors royalty of 10% based on wholesale price. Offers advances (average amount: $1,000-3,000). Pays illustrators by the project or royalty of 10% based on wholesale price. Sends galleys to authors; dummies to illustrators. Book catalog free; ms guidelines available for SASE.
Tips: "Include cover letter explaining why your manuscript is unique and important, why we should publish it, who will buy it, etc."

THE PLACE IN THE WOODS, Read, America!, 3900 Glenwood Ave., Golden Valley MN 55422. (612)374-2120. Book publisher. Publisher/Editor: Roger Hammer. Publishes 4 elementary-age titles/year and 2 middle readers/year; 2 young adult titles/year. 100% of books by first-time authors. Books feature primarily diversity/multicultural storyline and illustration.
Fiction: Picture books and young adults: adventure, multicultural, suspense/mystery. Young readers: adventure, animal, fantasy, folktales, hi-lo, humor, multicultural, sports, suspense/mystery. Middle readers: adventure, animal, fantasy, folktales, hi-lo, humor, multicultural, problem novels, sports, suspense/mystery. Average word length: young readers—no limits; middle readers—no limits.

Nonfiction: Picture books and young adults: history, multicultural, special needs. Young readers and middle readers: activity books, animal, hi-lo, history, hobbies, how-to, multicultural, self help, social issues, special needs. sports. Multicultural themes must avoid negative stereo types. Average word length: young readers—no limits; middle readers—no limits.

How to Contact/Writers: Fiction/Nonfiction: Submit complete ms. Reports on queries/mss in 1 week. "No multiple or simultaneous submissions. Please indicate a time frame for response."

Illustration: Works with 2 illustrators/year. Uses primarily b&w artwork only. Reviews ms/ illustration packages from authors. Query; submit ms with dummy. Contact: Roger Hammer, editor. Illustration only: Query with samples. Reports in 1 week. Samples with SASE. "We buy all rights."

Photography: Buys photos from freelancers. Contact: Roger Hammer, editor. Works on assignment only. Uses photos that appeal to children. Model/property releases required; captions required. Uses any b&w prints. Submit cover letter and samples.

Terms: Work purchased outright from authors ($10-250). Pays illustrators by the project (range: $10-250). Pays photographers by project (range $10-250). For all contracts, "initial payment repeated with each printing." Original artwork not returned at job's completion. Book available for #10 SAE and 1 first-class stamp; ms and art guidelines available for SASE.

PLANET DEXTER, One Jacob Way, Reading MA 01867. (617)944-3700. Imprint of Addison Wesley Longman Publishing Co. Book publisher. Contact: Editorial Department. Publishes 10-15 young readers, middle readers/year. 25% of books by first-time authors. Publishes nonfiction interactive books—mainly math and science. No fiction, poetry, whole language or early readers at all. "Looking for inventive, smart, quirky takes on any educational topic."

● To learn more about Planet Dexter, see the Insider Report with Liz Doyle in the 1996 edition of *Children's Writer's & Illustrator's Market*.

Nonfiction: Young readers, middle readers: history, hobbies, how-to, nature/environment, science, math. No curriculum-oriented or textbook-style manuscripts; no characters or narratives. Average word length: middle readers—15,000; young readers—10,000. Published *Planet Dexter's Calculator Mania* (comes with calculator); *Grossology*, by Sylvia Branzei (comes with fake vomit on the cover); and *Planet Dexter's Planet Ant*.

How to Contact/Writers: Query. Submit outline/synopsis and 2 sample chapters with SASE. Reports in 8-12 weeks. Publishes a book 18 months after acceptance.

Illustration: Works with 1-2 illustrators/year. Uses color artwork only.

Terms: Pay authors royalty, or work purchased outright from authors. Offers advances. Pays illustrators/photographers by the project. Ms guidelines available for SASE.

Tips: "The more thorough a proposal, the better. Include outline, competition analysis, marketing 'hooks,' etc. Children's publishing is as competitive as adult's, so preparation on the author's part is key. We want fun, hip, irreverent, educational titles—books that kids learn from without realizing it (we call it 'stealth learning')."

PLAYERS PRESS, INC., P.O. Box 1132, Studio City CA 91614. (818)789-4980. Book publisher. Estab. 1965. Vice President/Editorial: R. W. Gordon. Publishes 7-25 young readers dramatic plays and musicals/year; 2-10 middle readers dramatic plays and musicals/year; 4-20 young adults dramatic plays and musicals/year. 35% of books by first-time authors; 1% of books from agented writers.

Fiction: "We use all categories (young readers, middle readers, young adults) but only for dramatic plays and/or musicals. No novels or storybooks." Multicultural needs include plays and musicals. Recently published *Tower of London*, a play by William Hezlep; and *Punch and Judy*, a play by William-Alan Landes.

Nonfiction: "Any children's nonfiction pertaining to the entertainment industry, performing arts and how-to for the theatrical arts only." Needs include and activity, arts/crafts, how-to, music/dance, reference and textbook. Published *Stagecrafter's Handbook*, by I.E. Clark; and *New Monologues for Readers Theatre*, by Steven Porter.

How to Contact/Writers: Fiction/nonfiction: Submit plays or outline/synopsis and sample chapters of entertainment books. Reports on queries in 2 weeks; mss in 4-12 months. Publishes a book 10 months after acceptance. No simultaneous submissions.

Illustration: Works with 1-4 illustrators/year. Use primarily b&w artwork. Illustrations only: Submit résumé, tearsheets. Reports on art samples in 2 weeks only if interested. Samples returned with SASE; samples filed.

Terms: Pays authors in royalties of 6-12% based on wholesale price or by outright purchase. Pay illustrators by the project; royalties range from 2-5%. Sends galleys to authors; dummies to illustrators. Book catalog and ms guidelines available for SASE.

Tips: Looks for "plays/musicals and books pertaining to the performing arts only. Illustrators: send samples that can be kept for our files."

*PLEASANT COMPANY, 8400 Fairway Place, Middleton WI 53562. (608)836-4848. Fax: (608)836-1999. Website: http://www.pleasantco.com. Book publisher. Senior Editor: Jodi Evert. Art Director: Jane Varda. Imprints: The American Girls Collection (Jodi Evert, senior editor); American Girl Library (Michelle Watkins, senior editor); Bitty Baby Collection (Jodi Evert, senior editor). Publishes 3 picture books/year; 12 young readers/year; 12 middle readers/year. 10% of books by first-time authors. Publishes fiction and nonfiction for girls 7 and up.
● Pleasant Company publishes *American Girl* magazine.
Fiction: Young readers, middle readers: history. Recently published *Meet Addy*, by Connie Porter, illustrated by Melodye Rosales (ages 7-12, historical fiction); *Meet Felicity*, by Valerie Tripp, illustrated by Dan Andreasen (ages 7-12, historical fiction); and *Meet Molly*, by Valerie Tripp, illustrated Nick Backes (ages 7-12, historical fiction).
Nonfiction: Young readers, middle readers: activity books, arts/crafts, biography, cooking, geography, health, history, hobbies, how-to, sports. Recently published *More Help!*, by Nancy Holyoke, illustrated by Scott Nash (ages 8 and up, self help); *Crafts for Girls*, by Sally Seamans, illustrated by Judy Pelikan (ages 8 and up, craft); and *Felicity's Cookbook, Pleasant Company* (ages 7-12, cooking).
How to Contact/Writers: Fiction/nonfiction: Query. Reports on queries/mss in 1 month. Will consider simultaneous submissions, previously published work.
Illustration: Works with 3 illustrators/year. Reviews ms/illustration packages from artists. Query. Contact: Jodi Evert, senior editor. Illustrations only: Query with samples. Contact: Jane Varda, art director. Reports back only if interested. Samples returned with SASE; samples filed.
Photography: Buys stock and assigns work. Contact: Jane Varda, art director. Submit cover letter, published samples, promo piece.
Terms: Pays authors royalty or work purchased outright. Pays illustrators by the project. Pays photographers by the project. Sends galleys to authors; dummies to illustrators. Originals returned to artist at job's completion. Book catalog available for 8½×11 SAE and 4 first-class stamps. All imprints included in a single catalog.

POLYCHROME PUBLISHING CORPORATION, 4509 N. Francisco, Chicago IL 60625. (312)478-4455. Fax: (312)478-0786. Book publisher. Contact: Editorial Board. Publishes 2-4 picture books/year; 1-2 middle readers/year; and 1-2 young adult titles/year. 50% of books are by first-time authors. Books aimed at children of Asian ancestry in the United States.
Fiction: All levels: adventure, contemporary, history, multicultural, problem novels, suspense/mystery. Middle readers, young adults: anthology. Multicultural needs include Asian American children's experiences. Not interested in animal stories, fables, fairy tales, folk tales. Published *Nene and the Horrible Math Monster*, by Marie Villanueva; *Stella: On the Edge of Popularity*, by Lauren Lee.
Nonfiction: All levels: multicultural. Multicultural needs include Asian-American themes.
How to Contact/Writers: Fiction/Nonfiction: Submit complete manuscript along with an author's bio regarding story background. Reports on queries in 3-4 months; mss in 4-6 months. Publishes a book 1-2 years after acceptance. Will consider simultaneous submissions.
Illustration: Works with 4 illustrators/year. Reviews ms/illustration packages from artists. Submit ms with bio of author re story background and photocopies of sample illustrations. Contact: Editorial Board. Illustrations only: Query with résumé and samples (can be photocopies) of drawings of multicultural children. Reports back only if interested. Samples returned with SASE; samples filed "only if under consideration for future work."
Terms: Pays authors royalty of 2-10% based on wholesale price. Work purchased outright ($25 minimum). Pays illustrators 2-10% royalty based on wholesale price. Sends galleys to authors; dummies to illustrators. Book catalog available for #10 SAE and 52¢. Manuscript guidelines available for SASE.
Tips: Wants "stories about experiences that will ring true with Asian Americans."

*PREP PUBLISHING, Imprint of Prep Inc., 1110½ Hay St., Fayetteville NC 28305. (910)483-6611. (910)483-2439. Book publisher. Editor: Anne McKinney. Publishes 2 young readers/year; 2 middle readers/year. 15% of books by first-time authors.
Fiction: All levels: adventure, suspense/mystery. Picture books: sports. "Our middle readers and young adult/teens line is just beginning."

Nonfiction: All levels: biography, careers.
How to Contact/Writers: Fiction/Nonfiction: Query with SASE. Reports on queries in 3 months. Publishes a book 18 months after acceptance. Will consider simultaneous submissions.
Terms: Pays authors royalty of 6-15%. Sends galleys to authors. Originals returned to artist at job's completion. Book catalog and ms/art guidelines available for SAE and 1 first-class stamp.

PRICE STERN SLOAN, INC., 11835 Olympic Blvd., 5th Floor, Los Angeles CA 90064. (310)477-6100. A Member of The Putnam & Grosset Group. Imprints: Mad Libs, Crazy Games, Serendipity, Doodle Art, Troubador Press, Cybersurfers, Mad Mysteries, Funstations, Workstations, Sliding Surprise, Wee Sing. Book publisher. Contact: Submissions Editor. Publishes 20-40 young reader titles/year; 10-20 middle reader titles/year; 0-6 young adult titles/year. 35% of books by first-time authors; 65% of books from agented writers; 10% from packagers.
Fiction: Young readers, middle readers: novelty, graphic readers. Recently published *Giant Animal Fold-outs, Scary Mysteries for Sleep-Overs, I'm Sick of It* and *Bang on the Door.*
Nonfiction: Novelty, activity books, important issues for young adults, computer, topical subjects. Recently published *Internet for Kids, Tattoo You!, Take a Stand!, Marco! Polo!* and *Quest Role-Playing Games.*
How to Contact/Writers: Fiction/nonfiction: Query with SASE for guidelines. "Absolutely no multiple submissions."
Illustration: Reviews ms/illustration packages from artists. "Please *do not* send original artwork." Query; submit 1-3 chapters of ms with 1-2 pieces of final art (color copies—no original work). Illustrations only: Query with samples; provide résumé, promo sheet, portfolio, tearsheets to be kept on file. Reports in 2-3 months.
Photography: Contact: Art Department. Buys stock and assigns work. Model/property releases required.
Terms: Pays authors royalty or work purchased outright. Offers advances. Pays photographers by the project or per photo. Book catalog available for 9 × 12 SAE and 5 first-class stamps. Ms/artist's guidelines available.

PUFFIN BOOKS, 375 Hudson St., New York NY 10014-3567. (212)366-2000. An imprint of Penguin USA Children's Books.
• The majority of Puffin's list is now reprints, therefore they no longer accept unsolicited submissions.

THE PUTNAM & GROSSET GROUP, 200 Madison Ave., New York NY 10016. See listings for Grosset & Dunlap, G.P. Putnam's Sons, Philomel and Price Stern Sloan.

G.P. PUTNAM'S SONS, 200 Madison Ave., New York NY 10016. (212)951-8700. Imprint of The Putnam & Grosset Group. Book publisher. Executive Editor: Refna Wilkin. Art Director: Cecilia Yung. Publishes 25 picture books/year; 4 middle readers/year; 7 young adult titles/year. 5% of books by first-time authors; 50% of books from agented authors.
• Putnam's book *Officer Buckle and Gloria*, by Peggy Rathrman, received the Caldecott Medal in 1996.
Fiction: Picture books: adventure, contemporary, history, humor, special needs. Young readers: adventure, contemporary, folktales, history, humor, problem novels, special needs, sports, suspense/mystery. Middle readers: adventure, contemporary, history, humor, problem novels, special needs, sports, suspense/mystery. Young adults: contemporary, problem novels, special needs. "Multicultural books should reflect different cultures accurately but unobtrusively." Regarding special needs, "stories about physically or mentally challenged children should portray them accurately and without condescension." Does not want to see series, romances. Very little fantasy. Average word length: picture books—200-1,500; middle readers—10,000-30,000; young adults—40,000-50,000. Recently published *Officer Buckle and Gloria*, by Peggy Rathmann; *When Pigs Fly*, by June Rae Wood; and *Amber Brown Wants Extra Credit*, by Paula Danziger.
Nonfiction: Picture books: concept, multicultural, social issues, special needs. Young readers, middle readers: biography, history, multicultural, social issues, special needs. Young adult: social issues. No hard science, series. Average word length: picture books—200-1,500; middle readers: 10,000-30,000; young adults: 30,000-50,000. Recently published *A Fence Away from Freedom To See with the Heart*, by Ellen Levine; and *You Want Women to Vote, Lizzie Stanton?*, by Jean Fritz.
How to Contact/Writers: Fiction/nonfiction: Query; submit outline/synopsis and 3 sample chapters. Unsolicited picture book mss only. Reports on queries in 2-3 weeks; mss in 4-10 weeks.

Publishes a book 2 years after acceptance. Will consider simultaneous submissions on queries only.

Illustration: Works with 40 illustrators/year. Reviews ms/illustration packages from artists. Ms/illustration packages and illustration only: Query. Reports back only if interested. Samples returned with SASE; samples filed.

Terms: Pays authors royalty based on retail price. Pays illustrators by the project or royalty based on retail price. Sends galleys to authors. Original artwork returned at job's completion. Books catalog and ms and artist's guidelines available for SASE.

Tips: "Study our catalogs and get a sense of the kind of books we publish, so that you know whether your project is likely to be right for us."

QUESTAR PUBLISHERS, INC., 305 W. Adams, P.O. Box 1720, Sisters OR 97759. (503)549-1144. Imprint: Gold 'n' Honey. Book publisher. Editorial Coordinator: Melody Carlson. Publishes 3-5 picture books/year; 5-8 young readers/year; 6-9 middle readers/year; and 4-6 adult titles/year. Less than 10% of books by first-time authors. Publishes spiritual/religious titles.

How to Contact/Writers: Questar Publishers accepts unsolicited mss.

Illustration: Works with 10-15 illustrators/year. Uses color artwork only. Reviews ms/illustration packages from artists. Query. Illustrations only: Query with samples, résumé, promo sheet. Reports back only if interested. Samples filed.

Photography: Buys photos from freelancers. Contact: art director. Buys stock and assigns work. Uses children, animals and nature photos. Model/property releases required; captions required. Uses 35mm, $2\frac{1}{4} \times 2\frac{1}{4}$, 4×5 transparencies. Submit cover letter, résumé, published samples, color promo piece.

Terms: Pays royalty based on wholesale price. Pays illustrators by the project or royalty. Pays photographers by the project or per photo. Sends galleys to authors.

❤RAGWEED PRESS, P.O. Box 2023, Charlottetown, Prince Edward Island C1A 7N7 Canada. (902)566-5750. Fax: (902)566-4473. E-mail: editor@ragweed.com. Book publisher. Contact: Managing Editor or Designer. Publishes 1 picture book/year; 2 young adult titles/year. 20% of books by first-time authors.

• Ragweed accepts work from Canadian authors only.

Fiction: Young readers: adventure, multicultural, suspense/mystery. Middle readers, young adults: adventure, anthology, contemporary, history, multicultural. Average word length: picture books—1,000-24 pages (full color illustration); middle readers: 96 pages; young adults: 256 pages. Published *Next Teller, A Book of Canadian Storytelling*, collected by Dan Yashinsky (for ages 12 and up).

How to Contact/Writers: Fiction: Query. Submit outline/synopsis and 2 sample chapters. Reports on queries/mss in 5-6 months. Publishes a book 6 months from final ms, "up to 2 years before editorial process is completed." Will consider simultaneous submissions.

Illustration: Works with 1-2 illustrators/year. Uses color artwork only. Reviews ms/illustration packages from artists. Query. Submit ms only. Publisher will find illustrator. Contact: Janet Riopelle, designer. Illustrations only: Query with samples. Contact: Janet Riopelle, designer. Samples returned with SASE; samples filed.

Terms: Pays authors/illustrators royalty of 5-10% based on retail price. Sends galleys to authors. Original artwork returned at job's completion. Book catalog available for 9×12 SAE and 2 first-class stamps; ms and art guidelines available for SASE.

Tips: "Submit in writing—phone calls won't get results. We do look at everything we receive and make our decision based on our needs. Be patient."

*RAINBOW PUBLISHERS, P.O. Box 261129, San Diego CA 92196. (619)271-7600. Fax: (619)578-4795. Book publisher. Editor: Christy Allen. Imprints: Rainbow Books (Editor: Christy Allen); Daybreak Books (Editor: Christy Allen). Publishes 5 young readers/year; 5 middle readers/year; 5 young adult titles/year. 50% of books by first-time authors.

Nonfiction: Young readers, middle readers, young adult/teens: religion. Does not want to see traditional puzzles. Recently published *The Palm Tree Bible* (series of 4), various authors, illustrated by Arthur Baker (ages 3-12, Bible storybooks); *Creative Bible Crafts/Grades 5 & 6*, by Dyan Beller, illustrated by Roger Johnson (ages 10-12, craft book); and *52 Ways to Teach About Stewardship*, by Nancy Williamson, illustrated by Roger Johnson (ages 4-12, children's ministry book).

How to Contact/Writers: Nonfiction: Submit outline/synopsis and 1-2 sample chapters. Reports on queries in 1 month; mss in 3 months. Publishes a book 6-12 months after acceptance.

Will consider simultaneous submissions, electronic submissions via disk and previously published work.

Illustration: Works with 2-5 illustrators/year. Reviews ms/illustration packages from artists. Submit ms with 2-5 pieces of final art. Contact: Christy Allen, editor. Illustrations only: Query with samples. Contact: Christy Allen, editor. Reports in 6 weeks. Samples returned with SASE; samples filed.

Photography: Works on assignment only. Contact: Dan Miley, general manager. Uses scenes suitable for greeting cards. Model/property releases required. Uses color prints. Submit cover letter, color promo piece.

Terms: Pays authors royalty of 8-12% based on wholesale price or work purchased outright (range: $500-2,000). Offers advances (Average amount: $2,500). Pays illustrators by the project (range: $300-700). Pays photographers per photo. Sends galleys to authors. Book catalog available for 9×12 SAE and 2 first-class stamps; ms guidelines available for SASE.

Tips: "Our Rainbow imprint carries 64-page reproducible books for teachers of children in Christian ministries. Our Daybreak imprint (new in '96) will handle nonfiction titles for children and adults in the Christian realm, such as Bible story books, devotional books, and so on. Please write for guidelines and study the market before submitting material."

*RAINTREE STECK-VAUGHN, Imprint of Steck-Vaughn, 466 Southern Blvd., Chatham NJ 07928. (201)514-1525. Fax: (201)514-1612. Book publisher. Publishing Directors: Frank Sloan and Walter Kossman. Art Director: Joyce Spicer (Steck-Vaughn, 8701 N. Mopac Expressway, Austin TX 78759.) Publishes 30 young readers/year; 30 middle readers/year; 20 young adults/year.

Nonfiction: Picture books, young readers, middle readers: animal, biography, geography, health, history, multicultural, nature/environment, science, sports. Young adults: biography, careers, geography, health, history, sports. Multicultural needs include: biographies. Average word length: young readers—48; middle readers—32; young adults: 64-100. Recently published: Innovative Minds series (about famous scientists); World's Top Ten series (about famous geographical sites); and contemporary Hispanic and African-American biographies.

How to Contact/Writers: Nonfiction: query. Reports on queries/mss in 3-4 months.

Illustration: Contact Joyce Spicer at above Texas address.

Photography: Contact Joyce Spicer at above Texas address.

Terms: Pays authors royalty. Offers advance. Sends galleys to authors. Book catalog available for 9×12 SAE and $3 first-class postage. Ms guidelines available for SASE.

Tips: "Request a catalog so you're not proposing books similar to those we've already done. Always include SASE."

RANDOM HOUSE BOOKS FOR YOUNG READERS, 201 E. 50th St., New York NY 10022. (212)572-2600. Random House, Inc. Book publisher. Vice President/Publishing Director: Kate Klimo. Vice President/Associate Publishing Director: Cathy Goldsmith. Easy-to-Read Books (step-into-reading): Lori Haskins, Associate Editor. Nonfiction: Alice Torcutis, Editor. Picture Books: Mallory Loehr, Assistant Publishing Director. First Stepping Stones: Linda Hayward, Creative Director. Middle Grade Fiction: Lisa Banim, Creative Director. Fantasy & Science Fiction: Alice Alfonsi, Senior Editor. Young Adult: Ruth Koeppel, Senior Editor. Baby & Toddler Books: Elizabeth Rivlin, Associate Editor. 100% of books published through agents; 2% of books by first-time authors.

• Random House now accepts agented material only.

Fiction: Picture books: animal, easy-to-read, history, sports. Young readers: adventure, animal, easy-to-read, history, sports, suspense/mystery. Middle readers: adventure, history, science, sports, suspense/mystery.

Nonfiction: Picture books: animal. Young readers: animal, biography, hobbies. Middle readers: biography, history, hobbies, sports.

How to Contact/Writers: Fiction/Nonfiction: Submit through agent only. Publishes a book 12-18 months after acceptance. Will consider simultaneous submissions.

Illustration: Reviews ms/illustration packages from artists through agent only.

Terms: Pays authors in royalties; sometimes buys mss outright. Sends galleys to authors. Book catalog free on request.

❦REIDMORE BOOKS INC., 10109-106 St., 1200, Edmonton, Alberta T5J 3L7 Canada. (403)424-4420. Fax: (403)441-9919. E-mail: reidmore@compusmart.ab.ca. Website: http://www.reidmore.com. Book publisher. Editor-in-chief: Leah-Ann Lymer. Publishes 4 textbooks/year (grades 2-12). 25% of books by first-time authors.

INSIDER REPORT

Series nonfiction is good training ground for writers

As it did with most kids, the movie *Bambi* upset Frank Sloan when he saw it as a child. "But my mom sat me down and said 'You have to understand, Frank—it's not true.' " These days distinguishing fact from fiction is in Sloan's job description. Facts, in fact, are his specialty. As publishing director at Raintree Steck-Vaughn, he oversees the Thompson Learning line of children's and young adult nonfiction.

Thompson publishes series nonfiction (as opposed to trade). Series publishers' titles generally get less attention design-wise than trade books. The books fit rigidly into curriculum needs. Sloan says that series nonfiction houses often get undeserved bad press because of the "cookie cutter" look to

Frank Sloan

their books. "Nonfiction should get better press—it's essential to evaluate truths. And these houses supply a good training ground for writers."

Sloan's 25 years in publishing include stints as art director and production manager at Franklin Watts and editorial director at Crestwood House, Dillon Press, and New Discovery (nonfiction imprints of the Macmillan Children's Book Group) previous to his position at Raintree. At each house, he has remained dedicated to finding new authors. "Every time I get a submission, I see if there's a kernel of a new person to develop," he says. "What I hope to find are terrific new Milton Meltzers, new Jim Giblins, new Russell Freedmans."

Sloan dislikes receiving query letters that use manic language to grab his attention. Letters that begin "DO YOU KNOW THE LIFE CYCLE HABITS OF TREE SLOTHS? WELL, YOU SHOULD, AND HERE IT IS!" don't impress him. He'd rather have a more sedate approach, an honest, sincere request to do a topic that the writer thinks will make a viable book, one that's responsible and engages the reader. "I don't mean to put the writing last, because if it isn't well-written, I don't want to think about it."

Sloan has worked with a large number of writers over the years, and feels that in nonfiction, new writers grow in response to their editors' questions. He frequently receives manuscripts he's not happy with, and works with authors to improve their work. When authors submit their second books, they have often picked up on the problems that existed the first time around. "I think it's a terrific achievement for a writer to be able to take direction and then create direction on his or her own."

But Sloan admits that relationships with writers sometimes go sour. "Maybe

INSIDER REPORT, *Sloan*

writers don't deliver manuscripts when they say they're going to. Or when they deliver manuscripts, there are major problems. I'm not going to cancel a manuscript just because I'm not happy with it," he says. "We have to work on it. But if an author, by negligence or sloppy work, is creating extra work for me, it makes me nuts!"

Advances and royalties for series publishers such as Raintree Steck-Vaughn are admittedly less lavish than those of other publishers. Writers may not receive an advance or do work-for-hire. He says it's because they sell fewer copies, and strictly to a library market where the discount is higher. And nonfiction titles receive little or no promotion. So there is less money to be made overall.

Sloan feels that authors who have talent and inclination for speaking should do as much as they want to promote their own titles, but he advises them to be realistic. "One of the delusions is that most authors feel they should be on *The Oprah Winfrey Show*. They also feel they should be in the news media, and I don't think that's an effective way yet to sell children's books. I do think local school appearances sell books. I think they help authors create an image for themselves that can be valuable along the line."

The market for nonfiction is shrinking, Sloan says. Publishers of information books, both trade and educational, are cutting back. Bookstores, with only so much shelf space, are buying fewer titles, and libraries and schools are using part of their book money to buy multimedia. But Sloan says there's always going to be a variety of nonfiction. "There will be well-written, high-quality nonfiction that trade houses publish. And there will be good, but perhaps not as magical, writing that series publishers need."

—Anna Olswanger

Frank Sloan's first book for young readers, *Titanic* (Franklin Watts), was a Children's Choice title in 1988. The idea for the book came about by accident—Sloan was in London the day that the first remains of the Titanic were discovered. The topic has interested the author since he was a kid.

© 1988 Frank Sloan

Chao Yu's pen, ink and watercolor illustration of a boy reading the newspaper accompanied by his faithful friend was created specifically for a textbook on Canadian geography. Cathie Crooks, editor at Reidmore Books, says she enjoys working with Chao because of her flexibility. "She can do everything from cartoons to realistic-style drawings in a variety of media." Along with teaching at a fine arts college in China and working for several years with a children's publishing house, Chao has also received a national award in China for her children's illustrations.

● Reidmore Books is not looking at fiction titles this year. See their listing in the Multimedia section.

Nonfiction: Young readers: history. Middle readers, young adults/teens: geography, history, multicultural, nature/environment, science, textbooks. Does not want to see "material that is not directly tied to social studies, science or math curricula. No picture books, please." Recently published: *Beginnings: From the First Nations to the Great Migration*, by Marshall Jamieson (grades 5-6, history textbook).

How to Contact/Writers: Nonfiction: Query, submit complete ms, submit outline/synopsis. Reports on queries in 1 month, mss in 2 months. Publishes a book 18 months after acceptance. Will consider simultaneous submissions.

Illustration: Works with 1 illustrator/year. Uses color artwork only. Illustration only: Query with samples. Contact: Leah-Ann Lymer, editor-in-chief. Samples returned with SASE; samples filed.

Photography: Buys photos from freelancers. Buys stock images. Uses "content-rich photos, often geography-related." Photo captions required. Uses color prints and 35mm transparencies. Submit cover letter.

Terms: Pays authors royalty. Pays illustrators by the project. Pays photographers by the project or per photo. Sends galleys to authors. Book catalog available for 9×12 SAE and 2 first-class stamps.

Tips: "There are fewer titles being published in Canada. Call before submitting—it tends to speed up the process and saves everyone time, money and effort."

RHACHE PUBLISHERS, LTD., 9 Orchard Dr., Gardiner NY 12525. (914)883-5884. E-mail: chedlund@aol.com, rhadin@aol.com, rhache@aol.com. Book publisher. Publisher: Richard H. Adin. Associate Publisher: Carolyn H. Edlund. Publishes 1-5 middle readers/year; 1-5 young adult titles/year. 90% of books by first-time authors. "We are looking for books for children 10 and up. They need to be primarily nonfiction. By that, we mean the story line can be fiction (e.g., a mystery) but the story must teach and not too subtly why a 'clue' in the mystery can't be correct because it defies a natural law, with a good solid exploration of that natural law. We are not looking for stories of the 'Little Engine That Could' or the Peter Cottontail type. No books for very young or that are primarily illustration.''

Nonfiction: Middle readers, young adults: activity books, animal, arts/crafts, careers, concept, cooking, computer, health, history, hobbies, how-to, music/dance, nature/environment, reference, science, self help, special needs. Interested in books for (not about) challenged children in any of the above areas, especially self help and computers. Average word length: middle readers— 50,000 (minimum); young adults—50,000 (minimum).

How to Contact/Writers: Nonfiction: Query with résumé first. Submit outline/synopsis and 2-4 sample chapters. Reports on queries in 3-4 weeks; mss in 45-60 days. Anticipates publishing a book 6 months after acceptance.

Illustration: Uses both b&w and color artwork. Reviews ms/illustration packages from authors. Query. Submit ms with 4-5 pieces of final art. Contact: Carolyn Edlund, associate publisher. Illustration only: Query with samples, résumé. Reports in 4-5 weeks. Samples returned with SASE; samples filed.

Photography: Buys photos from freelancers. Contact: Carolyn Edlund, associate publisher. Buys stock and assigns work. Model/property releases required; captions required. Uses 3×5, 4×5 glossy, color or b&w prints; or 35mm, 4×5 transparencies. Submit cover letter, résumé, samples.

Terms: Pays authors royalty of 10-17.5% based on wholesale price. Pays illustrators royalty of 5-10% based on wholesale price. Pays photographers per photo. Sends galleys to authors. Original artwork is not returned. Ms guidelines available for SASE only with topic query and résumé.

Tips: "Do not send a form request for guidelines; do not send handwritten queries; be sure any correspondence is grammatically correct and spelling error-free; be sure query is targeted and clearly stated; always include a résumé."

RIZZOLI BOOKS FOR CHILDREN, 300 Park Ave. S., New York NY 10010. (212)387-3653. Fax: (212)387-3535. Book publisher.
  ● Rizzoli Books for Children has suspended publishing indefinitely.

THE ROSEN PUBLISHING GROUP, 29 E. 21st St., New York NY 10010. (212)777-3017. Book publisher. Estab. 1950. Editorial Contact: Gina Strazzabosco. Publisher: Roger Rosen. Publishes 50 juvenile readers/year; 25 middle readers/year; 50 young adults/year. 35% of books by first-time authors; 3% of books from agented writers.

Nonfiction: Young adults: careers, hi-lo, multicultural, special needs, psychological self-help. No fiction. Average word length: middle readers—10,000; young adults—40,000. Published *Everything You Need to Know When a Parent is in Jail*, (hi-lo, young adult, The Need to Know Library); *The Value of Trust*, by Rita Milios (young adult, The Encyclopedia of Ethical Behavior); *Careers as an Animal Rights Activist*, by Shelly Field (young adult, The Career Series).

How to Contact/Writers: Submit outline/synopsis and sample chapters. Reports on queries/mss in 1-2 months. Publishes a book 9 months after acceptance.

Photography: Buys photos from freelancers. Contact: Roger Rosen. Works on assignment only.

Terms: Pays authors in royalties or work purchased outright. Book catalog free on request.

Tips: "Target your manuscript to a specific age group and reading level and write for established series published by the house you are approaching."

*ROUSSAN PUBLISHERS INC., P.O. Box 321, Prairie du Chien WI 53821. (608)326-4687. Fax: (608)326-8404. Book publisher. Managing Director-U.S.: Judy Frydenlund. Publishes 4 middle readers/year; 2 young adults/year. 50% of books by first-time authors.

Fiction: Middle readers: adventure, fantasy, history, science fiction, sports. Young adult/teens: adventure, contemporary, fantasy, history, problem novels, science fiction, sports, suspense/mystery. Does not want to see picture books. Average word length: middle readers—20,000; young adult/teens—30,000. Recently published *Parents From Space*, by George Bowering (young adult fiction); *Dark of the Moon*, by Barbara Haworth-Attard (middle reader, contemporary/time travel); and *Night of the Aliens*, by Dayle Campbell Gaetz (middle reader, hi-lo/science fiction).

How to Contact/Writers: Submit outline/synopsis and 3 sample chapters. Publishes a book 1 year after acceptance. Will consider simultaneous submissions.

Illustration: Works with 4 illustrators/year. Uses color artwork only.

Terms: Pays authors royalty of 8-10% based on retail price. Pays illustrators by the project. Sends galleys to authors. Book catalog; ms guidelines available for SASE.

ST. ANTHONY MESSENGER PRESS, 1615 Republic St., Cincinnati OH 45210. (513)241-5615. Fax: (513)241-0399. E-mail: stanthony@americancatholic.org. Website: http://www.Ameri canCatholic.org. Book publisher. Managing Editor: Lisa Biedenbach. 25% of books by first-time authors. "All books nurture and enrich Catholic Christian life. We also look for books for parents and religious educators."

Nonfiction: Young readers, middle readers, young adults: religion. "We like all our resources to include anecdotes, examples, etc., that appeal to a wide audience. All of our products try to reflect cultural and racial diversity." Does not want to see fiction, story books, picture books for preschoolers. Recently published *The Wind Harp and Other Angel Tales*, by Ethel Pochocki (middle to adult readers); and *Can You Find Jesus? Introducing Your Child to the Gospel*, by Philip Gallery and Janet Harlow (ages 5-10).

How to Contact/Writers: Query; submit outline/synopsis and sample chapters. Reports on queries in 2-4 weeks; mss in 4-6 weeks. Publishes a book 12-18 months after acceptance.

Illustration: Works with 2 illustrators/year. "We design all covers and do most illustrations in-house." Uses primarily b&w artwork. Reviews ms/illustration packages from artists. Query with samples, résumé. Contact: Mary Alfieri, art director. Reports on queries in 2-4 weeks. Samples returned with SASE; or samples filed.

Photography: Purchases photos from freelancers. Contact: Mary Alfieri, art director. Buys stock and assigns work.

Terms: Pays authors royalties of 10-12% based on net receipts. Offers average advance payment of $600. Pays illustrators by the project. Pays photographers by the project. Sends galleys to authors. Book catalog and ms guidelines free on request.

Tips: "Know our audience—Catholic. We seek popularly written manuscripts that include the best of current Catholic scholarship. Parents, especially baby boomers, want resources for teaching children about the Catholic faith for passing on values. We try to publish items that reflect strong Catholic Christian values."

SASQUATCH BOOKS, 615 Second Ave., Suite 260, Seattle WA 98104. (206)467-4300. Fax: (206)467-4301. Book publisher. Editor: Kate Rogers. Art Director: Karen Schober. Publishes 2-3 picture books/year. 40% of books by first-time authors. "Most of our books have something to do with the greater Northwest (Northern California to Alaska) or the Pacific Rim. Most are nonfiction."

Fiction: Picture books, young readers: adventure, animal, folktales, multicultural, nature/environment, special needs. Multicultural needs include Native American, Pacific Rim, Black. Does not want to see science fiction, poetry or religion. Average word length: picture books—less than 200.

Nonfiction: Picture books, young readers: activity books, animal, arts/crafts, cooking, geography, how-to, multicultural, music/dance, nature/environment, special needs. Multicultural needs include Native American, Pacific Rim, Black. Average word length: picture books—less than 200. Recently published *Seya's Song*, by Ron Hirschi (ages 3 and up, Native American story that shows relationship of salmon to people and seasons); and *O is for Orca*, photographs by Art Wolfe, text by Andrea Helman (ages 3 and up, a Northwest alphabet book).

How to Contact/Writers: Fiction: Query; submit complete ms. Nonfiction: Query; submit outline/synopsis and 2 sample chapters. Include SASE. Reports on queries in 1 month; mss in 3 months. Publishes a book 1 year after acceptance. Will consider simultaneous submissions.

Illustration: Works with 3 illustrators/year. Reviews ms/illustration packages from artists. Send ms with dummy. Contact: Kate Rogers, editor. Illustrations only: Query with samples; provide resume, promo sheets and slides. Contact: Karen Schober, art director. Reports in 3 months. Samples returned with SASE; "good ones" filed. Original artwork returned at job's completion.

Photography: Buys photos from freelancers. Contact: Karen Schober, art director. Works on assignment only.

Terms: Pays authors royalty of 6-10% based on retail price (split with illustrator); negotiable. Offers advances (Average amount: $2,000.) Pays illustrators royalty of 6-10% based on retail price (split with author); negotiable. Pays photographers royalty of 6-10%; negotiable. Sends galleys to authors; dummies to illustrators. Book catalog available upon request; for SASE.

Tips: "We concentrate on publishing material with some sort of Northwest regional perspective."

SCHOLASTIC INC., 555 Broadway, New York NY 10012. (212)343-6100. See listings for Blue Sky Press and Scholastic Hardcover.

 • Scholastic's title, *The Great Fire*, by Jim Murphy, received the 1996 Orbis Pictus Award for Outstanding Nonfiction for Children.

Puzzled Polly Peacock, Plucky Peter Plum and Snoopy Samantha Scarlet search for clues to track down a missing turtle in Chuck Slack's illustration for Scholastic books. Slack's depiction of the spying sleuths was used as the cover for *The Case of the Runaway Turtle*, by Parker C. Hinter, one of the books in Scholastic's line of mysteries for children called Clue Jr. and based on the bestselling Parker Brothers game. Slack, who created this piece in designer color and pencil, also illustrated the Clue Jr. game box.

Illustration: Works with 50 illustrators/year. Does not review ms/illustration packages.Illustrations only: send promo sheet and tearsheets. Contact: Claire Counihan, art director or Marijka Kistiw, associate art director. Reports back only if interested. Samples not returned. Original artwork returned at job's completion.

Terms: All contracts negotiated individually. Sends galleys to author; dummies to illustrators.

SEEDLING PUBLICATIONS, INC., 4079 Overlook Dr. E., Columbus OH 43214-2931. Phone/fax: (614)451-2412. Vice President: Josie Stewart. Publishes 5-10 young readers/year. 20% of books by first-time authors. Publishes books for the beginning reader.

Fiction: Young readers: adventure, animal, fantasy, folktales, hi-lo, multicultural, nature/environment, special needs and sports. Multicultural needs include stories which include children from many cultures and Hispanic centered storylines. Does not want to see texts longer than 16 pages or over 150-200 words or stories in rhyme. Averge word length: young readers—100. Recently published *No Luck*, by L. Salem and J. Stewart (ages 3-7, paperback early reader); *Play Ball, Sherman*, by Betty Erickson (ages 3-7, paperback early reader).

Nonfiction: Young readers: animal, concept, hi-lo, multicultural, music/dance, nature/environment, science, sports. Does not want to see texts longer than 16 pages or over 150-200 words. Average word length: young readers—100. Recently published *Taking Care of Rosie*, by L. Salem and J. Stewart (ages 3-7, early reader).

How to Contact/Writers: Fiction/Nonfiction: Submit complete ms. Reports in 4-5 months. Publishes a book 1 year after acceptance. Will consider simultaneous submissions.

Illustration: Works with 5-10 illustrators/year. Uses color artwork only. Reviews ms/illustration packages from artists. Submit ms with dummy. Illustrations only: Arrange personal portfolio review. Contact: Josie Stewart, vice president. Reports in 4-5 months. Samples returned with SASE only; samples filed.

Photography: Buys photos from freelancers. Contact: Josie Stewart, vice president. Works on assignment only. Model/property releases required. Uses color prints and 35mm transparencies. Submit cover letter and color promo piece.

Terms: Pays authors royalty of 5% based on retail price or work purchased outright. Pays illustrators and photographers by the project. Book catalog available for 2 first-class stamps.

Tips: "Follow our guidelines carefully and test your story with children and educators."

SILVER BURDETT PRESS, 299 Jefferson Rd., Parsippany NJ 07054-0480. (201)236-7000. Fax: (201)326-8606. Simon & Schuster Education Group. Imprints: Crestwood House, Dillon Press, Julian Messner, New Discovery. Book publisher. Editor: Dorothy Goeller. Publishes 40 young readers/year and 40 young titles/year. 1% of books by first-time authors.

Fiction/Nonfiction: "Our list ranges from pre-school to young adult books, both fiction and nonfiction. This also includes Crestwood House which is a hi-lo nonfiction imprint." Considers all fiction and nonfiction categories. Recently published *Riddle by the River*, *The United States Holocaust Memorial Museum*, *The White Stallions* and *Insects*.

How to Contact/Writers: Fiction/Nonfiction: Submit outline/synopsis and 1 sample chapter. Reports on queries in 6 months; mss in 12 months. Publishes a book 1 year after acceptance. Will consider simultaneous and electronic submissions via disk or modem. Only interested in agented material.

Illustration: Only interested in agented material. Works with 40 illustrators/year. Reviews ms/illustration packages from artists. Submit ms with dummy. Contact: Dorothy Goeller, senior editor. Illustrations only: Submit résumé and portfolio. Reports only if interested. Samples returned with SASE.

Photography: Buys photos from freelancers. Contact: Debbie Biber, senior product editor. Buys stock and assigns work. Captions required. Uses color or b&w prints, ½-full page. Submit published samples and client list.

Terms: Pays authors royalty of 3-7½% based on wholesale or retail price or work purchased outright from authors. Offers advances (average amount: $4,000). Pays illustrators by the project (range: $500-10,000) or royalty of 3-7½% based on wholesale or retail price. Sends galleys to authors; dummies to illustrators. Book catalog available for 9×11 SAE and $2.60 postage.

ALWAYS INCLUDE a self-addressed, stamped envelope (SASE) with submissions within your own country. When sending material to other countries, include a self-addressed envelope (SAE) and International Reply Coupons (IRCs).

SILVER MOON PRESS, 160 Fifth Ave., New York NY 10010. (212)242-6499. Publisher: David Katz. Book publisher. Publishes 2 books for grades 1-3; 10 books for grades 4-6. 25% of books by first-time authors; 10% books from agented authors.
Fiction: All levels: historical and mystery. Average word length: varies. Recently published *The Conspiracy of the Secret Nine*, by Celia Bland (ages 10-12, historical fiction); and *Told Tales*, by Jo Sepha Sherman (ages 10-12, folktales).
Nonfiction: All levels. Recently published *Techno Lab*, by Robert Sheely (ages 8-12, science).
How to Contact/Writers: Fiction/Nonfiction: Query. Reports on queries in 2-4 weeks; mss in 1-2 months. Publishes a book 1-2 years after acceptance. Will consider simultaneous submissions, electronic submissions via disk or moden, previously published work.
Illustration: Reviews ms/illustration packages from artists. Query. Illustrations only: Query with samples, résumé, client list; arrange personal portfolio review. Reports only if interested. Samples returned with SASE. Original artwork returned at job's completion.
Photography: Buys photos from freelancers. Buys stock and assigns work. Uses archival, historical, sports photos. Captions required. Uses color, b&w prints; 35mm, 2¼×2¼, 4×5, 8×10 transparencies. Submit cover letter, résumé, published samples, client list, promo piece.
Terms: Pays authors royalty or work purchased outright. Pays illustrators by the project, royalty. Pays photographers by the project, per photo, royalty. Sends galleys to authors; dummies to illustrators. Book catalog available for SAE.

SIMON & SCHUSTER BOOKS FOR YOUNG READERS, 1230 Avenue of the Americas, New York NY 10022. (212)698-7200. Imprint of Simon & Schuster Children's Publishing Division. Vice President/Editorial Director: Stephanie Owens Lurie. Art Director: Lucille Chomowicz. Publishes 100 books/year.
 ● See First Books, page 28, for an interview with Simon & Schuster young adult novelist Rob Thomas, author of *Rats Saw God*.
Fiction: All levels: anthology, contemporary, history, humor, poetry. Picture books: animal, concept. Young readers: animal. Middle readers, young adult: fantasy, science fiction, suspense/mystery. Does not want to see rhyming verse; didactic stories; problem novels. Recently published *Zin! Zin! Zin! A Violin*, by Lloyd Moss, illustrated by Marjorie Priceman; *The Faithful Friend*, by Robert San Souci, illustrated by Brian Pinkney; *Prophecy Rock*, by Rob MacGregor; and *Rats Saw God*, by Rob Thomas.
Nonfiction: All levels: biography, nature/environment. Picture books: concept. Young readers, young adult: reference. "We're looking for innovative and accessible nonfiction for all age levels." Recently published *Smart Moves: A Kid's Guide To Self Defense*, by Christopher Goedecke and Rosemary Hausherr; and *Yuck! A Big Book of Little Horrors*, by Robert Snedden.
How to Contact/Writers: Accepting query letters only. Submit query to Submissions Editor. Reports in 2-3 months. Publishes book 2-4 years after acceptance. Will consider simultaneous submissions.
Illustration: Works with 75 illustrators/year. Do not submit original artwork. Editorial reviews ms/illustration packages from artists. Submit query letter to Submissions Editor. Illustrations only: Query with samples; provide promo sheet, tearsheets. Contact: Lucille Chomowicz, art director. Reports only if interested.
Terms: Pays authors royalty (varies) based on retail price. Pays illustrators by the project or royalty (varies) based on retail price. Photographers paid royalty. Original artwork returned at job's completion. Ms/artist's guidelines free on request.
Tips: "We're looking for picture books centered on a strong, fully-developed protagonist who grows or changes during the course of the story; YA novels that are challenging and psychologically complex; also imaginative and humorous middle fiction. And we want nonfiction that is as engaging as fiction. Send a query letter only. Take a look at what we're publishing to see if your work would fit in. The hardcore market is shrinking and so it is more difficult than ever to break in for the first time. Your work must sparkle with humor, imagination, wit and creativity."

SOUNDPRINTS, 353 Main Ave., Norwalk CT 06851. (203)838-6009. Fax: (203)866-9944. Book publisher. Editorial Assistant: Deirdre Langeland. Publishes 16 picture books/year. 10% of books by first-time authors; 10% of books from agented authors. Subjects published include oceanic and backyard wildlife, habitats and historical events represented in the Smithsonian Institution.
Fiction: Picture books, young readers: animal, history, nature/environment. No fantasy or anthropomorphic animals. Average word length: picture books—1,000. Recently published *Ladybug at Orchard Ave.*, by Kathleen Weidner Zoehfeld, illustrated by Thomas Buchs (grades PS-2, picture book); *Sea Turtle Journey*, by Lorraine A. Jay, illustrated by Katie Lee (grades PS-2

picture book); and *One Giant Leap*, by Dana Rau, illustrated by Thomas Buchs (grades 2-5, picture book).

Nonfiction: Picture books, young readers: animal, history. "Soundprints books are fiction, but based in research, with an intent to teach."

How to Contact/Writers: Query. Reports on queries/mss in 6-8 weeks. Publishing time "can vary from one to two years, depending on where it can fit in our publishing schedule." Will consider simultaneous submissions. "Do not send manuscripts without reading our guidelines first."

Illustration: Works with 8-10 illustrators/year. Uses color artwork only. Illustrations are usually full bleed 2-page spreads. Reviews ms/illustration packages from artists "if subject matter is appropriate." Query. Contact: Deirdre Langeland, editorial assistant. Illustrations only: Query with samples; provide résumé, portfolio, promo sheet, slides. "If interest is generated, additional material will be requested." Reports back only if interested. Samples returned with SASE.

Terms: Pays authors a flat fee. Pays illustrators by the project or royalty. Original artwork returned at job's completion. Book catalog for 8½×11 SAE and $1.05 postage; ms guidelines and artist guidelines for #10 SASE. "It's best to request both guidelines and catalog. Both can be sent in self-addressed envelope at least 8½×11 with $1.05 postage."

Tips: "We want books that educate children about the subject while capturing the interest of the reader/listener through an entertaining storyline. Authors should read one of our books in the relevant series *before* submitting. Soundprints has very specific guidelines and it is unlikely that a manuscript written by an author who is not familiar with our books will be acceptable."

*SOURCEBOOKS, INC., 121 N. Washington St., Naperville IL 60540. (630)961-3900. Fax: (630)961-2168. Book publisher. Editor: Todd Stocke. Publisher: Dominique Raccah.

How to Contact/Writers: Fiction/Nonfiction: Query. Submit outline/synopsis. Reports on queries/mss in 3 months. Publishes a book 6 months after acceptance. Will consider simultaneous submissions, electronic submissions via disk or modem and previously published work.

Illustration: Works with 10 illustrators/year. Reviews ms/illustration packages from artists. Query. Contact: Dominique Raccah, publisher. Illustrations only: Query with samples. Samples returned with SASE; samples filed.

Photography: Buys stock. Contact: Dominique Raccah, publisher.

Terms: Send galleys to authors. Originals returned to artist at job's completion. Book catalog for 9×12 SAE. All imprints included in a single catalog. Ms guidelines available for SASE.

*SOUTHWEST PARKS & MONUMENTS ASSOCIATION, 221 N. Court St., Tucson AZ 85701. (520)622-1999. Fax: (520)623-9519. E-mail: dgallagher@spma.org. Nonprofit association. Publishes 10 picture books/year; 2 middle readers/year. 50% of books by first-time authors. Publishes books to help children understand and appreciate national parks in the Southwest.

Nonfiction: Middle readers: animal, geography, history, nature/environment. Average word length: middle readers—2,000. Recently published *101 Questions About Desert Life*; and *101 Questions About Ancient Southwest Cultures*.

How to Contact/Writers: Nonfiction: Query. Reports on queries in 6 weeks; mss in 3 months. Publishes a book 1 year after acceptance. Will consider simultaneous submissions and electronic submissions via disk or modem.

Illustration: Works with 2 illustrators/year. Reviews ms/illustration packages from artists. Query. Contact: Derek Gallagher, director of publishing. Illustrations only: Query with samples. Contact: Derek Gallagher, director of publishing. Reports in 6 weeks. Samples returned with SASE; samples filed.

Photography: Buys stock and assigns work. Contact: Laura Symms-Wallace, production editor. Uses photographs of sites in national parks and monuments in the Southwest. General natural history photographs (for example, animals). Model/property releases required; captions required. Uses 2¼×2¼, 4×5 or 8×10 transparencies. Submit published samples, promo piece or other nonreturnable samples.

Terms: Work purchased outright from authors ($1,000-2,500). Pays illustrators by the project (range: $500-2,500). Pays photographers by the project (range: $1,000-5,000) or per photo (range: $50-250). Sends galleys to authors. Book catalog available for SAE and 55¢ postage. All imprints included in a single catalog.

Tips: "We are a nonprofit association (private) working with 53 national parks in the Southwest. Any work submitted to us should advance the understanding of visitors to the parks as to the resources the parks preserve and protect."

THE SPEECH BIN, INC., 1965 25th Ave., Vero Beach FL 32960. (407)770-0007. Fax: (407)770-0006. Book publisher. Senior Editor: Jan J. Binney. Publishes 10-12 books/year. 50% of books by first-time authors; less than 15% of books from agented writers. "Nearly all our books deal with treatment of children (as well as adults) who have communication disorders of speech or hearing or children who deal with family members who have such disorders (e.g., a grandparent with Alzheimer's disease or stroke)."

Fiction: Picture books: animal, easy-to-read, fantasy, health, special needs. Young readers, middle readers, young adult: health, special needs.

Nonfiction: Picture books, young readers, middle readers, young adults: activity books, health, textbooks, special needs. Published *Chatty Hats and Other Props*, by Denise Mantione; *Holiday Hoopla: Holiday Games for Language & Speech*, by Michele Rost; and *Speech Sports*, by Janet M. Shaw.

How to Contact/Writers: Fiction/Nonfiction: Query. Reports on queries in 4-6 weeks; mss in 2-3 months. Publishes a book 10-12 months after acceptance. "Will consider simultaneous submissions *only* if notified; too many authors fail to let us know if manuscript is simultaneously submitted to other publishers! We *strongly* prefer sole submissions."

Illustration: Works with 4-5 illustrators/year ("usually inhouse"). Reviews ms/illustration packages from artists. Ms/illustration packages and illustration only: "Query first!" Submit tearsheets (no original art). SASE required for reply or return of material.

Photography: Photographers should contact Jan J. Binney, senior editor. Buys stock and assigns work. Looking for scenic shots. Model/property releases required. Uses glossy b&w prints, 35mm or 2¼×2¼ transparencies. Submit résumé, business card, promotional literature or tearsheets to be kept on file.

Terms: Pays authors in royalties based on selling price. Pay illustrators by the project. Photographers paid by the project or per photo. Sends galleys to authors. Original artwork returned at job's completion. Book catalog for 4 first-class stamps and 9×12 SAE; ms guidelines for #10 SASE.

SRI RAMA PUBLISHING, Box 2550, Santa Cruz CA 95063. (408)426-5098. Book publisher. Estab. 1975. Secretary/Manager: Karuna K. Ault. Publishes 1 or fewer young reader titles/year.
 • Sri Rama is not accepting manuscripts for the 1997 book year.

Illustration: Illustrations used for fiction. Will review artwork for possible future assignments. Contact: James McElheron, graphic design director. Not reviewing at this time, however.

Terms: "We are a nonprofit organization. Proceeds from our sales support an orphanage in India, so we encourage donated labor, but each case is worked out individually." Pays illustrators $200-1,000. Sends galleys to authors; dummies to illustrators. Book catalog free on request.

STANDARD PUBLISHING, 8121 Hamilton Ave., Cincinnati OH 45231. (513)931-4050. Book publisher. Director: Diane Stortz. Children's Editor: Gus Holder. Creative Director: Coleen Davis. Number and type of books varies yearly. Many projects are written inhouse. No juvenile or young adult novels. 25-40% of books by first-time authors; 1% of books from agented writers. Publishes well-written, upbeat books with a Christian perspective.

Fiction: Adventure, animal, contemporary, Bible stories. Average word length: board/picture books—400-1,000.

Nonfiction: Bible background, nature/environment, sports devotions. Average word length: 400-1,000. Recently published *The Manger Where Jesus Lay*, by Martha Larghar, illustrated by Karen Clark (picture book); and *Baby's First Bible*, illustrated by Colin and Moira Macheam (novelty board book).

How to Contact/Writers: Fiction/Nonfiction: Send complete ms except for longer works. Reports on queries/mss in 2 months. Publishes a book 18 months after acceptance. Will consider simultaneous submissions.

Illustration: Works with 15-20 new illustrators/year. Illustrations only: Submit cover letter and photocopies. Contact: Coleen Davis, creative director. Reports on art samples only if interested. Samples returned with SASE; samples filed.

Terms: Pays authors royalties of 5-10% based on wholesale price or work purchased outright (range varies by project). Illustrators paid (mostly) by project. Photographers paid by the photo. Sends galleys to authors on some projects. Book catalog available for $2 and 8½×11 SAE; ms guidelines for letter-size SASE.

Tips: "We look for manuscripts that help draw children into a relationship with Jesus Christ; help children develop insights about what the Bible teaches; make reading an appealing and pleasurable activity."

STEMMER HOUSE PUBLISHERS, INC., 2627 Caves Rd., Owings Mills MD 21117. (410)363-3690. Fax: (410)363-8459. Book publisher. Estab. 1975. President: Barbara Holdridge. Publishes 1-3 picture books/year. "Sporadic" numbers of young reader, middle reader, young adult titles/year. 60% of books by first-time authors.

Fiction: Picture books: history, multicultural, nature/environment. Does not want to see anthropomorphic characters. Recently published *How Pleasant to Know Mr. Lear: Poems by Edward Lear*, illustrated by Bohdan Butenko; and *The Marvelous Maze*, by Maxine Rose Schur, illustrated by Robin DeWitt and Patricia DeWitt-Grush.

Nonfiction: Picture books: animal, biography, multicultural, nature/environment. Multicultural needs include Native American, African. Published *The Hawaiian Coral Reef Coloring Book*, by Katherine Orr; *The First Teddy Bear*, by Helen Kay, illustrations by Susan Kronz.

How to Contact/Writers: Fiction/Nonfiction: Query; submit outline/synopsis and sample chapters. Reports on queries/mss in 2 weeks. Publishes a book 18 months after acceptance. Will consider simultaneous submissions.

Illustration: Works with 2-3 illustrators/year. Uses color artwork only. Reviews ms/illustration packages from artists. Query first with several photocopied illustrations. Contact: Barbara Holdridge, president. Illustrations only: Submit tearsheets and/or slides (with SASE for return). Reports in 2 weeks. Samples returned with SASE.

Terms: Pays authors royalties of 4-5% based on wholesale price. Offers average advance payment of $300. Pays illustrators royalty of 4-5% based on wholesale price. Pays photographers 4-5% royalty. Sends galleys to authors. Original artwork returned at job's completion. Book catalog and ms guidelines for 9×12 SASE.

Tips: Writers: "Simplicity, literary quality and originality are the keys." Wants to see ms/illustration packages. "Don't forget the SASE!"

STERLING PUBLISHING CO., INC., 387 Park Ave. S., New York NY 10016. (212)532-7160. Fax: (212)213-2495. Book publisher. Acquisitions Director: Sheila Anne Barry. Publishes 30 middle readers/year. 10% of books by first-time authors.

Nonfiction: Middle readers: activity books, animal, arts/crafts, geography, ghosts, hobbies, music, how-to, humor, mini-mystery, true mystery, multicultural, nature/environment, puzzles, reference, science, sports, supernatural incidents. "Since our books are highly illustrated, word length is seldom the point. Most are 96-128 pages." Does not want to see fiction, poetry, story books or personal narratives. Recently published *Awesome Jokes*, by Charles Keller, illustrated by Jeff Sinclair (ages 8-12, riddle and joke book); and *Reptiles & Amphibians: Birth & Growth*, by Andres Llamas Ruiz, illustrated by Ali Garousi (ages 8-12, nature/animals).

How to Contact/Writers: Reports on queries in 1-2 weeks; mss in 2-12 weeks. "If we are interested it may take longer." Publishes a book 6-18 months after acceptance. Will consider simultaneous submissions.

Illustration: Works with 12 illustrators/year. Reviews ms/illustration packages from artists. "Query first." Illustrations only: "Send sample photocopies of line drawings; also examples of some color work." Reports only if interested. Samples returned with SASE; samples kept on file.

Terms: Pays authors in royalties of up to 10%; "standard terms, no sliding scale, varies according to edition." Usually pays illustrators and photographers flat fee/project or royalty. Sends galleys to authors. Original artwork returned at job's completion "if possible, but sometimes held for future needs." Ms guidelines for SASE.

Tips: Looks for "humor, hobbies, science books for middle-school children." Also, "mysterious occurrences, activities and fun and games books."

*✿STODDART PUBLISHING CO. LIMITED, 34 Lesmill Rd., North York, Ontario M3B 2T6 Canada. (416)445-3333. Fax: (416)445-5967. E-mail: kelly.jones@ccmailgw.genpub.com. Book publisher. Publisher: Kathryn Cole. Publishes 15 picture books/year; 6 young readers/year; 6 young adults/year. 20% of books by first-time authors.

Fiction: Picture books: adventure, animal, contemporary, folktales, history, humor, multicultural. Young readers: contemporary, folktales, history. Young adult: contemporary, history, multicultural, suspense/mystery. Does not want to see science fiction. Average word length: picture books—800; young readers—38,000; young adult/teens—70,000. Recently published *Fires Burning*, by Julie Lawson (young adult fiction); and *Pavlova's Gift*, by Maxine Trottier, illustrated by Victoria Berdichevsky (picture book, historical fiction for ages 4-7).

How to Contact/Writers: Fiction: submit outline/synopsis and 2 sample chapters. Reports on queries in 3 weeks; mss in 3 months. Publishes a book 18 months after acceptance. Will consider simultaneous submissions.

Illustration: Works with 18 illustrators/year. Reviews ms/illustration packages from artists. Submit ms and photocopied artwork (no originals) and SASE. Contact: Kathryn Cole, publisher. Illustrations only: Send photocopied artwork, SASE and query. Contact: Kathryn Cole, publisher. Reports in 2 months. Samples returned with SASE; samples filed "if desirable."
Terms: Author and illustrator payments vary with project size and type. Sends galleys to authors. Originals returned to artist at job's completion. Book catalog available for large SAE and 2 first-class stamps. Ms guidelines available to SASE.
Tips: "Stoddart Kids is interested in developing a strong Canadian publishing program and therefore encourages the submission of Canadian materials. However, topics that cover both American and Canadian markets are also welcome."

*STOREY COMMUNICATIONS, INC., Imprint of Storey Publishing, Garden Way Publishing, Schoolhouse Rd., Pownal VT 05261. (802)823-5200. Fax: (802)823-5819. Book publisher. Editorial Director: Gwen Steege. Managing Editor: Cathy Gee Graney. Publishes 2 young readers/year. 7% of books by first-time authors.
Nonfiction: Young readers, middle readers: animal, arts/crafts, gardening, hobbies, how-to, nature/environment. Does not want to see cooking or nonfiction with a story line. Recently published *Your Pony/Your Horse*, by Cherry Hill (ages 9 +, guide to care of horses); *Tooth Truth* and *Puddle Jumpers*, by Jennifer Storey Gillis (ages 5-10, projects); and *Everything You Never Knew About Birds*, by Rebecca Rupp (ages 9 and up, science).
How to Contact/Writers: Nonfiction: Query. Submit outline/synopsis and 1 sample chapter. Reports on queries/mss in 2 months. Publishes a book 1 year after acceptance. Will consider simultaneous and electronic submissions via disk or modem.
Illustration: Works with 24 illustrators/year. Reviews ms/illustration packages from artists. Send ms with dummy. Contact: Gwen Steege, editorial director. Illustrations only: Query with samples, résumé and portfolio. Contact: Cathy Gee Graney. Reports in 2 months. Samples returned with SASE; samples filed. "Return of originals subject to negotiation."
Photography: Buys stock and assigns work. Contact: Cathy Gee Graney, managing editor. Uses animals and children. Model/property releases required. Uses b&w glossy prints and 35mm, 2¼×2¼, 4×5 transparencies. Submit cover letter, résumé, published samples, stock photo list.
Terms: Offers advances. Sends galleys to authors. Book catalog available for 8½×11 SAE. Ms guidelines available for SASE.
Tips: "Review our catalog."

SUNBELT MEDIA, INC./EAKIN PRESS, P.O. Box 90159, Austin TX 78709. (512)288-1771. Fax: (512)288-1813. Book publisher. Estab. 1978. President: Ed Eakin. Publishes 1-2 picture books/year; 2-3 young readers/year; 9 middle readers/year; 2 young adult titles/year. 50% of books by first-time authors; 5% of books from agented writers.
Fiction: Picture books: animal. Middle readers, young adults: history, sports. Average word length: picture books—3,000; young readers—10,000; middle readers—15,000-20,000; young adults—20,000-30,000. "90% of our books relate to Texas and the Southwest."
Nonfiction: Picture books: animal. Middle readers and young adults: history, sports. Recently published *Sam and the Speaker's Chair*.
How to Contact/Writers: Fiction/Nonfiction: Query. Reports on queries in 2 weeks; mss in 6 weeks. Publishes a book 18 months after acceptance. Will consider simultaneous submissions.
Illustration: Reviews ms/illustration packages from artists. Query. Illustrations only: Submit tearsheets. Reports on art samples in 2 weeks.
Terms: Pays authors royalties of 10-15% based on net to publisher. Pays for separate authors and illustrators: "Usually share royalty." Pays illustrators royalty of 10-15% based on wholesale price. Sends galleys to authors. Book catalog, ms/artist's guidelines for $1.25 postage and SASE.
Tips: Writers: "Be sure all elements of manuscript are included—include bio of author or illustrator." Submit books relating to Texas only.

*☐SYNCHRONICITY BOOKS, Imprint of Gesture Graphic Book Design & Production Co., 3411 Garth #208, Baytown TX 77521. (713)422-6326. E-mail: gestureg@aol.com. Independent book producer/packager. Editor: G.G. Thomson. Art Director: Ms. Nile Lienad. Publishes 5 picture books, middle readers, young adults/year. 60% of books by first-time authors.
   • Synchronicity Books is a work-for-hire book producer working with both standard and independent book publishers.
Fiction: Picture books, young readers: adventure, animal, anthology, concept, contemporary, folktales, history, humor, multicultural, nature/environment, poetry, suspense/mystery. Middle

readers: folktales, history, humor, multicultural, nature/environment, poetry, problem novels, suspense/mystery. Young adult/teens: anthology, contemporary, folktales, history, humor, multicultural, nature/environment, poetry, problem novels, science fiction. Does not want to see religious material. Recently published *The Moon 'n' Me*, by Amanda Miles, illustrated by Nile Lienad (preschool, activity book); *Ballet Sticker Book*, published by Synchronicity for Dancing Jester Press (ages 5-8, arts/crafts); and *The Twin Ballet Mystery*, by Clementine Mathis (ages 12 and up, mystery).

Nonfiction: Average word length varies with project. Recently published *Low-Fat Bac Pac Cook Book*, illustrated by Jane McClarrey (ages 12+); and *Blue Sky Heartbeat Lullabies for HIV+ Babies, And Other Ailing Small Fry*, by Glenda Daniel (audio cassette and book).

How to Contact/Writers: Fiction/Nonfiction: Query; submit outline/synopsis. Reports on queries in 3 months; ms in 3-6 months. Publishes a book 38 weeks after acceptance. Will consider simultaneous submissions and previously published work.

Illustration: Works with 3-6 illustrators/year. Reviews ms/illustration packages from artists. Send ms with dummy. Contact: Ms. Nile Lienad, art director. Illustrations only: Query with samples; send résumé, promo sheet. Contact: Ms. Nile Lienad, art director. Reports in 2 weeks only if interested. Samples kept on file.

Photography: Buys stock and assigns work. Contact: Ms. Nile Lienad, art director. Model/property releases required. Uses various prints; 35 mm transparencies. Submit stock photo list and promo piece.

Terms: "We are a for-hire book production company." Pays illustrators/photographers variable rate per project or 10% royalty based on wholesale price. Sends galleys to authors; dummies to illustrators. Originals returned to artist at job's completion. Ms and art guidelines available for SASE.

Tips: "Synchronicity Books is in sync with your publishing vision and in time with your production needs: typesetting, illustration, printing, binding, editorial services. Short runs of 200-3,000 are our specialty."

✦THISTLEDOWN PRESS LTD., 633 Main St., Saskatoon, Saskatchewan S7H 0J8 Canada. (306)244-1722. Fax: (306)244-1762. E-mail: thistle@broadwaynet.com. Book publisher. Contact: Patrick O'Rourke. Publishes numerous middle reader and young adult titles/year. "Thistledown originates books by Canadian authors only, although we have co-published titles by authors outside Canada. We do not publish children's picture books."

Fiction: Middle readers, young adults: adventure, anthology, contemporary, fantasy, humor, poetry, romance, science fiction, suspense/mystery. Average word length: middle readers—35,000; young adults—40,000. Recently published *The Blue Jean Collection*, and *Notes Across the Aisle*, edited by Peter Carver (young adult, short story anthologies); *Takes: Stories for Young Adults*, edited by R.P. MacIntyre (anthology); *Fish House Secrets*, by Kathy Stinson (YA novel) and *The Blue Camaro*, by R.P. MacIntyre (YA short fiction).

How to Contact/Writers: Prefers agented writers but "not mandatory." Submit outline/synopsis and sample chapters. Reports on queries in 3-4 weeks, mss in 3-6 months. Publishes a book about one year after acceptance. No simultaneous submissions.

Illustration: Prefers agented illustrators but "not mandatory." Works with few illustrators. Illustrations only: Query with samples, promo sheet, slides, tearsheets. Contact: A.M. Forrie, art director. Reports back only if interested. Samples returned with SASE; samples filed.

Terms: Pays authors royalty of 10-15% based on retail price. Pays illustrators and photographers by the project (range: $250-750). Sends galleys to authors. Original artwork returned at job's completion. Book catalog free on request. Ms guidelines for #10 envelope and IRC.

Tips: "Send cover letter including publishing history and SASE."

TICKNOR & FIELDS, See Houghton Mifflin Co. listing.

TILBURY HOUSE, PUBLISHERS, 132 Water St., Gardiner ME 04345. (207)582-1899. Fax: (207)582-8227. Book publisher. Publisher: Jennifer Elliott. Publishes 1-3 young readers/year.

☐ **THE OPEN BLOCK** before a listing indicates that the listing is a book packager/producer.

Fiction: Young readers and middle readers: multicultural, nature/environment. Special needs include books that teach children about tolerance and honoring diversity.

Nonfiction: Young readers and middle readers: multicultural, nature/environment. Recently published *Talking Walls* and *Who Belongs Here?* both by Margy Burns Knight, illustrated by Anne Sibley O'Brien (grades 3-8).

How to Contact/Writers: Fiction/Nonfiction: Submit outline/synopsis. Reports on queries/mss in 1 month. Publishes a book 1-2 years after acceptance. Will consider simultaneous submissions "with notification."

Illustration: Works with 1-2 illustrators/year. Illustrations only: Query with samples. Contact: J. Elliott, associate publisher. Reports in 1 month Samples returned with SASE. Original artwork returned at job's completion.

Photography: Buys photos from freelancers. Contact: J. Elliott, associate publisher. Works on assignment only.

Terms: Pays authors royalty. Pays illustrators/photographers by the project; royalty. Sends galleys to authors. Book catalog available for 9 × 12 SAE and 78¢ postage.

Tips: "We are primarily interested in children's books that teach children about tolerance in a multicultural society and honoring diversity. We are also interested in books that teach children about environmental issues."

TIME-LIFE FOR CHILDREN, subsidiary of Time Life, Inc., 777 Duke St., Alexandria VA 22314.

* Time-Life no longer accepts unsolicited manuscripts. All books produced by them are conceived and developed inhouse.

TOR BOOKS, Forge, Orb, 175 Fifth Ave., New York NY 10010. Publisher, Children's and Young Adult Division: Kathleen Doherty. Children's, Young Adult Editor: Jonathan Schmidt. Educational Sales Coordinator: Nichole Stanka. Publishes 5-10 young readers/year; 10-15 middle readers/year; 20-25 young adults/year.

Fiction: Young readers: humor, multicultural, nature. Middle readers, young adult titles: adventure, contemporary, history, humor, multicultural, nature/environment, problem, suspense/mystery. "We are interested and open to books which tell stories from a wider range of perspectives. We are interested in materials that deal with a wide range of issues." Average word length: young readers—10,000; middle readers—10,000; young adults—30,000-60,000. Published *Mind Quakes: Stories to Shatter Your Brain* and *Scorpion Shards*, both by Neal Shusterman (ages 10-16, young adult novel).

Nonfiction: Young readers, middle readers: activity books, geography, history, how-to, multicultural, nature/environment, science, social issues. Young adult: geography, history, multicultural, nature/environment, social issues. Does not want to see religion, cooking. Average word length: young readers—6-10,000; middle readers—10,000-15,000; young adults—40,000. Published *Strange Unsolved Mysteries*, by Phyllis Rabin Emert; *Stargazer's Guide* (to the Galaxy), by Q.L. Pearce (ages 8-12, guide to constellations, illustrated).

How to Contact/Writers: Fiction/Nonfiction: Submit outline/synopsis and 3 sample chapters or complete ms. Reports on queries in 2 months; mss in 3-4 months.

Illustration: Works with 40 illustrators/year. Reviews ms/illustration packages from artists. Query with samples. Contact: Nichole Rajana or Jonathan Schmidt. Reports only if interested. Samples returned with SASE; samples kept on file.

Terms: Pays authors royalty. Offers advances. Pays illustrators by the project. Book catalog available for 9 × 12 SAE and 3 first-class stamps.

Tips: "Know the house your are submitting to, familiarize yourself with the types of books they are publishing. Get an agent. Allow him/her to direct you to publishers who are most appropriate. It saves time and effort."

*TRANSWORLD PUBLISHERS LIMITED, 61-63 Uxbridge Rd., London W5 5SA England. (081)579-2652. Fax: (081)579-5479. Imprints are Doubleday, Picture Corgi (ages 3-6), Corgi Pups (ages 5-8), Young Corgi (ages 6-9), Corgi Yearling (ages 8-11), Corgi (ages 10+), Corgi Freeway (ages 11+), Bantam Books and Bantam YA (ages 10+). Book publisher. Publisher, Children's and Young Adult Publishing: Philippa Dickinson. Publishes 6 picture books/year; 12 young readers/year; 12 middle readers/year; and 6 young adult titles/year.

Fiction: Picture books: adventure, animal, anthology, contemporary, fantasy, folktales, humor, multicultural, nature/environment, poetry, suspense/mystery. Young readers: adventure, animal, anthology, contemporary, fantasy, folktales, humor, multicultural, nature/environment, poetry, sports, suspense/mystery. Middle readers: adventure, animal, anthology, contemporary, fantasy, folktales, humor, multicultural, nature/environment, problem novels, romance, sports, suspense/mystery. Young adults: adventure, contemporary, fantasy, humor, multicultural, nature/environment, problem novels, romance, science fiction, suspense/mystery. Average word length: picture books—800; young readers—1,500-6,000; middle readers—10,000-15,000; young adults—20,000-45,000. Recently published *Hacker*, by Malorie Blackman (8 + computer assisted adventure); *The Suitcase Kid*, by Jacqueline Wilson (8-11 contemporary); and *Horse Pie*, by Dick King-Smith (6-8 animal novel).

How to Contact/Writers: Submit outline/synopsis and 3 sample chapters to Geraldine Parkins. Reports on queries in 1-2 months; mss in 2-3 months. Will consider simultaneous and previously published submissions.

Illustration: Works with 50 illustrators/year. Reviews ms/illustration packages from artists. Submit ms with dummy. Contact: Penny Walker. Illustrations only: Query with samples. Reports in 1 month. Samples are returned with SASE (IRC).

Photography: Buys photos from freelancers. Contact: Liz Masters, art department. Buys stock images. Photo captions required.Uses color or b&w prints. Submit cover letter, published samples.

Terms: Pays authors royalty. Offers advances. Pays illustrators by the project or royalty. Pays photographers by the project or per photo. Sends galleys to authors; dummies to illustrators.

TREASURE CHEST BOOKS, P.O. Box 5250, Tuscon AZ 85703. (520)623-9558. Fax: (520)624-5888. Book publisher. Publisher: Ross Humphreys. Publishes 2-4 picture books/year.

Fiction: Picture books: animal, contemporary, fantasy, folktales, history, humor, multicultural, nature/environment. Special needs include Southwestern US cultures. Average word length: picture books—1,200.

Nonfiction: Picture books: animal, multicultural, nature/environment. Special needs include Southwestern US cultures.

How to Contact/Writers: Fiction: Query. Submit complete ms. Reports on queries in 1 month; mss in 2 months. Publishes a book 1 year after acceptance. Will consider simultaneous submissions, electronic submissions via disk or modem, previously published work.

Illustration: Works with 2 illustrators/year. Reviews ms/illustration packages from artists. Send ms with dummy. Illustrations only: Query with samples. Reports in 2 months. Samples returned with SASE; samples filed.

Photography: Buys photos from freelancers. Contact: Ross Humphreys. Buys stock and assigns work. Model/property releases required; captions required. Submit cover letter.

Terms: Pays authors royalty. Pays illustrators by the project, royalty. Pays photographers by the project, per photo, royalty. Sends galleys to authors; dummies to illustrators. Original artwork returned at job's completion. Ms guidelines available for SASE.

*TREASURE PUBLISHING, 829 S. Shields St., MSC 1000, Fort Collins CO 80521. (970)484-8483. Fax: (970)495-6700. Book publisher.

Nonfiction: Picture books, young readers: Bible stories. Recently published *Sowing and Growing*; *Don't Stop Fill Every Pot!*; and *God's Happy Helpers*, all by Marilyn Lashbrook, all illustrated by Stephanie McFetridge Britt.

How to Contact/Writers: Submit complete ms. Reports on mss in 3 months. Publishes a book 1 year after acceptance.

Illustration: Works with 3 illustrators/year. Uses color artwork only. Reviews ms/illustration packages from artists. Send ms with dummy. Contact: Mark Steiner, president. Illustrations only: Send résumé, promo sheet. Contact: Mark Steiner, president. Reports back only if interested. Samples filed.

Terms: Work purchased outright from authors (average $1,000). Illustrators paid by the project. Book catalog for 9×12 SAE and 2 first-class stamps. Manuscript guidelines for SASE.

TRICYCLE PRESS, P.O. Box 7123, Berkeley CA 94707. Acquisitions Editor: Nicole Geiger. Publishes 7 picture books/year; 4 activity books/year. 30% of books by first-time authors.

Fiction: Picture books: concept, health, multicultural, nature/environment. Average word length: picture books-1,200. Recently published *Amelia Writes Again*, by Marissa Moss (ages 7-12, picture book); and *Sarah's Story*, by Bill Harley and Eve Aldridge (ages 6-8, picturebook).

Nonfiction: Picture books: Activity books, arts/crafts, concept, geography, health, how-to, nature/environment, science, self help, social issues. Young readers: Activity books, arts/crafts, health, how-to, nature/environment, science, self help, social issues. Recently published *Raptors,*

Fossils, Fins & Fangs, by Ray Troll and Brad Matsen (ages 7-11, picture book); *Lotions, Potions & Slime*, by Nancy Blakey (ages 2-12, activity book); and *Pretend Soup and Other Real Recipes: A Cookbook for Preschoolers and Up*, by Mollie Katzen and Ann Henderson (ages 3-6, children's cookbook).

How to Contact/Writers: Fiction: Submit complete ms for picture books. Nonfiction: Submit complete ms. Reports on queries/mss in 10-12 weeks. Publishes a book 1 year after acceptance. Will consider simultaneous submissions.

Illustration: Works with 6 illustrators/year. Reviews ms/illustration package from artists. Submit ms with dummy. Contact: Nicole Geiger, acquisitions editor. Illustrations only: Query with samples, promo sheet, tearsheets. Reports back only if interested. Samples returned with SASE; samples filed. Original artwork returned at job's completion unless work for hire.

Terms: Pays authors 15% royalty (but lower if illustrated ms) based on wholesale price. Offers advances. Pays illustrators by the project or royalty. Sends galleys to authors. Book catalog for 9×12 SASE ($1.01). Ms guidelines for SASE.

Tips: "We are looking for something a bit outside the mainstream and with lasting appeal (no one-shot-wonders). Lately we've noticed a sacrifice of quality writing for the sake of illustration."

TROLL COMMUNICATIONS, 100 Corporate Dr., Mahwah NJ 07430. Book publisher. Editor: Marian Frances.
- Troll Communications is not accepting unsolicited manuscripts.

Fiction: Picture books: animal, contemporary, folktales, history, nature/environment, poetry, sports, suspense/mystery. Young readers: adventure, animal, contemporary, folktales, history, nature/environment, poetry, science fiction, sports, suspense/mystery. Middle readers: adventure, anthology, animal, contemporary, fantasy, folktales, health-related, history, nature/environment, poetry, problem novels, romance, science fiction, sports, suspense/mystery. Young adults: problem novels, romance and suspense/mystery.

Nonfiction: Picture books: activity books, animal, biography, careers, history, hobbies, nature/environment, sports. Young readers: activity books, animal, biography, careers, health, history, hobbies, music/dance, nature/environment, sports. Middle readers: activity books, animal, biography, careers, health, history, hobbies, music/dance, nature/environment, sports. Young adults: health, music/dance.

How to Contact/Writers: Fiction: Query or submit outline/synopsis and 3 sample chapters. Nonfiction: Query. Reports in 4 weeks.

Illustration: Reviews ms/illustration packages from artists. Contact: Marian Frances, editor. Illustrations only: Query with samples; provide résumé, promotional literature or tearsheets to be kept on file. Reports in 4 weeks.

Photography: Interested in stock photos. Model/property releases required.

Terms: Pays authors royalty or work purchased outright. Pays illustrators by the project or royalty. Photographers paid by the project.

TROPHY BOOKS, 10 E. 53rd St., New York NY 10022. Fax: (212)207-7915. Subsidiary of HarperCollins Children's Books Group. Book publisher. Publishes 6-9 chapter books/year, 25-30 middle grade titles/year, 30 reprint picture books/year, 25-30 young adult titles/year.
- Trophy is primarily a paperback reprint imprint. They do not publish original illustrated manuscripts.

TYNDALE HOUSE PUBLISHERS, INC., 351 Executive Dr., P.O. Box 80, Wheaton IL 60189. (630)668-8300. Book publisher. Children's editorial contact: Karen Watson. Children's illustration contact: Marlene Muddell. Publishes approximately 20 children's titles/year.
- Tyndale House no longer reviews unsolicited manuscripts.

Fiction: Middle readers: adventure, religion, suspense/mystery.

Nonfiction: Picture books: religion. Young readers: Christian living, Bible.

How to Contact/Writers: "Request children's writer guidelines from (630)668-8310 ext. 836 for more information."

Illustration: Uses full-color for book covers, b&w or color spot illustrations for some nonfiction. Illustrations only: Query with photocopies (color or b&w) of samples, résumé. Contact: Marlene Muddell.

Photography: Buys photos from freelancers. Contact: Marlene Muddell. Works on assignment only.

Terms: Pay rates for authors and illustrators vary.

Tips: "All accepted manuscripts will appeal to Evangelical Christian children and parents."

UNIVERSITY CLASSICS, LTD. PUBLISHERS, One Bryan Rd., P.O. Box 2301, Athens OH 45701. (614)592-4543. Book publisher. President: Albert H. Shuster. Publishes 1 young readers/year; 1 middle readers/year; 1 young adult title/year. 50% of books by first-time authors.
● This publisher is "booked for the next two years" in children's fiction and nonfiction. Do not submit work (manuscripts or illustrations) to them at this time.
Fiction: Picture books: animal, concept, health, nature/environment. Young readers: concept, health, nature/environment, special needs. Middle readers: health, nature/environment, problem novels, special needs. Young adults: health, nature/environment, special needs. Average word length: young readers—1,200; middle readers—5,000. Published *Toodle D. Poodle*, by Katherine Dana and Dorathyre Shuster (grades 4-6, ages 10-12); *The Day My Dad and I Got Mugged*, by Howard Goldsmith (grades 5-8, ages 12-15).
Nonfiction: Picture books: activity books, animal, arts/crafts, concept, health, nature/environment, self help, special needs. Young readers: activity books, animal, arts/crafts, concept, health, nature/environment, self help, special needs, textbooks. Middle readers, young adults: arts/crafts, concept, health, nature/environment, self help, special needs, textbooks. Average word length: young readers—1,200; middle readers—5,000. Published *Fitness and Nutrition: The Winning Combination*, by Jane Buch (ages 13-17, textbook); *The Way We Live: Practical Economics*, by John Shaw (ages 13-adult, textbook); *Ride Across America: An Environmental Commitment*, by Lucian Spataro (ages 13-17, trade).
Illustration: Works with 2 illustrators/year.
Terms: Pays authors royalty of 5-12% based on retail price. Pays illustrators by the project. Book catalog available for #10 SAE and 2 first-class stamps.
Tips: "Consumers are looking more for educational than fictional books, and this will continue."

*VOLCANO PRESS, Box 270, Volcano CA 95689. (209)296-3345. Fax: (209)296-4515. E-mail: sales@volcanopress.com. Website: http://www.volcanopress.com. Book publisher. President: Ruth Gottstein.
Fiction: All levels: animals, folktales, multicultural, nature/environment, poetry, history.
Nonfiction: All levels: health, history, multicultural, nature/environment, self help. Sees too much "fiction, trite fantasy, didactic and moralistic material, bad fairy tales, anthropomorphic male animal heroes."
How to Contact/Writers: Nonfiction: Submit outline/synopsis and sample chapters. Reports on queries in 2-3 weeks; mss in 4-6 weeks. Publishes a book 1 year after acceptance. "Please always enclose SASE."
Terms: Pays authors royalty. Book catalog for #10 SASE.
Tips: Considers "non-racist, non-sexist types of books that are empowering to women."

WALKER AND CO., 435 Hudson St., New York NY 10014. (212)727-8300. Division of Walker Publishing Co. Inc. Book publisher. Estab. 1959. Editorial Director: Emily Easton. Publishes 10 picture books/year; 10-15 middle readers/year; 5 young adult titles/year. 5% of books by first-time authors; 65% of books from agented writers.
Fiction: Picture books: animal, history, multicultural, special needs. Young readers: animal, contemporary, history, multicultural. Middle readers: animal, contemporary, history, multicultural, humor. Young adults: history. Recently published *Miss Malarkey Doesn't Live in Room 10*, by J. Finchler (picture book); *Liar*, by W. Morris (young adult); and *Meet the Monsters*, by J. Yolen (middle grade).
Nonfiction: Young readers: animals. Middle readers: animal, biography, health, history, multicultural, reference, social issues. Young adults: biography, careers, health, history, multicultural, reference, social issues, sports. Published *Pilgrim Voices*, by C. and R. Roop (picture book history); *Red-Tail Angels*, by P. and F. McKissack (young adult history). Multicultural needs include "contemporary, literary fiction and historical fiction written in an authentic voice. Also high interest nonfiction with trade appeal."
How to Contact/Writers: Fiction/nonfiction: Submit outline/synopsis and sample chapters. Reports on queries/mss in 2-3 months. Will consider simultaneous submissions.
Illustration: Works with 4-6 illustrators/year. Uses color artwork only. Editorial reviews ms/illustration packages from artists. Query or submit ms with 4-8 samples. Illustrations only: Tearsheets. "Please do not send original artwork." Reports on art samples only if interested. Samples returned with SASE.
Terms: Pays authors in royalties of 5-10% based on wholesale price "depends on contract." Offers advance payment against royalties. Original artwork returned at job's completion. Pays illustrators by the project (range: $500-5,000); royalties from 50%. Sends galleys to authors. Book catalog available for 9×12 SASE; ms guidelines for SASE.

Tips: Writers: "Don't take rejections personally and try to consider them objectively. We receive more than 20 submissions a day. Can it be improved?" Illustrators: "Have a well-rounded portfolio with different styles." Does not want to see folktales, ABC books, genre fiction (mysteries, science fiction, fantasy).

✦**WEIGL EDUCATIONAL PUBLISHERS**, 1902 11th St. SE., Calgary, Alberta T2G 3G2 Canada. (403)233-7747. Fax: (403)233-7769. Book publisher. Publisher: Linda Weigl.
● Weigl Educational Publishers will not accept manuscripts in 1997.
Nonfiction: Young reader, middle reader, young adult: textbooks. Young reader, middle reader: careers, multicultural. Average length: young reader, middle reader, young adult—64 pages. Recently published *Career Connections Series II*, (middle readers); *Digging for Dinosaurs*, (young readers, middle readers); and *Introducing Japan*, (young readers, middle readers).
How to Contact/Writers: Nonfiction: Submit query and résumé. Reports on queries in 3 months; mss in 4 months. Publishes a book 2 years after acceptance. Will consider simultaneous submissions.
Illustration: Works with 1 illustrator/year. Uses color artwork only. Reviews ms/illustration packages from artists. Query first. Contact: A. Woodrow, project coordinator. Illustrations only: Query with samples. Reports back only if interested or when appropriate project comes in. Samples returned with SASE; samples filed. Original artwork returned at job's completion.
Photography: Buys photos from freelancers. Buys stock and assigns work. Wants political, juvenile, multicultural photos. Contact: A. Woodrow.
Terms: Pays authors royalty or work purchased outright. Pays illustrators/photographers by the project. Sends galleys to author; dummies to illustrator. Book catalog for SASE.
Tips: Looks for "a manuscript that answers a specific curriculum need, or can be applied to a curriculum topic with multiple applications (e.g. career education)."

DANIEL WEISS ASSOCIATES, INC., 11th Floor, 33 W. 17th St., New York NY 10011. (212)645-3865. Fax: (212)633-1236. Independent book producer/packager. Editorial Assistant: Kieran Scott. Publishes 30 young readers/year; 40 middle readers/year; and 70 young adults/year. 25% of books by first-time authors. "We do mostly series!"
Fiction: Middle readers: sports. Young adults: fantasy, romance.
Nonfiction: Young adults: history.
readers, young adults: adventure, anthology, contemporary, problem novels, romance, sports, suspense/mystery.
How to Contact/Writers: Submit outline/synopsis and 2 sample chapters. Reports on queries in 1-2 months; mss in 2 months. Publishes a book 1 year after acceptance. Will consider simultaneous submissions.
Illustration: Works with 20 illustrators/year. Reviews ms/illustration packages from artists. Submit query. Contact: Lou Malcangi, assistant art director. Illustrations only: Provide promo sheet. Contact: Paul Matarazzo, art director. Reports in 2 months. Samples returned with SASE. Original artwork returned at job's completion.
Terms: Pays authors royalty of 4%. Work purchased outright from authors, $1,000 minimum. Offers advances (average amount: $3,000). Pays illustrators by the project. Ms guidelines available if SASE sent.

WESTERN PUBLISHING CO., 850 Third Ave., New York, NY 10022. (212)753-8500. Fax (212)371-1091. See the listing for Golden Books.

WHISPERING COYOTE PRESS, INC., Suite 860, 300 Crescent Court, Dallas TX 75201. Editor/Publisher: Lou Alpert. Publishes 8 picture books/year. 40% of books from first-time authors.
Fiction: Picture books: adventure, animal, contemporary, fantasy, hi-lo, history, humor, poetry. Does not want to see number, alphabet, death, handicap and holiday books. Average word length: picture books—under 1,500. Recently published *I'm A Little Teapot*, written and illustrated by Iza Trapani (4-8, picture book); and *Africa Calling*, by Dan Adlerman, illustrated by Kim Adlerman.
How to Contact/Writers: Submit complete ms. Reports in 3 months. Publishes a book 1½-3 years after acceptance. Will consider simultaneous submissions. "Include SASE. If no SASE is included manuscript is destroyed *without* reading."
Illustration: Works with 6-8 illustrators/year. Uses color artwork only. Reviews ms/illustration packages from artists. Submit ms with dummy or 3-4 pieces of final art. Contact: Lou Alpert, editor/publisher. Illustrations only: Submit color copies or a half dozen pieces for file. "Do not

send originals." Reports back only if SASE is included. Samples returned with SASE; samples filed if instructed to do so by illustrator.

Terms: Pays authors royalty of 4-5% based on retail price. Offers advances. Pays illustrators royalty of 4-5%. Book catalog available for #10 SASE and 1 first-class stamp. Manuscript and art guidelines available for SASE.

Tips: "Look at what we do before submitting. Follow the guidelines. I think publishers are doing fewer books and are therefore more selective in what they agree to publish. We are having more luck with shorter books with a sense of humor."

WHITEBIRD BOOKS, 200 Madison Ave., New York NY 10016. An imprint of Putnam and Grosset Group. See G.P. Putnam's Sons.

*❧WHITECAP BOOKS, 351 Lynn Ave., North Vancouver, British Columbia V7J 2C4 Canada. (604)980-9852. E-mail: whitecap@pinc.com. Book publisher. Publisher: Colleen MacMillan. Publishes 2 young readers/year; 2 middle readers/year.

Nonfiction: Young readers, middle readers: animal, nature/environment. Does not want to see text that writes down to children. Recently published *Welcome to the World of Wolves*, by Diane Swanson (ages 5-7); *Buffalo Sunrise*, by Diane Swanson (ages 9-11); and *The Day of the Twelve-Story Wave*, illustrations by Laura Cook (ages 9-11).

How to Contact/Writers: Nonfiction: Query. Reports on queries in 2 weeks; ms in 3 months. Publishes a book 6 months after acceptance. Will consider simultaneous submissions.

Illustration: Works with 1-2 illustrators/year. Reviews ms/illustration packages from artists. Query. Contact: Colleen MacMillan, publisher. Illustrations only: Query with samples—"never send original art." Contact: Colleen MacMillan, publisher. Samples returned with SASE if requested.

Photography: Buys stock. Contact: Colleen MacMillan, publisher. "We are always looking for outstanding wildlife photographs." Uses 35mm transparencies. Submit cover letter, client list, stock photo list.

Terms: Pays authors a negotiated royalty or purchases work outright. Offers advances. Pays illustrators by the project or royalty (depends on project). Pays photographers per photo (depends on project). Sends galleys to authors; dummies to illustrators. Originals returned to artist at job's completion unless discussed in advance. Ms guidelines available for SASE with international postal voucher for Canada.

Tips: "Writers and illustrators should spend time researching what's already available on the market. Whitecap specializes in nonfiction for children and adults."

ALBERT WHITMAN & COMPANY, 6340 Oakton St., Morton Grove IL 60053-2723. (708)581-0033. Fax: (847)581-0039. Book publisher. Editor-in-Chief: Kathleen Tucker. Publishes 30 books/year. 15% of books by first-time authors; 15% of books from agented authors. "We publish various categories, but we're mostly known for our concept books—books that deal with children's problems or concerns."

Fiction: Picture books, young readers, middle readers: adventure, animal, concept, contemporary, folktales, health, history, humor, multicultural, nature/environment, special needs. Middle readers: problem novels, suspense/mystery. "We are mostly interested in contemporary multicultural stories, set both in the U.S. and in other countries. We publish a wide variety of topics, and are interested in stories that will help children deal with their problems and concerns. Does not want to see "religion-oriented, ABCs, pop-up, romance, counting or any book that is supposed to be written in." Published *Turkey Pox*, by Laurie Halse Anderson, illustrated by Dorothy Donohue; *The Dog Who Lost His Bob*, by Tom and Laura McNeal, illustrated by John Sandford; and *Mississippi Going North*, by Sanna Anderson Baker, illustrated by Bill Farnsworth.

Nonfiction: Picture books, young readers, middle readers: animal, biography, concept, geography, health, history, hobbies, multicultural, music/dance, nature/environment, special needs. Middle readers: careers. Middle readers, young adults: biography, social issues. Does not want to see "religion, any books that have to be written in, biographies of living people." Recently published *The Fragile Frog*, by William P. Mara, illustrated by John R. Quinn; *Small Steps: The Year I Got Polio*, by Peg Kehret; and *I'm Tougher Than Asthma*, by Siri M. Carter and Alden R. Carter, photographs by Dan Young.

How to Contact/Writers: Fiction/Nonfiction: Submit complete ms. Reports on queries in 4-6 weeks; mss in 2 months. Publishes a book 18 months after acceptance. Will consider simultaneous submissions "but let us know if it is one" and previously published work "if out of print." Samples returned with SASE; samples filed.

Illustration: Works with 30 illustrators/year. Uses more color art than b&w. Reviews ms/illustration packages from artists. Submit all chapters of ms with any pieces of final art. Contact: Editorial. Illustrations only: Query with samples. Send slides or tearsheets. Reports back in 2 months.

Photography: Photographers should contact Editorial. Publishes books illustrated with photos but not stock photos—desires photos all taken for project. "Our books are for children and cover many topics; photos must be taken to match text. Books often show a child in a particular situation (e.g., kids being home-schooled, a sister whose brother is born prematurely)." Photographers should query with samples; send unsolicited photos by mail.

Terms: Pays authors royalty. Offers advances. Pays illustrators and photographers royalty. Sends galleys to authors; dummies to illustrators. Original artwork returned at job's completion. Ms/artist's guidelines available for SASE.

Tips: "In both picture books and nonfiction, we are seeking stories showing life in other cultures and the variety of multicultural life in the U.S. We also want fiction and nonfiction about mentally or physically challenged children—some recent topics have been AIDS, asthma, cerebral palsy. Look up some of our books first, to be sure your submission is appropriate for Albert Whitman & Co."

JOHN WILEY & SONS, INC., 605 Third Ave., New York NY 10158. (212)850-6206. Fax: (212)850-6095. Book publisher. Editor: Kate Bradford. Publishes 18 middle readers/year; 2 young adult titles/year. 20% of books by first-time authors. Publishes educational, nonfiction primarily science, nature and activities.

Nonfiction: Middle readers: activity books, animal, arts/crafts, biography, cooking, geography, health, history, hobbies, how-to, nature/environment, reference, science, self help. Young adults: activity books, arts/crafts, health, hobbies, how-to, nature/environment, reference, science, self help. Average word length middle readers—20,000-40,000. Published *The New York Public Library Incredible Earth*, by Janice Van Cleave, (ages 10-14, science reference); and *Online Kids*, by Preston Gralla (ages 8-12, computers); and *Earth-Friendly Toys*, by George Pfiffner, (8-12, crafts).

How to Contact/Writers: Query. Submit outline/synopsis and 2 sample chapters. Reports on queries in 1 month; mss in 3 months. Publishes a book 1 year after acceptance. Will consider simultaneous and previously published submissions.

Illustration: Works with 10 illustrators/year. Uses primarily black & white artwork. Reviews ms/illustration packages from artists. Query. Illustrations only: Query with samples, résumé, client list. Reports back only if interested. Samples filed. Original artwork returned at job's completion.

Terms: Pays authors royalty of 10-15% based on wholesale price. Offers advances. Pays illustrators by the project. Sends galleys to authors. Book catalog available for SAE.

Tips: "We're looking for topics and writers that can really engage kids' interest—plus we're always interested in a new twist on time-tested subjects."

WILLIAMSON PUBLISHING CO., Box 185, Charlotte VT 05445. (802)425-2102. Fax: (802)425-2199. Website: http://williamsonbooks.com. Book publisher. Editorial Director: Susan Williamson. Publishes 12-15 young readers titles/year. 50% of books by first-time authors; 20% of books from agented authors. Publishes "very successful nonfiction series (Kids Can!® Series—2,000,000 sold) on subjects such as nature, creative play, arts/crafts, geography. Successfully launched Little Hands® series for ages 2-6 and *Tales Alive*® series (tales plus activities)."

Fiction: Picture books, young readers, middle readers: folktales, multicultural.

Nonfiction: Young readers: activity books, animal, arts/crafts, career, concept, geography, health, history, hobbies, how-to, multicultural, music/dance, nature/environment, science, self-help, social issues. Does not want to see textbooks, picture books, fiction. "We are looking for books in which learning and doing are inseparable." Recently published *Super Science Concoctions*, by Jill Hauser, illustrated by Michael Kline (ages 6-12, exploring science); *Shapes, Sizes and More Surprises*, by Mary Tomczyk, illustrated by Loretta Trezzo Braren (ages 2-6, early learning skills); and *Tales of the Shimmering Sky*, retold by Susan Milord, illustrated by JoAnn Kitchel (ages 4 and up, multicultural tales with activities).

How to Contact/Writers: Query; submit outline/synopsis and 2 sample chapters. Reports on queries in 3-4 months; mss in 6 months. Publishes book, "depending on graphics, about 1 year" after acceptance.

Illustration: Works with 4 illustrators/year. Uses primarily b&w artwork; some 4-color.
Photography: Buys photos from freelancers. Contact: Susan Williamson, editorial director.
Terms: Pays authors royalty based on wholesale price. Offers advances. Pays illustrators by the project. Sends galleys to authors. Book catalog available for 8½×11 SAE and 4 first-class stamps; ms guidelines available for SASE.
Tips: "We're interested in interactive learning books with a creative approach packed with interesting information, written for young readers ages 2-6 and 4-10. In nonfiction children's publishing, we are looking for authors with a depth of knowledge shared with children through a warm, embracing style. Our publishing philosophy is based on the idea that all children can succeed and have positive learning experiences. Children's lasting learning experiences involve participation."

*WILLOWISP PRESS, 801 94th Ave. N., St. Petersburg FL 33702-2426. A division of PAGES, Inc. Imprints: Worthington Press, Riverbank Press, Hamburger Press. Book publisher. Writers contact: Acquisitions Editor. Illustrators contact: Art Director. Publishes 15-20 picture books/year; 6-8 young readers/year; 6-8 middle readers/year. 25% of books by first-time authors.
Fiction: Picture books: adventure, animal, contemporary, folktales, history, humor, multicultural, nature/environment, rhymes, concept books for preschool. Young readers: adventure, animal, contemporary, fantasy, folktales, history, humor, multicultural, nature/environment, sports, suspense/mystery. Middle readers: adventure, animal, anthology, contemporary, folktales, history, humor, multicultural, nature/environment, problem novels, romance, sports, suspense/mystery. Young adults: adventure, animal, anthology, contemporary, folktales, history, humor, multicultural, nature/environment, problem novels, romance, sports, suspense/mystery. No religious or violence. Average word length: picture books—350-1,000; beginning chapter books—3,000-4,000; middle readers—14,000-18,000; young adult—20,000-24,000. Recently published *Corey's Fire*, by Lee Wardlaw (grades 5 and up, novel); *Boomer's Journal*, by Ruth E. Kelley (grades 4-7, novel); and *The Mystery Artist*, by Pleasant DeSpain (grades K-3, picture book).
Nonfiction: Picture books: activity books, animal, biography, geography, history, how-to, multicultural, nature/environment, reference, science. Young readers: activity books, animal, arts/crafts, biography, geography, history, how-to, multicultural, nature/environment, reference, science, sports. Middle readers: activity books, animal, biography, careers, geography, history, hobbies, how-to, multicultural, nature/environment, reference, science, social issues, sports. Young adults: animal, biography, careers, concept, geography, history, hobbies, how-to, multicultural, nature/environment, reference, science, social issues, sports. No religious. Recently published *A Look Around Coral Reefs*, by Tracey E. Dils (ages K-3, environment); *For the Love of Chimps: the Jane Goodall Story*, by Martha Kendall (grades 5 and up, biography); *Wonderful Wolves of the Wild*, by Arlene Erlbach (grades 1-3, animal).
How to Contact/Writers: Fiction: Query. Submit outline/synopsis and 3 sample chapters. Nonfiction: Query with outline/synopsis and 1 sample chapter. "Only *one* manuscript at a time! Do *not* send original work when querying." Reports on queries/mss in 6-8 weeks. Publishes a book 6-12 months after acceptance. Will consider simultaneous submissions (if so noted). "SASE a must."
Illustration: Works with 10-12 illustrators/year. Reviews ms/illustration packages from artists "though almost all art is assigned independent of manuscript." Query; submit ms with dummy. Query with samples that can be kept on file; provide résumé. Reports in 2-3 months. Samples returned with SASE (and on request). Original artwork not returned at job's completion.
Photography: Purchases photos from freelancers. Contact: Acquisitions Editor. Buys stock and assigns work. Seeking photos related to environment, sports, animals. Photo captions required. Uses color slides. Submit cover letter, résumé, published samples, stock photo list.
Terms: Pays authors royalty or work purchased outright. Offers advance. Pays illustrators by the project. Photographers paid by the project or per photo. "Our terms are highly variable, both in reference to royalties and outright purchase." Ms and art guidelines available for SASE.
Tips: "Our books are intended for children to be able to read *themselves*, so please make sure language, length and sentence structure are age-appropriate. And keep the adult voice out!"

*WORLD BOOK, INC., 525 W. Monroe St., Chicago IL 60661. (312)258-3700. Fax: (312)258-3950. Website: http://www.worldbook.com. Book publisher. Product Development Director: Paul A. Kobasa. Executive Art Director: Roberta Dimmer. Publishes 6-10 picture books/year; 6-10 young readers/year; 6-10 middle readers/year; 15-20 young adult titles/year. 20% of books by first-time authors.
Nonfiction: Picture books: animal, concept, reference. Young readers: activity books, animal, arts/crafts, careers, concept, geography, health, reference. Middle readers: activity books, animal,

arts/crafts, careers, geography, health, history, hobbies, how-to, nature/environment, reference, science. Young adult: arts/crafts, careers, geography, health, history, hobbies, how-to, nature/environment, reference, science. Average word length: picture books—10-20 words; young readers—20-100 words; middle readers—100-400 words; young adults—500-2,000 words. Recently published *World Book Looks at Insects and Spiders* (ages 8-12); *World Book Children's Illustrated Atlas* (ages 7-12); and *Me and My Pet Cat* (ages 6-10).

How to Contact/Writers: Nonfiction: Submit outline/synopsis. Reports on queries/mss in 1-2 months. Publishes a book 18 months after acceptance. Will consider simultaneous submissions.

Illustration: Works with 10-30 illustrators/year. Illustrations only: Query with samples. Contact: Roberta Dimmer, executive art director. Reports only if interested. Samples returned with SASE; samples filed "if extra copies and if interested."

Photography: Buys stock and assigns work. Contact: Roberta Dimmer, executive art director. Needs broad spectrum; editorial concept, specific natural, physical and social science spectrum. Model/property releases required; captions required. Uses color 8×10 gloss and matte prints, 35mm, $2\frac{1}{4} \times 2\frac{1}{4}$, 4×5, 8×10 transparencies. Submit cover letter, résumé, promo piece (color and b&w).

Terms: Payment negotiated on project-by-project basis. Sends galleys to authors. Book catalog available for 9×12 SAE. Manuscript and art guidelines for SASE.

ZINO PRESS CHILDREN'S BOOK, Division of Knowledge Unlimited, 2348 Pinehurst Dr., Middleton WI 53562. (608)836-6660. Fax: (608)831-1570. Website: http://www.ku.com. Book publisher. Acquisitions Editor: Dave Schreiner. Publishes 2 picture books/year. Publishes rhyming stories and multicultural books.

Fiction: Rhyming picture books, young readers, middle readers: adventure, animal, contemporary, multicultural. "Text and art that is original and unique, and not a retold folktale. Works must reflect a range of lifestyles accurately and without stereotyping, and should express values that lead to tolerance, greater awareness of self and others, kindness and compassion." Does not want to see folktales; books about colors, vegetables, the alphabet, etc. or books without a plot. Average length: picture books—32 pages. Recently published *The Contrary Kid*, by Matt Cibula, illustrated by Brian Strassburg; *Slumgullion, the Executive Pig*, by Matt Cibala, illustrated by Tamara Boudreau.

Nonfiction: Picture books, young readers: history, multicultural, special needs. For multicultural work, author should be of culture written about or author should work with consultant of that culture. Does not want to see biographies of famous people. Average length: picture books—32-48 pages. Recently published *Sweet Words So Brave: The Story of African-American Literature*, by Barbara Curry and James Brodie, illustrated by Jerry Butler.

How to Contact/Writers: Fiction/Nonfiction: Submit complete ms. Reports in 12 weeks. Publishes a book 12-16 months after acceptance. Will consider simultansous submissions. Must enclose SASE.

Illustration: Works with 2-3 illustrators/yearly. Uses color artwork only. Reviews ms/illustration packages from artists. Submit ms with dummy. Contact: Dave Schreiner, acquisitions editor. Illustrations only: Query with samples. Reports in 1 month. Samples returned with SASE; some samples filed.

Photography: Buys stock images.

Terms: Pays authors royalty based on wholesale price or work purchased outright. Pays illustrators by the project. Pays photographers per photo. Sends galleys to authors; dummies to illustrators. Ms and artist's guidelines available for SASE.

Tips: "Take a fresh approach in submitting rhyming material. We are *not* looking for familiar stories or whimsical lines. We *are* looking for offbeat humor."

Magazines

Children's magazines are a great place for unpublished writers and illustrators to break into the market. Writer Kelly Milner-Halls began getting magazine assignments from the likes of *Highlights for Children* and *Crayola Kids* with ideas she generated as she researched her book *Dino-Trekking*. (See the Insider Report with Milner-Halls on page 176.) Illustrators, photographers and writers alike may find it easier to get book assignments if they have tearsheets or clips from magazines. Having magazine work under your belt shows you're professional and have experience working with editors and art directors and meeting deadlines.

But magazines aren't merely a breaking-in point. Writing, illustration and photo assignments for magazines let you see your work in print quickly, and the magazine market can offer steady work and regular paychecks. And a number of them pay on acceptance—book authors, illustrators and photographers may have to wait a year or two before receiving royalties from a project.

There are now several hundred kids' magazines found in homes, libraries and classrooms, about 110 of which are listed in this section. Magazines devoted to licensed characters (such as Barney or Batman), or publications that serve as promotions for toys or movies (which are primarily produced inhouse) are not included. What you will find are diverse magazines aimed at children of all ages and interests.

A VARIETY OF CHOICES

Some of the listings in this section are religious-oriented or special interest publications; others are general interest magazines. Though large circulation, ad-driven publications generally offer better pay rates than religious or nonprofit magazines, smaller magazines are more open to reviewing the work of newcomers, and can provide an excellent source for clips and tearsheets as you work your way toward more lucrative markets.

Publishers have acknowledged that children—and their interests—are as varied as adults. In this section you'll find magazines targeting boys (such as *Boys' Life* and *Boys' Quest*) and magazines targeting girls (like *Girls' Life* and *Seventeen*) just as you might find newsstand publications specifically for men or women.

Magazines for young people affiliated with almost every religious denomination are listed. You'll also notice specialized magazines devoted to certain sports, such as *Soccer Jr.* and *Black Belt for Kids*. Publications addressing various world cultures like *Skipping Stones* and *Faces* supply readers with ethnically diverse stories and artwork. The need for multicultural material is also present in general interest magazines (many editors have indicated specific multicultural needs within their listings). If you're not a member of the group you're interested in writing about, make sure to thoroughly research your subject to insure authenticity. Better yet, pass your work by an expert on the culture before submitting it.

Another plus for the children's magazine industry is that teachers are using fact-based educational publications—such as those teaching history, math or science—as supplements in their classrooms. As a result, it's not unusual for children to want their own personal subscriptions after initially being exposed to the magazines at school.

Remember kids today are worldly and want to know what's going on around them.

More and more informational adult magazines (like *Time*, *Sports Illustrated* and *Consumer Reports*) are publishing versions for kids. Since magazines have the advantage of timeliness, they can relay information about current events or interests much more quickly than books—and at less cost. The average one-year subscription, in fact, is about the same as the cost of one hardcover picture book.

TARGETING YOUR MARKET

No matter what the trends in the magazine industry, writers and illustrators must know what appeals to today's kids and target their material appropriately. Stu Slayen, editor of *What! A Magazine* for Canadian teens says for his market, talking to teenagers is your best research tool. (See the Insider Report with Slayen on page 206.) Getting in touch with your audience will help you write what interests them—and editors.

While it's important to know the current interests of children, you must also know the topics typically covered by different children's magazines. To help you match your work with the right publications, a Subject Index is included at the back of this book. This index lists both book and magazine publishers by the fiction and nonfiction subjects they're seeking.

Also included is a Photography Index listing all the children's magazines which use photos from freelancers. Use this in combination with the Subject Index, and you can quickly narrow your search of markets that suit your work. For instance, if you photograph sports, compare the Magazine list in the Photography Index with the lists under Sports in the Subject Index. Highlight the markets that appear on both lists, then read those listings to decide which are best for your work.

Writers can use the Subject Index in conjunction with the Age-Level Index to narrow their list of markets. Targeting the correct age-group with your submission is an important consideration. The majority of rejection slips are sent because the writer has not targeted a manuscript to the correct age. Few magazines are aimed at children of all ages, so your manuscript must be written for the audience level of the particular magazine you're submitting to.

To ensure you're on target, study both the listings and the actual publications. Each magazine has a different editorial philosophy. Language usage also varies between periodicals, as does the length of feature articles and the use of artwork and photographs. Reading the magazines you're considering submitting to is the best way to determine if your material is appropriate. Also, because magazines targeted to specific age-groups have a natural turnover in readership every few years, old topics (with a new slant) can be recycled.

Since many kids' magazines sell subscriptions through direct mail or schools, you may not be able to find a particular publication at bookstores or newsstands. Check your local library, or send for copies of the magazines you're interested in. Most magazines in this section have sample copies available and will send them for a SASE or small fee.

It's not uncommon for juvenile magazines to purchase all rights to both stories and artwork. Though work for hire is generally frowned upon among freelancers, well-respected magazines like *Highlights* and the magazines published by the Children's Better Health Institute buy all rights. But any clips acquired through these reputable magazines will be valuable. Other publications, such as those produced by the Carus Publishing Co. purchase only first rights, allowing writers and illustrators to sell the work again, perhaps to a book publisher. Writers, illustrators and photographers must decide for themselves whether it's worth it to sell all rights to a piece.

It's important to carefully review the listings of markets you wish to target for their preferred method of receiving submissions. Some editors may wish to see an entire manuscript; others prefer a query letter and outline, especially for nonfiction articles (with which accompanying photographs are generally welcome). If you're an artist or photographer, review the listing for the types of samples the art director wants to see. Following a magazine's guidelines, and sending only your best work improves your chances of having work accepted in this competitive market.

ADVOCATE, PKA'S PUBLICATION, (formerly *PKA's Advocate*), PKA Publication, 301A Rolling Hills Park, Prattsville NY 12468. (518)299-3103. Articles/Fiction Editor: Remington Wright. Art Director/Photo Editor: CJ Karlie. Bimonthly tabloid. Estab. 1987. Circ. 12,000. "*Advocate* advocates good writers and quality writings. We publish art, fiction, photos and poetry. *Advocate*'s submitters are talented people of all ages who do not earn their livings as writers. We wish to promote the arts and to give those we publish the opportunity to be published through a for-profit means rather than in a not-for-profit way. We do this by selling advertising and offering reading entertainment."

Fiction: Middle readers and young adults/teens: adventure, animal, contemporary, fantasy, folktales, health, humorous, nature/environment, problem-solving, romance, science fiction, sports, suspense/mystery. Looks for "well written, entertaining work, whether fiction or nonfiction." Buys approximately 42 mss/year. Average word length: 1,500. Byline given. Wants to see more humorous material, nature/environment and romantic comedy.

Nonfiction: Middle readers and young adults/teens: animal, arts/crafts, biography, careers, concept, cooking, fashion, games/puzzles, geography, history, hobbies, how-to, humorous, interview/profile, nature/environment, problem-solving, science, social issues, sports, travel. Buys 10 mss/year. Average word length: 1,500. Byline given.

Poetry: Reviews poetry any length.

How to Contact/Writers: Fiction/nonfiction: send complete ms. Reports on queries in 4-6 weeks/mss in 6-8 weeks. Publishes ms 2-18 months after acceptance.

Illustration: Uses b&w artwork only. Uses cartoons. Reviews ms/illustration packages from artists. Submit a photo print (b&w or color), an excellent copy of work (no larger than 8 × 10) or original. Illustrations only: "Send previous unpublished art with SASE, please." Reports in 2 months. Samples returned with SASE; samples not filed. Credit line given.

Photography: Buys photos from freelancers. Model/property releases required. Uses color and b&w prints. Send unsolicited photos by mail with SASE. Reports in 2 months. Wants nature, artistic and humorous photos.

Terms: Pays on publication. Acquires first rights for mss, artwork and photographs. Pays in copies. Original work returned upon job's completion. Sample copies for $4. Writer's/illustrator/photo guidelines for SASE.

Tips: "Artists and photographers should keep in mind that we are a b&w paper."

AIM MAGAZINE, America's Intercultural Magazine, P.O. Box 20554, Chicago IL 60620. (312)874-6184. Articles Editor: Ruth Apilado. Fiction Editor: Mark Boone. Photo Editor: Betty Lewis. Quarterly magazine. Circ. 8,000. Readers are high school and college students, teachers, adults interested in helping, through the written word, to create a more equitable world. 15% of material aimed at juvenile audience.

Fiction: Young adults: history, multicultural, "stories with social significance." Wants stories that teach children that people are more alike than they are different. Does not want to see religious fiction. Buys 20 mss/year. Average word length: 1,000-4,000. Byline given.

Nonfiction: Young adults: interview/profile, multicultural, "stuff with social significance." Does not want to see religious nonfiction. Buys 20 mss/year. Average word length: 500-2,000. Byline given.

How to Contact/Writers: Fiction: Send complete ms. Nonfiction: Query with published clips. Reports on queries/mss in 1 month. Will consider simultaneous submissions.

Illustration: Buys 20 illustrations/issue. Preferred theme: Overcoming social injustices through nonviolent means. Reviews ms/illustration packages from artists. Query first. Illustrations only: Query with tearsheets. Reports on art samples in 2 months. Original artwork returned at job's completion "if desired." Credit line given.

Photography: Wants "photos of activists who are trying to contribute to social improvement."

Terms: Pays on publication. Buys first North American serial rights. Pays $15-25 for stories/articles. Pays in contributor copies if copies are requested. Pays $5-25 for b&w cover illustration. Photographers paid by the project (range: $10-15). Sample copies for $4.

Tips: "We need material of social significance, stuff that will help promote racial harmony and peace and illustrate the stupidity of racism."

AMERICAN CHEERLEADER, Lifestyle Publications LLC, 350 W. 50th St., Suite 2AA, New York NY 10019. (212)265-8890. Editor: Julie Davis. Bimonthly magazine. Estab. 1995. Circ. 125,000. Special interest teen magazine for kids who cheer.
Nonfiction: Young adults: careers, fashion, health, how-to, problem-solving, sports, cheerleading specific material. "We're looking for authors who know cheerleading." Buys 50 mss/year. Average word length: 200-1,000. Byline given.
How to Contact/Writers: Query with published clips. Reports on queries/mss in 3 months. Publishes ms 3 months after acceptance. Will consider electronic submission via disk or modem.
Illustration: Buys 6 illustrations/issue; 30-50 illustrations/year. Works on assignment only. Reviews ms/illustration packages from artists. Illustrations only: Query with samples; arrange portfolio review. Reports only if interested. Samples filed. Originals not returned at job's completion. Credit line given.
Photography: Buys photos from freelancers. Looking for cheerleading at different sports games, events, etc. Uses 35mm, 2¼×2¼ transparencies. Query with samples; provide résumé, business card, tearsheets to be kept on file. "After sending query, we'll set up an interview." Reports only if interested.
Terms: Pays on publication. Buy all rights for mss, artwork and photographs. Pays $100-1,000 for stories. Pays illustrators $50-200 for b&w inside, $100-300 for color inside. Pays photographers by the project $300-800; per photo (range: $25-100). Sample copies for $5.
Tips: "Authors: Absolutely must have cheerleading background. Photographers and illustrators must have teen magazine experience or high profile experience."

ASPCA ANIMAL WATCH, ASPCA, 424 E. 92nd St., New York NY 10128. (212)876-7700, ext. 4441. Fax: (212)410-0087. Art Director: Amber Alliger. Quarterly magazine. Estab. 1951. Circ. 200,000. Focuses on animal issues. 15% of publication aimed at juvenile market.
Nonfiction: Animal, multicultural, nature/environment.
Illustration: Buys 5 illustrations/issue; 12 illustrations/year. Works on assignment only. Reviews ms/illustration packages from artists. Send ms with dummy. Illustrations only: Send color tearsheets, quality photocopies to hold on file. Reports back only if interested. Samples returned with SASE or kept on file. Originals returned upon job's completion. Credit line given.
Photography: Looking for animal care, animal abuse, and animal protection. Model/property releases required. Uses 8×10, glossy color/b&w prints; 35mm, 2¼×2¼ and 4×5 transparencies. Photographers should send stock list. Reports in 2 months.
Terms: Pays on publication. Buys one-time rights for artwork/photographs. Pays illustrators $100-150 for color cover; $100-125 for b&w, $100-200 for color inside. Photographers paid per photo (range: $50-100). Sample copies for 9×12 SASE with $2 postage. Writer's guidelines not available. Illustrator's/photo guidelines for SASE.
Tips: Trends include "more educational, more interactive" material. Children's section is "Eye on Animals." Not interested in realism. "Only cartoon or creative work needed."

BABYBUG, Carus Publishing Company, P.O. Box 300, Peru IL 61354. (815)224-6656. Editor: Paula Morrow. Art Director: Suzanne Beck. Published 9 times/year (every 6 weeks). Estab. 1994. "A listening and looking magazine for infants and toddlers ages 6 to 24 months. *Babybug* is 6 ¼×7, 24 pages long, printed in large type (26-point) on high-quality cardboard stock with rounded corners and no staples."
Fiction: Looking for very simple and concrete stories, 4-6 short sentences maximum.
Nonfiction: Must use very basic words and concepts, 10 words maximum.
Poetry: Maximum length 8 lines. Looking for rhythmic, rhyming poems.
How to Contact/Writers: "Please do not query first." Send complete ms with SASE. "Submissions without SASE will be discarded." Reports in 6-8 weeks.
Illustration: Uses color artwork only. Works on assignment only. Reviews ms/illustration packages from artists. "The manuscripts will be evaluated for quality of concept and text before the art is considered." Contact: Paula Morrow, editor. Illustrations only: Send tearsheets or photo prints/photocopies with SASE. "Submissions without SASE will be discarded." Reports in 12 weeks. Samples filed.
Terms: Pays on publication for mss; after delivery of completed assignment for illustrators. Buys first rights with reprint option or (in some cases) all rights. Original artwork returned at job's completion. Rates vary ($25 minimum for mss; $250 minimum for art). Sample copy for $5. Guidelines free for SASE.
Tips: "*Babybug* would like to reach as many children's authors and artists as possible for original contributions, but our standards are very high, and we will accept only top-quality material.

Before attempting to write for *Babybug*, be sure to familiarize yourself with this age child." (See listings for *Cricket*, *Ladybug* and *Spider*.)

*BECKETT PUBLICATIONS, 15850 Dallas Parkway, Dallas TX 75248. (214)991-6657. Fax: (214)991-8930. Website: http://www.beckett.com. Articles Editor: Mike Payne. Art Director: Judi Smalling. Photo Editor: Doug Williams. Monthly magazine. Estab. 1984. "Articles in Beckett® are hobby-related and deal with the sports world's hottest superstars."
● Beckett Publications' magazines include *Beckett Baseball Card Monthly*, *Beckett Basketball Monthly*, *Beckett Football Card Monthly*, *Beckett Future Stars*, *Beckett Hockey Monthly* and *Beckett Racing Monthly*.
Fiction: Young adults/teens: fantasy, history, humorous, sports.
Nonfiction: Picture-oriented material: humorous, sports. Young readers, middle readers: hobbies, humorous, sports. Young adults/teens: history, hobbies, humorous, sports. Buys 8-10 mss/year. Average word length: 500-2,000. Byline sometimes given.
How to Contact/Writers: Fiction/Nonfiction: Query. Reports on queries/mss in 1 month. Publishes ms 2 months after acceptance. Will consider simultaneous submissions, electronic submissions via disk or modem and some previously published work.
Illustration: Buys 2 illustrations/issue; 24 illustrations/year. Reviews ms/illustration packages from artists. Query. Contact: Judi Smalling, art director. Illustrations only: Query with samples. Contact: Judi Smalling, art director. Reports in 1 month. Samples returned with SASE. Originals returned to artist at job's completion. Credit line given.
Photography: Looks for action sports photos (popular league players). Uses color prints and 35mm, 2¼×2¼ transparencies. Query with samples. Reports in 4-6 weeks.
Terms: Pays on acceptance. Buys first North American serial rights for mss. Buys one-time North American serial rights for photos. Pays $150-250 for stories and articles. Pays photographers per photo (range: $2.95). Writer's/illustrator's/photo guidelines free for SASE.

*BLACK BELT FOR KIDS, Rainbow Publications, P.O. Box 918, Santa Clarita CA 91380. (805)257-4066. Fax: (805)257-3028. Articles Editor: Robert Young. Bimonthly. Special insert in *Karate/Kung Fu Illustrated* magazine. Estab. 1995. Circ. 35,000. "We publish instructional, inspirational and philosophical pieces written for children who study martial arts."
Nonfiction: Picture-oriented material: health, history, humorous, sports, travel. Young readers: health, history, humorous, interview/profile, sports, travel. Middle readers, young adults/teens: health, history, how-to, humorous, interview/profile, sports, travel. Does not want to see profiles written by parents about their own kid. Buys 10-15 mss/year. Average word length: 800-1,500. Byline given.
How to Contact/Writers: Nonfiction: Query. Reports on queries/mss in 1 month. Publishes ms 6 months after acceptance. Will consider electronic submissions via disk or modem.
Terms: Pays on publication. Buys all rights for mss. Pays $100-200 for articles. Sample copies free for 9×12 SAE and 6 first-class stamps. Writer's guidelines free for SASE.
Tips: "Make it fun."

THE BLUFTON NEWS PUBLISHING AND PRINTING COMPANY, 103 N. Main St., Bluffton OH 45817. See listings for *Boys' Quest* and *Hopscotch*.

BOY SCOUTS OF AMERICA, 1325 W. Walnut Lane, P.O. Box 152079, Irving TX 75015-2079. See listings for *Boys' Life* and *Exploring*.

BOYS' LIFE, Boy Scouts of America, 1325 W. Walnut Hill Lane, P.O. Box 152079, Irving TX 75015-2079. (214)580-2000. Website: http://www.bsa.scouting.org. Managing Editor: J.D. Owen. Articles Editor: Michael Goldman. Fiction Editor: Shannon Lowry. Director of Design: Joseph P. Connolly. Art Director: Elizabeth Hardaway Morgan. Monthly magazine. Estab. 1911. Circ. 1,300,000. *Boys' Life* is "a general interest magazine for boys 8 to 18 who are members of the Cub Scouts, Boy Scouts or Explorers; a general interest magazine for all boys."

✱ THE ASTERISK before a listing indicates the listing is new in this edition.

● *Boys' Life* was ranked 13th on the 1996 *Writer's Digest* Fiction 50, the magazine's annual list of top fiction markets.

Fiction: Middle readers: adventure, animal, contemporary, fantasy, history, humor, problem-solving, science fiction, sports, spy/mystery. Does not want to see "talking animals and adult reminiscence." Buys 12 mss/year. Average word length: 1,000-1,500. Byline given.

Nonfiction: "Subject matter is broad. We cover everything from professional sports to American history to how to pack a canoe. A look at a current list of the BSA's more than 100 merit badge pamphlets gives an idea of the wide range of subjects possible. Even better, look at a year's worth of recent issues. Column headings are science, nature, earth, health, sports, space and aviation, cars, computers, entertainment, pets, history, music and others." Average word length: 500-1,500. Columns 300-750 words. Byline given.

How to Contact/Writers: Fiction: Send complete ms with SASE. Nonfiction: query with SASE for response. Reports on queries/mss in 6-8 weeks.

Illustration: Buys 5-7 illustrations/issue; 23-50 illustrations/year. Works on assignment only. Reviews ms/illustration packages from artists. "Query first." Illustrations only: Send tearsheets. Reports on art samples only if interested. Original artwork returned at job's completion.

Terms: Buys first rights. Pays $750 and up for fiction; $400-1,500 for major articles; $150-400 for columns; $250-300 for how-to features. Sample copies for $2.50 plus 9 × 12 SASE. Writer's/illustrator's/photo guidelines available for SASE.

Tips: "I strongly urge you to study at least a year's issues to better understand type of material published. Articles for *Boys' Life* must interest and entertain boys ages 8 to 18. Write for a boy you know who is 12. Our readers demand crisp, punchy writing in relatively short, straightforward sentences. The editors demand well-reported articles that demonstrate high standards of journalism. We follow *The New York Times* manual of style and usage. All submissions must be accompanied by SASE with adequate postage." (See listing for *Exploring*.)

*BOYS' QUEST, The Bluffton News Publishing and Printing Co., 103 N. Main St., Bluffton OH 45817. (419)358-4610. Fax: (419)358-5027. Articles Editor: Marilyn Edwards. Bimonthly magazine. Estab. 1995.

Fiction: Young readers, middle readers: adventure, animal, history, humorous, nature/environment, problem-solving, sports, jokes, building, cooking, cartoons, riddles. Does not want to see violence, teenage themes. Buys 15-20 mss/year. Average word length: 200-500. Byline given.

Nonfiction: Young readers, middle readers: animal, arts/crafts, biography, cooking, games/puzzles, history, how-to, humorous, math, problem-solving, science. No nonfiction with photos. Buys 15-20 mss/year. Average word length: 200-500. Byline given.

Poetry: Reviews poetry. Maximum length: 21 lines. Limit submissions to 6 poems.

How to Contact/Writers: Fiction/Nonfiction: Query; send complete ms. Reports on queries in 1-2 weeks; mss in 3 weeks (if rejected); 3-4 months (if scheduled). Publishes ms 3 months-3 years after acceptance. Will consider simultaneous submissions and previously published work.

Illustration: Buys 6 illustrations/issue; 36-45 illustrations/year. Uses b&w artwork only. Works on assignment only. Reviews ms/illustration packages from artists. Send ms with dummy. Contact: Marilyn Edwards, editor. Illustrations only: Query with samples, arrange portfolio review. Send portfolio, tearsheets. Contact: Becky Jackman, editorial assistant. Reports in 2 weeks. Samples returned with SASE; samples filed.Credit line given.

Photography: Looks mostly for animal and sport photos. Model/property releases required. Uses b&w, 5 × 7 or 3 × 5 prints. Query with samples; send unsolicited photos by mail. Reports in 2-3 weeks.

Terms: Pays on publication. Buys first North American serial rights for mss. Buys first rights for artwork. Pays 5¢/word for stories and articles. Additional payment for ms/illustration packages and for photos accompanying articles. Pays $150-200 for color cover; $25-35 for b&w. Pays photographers per photo (range: $5-10). Originals returned to artist at job's completion. Sample copies for $3. Writer's/illustrator's/photo guidelines free for SASE.

Tips: "Send SASE with correct postage. No faxed material."

BREAD FOR GOD'S CHILDREN, Bread Ministries, Inc., P.O. Box 1017, Arcadia FL 34265. (941)494-6214. Editor: Judith M. Gibbs. Monthly magazine. Estab. 1972. Circ. 10,000 (US and Canada). "*Bread* is designed as a teaching tool for Christian families." 85% of publication aimed at juvenile market.

Fiction: Young readers, middle readers, young adults/teens: adventure, contemporary, history, humorous, nature/environment, problem-solving, sports. Looks for "teaching stories that portray Christian lifestyles without preaching." Buys approximately 20 mss/year. Average word length: 900-1,500 (for teens); 600-900 (for young children). Byline given.

Nonfiction: Middle readers and young adult/teens: history, problem-solving, religion, sports, social issues. "We do not want anything detrimental of solid family values." Buys 3-4 mss/year. Average word length: 500-800. Byline given.

How to Contact/Writers: Fiction/nonfiction: Send complete ms. Reports on mss in 2 weeks-6 months "if considered for use." Will consider simultaneous submissions and previously published work.

Terms: Pays on publication. Pays $30-40 for stories; $10-20 for articles. Sample copies free for 9×12 SAE and 6 first-class stamps (for 3 copies).

Tips: "Know the readership . . . know the publisher's guidelines. Edit carefully for content and grammar."

CALLIOPE, World History for Young People, Cobblestone Publishing, Inc., 7 School St., Peterborough NH 03458. (603)924-7209. Managing Editor: Denise L. Babcock. Art Director: Ellen Klempner Beguin. Magazine published 5 times/year. "*Calliope* covers world history (East/West) and lively, original approaches to the subject are the primary concerns of the editors in choosing material."

Fiction: Middle readers and young adults: adventure, folktales, history, biographical fiction. Material must relate to forthcoming themes. Word length: up to 800.

Nonfiction: Middle readers and young adults: arts/crafts, biography, cooking, games/puzzles, history. Material must relate to forthcoming themes. Word length: 300-800.

Poetry: Maximum line length: 100. Wants "clear, objective imagery. Serious and light verse considered."

How to Contact/Writers: "A query must consist of the following to be considered (please use nonerasable paper): a brief cover letter stating subject and word length of the proposed article; a detailed one-page outline explaining the information to be presented in the article; an extensive bibliography of materials the author intends to use in preparing the article; a self-addressed stamped envelope. Writers new to *Calliope* should send a writing sample with query. If you would like to know if your query has been received, please also include a stamped postcard that requests acknowledgment of receipt. In all correspondence, please include your complete address as well as a telephone number where you can be reached. A writer may send as many queries for one issue as he or she wishes, but each query must have a separate cover letter, outline, bibliography and SASE. Telephone queries are not accepted. Handwritten queries will not be considered. Queries may be submitted at any time, but queries sent well in advance of deadline *may not be answered for several months*. Go-aheads requesting material proposed in queries are usually sent five months prior to publication date. Unused queries will be returned approximately three to four months prior to publication date."

Illustration: Illustrations only: Send tearsheets, photocopies. Original work returned upon job's completion (upon written request).

Photography: Buys photos from freelancers. Wants photos pertaining to any forthcoming themes. Uses b&w/color prints, 35 mm transparencies. Send unsolicited photos by mail (on speculation).

Terms: Buys all rights for mss and artwork. Pays 20-25¢/word for stories/articles. Pays on an individual basis for poetry, activities, games/puzzles. "Covers are assigned and paid on an individual basis." Pays photographers per photo ($15-100 for b&w; $25-100 for color). Sample copy for $3.95 and SAE with $1.05 postage. Writer's/illustrator's/photo guidelines for SASE. (See listings for *Cobblestone, The History Magazine for Young People; Faces, The Magazine About People*; and *Odyssey, Science That's Out of This World.*)

CARUS PUBLISHING COMPANY, (formerly Carus Corporation), P.O. Box 300, Peru IL 61354. See listing for *Babybug, Cricket, Ladybug* and *Spider*.

*CAT FANCY, The Magazine for Responsible Cat Owners, Fancy Publications, P.O. Box 6050, Mission Viejo CA 92690. (714)855-8822. Fax: (714)855-3045. Articles Editor: Debbie Phillips-Donaldson. Art Director: David Blum. Monthly magazine. Estab. 1965. Circ. 300,000. "Our magazine is for cat owners who want to know more about how to care for their pets in a responsible manner. We want to see stories and articles showing children relating to or learning about cats in a positive, responsible way. We'd love to see more craft projects for children." 3% of material aimed at juvenile audience.

Fiction: Middle readers, young adults: animal (all cat-related). Does not want to see stories in which cats talk. Buys 3-9 mss/year. Average word length: 750-1,000. Byline given. Never wants to see work showing cats being treated abusively or irresponsibly or work that puts cats in a negative light. Never use mss written from cats' point of view.

Nonfiction: Middle readers, young adults: animal, arts/crafts (all cat-related). Buys 3-9 mss/year. Average word length: 450-1,000. Byline given. Would like to see more crafts and how-to pieces for children.

Poetry: Reviews short poems only. "No more than 10 poems per submission please."

How To Contact/Writers: Fiction/nonfiction: Send query only. Reports on queries in 1-2 months; mss in 2-3 months. Publishes ms (juvenile) 4 months after acceptance.

Illustration: Buys 10-12 illustrations/year. "Most of our illustrations are assigned or submitted with a story. We look for realistic images of cats done with pen and ink (no pencil)." Illustration only: "Submit photocopies of work; samples of spot art possibilities." Reports in 1-2 months. Credit line given.

Photography: "Cats only, in excellent focus and properly lit. Send SASE for photo needs and submit according to them."

Terms: Pays on publication. Buys first North American serial rights. Buys one-time rights for artwork and photos. Originals returned to artist at job's completion. Pays $50-200 for stories; $100-400 for articles. Pays illustrators $20 for b&w inside; $50-200 for color inside. Photographers paid per photo (range: $35-200). Sample copies for $5.50. Writer's/artist's/photo guidelines free for #10 SAE and 1 first-class stamp.

Tips: "Our 'Kids for Cats' department is most open. Perhaps the most important tip I can give is: Consider what 9 to 11 year olds want to know about cats and what they enjoy most about cats, and address that topic in a style appropriate for them. Writers, keep your writing concise, and don't be afraid to try again after a rejection. Illustrators, we use illustrations mainly as spot art; occasionally we make assignments to illustrators whose spot art we've used before."

CHALLENGE, Brotherhood Commission, SBC, 1548 Poplar Ave., Memphis TN 38104. (901)272-2461. Fax: (901)726-5540. E-mail: compuserve70423,2340. Articles Editor: Jeno Smith. Art Director: Roy White. Monthly magazine. Circ. 30,000. Magazine contains youth interests, sports, crafts, sports personalities, religious.

Fiction: Young adults/teens: adventure, animal, contemporary, health, history, nature/environment, problem-solving, religious, sports.

Nonfiction: young adults/teens: animal, arts/crafts, biography, games/puzzles, history, interview/profile, problem-solving. Young men: career, geography, health, hobbies, how-to, humorous, multicultural, nature/environment, religion, science, social issues, sports, travel, youth issues. Looking for stories on sports heroes with Christian testimony. Buys 36 mss/year. Average word length: 700-900. Byline given.

How to Contact/Writers: Nonfiction: Send complete ms. Reports on queries/mss in 3-5 weeks. Will consider simultaneous submissions.

Illustration: Buys 1-2 illustrations/issue; 12-24 illustrations/year. Reports in 3-5 weeks. Samples returned with SASE; samples filed. Credit line given.

Photography: Purchases photography from freelancers. Wants b&w photos with youth appeal.

Terms: Pays on publication. Buys one-time and reprint rights. Pays $20-100 for articles and stories. $5-20 for b&w, $10-35 for color inside. Photographers paid per photo (range: $5-100) or by project (range: $20-200). Originals returned to artist at job's completion. Sample copies for $4. Writer's guidelines for SAE and 1 first-class stamp.

Tips: "We prefer photo essays and articles about teenagers and teen activities, interests and issues (sports, nature, health, hobbies). Most open to new writers are features on sports figures who offer good moral guidelines to youth, especially those with an effective Christian testimony. We appreciate articles that encourage Christ-like character."

✦CHICKADEE MAGAZINE, for Young Children from OWL, Owl Communications, 179 John St., Suite 500, Toronto, Ontario M5T 3G5 Canada. (416)971-5275. Fax: (416)971-5294. E-mail: owlcom@owl.on.ca. Website: http://www.owl.on.ca. Editor-in-Chief: Nyla Ahmad. Managing Editor: Carolyn Meredith. Art Director: Tim Davin. Magazine published 10 times/year. Estab. 1979. Circ. 100,000. "*Chickadee* is a hands-on publication designed to interest 3-8 year olds in science, nature and the world around them. It features games, stories, crafts, experiments."

🍁 **THE MAPLE LEAF** before a listing indicates that the market is Canadian.

Fiction: Picture-oriented material: young readers: animal, humorous, nature/environment. Does not want to see religious, anthropomorphic animal, romance material, material that talks down to kids. Buys 8 mss/year. Average word length: 800-900. Byline given.

Nonfiction: Picture-oriented material, young readers: animal (facts/characteristics), arts/crafts, games/puzzles, humorous, nature/environment, science. Does not want to see religious material. Buys 2-5 mss/year. Average word length: 300-800. Byline given.

Poetry: Limit submissions to 5 poems at a time.

How to Contact/Writers: Fiction/nonfiction: Send complete ms. SASE for answer and return of ms. Reports on mss in 3 months. Will consider simultaneous submissions. "We prefer to read complete manuscript on speculation."

Illustration: Buys 3-5 illustrations/issue; 40 illustrations/year. Preferred theme or style: realism/humor (but not cartoons). Works on assignment only. Illustration only: Send promo sheet. Reports on art samples only if interested. Samples returned with SASE. Credit line given.

Photography: Looking for animal (mammal, insect, reptile, fish, etc.) and nature photos. Uses 35mm and $2\frac{1}{4} \times 2\frac{1}{4}$ transparencies. Write to request photo package for $1 money order, attention Ekaterina Gitlin, researcher.

Terms: Pays on publication. Buys all rights for mss. Buys one-time rights for photos. Original artwork returned at job's completion. Pays $10-250 for stories. Pays illustrators $100-650 for color inside, pays photographers per photo (range: $100-350). Sample copies for $4. Writer's guidelines free.

Tips: "The magazine publishes fiction and nonfiction that encourages kids to read and learn more about the world around them. The majority of *Chickadee*'s content is stories, puzzles, activities and observation games for young kids to enjoy on their own. Each issue also includes a longer story or poem that can be enjoyed by older kids." (See listing for *OWL*.)

CHILD LIFE, Children's Better Health Institute, 1100 Waterway Blvd., P.O. Box 567, Indianapolis IN 46206. Parcels and packages: please send to 1100 Waterway Blvd., 46202. (317)636-8881. Editor: Lise Hoffman. Art Director: Rebecca Ray. Magazine published 8 times/year. Estab. 1921. Circ. 80,000. Targeted toward kids ages 9-11. Focuses on health, sports, fitness, nutrition, safety, general interests, and the nostalgia of *Child Life*'s early days.

Nonfiction: Middle readers: animal, arts/crafts, biography, careers, cooking, games/puzzles, health, humorous, interview/profile, sports. Buys 20-25 nonfiction mss/year. Maximum word length: 800. Byline given.

How to Contact/Writers: Nonfiction: Send complete ms. No queries please. Reports on mss in 3 months. Will not consider previously published material.

Illustration: Buys 3 illustrations/issue. "Need realistic styles especially." Works on assignment only. Illustrations only: Send query, résumé and portfolio to art director. Samples must be accompanied by SASE for response and/or return. Reports only if interested. Credit line given.

Photography: Purchases professional quality photos with accompanying ms only.

Terms: Pays on publication. Writers paid 10-12¢/word for stories/articles. Buys all rights. Pays illustrators $275/cover; $35-90 b&w inside; $70-155 color inside. For artwork, buys all rights. Pays photographers per photo (range: $25-30). Buys one-time rights for photographs. Writer's guidelines available for SASE.

Tips: "Follow the writers' guidelines and examples in the *current* magazines to the 'T.' Once that is achieved, it's much easier to catch the editor's attention. We need profiles of young athletes, aged 9-11, and their sports (1,000 words maximum) and short pieces on outdoor games/exercise (300 words maximum). Submit all material 8-10 months in advance. We have used adult profiles occasionally. Already covered golf, baseball, basketball, track, sailing, circus, sky diving, tennis, beach volleyball and hockey. We also need lowfat recipes for mini-meals and healthful snacks for monthly feature. Avoid sugar, whole eggs (egg whites acceptable), red meat, chocolate (alas!), and shortening (when possible). Test recipes before sending them. No dessert recipes, please. (See listings for *Children's Digest*, *Children's Playmate*, *Humpty Dumpty's Magazine*, *Jack And Jill*, *Turtle Magazine* and *U*S*Kids*.)

CHILDREN'S BETTER HEALTH INSTITUTE, 1100 Waterway Blvd., P.O. Box 567, Indianapolis IN 46206. See listings for *Child Life*, *Children's Digest*, *Children's Playmate*, *Humpty Dumpty's Magazine*, *Jack And Jill*, *Turtle* and *U*S* Kids*.

CHILDREN'S DIGEST, Children's Better Health Institute, 1100 Waterway Blvd., Box 567, Indianapolis IN 46206. (317)636-8881. Editor: Layne Cameron. Art Director: Mary Stropoli. Magazine published 8 times/year. Estab. 1950. Circ. 125,000. For preteens; approximately 33% of content is health-related.

Mary Engelbreit, whose fanciful illustrations of children are recognized worldwide, was approached by *Child Life* magazine to create a cover for their special 75th anniversary issue. "*Child Life* magazine covers from long ago influenced my style," she notes. "In my work, you'll see the black backgrounds and the 1920s-looking children. It was a real treat to be asked to create an image for *Child Life*, one of my favorite magazines!"

Fiction: Middle readers: adventure, animal, contemporary, fantasy, folktales, health, history, humorous, nature/environment, problem-solving, science fiction, sports, suspense/mystery. Buys 25 mss/year. Average word length: 500-1,500. Byline given.

Nonfiction: Middle readers: animal, arts/crafts, biography, cooking, education, games/puzzles, geography, health, history, hobbies, how-to, humorous, interview/profile, nature/environment, science, sports, travel. Buys 16-20 mss/year. Average word length: 500-1,200. Byline given.

Poetry: Maximum length: 20-25 lines.

How to Contact/Writers: Fiction/nonfiction: Send complete ms. SASE. Reports on mss in 10 weeks.

Illustration: Reviews ms/illustration packages from artists. Works on assignment only. Query first. Illustrations only: Send résumé and/or slides or tearsheets to illustrate work; query with samples. Reports on art samples in 8-10 weeks. Credit line given.

Photography: Purchases photos with accompanying ms only. Model/property releases required; captions required. Uses 35mm transparencies.

Terms: Pays on acceptance for illustrators, publication for writers. Buys all rights for mss and artwork; one-time rights for photos. Pays 12¢/word for accepted articles. Pays $275 for color cover illustration; $35-90 for b&w, $70-155 for color inside. Photographers paid per photo (range: $10-50). Sample copies for $1.25. Writer's/illustrator's guidelines for SAE and 1 first-class stamp. (See listings for *Child Life*, *Children's Playmate*, *Humpty Dumpty's Magazine*, *Jack And Jill*, *Turtle Magazine* and *U*S* Kids*.)

CHILDREN'S PLAYMATE, Children's Better Health Institute, 1100 Waterway Blvd., Box 567, Indianapolis IN 46206. (317)636-8881. Editor: Terry Harshman. Art Director: Chuck Horsman. Magazine published 8 times/year. Estab. 1929. Circ. 135,000. For children between 6 and 8 years; approximately 50% of content is health-related.

Fiction: Young readers: animal, contemporary, fantasy, folktales, history, humorous, science fiction, sports, suspense/mystery/adventure. Buys 25 mss/year. Average word length: 200-700. Byline given.

Nonfiction: Young readers: animal, arts/crafts, biography, cooking, games/puzzles, health, history, how-to, humorous, sports, travel. Buys 16-20 mss/year. Average word length: 200-700. Byline given.

Poetry: Maximum length: 20-25 lines.

How to Contact/Writers: Fiction/nonfiction: Send complete ms. Reports on mss in 8-12 weeks.

Illustration: Works on assignment only. Reviews ms/illustration packages from artists. Query first.

Photography: Buys photos with accompanying ms only. Model/property releases required; captions required. Uses 35mm transparencies. Send completed ms with transparencies.

Terms: Pays on publication for illustrators and writers. Buys all rights for mss and artwork; one-time rights for photos. Pays 17¢/word for assigned articles. Pays $275 for color cover illustration; $35-90 for b&w inside; $70-155 for color inside. Pays photographers per photo (range: $10-75). Sample copy $1.25. Writer's/illustrator's guidelines for SASE. (See listings for *Child Life*, *Children's Digest*, *Humpty Dumpty's Magazine*, *Jack And Jill*, *Turtle Magazine* and *U*S* Kids*.)

CLASS ACT, Class Act, Inc., P.O. Box 802, Henderson KY 42420. E-mail: rmthurman@hcc-uky.campus.mci.net. Articles Editor: Susan Thurman. Monthly, September-May. Newsletter. Estab. 1993. Circ. 300. "We are looking for practical, ready-to-use ideas for the English/language arts classroom (grades 5-12)."

Nonfiction: Middle readers and young adults: games/puzzles, how-to. Does not want to see esoteric material; no master's theses; no poetry (except articles about how to write poetry). Buys 35 mss/year. Average word length: 200-4,000. Byline given.

How to Contact/Writers: Send complete ms. Reports in 10-12 weeks. Publishes ms 3-12 months after acceptance. Will consider simultaneous submissions. Must send SASE.

Terms: Pays on acceptance. Pays $10-30 per article. Buys all rights. Sample copy for $3 and SASE.

Tips: "We're only interested in language arts-related articles for teachers and students. Writers need to realize teens often need humor in classroom assignments. In addition, we are looking for teacher-tested ideas that have already worked in the classroom. If sending puzzles, we usually need at least 20 entries per puzzle to fit our format."

COBBLESTONE, The History Magazine for Young People, Cobblestone Publishing, Inc., 7 School St., Peterborough NH 03458. (603)924-7209. Fax: (603)924-7380. Editor: Meg Chorlian. Art Director: Ann Dillon. Managing Editor: Denise L. Babcock. Magazine published 10 times/year. Circ. 38,000. *"Cobblestone* is theme-related. Writers should request editorial guidelines which explain procedure and list upcoming themes. Queries must relate to an upcoming theme. Fiction is not used often, although a good fiction piece offers welcome diversity. It is recommended that writers become familiar with the magazine (sample copies available)."

Fiction: Middle readers, young adults: history. "Authentic historical and biographical fiction, adventure, retold legends, etc., relating to the theme." Buys 6-10 mss/year. Average word length: 800. Byline given.

Nonfiction: Middle readers, young adults: activities, biography, games/puzzles (no word finds), history (world and American), interview/profile, science, travel. All articles must relate to the issue's theme. Buys 120 mss/year. Average word length: 800. Byline given.

Poetry: Up to 100 lines. "Clear, objective imagery. Serious and light verse considered." Pays on an individual basis. Must relate to theme.

How to Contact/Writers: Fiction/nonfiction: Query. "A query must consist of all of the following to be considered (please use nonerasable paper): a brief cover letter stating the subject and word length of the proposed article; a detailed one-page outline explaining the information to be presented in the article; an extensive bibliography of materials the author intends to use in preparing the article; a self-addressed stamped envelope. Writers new to *Cobblestone* should send a writing sample with query. If you would like to know if your query has been received, please also include a stamped postcard that requests acknowledgment of receipt. In all correspondence, please include your complete address as well as a telephone number where you can be reached. A writer may send as many queries for one issue as he or she wishes, but each query must have a separate cover letter, outline, bibliography and SASE. Telephone queries are not accepted. Handwritten queries will not be considered. Queries may be submitted at any time, but queries sent well in advance of deadline *may not be answered for several months*. Go-aheads requesting material proposed in queries are usually sent five months prior to publication date. Reports on queries/mss in 2 weeks. Unused queries will be returned approximately three to four months prior to publication date."

Illustration: Buys 3 illustrations/issue; 27 illustrations/year. Preferred theme or style: Material that is simple, clear and accurate but not too juvenile. Sophisticated sources are a must. Works on assignment only. Reviews ms/illustration packages from artists. Query. Contact: Meg Chorlian. Illustrations only: Send photocopies, tearsheets, or other nonreturnable samples. Contact: Ann Dillon, art director. "Illustrators should consult issues of *Cobblestone* to familiarize themselves with our needs." Reports on art samples in 2 weeks. Samples returned with SASE; samples not filed. Original artwork returned at job's completion (upon written request). Credit line given.

Photography: Contact: Meg Chorlian, editor. Photos must relate to upcoming themes. Send transparencies and/or color/b&w prints. Submit on speculation.

Terms: Pays on publication. Buys all rights to articles and artwork. Pays 20-25¢/word for articles/stories. Pays on an individual basis for poetry, activities, games/puzzles. Pays photographers per photo ($15-100 for b&w; $25-100 for color). Sample copy $3.95 with 7½ × 10½ SAE and 5 first-class stamps; writer's/illustrator's/photo guidelines free with SAE and 1 first-class stamp.

Tips: Writers: "Submit detailed queries which show attention to historical accuracy and which offer interesting and entertaining information. Be true to your own style. Study past issues to know what we look for. All feature articles, recipes, activities, fiction and supplemental nonfiction are freelance contributions." Illustrators: "Submit b&w samples, not too juvenile. Study past issues to know what we look for. The illustration we use is generally for stories, recipes and activities." (See listings for *Calliope, The World History Magazine for Young People; Faces, The Magazine About People;* and *Odyssey, Science That's Out of This World.*)

COBBLESTONE PUBLISHING, INC., 7 School St., Peterborough NH 03458. See listings for *Calliope, Cobblestone, Faces* and *Odyssey.*

*COGNIZ, Keeping the Gears Turning, New World Publishers, 600 W. 28th, Suite 205, Austin TX 78705. (512)495-9666. Fax: (512)495-9667. Science Editor: Rafiq Ladhani. Editor: Caroline Ladhani. Photo Editor: Bret Brookshire. Magazine published 8 times/year. "Our objectives are to highlight the diversity of human expression in different cultures through ideas, music, art and storytelling and to pique curiosity about the mysteries of nature which abound and surround us. 50% of editorial is about science, nature, mathematics."

Fiction: Young adults: adventure, contemporary, folktale, history, humorous, multicultural, science fiction, suspense/mystery. "A story is based upon characters and situations. Depending on the storyline the identity of a character may or may not be relevant to the story. Avoid multiculturalism for the sake of multiculturalism. There is a danger in making a character representative of a culture/tradition." Buys 8-10 mss/year. Average word length: 800-1,200. Byline given.

Nonfiction: Young adult: biography, concept, games/puzzles, geography, health, history, humorous, interview/profile, math, multicultural, nature/environment, problem-solving, science, social issues, travel and photo essay. Buys 12-15 mss/year. Average word length: 900-1,100. "We have several one-page regular departments."

Poetry: Maximum length: 16 lines. Limit submissions to 3 poems.

How to Contact/Writers: Fiction/nonfiction: send complete ms. Reports on mss in 2-3 months. Publishes ms 3 months after acceptance. Will consider simultaneous submissions, electronic submission via disk or modem and previously published work.

Illustration: Buys 3-4 illustrations/issue; 25-30 illustrations/year. Uses b&w artwork only. Works on assignment only. Reviews ms/illustration packages from artists. Send ms with dummy. Contact: Caroline Ladhani, editor. Illustrations only: Query with samples. Contact: Caroline Ladhani, editor. Reports in 2-3 months. Samples returned with SASE; samples filed. Credit line given.

Photography: "Photographs tell stories, and if they are relevant to our editorial objective then we are interested." Model/property release required; captions required. Uses color, b&w prints preferably at least 5×7; 35mm transparencies. Query with samples. Reports in 2-3 months.

Terms: Pays on publication. Buys one-time and reprint rights for mss. Buys one-time rights for artwork and photographs. Original artwork returned at job's completion. Pays $50-100 for stories; $35-150 for articles. Additional payment for ms/illustration packages and for photos accompanying articles. Pays illustrators $75-100 for b&w cover; $15-30 for b&w inside. Pays photographers per photo (range: $15-30). Sample copies for $5. Writer's/illustrator's/photo guidelines for SASE.

Tips: "Please review at least a couple of issues of the magazine before submitting anything. We are looking for interesting and entertaining fiction. In nonfiction we are looking for articles which are challenging and though-provoking." (See listing for *Explorer*.)

COOK COMMUNICATIONS MINISTRIES, (formerly Scripture Press Inc.), P.O. Box 36640, Colorado Springs CO 80936. See listings for *Counselor*, *Primary Days*, *Teen Power* and *Zelos*.

COUNSELOR, Cook Communications Ministries, P.O. Box 36640, Colorado Springs CO 80936. (719)536-0100 or (800)708-5550. Primary Editor: Janice K. Burton. Art Director: Blake Ebel. Newspaper distributed weekly; published quarterly. Estab. 1940. "Audience: children 8-12 years. Papers designed to present everyday living stories showing the difference Christ can make in a child's life. Must have a true Christian slant, not just a moral implication. Correlated with Scripture Press Sunday School curriculum."

Fiction: Middle readers: adventure, history, multicultural, nature/environment, problem-solving, sports (all with Christian context). "Actually, true stories preferred by far. I appreciate well-written fiction that shows knowledge of our product. I suggest people write for samples." Buys approximately 12 mss/year. Average word length: 900. Byline given.

Nonfiction: Middle readers: arts/crafts, biography, games/puzzles, history, interview/profile, nature/environment, problem-solving, religion, science, social issues, sports. Buys approximately 12 mss/year. Average word length: 900-1,100. Byline given.

How to Contact/Writers: Fiction/nonfiction: Send complete ms. Reports on mss in 3 months. Publishes ms 1-2 years after acceptance ("we work a year in advance"). Will consider previously published work. "We will accept no new manuscripts before March, 1997."

Illustration: Buys 24-30 illustrations/year. Reviews ms/illustration packages from artists, but not often.

Photography: Purchases photos from freelancers.

Terms: Pays on acceptance. Buys second (reprint) rights, one-time rights, or all rights for mss. Pays 7-10¢/word for stories or articles, depending on amount of editing required. Sample copies for #10 SAE and 1 first-class stamp. Writers/photo guidelines for SASE.

Tips: "Send copy that is as polished as possible. Indicate if story is true. Indicate rights offered. Stick to required word lengths. Include Social Security number or manuscript. Write for our tips for writers, sample copies and theme lists." (See listing for *Primary Days*, *Teen Power* and *Zelos*.)

*CRAYOLA KIDS, Family Time Fun, Meredith Custom Publishing, 1912 Grand Ave., Des Moines IA 50309-3379. (515)284-2170. Fax: (515)284-2064. Articles Editor: Mary Heaton. Art Director: Bob Riley. Bimonthly magazine. Estab. 1994. Circ. 400,000. Publication to "encourage a love of reading and share the magic of creativity in families with children ages 4-8.

Nonfiction: Picture-oriented material, young readers: arts/crafts, games/puzzles, how-to, humorous. "Seasonal tie-ins are a plus." Does not want to see biographies. Buys 20-30 mss/year. Average word length: 250. Byline given.

How to Contact/Writers: Nonfiction: Query. Reports on queries in 3-4 weeks.

Illustration: Only interested in agented material.

Terms: Pays on acceptance. Buys all rights for mss. Pays $15-400 for articles. "Depends on subject, length, complexity, originality." Sample copies for $2.95 plus SASE.

Tips: "Study the magazine. Query."

CRICKET MAGAZINE, Carus Publishing, Company, P.O. Box 300, Peru IL 61354. (815)224-6656. Articles/Fiction Editor-in-Chief: Marianne Carus. Editor: Deborah Vetter. Art Director: Ron McCutchan. Monthly magazine. Estab. 1973. Circ. 83,000. Children's literary magazine for ages 9-14.

● *Cricket* was ranked 31st in the 1996 *Writer's Digest* Fiction 50, the magazine's annual list of top fiction markets.

Fiction: Middle readers, young adults: adventure, animal, contemporary, fantasy, folk and fairy tales, history, humorous, multicultural, nature/environment, science fiction, sports, suspense/mystery. Buys 180 mss/year. Maximum word length: 2,000. Byline given.

Nonfiction: Middle readers, young adults: animal, arts/crafts, biography, environment, experiments, games/puzzles, history, how-to, interview/profile, natural science, problem-solving, science and technology, space, sports, travel. Multicultural needs include articles on customs and cultures. Requests bibliography with submissions. Buys 180 mss/year. Average word length: 1,200. Byline given.

Poetry: Reviews poems, 1-page maximum length. Limit submissions to 5 poems or less.

How to Contact/Writers: Send complete ms. Do not query first. Reports on mss in 2-3 months. Does not like but will consider simultaneous submissions. SASE required for response.

Illustration: Buys 35 illustrations (14 separate commissions)/issue; 425 illustrations/year. Uses b&w and full-color work. Preferred theme or style: "strong realism; strong people, especially kids; good action illustration; no cartoons. All media, but prefer other than pencil." Reviews ms/illustration packages from artists "but reserves option to re-illustrate." Send complete ms with sample and query. Illustrations only: Provide tearsheets or good quality photocopies to be kept on file. SASE required for response/return of samples. Reports on art samples in 2 months.

Photography: Purchases photos with accompanying ms only. Model/property releases required. Uses color transparencies, b&w glossy prints.

Terms: Pays on publication. Buys first publication rights in the English language. Buys first publication rights plus promotional rights for artwork. Original artwork returned at job's completion. Pays up to 25¢/word for unsolicited articles; up to $3/line for poetry. Pays $750 for color cover; $75-150 for b&w, $150-250 for color inside. Pays $750 for color cover; $75-150 for b&w, $150-250 for color inside. Writer's/illustrator's guidelines for SASE.

Tips: Writers: "Read copies of back issues and current issues. Adhere to specified word limits. *Please* do not query." Illustrators: "Edit your samples. Send only your best work and be able to reproduce that quality in assignments. Put name and address on *all* samples. Know a publication before you submit—is your style appropriate?" (See listings for *Babybug*, *Ladybug* and *Spider*.)

CRUSADER, Calvinist Cadet Corps, P.O. Box 7259, Grand Rapids MI 49510. (616)241-5616. Editor: G. Richard Broene. Art Director: Robert DeJonge. Magazine published 7 times/year. Circ. 13,000. "Our magazine is for members of the Calvinist Cadet Corps—boys aged 9-14. Our purpose is to show how God is at work in their lives and in the world around them."

Fiction: Middle readers, young adults: Considers all categories but science fiction and romance. Wants to see more adventure, nature and sports. Buys 12 mss/year. Average word length: 800-1,500.

Nonfiction: Middle readers, young adults: considers all categories but fashion. Buys 6 mss/year. Average word length: 400-900.

How to Contact/Writers: Fiction/nonfiction: Send complete ms. Reports on queries/mss in 3-5 weeks. Will consider simultaneous submissions.

Illustration: Buys 1 illustration/issue; buys 6 illustrations/year. Works on assignment only. Reviews ms/illustration packages from artists. Reports in 3-5 weeks. Credit line given.

Photography: Buys photos from freelancers. Wants nature photos and photos of boys.
Terms: Pays on acceptance. Buys first North American serial rights; reprint rights. Pays $10-100 for stories/articles. Pays illustrators $50-200 for b&w cover or inside. Sample copy free with 9 × 12 SAE and 3 first-class stamps.
Tips: Publication is most open to fiction: write for a list of themes (available yearly in January). See trends in children's magazines in "hard line, real world, to the point and action" material.

CURRENT HEALTH I, The Beginning Guide to Health Education, 900 Skokie Blvd., Suite 200, Northbrook IL 60062. (847)205-3000. Monthly (during school year September-May) magazine. "For classroom use by students, this magazine is curriculum-specific and requires experienced educators who can write clearly and well at fifth grade reading level."
Nonfiction: Middle readers: health, nature/environment. Buys 60-70 mss/year. Average word length: 1,000. "Credit given in staff box."
How to Contact/Writers: Nonfiction: Query with published clips and résumé. Publishes ms 6-7 months after acceptance.
Illustration: Works on assignments only. Query with samples. Samples returned with SASE; samples filed. Originals returned at job's completion. Credit line given.
Terms: Pays on publication. Buys all rights. Pays $100-150, "more for longer features." Writer's guidelines available for SASE.
Tips: Needs material about drug education, nutrition, fitness and exercise. Articles are assigned to freelance writers on specific topics.

CURRENT HEALTH 2, The Continuing Guide to Health Education, 900 Skokie Blvd., Suite 200, Northbrook IL 60062-1563. (847)205-3000. Fax: (847)564-8197. Editor: Carole Rubenstein. Monthly (during school year September-May). "For classroom use by students, this magazine is curriculum specific and requires experienced educators who can write clearly and well at a ninth grade reading level."
Nonfiction: Young adults/teens: health (psychology, disease, nutrition, first-aid and safety), health-related drugs, environment, problem solving, fitness and exercise. Buys 70-90 mss/year. Average word length: 1,000-2,500. Byline given.
How to Contact/Writers: Nonfiction: Query with published clips and résumé. Does not accept unsolicited mss. Reports on queries in 2 months. Publishes ms 6-7 months after acceptance.
Illustration: Buys 2-4 illustrations/issue; 20-40 illustrations/year. Works on assignment only. Query with samples, promo sheet, slides, tearsheets. Contact: Jill Sherman, suvervisor of art direction. Reports only if interested. Samples not returned; samples filed. Originals returned at job's completion. Credit line given.
Terms: Pays on publication. Buys all rights. Pays average $150 for assigned article, "more for longer features." Pays illustrators $200-300 for color cover; $50 for b&w inside; $75-125 for color inside. Sample copies for 9 × 12 SAE with 3 first-class stamps. Writer's guidelines available only if writers are given an assignment; photo guidelines for SASE.
Tips: Needs writers with background in drug education, first aid and safety.

***DISCOVERY**, The John Milton Society for the Blind, 475 Riverside Dr., Room 455, New York NY 10115. (212)870-3335. Fax: (212)870-3229. Assistant Editor: Ingrid Peck. Editor: Darcy Quigley. Quarterly braille magazine. Estab. 1935. Circ. 2,000. "*Discovery* is a free braille magazine for blind and visually impaired youth ages 8-18. 95% of material is reprinted from 20 Christian and other magazines for youth. Original pieces from individual authors must be ready to print with little or no editing involved. We cannot offer reprint fees. Christian focus."
Fiction: Middle readers, young adults/teens: all categories and issues pertaining to blind. Does not want stories in which blindness is described as a novelty. It should be part of a story with a larger focus. Buys less than 10 mss/year. Average word length: 1,500 words (maximum). Byline given.
Nonfiction: Middle readers, young adults: all categories. Buys less than 10 mss/year. Average word length: 1,500 words (maximum). Byline given.
Poetry: Reviews poetry. Maximum length: 500 words.
How to Contact/Writers: Fiction/nonfiction: Send complete ms. Reports on queries/mss in 6 weeks. Publishes ms 3-12 months after acceptance. Will consider simultaneous submissions, previously published work.
Terms: Acquires reprint rights. Authors do not receive payment.
Tips: "95% of the material in *Discovery* is reprinted from Christian and other magazines for youth. Previously unpublished material must therefore be ready to print with little or no editing

involved. Please send complete manuscripts or request our 'Writers' Guidelines' which includes a list of periodicals we reprint from."

DOLPHIN LOG, The Cousteau Society, 777 United Nations Plaza, New York NY 10017-3585. (212)949-6290. Fax: (212)949-6296. Editor: Lisa Rao. Bimonthly magazine for children ages 7-13. Circ. 80,000. Entirely nonfiction subject matter encompasses all areas of science, natural history, marine biology, ecology and the environment as they relate to our global water system. The philosophy of the magazine is to delight, instruct and instill an environmental ethic and understanding of the interconnectedness of living organisms, including people. Of special interest are articles on ocean- or water-related themes which develop reading and comprehension skills.

Nonfiction: Middle readers, young adult: animal, games/puzzles, geography, interview/profile, nature/environment, science, ocean. Multicultural needs include indigenous peoples, lifestyles of ancient people, etc. Does not want to see talking animals. No dark or religious themes. Buys 10 mss/year. Average word length: 500-700. Byline given.

How to Contact/Writers: Nonfiction: Query first. Reports on queries in 3 months; mss in 6 months.

Illustration: Buys 1 illustration/issue; buys 6 illustrations/year. Preferred theme: Biological illustration. Reviews ms/illustration packages from artists. Illustrations only: Query; send résumé, promo sheet, slides. Reports on art samples in 8 weeks only if interested. Credit line given to illustrators.

Photography: Wants "sharp, colorful pictures of sea creatures. The more unusual the creature, the better."

Terms: Pays on publication. Buys first North American serial rights; reprint rights. Pays $25-200 for articles. Pays $75-200/color photos. Sample copy $2.50 with 9×12 SAE and 3 first-class stamps. Writer's/illustrator's guidelines free with #10 SASE.

Tips: Writers: "Write simply and clearly and don't anthropomorphize." Illustrators: "Be scientifically accurate and don't anthropomorphize. Some background in biology is helpful, as our needs range from simple line drawings to scientific illustrations which must be researched for biological and technical accuracy."

DYNAMATH, Scholastic Inc., 555 Broadway, New York NY 10012-3999. (212)343-6432. Editor: Joe D'Agnese. Art Director: Joan Michael. Monthly magazine. Estab. 1981. Circ. 300,000. Purpose is "to make learning math fun, challenging and uncomplicated for young minds in a very complex world."

Nonfiction: All levels: animal, arts/crafts, cooking, fashion, games/puzzles, health, history, hobbies, how-to, humorous, math, multicultural, nature/environment, problem-solving, science, social issues, sports—all must relate to math and science topics.

How to Contact/Writers: Nonfiction: Query with published clips, send ms. Reports on queries in 1 month; mss in 6 weeks. Publishes ms 4 months after acceptance. Will consider simultaneous submissions.

Illustration: Buys 4 illustrations/issue. Illustration only: Query first; send résumé and tearsheets. Reports back on submissions only if interested. Credit line given.

Terms: Pays on acceptance. Buys all rights for mss, artwork, photographs. Originals returned to artist at job's completion. Pays $50-300 for stories. Pays artists $800-1,000 for color cover illustration; $100-800 for color inside illustration. Pays photographers $300-1,000 per project.

Tips: See listings for *Junior Scholastic*, *Scholastic Math Magazine*, *Science World* and *Supersci-ence Blue*.

*EXPLORER, The Magazine for Inquisitive Kids, New World Publishers, P.O. Box 7216, Austin TX 78713. (512)495-9666. Fax: (512)495-9667. Science Editor: Rafiq Ladhani. Editor: Caroline Ladhani. Photo Editor: Bret Brookshire. Magazine published 8 times/year. "Our objective is to highlight the diversity of human expression in different cultures through ideas, music, art and storytelling and to pique curiosity about the mysteries of nature which abound and surround us. 50% of editorial is about science, nature, mathematics."

Fiction: Middle readers: adventure, contemporary, folktale, history, humorous, multicultural, science fiction, suspense/mystery. "A story is based upon character and situations. Depending on the storyline the identity of a character may or may not be relevant to the story. Avoid multiculturalism for the sake of multiculturalism. There is a danger in making a character representative of a culture/tradition." Buys 8-10 mss/year. average word length: 750-1,100. Byline given.

A coral reef is home to lots of undersea creatures! Can you find five parrotfish, three pufferfish, four clownfish, two pipefish and one sting ray in this picture?

BONUS: Find the hidden diver!

parrotfish   pufferfish   clownfish   pipefish   sting ray

© 1996 Stephen Blue

Pufferfish, clownfish, a sting ray and a hidden diver, among other sea creatures, swim through the depths of this colorful illustration by Stephen Blue. Created using Adobe Illustrator, Blue's illustration appeared on the back cover of the July 1996 issue of *Dolphin Log*, a children's nature magazine published by the Cousteau Society.

Nonfiction: Middle readers: animal, biography, concept, games/puzzles, geography, history, humorous, interview/profile, math, multicultural, nature/environment, problem-solving, science, sports, travel and photo-essay. Buys 12-15 mss/year. Average word length: 850-1,000. "We have several one-page regular departments."

Poetry: Maximum length: 16 lines. Limit submissions to 5 poems.

How to Contact Writers: Fiction/nonfiction: Send complete ms. Reports on mss in 2-3 months. Publishes ms 3 months after acceptance. Will consider simultaneous submissions, electronic submission via disk or modem and previously published work.

Illustration: Buys 3-4 illustrations/issue; 25-30 illustrations/year. Uses b&w artwork only. Works on assignment only. Reviews ms/illustration packages from artists. Send ms with dummy. Contact: Caroline Ladhani, editor. Illustrations only: Query with samples. Contact: Caroline Ladhani, editor. Reports in 2-3 months. Samples returned with SASE; samples filed. Credit line given.

Photography: "Photographs tell stories, and if they are relevant to our editorial objective then we are interested." Model/property release required; captions required. Uses color and b&w preferably at least 5×7 prints and 35mm transparencies. Query with samples. Reports in 3 months.

Terms: Pays on publication. Buys one-time and reprint rights for mss. Buys one-time rights for artwork and photographs. Original artwork returned at job's completion. Pays $50-100 for stories; $35-150 for articles. Additional payment for ms/illustration packages and for photos accompanying articles. Pays illustrators $75-100 for b&w cover; $15-30 for b&w inside. Pays photographers per photo (range: $15-30). Sample copies for $5. Writer's/illustrator's/photo guidelines for SASE.

Tips: "Please review at least a couple of issues of the magazine before submitting anything. We are looking for interesting and entertaining fiction. In nonfiction we are looking for articles which are challenging and thought-provoking." (See listing for *Cogniz*.)

EXPLORING, Boy Scouts of America, 1325 W. Walnut Hill Lane, P.O. Box 152079, Irving TX 75015-2079. (214)580-2365. Executive Editor: Scott Daniels. Art Director: Joe Connally. Photo Editor: Stephen Seeger. Magazine published "four times a year (January, April, June and November)." *Exploring* is a 20-page, 4-color magazine published for Exploring program members of the Boy Scouts of America. These members are young men and women between the ages of 14-21. Interests include careers, computers, life skills (money management, parent/peer relationships, study habits), college, camping, hiking, canoeing.

Nonfiction: Young adults: interview/profile, outdoor adventure (hiking, camping, white water boating), problem-solving, travel. Buys 12 mss/year. Average word length: 600-1,200. Byline given.

How to Contact/Writers: Nonfiction: Query with published clips. Reports on queries/mss in 1 week.

Illustration: Buys 3 illustrations/issue; 12 illustrations/year. Works on assignment only. Illustration only: Reports on art samples in 2 weeks. Original artwork returned at job's completion.

Terms: Pays on acceptance. Buys first North American serial rights. Pays $350-800 for assigned/unsolicited articles. Pays $1,000 for color illustrated cover; $250-500 for b&w inside; $500-800 for color inside. Sample copy with 8½×11 SAE and 5 first-class stamps. Free writer's/illustrator's guidelines.

Tips: Looks for "short, crisp career profiles of 1,000 words with plenty of information to break out into graphics." (See listing for *Boys' Life*.)

FACES, The Magazine About People, Cobblestone Publishing, Inc., 7 School St., Peterborough NH 03458. (603)924-7209. Fax: (603)924-7380. Assistant Publisher: Carolyn P. Yoder. Picture Editor: Francelle Carapetyan. Magazine published 9 times/year (September-May). Circ. 15,000. "Although *Faces* operates on a by-assignment basis, we welcome ideas/suggestions in outline form. All manuscripts are reviewed by the American Museum of Natural History in New York before being accepted. *Faces* is a theme-related magazine; writers should send for theme list before submitting ideas/queries."

Fiction: Middle readers: anthropology. Young adults: contemporary, folktales, history, multi-cultural, religious. Does not want to see material that does not relate to a specific upcoming theme. Buys 9 mss/year. Maximum word length: 800. Byline given.

Nonfiction: Middle readers and young adults: anthropology, arts/crafts, games/puzzles, history, interview/profile, religious, travel. Does not want to see material not related to a specific upcoming theme. Buys 63 mss/year. Average word length: 300-800. Byline given.

How to Contact/Writers: Fiction/nonfiction: Query with published clips and 2-3 line biographical sketch. "Ideas should be submitted six to nine months prior to the publication date. Responses to ideas are usually sent approximately four months before the publication date."

Illustration: Buys 3 illustrations/issue; buys 27 illustrations/year. Preferred theme or style: Material that is meticulously researched (most articles are written by professional anthropologists); simple, direct style preferred, but not too juvenile. Works on assignment only. Roughs required. Reviews ms/illustration packages from artists. Illustrations only: Send samples of b&w work. "Illustrators should consult issues of *Faces* to familiarize themselves with our needs." Reports on art samples in 1-2 months. Original artwork returned at job's completion (upon written request).

Photography: Wants photos relating to forthcoming themes.

Terms: Pays on publication. Buys all rights for mss and artwork. Pays 20-25¢/word for articles/stories. Covers are assigned and paid on an individual basis. Pays photographers per photo ($15-100 for b&w; $25-100 for color). Sample copy $3.95 with 7½×10½ SAE and 5 first-class stamps. Writer's/illustrator's/photo guidelines free with SAE and 1 first-class stamp.

Tips: "Writers are encouraged to study past issues of the magazine to become familiar with our style and content. Writers with anthropological and/or travel experience are particularly encouraged; *Faces* is about world cultures. All feature articles, recipes and activities are freelance contributions." Illustrators: "Submit b&w samples, not too juvenile. Study past issues to know what we look for. The illustration we use is generally for retold legends, recipes and activities." (See listing for *Calliope, The World History Magazine for Young People*; *Cobblestone, The History Magazine for Young People*; and *Odyssey, Science That's Out of This World*.)

FALCON FOR KIDS, (formerly *Falcon Magazine*), Falcon Press, 48 Last Chance Gulch, P.O. Box 1718, Helena MT 59624. (406)449-1335. Fax: (406)442-2995. E-mail: graphicb@aol.com. Executive Editor: Kay Morton Ellerhoff. Editorial Director: Carolyn Zieg Cunningham. Design Editor: Bryan Knaff. Bimonthly magazine. Estab. 1993. Circ. 100,000. "A magazine for young conservationists."

Nonfiction: Middle readers: adventure (outdoor), animal, nature/environment, sports (outdoor recreation), travel (to parks, wildlife refuges, etc.). Average word length: 800 maximum. Byline given.

How to Contact/Writers: Fiction/nonfiction: Query. Reports in 6 months.

Illustration: Buys 2 illustrations/issue; 12-15 illustrations/year. Prefers work on assignment. Reviews ms/illustration packages from artists. Illustrations only: Query; send slides, tearsheets. Reports in 2 months. Samples returned with SASE; samples sometimes filed. Credit line given.

Photography: *Must* be submitted in 20-slide sheets and individual protectors, such as KYMAC. Looks for "children outdoors—camping, fishing, doing 'nature' projects." Model/property releases required. Photo captions required. Uses 35mm transparencies. Should query with samples. Contact: Theresa Morrow Rush, photo editor. Reports in 2 months.

Terms: Pays 30-60 days after publication. Buys one-time rights for mss. Purchases one-time rights for photographs. Original work returned at job's completion. Pays $25-200 for stories; $100-200 for articles. Pays illustrators variable rate for b&w inside; $250 color cover; $35-100 color inside. Pays photographers by the project ($35 minimum); per photo (range: $35-100); $250 for cover photo. Sample copies for $3.95 and 8½×11 SAE. Writer's/illustrator's/photo guidelines for SASE.

Tips: "We are seriously overloaded with manuscripts and do not plan to buy very much new material in the next year."

FIELD & STREAM, Times Mirror Magazines, 2 Park Ave., New York NY 10016. (212)779-5000. Fax: (212)725-3836. E-mail: fsmagazine@aol.com. Editor: Duncan Barnes. Design Director: Daniel J. McClain. Estab. 1989. Circ. 1.75 million. "Field & Stream Jr.," a special 3- to 4-page section of *Field & Stream*, is designed to teach young sportsmen about hunting, fishing and related topics. "We publish straightforward how-to pieces, crafts and projects, puzzles, adventure stories, and fillers about hunting and fishing."

Nonfiction: Middle readers: animal, concept, games/puzzles, how-to, interview/profile, nature/environment, sports (hunting/fishing). "We are looking for articles that are related to hunting and/or fishing. We see too many articles not connected to these topics, and too many 'my first fishing trip' type stories." Buys 25 mss/year. Average word length: 25 to 500 (25 for fillers). Byline given.

How to Contact/Writers: Nonfiction: Query with published clips. Reports on queries/mss in 1 month. Will consider electronic submissions via disk or modem.

Illustration: Buys 5 illustrations/issue; 30 illustrations/year. Works on assignment only. Reviews ms/illustration packages from artists. Query. Illustrations only: Send résumé, promo sheet and portfolio. Samples returned with SASE; samples filed. Credit line given.

Photography: Buys photos from freelancers. Uses 35mm transparencies. Query with samples. Reports in 1 month.

Terms: Pays on acceptance. Buys first North American serial rights for mss. Buys first North American serial rights for artwork and photographs. Original work returned at job's completion. Pays $75-600 for articles. Additional payment for ms/illustration packages and for photos accompanying articles. Pays photographers per photo ($450). Sample copies for $4. Writer's/photo guidelines for SASE.

This chaotic kitchen scene of a very excited boy and his prehistoric breakfast guest was created by artist Peter Grosshauser using gouache and colored pencils. This illustration appeared in an ad for subscriptions to *Falcon Magazine*, a nature magazine for young conservationists. "My little nephew thought the illustration was pretty cool," says Grosshauser.

© 1996 Peter Grosshauser

Tips: "Study back issues of magazines to see what kinds of articles we print and what topics we cover. For 'Field & Stream Jr.,' we are looking for manuscripts that cover hunting and fishing and related topics, such as conservation, natural history and sporting ethics. Most photos or illustrations are requested by the editors in order to complement and illustrate stories. We also include writing by children."

*THE FLICKER MAGAZINE, Hillview Publishing, P.O. Box 660544, Birmingham AL 35266-0544. (205)324-7111. Fax: (205)324-4035. E-mail: yellowhamr@aol.com. Articles Editor: Lynn Christmas. Art Director: Jimmy Bass. Bimonthly magazine. Estab. 1994. Circ. 7,000. *"The Flicker Magazine* is a publication that promotes balanced growth in all areas of life—physical, spiritual, social, mental and emotional. It includes nonfiction, fiction, poetry, interviews, etc."

Fiction: Middle readers: adventure, animal, folktale, health, history, humorous, multicultural, nature/environment, problem-solving, religious, sports. Does not want to see science fiction, fantasy or romance. Sees too much fantasy and didactic materials. Wants more adventure, humorous and multicultural submissions. Buys 75-80 mss/year. Average word length: 400-800. Byline given.

Nonfiction: Middle readers: animal, arts/crafts, biography, careers, concept, cooking, games/puzzles, geography, health, history, hobbies, how-to, humorous, interview/profile, multicultural, nature/environment, problem-solving, religion, science, social issues, sports, travel. Does not want to see fashion oriented submissions. See too many how-to articles. Would like more arts/crafts, multicultural, science and nature articles. Buys 15-25 mss/year. Average word length: 400-600. Byline given.

Poetry: Reviews poetry. Maximum length: 4-24 lines.

How to Contact/Writers: Fiction/Nonfiction: Send complete ms. Reports on queries/mss in 1-2 months. Publishes ms 2-12 months after acceptance. Will consider simultaneous submissions and sometimes previously published work.

Illustration: Only interested in agented material. Buys 5 illustrations/issue; 30 illustrations/year. Uses color artwork only. Works on assignment only. Reviews ms/illustration packages from artists. Send ms with dummy. Contact: Jimmy Bass, art director. Illustrations only: send promo sheet and tearsheets. Samples returned with SASE; samples filed. Credit line sometimes given.

Photography: Buys photos from freelancers. Looking for action photos. Model/property releases required; captions required. Uses color, 8½×11 matte prints and 35mm transparencies, 2¼×2¼ transparencies. Send unsolicited photos by mail. Reports only if interested.

Terms: Pays on acceptance. Buys all rights for mss, artwork and photos. Pays 8-12¢/word for stories; 8-12¢/word for articles. Pays illustrators $50-250 for color inside. Pays photographers by the project (range: $50-200). Sample copies for $2.95. Writer's/illustrator guidelines free for SASE.

Tips: "If you are submitting photos or illustrations, please do not send originals unless otherwise specified. Call and inquire about future issues. The magazine usually has a central theme. Also call for guidelines."

FLORIDA LEADER, for high school students, Oxendine Publishing, Inc., P.O. Box 14081, Gainesville FL 32604-2081. (352)373-6907. Fax: (352)373-8120. E-mail: 75143.2043@compuse rve.com. Articles Editor: Sarah Beavers. Art Director: Jeff Riemersma. Quarterly magazine. Estab. 1992. Circ. 50,000. Audience includes ages 14-17. Aimed at the juvenile market.

Nonfiction: Young adult: careers, social issues, travel. Looking for "more advanced pieces on college preparation—academic skills, career exploration and general motivation for college." Buys 6-8 mss/year. Average word length: 800-1,000. 200-300 for columns.

How to Contact/Writers: Nonfiction: Query with published clips. Reports on queries in 3-5 weeks; mss in 6 months. Publishes ms 3-5 months after acceptance. Will consider simultaneous submissions, electronic submissions, previously published work.

Illustration: Buys 5 illustrations/issue; 20 illustrations/year. Uses color artwork only. Works on assignment only. Reviews ms/illustration packages from artists. Query. Contact: Jeff Riemersma, art director. Illustrations only: query with samples; send résumé, promo sheet, tearsheets. Contact: Jeff Riemersma, art director. Reports only if interested. Samples returned with SASE; samples filed. Credit line given.

Photography: Buys photos from freelancers. Buys photos separately. Works on assignment only. Model/property release required. Uses color prints and 35mm, 2¼×2¼, 4×5 transparencies. Query with samples. Reports only if interested.

Terms: Pays on publication. Buys first North American serial rights, reprint rights for mss. Buys first time rights for artwork; first time rights for photos. Originals returned at job's completion. Pays $35-50 for articles. Pays first-time or less experienced writers or for shorter items with contribution copies or other premiums. Pays illustrators $50-75 for color inside. Pays photographers by the project (range: $150-300). Sample copies for $3.50. Writer's guidelines free for SASE.

Tips: "Query first and review past issues for style and topics."

FOCUS ON THE FAMILY CLUBHOUSE; FOCUS ON THE FAMILY CLUBHOUSE JR., Focus on the Family, 8605 Explorer Dr., Colorado Springs CO 80920. (719)531-3400. Editor: Lisa Brock. Art Director: Timothy Jones. Monthly magazine. Estab. 1987. Combined circulation is 250,000. "*Focus on the Family Clubhouse* is a 16-page Christian magazine, published monthly, for children ages 8-12. Similarly, *Focus on the Family Clubhouse Jr.* is published for children ages 4-8. We want fresh, exciting literature that promotes biblical thinking, values and behavior in every area of life."

Fiction: Picture-oriented material, young readers, middle readers: adventure, animal, health, nature/environment, religious, sports. Picture-oriented material, young readers: multicultural. Multicultural needs include: "interesting, informative, accurate information about other cultures to teach children appreciation for the world around them." Buys approximately 6-10 mss/year. Average word length: *Clubhouse*, 500-1,400; *Clubhouse Jr.*, 250-1,100. Byline given on all fiction; not on puzzles.

Nonfiction: Picture-oriented material, young readers, middle readers: animal, arts/crafts, cooking, games/puzzles, health, hobbies, how-to, multicultural, nature/environment, science. Middle readers: humorous, interview/profile, sports. Buys 3-5 mss/year. Average word length: 200-1,000. Byline given.

Poetry: Wants to see "humorous or biblical" poetry. Maximum length: 25 lines.

How to Contact/Writers: Fiction/nonfiction: send complete ms. Reports on queries/mss in 4-6 weeks. Publishes ms 6-8 months after acceptance.

Illustration: Buys 8 illustrations/issue. Uses color artwork only. Works on assignment only. Reviews ms/illustration packages from artists. Submit ms with rough sketches. Contact: Tim Jones, art director. Illustrations only: Query with samples, arrange portfolio review or send tearsheets. Contact: Tim Jones, art director. Reports in 2-3 months. Samples returned with SASE; samples kept on file. Credit line given.

Photography: Buys photos from freelancers. Uses 35mm transparencies. Photographers should query with samples; provide résumé and promotional literature or tearsheets. Reports in 2 months.

Terms: Pays on acceptance. Buys first North American serial rights for mss. Buys first rights or reprint rights for artwork and photographs. Original artwork returned at job's completion.

Additional payment for ms/illustration packages. Pays writers $100-300 for stories; $50-150 for articles. Pays illustrators $300-700 for color cover; $200-700 for color inside. Pays photographers by the project or per photo. Sample copies for 9 × 12 SAE and 3 first-class stamps. Writer's/illustrators/photo guidelines for SASE.

Tips: "Test your writing on children. The best stories avoid moralizing or preachiness and are not written *down* to children. They are the products of writers who share in the adventure with their readers, exploring the characters they have created without knowing for certain where the story will lead. And they are not always explicitly Christian, but are built upon a Christian foundation (and, at the very least, do not contradict biblical views or values)."

FOR SENIORS ONLY, Campus Communications, Inc., 339 N. Main St., New City NY 10956. (914)638-0333. Publisher: Darryl Elberg. Articles/Fiction Editor: Judi Oliff. Art Director: David Miller. Semiannual magazine. Estab. 1971. Circ. 350,000. Publishes career-oriented articles for high school students, college-related articles, and feature articles on travel, etc.

Fiction: Young adults: health, humorous, sports, travel. Byline given.

Nonfiction: Young adults: careers, games/puzzles, health, how-to, humorous, interview/profile, social issues, sports, travel. Buys 4-6 mss/year. Average word length: 1,000-2,500. Byline given.

How to Contact/Writers: Fiction/nonfiction: Query; query with published clips; send complete ms. Publishes ms 2-4 months after acceptance. Will consider simultaneous submissions, electronic submissions via disk or modem and previously published work.

Illustration: Reviews ms/illustration packages from artists. Query; submit complete package with final art; submit ms with rough sketches. Illustrations only: Query; send slides. Reports back only if interested. Samples not returned; samples kept on file. Original work returned upon job's completion. Credit line given.

Photography: Model/property release required. Uses 5½ × 8½ and 4⅞ × 7⅜ color prints; 35mm and 8 × 10 transparencies. Query with samples; send unsolicited photos by mail. Reports back only if interested.

Terms: Pays on publication. Buys exclusive magazine rights. Payment is byline credit. Writer's/illustrator's/photo guidelines for SASE.

THE FRIEND MAGAZINE, The Church of Jesus Christ of Latter-day Saints, 50 E. North Temple, Salt Lake City UT 84150. (801)240-2210. Managing Editor: Vivian Paulsen. Art Director: Richard Brown. Monthly magazine. Estab. 1971. Circ. 350,000. Magazine for 3-11 year olds.

Fiction: Picture material, young readers, middle readers: adventure, animal, contemporary, folktales, history, humorous, problem-solving, religious, ethnic, sports, suspense/mystery. Does not want to see controversial issues, political, horror, fantasy. Average word length: 400-1,000. Byline given.

Nonfiction: Picture material, young readers, middle readers: animal, arts/crafts, biography, cooking, games/puzzles, history, how-to, humorous, problem-solving, religious, sports. Does not want to see controversial issues, political, horror, fantasy. Average word length: 400-1,000. Byline given.

Poetry: Reviews poetry. Maximum length: 20 lines.

How to Contact/Writers: Fiction/nonfiction: Send complete ms. Reports on mss in 2 months.

Illustration: Illustrations only: Query with samples; arrange personal interview to show portfolio; provide résumé and tearsheets for files.

Terms: Pays on acceptance. Buys all rights for mss. Pays 9-11¢/word for unsolicited articles. Contributors are encouraged to send for sample copy for $1.50, 9 × 11 envelope and $1 postage. Free writer's guidelines.

Tips: "*The Friend* is published by The Church of Jesus Christ of Latter-day Saints for boys and girls up to twelve years of age. All submissions are carefully read by the *Friend* staff, and those not accepted are returned within two months when a self-addressed, stamped envelope is enclosed. Submit seasonal material at least eight months in advance. Query letters and simultaneous submissions are not encouraged. Authors may request rights to have their work reprinted after their manuscript is published."

GIRLS' LIFE, Monarch Avalon, 4517 Harford Rd. Baltimore MD 21214. Fax: (410)254-0991. Articles Editor: Kelly White. Art Director: Chun Kim. Bimonthy magazine. Estab. 1994. General interest magazine for girls, ages 7-14.

Nonfiction: Accepts articles on any subject except religion. Buys appoximately 25 mss/year. Word length varies. Byline given. "No fiction!"

How to Contact/Writers: Nonfiction: Query with published clips. Send complete ms on spec only. Reports in 4 months. Publishes ms 3 months after acceptance. Will consider simultaneous submissions.

Illustration: Buys 40 illustrations/issue. Uses color artwork only. Works on assignment only. Reviews ms/illustration packages from artists. Send ms with dummy. Contact: Kelly White, senior editor. Illustration only: Query with samples; send tearsheets. Contact: Chun Kim, art director. Reports back only if interested. Samples filed. Credit line given.

Photography: Buys photos from freelancers. Uses 35mm transparencies. Provide samples. Reports back only if interested.

Terms: Pays on publication. Sample copies available for $5. Writer's guidelines for SASE.

THE GOLDFINCH, Iowa History for Young People, State Historical Society of Iowa, 402 Iowa Ave., Iowa City IA 52240. (319)335-3916. Fax: (319)335-3935. Editor: Amy Ruth. Quarterly magazine. Estab. 1975. Circ. 2,500. "The award-winning *Goldfinch* consists of 10-12 nonfiction articles, short fiction, poetry and activities per issue. Each magazine focuses on an aspect or theme of history that occurred in or affected Iowa."

Fiction: Middle readers: historical fiction only. "Study past issues for structure and content. Most manuscripts written inhouse." Average word length: 500-1,500. Byline given.

Nonfiction: Middle readers: arts/crafts, biography, games/puzzles, history, interview/profile, "all tied to an Iowa theme." Uses about 10 freelance mss/year. Average word length: 500-800. Byline given.

Poetry: Reviews poetry. No minimum or maximum word length; no maximum number of submissions. "All poetry must reflect an Iowa theme."

How to Contact/Writers: Fiction/nonfiction: Query with published clips. Reports on queries/mss in up to 2 months. Publishes ms 1 month-1 year after acceptance. Will consider electronic submissions via disk or modem.

Illustration: Buys 8 illustrations/issue; 32 illustrations/year. Works on assignment only. Prefers cartoon, line drawing. Illustrations only: Query with samples. Reports in up to 2 months. Samples returned with SASE.

Photography: Types of photos used vary with subject. Model/property releases required with submissions. Uses b&w prints; 35mm transparencies. Query with samples. Reports in 2-4 weeks.

Terms: Pays on publication. Buys all rights. Payment for mss is in copies at this time. Pays illustrators $10-150. Sample copy for $4. Writer's/illustrator's guidelines free for SASE.

Tips: "The editor researches the topics and determines the articles. Writers, most of whom live in Iowa, work from primary and secondary research materials to write pieces. The presentation is aimed at children 8-14. All submissions must relate to an upcoming Iowa theme. Please send SASE for our writer's guidelines and theme lists before submitting manuscripts."

GUIDE MAGAZINE, Review and Herald Publishing Association, 55 W. Oak Ridge Dr., Hagerstown MD 21740. (301)791-7000. Articles Editor: Carolyn Rathbun. Art Director: Bill Kirstein. Weekly magazine. Estab. 1953. Circ. 34,000. "Ours is a weekly Christian journal written for middle readers and young adults, presenting true stories relevant to the needs of today's young person, emphasizing positive aspects of Christian living."

Nonfiction: Middle readers, young adults: adventure, animal, biography, character-building, contemporary, games/puzzles, humorous, nature/environment, problem-solving, religious, social issues, sports. "We need true, or based on true, happenings, not merely true-to-life. Our stories and puzzles must have a spiritual emphasis." No violence. No articles. "We always need humorous adventure stories." Buys 150 mss/year. Average word length: 500-600 minimum, 1,000-1,200 maximum. Byline given.

How to Contact/Writers: Nonfiction: Send complete ms. Reports in 1-2 weeks. Will consider simultaneous submissions. "We can only pay half of the regular amount for simultaneous submissions." Reports on queries/mss in 1 week. Credit line given.

Terms: Pays on acceptance. Buys first North American serial rights; first rights; one-time rights; second serial (reprint rights); simultaneous rights. Pays 3-6¢/word for stories and articles. "Writer receives several complimentary copies of issue in which work appears." Sample copy free with 5×9 SAE and 2 first-class stamps. Writer's guidelines for SASE.

Tips: Children's magazines "want mystery, action, discovery, suspense and humor—no matter what the topic."

GUIDEPOSTS FOR KIDS, P.O. Box 538 A, Chesterton IN 46304. Editor: Mary Lou Carney. Articles Editor: Sailor Metts. Fiction Editor: Lurlene McDaniel. Art Director: Mike Lyons. Photo

Editor: Wendy Marciniak. Bimonthly magazine. Estab. 1990. Circ. 200,000. *"Guideposts for Kids* is published bimonthly by Guideposts for kids 7-12 years-old (emphasis on upper end of that age bracket). It is a value-centered, direct mail magazine that is *fun* to read. It is *not* a Sunday school take-home paper or a miniature *Guideposts.*"

Fiction: Middle readers: adventure, animal, contemporary, fantasy, folktales, health, historical, humorous, multicultural, nature/environment, problem-solving, religious, romance, science fiction, sports, suspense/mystery, travel. Multicultural needs include: Kids in other cultures—school, sports, families. Does not want to see preachy fiction. "We want real stories about real kids doing real things—conflicts our readers will respect; resolutions our readers will accept. Problematic. Tight. Filled with realistic dialogue and sharp imagery. No stories about 'good' children always making the right decision. If present at all, adults are minor characters and *do not* solve kids' problems for them." Buys approximately 10 mss/year. Average word length: 500-1,300. Byline given.

Nonfiction: Middle readers: animal, biography, careers, concept, cooking, current events, fashion, games/puzzles, geography, health, history, how-to, humorous, interview/profile, math, multicultural, nature/environment, problem-solving, profiles of kids, religious, science, seasonal, social issues, sports, travel. "Make nonfiction issue-oriented, controversial, thought-provoking. Something kids not only *need* to know, but *want* to know as well." Buys 20 mss/year. Average word length: 200-1,300. Byline usually given.

How to Contact/Writers: Fiction: Send complete ms. Nonfiction: Query. Reports on queries/mss in 6 weeks.

Illustration: Buys 7 illustrations/issue; 40 illustrations/year. Uses color artwork only. Works on assignment only. Reviews ms/illustration packages from artists. Contact: Mike Lyons, art director. Illustration only: Query; send résumé, tearsheets. Reports only if interested. Credit line given.

Photography: Looks for "spontaneous, *real* kids in action shots."

Terms: Pays on acceptance. Buys all rights for mss. Buys first rights for artwork. "Features range in payment from $250-600; fiction from $250-600. We pay higher rates for stories exceptionally well-written or well-researched. Regular contributors get bigger bucks, too." Additional payment for ms/illustration packages "but we prefer to acquire our own illustrations." Pays illustrators $400-800/page. Pays photographers by the project (range: $300-1,000) or per photo (range: $100-500). Sample copies for $3.25. Writer's guidelines free for SASE.

Tips: "Make your manuscript good, relevant and playful. No preachy stories about Bible-toting children. *Guideposts for Kids* is not a beginner's market. Study our magazine. (Sure, you've heard that before—but it's *necessary!*) Neatness *does* count. So do creativity and professionalism. SASE essential."

HIGHLIGHTS FOR CHILDREN, 803 Church St., Honesdale PA 18431. (717)253-1080. Manuscript Coordinator: Beth Troop. Art Director: Janet Moir. Monthly magazine. Estab. 1946. Circ. 2.8 million. "Our motto is 'Fun With a Purpose.' We are looking for quality fiction and nonfiction that appeals to children, encourages them to read, and reinforces positive values. All art is done on assignment."

 • *Highlights* was ranked 6th in the 1996 *Writer's Digest* Fiction 50, the magazine's annual list of top fiction markets.

Fiction: Picture-oriented material, young readers, middle readers: adventure, animal, contemporary, fantasy, folktales, history, humorous, multicultural, nature/environment, science fiction, sports. Multicultural needs include first person accounts of children from other cultures and first-person accounts of children from other countries. Does not want to see war, crime, violence. "We see too many stories with overt morals." Would like to see more suspense/stories/articles with world culture settings, sports pieces, action/adventure. Buys 150 mss/year. Average word length: 400-800. Byline given.

Nonfiction: Picture-oriented material, young readers, middle readers: animal, arts/crafts, biography, careers, games/puzzles, geography, health, history, hobbies, humorous, interview/profile, multicultural, nature/environment, problem solving, religion, science, sports, travel. Young readers, middle readers: careers, foreign, geography, interview/profile, problem-solving, social issues. Multicultural needs include articles set in a country *about* the people of the country. "We have plenty of articles with Asian and Spanish settings. We also have plenty of holiday articles." Does not want to see trendy topics, fads, personalities who would not be good role models for children, guns, war, crime, violence. "We'd like to see more nonfiction for younger readers—maximum of 600 words. We still need older-reader material, too—600-900 words." Buys 75 mss/year. Maximum word length: 900. Byline given.

INSIDER REPORT

Conquer the magazine market with multiple sales

For Kelly Milner-Halls, author of *Dino Trekking, The Ultimate Dinosaur Lover's Travel Guide* and numerous magazine articles, writing for children comes easily. "I have always seen myself as a big kid—stayed in close contact with the fun-loving aspects of life that keep the child alive in us all. Factor in my 'Mom' status (two daughters, 6 and 13) and it's a natural pairing."

Motivated by a strong desire to make a living as a writer, Milner-Halls carved out an enjoyable career, dividing her time between book and maga-zine assignments. "The two markets very nicely

Kelly Milner-Halls

complement one another," she says. "Just as I wrap up a book assignment, I'm really longing for those short-term assignments again. It offers a real sense of balance."

But while many writers enter the magazine market to help them break into books, Milner-Halls's first article ideas arose as a bi-product of her first book. "Researching *Dino-Trekking* was exhaustive work, but the act of doing that re-search brought me in touch with dozens of good story ideas. I'd go to sleep thinking how great a story would be, how fun it would be for me to research a specific topic, and so, how fun it might be for a young person to read the end results." When she read about Vince Santucci, a pistol-packing paleontologist who fought against fossil thieves at Arizona's Petrified Forest National Park, she made up her mind to give magazine writing a try.

Milner-Halls discovered the key to thriving as a writer is learning how to recycle your research and material. By slanting it to appeal to various publica-tions, one interview can result in multiple sales. While researching a feature for *Highlights for Children* about a natural science artist who reconstructed the face of a 5,000-year-old mummy, Milner-Halls discovered the artist also illustrated dinosaurs. Though the information didn't fit the focus of her *Highlights* piece, she used it to write an article about dinosaur illustrations for *Crayola Kids*. But that's not all. During that same interview, the artist mentioned he created sketches for the film *Jurassic Park*. "I took careful notes, and eventually sold a story based on that part of my interview to the Dinosaur Society's *Dino Times*. By keeping several publications with special needs in mind, I was able to sell three stories without compromising any of my editors' needs."

Milner-Halls finds story ideas everywhere. "I read newspapers, magazines, fliers, brochures. If I'm sitting in a car repair shop, I'll leaf through the auto mechanics trades. If I'm at the pediatrician's, I'll read up on medical issues. If

INSIDER REPORT, *Milner-Halls*

I'm watching TV, a part of my brain is taking notes, collecting story ideas. I keep my eyes open virtually every waking minute. When I see an idea that appeals to me, I write the topic on a 3×5 card. As I collect details, I jot the basics down on the card."

Finding and writing stories is easy compared to selling them to editors. "It took me two years to place that first article. I realize now it wasn't the quality of the writing that held me back as much as it was my ability (or lack of ability) to read the market." After several dozen rejections, Milner-Halls re-read writer's

DINO-TREKKING

The Ultimate Dinosaur Lover's Travel Guide

The 300 Best Dino-Sites in the U.S. and Canada

Includes Complete Dino-Shopping Guide & Detailed Dino-Identifier

Kelly Milner Halls

Illustrations by Rick Spears

Writer Kelly Milner-Halls gets the most mileage out of every assignment. As Milner-Halls researched her first book *Dino Trekking* (John Wiley & Sons), for example, she got ideas for several stories which she sold to magazines like *Crayola Kids* and *Highlights*.

INSIDER REPORT, *continued*

guidelines and thoroughly studied issues of her target publications to determine each editor's needs. "When I sold that pistol-packing paleontologist piece it was because I finally successfully married the work to the right publication and editor."

As a beginner, Milner-Halls had better luck submitting a completed manuscript instead of a query letter. "Editors have to know they will get the product in the end. And how can they know that from a query submitted by an unknown newbie?" She figured that at first, editors needed to see her writing style and research ability before they'd be willing to take a chance on a new writer.

These days Milner-Halls lands most of her assignments by sending a query letter and clips. She completes a good portion of her research before composing her letter so it reflects some level of expertise on the topic. "I'll outline how I'll track and bag my interviews and [describe] accompanying photographs. And I include clips that illustrate my ability to write the kind of article about which I'm querying."

Once you have successfully worked with editors, they will call you to discuss future assignments. "Editors will often call me and say, 'Kelly, I need a piece with a beach theme . . . any ideas?' " When that happens, it pays to be prepared. "I'll pull out my index cards. More often than not I have an idea registered in my file. If I don't, my cards often inspire new ideas as I riffle through them."

Milner-Halls advises beginning writers not to take rejection personally. The lessons you learn as you climb the freelancing ladder are invaluable. "Consider the lean times paying your dues—a freelance education. Every low budget piece you publish brings you that much closer to the brass ring. If you approach rejections the right way, they are very helpful. One, they help you understand what an editor wants or doesn't want. Two, if critical comments are offered, they help you improve your work. Three, even rejections help make your work known at various editorial offices."

If you are persistent in submitting to the same publications, editors will eventually offer a little guidance. "Take it with a joyous and thankful heart. It's a gift." Willingly offer up a rewrite. "It took me two years and a dozen rejection slips to sell my first article. But I did sell it. I didn't give up. If you really want to write for a living, you shouldn't either. If you work hard, really pour on the steam, and network effectively, you can make a reasonable living." Though you probably won't get rich, the payoff is more than financial gain. You'll enjoy the luxury of doing what you love every day.

—*Mary Cox*

How to Contact/Writers: Send complete ms. Reports on queries in 4-6 weeks; mss in 2 months.

Illustration: Buys 25-30 illustrations/issue. Preferred theme or style: Realistic, some stylization, cartoon style acceptable. Works on assignment only. Reviews ms/illustration packages from artists. Send ms and sample illustrations. Contact: Beth Troop, manuscript coordinator. Illustrations only: photocopies, promo sheet, tearsheets, or slides. Résumé optional. Portfolio only if requested. Contact: Janet Moir, art director. Reports on art samples in 4-6 weeks. Samples returned with SASE; samples filed. Credit line given.

Terms: Pays on acceptance. Buys all rights for mss. Pays 14¢/word and up for unsolicited articles. Pays illustrators $1,000 for color cover; $25-200 for b&w, $100-500 for color inside. Sample copies $3.95 and 9×11 SASE with 4 first-class stamps.Writer's/illustrator's guidelines free on request.

Tips: "Know the magazine's style before submitting. Send for guidelines and sample issue if necessary." Writers: "At *Highlights* we're paying closer attention to acquiring more nonfiction for young readers than we have in the past." Illustrators: "Fresh, imaginative work encouraged. Flexibility in working relationships a plus. Illustrators presenting their work need not confine themselves to just children's illustrations as long as work can translate to our needs. We also use animal illustrations, real and imaginary. We need party plans, crafts and puzzles—any activity that will stimulate children mentally and creatively. We are always looking for imaginative cover subjects."

HOBSON'S CHOICE, P.O. Box 98, Ripley OH 45167. (513)392-4549. Editor: Susannah C. West. Bimonthly magazine. Estab. 1974. Circ. 2,000. *"Hobson's Choice* is a science fiction magazine which also publishes science and technology-related nonfiction along with stories. Although the magazine is not specifically aimed at children, we do number teenagers among our readers. Such readers are the type who might enjoy reading science fiction (both young adult and adult), attending science fiction conventions, using computers, and be interested in such things as astronomy, the space program, etc."

Fiction: Young adults: fantasy, science fiction. "I'm really not interested in seeing fiction other than science fiction and fantasy. Nor am I interested in horror and cyberpunk, although these can be considered subgenres of fantasy and science fiction. I also see too much hackneyed science fiction and fantasy." Buys 12-15 mss/year. Average word length 2,000-10,000.

Nonfiction: Young adults: how-to (science), interview/profile, science. Does not want to see crafts. Buys 8-10 mss/year. Average word length: 1,500-5,000. Byline given.

How to Contact/Writers: Fiction: Send complete ms. Nonfiction: Query first. Reports on queries/mss in 4 months maximum. ("After 4 months, author should feel free to withdraw ms from consideration.") Will consider submissions via disk (Macintosh MacWrite, WriteNow, IBM PC or compatible on 3½ disks).

Illustration: Buys 2-5 illustrations/issue; 20-30 illustrations/year. Uses b&w artwork only. Prefers to review "science fiction, fantasy or technical illustration." Reviews ms/illustration packages; reviews artwork for future assignments.

How to Contact/Illustrators: Ms/illustration packages: "Would like to see clips to keep on file (b&w only, preferably photocopies)." Illustrations only: Query with tearsheets to be kept on file. "If we have an assignment for an artist, we will contact him/her with the ms we want illustrated. We like to see roughs before giving the go-ahead for final artwork." Reports in 4 months "if requested and if request accompanied by SASE." Original artwork returned at job's completion, "sometimes, if requested. We prefer to retain originals, but a high-quality PMT or Velox is fine if artist wants to keep artwork." Credit line given.

Photography: Purchases photos with accompanying ms only. Uses b&w prints. Wants photos for nonfiction.

Terms: Pays 25% on acceptance, 75% on publication. Buys first North American serial rights for mss, artwork and photographs. Pays $20-100 for stories/articles. Pay illustrators $25-50 for b&w cover; $5-25 for b&w inside. Pays photographers per photo (range: $5-25). Sample copies for $2.75. Writer's/illustrator's guidelines free with business-size SAE and 1 first-class stamp. "Specify fiction or nonfiction guidelines, or both." Tip sheet package for $1.25 and business-size envelope with 1 first-class stamp (includes all guidelines and tips on writing science fiction and nonfiction).

Tips: Writers: "Read lots of children's writing in general, especially specific genre if you're writing a genre story (science fiction, romance, mystery, etc.). We list upcoming needs in our guidelines; writers can study these to get an idea of what we're looking for. We're always looking for nonfiction." Illustrators: "Study illustrations in back issues of magazines you're interested in illustrating for, and be able to work in a genre style if that's the type of magazine you want to publish your work. Everything is open to freelancers, as almost all our artwork is done out-of-house. (We occasionally use public domain illustrations, copyright-free illustrations and photographs.)"

HOLIDAYS & SEASONAL CELEBRATIONS, Teaching & Learning Company, 1204 Buchanan, P.O. Box 10, Carthage IL 62321. (217)357-2591. Fax: (217)357-6789. Contact: Articles Editor or Art Director. Quarterly magazine. Estab. 1995. Every submission must be seasonal or holiday-related. Materials need to be educational and consistent with grades Pre K-3 development and curriculum.

Fiction: Young readers: must be holiday or seasonal related; health, multicultural, nature/environment. Buys 8 mss/year. Byline given.

Nonfiction: Young readers: animal, arts/crafts, biography, concept, cooking, games/puzzles, geography, health, history, math, multicultural, nature/environment, science. "We need holiday and seasonally-related ideas from all cultures that can be used in the classroom." Buys 150 mss/year. Byline given.

Poetry: Reviews holiday or seasonal poetry.

How to Contact/Writers: Fiction: Query. Nonfiction: Send complete ms. Reports on queries in 2 months; mss in 3 months. Publishes ms 4-12 months after acceptance. Will consider electronic submissions via disk or modem.

Illustration: Buys 70 illustrations/issue; 300 illustrations/year. Uses b&w and color artwork. Works on assignment only. "Prefers school settings with lots of children; b&w sketches at this time." Reviews ms/illustration packages from artists. Submit ms with rough sketches. Illustrations only: submit résumé, promo sheet, tearsheets, sketches of children. Reports in 1 month. Samples returned with SASE; samples filed. Credit line sometimes given.

Photography: Buys photos from freelancers. Looking for photos of children. Model/property releases required. Uses 35mm transparencies. Send unsolicited photos by mail or submit portfolio for review. Reports in 2 months.

Terms: Pays on publication. Buys all rights. Pays $20-75 for stories; $10-125 for articles. Additional payment for ms/illustration packages. Pays illustrators $150-300 for color cover; $10-15 for b&w inside. Pays photographers per photo. Sample copy available for $4.50. Writer's/illustrator's guidelines for SASE.

Tips: "95% of our magazine is written by freelancers. Writers must know that this magazine goes to teachers for use in the classroom, grades pre-K through 3. Also 90% of our magazine is illustrated by freelancers. We need illustrators who can provide us with 'cute' kids grades pre-K through 3. Representation of ethnic children is a must. Because our magazine is seasonal, it is essential that we receive manuscripts approximately 8-12 months prior to the publication of that magazine. Too often we receive a holiday-related article way past the deadline."

HOPSCOTCH, The Magazine for Girls, The Bluffton News Publishing and Printing Company, 103 N. Main St., Bluffton OH 45817. (419)358-4610. Editor: Marilyn Edwards. Bimonthly magazine. Estab. 1989. Circ. 10,000. For girls from 6 to 12 years, featuring traditional subjects—pets, games, hobbies, nature, science, sports, etc.—with an emphasis on articles that show girls actively involved in unusual and/or worthwhile activities."

Fiction: Picture-oriented material, young readers, middle readers: adventure, animal, history, humorous, nature/environment, science fiction, sports, suspense/mystery. Does not want to see stories dealing with dating, sex, fashion, hard rock music. Buys 24 mss/year. Average word length: 300-700. Byline given.

Nonfiction: Picture-oriented material, young readers, middle readers: animal, arts/crafts, biography, cooking, games/puzzles, geography, hobbies, how-to, humorous, math, nature/environment, science. Does not want to see pieces dealing with dating, sex, fashion, hard rock music. "Need more nonfiction with quality photos about a Hopscotch-age girl involved in a worthwhile activity." Buys 46 mss/year. Average word length: 400-700. Byline given.

"PICTURE-ORIENTED MATERIAL" is for preschoolers to 8-year-olds; "Young readers" are for 5- to 8-year-olds; "Middle readers" are for 9- to 11-year-olds; and "Young adults" are for those ages 12 and up.

Poetry: Reviews traditional, wholesome, humorous poems. Maximum word length: 300; maximum line length: 20. Will accept 6 submissions/author.

How to Contact/Writers: Fiction: Send complete ms. Nonfiction: Query, send complete ms. Reports on queries in 2 weeks; on mss in 2 months. Will consider simultaneous submissions.

Illustration: Buys illustrations for 6-8 articles/issue; buys 50-60 articles/year. "Generally, the illustrations are assigned after we have purchased a piece (usually fiction). Occasionally, we will use a painting—in any given medium—for the cover, and these are usually seasonal." Uses b&w artwork only for inside; color for cover. Review ms/illustration packages from artists. Query first or send complete ms with final art. Illustrations only: Send résumé, portfolio, client list and tearsheets. Reports on art samples with SASE in 2 weeks. Credit line given.

Photography: Purchases photos separately (cover only) and with accompanying ms only. Looking for photos to accompany article. Model/property releases required. Uses 5×7, b&w prints; 35mm transparencies. Black and white photos should go with ms. Should have girl or girls ages 6-12.

Terms: For manuscripts, pays a few months ahead of publication. For mss, artwork and photos, buys first North American serial rights; second serial (reprint rights). Original artwork returned at job's completion. Pays 5¢ word and $10/photo used ($5/photo if it is a slide). "We always send a copy of the issue to the writer or illustrator." Text and art are treated separately. Pays $150-200 for color cover; $25-35 for b&w inside. Photographers paid per photo (range: $5-15). Sample copy for $3. Writer's/illustrator's/photo guidelines free for #10 SASE.

Tips: "Please look at our guidelines and our magazine . . . and remember, we use far more nonfiction than fiction. If decent photos accompany the piece, it stands an even better chance of being accepted. We believe it is the responsibility of the contributor to come up with photos. Please remember, our readers are 6-12 years—most are 7-10—and your text should reflect that. Many magazines try to entertain first and educate second. We try to do the reverse of that. Our magazine is more simplistic like a book, to be read from cover to cover. We are looking for wholesome, non-dated material." (See listing for *Boys' Quest*.)

HUMPTY DUMPTY'S MAGAZINE, Children's Better Health Institute, 1100 Waterway Blvd., P.O. Box 567, Indianapolis IN 46206. (317)636-8881. Fax: (317)684-8094. Editor: Sandy Grieshop. Art Director: Rebecca Ray. Magazine published 8 times/year—Jan/Feb; Mar; April/May; June; July/Aug; Sept; Oct/Nov; Dec. *HDM* is edited for children approximately ages 4-6. It includes fiction (easy-to-reads; read alouds; rhyming stories; rebus stories), nonfiction articles (some with photo illustrations), poems, crafts, recipes and puzzles. Much of the content encourages development of better health habits. "We especially need material promoting fitness."

Fiction: Picture-oriented material: adventure, animal, contemporary, fantasy, folktales, health, history, humorous, multicultural, nature/environment, problem-solving, sports. Does not want to see "bunny-rabbits-with-carrot-pies stories! Also, talking inanimate objects are very difficult to do well. Beginners (and maybe everyone) should avoid these." Buys 25-40 mss/year. Maximum word length: 500. Byline given.

Nonfiction: Picture-oriented material: animal, arts/crafts, concept, cooking, games/puzzles, health, hobbies, how-to, humorous, nature/environment, science, sports, health-related. Does not want to see long, boring, encyclopedia rehashes. "We're open to almost any subject (although most of our nonfiction has a health angle), but it must be presented creatively. Don't just string together some facts." Looks for a fresh approach. Buys 6-10 mss/year. Prefers very short nonfiction pieces—350 words maximum. Byline given.

How to Contact/Writers: Send complete ms. Nonfiction: Send complete ms with bibliography if applicable. "No queries, please!" Reports on mss in 3 months.

Illustration: Buys 13-16 illustrations/issue; 90-120 illustrations/year. Preferred theme or style: Realistic or cartoon. Works on assignment only. Illustrations only. Query with slides, printed pieces or photocopies. Contact: Rebecca Ray, art director. Samples are not returned; samples filed. Reports on art samples only if interested. Credit line given.

Terms: Writers: Pays on publication. Artists: Pays within 1-2 months. Buys all rights. "One-time book rights may be returned if author can provide name of interested book publisher and tentative date of publication." Pays up to 22¢/word for stories/articles; payment varies for poems and activities. 10 complimentary issues are provided to author with check. Pays $250 for color cover illustration; $35-90 per page b&w inside; $70-155 for color inside. Sample copies for $1.25. Writer's/illustrator's guidelines free with SASE.

Tips: Writers: "Study current issues and guidelines. Observe, especially, word lengths and adhere to requirements. It's sometimes easier to break in with recipe or craft ideas, but submit what you do best. Don't send your first, second, or even third drafts. Polish your piece until it's as perfect as you can make it." Illustrators: "Please study the magazine before contacting us. Your art must have appeal to three- to seven-year-olds." (See listings for *Child Life, Children's Digest, Children's Playmate, Jack And Jill, Turtle Magazine* and *U*S* Kids*.)

HYPE HAIR, Word Up Publication, 210 Route 4 East, Suite 401, Paramus NY 07652. (201)843-4004. Editor: Adrienne Moore. Bimonthly magazine. Estab. 1990. Publishes articles about fashion, hair trends, health, grooming, entertainment. Features celebrities (TV, movies, entertainment, fashion).
Nonfiction: Young adults: careers, fashion, games/puzzles, health, hobbies, how-to, interview/profile, problem-solving. Byline given.
How to Contact/Writers: Nonfiction: Query with published clips. Publishes ms 5 months after acceptance. Will consider electronic submissions via disk or modem.
Illustration: Buys 10 illustrations/issue. Illustrations should be done on 8½×11 paper. Works on assignment only. Reviews ms/illustration packages from artists. Submit complete package with final art. Illustrations only: Send promo sheet, portfolio, tearsheets. Reports back only if interested. Samples not filed. Original work returned upon job's completion. Credit line given.
Photography: Model/property releases and photo captions required. Uses b&w and color prints. Photographers should send unsolicited photos by mail. Reports back only if interested.
Terms: Pays on publication. Buys one-time rights to mss. Pays $75-100 for articles. Additional payment for ms/illustration packages. Pays illustrators $50-75. Photographers paid per photo (range $35-150). Writer's/illustrator's/photo guidelines free for SASE.
Tips: "Send fun ideas."

JACK AND JILL, Children's Better Health Institute, 1100 Waterway Blvd., P.O. Box 567, Indianapolis IN 46206. (317)636-8881. Editor: Daniel Lee. Art Director: Mary Rivers. Magazine published 8 times/year. Estab. 1938. Circ. 360,000. "Write entertaining and imaginative stories *for* kids, not just *about* them. Writers should understand what is funny to kids, what's important to them, what excites them. Don't write from an adult 'kids are so cute' perspective. We're also looking for health and healthful lifestyle stories and articles, but don't be preachy."
Fiction: Young readers: animal, contemporary, fantasy, history, humorous, problem-solving. Middle readers: contemporary, humorous. Buys 30-35 mss/year. Average word length: 900. Byline given.
Nonfiction: Young readers: animal, history, how-to, humorous, interview/profile, problem-solving, travel. Buys 8-10 mss/year. Average word length: 1,000. Byline given.
Poetry: Reviews poetry.
How to Contact/Writers: Fiction/nonfiction: Send complete ms. Reports on mss in 3 months.
Terms: Pays on publication; minimum 10¢/word. Buys all rights.
Tips: See listings for *Child Life, Children's Digest, Children's Playmate, Humpty Dumpty's Magazine, Turtle Magazine* and *U*S* Kids*.

*JUNIOR LEAGUE BASEBALL, 2D Publishing, P.O. Box 9099, Canoga Park CA 91309. (818)710-1234. Fax: (818)710-1877. E-mail: jlbmag.com. Articles Editor/Art Director: Dave Destler. Monthly magazine. Estab. 1996. Circ. 60,000. *Junior League Baseball* is devoted to youth baseball players, their parents, coaches and associated organizations regardless of league, park or school affiliation. 85% of publication aimed at juvenile market.
Nonfiction: Young readers, middle readers, young adults/teens: sports (baseball). Buys about 12 mss/year. Average word length: 1,000-1,500. Byline given.
How to Contact/Writers: Nonfiction: Query with published clips or send complete ms. Reports on queries/mss in 2 weeks. Publishes ms 3 months-1 year after acceptance.Will consider simultaneous submissions or electronic submission via disk.
Illustration: Buys 3-4 illustrations/issue. "Must be professional quality." Reviews ms/illustration packages from artists. Send ms with dummy. Contact: D. Destler, publisher/editor. Illustrations only: Query with samples. Send promo sheet, tearsheets. Contact: D. Destler, publisher/editor. Reports in 2 weeks. Samples returned with SASE; samples filed. Credit line sometimes given.
Photography: Buys photos with accompanying ms only. Looks mostly for photos featuring youth baseball action. "Must be professional quality." Model/property release required; captions required. Uses color 5×7-8×10 glossy prints and 35mm 2¼×2¼ transparencies. Query with samples. Reports in 2 weeks.
Terms: Pays on publication. Buys all rights for mss/artwork/photos. Originals sometimes returned. Pays $50 for stories; 20¢/word for articles "unless other arrangements are made." Addi-

tional payment for ms/illustration packages and for photos accompanying articles. Pays photographers per photo. Sample copies for $4 with 8½×11 SAE and 4 first-class stamps. Writers/photo guidelines free for SASE.

Tips: "You must know youth baseball well, either by being a parent, coach, instructor, etc., of young baseball players. Avoid cliché articles about how little Johnny was the last picked for the team, and ended up winning the game with a home run. We prefer writers very knowledgeable on youth baseball, not just parents in the stands."

JUNIOR SCHOLASTIC, Scholastic Inc., 555 Broadway, New York NY 10012-3999. (212)343-6295. Articles Editor: Lee Baier. Art Director: Glenn Davis. Photo Editor: Donna Frankland Magazine published biweekly during school year. Estab. 1937. Circ. 500,000. Social studies and current events classroom magazine for students in grades 6-8.

Nonfiction: Middle readers, young adults: geography, history, interview/profile, multicultural, nature/environment, social issues, foreign countries. "We mainly buy stories on countries in the news, that include interviews and profiles of kids 11-14." Buys 20 mss/year. Average word length: 500-1,000. Byline given.

How to Contact/Writers: Nonfiction: Query with published clips. Reports on queries in 2 months; mss in 6 months. Publishes ms 2 months after acceptance.

Illustration: Buys 1 illustration/issue; 20 illustrations/year. Works on assignment only. Reviews ms/illustration packages from artists. Illustrations only: send portfolio. Reports back only if interested. Samples returned with SASE; samples filed. Credit line given.

Photography: Buys photos from freelancers. Wants "photos of young teens in foreign countries; teens relating to national issues." Uses b&w/color prints and 35mm transparencies. Query with samples. Reports back only if interested.

Terms: Pays on publication. Buys all rights. Pays $300-600 for articles. Additional payment for photos accompanying articles. Pays illustrators $800 for color cover; $600 for color inside. Sample copies for 9×11 SAE. Writers/photo guidelines for SASE.

Tips: See listings for *Dynamath, Scholastic Math Magazine, Science World,* and *Superscience Blue.*

KEYNOTER, Key Club International, 3636 Woodview Trace, Indianapolis IN 46268. (317)875-8755. Articles Editor: Julie A. Carson. Art Director: James Patterson. Monthly magazine. Estab. 1915. Circ. 133,000. "As the official magazine of the world's largest high school service organization, we publish nonfiction articles that interest teenagers and will help our readers become better students, better citizens, better leaders."

Nonfiction: Young adults: careers, health, hobbies, how-to, problem-solving, social issues, travel. Does not want to see first-person accounts; short stories. Buys 15 mss/year. Average word length: 1,500-1,800. Byline given.

How to Contact/Writers: Nonfiction: Query. Reports on queries/mss in 1 month. Will consider simultaneous submissions.

Illustration: Buys 2-3 illustrations/issue; 15 illustrations/year. Works on assignment only. Reviews ms/illustration packages from artists. Ms/illustration packages and illustration only: "Because of our publishing schedule, we prefer to work with illustrators/photographers within Indianapolis market." Reports on art samples only if interested. Samples returned with SASE. Credit line given.

Terms: Pays on acceptance. Buys first North American serial rights. Pays $150-350 for assigned/unsolicited articles. Original artwork returned at job's completion if requested. Sample copy free with 8½×11 SAE and 65¢ postage. Writer's guidelines free with SAE and 1 first-class stamp.

Tips: "We are looking for light or humorous nonfiction, self-help articles." Also looking for articles about education reform, national concerns and trends, teen trends in music, fashion, clothes, ideologies, etc.

*KIDS AT HOME, the magazine written by and for homeschoolers, Kids at Home, Inc., P.O. Box 9148, Bend OR 97708. (541)389-8549. Fax: (541)389-8549. E-mail: kidshome@transport.com. Articles Editor/Fiction Editor: Joann Lum. Bimonthly magazine. Estab. 1995. Circ. 5,000. "We are dedicated to publishing a quality magazine that gives homeschoolers a purpose for writing—not just self-expression, but for sharing their works with others across the country."

Fiction: Picture-oriented material, young readers, middle readers, young adults/teens: adventure, animal, contemporary, folktale, history, multicultural, nature/environment, science fiction, sports, suspense/mystery. "We accept works, writing and art, from homeschoolers, ages 4-13." Name, age, city state given.

Nonfiction: Picture-oriented material, young readers, middle readers, young adults/teens (up to age 13): animal, arts/crafts, careers, geography, history, hobbies, multicultural, nature/environment, science, sports, travel. Looks for nonfiction contributions from home schoolers ages 4-13. Average word length: 35-1,500.

Poetry: Reviews all poetry. Maximum length: 20 lines.

How to Contact/Writers: Fiction/Nonfiction: Send complete ms. Reports on mss in 1 week. Publishes ms 1-6 months after acceptance. Will consider simultaneous submissions and electronic submission via disk or modem.

Illustration: Uses b&w artwork only. Illustration only: Query with samples. Send résumé. Contact: Joann Lum, editor. Reports in 1 week. Samples returned with SASE; samples filed. Child's name, age, city, state given.

Terms: Pays on publication. Originals returned to artist at job's completion. Sample copy $4. Writer's/illustrator's/photo guidelines free with SASE.

Tips: "We feature a published children's author or illustrator in every issue. We also have an author contest which enables homeschoolers to win an autographed copy of the featured author! We *only* publish writing/art/photos by homeschooled children, ages 4-13. Payment is issue of *Kids at Home.*"

*❧KIDS WORLD MAGAZINE, MIR Communications Inc., 108-93 Lombard Ave., Winnipeg, Manitoba R3B 3B1 Canada. (204)942-2214. Fax: (204)943-8991. E-mail: kidsworld@kidsw orld~online.com. Website: http://www.kidsworld~online.com. Articles Editor: Stuart Slayen. Fiction Editor: Leslie Malkin. Art Director: Brian Kauste. Magazine published 6 times/year. Estab. 1993. Circ. 225,000. *Kids World Magazine* aims to give its 9-12-year-old readers an entertaining, interactive and empowering publication with a global perspective.

• See Insider Report with Stu Slayen, editor of *Kids World* and *What! A Magazine*, later in this section.

Fiction: Middle readers: adventure, contemporary, folktale, humorous, multicultural, nature/environment, problem-solving, science fiction, sports, suspense/mystery, relationships. Multicultural needs include relationships/learning between kids of different backgrounds. "I get too many serious submissions." Buys 8 mss/year. Average word length: 550-1,000. Byline given.

Nonfiction: Middle readers: animal, biography, careers, concept, games/puzzles, history, hobbies, how-to, humorous, interview/profile, multicultural, nature/environment, problem-solving, science, social issues, sports. Multicultural needs include stories of an international nature—kids relating with schools/kids in other countries. Buys 12 mss/year. Average word length: 550-1,200. Byline given.

How to Contact/Writers: Fiction: Send complete ms. Nonfiction: Query with published clips. Reports on queries/mss in 2 months. Publishes ms 2 months after acceptance.

Terms: Pays on publication plus 30 days. Buys first rights for mss. Pays $100-200 (Canadian) for stories; $100-400 (Canadian) for articles. Sample copies when available for 9×12 SAE and $1.45 (Canadian). Writer's guidelines for SASE.

Tips: "We're beginning to run stories with an international flavor. We want our readers to feel part of the world and we encourage them to interact with kids in other countries via the Internet. We treat our readers with respect and dignity. We avoid cliché and we try to create a fun and responsible publication." (See listing for *What! A Magazine.*)

LADYBUG, THE MAGAZINE FOR YOUNG CHILDREN, Carus Publishing Company, P.O. Box 300, Peru IL 61354. (815)224-6656. Editor-in-Chief: Marianne Carus. Editor: Paula Morrow. Art Director: Suzanne Beck. Monthly magazine. Estab. 1990. Circ. 130,000. Literary magazine for children 2-6, with stories, poems, activities, songs and picture stories.

• *Ladybug* ranked 44th in the 1996 *Writer's Digest* Fiction 50, the magazine's annual listing of top fiction markets.

Fiction: Picture-oriented material: adventure, animal, fantasy, folktales, humorous, multicultural, nature/environment, problem-solving, science fiction, sports, suspense/mystery. "Open to any easy fiction stories." Buys 50 mss/year. Average word length 300-850 words. Byline given.

Nonfiction: Picture-oriented material: activities, animal, arts/crafts, concept, cooking, humorous, math, nature/environment, problem-solving, science. Buys 35 mss/year.

Poetry: Reviews poems, 20-line maximum length; limit submissions to 5 poems. Uses lyrical, humorous, simple language.

How to Contact/Writers: Fiction/nonfiction: Send complete ms. Queries not accepted. Reports on mss in 3 months. Publishes ms up to 2 years after acceptance. Does not like, but will consider simultaneous submissions.

Illustration: Buys 12 illustrations/issue; 145 illustrations/year. Prefers "bright colors; all media, but use watercolor and acrylics most often; same size as magazine is preferred but not required." To be considered for future assignments: Submit promo sheet, slides, tearsheets, color and b&w photocopies. Reports on art samples in 3 months.

Terms: Pays on publication for mss; after delivery of completed assignment for illustrators. For mss, buys first publication rights; second serial (reprint rights). Buys first publication rights plus promotional rights for artwork. Original artwork returned at job's completion. Pays up to 25¢/word for prose; $3/line for poetry; $25 minimum for articles. Pays $750 for color (cover) illustration, $50-100 for b&w (inside) illustration, $250/page for color (inside). Sample copy for $4. Writer's/illustrator's guidelines free for SASE.

Tips: Writers: "Get to know several young children on an individual basis. Respect your audience. Wants less cute, condescending or 'preach-teachy' material. Less gratuitous anthropomorphism. More rich, evocative language, sense of joy or wonder. Set your manuscript aside for at least a month, then reread critically." Illustrators: "Include examples, where possible, of children, animals, and—most important—action and narrative (i.e., several scenes from a story, showing continuity and an ability to maintain interest). Keep in mind that people come in all colors, sizes, physical conditions. Be inclusive in creating characters." (See listings for *Babybug*, *Cricket* and *Spider*.)

LIGHTHOUSE, Lighthouse Publications, Box 1377, Auburn WA 98071-1377. Editor/Publisher: Tim Clinton. Quarterly magazine. Estab. 1986. Circ. 300. Magazine contains timeless stories and poetry for family reading. 25% of material aimed at juvenile audience.

Fiction: Young readers, middle readers, young adults: adventure, history, humorous, nature, problem-solving, sports, suspense/mystery (not murder). Young adults: romance. Does not want to see anything not "G-rated," any story with a message that is not subtly handled or stories without plots. Buys 36 mss/year. Average word length: 2,000. Byline given.

Poetry: Reviews poetry. Maximum line length: 50. Limit submissions to 5 poems.

How to Contact/Writers: Fiction: Send complete ms and SASE with sufficient postage for return of ms. Reports on mss in 3-4 months.

Terms: Pays on publication. Buys first North American serial rights; first rights. Pays $5-50. Sample copy for $3 (includes guidelines). Writer's guidelines free with regular SAE and 1 first-class stamp.

Tips: "All sections are open to freelance writers—just follow the guidelines and stay in the categories listed above. Try to think of a *new* plot (see so many stories on bullies, storms and haunted houses)."

MAGIC REALISM, Pyx Press, P.O. Box 922648, Sylmar CA 91392-2648. Editor and Publisher: C. Darren Butler. Editor: Julie Thomas. Associate Editor: Patricia Hatch. Associate Publisher: Lisa S. Laurencot. Quarterly magazine. Estab. 1990. Circ. 600. "We publish magic, realism, exaggerated realism, literary fantasy; glib fantasy of the sort found in folktales, fables, myth." 10% of publication aimed at juvenile market.

● *Magic Realism* was ranked 7th on the 1996 *Writer's Digest* Fiction 50, the magazine's annual list of the top fiction markets.

Fiction: Middle readers and young adults: "primarily folktales and glib fantasy." Sees too much of wizards, witches, card readings, sword-and-sorcery, silly or precious tales of any sort, sleight-of-hand magicians. Especially needs short-shorts. Buys approximately 80 mss/year. Byline given.

Poetry: Reviews poetry. Length: prefers 3-30 lines. Limit submissions to 3-8 poems.

How to Contact/Writers: Fiction: send complete ms. Reports on queries in 1 month; mss in 3-6 months. Publishes ms 4 months-2 years after acceptance. "Simultaneous and previously published submissions are welcome if clearly labeled as such."

Illustration: Uses b&w or color covers; b&w inside. Reviews ms/illustration packages from artists. Query; submit complete package with final art or submit ms with rough sketches. Illustrations only: Query or send résumé and portfolio. Reports in 3 months. Samples returned with SASE. Original work returned at job's completion. Credit line given.

Photography: "We consider photos, but have received very few submissions." Model/property releases preferred. Photographers should query with samples and résumé of credits; submit portfolio for review.

Terms: Pays on acceptance. Buys first North American serial rights or one-time rights and reprint rights for ms, artwork and photographs; also buys worldwide Spanish language rights for Spanish edition published 1-2 years after English edition. Pays ¼¢/word plus 3 copies for stories; $3 per magazine page and 1 copy for poetry. Pays illustrators $50 for b&w or $100 for color cover; $3-10 for b&w inside. Photographers paid per photo (range: $3-10). Sample copies for $4.95 (back issue); $5.95 (current issue). Writer's guidelines for SASE.

Tips: "Only a fraction of the material we publish is for children. We rarely use anthropomorphic tales. Most material for children is related to folklore.

MY FRIEND, The Catholic Magazine for Kids, Pauline Books & Media, 50 St. Paul's Ave., Jamaica Plain, Boston MA 02130. (617)522-8911. Articles/Fiction Editor: Sister Anne Joan Flanagan, fsp. Art Director: Sister Helen Rita Lane, fsp. Magazine published 10 times/year. Estab. 1979. Circ. 12,000. "*My Friend* is a magazine of inspiration and entertainment for a predominantly Catholic readership. We reach ages 6-12."

Fiction: Young readers, middle readers: adventure, animal, Christmas, contemporary, humorous, nature/environment, religious. Does not want to see poetry, animals as main characters in religious stories, stories whose basic thrust would be incompatible with Catholic values. Buys 50 mss/ year. Average word length: 450-750. Byline given.

Nonfiction: Young readers: arts/crafts, games/puzzles, health, history, hobbies, humorous, problem-solving, religious, science. Middle readers: arts/crafts, games/puzzles, health, history, hobbies, how-to, humorous, interview/profile, media literacy, nature/environment, problem-solving, religion, science, sports. Does not want to see material that is not compatible with Catholic values; no "New Age" material. Buys 10 mss/year. Average word length: 450-750. Byline given.

How to Contact/Writers: Fiction/nonfiction: Send complete ms. Reports on queries/mss in 2 months.

Illustration: Buys 8 illustrations/issue; buys 60-80 illustrations/year. Preferred theme or style: Realistic depictions of children, but open to variety! "We'd just like to hear from more illustrators who can do *humans*! (We see enough of funny cats, mice, etc.)" Looking for a "Bible stories" and comic book style artist, too. Reviews ms/illustration packages from artists. Send complete ms with copy of final art. Contact: Sister Helen Rita Lane, art director. Illustrations only: Query with samples. Send résumé, promo sheet and tearsheets. Contact: Sister Helen Rita Lane. Reports only if interested. Credit line given.

Photography: Wants photos of "children at play or alone; school scenes; also, sports."

Terms: Pays on acceptance for mss. Buys first rights for mss; variable for artwork. Original artwork returned at job's completion. Pays $35-100 for stories/articles. Pays illustrators $50-150/ b&w (inside); $50-200/color (inside). Sample copy $2 with 9 × 12 SAE and 4 first-class stamps. Writer's guidelines free with SAE and 1 first-class stamp.

Tips: Writers: "Right now, we're especially looking for articles and activities on media literacy. We are not interested in poetry unless it is humorous. Fiction needs are *amply* provided for already." Illustrators: "Please contact us! For the most part, we need illustrations for fiction stories." In the future, sees children's magazines "getting more savvy, less sappy. Suspect that electronic media styles will penetrate a greater number of magazines for kids and adults alike; literary or intellectual publications would be less affected."

*NATIONAL GEOGRAPHIC WORLD, National Geographic Society, 1145 17th St. NW, Washington DC 20036-4688. (202)857-7000. Fax: (202)425-5712. Editor: Susan Tejada. Art Director: Ursula Vosseler. Photo Editor: Chuck Herron. Monthly magazine. Estab. 1975. Circ. 1.1 million.

Nonfiction: Young readers, middle readers, young adult/teens: animal, arts/crafts, biography, cooking, games/puzzles, geography, history, hobbies, how-to, interview/profile, multicultural, nature/environment, science, sports, travel. Middle readers, young adult/teens: social issues. "We do not review or buy unsolicited manuscripts, but do use freelance writers."

Illustration: Buys 100% of illustrations from freelancers. Works on assignment only. Query. Contact: Ursula Vosseler, art director. Illustrations only: Query with samples. Contact: Ursula Vosseler, art director. Reports in 2 months. Samples returned with SASE; samples filed. Credit line given.

Photography: Buys photos separately. Looking for active shots, funny, strange animal close-ups. Uses 35mm transparencies. Query with samples. Reports in 2 months.

Terms: Pays on acceptance. Buys all rights for mss and artwork. Originals returned to artist at job's completion. Writers get 3 copies of issue their work appears in. Pays photographers by the project. Sample copies free for 9 × 12 SAE and 2 first-class stamps; photo guidelines available free for SASE.

Tips: "Most story ideas are generated inhouse and assigned to freelance writers. Query with cover letter and samples of your writing for children or young adults. Keep in mind that *World* is a visual magazine. A story will work best if it has a very tight focus and if the photos show children interacting with their surroundings as well as with each other."

NATURE FRIEND MAGAZINE, Pilgrim Publishers, 22777 State Road 119, Goshen IN 46526. (219)534-2245. Articles Editor: Stanley Brubaker. Monthly magazine. Estab. 1983. Circ. 9,000.
Nonfiction: Picture-oriented material, young readers, middle readers, young adults: animal, nature. Does not want to see evolutionary material. Buys 50-80 mss/year. Average word length: 350-1,500. Byline given.
How to Contact/Writers: Nonfiction: Send complete ms. Reports on mss in 1-4 months. Will consider simultaneous submissions.
Illustration: Works on assignment only.
Terms: Pays on publication. Buys one-time rights. Pays $15-75. Payment for illustrations: $15-80/b&w inside. Two sample copies for $5 with 7 × 10 SAE and 85¢ postage. Writer's/illustrator's guidelines for $2.50.
Tips: Looks for "main articles, puzzles and simple nature and science projects. Please examine samples and writer's guide before submitting."

NEW ERA MAGAZINE, Official Publication for Youth of the Church of Jesus Christ of Latter-Day Saints, 50 E. North Temple St., Salt Lake City UT 84150. (801)240-2951. Articles/Fiction Editor: Richard M. Romney. Art Director: B. Lee Shaw. Monthly magazine. Estab. 1971. Circ. 200,000. General interest religious publication for youth ages 12-18 who are members of The Church of Jesus Christ of Latter-Day Saints (Mormons).
Fiction: Young adults: contemporary, humorous, religious, romance, science fiction, sports. "All material must relate to Mormon point of view." Does not want to see "formula pieces, stories not sensitive to an LDS audience." Buys 20 mss/year. Average word length: 250-2,500. Byline given.
Nonfiction: Young adults: biography, games/puzzles, history, religion, social issues, travel, sports; "general interest articles by, about and for young Mormons. Would like more about Mormon youth worldwide." Does not want to see "formula pieces, articles not adapted to our specific voice and our audience." Buys 150-200 mss/year. Average word length: 250-2,000. Byline given.
Poetry: Reviews poems, 30-line maximum. Limit submissions to 10 poems.
How to Contact/Writers: Fiction/nonfiction: Query. Reports on queries/mss in 2 months. Publishes ms 1 year or more after acceptance. Will consider electronic submissions via disk.
Illustration: Buys 5 illustrations/issue; 50-60 illustrations/year. "We buy only from our pool of illustrators. We use all styles and mediums." Works on assignment only. Illustrations only: Query with samples or to arrange portfolio review. Send résumé, promo sheet, slides and tearsheets. Samples returned with SASE; samples filed. Originals returned at job's completion. Reports only if interested. Original artwork returned at job's completion. Credit line given.
Terms: Pays on acceptance. For mss, buys first rights; right to publish again in other church usage (rights reassigned on written request). Buys all or one-time rights for artwork and photos. Pays $25-375 for stories; $25-350 for articles. Pays illustrators and photographers "by specific arrangements." Sample copies for $1. Writer's guidelines free for #10 SASE.
Tips: Open to "first-person and true-life experiences. Tell what happened in a conversational style. Teen magazines are becoming more brash and sassy. We shy away from the outlandish and trendy, but still need a contemporary look."

NEW MOON: The Magazine For Girls & Their Dreams, New Moon Publishing, Inc., P.O. Box 3620, Duluth MN 55803-3620. (218)728-5507. Fax: (218)728-0314. E-mail: newmoon @newmoon.duluth.mn.us. Website: http://newmoon.duluth.mn.us/~newmoon. Articles Editors/ Art Director: Barbara Stretchberry, Tya Ward. Bimonthly magazine. Estab. 1992. Circ. 25,000. *New Moon* is for every girl who wants her voice heard and her dreams taken seriously. *New Moon* portrays strong female role models of all ages, backgrounds and cultures now and in the past. 100% of publication aimed at juvenile market.

 A BULLET within a listing introduces special comments by the editor of *Children's Writer's & Illustrator's Market.*

• To learn more about *New Moon*, see the Insider Report with Joe Kelly in the 1996 edition of *Children's Writer's & Illustrator's Market*.

Fiction: Middle readers, young adults: adventure, animal, contemporary, fantasy, folktales, health, history, humorous, multicultural, nature/environment, problem-solving, science fiction, sports, suspense/mystery, travel. Buys 6 mss/year. Average word length: 300-1,200. Byline given.

Nonfiction: Middle readers, young adults: animal, arts/crafts, biography, careers, concept, games/puzzles, health, history, hobbies, humorous, interview/profile, math, multicultural, nature/environment, problem-solving, science, social issues, sports, travel, stories about real girls. Does not want to see how-to stories. Wants more stories about real girls doing real things. Buys 6 mss/year. Average word length: 300-900. Byline given.

Poetry: Reviews poetry.

How to Contact/Writers: Fiction/Nonfiction: send complete ms. Reports on queries/mss in 2-4 months. Will consider simultaneous submissions, electronic submissions via disk or modem, previously published work.

Illustration: Buys 15 illustrations/year from freelancers. *New Moon* seeks 4-color cover illustrations as well as b&w illustrations for inside. They also seek small graphics, borders and other illustrations which are multicultural, whimsical and positively portray girls. Reviews ms/illustrations packages from artists. Query. Submit ms with rough sketches. Illustration only: Query; send résumé. Samples returned with SASE; samples filed. Reports only if interested. Credit line given.

Photography: Buys photos from freelancers. Model/property releases required; captions required. Uses color, b&w, glossy prints. Query with samples. Reports only if interested.

Terms: Pays on publication. Buys first rights, one-time rights, reprint rights for mss. Buys one-time rights, reprint rights, first rights for artwork and photographs. Original artwork returned at job's completion. Pays 4-8¢/word for stories; 4-8¢/word for articles. Pays in contributor's copies. Additional payment for ms/illustration packages and for photos accompanying articles. Pays illustrators $200 for color cover; $15-60 for b&w inside. Pays photographers $15-25 per photo. Sample copies for $6.50. Writer's/illustrator's/photo/cover art guidelines for SASE.

Tips: "Please refer to a copy of *New Moon* to understand the style and philosophy of the magazine. Writers and artists who comprehend our goals have the best chance of publication. We're looking for stories about real girls; women's careers, and articles for our Global Village feature on the lives of girls from other countries." Publishes writing/art/photos by children.

ODYSSEY, Science That's Out of This World, Cobblestone Publishing, Inc., 7 School St., Peterborough NH 03458. (603)924-7209. Editor: Elizabeth E. Lindstrom. Managing Editor: Denise L. Babcock. Art Director: Ann Dillon. Magazine published 10 times/year. Estab. 1979. Circ. 35,000. Magazine covers astronomy and space exploration for children ages 8-14. All material must relate to the theme of a specific upcoming issue in order to be considered.

Fiction: Middle readers and young adults: adventure, folktales, history, biographical fiction. Does not want to see anything not theme-related. Average word length: 750 maximum.

Nonfiction: Middle readers and young adults: arts/crafts, biography, cooking, games/puzzles (no word finds), science (space). Don't send anything not theme-related. Average word length: 200-750, depending on section article is used in.

How to Contact/Writers: "A query must consist of all of the following to be considered (please use nonerasable paper): a brief cover letter stating the subject and word length of the proposed article; a detailed one-page outline explaining the information to be presented in the article; an extensive bibliography of materials the author intends to use in preparing the article; a SASE. Writers new to *Odyssey* should send a writing sample with query. If you would like to know if your query has been received, please also include a stamped postcard that requests acknowledgment of receipt. In all correspondence, please include your complete address as well as a telephone number where you can be reached. A writer may send as many queries for one issue as he or she wishes, but each query must have a separate cover letter, outline, bibliography, and SASE. Telephone queries are not accepted. Handwritten queries will not be considered. Queries may be submitted at any time, but queries sent well in advance of deadline *may not be answered for several months*. Go-aheads requesting material proposed in queries are usually sent five months prior to publication date. Unused queries will be returned approximately three to four months prior to publication date."

Illustration: Buys 3 illustrations/issue; 27 illustrations/year. Works on assignment only. Reviews ms/illustration packages from artists. Query. Contact: Beth Lindstrom, editor. Illustration only: Query with samples. Send tearsheets, photocopies. Contact: Ann Dillon, art director. Reports in 2 weeks. Samples returned with SASE; samples not filed. Original artwork returned upon job's completion (upon written request).

Photography: Wants photos pertaining to any of our forthcoming themes. Uses b&w and color prints; 35mm transparencies. Photographers should send unsolicited photos by mail on speculation.

Terms: Pays on publication. Buys all rights for mss and artwork. Pays 20-25¢/word for stories/ articles. Covers are assigned and paid on an individual basis. Pays photographers per photo ($15-100 for b&w; $25-100 for color). Sample copy for $3.95 and SASE with $1.05 postage. Writer's/ illustrator's/photo guidelines for SASE. (See listings for *Calliope, The World History Magazine for Young People*; *Cobblestone, The History Magazine for Young People*; and *Faces, The Magazine About People*.)

ON COURSE, A Magazine for Teens, General Council of the Assemblies of God, 1445 Boonville Ave., Springfield MO 65802-1894. (417)862-2781. Fax: (417)866-1146. E-mail: oncou rse@ag.org. Editor: Melinda Booze. Assistant Editor: Valorie Hurd. Quarterly magazine. Estab. 1991. Circ. 162,000. *On Course* is a religious quarterly for teens "to encourage Christian, biblical discipleship; to promote denominational post-secondary schools; to nurture loyalty to the denomination."

Fiction: Young adults: adventure, contemporary, history, humorous, religious, Christian discipleship, sports. Average word length: 1,000. Byline given.

Nonfiction: Young adults: careers, hobbies, humorous, interview/profile, religion, social issues, sports, college life, Christian discipleship.

How to Contact/Writers: Fiction/nonfiction: Send complete ms. Reports on mss in 2 months. Publishes ms 6-24 months after acceptance. Will consider simultaneous submissions, electronic submissions via disk or modem and previously published work.

Illustration: Buys 4 illustrations/issue; 16 illustrations/year. Uses color artwork only. Reviews ms/illustration packages from artists. Query. Contact: Melinda Booze, editor. Illustration only: Query with samples or send résumé, promo sheet, slides, client list and tearsheets. Contact Melinda Booze, editor. Reports in 2 months. Samples returned with SASE; samples filed. Originals not returned at job's completion. Credit line given.

Photography: Buys photos from freelancers. "Teen life, church life, college life; unposed; often used for illustrative purposes." Model/property releases required. Uses color glossy prints and 35mm or 2¼ × 2¼ transparencies. Query with samples; send business card, promotional literature, tearsheets or catalog. Reports only if interested.

Terms: Pays on acceptance. Buys first or reprint rights for mss. Buys one-time rights for photographs. Pays 6¢/word for stories/articles. Pays illustrators and photographers "as negotiated." Sample copies free for 9 × 11 SAE. Writer's guidelines for SASE.

Tips: Also publishes writing by teens.

ON THE LINE, Mennonite Publishing House, 616 Walnut Ave., Scottdale PA 15683. (412)887-8500. Editor: Mary Clemens Meyer. Magazine published monthly. Estab. 1970. Circ. 6,500.

Fiction: Young adults: contemporary, history, humorous, problem-solving, religious, sports and suspense/mystery. "No fantasy or fiction with animal characters." Buys 60 mss/year. Average word length: 1,000-1,800. Byline given.

Nonfiction: Middle readers, young adults: animal, arts/crafts, biography, cooking, games/puzzles, health, history, hobbies, how-to, humorous, nature/environment, problem-solving. Does not want to see articles written from an adult perspective. Average word length: 200-600. Byline given.

Poetry: Wants to see light verse, humorous poetry. Maximum length: 12 lines.

How to Contact/Writers: Fiction/nonfiction: Send complete ms. Reports on queries/mss in 1 month. Will consider simultaneous submissions.

Illustration: Buys 5-6 illustrations/issue; buys 65-70 illustrations/year. "Inside illustrations are done on assignment only, to accompany our stories and articles—our need for new artists is very limited." Looking for new artists for cover illustrations—full-color work. Illustrations only: "Prefer samples they do not want returned; these stay in our files." Reports on art samples only if interested. Original art work returned at job's completion.

Photography: Looking for photography showing ages 12-14, both sexes, good mix of races, wholesome fun. Uses 8 × 10 glossy b&w prints (1-2 per issue). Photographers should send unsolicited photos by mail.

Terms: Pays on acceptance. For mss buys one-time rights; second serial (reprint rights). Buys one-time rights for artwork and photos. Pays 2-5¢/word for assigned/unsolicited articles. Pays $25-50 for 2- or 3-color inside illustration; $150 for full-color cover illustration. Photographers are paid per photo, $25-50. Sample copy free with 7 × 10 SAE. Free writer's guidelines.

Tips: "We will be focusing on the age 12-13 group of our age 9-14 audience. (Focus was somewhat younger before.)"

❖**OWL COMMUNICATION**, 179 John St., Suite 500, Toronto, Ontario M5T 3G5 Canada. See listings for *Chickadee* and *OWL*.

❖**OWL MAGAZINE, The Discovery Magazine for Children**, Owl Communication, 179 John St., Suite 50, Toronto, Ontario M5T 3G5 Canada. (416)971-5275. Fax: (416)971-5294. E-mail: owlcom@owl.on.ca. Website: http://www.owl.on.ca. Editor: Nyla Ahmad. Art Director: Tim Davin. Photo Editor: Ekaterina Gitlin. Monthly magazine. Circ. 110,000. "*OWL* helps children over eight discover and enjoy the world of science, nature and technology. We look for articles that are fun to read, that inform from a child's perspective, and that motivate hands-on interaction. *OWL* explores the reader's many interests in the natural world in a scientific, but always entertaining, way."
Nonfiction: Middle readers: animal, arts/craft, biology, games/puzzles, high-tech, humor, nature/environment, science, social issues, sports, travel. Especially interested in puzzles and game ideas: logic, math, visual puzzles. Does not want to see religious topics, anthropomorphizing. Buys 20 mss/year. Average word length: 500-1,500. Byline given.
How to Contact/Writers: Nonfiction: Query with published clips. Reports on queries in 3 months.
Illustration: Buys 3-5 illustrations/issue; 40-50 illustrations/year. Uses color artwork only. Preferred theme or style: lively, involving, fun, with emotional impact and appeal. "We use a range of styles." Works on assignment only. Illustrations only: Send tearsheets and slides. Reports on art samples only if interested. Original artwork returned at job's completion.
Photography: Looking for shots of animals and nature. "Label the photos." Uses 2¼×2¼ and 35mm transparencies. Photographers should query with samples.
Terms: Pays on publication. Buys first North American and world rights for mss, artwork and photos. Pays $200-500 (Canadian) for assigned/unsolicited articles. Pays up to $650 (Canadian) for illustrations. Photographers are paid per photo. Sample copies for $4. Free writer's guidelines.
Tips: Writers: "*OWL Magazine* is dedicated to entertaining kids with contemporary and accurate information about the world around them. *OWL* is intellectually challenging but is never preachy. Ideas should be original and convey a spirit of humor and liveliness." (See listing for *Chickadee Magazine*.)

***PARENTS AND CHILDREN TOGETHER ONLINE, A magazine for parents and children on the World Wide Web**, EDINFO Press/Family Literary Centers, 2805 East 10th St., Suite 150, Bloomington IN 47408. (800)759-4723. E-mail: disted@indiana.edu. Website: http://www.indiana.edu/~eric_rec/fl/pcto/menu.html. Editor-in-Chief: Christopher Essex. Quarterly online magazine. Estab. 1990 (in print format). Circ. 9,000 via worldwide web. "Our magazine seeks to promote family literacy by providing original articles and stories for parents and children via the worldwide web." 50% of publication aimed at juvenile market.
Fiction: We accept all categories except the overtly religious. Would like to see more humorous stories. We welcome stories from all cultural backgrounds. Buys 32 mss/year. Byline given.
Nonfiction: All categories are looked at and considered. We especially look for articles with photographs and/or illustrations included. We welcome articles about children and subjects that children will find interesting, that reflect diverse cultural backgrounds. We like articles about animals, but we do get quite a few of them. Buys 24 mss/year. Byline given.
Poetry: Reviews poetry. Limit submissions to 3 poems. "We accept poems written for children that children will enjoy—not poems about childhood by an adult looking back nostalgically. Humorous, but not just silly, poems especially appreciated."
How to Contact/Writers: Fiction/nonfiction: Send complete ms. Reports on queries in 1 week; mss in 3 months. Publishes ms 3-6 months after acceptance. Will consider simultaneous submissions, electronic submissions via disk or modem and previously published work.
Illustration: Buys 12 illustrations/issue; 48 illustrations/year. Uses color artwork only. Reviews ms/illustration packages from artists. Query with ms dummy. Contact: Christopher Essex, editor. Illustrations only: Query with samples. Contact: Christopher Essex, editor. Reports on art samples in 1 month. Samples returned with SASE. Credit line given.
Photography: Looking for children and parents together, either reading together or involved in other interesting activities. Also, children with grandparents. Uses color prints and 35mm transparencies. Query with samples. Send unsolicited photos by mail. Reports in 1 month.
Terms: Buys first North American serial rights for mss. Art/photos use on web with copyright retained by artist/photographer. "We are a free online publication, and cannot afford to pay our

contributors at present." Sample copies for $9. Writer's guidelines free for SASE.

Tips: "We are a good market for writers, artists and photographers who want their material to reach a wide audience. Since we are a free publication, available without charge to anyone with a web browser, we cannot offer our contributors anything more than a large, enthusiastic audience for their work. Our stories and articles are read by thousands of children and parents every month via their families' internet-connected computer."

POCKETS, Devotional Magazine for Children, The Upper Room, 1908 Grand, P.O. Box 189, Nashville TN 37202. (615)340-7333. Articles/Fiction Editor: Janet R. Knight. Art Director: Chris Schechner, Suite 207, 3100 Carlisle Plaza, Dallas TX 75204. Magazine published 11 times/year. Estab. 1981. Circ. 96,000. "Stories should help children 6 to 12 experience a Christian lifestyle that is not always a neatly wrapped moral package but is open to the continuing revelation of God's will."

• *Pockets* was ranked 26th on the 1996 *Writer's Digest* Fiction 50, the magazine's annual list of top fiction markets.

Fiction: Picture-oriented, young readers, middle readers: contemporary, folktales, multicultural, nature/environment, problem-solving, religious. Does not want to see violence or talking animal stories. Buys 40-45 mss/year. Average word length: 800-1,600. Byline given.

Nonfiction: Picture-oriented, young readers, middle readers: cooking, games/puzzles, interview/profile, multicultural, nature/environment, problem-solving. Does not want to see how-to articles. "Our nonfiction reads like a story." Multicultural needs include: stories that feature children of various racial/ethnic groups and do so in a way that is true to those depicted. Buys 10 mss/year. Average word length: 800-1,600. Byline given.

How to Contact/Writers: Fiction/nonfiction: Send complete ms. "Prefer not to deal with queries." Reports on mss in 2-4 weeks. Will consider simultaneous submissions.

Illustration: Buys 50 illustrations/issue. Preferred theme or style: varied; both 4-color and 2-color. Works on assignment only. Illustrations only: Send promo sheet, tearsheets and slides to Chris Schechner, Suite 207, 3100 Carlisle Plaza, Dallas TX 75204. "Include samples of both 2-color and 4-color, if you have them." Reports on art samples in 3 months. Samples returned with SASE. Original artwork returned at job's completion. Credit line given.

Photography: Purchases photography from freelancers. Buys photos with accompanying ms only.

Terms: Pays on acceptance. Buys first North American serial rights for mss; one-time rights for artwork and photos. Pays 12-15¢/word for stories/articles. Pays $500-600 for color cover illustration; $50-400 for color inside; $50-250 (2-color). Pays $25 for color transparencies accompanying articles; $500 for cover photos. Sample copy free with 8 × 10 SAE and 4 first-class stamps. Writer's/illustrator's guidelines free with SASE.

Tips: "Ask for our themes first. They are set yearly in the fall. Also, we are looking for articles about real children involved in environment, peace or similar activities. We have added a 2-page story, about 600 words, for beginning readers. Become familiar with *Pockets* before submitting. So much of what we receive is not appropriate for our publication."

POWER AND LIGHT, Children's Ministries, 6401 The Paseo, Kansas City MO 64131. (816)333-7000. Fax: (816)333-4439. E-mail: mhammer@nazarene.org. Editor: Beula Postlewait. Associate Editor: Melissa Hammer. Weekly story paper. "*Power and Light* is a leisure reading piece for fifth and sixth graders. It is published weekly by the Department of Children's Ministries of the Church of the Nazarene. The major purposes of *Power and Light* are to provide a leisure reading piece which will build Christian behavior and values; provide reinforcement for Biblical concepts taught in the Sunday School curriculum. The focus of the reinforcement will be life-related, with some historical appreciation. *Power and Light*'s target audience is children ages 11-12 in grades five and six."

Fiction: Middle readers: adventure, contemporary, multicultural, religious. "Avoid fantasy, science fiction, abnormally mature or precocious children, personification of animals. Also avoid extensive cultural or holiday references, especially those with a distinctly American frame of reference. Our paper has an international audience. We need stories involving multicultural pre-teens in realistic settings dealing with realistic problems with God's help." Average word length: 500-700. Byline given.

Nonfiction: Middle readers: archaeological religions, multicultural, religion. Multicultural needs include: ethnics and cultures—other world areas especially English-speaking.

How to Contact/Writers: Send complete ms. Reports on queries in 1 month; mss in 2 months. Publishes ms 2 years after acceptance.

Illustration: Buys 1 illustration/issue; 14 illustrations/year. *Power and Light* publishes a wide variety of artistic styles, i.e., cartoon, realistic, montage, etc., but whatever the style, artwork must appeal to 11-12 year old children. Illustrations only: Query; send résumé, promo sheet and portfolio. Reports back only if interested. Credit line given.

Photography: Buys "b&w archaeological/Biblical for inside use and color preteen/contemporary/action for cover use."

Terms: Pays on publication. "Payment is made approximately one year before the date of issue." Buys multiple use rights for mss. Purchases all rights for artwork and first/one-time rights for photographs. Pays 5¢/word for stories/articles. Pays illustrators $40 for b&w, $75 for color cover; $40 for b&w, $50-75 for color inside. Photographers paid per photo (range: $35-45; $200 maximum for cover color photo). Writer's/illustrator's guidelines for SASE.

Tips: "Themes and outcomes should conform to the theology and practices of the Church of the Nazarene, Evangelical Friends, Free Methodist, Wesleyan and other Bible-believing Evangelical churches." Looks for "bright, colorful illustrations; concise, short articles and stories. Keep it realistic and contemporary. Request guidelines first!" (See listing for *Discoveries*.)

PRIMARY DAYS, Cook Communication Ministries, P.O. Box 36640, Colorado Springs CO 80936. (719)536-0100. Editor: Janice K. Burton. Distributed weekly; published quarterly. Estab. 1935. "Our audience is children 6-8 years old." All materials attempt to show God's working in the lives of children. Must have a true Christian slant, not just a moral implication.

Fiction: Young readers: adventure, multicultural, nature/environment, problem-solving, religious, sports (Christian concepts only). Average word length: 300-350.

Nonfiction: Young readers: arts/crafts, biography, games/puzzles, history, interview/profile, multicultural, hobbies, how-to, nature/environment, problem-solving, religion, sports (all need Christian slant). Multicultural needs include: stories that have their settings in other countries and deal with ethnic family situations. Average word length: 100-200.

How to Contact/Writers: Fiction/nonfiction: Send complete ms. Reports on mss in 3 months. Publishes ms 1-2 years after acceptance. ("We work one year ahead.") Will consider previously published work. "We will not accept new manuscripts before March, 1997."

Illustration: Buys 24-30 illustrations/year. Credit line sometimes given.

Photography: Buys photos from freelancers.

Terms: Pays on acceptance. Buys all rights, one-time rights and second (reprint) rights for mss. Pays 7-10¢/word for stories/articles depending on amount of editing required. Sample copies for #10 SASE. Writer's/photo guidelines for SASE.

Tips: "I'm not interested in material that lacks any spiritual element. Stories/articles must be appropriate for a Sunday School take-home paper. Write for Tips to Writers, sample copies, theme lists. Include Social Security number on manuscript." (See listings for *Counselor*, *Teen Power* and *Zelos*.)

R-A-D-A-R, Standard Publishing, 8121 Hamilton Ave., Cincinnati OH 45231. (513)931-4050. Fax: (513)931-0904. Editor: Elaina Meyers. Weekly magazine. Circ. 120,000. *R-A-D-A-R* is a weekly take-home paper for boys and girls who are in grades 3-6. "Our goal is to reach these children with the truth of God's Word, and to help them make it the guide of their lives. Most of our features, including our stories, correlate with the Sunday school lesson themes. Send SASE for a quarterly theme list and sample copies of *R-A-D-A-R*."

● *R-A-D-A-R* was ranked 43rd on the 1996 *Writer's Digest* Fiction 50, the magazine's annual list of top fiction markets.

Fiction: Young readers and middle readers: adventure, animal, contemporary, history, humorous, nature/environment, problem-solving, religious, sports, suspense/mystery, travel. Does not want to see fantasy or science fiction. Buys 52 mss/year. Average word length: 400-1,000. Byline given.

Nonfiction: Young readers and middle readers: animal, arts/crafts, biography, cooking, games/puzzles, geography, health, history, hobbies, how-to, humorous, interview/profile, math, nature/environment, problem-solving, religious, science, social issues, sports, travel. Buys 50 mss/year. Average word length: 400-500. Byline given.

Poetry: Reviews poetry. Maximum length: 16 lines.

How to Contact/Writers: Fiction/nonfiction: Send complete ms. Reports on queries/mss in 1-2 weeks. Will consider simultaneous submissions (but prefers not to). "No queries or ms submissions via fax, please."

Illustration: Buys 3 illustrations/issue; 156 illustrations/year. Works on assignment only. Illustrations only: Send résumé, tearsheets or promo sheets; samples of art can be photocopied.

Contact: Elaina Meyers, editor. Reports in 1-2 weeks. Samples returned with SASE; samples filed. Credit line given. Send SASE for artists' guidelines.

Terms: Pays on acceptance. Buys first rights, one-time rights, second serial, first North American rights for mss. Purchases all rights for artwork. Originals not returned at job's completion. Pays 3-7¢/word for unsolicited articles. Contributor copies given not as payment, but all contributors receive copies of their art/articles. Pays $150 for color (cover); $70-100 for color (inside). Sample copy and writer's guidelines free with business SASE.

Tips: "Write about current topics, issues that elementary-age children are dealing with. Keep illustrations/photos current. Children are growing up much more quickly these days than ever before. This is seen in illustrations and stories. Times are changing and writers and illustrators should keep current with the times to be effective. Send an SASE for sample copies, guidelines, and theme sheet. Be familiar with the publication for which you wish to write." (See listing for *Straight*.)

Photographer John H. Leeser has sold this charming photo of a girl with a bird perched atop her head to six different publications, including *Ranger Rick* and *National Wildlife*. "After the photo was published in *Ranger Rick*, other publications called me to use it again," says Leeser. Using an Olympus OM-1 camera with Kodachrome film, Leeser captured one of his fifth grade students, Erin Shellaway, as she attracted a tufted titmouse to her cap by enticing it with some tasty sunflower seeds.

© John H. Leeser

RANGER RICK, National Wildlife Federation, 8925 Leesburg Pike, Vienna VA 22184. (703)790-4000. Editor: Gerald Bishop. Design Director: Donna Miller. Monthly magazine. Circ. 850,000. "Our audience ranges from ages six to twelve, though we aim the reading level of most material at nine-year-olds or fourth graders."

Fiction: Middle readers: animal (wildlife), fantasy, humorous, science fiction. Buys 4-6 mss/year. Average word length: 900. Byline given.

Nonfiction: Middle readers: animal (wildlife), conservation, outdoor adventure, humorous. Buys 20-30 mss/year. Average word length: 900. Byline given.

How to Contact/Writers: Fiction: Query with published clips; send complete ms. Nonfiction: Query with published clips. Reports on queries/mss in 6 weeks.

Illustration: Buys 6-8 illustrations/issue; 75-100 illustrations/year. Preferred theme: nature, wildlife. Works on assignment only. Illustrations only: Send résumé, tearsheets. Reports on art samples in 6 weeks. Original artwork returned at job's completion.

Terms: Pays on acceptance. Buys all rights (first North American serial rights negotiable). Pays up to $575 for full-length of best quality. For illustrations, buys one-time rights. Pays $250-1,000 for color (inside, per page) illustration. Sample copies for $2. Writer's guidelines free with SASE.

Tips: "Fiction and nonfiction articles may be written on any aspect of wildlife, nature, outdoor adventure and discovery, domestic animals with a 'wild' connection (such as domestic pigs and wild boars), science, conservation or related subjects. To find out what subjects have been covered recently, consult our annual indexes and the *Children's Magazine Guide*. These are available in many libraries. The National Wildlife Federation (NWF) discourages the keeping of wildlife as pets, so the keeping of such pets should not be featured in your copy. Avoid stereotyping of any group. For instance, girls can enjoy nature and the outdoors as much as boys can, and mothers can be just as knowledgeable as fathers. The only way you can write successfully for *Ranger Rick* is to know the kinds of subjects and approaches we like. And the only way you can do that is to read the magazine. Recent issues can be found in most libraries or are available from our office for $2 a copy."

REACT MAGAZINE, The magazine that raises voices, Parade Publications, 711 Third Ave., New York NY 10017. Fax: (212)450-0978. Art Director: Lynda Rubes. Photo Editor: Nancy Iacoi. Weekly magazine. Estab. 1995. Circ. 4 million. 100% publication aimed at juvenile market.
Nonfiction: Young adult: animal, entertainment, games/puzzles, health, hobbies, interview/profile, nature/environment, news, science, social issues, sports. Average word length: 250-600. Byline sometimes given.
How to Contact/Writers: Query with published clips.
Illustration: Works on assignment only. Illustration only: arrange portfolio review. Contact: Lynda Rubes, art director. Credit sometimes given.
Photography: Query with résumé or credits.. Reports only if interested.
Terms: Pays on acceptance. Buys all rights for mss, artwork and photographs. Pays $250-2,000 for stories. Additional payment for photos accompanying articles. Pays photographers by the project. Writer's guidelines and sample issue for SAE and 80¢ postage.
Tips: "*Do not submit work. Query with clips only.*"

SCHOLASTIC INC., 555 Broadway, New York NY 10012-3999. See listings for *Dynamath*, *Junior Scholastic*, *Scholastic Math Magazines*, *Science World* and *Superscience Blue*. Scholastic publishes 40 children's magazines. Contact them for more information.

SCHOLASTIC MATH MAGAZINE, Scholastic Inc., 555 Broadway, New York NY 10012-3999. (212)343-6100. Fax: (212)343-6333. E-mail: mathmag@scholastic.com. Editor: Sarah Jane Brian. Art Director: Joan Michael. Magazine published 14 times/year, September-May. Estab. 1980. Circ. 230,000. "We are a math magazine for seventh, eighth and ninth-grade classrooms. We present math in current, relevant, high-interest (to teens) topics. Math skills we focus on include whole number, fraction and decimal computation, percentages, ratios, proportions, geometry."
Nonfiction: Young adults: animal, arts/crafts, careers, games/puzzles, health, history, hobbies, how-to, humorous, interview/profile, math, multicultural, nature/environment, problem solving, science, sports. No fiction. Does not want to see "anything dealing with *very* controversial issues—e.g., teenage pregnancy, etc. Multicultural submissions must feature a math application, such as math games from around the world." Buys 20 mss/year. Byline given.
How to Contact/Writers: Query. Reports on queries/mss in 6 weeks. Will consider simultaneous submissions. Please include clips of previously published writing for teenagers.
Illustration: Buys 3 illustrations/issue; 42 illustrations/year. Prefers to review "humorous, young adult sophistication" types of art. Works on assignment only. Reviews ms/illustration packages from artists. Query first. Illustrations only: Query with samples; submit portfolio for review. Reports back only if interested. Credit line given.
Terms: Pays on publication. Buys all rights for mss. Original artwork returned at job's completion. Pays $25 for puzzles and riddles; maximum of $350 for stories/articles. Photographers are paid by the project. Samples copies are free for 8½×11 SASE.
Tips: "For our magazine, stories dealing with math concepts and applications in the real world are sought. We are a unique magazine with extremely specific needs. Most of the submissions we receive are wildly inappropriate because the freelancer who has sent the submission has never seen the magazine. Writers should get a copy of the magazine first, and then send a query rather than a complete article." (See listings for *Dynamath*, *Junior Scholastic*, *Science World* and *Superscience Blue*.)

SCHOOL MATES, USCF's Magazine for Beginning Chess Players, United States Chess Federation, 186 Rt. 9W, New Windsor NY 12553. (914)562-8350. Fax: (914)561-CHES. Contact:

Articles Editor. Bimonthly magazine. Estab. 1987. Circ. 30,000. Magazine for beginning chess players. Offers instructional articles, features on famous players, scholastic chess coverage, games, puzzles, occasional fiction, listing of chess tournaments.

Fiction: Young readers, middle readers, young adults: chess. Middle readers: humorous (chess-related). Average word length: 500-2,500 words.

Nonfiction: Young readers, middle readers, young adults: games/puzzles, chess. Middle readers, young adults: interview/profile (chess-related). "No *Mad Magazine* type humor. No sex, no drugs, no alcohol, no tobacco. No stereotypes. We want to see chess presented as a wholesome, non-nerdy activity that's fun for all. Good sportsmanship, fair play, and 'thinking ahead' are extremely desirable in chess articles. Also, celebrities who play chess."

Poetry: Infrequently published. Must be chess related.

How to Contact/Writers: Send complete ms. Reports on queries/mss in 5 weeks.

Illustration: Buys 10-25 illustrations/year. Prefers b&w and ink; cartoons OK. Illustration only: Query first. Reports back only if interested. Credit line sometimes given. "Typically, a cover is credited while an illustration inside gets only the artist's signature in the work itself."

Photography: Purchases photos from freelancers. Wants "action shots of chess games (at tournament competitions), well-done portraits of popular chess players."

Terms: Pays on publication. Buys one-time rights for mss, artwork and photos. For stories/articles, pays $20-100. Pays illustrators $50-75 for b&w cover; $20-50 for b&w inside. Pays photographers per photo (range: $25-75). Sample copies free for 9×12 SAE and 2 first-class stamps. Writer's guidelines free on request.

Tips: Writers: "Lively prose that grabs and sustains kids' attention is desirable. Don't talk down to kids or over their heads. Don't be overly 'cute.' " Illustration/photography: "Whimsical shots are often desirable."

SCIENCE WEEKLY, Science Weekly Inc., P.O. Box 70638, Chevy Chase MD 20813. (301)680-8804. Fax: (301)680-9240. Editor: Deborah Lazar. Magazine published 16 times/year. Estab. 1984. Circ. 250,000.

- *Science Weekly* uses freelance writers to develop and write an entire issue on a single science topic. Send résumé only, not submissions.

Nonfiction: Young readers, middle readers, (K-8th grade): science/math education, education, problem-solving. "Author must be within the greater DC, Virginia, Maryland area." Works on assignment only.

Terms: Pays on publication. Prefers people with education, science and children's writing background. *Send résumé.*

*SCIENCE WORLD, Scholastic Inc., 555 Broadway, New York NY 10012-3999. (212)343-6456. Fax: (212)343-6333. E-mail: scienceworld@scholastic.com. Articles Editor: Karen McNulty. Art Director: Susan Kass. Photo Editor: Daniella Jo Nilva. Magazine published biweekly during the school year. Estab. 1959. Circ. 350,000. Publishes articles in Life Science/Health, Physical Science/Technology, Earth Science/Environment/Astronomy for students in grades 7-10. The goal is to make science relevant for teens.

- *Science World* publishes a separate teacher's edition with lesson plans and skills pages to accompany feature articles.

Fiction: Young adults/teen: science fiction. Buys 1-2 mss/year. Average word length: 1,000. Byline sometimes given.

Nonfiction: Middle readers, young adults/teens: animal, biography, careers, health, how-to, humorous, interview/profile, multicultural, nature/environment, problem solving, science, sports (science), "anything with a science theme." Multicultural needs include: minority scientists as role models. Does not want to see stories without a clear news hook. Buys 20 mss/year. Average word length: 500-1,000. Byline sometimes given.

How to Contact/Writers: Nonfiction: Query with published clips. Reports on queries in 2 months. Publishes ms 2 months after acceptance.

Illustration: Buys 2 illustrations/issue; 28 illustrations/year. Works on assignment only. Illustration only: Query with samples, tearsheets. Contact: Susan Kass, art director. Reports back only if interested. Samples returned with SASE; samples filed "if we use them." Credit line sometimes given.

Photography: Model/property releases required; captions required including background information. Provide résumé, business card, promotional literature or tearsheets to be kept on file. Reports back only if interested.

Terms: Pays on acceptance. Buys all right for mss/artwork. Originals returned to artist at job's completion. For stories/articles, pays $200. Pays photographers per photo. Sample copies free for 9×12 SAE and 2 first-class stamps. Writer's guidelines free for SASE.

SCIENCELAND, To Nurture Scientific Thinking, Scienceland Inc., 501 Fifth Ave., #2108, New York NY 10017-6165. (212)490-2180. Fax: (212)490-2187. Editor/Art Director: Al Matano. Magazine published 8 times/year. Estab. 1977. Circ. 16,000. This is "a content reading picture-book for the preschool youngster being read to, the first-grader learning to read and for the second and third grader beginning to read independently."

Nonfiction: Picture-oriented material, young readers: animal, art/crafts, biography, careers, cooking, education, games/puzzles, health, history, how-to, nature/environment, problem-solving. Does not want to see unillustrated material; All material must be illustrated in full color.

How to Contact/Writers: *Must* be picture or full-color illustrated stories.

Illustration: Uses color artwork only. Prefers to review "detailed, realistic, full color art. No abstracts or fantasy." Reviews captioned/illustration packages from artists. "Query first." Illustrations only: Send unsolicited art by mail; provide résumé, promotional literature or tearsheets to be kept on file. Reports back in 3-4 weeks. "Exclusively contracted original artwork retained at our option for exhibits, etc. Others returned at job's completion."

Photography: Wants to see "physical and natural science photos with children in scenes whenever possible." Model/property release and photo captions required where applicable. Uses 35mm transparencies. Photographer should submit portfolio for review; provide résumé, promotional literature or tearsheets to be kept on file.

Terms: Pays on publication. Buys nonexclusive rights to artwork and photos. Payment for captioned/illustration packages: $50-500 and up. Payment for illustrations: $25-300 and up for color cover; $25-300 and up for color inside. Photographers paid by the project. Sample copy free with 9×12 SASE.

Tips: "Must be top notch illustrator or photographer. No amateurs."

SEVENTEEN MAGAZINE, K-III Magazines, 850 Third Ave., New York NY 10022. (212)407-9700. Editor-in-Chief: Caroline Miller. Fiction Editor: Susan Brenna. Senior Editor: Heidi Parker. Art Director: Florence Sicard. Monthly magazine. Estab. 1944. Circ. 2 million. "General interest magazine for teenage girls."

Fiction: Young adults: animal, contemporary, fantasy, folktales, health, history, humorous, religious, romance, science fiction, sports, spy/mystery/adventure. "We consider all good literary short fiction." Buys 12-20 mss/year. Average word length: 1,000-4,000. Byline given.

Nonfiction: Young adults: animal, fashion, careers, health, hobbies, how-to, humorous, interview/profile, multicultural, religion, social issues, sports. Buys 150 mss/year. Word length: Varies from 800-1,000 words for short features and monthly columns to 800-2,500 words for major articles. Byline given.

How to Contact/Writers: Fiction: Send complete ms. Nonfiction: Query with published clips or send complete ms. "Do not call." Reports on queries/mss in 1 month. Will consider simultaneous submissions.

Terms: Pays on acceptance. Writer's guidelines available for SASE.

SHOFAR, 43 Northcote Dr., Melville NY 11747. (516)643-4598. Managing Editor: Gerald H. Grayson. Magazine published monthly October through May—double issues December/January and April/May. Circ. 17,000. For Jewish children ages 8-13.

Fiction: Middle readers: cartoons, contemporary, humorous, poetry, religious, sports. All material must be on a Jewish theme. Buys 10-20 mss/year. Average word length: 500-700. Byline given.

Nonfiction: Middle readers: history, humorous, interview/profile, puzzles, religious. Buys 10-20 mss/year. Average word length: 500-1,000. Byline given.

How to Contact/Writers: Fiction/nonfiction: Send complete ms (preferred) with SASE. Queries welcome. Publishes special holiday issues. Submit holiday theme pieces at least 4 months in advance. Reports on queries/mss in 1 month. Will consider simultaneous submissions.

● **A BULLET** within a listing introduces special comments by the editor of *Children's Writer's & Illustrator's Market*.

Illustration: Buys 3-4 illustrations/issue; buys 15-20 illustrations/year. Works on assignment only. Reviews ms/illustration packages from artists. Query first. Illustrations only: Send tearsheets. Works on assignment only. Reports on art samples only if interested. Original artwork returned at job's completion.

Terms: Buys first North American serial rights or first serial rights for mss and artwork. Pays on publication. Pays 10¢/word plus 5 contributor's copies. Photos purchased with mss at additional fees. Pays $25-100/b&w cover illustration; $50-150/color (cover). Sample copy free with 9×12 SAE and 98¢ postage. Free writer's/illustrator's guidelines.

SKIPPING STONES, A Multicultural Children's Magazine, P.O. Box 3939, Eugene OR 97403. (541)342-4956. Website: http://www.nonviolence.org/~hvweb/skipping/. Articles/Photo Editor: Arun N. Toké. Fiction Editor: Rachel Johnson. Bimonthly magazine. Estab. 1988. Circ. 3,000. *"Skipping Stones* is a multicultural, nonprofit children's magazine designed to encourage cooperation, creativity and celebration of cultural and environmental richness. We encourage submissions by minorities and under-represented populations."

Fiction: Middle readers, young adult/teens: animal, contemporary, humorous. All levels: folktales, multicultural, nature/environment. Multicultural needs include: bilingual or multilingual pieces; use of words from other languages; settings in other cultures or multi-ethnic communities.

Nonfiction: All levels: animal, biography, cooking, games/puzzles, history, humorous, interview/profile, multicultural, nature/environment, creative problem-solving, religion and cultural celebrations, sports, travel, multicultural and environmental awareness. Does not want to see preaching or abusive language; no poems by authors over 18 years old; no suspense or romance stories for the sake of the same. Average word length: 500-750. Byline given.

How to Contact/Writers: Fiction: Query. Nonfiction: Send complete ms. Reports on queries in 1 month; mss in 4 months. Will consider simultaneous submissions; reviews artwork for future assignments. Please include your name on each page.

Illustration: Prefers b&w drawings especially by young adults. Will consider all illustration packages. Ms/illustration packages: Query; submit complete ms with final art; submit tearsheets. Reports back in 4 months. Original artwork returned at job's completion. Credit line given.

Photography: Black & white photos preferred, but color photos will be considered. Children 7-15, international, nature, celebration.

Terms: Pays on publication. Buys first or reprint rights for mss and artwork; reprint rights for photographs. Pays in copies for authors, photographers and illustrators. Sample copies for $5 with SAE and 4 first-class stamps. Writer's/illustrator's guidelines for 4×9 SASE.

Tips: Wants material "meant for children" with multicultural or environmental awareness theme. "Think, live and write as if you were a child. Let the 'inner child' within you speak out— naturally, uninhibited." Wants "material that gives insight on cultural celebrations, lifestyle, custom and tradition, glimpse of daily life in other countries and cultures. Photos, songs, artwork are most welcome if they illustrate/highlight the points. Translations are welcome if your submission is in a language other than English. In 1997, our themes will include homeless and street children, world religions and cultures, life in the innercity, celebrations in various cultures, creative problem-solving approaches, grandparents and elders in your life. How I am Making a Difference in the World, cycles of change, Native American cultures, cooperative games, recipes for healthy living (from home kitchens around the world), music."

SOCCER JR., The Soccer Magazine for Kids, Triplepoint Inc., 27 Unquowa Rd., Fairfield CT 06430. (203)259-5766. Articles/Fiction Editor: Owen Lockwood. Bimonthly magazine. Estab. 1992. Circ. 100,000. *Soccer Jr.* is for soccer players 8-16 years-old. It offers "instruction, inspiration and fun."

Fiction: Middle readers, young adults: sports (soccer). Does not want to see "cute," preachy or "moralizing" stories. Buys 3-4 mss/year. Average word length: 1,000-2,000. Byline given.

Nonfiction: Young readers, middle readers, young adults: games/puzzles—soccer-themed. Buys 10-12 mss/year.

How to Contact/Writers: Fiction/nonfiction: Send complete ms. Reports on mss in 2-3 months. Publishes ms 3-12 months after acceptance. Will consider simultaneous submissions.

Illustration: Uses color artwork only. Works on assignment only. Illustrations only: Send samples to be filed. Samples not returned. "We have a small pool of artists we work from, but look for new freelancers occasionally, and accept samples for consideration."

Terms: Pays on acceptance. Buys first rights for mss. Sample copies for 9×12 SAE and 5 first-class stamps.

Tips: "Read *Soccer Jr.*. An astonishing number of manuscripts are submitted either by people who've never seen the publication or who send non-soccer-related material." The magazine also accepts stories written by children.

SPIDER, The Magazine for Children, Carus Publishing Company, P.O. Box 300, Peru IL 61354. Editor-in-Chief: Marianne Carus. Associate Editor: Christine Walske. Art Director: Ron McCutchan. Monthly magazine. Estab. 1994. Circ. 85,000. *Spider* publishes high-quality literature for beginning readers, primarily ages 6-9.
Fiction: Young readers: adventure, animal, contemporary, fantasy, folktales, history, humorous, multicultural, nature/environment, problem-solving, science fiction, sports, suspense/mystery. "Authentic, well-researched stories from all cultures are welcome. We would like to see more multicultural material. No didactic, religious, or violent stories, or anything that talks down to children." Average word length: 300-1,000. Byline given.
Nonfiction: Young readers: animal, arts/crafts, cooking, games/puzzles, geography, history, math, multicultural, nature/environment, problem-solving, science. "Well-researched articles on all cultures are welcome. Would like to see more games, puzzles and activities, especially ones adaptable to *Spider*'s takeout pages. No encyclopedic or overtly educational articles." Average word length: 300-800. Byline given.
Poetry: Serious, humorous, nonsense rhymes. Maximum length: 20 lines.
How to Contact/Writers: Fiction/nonfiction: Send complete ms. Reports on mss in 3 months. Publishes ms 1-2 years after acceptance. Will consider simultaneous submissions and previously published work.
Illustration: Buys 20 illustrations/issue; 240 illustrations/year. Uses color artwork only. "Any medium—preferably one that can wrap on a laser scanner—no larger than 20 × 24. We use more realism than cartoon-style art." Works on assignment only. Reviews ms/illustration packages from artists. Submit ms with rough sketches. Illustrations only: Send promo sheet and tearsheets. Reports in 6 weeks. Samples returned with SASE; samples filed. Credit line given.
Photography: Buys photos from freelancers. Buys photos with accompanying ms only. Model/property releases required; captions required. Uses 35mm or 2¼ × 2¼ transparencies. Send unsolicited photos by mail; provide résumé and tearsheets. Reports in 6 weeks.
Terms: Pays on publication for text; within 45 days from acceptance for art. Buys first, one-time or reprint rights for mss. Buys first and promotional rights for artwork; one-time rights for photographs. Original artwork returned at job's completion. Pays 25¢/word for stories/articles. Authors also receive 2 complimentary copies of the issue in which work appears. Additional payment for ms/illustration packages and for photos accompanying articles. Pays illustrators $750 for color cover; $200-300 for color inside. Pays photographers per photo (range: $25-75). Sample copies for $4. Writer's/illustrator's guidelines for SASE.
Tips: "Writers: Read back issues before submitting." (See listings for *Babybug*, *Cricket*, and *Ladybug*.)

STANDARD PUBLISHING, 8121 Hamilton Ave., Cincinnati OH 45231. See listings for *R-A-D-A-R* and *Straight*.

STORY FRIENDS, Mennonite Publishing House, 616 Walnut Ave., Scottdale PA 15683. (412)887-5181. Fax: (412)887-3111. E-mail: rstutz%5904477@mcimail.com. Editor: Rose Mary Stutzman. Art Director: Jim Butti. Magazine published monthly in weekly issues. Estab. 1905. Circ. 7,000. Story paper that reinforces Christian values for children ages 4-9.
Fiction: Picture-oriented material: contemporary, humorous, multicultural, nature/environment, problem-solving, religious, relationships. Multicultural needs include fiction or nonfiction pieces which help children be aware of cultural diversity and celebrate differences while recognizing similarities. Buys 45 mss/year. Average word length: 300-800. Byline given.
Nonfiction: Picture-oriented: animal, humorous, interview/profile, multicultural, nature/environment. Buys 10 mss/year. Average word length: 300-800. Byline given.
Poetry: "I like variety—some long story poems and some four-lines."
How to Contact/Writers: Fiction/nonfiction: Send complete ms. Reports on mss in 5-6 weeks. Will consider simultaneous submissions.
Illustration: Works on assignment only. Send tearsheets with SASE. Reports in 2 months. Samples returned with SASE; samples filed. Credit line given.
Photography: Occasionally buys photos from freelancers. Wants photos of children ages 4-8.
Terms: Pays on acceptance. Buys one-time rights or reprint rights for mss and artwork. Original artwork returned at job's completion. Pays 3-5¢/word for stories and articles. Pays $20-30 for

b&w cover; $50 for color cover; $20-30 for b&w inside; $50 for color inside. Writer's guidelines free with SAE and 2 first-class stamps.
Tips: "Become immersed in high quality children's literature."

STRAIGHT, Standard Publishing, 8121 Hamilton Ave., Cincinnati OH 45231. (513)931-4050. Articles/Fiction Editor: Heather Wallace. Magazine published quarterly in weekly parts. Circ. 40,000. *Straight* is a magazine designed for today's Christian teenagers.
  • *Straight* was ranked 24th in the 1996 *Writer's Digest* Fiction 50, the magazine's annual list of top fiction markets.
Fiction: Young adults: contemporary, health, humorous, problem solving, religious, sports. Does not want to see science fiction, fantasy, historical. "All should have religious perspective." Buys 100-115 mss/year. Average word length: 1,100-1,500. Byline given.
Nonfiction: Young adults: health, hobbies, humorous, interview/profile, problem-solving, religion, social issues, sports. Does not want to see devotionals. Buys 24-30 mss/year. Average word length: 500-1,000. Byline given.
Poetry: Reviews poetry from teenagers only.
How to Contact/Writers: Fiction/nonfiction: Query or send complete ms. Reports on queries in 1-2 weeks; mss in 1-2 months. Will consider simultaneous submissions.
Illustration: Buys 40-45 illustrations/year. Uses color artwork only. Preferred theme or style: Realistic, cartoon (full-color only). Works on assignment only. Reviews ms/illustration packages from artists. Query first. Illustrations only: Submit promo sheets or tearsheets. Samples kept on file. Reports back only if interested. Credit line given.
Photography: Buys photos from freelancers. Looking for photos of contemporary, modestly-dressed teenagers. Model/property release required. Uses 35mm transparencies. Photographer should send unsolicited photos by mail.
Terms: Pays on acceptance. Buys first rights and second serial (reprint rights) for mss. Buys full rights for artwork; one-time rights for photos. Pays 5-7¢ per word for stories/articles. Pays illustrators $150-325/color inside. Pays photographers per photo (range: $75-125). Sample copy free with business SASE. Writer's/illustrator's guidelines free with business SASE.
Tips: "Remember we are a publication for Christian teenagers. Each fiction or nonfiction piece should address modern-day issues from a religious perspective. We are trying to become more racially diverse. Writers, illustrators and photographers should keep this in mind and submit more material with African-Americans, Hispanics, Asian-Americans, etc. as the focus. The main characters of all pieces should be contemporary teens who cope with modern-day problems using Christian principles. Stories should be uplifting, positive and character-building, but not preachy. Conflicts must be resolved realistically, with thought-provoking and honest endings. Accepted length is 1,100 to 1,500 words. Nonfiction is accepted. We use articles on current issues from a Christian point of view and humor. Nonfiction pieces should concern topics of interest to teens, including school, family life, recreation, friends, part-time jobs, dating and music." (See listing for *R-A-D-A-R*.)

STREET TIMES, Outside In, 1236 SW Salmon, Portland OR 97205. (503)223-4121, ext. 31. Fax: (503)223-6837. Editor: Deborah Abela. Monthly newsletter. Estab. 1987. Circ. 800. Contains "resources, street life stories, poetry and art—designed as a pre-employment training tool for Portland street youth." 70% of publication aimed at juvenile market.
Fiction: Young adult: adventure, contemporary, fantasy, folktales, history, humorous, multicultural, problem-solving.
Nonfiction: Young adult: arts/crafts, careers, concepts, history, interview/profile, multicultural, problem-solving. Wants experiences of "other street youth or former street youth; difficulties of getting off the street."
Poetry: Reviews poetry.
How to Contact/Writers: Nonfiction: Send complete ms. Reports on queries/mss in 6 months. Will consider simultaneous submissions and previously published work.

MARKET CONDITIONS are constantly changing! If you're still using this book and it is 1998 or later, buy the newest edition of *Children's Writer's & Illustrator's Market* at your favorite bookstore or order directly from Writer's Digest Books.

Terms: Sample copies free for SASE.

STUDENT LEADERSHIP JOURNAL, InterVarsity Christian Fellowship, P.O. Box 7895, Madison WI 53707. (608)274-9001, ext. 425. Editor: Jeff Yourison. Quarterly magazine. Estab. 1988. Circ. 10,000.

Fiction: Young adults (collegiate): multicultural, religious. Multicultural themes include: Forming campus fellowships that reflect the ethnic makeup of the campus and demonstrating *reconciliation* beyond celebrating difference. "I see too much aimed at young teens. Our age group is 18-30 years old." Buys 4 mss/year. Average word length: 300-1,800. Byline given.

Nonfiction: Young adults: history, interview/profile, multicultural, nature/environment, religion, social issues. Multicultural themes include: Affirming the need for ethnic validation and reconciliation. "We don't affirm all lifestyles—therefore we are promoting multi-ethnicity but not full-orbed multiculturalism. We prefer articles on issues, leadership, spiritual growth, sexual healing, campus ministry, etc." Buys 6-8 mss/year. Average word length: 1,100-2,200. Byline given.

Poetry: Wants to see free verse; lots of good imagery. Maximum length: 18 lines. Limit submissions to 5 poems.

How to Contact/Writers: Fiction/nonfiction: Send complete ms. Reports on queries/mss in 6 months. Publishes ms 1-2 years after acceptance. Accepts IBM-compatible word processing files on diskettes.

Illustration: Buys 5 illustrations/issue; 20 illustrations/year. Uses b&w line art only. Prefers cartoon pen & ink 5×7 or 8×10 stand alone campus/religious humor. Illustrations only: Send promo sheet, portfolio and tearsheets. Reports only if interested. Samples not returned; samples kept on file. Credit line given.

Photography: Looks for campus shots—all types: single faces, studying, thinking, "mood"—pairs and groups: praying, studying, talking, playing. 18-22 year old subjects or professor-types. Model/property release preferred. Uses color and b&w 5×7 glossy prints; 2¼×2¼, 4×5 or 35mm transparencies. Photographers should query with samples; send unsolicited photos by mail; provide business card, promotional literature or tearsheets. "Send photocopies I can keep. I'll call for the print." Reports only if interested.

Terms: Pays on acceptance for ms; on publication for photos and cartoons. Buys first North American serial rights, first rights and reprint rights for ms. Purchases first rights for artwork; one-time rights for photographs. Original work returned at job's completion. Pays $50-75 for stories; $50-125 for articles; and contributor's copies. Pays illustrators $50-100 for b&w cover; $25-75 for b&w inside. Photographers paid per photo (range: $25-50). Sample copies for $3. Writer's guidelines for SASE.

Tips: "Please write and photograph according to the audience. Research the age group and the subculture. Older teens are really sensitive to tokenism and condescension toward their generation. They want to be treated as sophisticated even though they are frequently uninformed and hurting. To reach this audience requires credibility, vulnerability, transparency and confidence!"

SUPERSCIENCE BLUE, Scholastic Inc., 555 Broadway, New York NY 10012-3999. (212)343-6100. Editor: Kathy Burkett. Art Director: Susan Kass. Monthly (during school year) magazine. Estab. 1989. Circ. 375,000. "News and hands-on science for children in grades 4-6. Designed for use in a class setting; distributed by teacher. Articles make science fun and interesting for a broad audience of children. Issues are theme-based."

• *Superscience Blue* is not currently accepting submissions.

Nonfiction: Middle readers: animal, how-to (science experiments), nature/environment, problem-solving, science topics. Does not want to see "general nature stories. Our focus is science with a *news* or *hands-on* slant. To date we have never purchased an unsolicited manuscript. Instead, we assign articles based on clips—and sometimes queries." Average word length: 250-800. Byline sometimes given.

How to Contact/Writers: Nonfiction: Query with published clips. (Most freelance articles are assigned.)

Illustration: Buys 2-3 illustrations/issue; 10-12 illustrations/year. Works on assignment only. Illustrations only: Send résumé and tearsheets. Reports on art samples only if interested. Original artwork returned at job's completion.

Tips: Looks for "news articles and photo essays. Good journalism means always going to *primary* sources—interview scientists in the field, for example, and *quote* them for a more lively article." (See listings for *Dynamath, Junior Scholastic, Scholastic Math Magazine* and *Science World*.)

TEEN LIFE, Gospel Publishing House, 1445 Boonville Ave., Springfield MO 65802-1894. (417)862-2781, ext. 4359. Fax: (417)862-6059. E-mail: tbicket@publishing.ag.org. Articles/Fiction Editor: Tammy Bicket. Art Director: Sonny Carder. Photo Editor: Carol Arnold. Quarterly newspaper (Sunday school take-home paper). Estab. 1920. Circ. 80,000. "Slant articles toward the 15- to 19-year-old teen. We are a Christian publication, so all articles should focus on the Christian's responses to life. Fiction should be realistic, not syrupy nor too graphic. Fiction should have a Christian slant also."

Fiction: Young adults: adventure, contemporary, history, humorous, religious, sports (all with Christian slant). Also wants fiction based on true stories. Buys 50 mss/year. Average word length 700-1,500. Byline given.

Nonfiction: Young adults: biography, careers, history, humorous, interview/profile, multicultural, religion, social issues, sports, "thoughtful treatment of contemporary issues (i.e., racism, preparing for the future); interviews with famous Christians who have noteworthy stories to tell. Multicultural needs include: material on missions. Buys 50 mss/year. "Looking for more articles and fewer stories." Average word length: 1,000. Byline given.

How to Contact/Writers: Fiction/nonfiction: Send complete ms. Do *not* send query letters. Reports on mss in 2-3 months. Will consider simultaneous submissions.

Illustration: Buys 50-200 illustrations/issue, 200 illustrations/year. Uses color artwork only. Prefers to review youth-oriented styles. Art director will assign freelance art. Works on assignment only. Reviews ms/illustration packages from artists. Send portfolio. "We are Mac literate." Contact: Sonny Carder, art director. Illustration only: arrange portfolio review or send promo sheet, slides, client list, tearsheets or on disk (Mac). Contact: Sonny Carder, art director. Illustrations and design: "We are interested in looking at portfolios consisting of illustration and design work that is teen-oriented." Reports in 3-4 weeks. Samples filed. Originals returned to artist at job's completion. Credit line given.

Photography: Buys photos from freelancers. Wants "teen photos that look spontaneous. Ethnic and urban photos urgently needed." Uses color prints, 35mm, 2¼×2¼, 4×5 transparencies. Send unsolicited photos by mail.

Terms: Pays on acceptance. For mss, buys first North American serial rights, first rights, one-time rights, second serial (reprint rights), simultaneous rights. For artwork, buys one-time rights for cartoons; one-time rights for photos. Rights for illustrations negotiable. Pays $25-75 for stories; $25-100 for articles. Pays illustrators: $200-300 for color cover or inside. Pays photographers $75-100/color cover photo; $35-45/b&w inside photo; $50-60/color inside photo. Sample copies free (2) with 9×12 SASE with 3 first-class stamps. Writer's/photo guidelines free with SASE.

Tips: "We want contemporary, real life articles, or fiction that has the same feel. Try to keep it teen-oriented—trendy, hip, interesting perspectives; current, topical situations that revolve around teens. We work on specific themes for each quarter, so interested writers should request current writers guidelines and topic list."

TEEN POWER, Cook Communications Ministries, P.O. Box 36640, Colorado Springs CO 80936. (719)536-0100, ext. 3991. Editor: Chris Lyon. Quarterly magazine. Estab. 1965. "*Teen Power* is an eight-page Sunday School take-home paper aimed at 11-16 year olds in a conservative Christian audience. Its primary objective is to help readers see how principles for Christian living can be applied to everyday life. We are looking for fresh, creative true stories, true-to-life, and nonfiction articles. All must show how God and the Bible are relevant in the lives of today's teens. All manuscripts must have a clear, spiritual emphasis or 'take away value.' We don't use stories which merely have a good moral. Be careful not to preach or talk down to kids. Also, be realistic. Dialogue should be natural. Resolutions should not be too easy or tacked on. We are a specialized market with a distinct niche, but we do rely heavily on freelance writers. We are open to any new writer who grasps the purpose of our publication."

Fiction: Young adults: adventure, contemporary, humorous, multicultural, problem-solving, religious, sports. Buys 75 mss/year. Average word length: 600-1,200. Byline given.

Nonfiction: Young adults: biography, games/puzzles, how-to, humorous, interview/profile, multicultural, problem-solving, religion, social issues, sports. Multicultural themes include: Christian teens in foreign countries, missions, missionary kids, ethnic Christian teens in US and Canada. Does not want to see "articles with no connection to Christian principles." Buys 75 mss/year. Average word length: 300-1,000. Byline given.

How To Contact/Writers: Fiction/nonfiction: Send complete ms. Reports on mss in 3-4 months. Publishes ms "at least one year" after acceptance. Will consider simultaneous submissions. Please include Social Security number on mss.

Illustration: Send résumé, promo sheet, tearsheets. Reports back only if interested. Credit line given.

Photography: Buys photos from freelancers. Looks for mood shots: teen fads and hang outs; sport and school activities shots.

Terms: Pays on acceptance. Buys one-time rights. Pays $25-120 for stories/articles. Negotiates illustrators' fees. Photographers paid per photo. Sample copies and writer's guidelines for #10 SAE and 1 first-class stamp.

Tips: "Take-home papers are a great 'break-in' point. Each weekly issue contains at least two freelance-written features. However, we are very specific about the type of material we are looking for. We want stories and articles to reinforce our Sunday School lessons and help our readers apply what they learned in Sunday School throughout the week. All submissions must have a spiritual emphasis—not merely a moral lesson." (See listings for *Counselor*, *Primary Days* and *Zelos*).

3-2-1 CONTACT, Children's Television Workshop, One Lincoln Plaza, New York NY 10023. (212)595-3456.
• This magazine no longer needs freelancers.

TIME FOR KIDS, 1271 Avenue of the Americas, 23rd Floor, New York NY 10020-1393. (212)522-1212. Estab. 1995. News magazine for kids from the publishers of TIME.
• This magazine no longer uses freelancers.

TOTALLY FOX KIDS MAGAZINE, Peter Green Design/Fox Kids Network, 4219 W. Burbank Blvd., Burbank CA 91505. (818)953-2210. E-mail: bananadog@aol.com. Articles Editor: Scott Russell. Art Director: Debra Hintz. Quarterly magazine. Estab. 1990. Circ. 4 million. Features "fun and hip articles, games and activities for Fox Kids Club members ages 6-13, promoting Fox Kids shows."

Nonfiction: Picture-oriented material, young readers, middle readers: Any material tied in to a Fox Kids Network show or one of our other features (no religious material). Buys 16 mss/year. Average word length: 200-500.

How to Contact/Writers: Nonfiction only: Query with published clips. Reports on queries/mss in 2-3 months. Publishes mss 2-6 months after acceptance. Will consider simultaneous submissions and electronic submissions via disk or modem.

Illustration: Buys 5 illustrations/issue. Uses color artwork only. Works on assignment only. Prefers "cartoon character work, must be *on model*." Reviews ms/illustration packages from artists. Query. Illustrations only: Send résumé, promo sheet, tearsheets. Reports only if interested. Samples returned with SASE; samples filed. Original work returned at job's completion. Credit line given.

Photography: Buys photos from freelancers. Uses a variety of subjects, depending on articles. Model/property release required. Uses color prints and 4×5 or 35mm transparencies. Query with résumé, business card, tearsheets. Reports only if interested.

Terms: Pays 30 days from acceptance. Buys all rights. Pays $100-400 for stories/articles. Additional payment for ms/illustration packages and for photos accompanying articles. Sample writer's guidelines for SASE.

Tips: "Practice. Read. Come up with some new and creative ideas. Our articles are almost always humorous. We try to give kids cutting edge information. All of our articles are tied into Fox Kids shows."

TOUCH, GEMS Girls' Clubs, Box 7259, Grand Rapids MI 49510. (616)241-5616. Managing Editor: Carol Smith. Art Director: Joan Hall. Monthly (with combined issues May/June, July/August) magazine. Circ. 16,000. "*Touch* is designed to help girls ages 9-14 see how God is at work in their lives and in the world around them."

Fiction: Middle readers: adventure, animal, folktales, health, humorous, multicultural, problem-solving, religious, romance, sports. Does not want to see unrealistic stories and those with trite, easy endings. Buys 40 mss/year. Average word length: 400-1,000. Byline given.

Nonfiction: Middle readers, teens: animal, careers, fashion, games/puzzles, hobbies, how-to, humorous, interview/profile, multicultural, problem-solving, religious, social issues, sports, travel. Buys 9 mss/year. Average word length: 200-800. Byline given.

How to Contact/Writers: Send for biannual update for publication themes. Fiction/nonfiction: Send complete ms. Reports on mss in 2 months. Will consider simultaneous submissions.

Illustration: Buys 3 illustrations/year. Prefers ms/illustration packages. Works on assignment only. Reports on submissions only if interested. Samples returned with SASE. Credit line given.

Anyone who watches early morning cartoons will recognize Bobby, the daydreaming troublemaker from *Bobby's World* on Fox Television. Artist Kelley Kennedy illustrated Bobby's weird thoughts for *Totally Fox Kids*, a magazine designed for Fox Kids Club members. "Kelley helps come up with the ideas for the features," says Articles Editor Scott Russell. "His mind is fittingly twisted to this purpose, and he's fast!"

Terms: Pays on publication. Buys first North American serial rights, first rights, second serial (reprint rights) or simultaneous rights. Original artwork not returned at job's completion. Pays $20-50 for assigned articles; $5-30 for unsolicited articles. "We send complimentary copies in addition to pay." Pays $50-75 for color cover illustration; $25-40 for color inside illustration. Pays photographers by the project ($35-50 per photo). Writer's guidelines free with SASE.
Tips: Writers: "The stories should be current, deal with adolescent problems and joys, and help girls see God at work in their lives through humor as well as problem-solving."

TURTLE MAGAZINE, For Preschool Kids, Children's Better Health Institute, 1100 Waterway Blvd., P.O. Box 567, Indianapolis IN 46206. (317)636-8881. Editor: Nancy S. Axelrad. Art Director: Bart Rivers. Monthly/bimonthly magazine published January/February, March, April/May, June, July/August, September, October/November, December. Circ. 300,000. *Turtle* uses read-aloud stories, especially suitable for bedtime or naptime reading. Also uses poems, simple science experiments, and health-related articles. All but 2 pages aimed at juvenile audience.

Fiction: Picture-oriented material: adventure, animal, contemporary, fantasy, folktales, health-related, history, holiday themes, humorous, multicultural, nature/environment, problem-solving, sports, suspense/mystery. "Need very simple experiments illustrating basic science concepts. Also needs action rhymes to foster creative movement." Do not want stories about monsters or scary things. Avoid stories in which the characters indulge in unhealthy activities like eating junk food. Buys 50 mss/year. Average word length: 150-300. Byline given.

Nonfiction: Picture-oriented material: animal, arts/crafts, cooking, games/puzzles, geography, health, multicultural, nature/environment, science, sports. Buys 20 mss/year. Average word length: 150-300. Byline given.

How to Contact/Writers: Fiction/nonfiction: "Prefer complete manuscript to queries." Reports on mss in 8-10 weeks.

Photography: Buys photos from freelancers with accompanying ms only.

Terms: Pays on publication. Buys all rights for mss/artwork; one-time rights for photographs. Pays up to 22¢/word for stories and articles (depending upon length and quality) and 10 complimentary copies. Pays $30-70 for b&w inside. Sample copy $1.25. Writer's guidelines free with SASE.

Tips: "We're beginning to edit *Turtle* more for the very young preschooler, so we're looking for stories and articles that are written more simply than those we've used in the past. Our need for health-related material, especially features that encourage fitness, is ongoing. Health subjects must be age-appropriate. When writing about them, think creatively and lighten up! Fight the tendency to become boringly pedantic. Nobody—not even young kids—likes to be lectured. Always keep in mind that in order for a story or article to educate preschoolers, it first must be entertaining—warm and engaging, exciting, or genuinely funny. Understand that writing for *Turtle* is a difficult challenge. Study the magazine to see if your manuscript is right for *Turtle*. Magazines have distinct personalities which can't be understood by only reading market listings. Here the trend is toward leaner, lighter writing. There will be a growing need for interactive activities. Writers might want to consider developing an activity to accompany their concise manuscripts." (See listings for *Child Life, Children's Digest, Children's Playmate, Humpty Dumpty's Magazine, Jack And Jill* and *U*S* Kids*.)

U*S* KIDS, Children's Better Health Institute, 1100 Waterway Blvd., P.O. Box 567, Indianapolis IN 46206. (317)636-8881. Editor: Beth Struck. Art Director: Matthew Brinkman. Magazine published 8 times a year. Estab. 1987. Circ. 250,000.

Fiction: Young readers and middle readers: adventure, animal, contemporary, health, history, humorous, multicultural, nature/environment, problem-solving, sports, suspense/mystery. "We see too many stories with no real story line. We'd like to see more mysteries and contemporary humor stories." Buys approximately 8-16 mss/year. Average word length: 500-800. Byline given.

Nonfiction: Young readers and middle readers: animal, arts/crafts, cooking, games/puzzles, health, history, hobbies, how-to, humorous, interview/profile, multicultural, nature/environment, science, social issues, sports, travel. Wants to see interviews with kids ages 5-10, who have done something unusual or different. Buys 30-40 mss/year. Average word length: 500-600. Byline given.

Poetry: Maximum length: 32 lines.

How to Contact/Writers: Fiction: Send complete ms. Nonfiction: Query. Reports on queries and mss in 1 month. Publishes ms 6 months after acceptance. Will consider simultaneous submissions, electronic submissions via disk or modem and previously published work.

Illustration: Buys 8 illustrations/issue; 70 illustrations/year. Color artwork only. Works on assignment only. Reviews ms/illustration packages from artists. Query. Illustrations only: Send résumé and tearsheets. Reports back only if interested. Samples returned with SASE; samples kept on file. Does not return originals. Credit line given.

Photography: Purchases photography from freelancers. Looking for photos that pertain to children ages 5-10. Model/property release required. Uses color and b&w prints; 35mm, 2¼×2¼, 4×5 and 8×10 transparencies. Photographers should provide résumé, business card, promotional literature or tearsheets to be kept on file. Reports back only if interested.

Terms: Pays on publication. Buys all rights for mss. Purchases all rights for artwork. Purchases one-time rights for photographs. Pays 10¢/word minimum. Additional payment for ms/illustration packages. Pays illustrators $140/page for color inside. Photographers paid by the project or per photo (negotiable). Sample copies for $2.50. Writer's/illustrator/photo guidelines for SASE.

Tips: "Write clearly and concisely without preaching or being obvious." (See listings for *Child Life*, *Children's Digest*, *Children's Playmate*, *Humpty Dumpty's Magazine*, *Jack And Jill* and *Turtle Magazine*.)

*✹WHAT! A MAGAZINE, What! Publishers Inc. 108-93 Lombard Ave., Winnipeg, Manitoba R3B 3B1 Canada. (204)942-2214. Fax: (204)943-8991. E-mail: what@fox.nstn.ca. Articles Editor: Stuart Slayen. Art Director: Brian Kauste. Magazine published 5 times/year. Estab. 1987. Circ. 200,000. "Informative and entertaining teen magazine for both genders. Articles deal with issues and ideas of relevance to Canadian teens. The magazine is distributed through schools so we aim to be cool and responsible at the same time."
Nonfiction: Young adults (14 and up): biography, careers, concept, health, how-to, humorous, interview/profile, nature/environment, science, social issues, sports. "No cliché teen stuff. Also, we're getting too many heavy pitches lately on teen pregnancy, AIDS, etc." Buys 8 mss/year. Average word length: 675-2,100. Byline given.
How to Contact/Writers: Nonfiction: Query with published clips. Reports on queries/mss in 2 months. Publishes ms 2 months after acceptance.
Terms: Pays on publication plus 30 days. Buys first rights for mss. Pays $100-500 (Canadian) for articles. Sample copies when available for 9 × 12 and $1.45 (Canadian). Writer's guidelines free for SASE.
Tips: "Teens are smarter today than ever before. Respect that intelligence in queries and articles. Aim for the older end of our age-range (14-19) and avoid cliché. Humor works for us almost all the time." (See listing for *Kids World Magazine*.)

WITH, The Magazine for Radical Christian Youth, Faith & Life Press, 722 Main, P.O. Box 347, Newton KS 67114. (316)283-5100. Editors: Eddy Hall, Carol Duerksen. Published 8 times a year. Circ. 6,100. Magazine published for teenagers, ages 15-18, in Mennonite, Brethren and Mennonite Brethren congregations. "We deal with issues affecting teens and try to help them make choices reflecting a radical Christian faith."
Fiction: Young adults: contemporary, fantasy, folktales, humorous, multicultural, problem-solving, religious, sports. Multicultural needs include: race relations, first-person stories featuring teens of ethnic minorities. "Stories, fiction or nonfiction, in which high-school-age youth of various cultures/ethnic groups, are the protaganist. Stories may or may not focus on cross-cultural relationships. Also, would like to see more humor and parables/allegories." Buys 15 mss/year. Average word length: 1,000-2,000. Byline given.
Nonfiction: Young adults: first-person teen personal experience (as-told-to), how-to, humorous, multicultural, problem-solving, religion, social issues. Buys 15-20 mss/year. Average word length: 1,000-2,000. Byline given.
Poetry: Wants to see religious, humorous, nature. "Buys 1-2 poems/year." Maximum length: 50 lines.
How to Contact/Writers: Send complete ms. Query on first-person teen personal experience stories and how-to articles. (Detailed guidelines for first-person stories, how-tos, and fiction available for SASE.) Reports on queries in 1 month; mss in 6 weeks. Will consider simultaneous submissions.
Illustration: Buys 6-8 illustrations/issue; buys 50-60 illustrations/year. Uses b&w and 2-color artwork only. Preferred theme or style: candids/interracial. Reviews ms/illustration packages from artists. Query first. Illustrations only: Query with portfolio (photocopies only) or tearsheets. Reports only if interested. Original artwork returned at job's completion upon request. Credit line given.
Photography: Buys photos from freelancers. Looking for candid photos of teens (ages 15-18), especially ethnic minorities. Uses 8 × 10 b&w glossy prints. Photographers should send unsolicited photos by mail.
Terms: Pays on acceptance. For mss buys first rights, one-time rights; second serial (reprint rights). Buys one-time rights for artwork and photos. Pays 5¢/word for unpublished manuscripts; 3¢/word for reprints. Will pay more for assigned as-told-to stories. Pays $50-60 for b&w cover illustration and b&w inside illustration. Pays photographers per photo (range: $25-50, cover only). Sample copy for 9 × 12 SAE and 5 first-class stamps. Writer's/illustrator's guidelines free with SASE.
Tips: "We're hungry for stuff that makes teens laugh—fiction, nonfiction and cartoons. It doesn't have to be religious, but must be wholesome."

WONDER TIME, WordAction Publications, 6401 The Paseo, Kansas City MO 64131. (816)333-7000. Editor: Lois Perrigo. Weekly magazine. Circ. 45,000. "*Wonder Time* is a full-

INSIDER REPORT

Maintaining the balance between cool and responsible

Your assignment: Write an article for a teen magazine. Sound easy? Okay, here's a pop quiz: What's hip with today's teens? What are they into? What's important to them? What are they talking about? You can't find answers by paging through a few issues of *Seventeen* or watching reruns of *My So-Called Life*. Try following the advice of Stu Slayen, editor of the cool Canadian teen mag *What! A Magazine*—talk to teenagers.

Slayen not only preaches, but also practices this advice. He and the staff of *What!* annually assemble what's called the National Editorial Advisory Committee, made up of 10-13 teens from across Canada, chosen through an application process to represent the diversity of the country's teen population. The committee provides feedback and opinions on story ideas.

Stu Slayen

"There are a lot of intelligent teens out there, and I don't think the adult media portray teens in a positive or objective light. It's really good for us to hear what they're saying because we think we get a more accurate snapshot than a large TV network or a daily newspaper would."

Slayen's second piece of advice is "talk to teachers. Teachers see teens in their very real light. At least they have the opportunity to, whether or not they choose to take advantage of it. And I think they can provide an objective opinion," he says.

Though he also advises writers to read teen magazines, Slayen cautions against using them as a research tool and getting caught up in the cliches of what adults think teen magazines are all about—fashion, makeup and what to wear to the prom. "I think there's a lot of room for improvement in youth media. I was interviewed recently by a Canadian youth cable channel, and the reporter asked me to describe the typical teen. To me, that is the most inane question, because there's no such thing. And I think that a lot of mainstream media assume there is."

Slayen feels that teens are interested in many of the same things adult are, but from a perspective relevant to them. "If you want to talk about something as obscure as the International Monetary Fund, I think you can do that as long as you write about it in such a way that there are applications to what it means to a teenager," he says.

For example, *What!* did an article on problem gambling. "That story's been done a thousand times, but we did it from the perspective of teens who have problems. That's not cliche teen journalism—that's what they want to read. My

INSIDER REPORT, *Slayen*

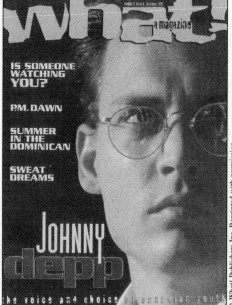

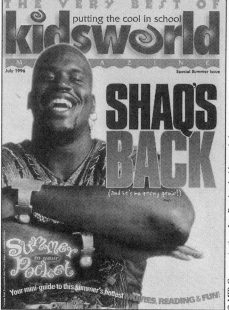

Stu Slayen edits two hip magazines for Canadian youth—*What! A Magazine* for teens, and *Kids World Magazine* for preteens. Both the magazines are distributed almost exclusively through Canadian classrooms.

INSIDER REPORT, *continued*

recommendation to writers is whatever you think teen writing should be, stop and start again."

What! often addresses topics which you may be surprised to find in a teen magazine. They kept readers up-to-date on the Quebec Referendum. They put together a piece on starting your own business. They ran an article on buying your first car. They even tackled the search for spiritual fulfillment (for which they received great response from their young readership). Slayen feels this type of intelligent journalism is important for teen publications. "We try to be interactive, empowering, and entertaining. I know these are all buzzwords, but we really try to do that in every issue."

Recurring entertainment features in *What!* include music and movie reviews, sports news, and interviews with celebrities in music, movies and TV (such as Alanis Morrisette, Tori Amos, Stone Temple Pilots, the Kids in the Hall, Scott Wolf and Johnny Depp). But *What!* mainly uses freelancers for feature articles.

There is something special about *What! A Magazine* that writers should keep in mind—it's distributed almost solely through Canadian high schools (about 1,000, who must request the mag) at no charge. The editorial staff, therefore, has two masters: "the readers and the environment in which we distribute." So Slayen and his staff strive to produce a "cool yet responsible" publication. Maintaining that balance is a bit instinctive, says Slayen. It's having the right story idea, combined with common sense; providing editorial that excites the readers, that is in keeping with societal and entertainment trends, but is still sensitive to the school environment.

"We did a story on body piercing last year, and we had a couple of photos that were graphic [descriptive], and we had a few schools cancel because of the shocking nature of seeing someone with a pierced neck or a pierced navel." But cases like this, says Slayen, are few and far between. "Canadian educators are very hip, very modern, very progressive, very respectful of what their students are reading, and still happy to distribute the magazine."

Audience gender is a consideration when working for teen publications. *What!*'s editors try to achieve gender balance. "We're in schools. It would be a huge error to target one gender," says Slayen. "If we feel an issue is leaning a little feminine, we try to put something in that might be a little more male-oriented, and vice versa. But a lot of things could appeal to either."

In terms of writing style, Slayen urges freelancers writing for teens not to change how they write. "Just be conversational, chatty, use humor when appropriate. The basic tenets of journalism still apply—accuracy and balance are absolutely crucial." But most important, don't talk down to the readers. "If you use a condescending lead in a story, [teenagers] probably won't read the rest of the story. They might not read the rest of the issue."

—*Alice P. Buening*

color story paper for first and second graders. It is designed to connect Sunday School learning with the daily living experiences and growth of the primary child. Since *Wonder Time*'s target audience is children ages six to eight, the readability goal is to encourage beginning readers to read for themselves. The major purposes of *Wonder Time* are to: Provide a life-related paper which will build Christian values and encourage ethical behavior and provide reinforcement for the biblical concepts taught in the WordAction Sunday School curriculum."

Fiction: Picture-oriented material: adventure, contemporary, multicultural, nature/environment, religious. "We need ethnic balance—stories and illustrations from a variety of ethnic experiences." Buys 52 mss/year. Average word length: 300-400. Byline given.

Nonfiction: Picture-oriented material: problem solving, religious, social issues.

How to Contact/Writers: Fiction/nonfiction: Send complete ms. Reports on queries/mss in 6 weeks. Will consider simultaneous submissions.

Illustration: Buys 50 illustrations/year. Works on assignment only. Reviews ms/illustration packages from artists. Query. Contact: Lois Perrigo, *Wonder Time* editor. Illustrations only: Submit samples of work. Reports on art samples in 6 weeks. Samples returned with SASE; samples kept on file. Credit line given.

Terms: Pays on acceptance. Original artwork not returned. Pays $25 per story for rights which allow the publisher to print the story multiple times in the same publication without repayment. Pays illustrators $40 for b&w cover or inside; $75 for color cover or inside. Photographers paid per photo (range: $25-75). Sends complimentary contributor's copies of publication. Sample copy and writer's guidelines with 9½×12 SAE and 2 first-class stamps.

Tips: "Basic themes reappear regularly. Please write for a theme list. Also be familiar with what *Wonder Time* is all about. Ask for guidelines, sample copies, theme list *before* submitting."

WRITER'S INTERNATIONAL FORUM, Bristol Services International, P.O. Box 516, Tracyton WA 98393. Bimonthly magazine. Estab. 1990. Up to 25% aimed at juvenile market. Some issues "Special Juniors Editions" include 100% material aimed at juvenile market.

Fiction: Middle readers, young adults: adventure, animal, contemporary, fantasy, folktales, humorous, mystery, nature/environment, problem-solving, romance, science fiction, suspense/mystery. "No experimental formats; no picture books; no poetry. No stories for children under age 8. We see too many anthropomorphic characters. We would like to see more mysteries, problem-solving and adventures." Buys approximately 48-54 mss/year. Average word length: 400-2,000. Byline given.

How to Contact/Writers: Fiction: Reports on mss in 2 months. Publishes ms 4-6 months after acceptance.

Illustration: Uses illustration "only to accompany a story." Reports on submission in 2 months. Samples returned with SASE. Credit line given.

Terms: Pays on acceptance. Buys first North American serial rights. Original artwork returned at job's completion. Pays $5 minimum for stories and illustrations. Sample copies for $3.50 standard edition; $5 for Juniors Edition.

Tips: "All the stories accepted for publication in *Writers' International Forum* are open to comments by our readers. Many of our readers write exclusively for children and/or are school teachers. The most often noted critique on our children's pieces is that writers fail to clearly write for a specific age group. Determine your audience's age, then write every word, description and action to that audience. Each issue includes lessons and tips on writing. Our 'Writer to Writer' column uses tips on the writing process and is our most open area; limit is 300 words and payment is one contributor copy."

*YOUNG JUDAEAN, Young Judaea-Hadassah Zionist Youth Commission, 50 West 58th St., New York NY 10019. (212)303-4588. Fax: (212)303-4572. Articles Editor: Jonathan Mayo. Quarterly magazine. Circ. 5,000. Children's magazine with Jewish/Zionist theme.

Fiction: Middle readers: religious; any subject with Jewish relevance. Does not want to see preachy/moral stories. Buys 4 mss/year. Average word length: 600-1,200. Byline given.

Nonfiction: Middle readers: history, religion, social issues; any subject with Jewish theme. Buys 2-3 mss/year. Average word length: 1,000-1,500. Byline given.

♣ **THE MAPLE LEAF** before a listing indicates that the market is Canadian.

How to Contact/Writers: Fiction/nonfiction: send complete ms. Reports on queries in 1 month; mss in 6 months. Publishes ms 2-3 months after acceptance. Will consider simultaneous submissions and previously published work.
Illustrations: Uses b&w artwork only. Illustrations only: Query with samples. Contact: Jonathan Mayo, editor. Reports back only if interested. Samples returned with SASE. Credit line given.
Photography: Reports back only if interested.
Terms: "No payment—just copies of publication." Sample copies free for SAE. Writer's guidelines free for SASE.

YOUNG SALVATIONIST, The Salvation Army, 615 Slaters Lane, P.O. Box 269, Alexandria VA 22313. (703)684-5500. Published 10 times/year. Estab. 1984. Circ. 50,000. "We accept material with clear Christian content written for high school age teenagers. *Young Salvationist* is published for teenage members of The Salvation Army, an evangelical part of the Christian Church."
Fiction: Young adults: contemporary religious. Buys 12-20 mss/year. Average word length: 750-1,200. Byline given.
Nonfiction: Young adults: religious—careers, health, interview/profile, social issues, sports. Buys 40-50 mss/year. Average word length: 750-1,200. Byline given.
How to Contact/Writers: Fiction/nonfiction: Query with published clips or send complete ms. Reports on queries/mss in 1 month. Will consider simultaneous submissions.
Illustrations: Buys 3-5 illustrations/issue; 20-30 illustrations/year. Reviews ms/illustration packages from artists. Send ms with art. Contact: Lesa Davis, production manager. Illustrations only: Query; send résumé, promo sheet, portfolio, tearsheets. Reports back only if interested. Samples returned with SASE; samples filed. Credit line given.
Photography: Purchases photography from freelancers. Looking for teens in action.
Terms: Pays on acceptance. Buys first North American serial rights, first rights, one-time rights or second serial (reprint) rights for mss. Purchases one-time rights for artwork and photographs. Original artwork returned at job's completion "if requested." For mss, pays 15¢/word; 10¢/word for reprints. Pays $100-150 color (cover) illustration; $50-100 b&w (inside) illustration; $100-150 color (inside) illustration. Sample copy for 9 × 12 SAE and 4 first-class stamps. Writer's guidelines free for #10 SASE.
Tips: "Ask for theme list/sample copy! Write 'up,' not down to teens. Aim at young *adults*, not children." Wants "less fiction, more 'journalistic' nonfiction."

*YOUR BIG BACKYARD, National Wildlife Federation, 8925 Leesburg Pike, Vienna VA 22184. (703)790-4515. Fax: (703)827-2585. E-mail: johnsond@nwf.org. Articles/Fiction Editor: Donna Johnson. Art Director: Tamara Tylenda. Photo Editor: Stephen B. Freligh. Monthly magazine (includes a parents' newsletter bound into the center to be pulled out). Estab. 1980. Circ. 400,000. Purpose of the magazine is to educate young children (ages 3-6) about nature and wildlife in a fun, interactive and entertaining way. 90% of publication aimed at juvenile market (10% is parents' newsletter).
Fiction: Picture-oriented material: animal, fantasy, humorous, multicultural, nature/environment. Young readers: adventure, animal, humorous, multicultural, nature/environment. "We do not want fiction that does not involve animals or nature in some way." Buys 12 mss/year. Average word length: 200-1,000. Byline given.
Nonfiction: Picture-oriented material, young readers: animal, arts/crafts, games/puzzles, nature/environment. Wants no articles that deal with subjects other than nature. Buys 2 mss/year. Average word length: 50-100.
Poetry: Reviews poetry. Maximum length: 15 words or 25 lines.
How to Contact/Writers: Fiction: send complete ms. Nonfiction: Query with published clips; send complete ms. Reports on queries/mss in 2 weeks. Publishes ms 4 months after acceptance. Will consider simultaneous submissions, electronic submission via disk or modem and previously published work.
Illustration: Buys 5 illustrations/issue 60 illustrations/year. Uses color artwork only. Reviews ms/illustration packages from artists. Send ms with dummy. Contact: Donna Johnson, art director. Illustrations only: Send promo sheet, portfolio, slides, tearsheets. Contact: Tammy Tylenda, art director. Reports back only if interested. Samples not returned; filed. Credit line given.
Photography: Wants animal photos. Uses 35mm transparencies. Send unsolicited photos by mail. Reports in 2 months.
Terms: Pays on acceptance. Buys one-time rights, reprint rights for mss. Buys one-time rights for artwork and photographs. Original artwork returned at job's completion. Pays $250-750 for

stories; $50-200 for articles. Additional payment for ms/illustration packages and for photos accompanying articles. Pays illustrators $200-500 for color inside. Pays photographers per photo (range: $200-600). Sample copies for $1.

Tips: "With regard to fiction, we accept stories in which the main characters are talking animals; however, the storyline should deal with some aspect of the animal's natural history or habitat. The book *Stellaluna* is an example of the type or good fiction we want to see more of."

YOUTH UPDATE, St. Anthony Messenger Press, 1615 Republic St., Cincinnati OH 45210. (513)241-5615. Articles Editor: Carol Ann Morrow. Art Director: June Pfaff. Monthly newsletter. Estab. 1982. Circ. 23,000. "Each issue focuses on one topic only. *Youth Update* addresses the faith and Christian life questions of young people and is designed to attract, instruct, guide and challenge its audience by applying the gospel to modern problems and situations. The students who read *Youth Update* vary in their religious education and reading ability. Write for average high school students. These students are 15-year-olds with a C+ average. Assume that they have paid attention to religious instruction and remember a little of what 'sister' said. Aim more toward 'table talk' than 'teacher talk.' "

Nonfiction: Young adults/teens: religion. Buys 12 mss/year. Average word length: 2,200-2,300. Byline given.

How to Contact/Writers: Nonfiction: Query. Reports on queries/mss in 6 weeks. Will consider computer printout and electronic submissions via disk.

Photography: Buys photos from freelancers. Uses photos of teens (high-school age) with attention to racial diversity and with emotion.

Terms: Pays on acceptance. Buys first North American serial rights for mss. Buys one-time rights for photographs. Pays $325-400 for articles. Pays photographers per photo ($40 minimum). Sample copy free with #10 SASE. Writer's guidelines free on request.

Tips: "Read the newsletter yourself—3 issues at least. In the past, our publication has dealt with a variety of topics including: dating, Lent, teenage pregnancy, baptism, loneliness, violence, confirmation and the Bible. When writing, use the *New American Bible* as translation. Interested in church-related topics."

ZELOS, Cook Communications Ministries, P.O. Box 36640, Colorado Springs CO 80936. (719)536-0100, ext. 3991. Editor: Chris Lyon. Quarterly spiral-bound Sunday School curriculum book. Estab. 1995. *Zelos* is a Christain lifestyle notebook which helps high school-aged students grow in their relationship with God. Each weekly section contains a calendar; a personal introduction to the topic of the week by author, speaker and youth leader Dewey Bertolini; daily journal activities; and one freelance-written feature which correlates with the weekly topic.

Fiction: Young adults: humorous, religious, slice-of-life vignettes. Buys 20 mss/year. Average word length: 400-1,000. Byline given.

Nonfiction: Young adult: humorous, interview/profile, religion, inspirational, personal experience. Buys 40 mss/year. Average word length: 400-1,000. Byline given.

Poetry: Reviews poetry. Wants free verse, light verse and traditional. Maximum length: 5-30 lines. Limit submissions to 3 poems.

How to Contact/Writers: Fiction/nonfiction: Send complete ms. Reports on mss in 2-3 months. Publishes ms 12-18 months after acceptance. Will consider simultaneous submissions, previously published work.

Photography: Buys photos from freelancers. Model/property release required.

Terms: Pays on acceptance. Buys one-time rights for magazines. Pays $30-120 for stories and articles. Sample copies of articles free (#10 envelope stamped for 2 oz.); sample publication for $4.99.

Tips: "Whenever possible, we use true stories: personal experiences, 'as told tos,' profiles and interviews. Subjects can be everyday teens or celebrities with strong, Christian testimonies. We're looking for fresh, motivating, hard-hitting stories to challenge our readers. All material must have a clear, Christian perspective. We use some fiction—usually contemporary, true-to-life. Stories should be realistic. Resolutions should be natural and characters and subjects should not be too good to be true. *Zelos* is an exciting new product. We are looking for writers who will dig up interesting stories to challenge today's teens." (See listings for *Counselor*, *Primary Days* and *Teen Power*.)

*ZILLIONS For Kids From Consumer Reports, Consumers Union, 101 Truman Ave., Yonkers NY 10703-1057. (914)378-2551. Fax: (914)378-2904. Articles Editor: Moye Thompson. Art Director: Rob Jenter. Bimonthly magazine. Estab. 1980. Circ. 300,000. "*Zillions* is the consumer reports for kids (with heavy emphasis on fun!) We cover products, advertising, money matters, etc."

• *Zillions* does not accept unsolicited manuscripts; query first.

Nonfiction: Young adults/teens: arts/crafts, careers, games/puzzles, health, hobbies, how-to, humorous, nature/environment, problem-solving, social issues, sports. "Will consider story ideas on kid money matters, marketing to kids and anything that educates kids to be smart consumers." Buys 10 mss/year. Average word length: 800-2,000.

How to Contact/Writers: Nonfiction: Query with published clips. "We'll contact if interested (within a few months probably)." Publishes ms 2 months after acceptance.

Terms: Pays on publication. Buys all rights for ms. Pays $1,000 for articles. Writer's guidelines free for SASE.

Tips: "Read the magazine!"

Multimedia

Welcome to the world of multimedia! This brand new section is devoted to producers and developers of CD-ROMs and software for children. Some of the companies will be familiar to you. For instance, we have listings for Houghton Mifflin Interactive and Reidmore Books. Much of the work they produce ties into their book titles. Other companies such as Creative Wonders were developed independently. They produce work such as *Sesame Street*-related titles.

All of the companies listed here need freelance illustration, writing, or even project proposals. Writers and illustrators should submit to them in much the same way they submit to book publishers. A difference is that these companies may want samples of previous multimedia work submitted on disk. It's not always necessary, however, that writers and illustrators have experience working on CD-ROM or software titles. According to CD-ROM writer and developer Annie Fox, the newness of the multimedia industry may make it easier to break into than book publishing. See the Insider Report with Fox on page 214 for more information and a lesson in CD-ROM design.

The listings here are just the tip of the iceberg in a sea of multimedia producers. There are hundreds of companies that produce CD-ROMs and software for kids. In the future the number of multimedia listings in the section should grow and grow as the industry expands and stabilizes. There are a number of sources available if you'd like to find additional multimedia producers to query. The Society of Children's Book Writers and Illustrators has a Guide to Multimedia Markets compiled by Bruce Balan, available to members for an $8\frac{1}{2} \times 11$ SAE and $1.01 postage. You can also consult the 6th edition of *The Multimedia Directory* (The Corronade Group). Also refer to Get Plugged In! Opportunities in the Children's Multimedia Market, by Kelly Quiroz on page 19 for more information on this growing market.

*CREATIVE WONDERS, 595 Penobscot Dr., Redwood City CA 94063. (415)482-2300. Fax: (415)482-2301. Website: http://www.cwonders.com. Estab. 1994. 23 titles currently in distribution.
Software: Produces early learning, creativity tools, problem solving, math, social studies, language arts and science software (for grades pre-K and up). Recently produced *Sesame Street: Elmo's Preschool* (preschool, ages 3-6); and *School House Rock: Grammar Rock* (ages 6-10).
Writing: Submit cover letter, résumé, writing samples: hard copy, on disk (Mac, Windows); demo disk of previous projects. Submissions not returned; submissions filed. Reports only if interested. Requires previous multimedia experience. Does not require writers be available for on-site consultation.
Illustration: Needs freelancers for various assignments. Submit cover letter, résumé and demo disk of previous projects (Mac, Windows). Samples not returned; samples filed. Does not require artist to be available for on-site consultation.
Proposals: Accepts proposals directly from individuals, from agents and from book publishers. Contact: Maryann Duringer, product submissions. Submission guidelines free on request. Requires signed submission before reviewing proposal. Submission agreement free on request. Submit résumé, submission agreement, storyboard (hardcopy), script (hard copy), videotape, original book (if based on published work), computer presentation, demo of product, complete product, all available materials relevant to proposal. Prefers project proposal presented by regular mail. Reports back only if interested. Product development varies.
Terms: Payment determined on individual basis. Product catalogs free on request.
Tips: "Be knowledgeable about the market you are trying to serve: look at and be familiar with all current software 'hits.' Don't 'hound' publishers. Persistence can be irritating."

INSIDER REPORT

Take a crash course in CD-ROM design

In 1990 Annie Fox and writing partner Laurie Arnold Bauman were unpublished screenwriters with hopes of breaking into Hollywood. "Writing dialogue, creating characters and stories were what I loved to do, and I didn't see another format to do it in," says Fox.

Then they got a call from a friend who was president of ICOM Simulations, a company working on a CD-ROM project called *Sherlock Holmes Consulting Detective*. "Because he knew we had been writing screenplays and we knew how to create characters and write dialogue, he wanted us to work on the CD-ROM."

Sherlock Holmes got a lot of publicity because

Annie Fox

it was the first project that used digitized video. And it was the transitional project for Fox and Arnold to move from screenwriting into CD-ROM. "When people heard we worked on *Sherlock Holmes*, they'd say 'Wow, that was really good writing.' Most of the people who were designing computer games in those days were not writers, and that's why there were no real characters emerging, just the same kind of shoot-em-up games."

In 1992, Fox and Arnold worked with Ron Gilbert of Humongous Entertainment on a CD-ROM-based graphic adventure game for kids ages 4-7—starring a little car named Putt-Putt. "Once the Putt-Putt CD-ROMs came out, everyone said 'Wow! So this is what kids' software should be.' Since then we've worked as much as we've wanted to on all sorts of projects, together and separately. Everything from *Madeline and the Magnificent Puppet Show* to *Mr. Potato Head Saves Veggie Valley*," for companies including Disney, IBM, Broderbund, Microsoft and Mattel.

Most of the characters for which Fox has designed or scripted CD-ROMs have been licensed characters like Madeline or Charlie Brown. "The kids' market is so crowded now that to come up with something original and actually have a publisher say 'Sure—let's develop this' is relatively rare."

To begin the process of designing a CD-ROM game, Fox and Bauman sit down and map out the whole environment of the game. "There may be as many as 45 different screen locations. Say screen 12 is an apple orchard, we'll link it to two or three different screens. If you click on the far right edge of the screen, there's usually a blackout or transition screen, and when the next screen comes up, you're in a location adjacent to the apple orchard." What this is depends on what is mapped out ahead of time.

INSIDER REPORT, *Fox*

The CD-ROM environment is a world with locations that are connected as if they were rooms. It must make sense to players moving through the environment. They must have a sense that when they turn right at point A, the apple orchard, they get to point B, the grassy hill. "In a way we make a floor plan, after thinking about what the story is, who the characters are, and what the goal of the game is. In the adventure game genre, there is a quest for the character, something that needs to be accomplished, and there are obstacles along the way for the protagonist to overcome."

Since designing CD-ROMs was something new for Fox and Bauman, they created a system using some of their screenplay formats. "In CD-ROMs, you've got screens instead of scenes and you've got to describe what each screen looks like. For example, you've got 'screen 12, exterior, apple orchard.' " The writers then provide a description of what the player will see on the screen. "Like three apple trees, one covered with yellow apples, one with green, one with red. There's a large barrel under the green apple tree and it's overflowing with pickles."

They also list objects which will be "hotspots"—items a player can click on to make something happen. "When you click on the pickle barrel for the first time, the pickles will jump up and do somersaults. Click on it a second time and

This scene from the *Madeline and the Magnificent Puppet Show* CD-ROM (Creative Wonders) shows an activity to teach French names for objects in a classroom. *Madeline*, which also teaches English and Spanish vocabulary, problem solving, critical thinking and creativity through interaction, was a special project for CD-ROM designers Annie Fox and partner Laurie Arnold Bauman. "Madeline was a little girl in literature who was gutsy, funny and smart. She was a positive role model for girls when we grew up in the '50s. There was much less awareness back then that girls needed role models that did more than bake cookies and dress up dolls," says Fox.

INSIDER REPORT, *continued*

something else might happen. There might be something random that says 'click here and one of the following might happen,' in which case the computer will randomly choose on each click one of the possibilities,'' says Fox.

Fox and Arnold must also write a script for the characters in the CD-ROM game. "It reads like a screenplay, and we set it up that way, so that every single kind of action that can take place, initiated by the player, is anticipated and described." This way, says Fox, when the developers actually build the game, they know what to take into account. "I guess it's the equivalent of a shooting script for a movie—it's all there and the developers build it in modules, then link it all together and make sure it flies."

It's very important, says Fox, that they design "replayability" into the games. "If parents pay $40 or $50 for a CD-ROM, they want to know that the kid is going to enjoy it for more than a few hours. That he or she will be happy to go back and replay the game. It's something we have to take into account as game designers in addition to coming up with a story and characters, which was mostly all we needed to do writing in a linear medium."

Writers interested in getting into multimedia need not be put off by what seems like a complicated design process. "I think it's really good to be able to get involved in a multimedia project on any level, just so that you can say on your résumé 'I worked on this project.' Because the industry is still new, a lot of people, especially producers, come from other fields anyway. They didn't know about nonlinear work before they got in, but they used their producer skills to get into the field. I think writers can do that as well."

Fox suggests writers first take a look at what is out there, find a company whose work they admire, and contact the publisher. "Say, 'I'm a writer and this is what I do. Maybe I don't have any nonlinear writing experience, but I'm great at X, Y and Z. Here are some writing samples.' I think that anybody who wants to get into this field should use what they already do well as leverage. If someone has written for children before, but hasn't done anything for multimedia, that's fine.

"The truth is that the children's book publishing industry is very tight, and the risks are very high for the publishers. I find with multimedia, because it's so much more wide open and not as established, it's easier to get your foot in the door without having a body of published work. All you need to do is prove that you can write and that you could get things handed in on schedule."

—*Alice P. Buening*

*DYNACOMP, INC., 4560 E. Lake Rd., Livonia NY 14487. (716)346-9788. Estab. 1978. 800 titles currently in distribution; 800 titles currently in production.
Software: Produces interactive storybooks in Mac, MS-DOS on floppy (for ages preschool and up); produces early learning, reading/language arts, science, math and reference software in MS-DOS on floppy (for ages preschool and up). Games: produces mystery/puzzle and horror software in Mac, MS-DOS on floppy (for ages preschool and up). Recently produced *Children's Carrousel* (early learning, ages 2-6); *Hodge Podge* (early learning, ages 2-6).
Writing: "Submit full documentation with software—no partial products or 'ideas.' " Contact: Marketing Director. Submissions returned with SASE; submissions filed. Reports in 1 week.
Terms: Writers paid royalty of 5-15%. Product catalogs available for 9×12 SAE with $1.93 postage.

*HEARTSOFT, INC., 3101 N. Hemlock, Broken Arrow OK 74012. (918)251-1066. Fax: (918)251-4018. Website: http://www.heartsoft.com. Estab. 1986. 50 titles currently in distribution; 50 titles currently in production.
Software: Produces early learning, reading/language arts, science, math, creativity tools software in Mac, Windows on floppy (for ages preschool and up). Games: produces mystery/puzzle in Mac and Windows on floppy for ages preschool and up. Recently produced *Tommy the Time Turtle* (math, grades 2-4); *Reading Rodeo* (early learning, grades K-2).
Illustration: Needs freelancers for storyboarding, animation, backgrounds and textures. Submit cover letter, résumé, samples (color copies, Website, original art, Mac), demo disk of previous projects (Mac). Contact: Jimmy Butler, vice president of development. Samples filed; samples returned. Reports only if interested. Requires previous multimedia experience. Requires artists to be available for on-site consultation.
Terms: Work purchased outright.

*HOUGHTON MIFFLIN INTERACTIVE, 120 Beacon St., Somerville MA 02143. (617)503-4800. Fax: (617)503-4900. E-mail: hmi@hmco.com. Website: http://www.hminet.com. Estab. 1994. Produced 7 titles last year; 9 titles currently in distribution; 9 titles currently in production.
Software: Produces interactive storybooks, early learning, reading/language arts, science, math, creativity tools, reference and online content software in Mac or Windows on CD-ROM (for ages preschool and up). Recently produced *Curious George Comes Home* (interactive storybook/ early learning, ages 3-6); and *Awesome Animated Monster Maker* (creative play/early learning, ages 3-adult).
Writing: "When submitting, you might start with just a summary, or give as much as you are comfortable with; the more we see, the better idea we'll have, but some of the most compelling materials have been a simple cover letter and résumé." Submit cover letter, résumé, writing samples: hard copy, Website, on disk (Mac or Windows), demo disk (Mac or Windows). Submissions returned with SASE; submissions filed. Contact: Anne Hoyt, assistant to the publisher. Reports in 6 weeks only if interested. Generally requires previous experience. "We're very open to all levels of experience. It never hurts to submit. We work with people all over the U.S., although it is nice if we can meet people from time to time. We believe in making learning fun. Our products are high quality, with a sincere commitment to children's entertainment. The best submission will demonstrate a fun attitude, intelligent thinking, and creativity—nothing outlandish, just out of the ordinary."
Illustration: "If we like your work, we'll find a way to use it. Send us what you can do." Submit cover letter, résumé, samples (color copies, Website, original art, Mac or Windows), computer presentation, demo disk (Mac or Windows) or demo reel (video) of previous projects. "Send us as much or as little as you like. We don't need much to get an idea of what your work is like, and sometimes, anything beyond color copies is too expensive for the artist. We do need to see *something*." Contact: Anne Hoyt, assistant to the publisher. Samples filed; samples returned with SAE. Reports back only if interested. Generally requires experience. "We're open to all levels of experience. If we like someone's work, we'll use it. Look at some of our titles; we have

---

✱ **THE ASTERISK** before a listing indicates the listing is new in this edition.

a wide variety of styles, but they may help to indicate styles we do not use. Send us samples that will indicate what you can do for us, not necessarily everything you can do."

Proposals: Accepts proposals directly from individuals, from agents and from book publishers. Submission guidelines not available. Submission agreement free on request. Submit résumé, submission agreement, storyboard (hardcopy), script (hardcopy), videotape, original book (if based on published work), computer presentation, demo of product (Mac or Windows) or complete product (Mac or Windows). "The more you send, the better idea we'll get of the product. You may want to start with an introductory letter and summary, but we'll take as much or as little as a person desires to send." Contact: Anne Hoyt, assistant to the publisher. "To begin with, we prefer any contact that is not a physical meeting. As our interest develops, we will meet in person." Reports back in 6 weeks. Product developed by creator, varies. "Visit our Website or call and request a catalog. We're very open to all sorts of ideas but are very focused on certain areas. The more information you can give us, the more likely we are to understand your concept."

Terms: Payment varies depending on the project. Offers an advance (amount varies). Product catalogs free on request.

Tips: "The children's multimedia market will probably continue to grow, although products will be more and more improved. HMI is committed to high-quality products. We are examining and exploring taking multimedia into a fuller experience, providing aspects that children can take away from the computer, whether it be their own personalized storybook or their new monster friend. Our products and the heritage of Houghton Mifflin respect books, learning and education. We are also taking children's multimedia online. More and more will be done on the Worldwide Web, with more sites for children to learn and explore in. Successful artists, writers and developers will be aware of the market, as well as its latest fads and hottest hits. They will push their creativity and attempt to be 'on the cutting edge.' To be successful, they will also know facts outside of the software arena—the latest toys, books, movies, etc. To be successful with HMI, they will be excited about finding fun new ways to make kids want to learn."

*LAREDO PUBLISHING CO., 8907 Wilshire Blvd., Beverly Hills CA 90211. (310)358-5288. Fax: (310)358-5282. E-mail: laredo@online2000.com. Estab. 1991. Produced 15 titles last year; 150 titles currently in distribution; 10 titles currently in production.

Software: Produces interactive storybooks, early learning and reading/language arts software.

Writing: Submit writing samples (Mac), demo disk of previous projects (Mac). Contact: Sam Laredo, president. Submissions returned with SASE; submissions filed. Reports in 2 weeks. Requires previous multimedia experience. "We specialize in language development tools and English as a second language (ESL) material."

Illustration: Needs storyboarding, animation and 3-D modeling. Submit samples (color copies), demo disk of previous projects (Mac). Contact: Sam Laredo, president. Samples returned with SASE; submissions filed. Reports on submissions in 2 weeks.

Proposals: Accepts proposals directly from individuals. Submission guidelines not available. Contact: Sam Laredo, president.

Terms: Writers paid royalty of 7-10% or work purchased outright for $1,000-5,000. Artists paid royalty or work purchased outright for $1,000-5,000. Work purchased outright for $1,000-5,000 from creators. Offers advance (depends on project).

*MEMOREX SOFTWARE N-TK ENTERTAINMENT TECHNOLOGY, 18000 Studebaker Rd., #200, Cerritos CA 90703. (310)403-0039. Fax: (310)403-0049. Estab. 1995. Produced 32 titles last year; 32 titles currently in distribution; 2 titles currently in production.

Software: Produces interactive storybooks, early learning, reference software in Windows on CD-ROM (for ages preschool and up). Games: produces action/adventure, fantasy, mystery/puzzle and arcade software in Windows on CD-ROM (for ages preschool and up). Recently produced *Bug Explorers* (entertainment, ages 4 and up); *Aladdin & His Wonderful Lamp* (storybook, 6 and up).

Writing: Submit demo disk of previous projects (Windows, hybrid) or finished product (previously published). Submissions returned with SASE; submissions filed. Reports in 2 months. Requires previous multimedia experience. Requires writers to be available for on-site consultations.

Proposals: Accepts proposals directly from individuals, from agents and from book publishers. Submission guidelines not available. Submit storyboard (hardcopy), videotape, original book (if based on published work), demo of product (Windows, hybrid), complete product (Windows, hybrid). Contact: Olivier Vabois, acquisition coordinator. Prefers project proposal presented by fax or by regular mail. Reports in 2 months. Development of product varies.

Terms: Writers paid royalty or work purchased outright. Creators paid royalty of 50% or purchased outright. Advance amount varies. Product catalogs free on request.

*NORDIC SOFTWARE, P.O. Box 6007, Lincoln NE 68506. (402)488-5086. Fax: (402)488-2914. Website: www.nordicsoftware.com. Estab. 1983. Produced 6 titles last year; 12 titles currently in distribution; 5 titles currently in production.
Software: Produces early learning, reading/language arts and math software in Mac or Windows on floppy or CD-ROM (for ages preschool and up). Recently produced *Turbo Math Facts 3.0* (math, ages 5-8); *Noah's Ark* (early learning, preschool).
Writing: Submit cover letter, résumé, writing samples (Mac), demo disk of previous projects (Mac). Contact: Kent Porter, director of development. Submissions returned with SASE; submissions filed. Reports back only if interested. Does not require writers to be available for on-site consultation.
Illustration: Needs freelancers for storyboarding, animation and 3-D modeling. Submit cover letter, résumé, samples (Mac), demo disk of previous projects (Mac). Contact: Kent Porter, director of development. Samples returned with SASE; samples filed. Reports only if interested. Does not require previous multimedia experience. Requires artists to be available for on-site consultation.
Terms: Writers/artists paid royalty of 1-10% or work purchased outright (varies from project to project). Advance amount varies.

*NTC/CONTEMPORARY PUBLISHING CO., 4255 W. Touhy, Lincolnwood IL 60646-1975. (847)679-5500. Fax: (847)679-2494. E-mail: ntcpub2@aol.com. Estab. 1967. Produced 400 titles last year; 4,000 titles currently in distribution; 400 titles currently in production.
Software: Produces interactive storybooks in Mac or Windows on floppy or CD-ROM (for preschool and up); produces reference and foreign language software in Mac and Windows on CD-ROM (for preschool and up). Recently produced *Let's Learn French* (foreign language/early learning, ages 5-11); *Let's Learn Spanish* (foreign language, early learning, ages 5-11).
Writing: Submit cover letter, résumé and formal proposal. Contact: Joyous Masco, editorial department assistant. Submissions returned with SASE; submissions not filed. Reports in 3-4 months. Requires previous multimedia experience. Requires writers to be available for on-site consultations.
Illustrations: Needs animation and box design. Submit cover letter, résumé, samples (color copies), demo disk (Mac, Windows). Contact: Karen Christoffersen, art director. Samples returned with SASE; samples filed. Reports only if interested. Requires previous multimedia experience. Does not require artists to be available for on-site consultation.
Proposals: Accepts proposals directly from individuals. Submission guidelines for proposals free on request. Submit résumé. Contact: Joyous Masco, editorial department assistant. Prefers project proposal presented by regular mail. Reports back in 3-4 months. Development of product varies. "Our primary area of interest is foreign language, ESL, and English language arts, both educational and trade products."
Terms: Writers paid royalty or work purchased outright. Works purchased outright from artists. Creators paid royalty or work purchased outright. Product catalogs free on request.

*ORION/MPCA PICTURES—INTERACTIVE, 1401 Ocean Ave., Suite 301, Santa Monica CA 90401. (310)319-9500. Fax: (310)576-1807. E-mail: drcperjean@aol.com. Interactive Division established 1993; film division active since 1986. Produced 3 titles last year; 1 title currently in distribution; 2 titles currently in production.
Software: Produces reading/language arts and math software in Windows on CD-ROM (for ages preschool and up). Games: produces action/adventure, horror and arcade software in Windows on CD-ROM (for ages preschool and up). Recently produced *Bloodwings* and *Pumpkinhead's Revenge* (horror, ages 16 and up).
Writing: Submit cover letter, résumé, writing samples (hard copy, Website and Windows), demo disk of previous projects (Windows). Contact: Jeanette Draper, vice president creative affairs. Submissions returned with SASE; submissions filed. Reports in 2-4 weeks. Generally requires previous experience. "Exceptions can be granted for a superb portfolio." Strongly prefers writers to be available for on-site consultations. "Come in with a good proof at concept. Commitment to excellent work. Adaptability, sense of humor, brilliance, creativity, good aim, ability to take initiative and develop ideas through to production are qualities we look for."
Illustration: Needs freelancers for storyboarding, animation, 3-D modeling, backgrounds, textures and web design. Submit cover letter, résumé, samples (color copies, Website, original art

INSIDER REPORT

Creative risks necessary in a world of multiple media

Deborah Forte rejects the term "multimedia." As senior vice-president of Scholastic, Inc. and head of Scholastic Productions, the branch of the company responsible for expanding Scholastic's book offerings into the realms of video, television, and CD-ROM, she considers herself simply "a media person. I think media in general is in a state of transition and I think new media, multimedia—people don't even really know what that means."

Deborah Forte

As consumers begin to sort out the expanding universe of media available for entertainment and education, Forte feels writers must be open to the various platforms as well. "I think one of the things that will be important for the creative community moving forward is to be able to visualize and work across multiple media platforms. People are going to be depending on their success from multiple markets rather than a single marketplace," she says. "And the better projects will be those that maintain their integrity across all media platforms. Writers must be creative, take risks and not think in terms of a single media platform."

Taking creative risks is not merely Forte's advice—it seems to be her job description. In 1984, she began at Scholastic working in what was then a new format, home video. From there Scholastic Productions developed into a producer of multiple media projects for kids, such as the successful public television series "The Magic School Bus," and a number of *Goosebumps*-related projects, which evolved from the phenomenally successful line of creepy tales for kids by R.L. Stine. The company is also developing original alternative media projects (work that was not first published in book form).

When she took on production of "Goosebumps" as a weekly anthology TV series, Forte says everyone in the television business told her such series don't work, that kids don't like them. "They said if there are not repeating characters and locations that are continually familiar to the audience, that your audience won't stick with your show. Everyone told me that."

But since its debut in November of 1995, "Goosebumps" has consistently been the top-rated kids' show on TV. "I believe to be good in this business, you must take creative risks. You must be willing to do things differently."

Forte says successful shows like *Mighty Morphin Power Rangers* or *Barney & Friends* weren't like anything else on television when they started. "They broke the mold. A lot of the media marketplace is characterized by imitation.

INSIDER REPORT, *Forte*

photo © Scholastic Productions. Reprinted with permission

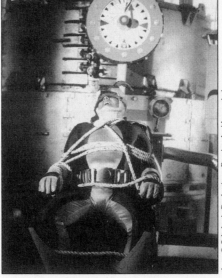

photo © Scholastic Productions. Reprinted with permission

The outrageously popular, spooky *Goosebumps* books by R.L. Stine spawned a top-rated *Goosebumps* TV show produced by Protocol Entertainment in association with Scholastic Productions under the direction of producer Deborah Forte. The top scene from the 1996 fall season premiere "Attack of the Mutant" features young Skipper (played by Dan Warry-Smith) and the Mutant (Scott Wickware). Skipper must rescue the Galloping Gazelle (Adam West, of *Batman* fame, bottom photo) from the evil Mutant in a special one-hour episode.

INSIDER REPORT, *continued*

People tend to want to develop and produce things that are like other things that have been successful. I would not spend my time imitating successful things," she says. "The real challenge and the real excitement about being in this business is the opportunity to make something new that is unique that people will respond to."

The success of "Goosebumps" on TV led to a partnership with Steven Spielberg's Dreamworks SKG to develop a "Goosebumps" CD-ROM. (Microsoft also produces CD-ROMs for Scholastic.) In its early development, Dreamworks interviewed interactive writers to script the CD-ROM. "But our inclination was to go with a writer of filmed entertainment because we felt that, although the interactivity in the CD-ROM would be very different from the linear characteristics of television, we still wanted there to be story and characters," says Forte. "We all conferred and agreed to hire a feature film writer for the CD-ROM. That was a risk." But it was a way to combine the best of filmed entertainment with the best of interactivity.

Story and characters are indeed important factors in deciding which books will translate well into alternative media. Uniqueness is another. "I don't think 'Goosebumps' would have been successful if there were four other things out there that were scary, funny series. And I don't think I would have done it. But it's unique and had a reason to be. 'Magic School Bus' is the same way."

"Magic School Bus," like "Goosebumps," is an example of an idea that worked in multiple media platforms. The successful book series spawned the PBS series. Traveling "Magic School Bus" exhibits are seen by young museum-goers throughout the U.S. as well as "Magic School Bus" science activity trunks, CD-ROMs, videos, and magazine tie-ins.

"The whole idea is that when you have a franchise, you can develop it so that it works across all media platforms as an interactive experience. The CD-ROMs we do with Microsoft and Dreamworks are electronic interactive experiences. And the television is a different kind of experience. They all complement each other. And that's what, more and more, the world of media will be about."

But, Forte points out, each medium cannibalizes the others to some extent in terms of audience. "There are fewer people doing any one thing at one time because there are so many new media platforms. People only have a specific amount of leisure time to do all these things. Even children. Especially children."

—*Alice P. Buening*

and Windows), demo disk of previous projects (Windows) or demo reel. Samples returned with SASE; samples filed. Reports in 2-4 weeks. "Again, unexperienced miracle-workers are accepted." Strongly prefers artists be available for on-site consultation. "We look for a solid portfolio and its ability to push the creative envelope in pursuit of aesthetic brilliance. Be dazzling."
Proposals: Accepts proposals directly from individuals, agents and book publishers. Submission guidelines for proposals not available. Requires signed submission before reviewing proposal. Submission agreement free on request. Submit résumé, submission agreement, storyboard, script (hard copy), videotape, original book (if based on published work), computer presentation (Windows). Contact: Jeanette Draper, vice president creative affairs. Prefers project proposal presented by e-mail, in person or by regular mail. Reports in 2-4 weeks. Product development varies.

*POWER INDUSTRIES, INC., 37 Walnut St., Wellesley Hills MA 02181. (617)235-7733. Fax: (617)235-0084. E-mail: 71107.1111@compuserve.com. Estab. 1990. Produced 1 title last year; 20 titles currently in distribution; 1 title currently in production.
Software: Produces interactive storybooks, early learning, reading/language arts, science, math, creativity tools, reference software in Mac, Windows, on floppy and CD-ROM (for ages 4-12).
Proposals: Accepts proposals directly from individuals, from agents and from book publishers. Submit demo of product (Mac or Windows) and complete product (Mac or Windows). Contact: New Product Submission Department. Prefers project proposal presented by regular mail. Reports back only if interested. Product developed by the creator.
Terms: Creators paid royalty or work purchased outright. Product catalogs not available.

*BYRON PREISS MULTIMEDIA CO., INC., 24 W. 25th St., New York NY 10010. (212)989-6252. Fax: (212)989-6550. E-mail: welcome@bpmc.com. Website: http://www.byronp reiss.com. Estab. 1992. Produced 17 titles last year; 24 titles currently in distribution; 18 titles currently in production.
Software: Produces interactive storybooks, early learning, reading/language arts, math, creative tools software in Mac and Windows on CD-ROM (for ages preschool and up); produces reference software in Windows on CD-ROM (for ages preschool and up); produces fantasy and nursery puzzle software in Mac and Windows (for ages preschool and up).
Writing: Contact: Clarice Levin. Submit cover letter, résumé, writing samples: hard copy; demo disk of previous projects in Mac or Windows. Submissions returned with SASE; submissions filed. Reports only if interested. Experience in writing for children is requested. "Know the products out on the market (not just ours). Be familiar with the technology."
Illustration: Needs freelancers for storyboarding, animation, 3-D modeling and backgrounds. Contact: Clarice Levin. Submit cover letter, résumé, samples (color copies, Website, original art, demo disk on Mac or Windows), computer presentation (self running demo in Director or other language). Samples filed; samples returned. Reports only if interested. Requires previous multimedia experience. Requires artists to be available for on-site consultation. "Be familiar with the medium. Be flexible with the types of platforms and programs you work in."
Terms: Writers'/artists' payment depends on project and type of work.
Tips: "It is important to know your audience as well as your medium. Hang out with kids, watch them play. They're the experts. Be flexible with the platforms you create for and the tools you work with. Not only is every company different in what they require, but the market (and technology) is changing so rapidly, you need to be prepared for the next hot new wave of technology to hit."

*❋REIDMORE BOOKS INC., 1200, 10109-106th St., Edmonton, Alberta T5J 3L7 Canada. (403)424-4420. Fax: (403)441-9919. E-mail: reidmore@compusmart.ab.ca. Website: http://www .reidmore.com. Estab. 1979. Produced 1 title last year; 1 title currently in distribution; 2 titles currently in production.
Software: Produces reference software in Mac and Windows on CD-ROM (for ages 10-adult). Recently produced *From Mountain to Plain* (reference, middle readers to teens).
Writing: "We don't subcontract writing. We're looking for authors with experience in developing software packages. Contact for this is Cathie Crooks, director of marketing/sales." Query. Submissions returned with SASE; submissions filed (if worthwhile). Requires previous multimedia experience. Does not require writers to be available for on-site consultation. "We're looking for people to come to us with ideas for nonfiction works, preferably saleable to elementary or junior high schools for use in social studies programs. Call first. We definitely are not interested in trade titles, fiction or children's 'picture book' style products."
Illustration: Needs storyboarding, animation, 3-D modeling, backgrounds, textures, box design and C + + programmers. Submit cover letter, and samples (Mac or Windows). "Any format for

submission, other than original art, is acceptable." Contact: James Manis, manager, production and design. Samples returned with SASE; samples filed. Reports only if interested. Requires previous multimedia experience. "We prefer to work with local artists due to convenience, but will sometimes work long distance. We need to work with artists willing to make revisions based on feedback from editors and reviewers. We sell to the educational (nonfiction) market, and accuracy is essential. We do very little work with new artists, but are always interested in learning about who is out there and their work. Don't have high expectations!"

Proposals: Accepts proposals directly from individuals, from agents and from book publishers. Call first to discuss project and how material should be submitted. Contact: Cathie Crooks, director of marketing/sales. Prefers project proposal presented by phone, e-mail or regular mail. Reports back in 2 months. Product development varies. "We prefer that project personnel be experienced in the field; previously published is best. Call first."

Terms: Writers paid royalty or work purchased outright. Artists paid royalty or work purchased outright. Creators paid royalty. Product catalogs free on request.

*RIEDEL SOFTWARE PRODUCTIONS, INC., 1840 E. River Rd., #100, Tucson AZ 85718. (520)577-0321. Fax: (520)577-8670. E-mail: vdesire@rspring.com. Estab. 1986. Produced 12 titles last year; 15 titles currently in distribution; 4 titles currently in production.

Software: Produces interactive, early learning, reading/language arts, science and math software in Mac and Windows on CD-ROM (for preschool and up). Games: produces action/adventure and arcade software in Mac and Windows on CD-ROM (for preschool and up). Recently produced *The Muppet CD-ROM* (entertainment, "99 and younger"); *Aesop's Fables* (entertainment, ages 3-8).

Writing: Submit cover letter, résumé, writing samples: hard copy, Website, on disk (Windows), demo disk of previous projects (Mac and Windows). Contact: Vince Desiderio, vice president. Submissions not returned; submissions filed. Reports only if interested. Does not require previous multimedia experience. Requires writers to be available for on-site consultations. "Be real and honest" when submitting.

Illustration: Needs storyboarding, animation, 3-D modeling, backgrounds, textures and box design. Submit cover letter, résumé, samples (color copies), Website, original art, on disk (Mac or Windows), demo disk of previous projects (Mac or Windows) or demo reel. Samples not returned; samples filed. Reports only if interested. Does not require previous multimedia experience. Requires artists to be available for on-site consultation.

Proposals: Accepts proposals directly from individuals, from agents or from book publishers. Submission guidelines for proposals not available. Requires signed submission agreement before reviewing proposal. Submit résumé, submission agreement, storyboard (hard copy), script (hard copy), videotape, original book (if based on published work), computer presentation, demo of product or complete product. Contact: Vince Desiderio, vice president. Prefers project proposal presented by phone, by fax, by e-mail, in person or by regular mail. Reports back only if interested. Product developed in house with the input of the creator.

Terms: Writer's/artist's work purchased outright. Creators paid royalty or purchased outright.

Tips: "Make sure your work is ready. Be willing to work on a sample on spec."

*✦TIMEBOX INC., P.O. Box 3060, Station D, Ottawa, Ontario K1P 6H6 Canada. (613)256-7338. Fax: (613)256-7340. E-mail: timebox@magi.com. Website: http://www.infoweb.magi.com/~timebox/. Estab. 1992. Produced 1 title last year; 5 titles currently in distribution; 2 titles currently in production.

Software: Produces interactive storybooks, science and reference software in Mac on CD-ROM (for ages 7-adult). Games: produces fantasy software in Mac on CD-ROM (for ages 7-adult). Recently produced *Adventure Book of Christopher Columbus* (education, ages 7-14); *Dreambuilders* (reference, 8 and up).

Writing: Submit cover letter, résumé, writing samples: Website and on disk (Mac). Contact: Colette Dionne, president. Submissions not returned; submissions filed. Reports only if interested.

MARKET CONDITIONS are constantly changing! If you're still using this book and it is 1998 or later, buy the newest edition of *Children's Writer's & Illustrator's Market* at your favorite bookstore or order directly from Writer's Digest Books.

Does not require previous multimedia experience. Usually requires writers to be available for on-site consultations. "Just do it! and don't try to find a recipe on how to do it. There isn't any—(yet!)"

Illustration: Needs freelancers for animation, 3-D modeling and box design. Submit cover letter, résumé, samples (color copies), Website or on disk (Mac) or demo disk (1 or 2 of the above). Contact: Colette Dionne, president. Samples not returned; samples filed. Reports only if interested. Requires previous multimedia experience. Does not require artists to be available for on-site consultation.

Proposals: Accepts proposals directly from individuals. Submission guidelines for proposals not available. Submit résumé, script (hard copy) and computer presentation (PowerPoint) ("one or two samples"). Contact: Colette Dionne, president. Prefers project proposal presented by regular mail. Reports only if interested. Product developed in house with the input of the creator (varies).

Terms: Writers paid royalty of 15-25%. Artist's work purchased outright. Creators paid royalty of 15-25%. Product catalogs available on website listed above.

Tips: "To be successful in multimedia, do the same things you do to be successful elsewhere—work and be creative. Ideas are not as valuable as you think. The market needs to have distribution ideas. Creative ones are not lacking."

*VORTEX MEDIA ARTS, 508 S. Verduga Dr., Suite 200, Burbank CA 91502. (818)557-2929. Fax: (818)557-2930. E-mail: giolito@vortexmedia.com. Website: http//www.prtment.com/~vma. Estab. 1994. Produced 2 titles year; 2 titles currently in distribution; 5 titles currently in production.

Software: Produces interactive storybooks software in online; produces early learning, reading/language arts, science, math and creativity tools software in Mac and Windows; produces online content in Mac, Windows and online. Games: produces action/adventure, fantasy and simulation software in Mac, Windows and Set Top. Recently produced *Madeline and the Magnificent Puppet Show* (early learning, ages 4-8); *Tonka Construction* (creativity, 4-10).

Writing: Submit cover letter, résumé and writing samples: hard copy. Contact: Fritz Bronner, president. Submissions filed. Reports only if interested. Requires writers to be available for on-site consultation.

Illustration: Needs freelancers for storyboarding, animation, 3-D modeling, backgrounds, textures and box design. Submit cover letter, résumé, samples (color copies), original art, on disk (Mac and Windows), demo disk of previous projects or demo reel ("any of the above.") Contact: Chris Takami, vice president creative development. Samples not returned; samples filed. Reports only if interested. Does not require previous multimedia experience. Does not require artist to be available for on-site consultation. "Must have multimedia experience for out-of-house."

Proposals: Accepts proposals directly from individuals, from agents and from book publishers. Submission guidelines for proposals not available. Requires signed submission agreement before reviewing proposal. Submission agreement free on request. Submit submission agreement, script (hard copy), demo of product (Mac and Windows). Contact: Rick Giocito, vice president business. Prefers project proposal presented by phone or in person. Reports in 2 months. Product development varies. "Have a well-thought-out, cohesive idea preferably in preliminary script form."

Terms: Writer's paid royalty of 2-50%. Artists paid on a per piece basis. Creators paid royalty of 2-50%. Product catalogs not available.

Tips: "The market is shrinking. Creators should think about products that are attached to existing content in order to insure a greater chance of success."

Audiovisual & Audiotape

The business of kids' audio and video has gained respectability in the past few years. In September of 1995, *Billboard* magazine debuted *Billboard*'s Top Kid Audio Chart. The National Academy of Recording Arts and Sciences created separate categories for children's music and spoken work. And children's audio and video are enjoying healthy sales.

Just as in the children's book industry, the use of licensed characters in children's audio and video is commonplace. The sales charts are littered with Disney characters from Mickey Mouse to the Hunchback of Notre Dame to Winnie the Pooh, and Barney the dinosaur is still enjoying popularity.

And though the market is flooded with these character-driven products, this should help the sales of other audio and video titles. Stocking hundreds of items on store shelves featuring the Hunchback, for example, brings consumers into the stores who will ultimately buy other audio and video products.

With a lot happening in the world of children's entertainment, there are growing opportunities for a great many talents. In the Audiovisual and Audiotape sections that follow, you'll find record companies, book publishers, video production houses and more. Many of the companies listed work with a variety of projects and may need anything from songs and short stories to illustration and clay animation.

To keep up on the dynamic world of children's entertainment, read "Child's Play," Moira McCormick's *Billboard* magazine column, as well as *Publishers Weekly*, which often covers and reviews audio and video in its children's section. Industry publications such as *Variety* and *Hollywood Reporter* may also offer useful information on kids' video.

AUDIOVISUAL

The production houses listed here don't produce just video cassettes. Many also create filmstrips, slide sets, multimedia productions—even television shows. These studios and production houses are in need of illustration, video graphics, special effects, and a variety of animation techniques, including stop motion, cell, clay and computer animation. They also need the work of writers for everything from animation scripts to educational filmstrips, but be aware that audiovisual media rely more on the "visual" to tell the story.

Also note that technology in the world of video production is advancing. Many companies are producing CD-ROM and interactive titles for kids, and computer imaging is becoming the norm in kids' video, so it's important that illustrators stay up-to-date on emerging techniques. (For a list of CD-ROM and software producers, see our new Multimedia section on page 213.)

BRIDGESTONE MULTIMEDIA GROUP, 300 North McKerny Ave., Chandler AZ 85226-2618. (602)438-2717. Fax: (602)940-8924. Estab. 1986. Video management, license and distribution, software publisher. Audience: Family, children. Produces multimedia productions. **Illustration:** Submit demo tape (VHS). Guidelines/catalog free on request.

BROADCAST QUALITY, INC., 2334 Ponce de Leon Blvd., #200, Coral Gables FL 33143. (305)461-5416. Fax: (305)446-7746. E-mail: bqiaix.netcom.com. President: Diana Udel. Estab. 1978. Video production and post production house. Produces videotapes. Children's productions:

"It's Ours to Save—Biscayne National Park," written by Jack Moss, produced by Diana Udel/ BQI, Betacam SP/1″ Master, (Environmental awareness for grades 4-7); "The Wildlife Show at Parrot Jungle," written by Amy Smith, produced by BQI, Betacam SP/1″ Master, (Hands on to Florida's Wildlife for K-8th grade). Uses 2-5 freelance writers/year; purchases various projects/ year.
Tips: "Send a résumé and demo reel. Seeks variety, knowledge of subject and audience."

CENTRE COMMUNICATIONS, 1800 30th St., Suite #207, Boulder CO 80301. (303)444-1166. Contact: Deborah O'Grady. Estab. 1975. Production and distribution company. Audience: schools, libraries and television. Produces films and videotapes. Children's productions: "Violence: Dealing with Anger," (educational video for ages 10-12); "A Norman Rockwell Christmas Story"; and "Pepper and All the Legs," written by Dick Gackenbach (children's story video for ages 4-8). Uses 2-3 freelance writers/year; purchases 5-6 writing projects/year.
Children's Writing: Needs: educational material, documentaries and live action. "We only commission work or distribute finished products." Reports back only if interested. Buys material outright. Guidelines free on request.

EDUCATIONAL VIDEO NETWORK, 1401 19th St., Huntsville TX 77340. (409)291-2860. Fax: (409)295-4360. E-mail: pop123@tcac.com. Website: http://www.infsol.com/amn/. Production Manager: Anne Russell. Estab. 1954. Production house. Audience: educational (school). Uses videotapes. 20% of writing by freelancers; 20% of illustrating/animating is by freelancers. Recent children's productions: "The History of Ancient Egypt," written by Mary Lee Nolan (history video for junior high-college); and "Teenage Alcohol Abuse," written and illustrated by Christina Vuckovic (junior high-college). Uses 1-2 freelance artists/year; buys 2-3 art projects/ year.
Children's Writing: Needs: "Curriculum-oriented educational material" for junior high through college audiences. Query. Submissions returned with proper SASE. Reports in 2-6 months. Guidelines/catalog free. Pays writers royalties of 3% or buys material outright.
Illustration/Animation: Hires illustrators for animation. Types of animation produced: video graphics, extensive computer animation. To submit, send cover letter and VHS demo tape. Art samples returned with proper SASE. Reports in 2-6 months. Guidelines/catalog free. Pays $10-30/cel for animation work.
Tips: "Materials should fill a curriculum need for junior high to college. We seldom assign projects to freelancers. We want to be approached by people who know a particular subject and who have a plan for getting that information across to students. Programs should feature professional production techniques and involve the viewers in the message."

FILM CLASSIC EXCHANGE, 143 Hickory Hill Circle, Osterville MA 02655. (508)428-7198. Fax: (508)420-0121. President: J.H. Aikman. Estab. 1916. Distribution/production house. Audience: pre-school through college. Produces films, videotapes. Children's productions: "The Good Deed," written by William P. Pounder, illustrated by Karen Losaq (film on family values aimed at preschool); "Willie McDuff's Big Day," written and illustrated by Joe Fleming (anti-drug film aimed at ages 12 and up). Uses 6 freelance writers and artists/year. Purchases 6 writing and 6 art projects/year.
Children's Writing: Needs: preschool. Subjects include: anti-drug. Query with synopsis or submit completed script. Submissions are returned with proper SASE. Reports back only if interested. Buys material outright.
Illustration/Animation: Hires illustrators for cel/video animation, storyboarding, character development, live action, comprehensives, pencil testing. Types of animation produced: cel animation, clay animation, stop motion, special effects, computer animation, video graphics, motion control, live action. To submit, send cover letter, résumé, demo tape (VHS), color print samples. Art samples returned with proper SASE. Reports back only if interested.
Tips: "Keep sending updated résumés/samples of work."

MARKET CONDITIONS are constantly changing! If you're still using this book and it is 1998 or later, buy the newest edition of *Children's Writer's & Illustrator's Market* at your favorite bookstore or order directly from Writer's Digest Books.

FILMS FOR CHRIST, INC., (aka, "Eden Communications"), 1044 N. Gilbert Rd., Gilbert AZ 85234. (602)497-8200. Fax: (602)497-8001. Executive Director: Paul S. Taylor. Estab. 1961. Producer/distributor of films, videos, books and software. Audience: Christian families and church audiences. Produces multimedia productions, films, videotapes, books and software. Children's productions: "The Great Dinosaur Mystery," written by Paul S. Taylor, illustrated by Charles Zilch, Gary Webb, Paul S. Taylor (documentary on creation vs. evolution, 7-adult); and "The Great Dinosaur Mystery and the Bible," written by Paul S. Taylor, illustrated by C. Zilch, G. Webb, T. Tennant, J. Chong, P.S. Taylor (creation vs. evolution book, 7-adult). Uses 0-1 freelancer/year. Uses 1-2 artists/year; buys 3-8 art projects/year.
Children's Writing: Needs: documentaries, books, software and projects (ages 5-8, 9-12, adult). Subjects include: Christianity and creation vs. evolution. Query with synopsis; submit résumé. Submissions cannot be returned; submissions filed. Reports only if interested. Catalog free on request. Pays royalty or buys material outright.
Illustration: Hires illustrators for animation, live action, detailed renderings. Types of animation produced: cel animation, special effects, computer animation, video graphics. Submit cover letter, résumé, demo tape if available (VHS), color print samples. Art samples are filed if interested. Reports only if interested. Catalog is free on request. Rates negotiable, based on anticipated marketability of each project.
Tips: "As a nonprofit, evangelical ministry, we are most interested in developing working relationships with artists and illustrators who are anxious to use their gifts and talents to help propagate the life-changing truths of the Bible."

I.N.I. ENTERTAINMENT GROUP, INC., Suite 700, 11845 W. Olympic Blvd., Los Angeles CA 90064. (310)479-6755. Fax: (310)479-3475. Chairman of the Board/CEO: Irv Holender. President: Michael Ricci. Estab. 1985. Producer/International Distributor. Audience: children of all ages. Uses films. Children's productions: "The Adventures of Oliver Twist," screenplay written by Fernando Ruiz (updated version of the Dickens' tale for ages 4-12); "Alice Through the Looking Glass," screenplay written by James Brewer (updated and upbeat version of Carroll's book for ages 4-12). 100% of writing is by freelancers; 100% of illustrating/animating is by freelancers.
Children's Writing: Needs: animation scripts. "Anything from fantasy to fable." To submit, query with synopsis. Submit synopsis/outline, completed script, résumé. Submissions returned with proper SASE. Reports back only if interested. Pay varies.
Illustration/Animation: Type of animation produced: computer animation. To submit, send cover letter, résumé, demo tape (VHS), color print samples, business card. Art samples are filed, returned with proper SASE or not returned. Reports back only if interested.
Tips: "We are gearing to work with fairytales or classic stories. We look for concise retelling of older narratives with slight modifications in the storyline, while at the same time introducing children to stories that they would not necessarily be familiar with. We are currently in production doing "International Family Classics, Part II." We don't hire illustrators for animation. We hire the studio. The illustrators who we hire are used to create the advertising art."

KIDVIDZ: Special Interest Video for Children, 618 Centre St., Newton MA 02158. (617)965-3345. Fax: (617)965-3640. Website: http://www.kidvidz.com. Partner: Jane Murphy. Estab. 1987. Home video publisher and family media consultants. Audience: pre-school and primary-age children, 2-12 years. Produces videotapes. Children's productions: "Let's Get a Move On! A Kid's Video Guide to a Family Move" (VHS video, a family move, 4-12 year olds); "Squiggles Dots & Lines, A Kid's Video Guide to Art & Creativity (art video on creativity for 5-12 year olds). Uses 2 freelance writers/year. Uses 3 freelance artists/year. Submissions filed.
 • Kidvidz has just published a book, *Raising Media: Save Kids in the Age of the Channel Surfing Couch Potato* (Doubleday).
Tips: "Submit material strong on dialogue using a child-centered approach. Be able to write shooting scripts."

KJD TELEPRODUCTIONS, 30 Whyte Dr., Voorhees NJ 08043. (609)751-3500. Fax: (609)751-7729. President: Larry Scott. Creative Director: Kim Davis. Estab. 1989. Location production services (Betacam SP) plus interformat edit and computer animation. Audience: industrial and broadcast. Uses slide sets, multimedia productions, videotapes. Recent children's productions: "Aluminations," (about recycling super heros). 10% of writing is by freelancers; 25% of animating/illustrating by freelancers.

Children's Writing: Needs: animation. To submit, query. Submissions are filed. Reports in 3 months. Pays royalty or buys material outright.

Illustration/Animation: Hires illustrators for animation. Types of animation produced: computer animation. To submit, send cover letter, résumé, demo tape (VHS or ¾″), b&w print samples, tearsheets, business card. Art samples are filed. Reports in 3 months. Pay varies.

Tips: "Keep us up to date with work; we inquire on projects. Stay diligent."

NEW & UNIQUE VIDEOS, 2336 Sumac Dr., San Diego CA 92105. (619)282-6126. Fax: (619)283-8264. Acquisitions Managers: Candy Love, Mark Schulze. Estab. 1985. Video production and distribution services. "Audience varies with each title." Uses films and videotapes. Children's productions: "Battle at Durango: The First-Ever World Mountain Bike Championships," written by Patty Mooney, produced by Mark Schulze (VHS video mountain bike race documentary for 12 and over); "John Howard's Lessons in Cycling," written by John Howard, direction and camera by Mark Schulze (VHS video on cycling for 12 and over). 50% of writing is by freelancers; 85% of illustrating/animating is by freelancers.

Children's Writing: Needs: Completed and packaged videotape productions (45 minutes to one hour in length) whose intended audiences may range from 1 and older. "No scripts or treatments, please. Any subject matter focusing on a special interest that can be considered 'new and unique.' " Query. Submissions are returned with proper SASE. Reports in 2-3 weeks. Payment negotiable.

Illustration/Animation: Hires illustrators for film or video animation. Types of animation produced: computer animation and video graphics. To submit, send cover letter. Art samples returned with proper SASE. Reports back in 2-3 weeks. Payment negotiable.

Tips: "As more and more video players appear in homes across the world, and as the interest in special interest videos climbs, the demand for more original productions is rising meteorically."

RARE MEDIA WELL DONE, 1110 Washington St., Boston MA 02124. (617)296-7000. Fax: (617)296-7001. E-mail: m.sand@aol.com. President: Michael Sand. Estab. 1964. Museum planning consultants. Audience: museum visitors. Produces multimedia productions, films, videotapes and interactive video disks. Children's productions: "The Water Course," written by Kathy Suter, illustrated by Valentin Sahleanu (interactive touch-screen exhibit); and "Transformations Exhibit," written by Michael Sand, illustrated by Frank Constantine (multimedia exhibit renderings on art evaluation for 8-year-olds). Uses 4 freelance writers/year; buys 12 writing projects/year. Uses 8 freelance artists/year; buys 30 art projects/year.

Children's Writing: Needs: animation scripts, educational material, documentaries (ages 5-8, 9-11, 12 and older). Subjects include: history, science, art. To submit, query with synopsis, completed script, résumé, samples. Submissions are returned with proper SASE; submissions sometimes filed. Reports in 1 month. Buys material outright (pay varies).

Illustration: Hires illustrators for computer-based animation, storyboarding, character development, comprehensives, pencil testing, exhibit renderings, models, 3-D illustration. Type of animation produced: cel animation, stop motion, special effects, computer animation, video graphics, motion control, live action. Submit cover letter, résumé, demo tape (VHS), b&w print samples, color print samples, tearsheets, slides, promo sheet. Samples somtetimes filed. Reports in 1 month if interested. Pays minimum $25/hour.

Tips: "Submit one or more examples of your most imaginative work. Kids expect cute. We prefer authentic themes, pertinent to their lives."

*ST. ANTHONY MESSENGER PRESS AND FRANCISCAN COMMUNICATIONS, 1615 Republic St., Cincinnati OH 45210. (513)241-5615. Fax: (513)241-0399. E-mail: gregf@a mericancatholic.org. Website: http://www.americancatholic.org. Executive Producer: Greg Friedman, OFM. Estab. 1893. Supplier of resources (print, audio and video) for education within the Catholic Church. Audience: Catholic religious educators and Catholics at large. Produces videotapes. "We are just beginning our video department productions in this area." Uses 1-2 freelance writers/year. Uses 1-2 freelance artists/year.

Children's Writing: Needs: short dramatic stories (maximum 10 minutes). Subjects include: life issues told in dramatic/story form. Query. Submissions are returned with proper SASE. Submissions are filed. Reports in 2 weeks. Guidelines/catalog free on request. Buys material outright; pays $100-250.

Illustration: Hires illustrators for animation (limited—"photomation" from stills). Types of animation produced: motion control. Send cover letter, résumé, b&w print samples, color print samples. Art samples returned with proper SASE. Reports in 2 weeks. Guidelines/catalog free on request.

Tips: "We are a very specialized producer, so would be interested in writers willing to work with our direction and goals. For artists, we are more flexible, and are interested to build a file of potential illustrators to work with."

SEA STUDIOS, INC., 810 Cannery Row, Monterey CA 93940. (408)649-5152. Fax: (408)649-1380. E-mail: seastudios@seastudios.com. Website: http://www.seastudios.com. Office Manager: Melissa Lewington. Estab. 1985. Natural history video production company. Audience: general. Recent children's productions: "Jellies & Other Ocean Drifters," written by Robin Burnett, illustrated by Heather Weyers (general video on jellyfish). Uses multimedia productions, videotapes. 50% of writing is by freelancers; 50% of illustrating/animating is by freelancers.
Children's Writing: Needs: educational material—target age dependent on project. Send résumé (no phone calls, please). Submissions returned with proper SASE. Reports back in 3 months. Pay negotiable.
Illustration/Animation: Send cover letter, résumé (no phone calls please). Art samples returned with proper SASE. Reports back in 3 months.

*CHIP TAYLOR COMMUNICATIONS, 15 Spollett Dr., Derry NH 03038. (603)434-9262. Fax: (603)432-2723. E-mail: chiptaylor@delphi.com. President: Chip Taylor. Estab. 1985. Production house. Audience: all ages. Produces multimedia productions, videotapes. Recent children's productions: "I've Got Your Nose," written by Nancy Bentley, illustrated by Don Madden (video on values aimed at preschool to 3rd-grade audience); "Picking Pens for a Penny," written by Angela Shelf Medlearis, illustrated by Charles Shaw (video about growing up during the depression for 2nd- to 5th-grade audience). Uses 12-20 freelance writers/year; buys 12-20 writing projects/year. Uses 1-2 freelance artists/year; buys 10-20 art projects/year.
Children's Writing: Needs: scripts and already-written picture books. Subjects include educational content—values. Submit sample of books. Submissions returned with proper SASE; submissions filed. Reports in 3 weeks. Guidelines/catalog for 9×12 SAE and 3 first-class stamps. Pays royalty of 2-10%.
Illustration: Hires illustrators for character development, live action. Types of animation produced: computer animation, video graphics, live action. Send color print samples, demo tape. Art samples returned with proper SASE; art samples filed. Reports in 3 weeks. Guidelines/catalog for 9×12 SAE and 3 first-class stamps. Payment varies with project.

TREEHAUS COMMUNICATIONS, INC., 906 W. Loveland Ave., P.O. Box 249, Loveland OH 45140. (513)683-5716. Fax: (513)683-2882. President: Gerard A. Pottebaum. Estab. 1968. Production house. Audience: preschool through adults. Produces film strips, multimedia productions, videotapes. Recent children's production: "The Little Grain of Wheat," written by Gerard Pottebaum, illustrated by Robert Strobridge (Biblical parable video, for ages 4-9). 30% of writing is by freelancers; 30% of illustrating/animating is by freelancers.
Children's Writing: Needs: educational material/documentaries, for all ages. Subjects include: "social studies, religious education, documentaries on all subjects, but primarily about people who live ordinary lives in extraordinary ways." Query with synopsis. Submissions returned with proper SASE. Reports in 1 month. Guidelines/catalog for SASE. Pays writers in accordance with Writer's Guild standards.
Tips: Illustrators/animators: "Be informed about movements and needs in education, multicultural sensitivity." Looks for "social values, originality, competency in subject, global awareness."

AUDIOTAPE

Among these listings you'll find companies with a range of offerings. Some publish exclusively story tapes; more often the companies listed publish and produce music as well as stories. In either case, these companies provide opportunities for songwriters and writers to showcase their work on tape or compact disk.

Among the record companies listed you'll find both large producers and distributors, and smaller independent studios. For more information about the children's entertainment industry, see the Audiovisual & Audiotape introduction on page 226.

*AMERICATONE INTERNATIONAL—USA, 1817 Loch Lomond, Las Vegas NV 89102-4437. (702)384-0030. Fax: (702)382-1926. President/CEO: Joe Jan Jaros. Music publisher, record

company. Record labels include Americatone Records International and Christy Records International. Estab. 1983.
Music: Releases 5-10 singles/year (CDs and cassettes). Member of BMI. Hires staff writers for children's music. For music published, pays standard royalty of 50%; for songs recorded, pays musicians on salary for inhouse studio work, and songwriters on royalty contract (10%). Submit demo tape by mail; unsolicited submissions OK. Submit demo cassette. Submissions returned with SASE.

BARRON'S EDUCATIONAL SERIES, 250 Wireless Blvd., Hauppauge NY 11788. (516)434-3311. Fax: (516)434-3723. Managing Editor/Director of Acquisitions: Grace Freedson. Book publisher. Estab. 1940.
Stories: Publishes 1 book/cassette package/year. 100% of stories are fiction. For fiction, will consider foreign language. Pays authors royalty. Query. Catalog free for SAE. Ms guidelines free for SASE. Recently recorded story tapes: *Un, Deux, Trois—My First French Rhymes*, by Opal Dunn, illustrated by Patricia Aggs (ages 4-8 foreign language).

BRIGHT IDEAS PRODUCTIONS, 31220 La Baya Dr., West Lake Village CA 91362. (818)707-7127. Fax: (818)707-0889. E-mail: brightidea@aol.com. President: Lisa Marie Nelson. Music publisher, book publisher, record company (Bright Ideas Productions), interactive media. Estab. 1990.
Music: Releases 1 LP/cassette/year; 1 CD/year. Member of ASCAP. Publishes and records 14 children's songs/year. Works with composers, lyricists and team collaborators. For music published, pays usually on a per-project basis. Write for permission to submit material. Submit demo cassette with 3 songs and lyric sheet. Submissions returned with SASE. Recently produced and published songs: "Express Yourself," by Nelson/Shur, recorded by Andre Garner on Bright Ideas (pop for elementary school ages); and "Lucky Day," by Nelson/Shur, recorded by Curt Skinner on Bright Ideas (pop for elementary school ages).
Tips: Write first and ask permission to submit.

*BRILLIANCE AUDIO, P.O. Box 887, Grand Haven MI 49417. (616)846-5256. Fax: (616)846-0302. Vice President, Editorial: Eileen A. Hutton. Spoken audio publisher. Estab. 1984.
Stories: Publishes 12 cassette packages/year. 100% of stories are fiction. "Any established young adult series considered (ages 7-19)." Pays authors 10% based on wholesale price. Offers $1,000 average advance. Submit complete ms through agent only. Reports on mss in 6 weeks. Catalog free on request. Recently published/recorded *Strange Matter #1-12*, by Engle and Barnes, narrated by a multi-voice cast (for ages 7-up. "Think *Goosebumps* with a better vocabulary.")

BROADCAST PRODUCTION GROUP, 1901 S. Bascom Ave., 9th Floor, Campbell CA 95008. (408)559-6300. Fax: (408)559-6382. Vice President, Film/Video: Kevin Sullivan. Video and film production and multimedia group. Estab. 1986.
Music: Hires staff writers for children's music. Works with composers and/or lyricists, team collaborators. "Our projects are on a single-purchase basis." Pays per project for songs recorded. Submit demo tape by mail; unsolicited submissions okay. Submit demo cassette, résumé and videocassette if available. Not necessary to include lyric or lead sheets. Reports in 3 weeks.

CENTER FOR THE QUEEN OF PEACE, Suite 412, 3350 Highway 6, Houston TX 77478. Music publisher, book/video publisher and record company. Record labels include Cosmotone Records, Cosmotone Music. Estab. 1984.
  ● Does not review material at this time.
Music: Releases 1 single, 1 12-inch single and 1 LP/year. Member of ASCAP. Works with team collaborators. For music published, pays negotiable royalty; for songs recorded, pays musicians on salary for inhouse studio work, songwriters on royalty contract.

✳ THE ASTERISK before a listing indicates the listing is new in this edition.

CHILDREN'S MEDIA PRODUCTIONS, P.O. Box 40400, Pasadena CA 91114. (818)797-5462. Fax: (818)797-7524. President: C. Ray Carlson. Video publisher. Estab. 1983.
Music: Works with composers and/or lyricists. For songs recorded, pays musicians/artists on record contract. Write for permission to submit material.
Tips: "We use only original music and songs for videos.We serve markets worldwide and must often record songs in foreign languages. So avoid anything provincially *American*. Parents choose videos that will *'teach* for a lifetime' (our motto) rather than entertain for a few hours. State concisely what the 'message' is in your concept and why you think parents will be interested in it. How will it satisfy new FCC regulations concerning 'educational content?' We like ethnic and/or multi-racial stories and illustrations."

CHOO CHOO RECORDS, 13119 Garden Land Rd., Los Angeles CA 90049. (310)472-4211. Fax: (310)472-3436. Director: Richard Perlmutter. Music publisher, record company (Choo Choo Records). Estab. 1992.
Music: Releases 3-5 LPs-cassettes/year; 3-5 CDs/year. Member of ASCAP and BMI. Publishes 10-20 and records 50 songs/year. Works with composers and lyricists. For music published, pay varies; for songs recorded, pays musicians/artists on record contract, songwriters on royalty contract (percentage royalty paid: statutory rate or less). Submit demo tape by mail; unsolicited submissions OK. Submit demo cassette with 3-10 songs. Cannot return material. Reports in 2-4 weeks. Recorded songs: "When The Cat's Away," by Will Ryan, recorded by Victoria Jackson on Choo Choo Records (swing music for ages 2-10); and "Don't Fence Me In," by Cole Porter, recorded by Nickel Creek Band on Choo Choo Records (country western swing for ages 2-10).

*THE CHRISTIAN SCIENCE PUBLISHING SOCIETY, One Norway Street, Boston MA 02115. (617)450-2033. Fax: (617)450-2797. General Publications Product Development Manager: Martha S. Gordon. Book publisher, "but we do issue some recordings." Estab. 1898.
Music: Works with team collaborators on audiocassettes. Submit query letter with proposal, references, résumé. Does not return unsolicited submissions unless requested. Reports in 3-4 months.
Stories: 100% of stories are nonfiction. Will consider nonfiction for beginning readers, juveniles, teens based on the Bible (King James Version). Authors are paid royalty or work purchased outright, "negotiated with contract." Submit query letter with proposal, references and résumé. Include Social Security number. Reports on queries in 3-4 months.
Tips: "Since we are part of The First Church of Christ, Scientist, all our publications are in harmony with the teachings of Christian Science."

*CROSSPOINT INTERNATIONAL, INC., 30 Monument Square #150B-2, Concord MA 01742. (508)371-2300. Fax: (508)287-5325. Product Developer: Noah Tier. Music publisher, book publisher, record company. Estab. 1995.
Music: Releases 6 LPs/year. Publishes and records 38 children's songs/year. Hires staff writers for children's music. Works with composers, lyricists and teams collaborators. Payment is negotiable. Submit demo tape by mail; unsolicited submissions OK. Include demo cassette with 1-30 songs and VHS videocassette. "We focus on self-esteem-building music for children." Cannot return material. Reports in 4 months. Recently published and recorded "Tricky Ricky" (ages 2-6); and "To The Zoo-ey" both recorded by John and Sara on John & Sara's FunTapes (children's music for ages 2-10).
Music Tips: "Concentrate on fun, self-esteem-building content."
Stories: Publishes 4 book/cassette packages/year. 100% of stories are fiction. For fiction/nonfiction, will consider ages 1-8. Payment negotiable. Submit complete ms. Reports on queries/mss in 4 months. Recently published and recorded *Tricky Ricky* and *Wintertime*, both by John and Sara, narrated by John Garland (ages 1-8).

ROY EATON MUSIC INC., 595 Main St., Roosevelt Island NY 10044. (212)980-9046. Fax: (212)980-9068. President: Roy Eaton. Music publisher, TV and radio music production company. Estab. 1982.
Music: Member of BMI. Hires staff writers for children's TV commercial music only. Works with composers, lyricists, team collaborators. Write or call for permission to submit material. Submit demo cassette with lyric sheet.
Tips: "Primarily interested in commericals for children."

FINE ART PRODUCTIONS, 67 Maple St., Newburgh NY 12550-4034. (914)561-5866. E-mail: rs7.fap@mhv.net. Websites: http://www.audionet.com/pub/books/fineart/fineart.htm or

http://www.geocites.com/Hollywood/1077. Contact: Richie Suraci. Music publisher, record company, book publisher. Estab. 1989.
Music: Member of ASCAP and BMI. Publishes and records 1-2 children's songs/year. Hires staff writers for children's music. Works with composers, lyricists, team collaborators. For music published, pays standard royalty of 50% or other amount; for songs recorded, pays musicians/artists on record contract, musicians on salary for inhouse studio work, songwriters on varying royalty contract. Submit ½″ demo tape by mail; unsolicited submissions OK. Submit demo cassette. Not neccessary to include lyric or lead sheets. Submissions returned with SASE. Reports in 3-4 months. Include SASE with all submissions.
Stories: Publishes 1 book/cassette package and 1 audio tape/year. 50% of stories are fiction; 50% nonfiction. Will consider all genres for all age groups. Authors are paid varying royalty on wholesale or retail price. Submit both cassette tape and ms. Reports in 3-4 months. Ms guidelines free with SASE.

*LINDSEY PUBLISHING, INC., 117 W. Harrison, #L220, Chicago IL 60605. (312)660-9528. Fax: (312)660-0106. President/Publisher: Donna Carter. Book publisher. Estab. 1992.
Stories: Publishes 1 cassette/year. 100% of stories are fiction. For fiction will consider African-American focus in history, adventure, sports, mystery (ages 3-13). For nonfiction will consider self-help, biography (ages 3-18). Pays authors 5-10% royalty based on wholesale price. Query. Reports on queries in 6-8 weeks. Recently published and recorded *Music In The Family*, by Donna Renee Carter, narrated by Isaiah Robinson (ages 3-7, story of boy growing up in musical family).
Tips: "Submit query for upbeat stories that feature African-Americans in positive roles and relationships."

*LOLLIPOP FARM ENTERTAINMENT, P.O. Box 460086, Garland TX 75046. (214)497-1616. President: Lonny J. Schonfeld. Record company, live performance videotape producer. Record labels include Lollipop Farm.
Music: Releases 4-6 singles/year; 2-3 LPs/year; 2-3 CDs/year. Member of BMI. Publishes and records 10-12 songs/year. Works with composers and/or lyricists and teams collaborators. For music published, pays standard royalty of 50%; for songs recorded, pays musicians on salary for inhouse studio work, and songwriters on royalty contract (50%). Submit demo tape by mail; unsolicited submissions OK. Submit demo cassette, VHS videocassette if available with 3-5 songs and lyric sheet. "Be original and have material with a positive attitude or message. No violent material accepted." Submissions returned with SASE. Reports in 4-6 weeks. Recently published and recorded songs: "The Little Bitty Chicken," by The Warmer Brothers, recorded by Scudler and Friends on the Lollipop Farm label (pop for ages 4-10); and "You Put the Merry in My Christmas," by The Warmer Brothers, recorded by Mary Massey on the Lollipop Farm label (pop/Christmas for ages 4-18).
Music Tips: "Keep in mind that our philosophy is that even though society has changed since the 1950s, we still believe that values such as family, education, decency, respect, and manners should be a large part of children's entertainment."
Stories: Publishes 2-4 book/cassette packages/year. 50% of stories are fiction; 50% nonfiction. For fiction and nonfiction, will consider animal, fantasy, history, sports, spy/mystery/adventure, education, human relationships (ages 4-12). Pays negotiable royalty based on wholesale price. Submit both cassette tape and ms. Reports on queries/mss in 4-6 weeks. Catalog not available. Submission guidelines free with SASE. Recently published and recorded "Did You Know?," by various writers, narrated by Larry Stones (ages 4-12, educational facts, amusing stories, fun songs); "Did You Know II?," by various writers, narrated by Robert Styx (ages 4-12, educational facts, amusing stories, fun songs).

OMNI 2000 INC., 413 Cooper St., Camden NJ 08102. (609)963-6400. Fax: (609)964-3291. President: Michael Nise. Music publisher, book publisher (audio books), record company. Record labels include Power Up Records. Estab. 1995. Member of BMI. Works with composers, lyricists and team collaborators. For music published, pays standard royalty of 50%; for songs recorded, pays musicians/artists on record contract, musicians on salary for inhouse studio work. "Include SASE for artist's release form. Completion is required prior to (or with) submission." Submit demo cassette with 3 songs. "Make sure product is protected and you have our release signed and returned. Don't send original masters." Reports within 3 months.
Stories: For fiction and nonfiction submissions, will consider all formats (ages 2-11 and 12-17). Pays authors negotiable royalty; or outright purchase to be negotiated. Submit cassette tape of story. Reports on queries in approximately 3 months.

*PEOPLE RECORDS, 8929 Apache Dr., Beulah CO 81023. (719)485-3191. Fax: (719)485-3500. E-mail: dvanman@aol.com. Contact: Helene Van Manen. Music publisher, record company. Record labels include People Records. Estab. 1986.
Music: Releases 1 LP/year; 1 CD/year. Member of BMI. Publishes and records 10 children's songs/year. For music published, pays standard royalty of 50%. Submit demo tape by mail—unsolicited submissions OK. Submit demo cassette with 3 songs and lyric sheet. Submission returned with SASE. Reports in 3 months. Recently published and recorded "Don't Whine," by Dave and Helene Van Manen, recorded by The Van Manens on the People Records label (folk music for ages 3-12); "Get Out," by Dave and Helene Van Manen, recorded by The Van Manens on the People Records label (bluegrass music for ages 3-12).
Music Tips: "Songs for children should be singable, fun and catchy. Do not be afraid of simplicity—some of the best songs for kids (and even adults) are very simple songs."

*PERIDOT RECORDS, P.O. Box 8846, Cranston RI 02920. (401)785-2677. Owner/President: Amy Parravano. Music publisher, record company. Record labels include Peridot. Estab. 1992.
Music: Releases 2 singles/year; 2 LPs/year; 1 CD/year. Member of ASCAP, BMI. Publishes 1-4 and records 2-6 children's songs/year. Works with composers and/or lyricists and team collaborators. For music published, pays standard royalty of 50%; for songs recorded, pays songwriters on royalty contract. Submit demo tape by mail; unsolicited submissions OK. Submit demo cassette with 1-10 songs and lyric sheet. Reports in 2-3 months. Recently recorded songs: "The Whale Rap" and "Pop-A-Dop-A-Doo," written and recorded by Amy Parravano on the Peridot label (children's rap music for ages 1-10).
Music Tips: "Send something with 'commercial-novelty' flair."
Stories: For nonfiction, will consider biography, education, history.

PRAKKEN PUBLICATIONS, INC., P.O. Box 8623, 275 Metty Dr., Suite 1, Ann Arbor MI 48107. (313)769-1211. Fax: (313)769-8383. Publisher: George Kennedy. Magazine publisher. Estab. 1934.
Stories: Publishes 3-4 books/videos/year. 100% nonfiction. Will consider any genre of nonfiction (ages 3-8). Authors are paid 10% royalty based on net sales. Other payment negotiable. Advance not standard practice but possibly negotiable. Submit outline/synopsis and sample chapters. Reports on queries in 2 weeks; mss in 6 weeks if return requested and SASE enclosed. Catalog free on request. Submission free with SASE.
Tips: "We are presently a publisher of magazines and books for educators. We are now seriously considering expanding into such areas as children's books and other than print media."

*RADIO AAHS, 5501 Excelsior Blvd., Minneapolis MN 55416. (612)926-1280. Fax: (612)926-8014. Music Director: Don Michaels. Radio network. Estab. 1990.
Stories: Submit cassette tape of story.

RHYTHMS PRODUCTIONS/TOM THUMB MUSIC, P.O. Box 34485, Los Angeles CA 90034-0485. President: R.S. White. Multimedia production cassette and book packagers. Record label, Tom Thumb—Rhythms Productions. Estab. 1955.
Music: Member of ASCAP. Works with composers and lyricists. For songs recorded pays musicians/artists on record contract, songwriters on royalty contract. Submit a cassette demo tape or VHS videotape by mail—unsolicited submissions OK. Requirements: "We accept musical stories. Must be produced in demo form, and must have educational content or be educationally oriented." Reports in 2 months. Recorded songs: "Adventures of Professor Whatzit & Carmine Cat," by Dan Brown and Bruce Crook (6 book and cassette packages); "First Reader's Kit" (multimedia learning program); and "Learn About" cassettes; all on Tom Thumb label.

ALWAYS INCLUDE a self-addressed, stamped envelope (SASE) with submissions within your own country. When sending material to other countries, include a self-addressed envelope (SAE) and International Reply Coupons (IRCs).

"WE WANT TO PUBLISH YOUR WORK."

You would give anything to hear an editor speak those 6 magic words. So you work hard for weeks, months, even years to make that happen. You create a brilliant piece of work and a knock-out presentation, but there's still one vital step to ensure publication. You still need to submit your work to the right buyers. With rapid changes in the publishing industry it's not always easy to know who those buyers are. That's why each year thousands of writers and illustrators turn to the most current edition of this indispensable market guide.

Keep ahead of the changes by ordering *1998 Children's Writer's & Illustrator's Market* today! You'll save the frustration of getting your work returned in the mail stamped MOVED: ADDRESS UNKNOWN. And of NOT submitting your work to new listings because you don't know they exist. All you have to do to order the upcoming 1998 edition is complete the attached order card and return it with your payment. Order now and you'll get the 1998 edition at the 1997 price—just $22.99—no matter how much the regular price may increase! *1998 Children's Writer's & Illustrator's Market* will be published and ready for shipment in January 1998.

Keep on top of the ever-changing industry and get a jump on selling your work with help from the *1998 Children's Writer's & Illustrator's Market*. Order today—you deserve it!

Turn Over for More Great Books to Help Get Your Children's Works Published!

Get Your Children's Stories Published with help from these Writer's Digest Books!

Writing and Illustrating Children's Books for Publication

Create a good, publishable manuscript in eight weeks using this self-taught writing course. Easy-to-follow lessons and exercises cover everything from getting ideas to writing, polishing and publishing. #10448/$24.95/128 pages/200 illus.

How To Write and Sell Children's Picture Books

If you yearn to put smiles on little faces, you need this charming guide. You'll discover how to put your picture book on paper and get it published—whether you're retelling a wonderful old tale, or spinning a splendid new yarn. #10410/$16.99/192 pages

How To Write and Illustrate Children's Books and Get Them Published

Find everything you need to break into the lucrative children's market. You'll discover how to write a sure-fire seller, create captivating illustrations, get your manuscript into the right buyer's hands and more! #30082/$23.99/144 pages/115 illus.

Children's Writer's Word Book

Even the most original children's story won't get published if its language usage or sentence structure doesn't speak to young readers. You'll avoid these pitfalls with this quick-reference guide full of word lists, reading levels for synonyms and more! #10316/$19.99/352 pages

The Very Best of Children's Book Illustration

Feast your eyes on this wonderful collection of the best in contemporary children's book illustration. You'll see nearly 200 full-color illustrations sure to spark your creativity. #30513/$29.95/144 pages/198 illus.

Fill out order card on reverse side and mail today!

RODELL RECORDS, INC., P.O. Box 93457, Hollywood CA 90093. (714)434-7730. Fax: (714)434-7756. President: Adam Rodell. Music publisher, record company. Record labels include Rodell Records, Inc. Estab. 1989.

Music: Releases 25-50 singles/year; 5 CDs/year. Member of BMI and ASCAP. Publishes and records 1-3 children's songs/year. Works with composers, lyricists and team collaborators. For music published, pays standard royalty of 50%. Submit demo tape by mail; unsolicited submissions OK. Submit cassette, VHS videocassette, DAT or CD with 1-3 songs and lyric sheet. "Include accurate contact information." Reports in 1 month.

Music Tips: "If we like what we hear, we'll talk! Be patient!"

SATURN, A division of Rock Dog Records, P.O. Box 3687, Hollywood CA 90028. (213)661-0259. Fax: (310)641-5074. VP A&R: Gerry North. Record company. Estab. 1987.

Stories: Publishes 2 book/cassettes and 2 cassette/CDs/year. 99% of stories are fiction; 1% nonfiction. For fiction, will consider fantasy, adventure, mystery, animal (ages 3-5). Payment negotiable. Query. "No phone calls please." Reports on queries in 1 month. Published songs: "Four Eyed Freddie" and "The Green Grickled Monster," both recorded at Saturn Studio (children's stories).

Tips: "Send typed script. If you want a reply or your materials returned, be sure to include SASE."

CHARLES SEGAL MUSIC, 16 Grace Rd., Newton MA 02159. (617)969-6196. Fax: (617)969-6114. Contact: Charles Segal. Music publisher and record company. Record labels include Spin Record. Estab. 1980.

Music: Publishes 24 children's songs/year. Works with composers and/or lyricists, team collaborators. For music published, pays standard royalty of 50%; for songs recorded, pays musicians/artists on record contract. Submit demo tape by mail; unsolicited submissions OK. Submit demo cassette if available with 1-3 songs and lyric or lead sheets. Reports in 6-7 weeks. Recorded songs: "Animal Concert," by Colleen Hay, recorded by Concert Kids on CBS label (sing along for ages 4-13); "Everyday Things," recorded by Charles Segal on MFP label (pop music for ages 6-15).

Music Tips: "Must be of educational value, entertaining, easy listening. The lyrics should not be focused on sex, killing, etc."

Stories: Publishes 6 book/cassette packages/year. 50% of stories are fiction; 50% nonfiction. Will consider all genres aimed at ages 6-15. For nonfiction, considers all aimed at ages 6-15. Authors are paid royalty. Submit complete ms or submit both cassette tape and ms. Reports on queries in 6 weeks; mss in 2 months.

Story Tips: "I always look for the experienced writer who knows where he's going and not beating around the bush; in other words, has a definite message—a simple, good storyline."

*SMARTY PANTS AUDIO/VIDEO, 15104 Detroit, Suite #2, Lakewood OH 44107. (216)221-5300. Fax: (216)221-5348. President: S. Tirk. Music publisher, book publisher, record company. Record labels include Smarty Pants, Smarty Time, High Note, S.P.I. Estab. 1988.

Music: Releases 25 LPs/year; 25 CDs/year. Member of BMI. Publishes 5-10 songs/year; records 10-20 songs and stories/year. Hires staff writers for children's music. Works with composers, lyricists, team collaborators. Buys all rights to material. Call first and obtain permission to submit material. Submit demo cassette and videocassette if available; 3 or 4 songs and lyric sheet. Material must be copyrighted. SASE/IRC for return of submission. Reports in 2 weeks. Recorded songs: "Beatrix Potter," by S. Tirk/Kathy Garver, recorded by Kathy Garver on the Smarty Pants label (children's music for ages 3-8); "Flopsy Bunnies," by S. Tirk/Kathy Garver, recorded by Kathy Garver on the Smarty Pants label (children's music for ages 3-8).

Music Tips: "Keep it upbeat, topical and clear." Sees big name artists trying to crack children's market.

Stories: Publishes 8 book/cassette packages/year; 2 cassettes/CDs/year. 100% of stories are fiction. Considers animal, fantasy aimed at ages 3-8. Work purchased outright. Submit both cassette tape and manuscript. Reports on queries/mss in 2 weeks. Catalog free on request. Call for guidelines. Published and recorded story tapes: *The Tale of Squirrel Nutkin*, by Beatrix Potter, narrated by Kathy Garver (ages 3-8); *The Tale of Benjamin Bunny*, by Blanche Fisher Wright, narrated by Kathy Garver (ages 3-8).

SOUNDPRINTS, 353 Main Ave., Norwalk CT 06851. (203)838-6009. Fax: (203)866-9944. Editorial Assistant: Deirdre Langeland. Book publisher. Estab. 1988.

Stories: Publishes 16 book/cassette packages/year. Almost 100% of stories are fiction. Will consider realistic animal stories for preschool-3rd grade. Query with SASE. Reports on queries in 2 weeks; mss in 1 month. Catalog for SASE. Ms guidelines free with SASE. Recently published and recorded story tapes: *Sea Turtle Journey*, by Lorraine A. Jay, narrated by Peter Thomas (for preschool-2nd grade); *Screech Owl at Midnight Hollow*, by C. Drew Lamm, narrated by Alexi Komisar (for preschool-2nd grade).
Tips: "Stories should be realistic and not anthropomorphic. But they should not be dry nonfiction. We are looking for well-crafted storylines."

STEMMER HOUSE PUBLISHERS, 2627 Caves Rd., Owings Mills MD 21117. (410)363-3690. Fax: (410)363-8459. President: Barbara Holdridge. Book publisher.
Stories: Catalog for 9×12 SAE and $1.01 postage. Ms guidelines for SASE. "We only record selected books previously published by Stemmer House. Therefore it's necessary to submit a manuscript rather than a tape." Recorded story tapes: *The Wily Witch*, by Godfried Bomans, narrated by Tammy Grimes, John Houseman (ages 5-10, fairy tales).

*TOOTER SCOOTER MUSIC, 195 S. 26th St., San Jose CA 95116. (408)286-9840. Fax: (408)286-9845. A&R: Gradie O'Neal. Music publisher, record company. Record labels include Rowena Records. Estab. 1969.
Music: Releases 6 CDs/year. Member of BMI, ASCAP. Works with composers, lyricists. For music published, pays standard royalty of 50%; for songs recorded, pays musicians/artists on record contract. Submit demo tape by mail; unsolicited submissions OK. Submit demo cassette with 1-4 songs, lyric sheet and SASE. Submissions returned with SASE. Reports in 2 weeks. Recently recorded songs: "It's Good to Read," by Johnny Gitar, recorded by Johnny Gitar on Rowena label (English and Spanish for ages 6-12).

*TREEHOUSE RADIO®, P.O. Box 13272, Ft. Wayne IN 46868-3272. (217)356-2400. Executive Producer: Cherie Lyn. Weekly children's radio show hosted by kids. Estab. 1990.
Tips: "We give priority to songs done from a kids' perspective, and/or written by kids."

TVN-THE VIDEO NETWORK, 31 Cutler Dr., Ashland MA 01721. (508)881-1800. Fax: (508)881-1800. Producer: Gregg C. McAllister. Video publisher. Estab. 1986.
Music: Publishes and records 8 children's songs/year for video and multimedia projects. Member of ASCAP and BMI. Hires staff writers for children's music. Pays on a work-for-hire basis. Pays musicians on salary for inhouse studio work. Submit demo cassette, VHS videocassette if available. "Reports on an as needed basis only." Recorded "Tugboat" and "My Dad and Me."

TWIN SISTERS PRODUCTIONS, INC., Suite D, 1340 Home Ave., Akron OH 44310. (216)633-8900. Fax: (216)633-8988. President: Kim Thompson. CEO: Karen Hilderbrand. Music publisher, record company. Estab. 1987.
Music: Releases 12 singles/year; 12 LPs-cassettes/year. Publishes and records 120 children's songs/year. Works with composers and teams collaborators. Pays musicians on salary for inhouse studio work. Call first and obtain permission to submit material. Submit demo cassette with lyric sheet and VHS videocassette. Not necessary to include lyric or lead sheets. List past history of successes. SASE/IRC for return of submission. Reports in 1 month. Recorded songs: "Did You Know That Monkeys Like to Swing?," by Kim Thompson and Karen Hilderbrand, recorded by Greg Fortson on the Twin Sisters Productions label (children's music for ages 2-7); "The Tiger's Loose" by Kim Thompson and Karen Hilderbrand, recorded by Greg Forston on the Twin Sisters Productions label (children's, music for ages 2-7).
Tips: "Send a professional-sounding recording, labelled with all information—name, phone number, etc. Children's music is starting to be widely recognized in mainstream music. Independent labels are major contributors."

WATCHESGRO MUSIC PUBLISHING CO., Watch Us Climb, 9208 Spruce Mountain Way, Las Vegas NV 89134-6024. (702)363-8506. President: Eddie Lee Carr. Music publisher, record company. Record labels include Interstate 40 Records, Tracker Records. Estab. 1970.
Music: Releases 10 singles/year; 5 12-inch singles/year; 1 LP/year; 1 CD/year. Member of BMI. Publishes 15 and records 4 children's songs/year. Works with composers, lyricists. For music published, pays standard royalty of 50%; for songs recorded, pays musicians/artists on record contract, musicians on salary for inhouse studio work. Write or call first and obtain permission to submit a cassette tape. Does not return unsolicited material. Reports in 1 week.

WE LIKE KIDS!, produced by KTOO-FM, 360 Egan Dr., Juneau AK 99801. (907)586-1670. Fax: (907)586-3612. Producer: Jeff Brown. Producer of children's radio show.
Music: Releases 50 programs/year. Member of Children's Music Network; National Storytelling Association. Submit demo tape by mail; unsolicited submissions OK. Submit demo cassette, vinyl, CD.
Music Tips: "The best advice we could give to anyone submitting songs for possible airplay is to make certain that you give your best performance and record it in the best way possible. A mix of well-honed songwriting skills, an awareness of a variety of international musical styles, and the advent of home studios have all added up to a delightful abundance of quality songs and stories for children."
Stories: "Our show is based on themes most of the time. Send us your *recorded* stories. We play an average of one story per show, *all* from pre-recorded cassettes, LPs and CDs. Please do not send us *written* stories. Many storytellers have discovered We Like Kids! as a way of sharing their stories with a nationwide audience."

*WORLD LIBRARY PUBLICATIONS A division of J.S. Paluch Co., 3815 N. Willow Rd., Schiller Park IL 60176. (708)678-0621. General Editor: Laura Dankler. Music publisher. Estab. 1945.
Music: Publishes 75-100 children's songs/year. Works with composers. For music published pays 10% of sales. Making contact: Submit demo cassette tape and lead sheet by mail; unsolicited submissions OK. "Please submit no more than five works at one time. If it is not a full score, we do require a cassette. Should be liturgical. We are primarily a Roman Catholic publisher." Reports in 3 months. Published children's songs and collections by Jim Marchionda, Julie Howard and the Crayons, Joe Mattingly and the Newman Singers, Steve Warner and the Notre Dame Folk Choir, Ed Bolduc, Paul Tate, Dolores Hruby, Mary Kay Beall, Carl Schalk, Jeffrey Honore and many others.

*WUVT-FM; HICKORY DICKORY DOCK SHOW, P.O Box 99, Pilot VA 24138. (703)382-4975. Producer: Linda DeVito. Radio producer of children's show which features music, stories, poems. Estab. 1989.
Music: Submit demo cassette. SASE/IRC for return of submission.
Music Tips: "Write material that the whole family can enjoy. Sing-songy is out. Current topics and acoustic/folk melodies are great!"
Stories: Will consider animal, fantasy, sports, adventure. For nonfiction, considers animal, sports (ages 4-10).

Greeting Cards,
Puzzles & Games

We've changed the name of this section from Special Markets to better describe what you'll find here—companies that produce puzzles, games, greeting cards and other items (like coloring books, stickers and giftwrap) especially for kids. These are items you'll find in children's sections of bookstores, toy stores, department stores and card shops.

Because these markets create an array of products, their needs vary greatly. Some may need the service of freelance writers for greeting card copy or slogans for buttons and stickers. Others are in need of illustrators for coloring books or photographers for puzzles. Carefully read through the listings to find a company's needs, and send for guidelines if they're offered, just as you would for a book or magazine publisher.

*S.S. ADAMS COMPANY, P.O. Box 850, Neptune NJ 07754. E-mail: ssadams@monmouth.com Contact: C.S. Adams. Estab. 1906. Novelty company. Manufactures practical joke and magic items. 100% of products are made for kids or have kids' themes.
Illustration: Needs comic illustrations for practical jokes and magic tricks. Looking for 1930s-'50s style comic illustrations that reproduce well in 1×1" area. To contact, send cover letter, b&w photocopies. Reports in 1 month. Materials not returned. Pays on acceptance. Buys all rights.

*AMCAL, 2500 Bisso Lane, #500, Concord CA 94520. (415)689-9930. Fax: (415)689-0108. Editor/Art Director: Judy Robertson. Estab. 1975. Greeting cards, calendars, desk diaries, boxed Christmas cards, limited edition prints and more.
Illustration: Receives over 150 submissions/year. "AMCAL publishes high quality full color, narrative and decorative art for a wide market from traditional to contemporary. "Currently we are very interested in country folkart styles. Know the trends and the market. Juvenile illustration should have some adult appeal. We don't publish cartoon, humorous or gag art, or bold graphics. We sell to small, exclusive gift retailers. Submissions are always accepted for future lines." To contact, send samples, photocopies, slides and SASE for return of submission. Reports in 1 month. Pays on publication. Pay negotiable/usually advance on royalty. Rights purchased negotiable. Guideline sheets for #10 SASE and 1 first-class stamp.

ARISTOPLAY, LTD., P.O. Box 7028, Ann Arbor MI 48107. (313)995-4353. Fax: (313)995-4611. E-mail: aristo@chamber.ann-arbor.mi.vs. Product Development Director: Lorraine Hopping Egan. Art Director: Jack Thompson. Estab. 1979. Produces educational board games and card decks, activity kits—all educational subjects. 100% of products are made for kids or have kids' themes.
Illustration: Needs freelance illustration and graphic designers (including art directors) for games and card decks. Makes 2-4 illustration assignments/year. To contact, send cover letter, résumé, published samples or color photocopies. Reports back in 1 month if interested. For artwork, pays by the project, $500-5,000. Pays on acceptance (½-sketch, ½-final). Buys all rights. Credit line given.
Photography: Buys photography from freelancers. Wants realistic, factual photos.
Tips: "Creating board games requires a lot of back and forth in terms of design, illustration, editorial and child testing; the more flexible you are, the better. Also, factual accuracy is important." Target age group 4-14. "We are an educational game company. Writers and illustrators working for us must be willing to research the subject and period of focus."

A/V CONCEPTS CORP., 30 Montauk Blvd., Oakdale NY 11769. (516)567-7227. Fax: (516)567-8745. Editor: Laura Solimene. President: Philip Solimene. Estab. 1969. "We are an educational publisher. We publish books for the K-12 market—primarily language arts and math and reading." 20% of products are made for kids or have kids' themes.

Writing: Needs freelance writing for classic workbooks only: adaptations from fine literature. Makes 5-10 assignments/year. To contact, send cover letter and writing samples and 9×12 SASE. Reports in 3 weeks. For writing assignments, pays by the project ($700-1,000). Pays on publication. Buys all rights.

Illustration: Needs freelance illustration for classic literature adaptations, fine art, some cartoons, super heroes. Makes 15-20 illustration assignments/year. Needs "super hero-like characters in four-color and b&w." To contact, send cover letter and photocopies. Reports back in 3 weeks. For artwork, pays by the project (range: $200-1,000). Pays on publication. Buys all rights.

Tips: Submit seasonal material 4 months in advance. "We're getting into CD-ROM development."

THE AVALON HILL GAME CO., 4517 Harford Rd., Baltimore MD 21214. (410)254-9200. Fax: (410)254-0991. President: Jackson V. Dott. Editor: A. Eric Dott. Art Director: June Kim. Estab. 1958. Produces *Girl's Life* magazine for girls ages 7-14. *Girl's Life* is promoted through the Girl Scouts of America. 50% of material written and illustrated by freelancers. Buys 50 freelance projects/year; receives 500 submissions annually.

Writing: Makes 6 writing assignments/month; 36/year. To contact send cover letter, résumé, client list, writing samples. Reports back only if interested. Pays on publication. Buys all rights. Credit line given.

Illustration: Makes 12 illustration assignments/month. Prefers styles pertaining to general interest topics for girls. To contact send cover letter, résumé, published samples, portfolio. Reports in 1 month. Pays on acceptance. Buys all rights. Credit line given.

THE BEISTLE COMPANY, P.O. Box 10, Shippensburg PA 17257. (717)532-2131. Fax: (717)532-7789. Product Manager: C. Michelle Luhrs-Wiest. Art Director: Brad Clever. Estab. 1900. Paper products company. Produces decorations and party goods, bulletin board aides, posters—baby, baptism, birthday, holidays, educational. 50% of products are made for kids' or have kids' themes.

Illustration: Needs freelance illustration for decorations, party goods, school supplies, point-of-purchase display materials and educational aides. Makes 20 illustration assignments/year. Prefers fanciful style, cute 4- to 5-color illustration in gouache. To contact, send cover letter, résumé, client list, promo piece. To query with specific ideas, phone or write. Reports only if interested. Materials returned with SASE; materials filed. Pays by the project or by contractual agreement; price varies according to type of project. Pays on acceptance. Buys all rights. Artist's guidelines available for SASE.

Photography: Buys photography from freelancers. Buys stock and assigns work. Makes 30-50 assignments/year. Uses 35mm, 2¼×2¼, 4×5 transparencies. To contact, send cover letter, résumé, slides, client list, promo piece. Reports only if interested. Materials returned if accompanied with SASE; materials filed. Pays on acceptance. Buys first rights. Credit line sometimes given—depends on project. Guidelines available for SASE.

Tips: Submit seasonal material 6-8 months in advance.

*BEPUZZLED/LOMBARD MARKETING, INC., 22 E. Newberry Rd., Bloomfield CT 06002. (860)769-5723. Fax: (860)769-5799. Creative Services Manager: Sue Tyska. Estab. 1987. Publishes mystery jigsaw puzzles, mystery dinner games. 30% of products are for kids or have kids' themes.

Writing: Needs freelance writing for short mystery stories. Makes 15-20 writing assignments/year. To contact, send cover letter and writing samples. Reports back in 3 weeks. Pays by the project ($1,800). Pays on publication. Buys all rights. No credit line given.

Photography: Needs freelance photographers for mystery jigsaw puzzles. Makes 20-30 photography assignments/year. Preferences announced when needed. To contact, send cover letter, résumé, client list and color promo pieces. Reports back in 2 months. Pays by the project. Pays on publication. Buys all rights.

Tips: "Send seasonal material six months in advance. Send SASE for guidelines. Submissions should be short and include idea of writing style, and an outline of ideas for visual and literal clues (six each, some with red herrings)."

RUSS BERRIE & COMPANY, INC., 111 Bauer Dr., Oakland NJ 07436. (201)337-9000. Fax: (201)405-2544. Director, Greeting Cards: Angelica Urra. Estab. 1963. Greeting card and paper products company. Manufactures "all kinds of paper products and impulse gifts—photo frames, mugs, buttons, baby gift products, cards, plaques, plush, ceramics, toys, bibs, booties, etc." One-third of products are for kids or have kids' themes.

Writing: Makes 4-8 writing assignments/month; unlimited/year. Needs freelance writing for children's books, booklets, greeting cards and other children's products (T-shirts, buttons, book-marks, stickers, diaries, address books, plaques, perpetual (undated) calendars). To contact, send writing samples to Angelica Urra, director of greeting cards. Reports in 2 months. Materials returned with SASE; files materials "if we think there may be interest later." For greeting cards, pays flat fee of $50-100 per piece of copy. For books, plaques and other writing, pays more, depending on the project. Pays on acceptance. Buys all rights or exclusive product rights. Writer's guidelines for SASE.

Illustration: Needs freelance illustration for children's greeting cards and other children's products. Makes 6-8 illustration assignments/month. Artwork should be "contemporary, eye catching, colorful—professional. Because we also do products for parents and parents-to-be, we seek both juvenile *and* adult looks in products about children." To contact, send client list, published samples, photocopies, slides and/or promo piece. To query with specific ideas, send tight roughs. Reports in 2 months. Returns material with SASE; files material "if future interest is anticipated." For greeting cards, pays flat fee of $250-500. Pays on acceptance. Buys all rights or exclusive product rights. Credit line sometimes given.

Tips: "Send best samples of your style in portfolio with SASE for review. Seasonal material should be submitted 18 months in advance. We're using more freelance illustrators and freelance writers who can submit a concept rather than single piece of writing. We are upbeat, with a large, diverse baby/children's line. Send all material to greeting card director—if it is for another product it will be passed along to the appropriate department."

CONTEMPORARY DESIGNS, 213 Main St., Gilbert IA 50105. (515)232-5188. Fax: (515)232-3380. Editor and Art Director: Sallie Abelson. Estab. 1977.
● Contemporary Designs wants greeting cards for campers and Jewish markets only. Puzzles, games and coloring books should be Judaic in theme.

Writing/Illustration: Publishes greeting cards, coloring books and puzzles and games. "Greeting cards should be funny—for children who go to camp." 25% of material is written by freelancers; 20% illustrated by freelancers. Buys 50 freelance projects/year; receives 150 submissions/year. Materials returned with SASE. Reports in 1 month. Pays $40 for greeting cards. Pays on acceptance. Buys all rights on accepted material; negotiable amount for coloring books and puzzles. Writer's/illustrator's guidelines for SASE.

Tips: Submit seasonal material 1 year in advance.

CREATE-A-CRAFT, P.O. Box 330008, Fort Worth TX 76163-0008. Contact: Editor. Estab. 1967. Produces greeting cards, giftwrap, games, calendars, posters, stationery and paper table-ware products for all ages.

Illustration: Works with 3 freelance artists/year. Buys 3-5 designs/illustrations/year. Prefers artists with experience in cartooning. Works on assignment only. Buys freelance designs/illustrations mainly for greetings cards and T-shirts. Also uses freelance artists for calligraphy, P-O-P displays, paste-up and mechanicals. Considers pen & ink, watercolor, acrylics and colored pencil. Prefers humorous and "cartoons that will appeal to families. Must be cute, appealing, etc. No religious, sexual implications or off-beat humor." Produces material for all holidays and seasons. Contact only through artist's agent. Some samples are filed; samples not filed are not returned. Reports only if interested. Write for appointment to show portfolio of original/final art, final reproduction/product, slides, tearsheets, color and b&w. Original artwork is not returned. "Payment depends upon the assignment, amount of work involved, production costs, etc. involved in the project." Buys all rights. For guidelines and sample cards, send $2.50 and #10 SASE.

Tips: Submit 6 months in advance. "Demonstrate an ability to follow directions exactly. Too many submit artwork that has no relationship to what we produce. No phone calls accepted."

 A BULLET within a listing introduces special comments by the editor of *Children's Writer's & Illustrator's Market.*

CREATIF LICENSING CORP., 31 Old Town Crossing, Mt. Kisco NY 10549. (914)241-6211. E-mail: jahee@aol.com. President: Pat Cohen. Estab. 1975. Gift industry licensing agency. Publishes greeting cards, comic books, puzzles, posters, calendars, fabrics, home furnishings, all gifts. 75% of products are made for kids or have kids' themes.

Illustration: Needs freelance illustration for children's greeting cards, all gift and home furnishings. Makes many illustration assignments/month. Uses both color and b&w artwork. To contact, send cover letter, résumé, client list, published samples, photocopies, portfolio, promo piece and SASE. Reports in 1 month. Materials returned with SASE; materials filed. For greeting cards, pays royalty and advance. For other artwork, pays royalty and advance. Pays on acceptance or publication. Buys reprint rights. Artist's guidelines available for SASE.

Tips: Submit seasonal material 8-12 months in advance.

DESIGN DESIGN INC., P.O. Box 2266, Grand Rapids MI 49501. (616)774-2448. President: Don Kallil. Creative Director: Tom Vituj. Estab. 1986. Greeting card company.

Writing: Needs freelance writing for children's greeting cards. For greeting cards, prefers both rhymed and unrhymed verse ideas. To contact, send cover letter and writing samples. Reports in 3 weeks. Materials returned with SASE; materials not filed. For greeting cards, pays flat fee. Buys all rights or exclusive product rights; negotiable. No credit line given. Writer's guidelines for SASE.

Illustration: Needs freelance illustration for children's greeting cards, notecards, wrapping paper. Makes 30 illustration assignments/month. Uses color artwork only. To contact, send cover letter, published samples, color or b&w photocopies, color or b&w promo pieces or portfolio. Reports in 3 weeks. Returns materials with SASE. Pays by the project or royalty. Buys all rights or exclusive product rights; negotiable. Artist's guidelines available for SASE.

Photography: Purchases photography from freelancers. Buys stock and assigns work. Uses 4×5 transparencies or high quality 35mm slides. To contact, send cover letter with slides, stock photo list, published samples and promo piece. Reports in 3 weeks. Materials returned with SASE; materials not filed. Pays per photo or royalties. Pays on usage. Buys all rights or exclusive product rights; negotiable. Photographer's guidelines for SASE.

EPI GROUP LIMITED, 250 Pequot Ave., Southport CT 06490. (203)255-1112. Vice President: Merryl Lambert. Estab. 1989. Paper products company. Publishes puzzles, activity kits, nature kits, games, books and plush toys, posters for nature and educational markets. 80% of products are made for kids or have kids' themes.

Writing: Needs freelance writing for children's books. Makes "hundreds of" freelance writing assignments/year. To contact, send cover letter and writing samples. To query with specific ideas, submit overview with sample. Reports back only if interested. Materials returned with SASE; materials filed. Pays on acceptance. Buys all rights; negotiable. Credit line given.

Illustration: Needs freelance illustration for books/activity kits. Makes "hundreds of" illustration assignments/year. Prefers animal/nature illustrations for packaging, posters, activity books, games, etc. Uses both b&w and color artwork. To contact, send photocopies and promo pieces. To query with specific ideas, submit samples with overview. Reports only if interested. Materials returned with SASE; materials filed. Pays on acceptance. Buys all rights; negotiable. Credit line given.

Photography: Buys stock and assigns work. Buys stock infrequently. Makes "hundreds of" assignments/year. Uses 4×5 prints. To contact, send promo piece. Reports only if interested. Returns material with SASE; materials filed. Pays on acceptance. Buys all rights; negotiable. Credit line given.

Tips: Submit seasonal material six months in advance.

EVERYTHING GONZO!, P.O. Box 1322, Roslyn Heights NY 11577. (516)623-9477. Fax: (516)546-5535. Owner: H.J. Fleischer. Toy designer and manufacturer. Designs, licenses, manufactures toys, gifts and related products. Manufactures novelties (educational, impulse, creative), puzzles, games; publishes booklets. 100% of products are made for kids or have kids' themes.

Illustration: Needs freelance illustration for toy concepts. Makes 2 illustration assignments/year. Uses both color and b&w artwork. To contact, send cover letter, résumé, published samples, portfolio, photocopies, promo pieces. To query with specific ideas, write to request disclosure form first. Reports only if interested. Materials returned with SASE; materials filed. For other artwork, pays by the hour($10); negotiable royalty. Pays on acceptance. Credit line sometimes given.

Photography: Buys photography from freelancers. Works on assignment only. Uses transparencies. To contact, send cover letter, published samples, portfolio, promo piece. Reports only if

These comfy mice sitting beside the fire with their tails intertwined were rendered in watercolor by British artist Betty Davis. The cozy couple has appeared on stationery, socks and cross stitch and needlework kits created by Creatif Licensing Corp., a company that licenses gift products.

interested. Materials returned; materials filed. Pays on acceptance. Credit line sometimes given. **Tips:** Submit seasonal material 6 months in advance.

FAX-PAX USA, INC., 37 Jerome Ave., Bloomfield CT 06002. (203)242-3333. Fax: (203)242-7102. Editor: Stacey L. Savin. Estab. 1990. Buys 1 freelance project/year. Publishes art and history flash cards. Needs include US history, natural history.

Writing/Illustration: Buys all rights. Pays on publication. Cannot return material.
Tips: "We need concise, interesting, well-written 'mini-lessons' on various subjects including U.S. and natural history."

FOTOFOLIO/ARTPOST, 536 Broadway, New York NY 10012. (212)226-0923. Editorial Director: JoAnne Seador. Estab. 1976. Greeting card company. Also publishes fine art and photographic postcards, notecards, posters, calendars. New children's line.
Illustration: Needs freelance illustration for children's greeting cards, calendars and coloring books. To contact, send cover letter, published samples, photocopies, slides, promo piece. Reports back only if interested. Returns materials with SASE. Buys materials not filed. Rights negotiable. Credit line given. Artist's guidelines not available.
Photography: Buys photography from freelancers. Buys stock. To contact, send cover letter, slides, stock photo list, published samples and promo piece. Reports back only if interested. Returns material with SASE. Pays on usage. Rights negotiable. Credit line given.

GALISON BOOKS, 36 W. 44th St., Suite 910, New York NY 10036. (212)354-8840. Estab. 1978. Paper products company. Publishes museum-quality gift products, including notecards, journals, address books and jigsaw puzzles. Publishes children's jigsaw puzzles with images licensed from popular children's books.
Illustration: Needs freelance illustration for greeting cards, jigsaw puzzles, journals, address books and recipe notecards. Makes 30 illustration assignments/year. Uses color artwork only. To contact, send cover letter, published samples and color promo piece. Reports back only if interested. Returns materials with SASE; materials filed. Pays flat fee. Credit line given. Artist's guidelines not available.
Photography: Buys photography from freelancers. Buys stock. Uses 4×5 or larger transparencies. To contact, send cover letter, stock photo list, published samples or duplicate slides. Reports back only if interested. Returns materials with SASE; materials filed. Pays flat fee. Pays on publication. Credit line given. Photographer's guidelines available for SASE.
Tips: Christmas images should be submitted 1 year in advance. Submit materials to the attention of Heather Zschock, design director.

GREAT AMERICAN PUZZLE FACTORY, INC., 16 S. Main St., S. Norwalk CT 06854. (203)838-4240. Fax: (203)838-2065. Art Director: Anne Mulligan. Estab. 1976. Produces puzzles.
Illustration: Needs freelance illustration for puzzles. Makes over 30 freelance assignments/year. To contact, send cover letter, color photocopies and color promo pieces (no slides or original art) with SASE. Reports in 2 months. Artists guidelines available for SASE. Rights purchased vary. Buys all rights to puzzles. Pays on publication. Pay varies.
Photography: Needs local cityscapes for regional puzzles.
Tips: Wants "whimsical, fantasy" material. Targets ages 4-12 and adult. "No slides. Send color copies (3-4) for style. Looking for whimsical, fantasy and nature themes with a bright, contemporary style. Not too washy or cute. We often buy reprint rights to existing work."

GREAT SEVEN, INC., Unit 503, 3870 Del Amo Blvd., Torrance CA 90503. (310)371-4555. Vice President: Ronald Chen. Estab. 1984. Paper products company. Publishes educational and fun stickers for children and teenage markets. 100% of products are made for kids or have kids' themes.
Illustration: Needs freelance illustration for children's fun stickers. Makes 120 illustration assignments/year. Wants "kid themes." To contact, send published samples and b&w photocopies. To query with specific ideas, write to request disclosure form first. Reports back only if interested. Returns material with SASE; materials filed. Pays on acceptance. Buys all rights. No credit line given. Artist's guidelines not available.
Tips: Seasonal material should be submitted 10 months in advance.

HANDPRINT SIGNATURE, INC., P.O. Box 22682, Portland OR 97269. (503)295-1925. Fax: (503)295-3673. President: Paula Carlson. Greeting card company. "Manufacturer of greeting cards especially designed for kids to send. Each card to be 'signed' with a child's handprint or footprint." 100% of products are made for kids or have kids' themes.
Illustration: Needs freelance illustration for children's greeting cards. "All art must tie in with general theme of Handprint Signature—cards for kids to send. Pure colors." To contact, send cover letter, résumé, published samples and acknowledgement that he/she has seen and under-

A basket full of happy chirping chicks, a smiling dog and a somewhat befuddled cat are greeted by a hopping Easter Bunny in this bright, contemporary illustration by Mary Grace Eubank. The Great American Puzzle Factory used Eubank's illustration, which was created using gouache with airbrush, for a 100-piece children's jigsaw puzzle entitled *Easter Morning*.

stands Handprint Signature card line. Reports in 1 month. Returns materials with SASE. For greeting cards, pays $250/image. Pays on publication. Credit line given. Artist's guidelines available.

Tips: "Even though an artist's work must tie in with other artists already published, the design and presentation must stand out as his or her own unique interpretation. The card design and the text should be harmonious and always conscious that even though the parent (adult) is buying the card, the card is from a child. The cards are viewed as gifts and are primarily marketed in toy and gift stores. It is a bigger market than stationery/children's cards."

*INNOVA, P.O. Box 36, Redmond WA 98073. (206)746-7774. Fax: (206)451-3959. E-mail: kenesa@aol.com. Owner: Ken Jacobson. Estab. 1981. Paper products company and producer of educational and strategic games. Publishes coloring books, games, books. 10% of products are made for kids or have kids' themes.

Writing: To contact, send cover letter and writing samples. Reports in 3 months only if interested. Materials returned with SASE; materials filed. Payment is negotiated. Buys all rights. Credit line given.

Illustration: Makes 1-2 illustration assignments/year. To contact, send cover letter and published samples. Reports in 3 months. Materials returned with SASE. Payment is negotiated. Pays on publication. Buys all rights. Credit line given.

Photography: Buys stock and assigns work. To contact, send cover letter and published samples. Reports in 3 months. Material returned if accompanied with SASE; materials filed. Payment is negotiated. Buys all rights. Credit line given.

---

*   THE ASTERISK before a listing indicates the listing is new in this edition.

INTERCONTINENTAL GREETINGS LTD., 176 Madison Ave., New York NY 10016. (212)683-5830. Contact: Robin Lipner. Estab. 1964. 100% of material freelance written and illustrated. Produces greeting cards, scholastic products (notebooks, pencil cases), novelties (gift bags, mugs), tin gift boxes, shower and bedding curtains.

Writing: "We use very little writing except for humor." Makes 4 writing assignments/year. To contact, send cover letter, résumé, client list and writing samples with SASE. Reports in 4-6 weeks. Pays advance of $20-100 and royalty of 20% for life. Pays on publication. Contracts exclusive product rights. Credit line sometimes given.

Illustration: Needs children's greeting cards, notebook cover, photo albums, gift products. Makes 15 illustration assignments/month. Prefers primarily greeting card subjects, suitable for gift industry. To contact, send cover letter, résumé, client list, published samples, photocopies, slides and promo piece with SASE. Reports in 4-6 weeks. For greeting cards pays advance of $75 against 20% royalty for life. For other artwork pays 20% royalty for life. Pays on publication. Buys exclusive product rights. Credit line sometimes given.

Photography: Needs stylized and interesting still lifes, studio florals, all themed toward the paper and gift industry.

Tips: Target group for juvenile cards: ages 1-10. Illustrators: "Use clean colors, not muddy or dark. Send a neat, concise sampling of your work. Include some color examples, a SASE to issue return of your samples if wanted."

INTERNATIONAL PLAYTHINGS, INC., 120 Riverdale Rd., Riverdale NJ 07457. (201)831-1400. Fax: (201)616-7775. Assistant Product Manager: Kim McCue. Estab. 1968. Toy/game company. Distributes and markets children's toys, games and puzzles in specialty toy markets. 100% of products are made for kids or have kids' themes.

Illustration: Needs freelance illustration for children's puzzles and games. Makes 20-30 illustration assignments/year. Prefers fine-quality, original illustration for children's puzzles. Uses color artwork only. To contact, send published samples, slides, portfolio, or color photocopies or promo pieces. Reports in 1 month only if interested. Materials filed. For artwork, pays by the project (range: $1,000-3,000). Pays on publication. Buys one-time rights, negotiable.

Tips: "Mail correspondence only, please."

JILLSON & ROBERTS GIFTWRAP, INC., 5 Watson Ave., Irvine CA 92718. (714)859-8781. Art Director: Josh Neufeld. Estab. 1973. Paper products company. Makes giftwrap/giftbags. 20% of products are made for kids or have kids' themes.

Illustration: Needs freelance illustration for children's giftwrap. Makes 6-12 illustration assignments/year. Wants children/baby/juvenile themes. To contact, send cover letter. Reports in 1 month. Returns material with SASE; materials filed. For wrap and bag designs, pays flat fee of $250. Pays on publication. Rights negotiable. No credit line given. Artist's guidelines for SASE.

Tips: Seasonal material should be submitted up to 1 month in advance. "We produce two lines of giftwrap per year: one everyday line and one Christmas line. The closing date for everyday is June 30th and Christmas is September 15th."

LOVE GREETING CARD CO. INC., 1717 Opa-Locka Blvd., Opa-Locka FL 33054. (305)685-5683. Editor: Norman Drittel. Estab. 1980. Greeting card, paper products and children's book company. Publishes greeting cards (Muffy 'N' Pebbles), posters, small books. 20% of products are made for kids or have kids' themes.

Writing: Needs freelance writing for children's greeting cards. Makes 2 writing assignments/month; 12/year. Prefers rhymed verse ideas. To contact, send writing samples. To query with specific ideas, contact Norman Drittel. Reports in 2 months. Materials returned with SASE; materials filed. For greeting cards, pays flat fee of $50-100. Pays on acceptance. Buys one-time rights, reprint rights; negotiable. Credit line given. Writer's guidelines available for SASE.

Illustration: Needs freelance illustration for children's greeting cards, book material. Makes 2 illustration assignments/month; 12/year. Prefers 8-10 page books. Uses color artwork only. To contact, send published samples, portfolio. Reports in months. Materials returned with SASE; materials filed. For greeting cards, pays flat fee of $100-250. For other artwork, pays by the project (range: $500-2,500). Pays on acceptance. Rights negotiable. Credit line given. Artist's guidelines available for SASE.

Photography: Buys photography from freelancers. Buys stock and assigns work. Buys 20 stock images/year. Makes 5 assignments/year. Wants children, any subject. Uses color prints; 8×10 transparencies. To contact, send slides, portfolio. Reports in 2 months. Materials returned with SASE; materials filed. Pays per photo (range for $100-150) for b&w/color. Pays on acceptance.

Rights negotiable. Credit line given. Guidelines available for SASE.
Tips: Submit seasonal material 6 months in advance.

MARCEL SCHURMAN COMPANY, 2500 N. Watney Way, Fairfield CA 94533. Editor: Meg Schutte. Creative Director: Diana Ruhl. Greeting card company. Publishes greeting cards, gift wrap, stationery, bags, journals and note cards. 20% of products are made for kids or have kids' themes.
Writing: Needs freelance writing for children's greeting cards. Makes 2-3 writing assignments/month; 50/year. For greeting cards, prefers unrhymed verse ideas. To query with specific ideas, write to request disclosure form first. Reports in 6 weeks. Materials returned with SASE; sometimes files material. For greeting cards, pays flat fee of $75-125 on acceptance. Writer's guidelines available for SASE.
Illustration: Needs freelance illustration for children's greeting cards. Makes 60 illustration assignments/month; 800/year. Uses color artwork only. To contact, send color photocopies. To query with specific ideas, send letter with or without samples. Reports in 1 month. Materials returned if accompanied by SASE; materials filed. For greeting cards pays advance of $300 against 5% royalty for 3 years. Pays "when final art is approved." Credit line given. Artist's guidelines available for SASE.
Photography: Buys photography from freelancers. Buys stock and assigns work. Uses 4×5 transparencies. To contact, send slides. Reports in 1 month. Materials returned with SASE. Materials returned or filed. Pays advance of $300 and 5% royalties. Pays "when final art is approved." Buys exclusive product rights, worldwide, 3-year period. Credit line given. Guidelines for SASE.
Tips: Submit seasonal ideas 6-8 months in advance.

*NOVO CARD PUBLISHERS, INC., 4513 N. Lincoln, Chicago IL 60625. (312)769-6880. Fax: (312)769-6769. Freelance writers contact: Sheri Cline. Freelance photographers contact: Thomas Benjamin. Estab. 1926. Greeting card company. Company publishes greeting cards, note/invitation packs and gift envelopes for middle market. Publishes greeting cards (Novo Card/Cloud-9). 20% of products are made for kids or have kids' themes.
Writing: Needs freelance writing for children's greeting cards. Makes 400 writing assignments/year. Other needs for freelance writing include invitation notes. To contact send writing samples. To query with specific ideas, write to request disclosure form first. Reports back in 1 month only if interested. Materials returned only with SASE; materials filed. For greeting cards, pays flat fee of $2/line. Pays on acceptance. Buys all rights. Credit line sometimes given. Writer's guidelines available for SASE.
Illustration: Needs freelance illustration for children's greeting cards. Makes 1,000 illustration assignments/year. Prefers just about all types: traditional, humor, contemporary, etc. To contact, send published samples, slides and color photocopies. To query with specific ideas write to request disclosure form first. Reports in 1 month. Materials returned with SASE; materials filed. For greeting cards, pay negotiable. Pays on acceptance. Rights negotiable. Credit line sometimes given. Artist's guidelines available for SASE.
Photography: Buys stock and assigns work. Buys 30-40 stock images/year. Wants all types: prefers contemporary images for the time being. Uses color and b&w prints; 35mm transparencies. To contact, send slides, stock photo list, published samples, paper copies acceptable. Reports in 1 month. Materials returned with SASE; materials filed. Pays negotiable rate. Pays on acceptance. Rights negotiable. Credit line sometimes given. Guidelines for SASE.
Tips: Submit seasonal material 10-12 months in advance. "Novo has extensive lines of greeting cards: everyday, seasonal (all) and alternative lives (over 24 separate lines of note card packs and gift enclosures). Our lines encompass all types of styles and images."

P.S. GREETINGS/FANTUS PAPER PRODUCTS, 5060 N. Kimberly Ave., Chicago IL 60630. (312)725-9308. Art Director: Bill Barnes. Greeting card company. Publishes boxed and individual counter cards. Publishes greeting cards (Kards for Kids—counter; Kids Kards—boxed; Christmas). "Only 7% of products are made for kids or have kids' themes, so it needs to be great stuff!"
Writing: Needs freelance writing for children's greeting cards. Makes 1-10 writing assignments/year. Looks for writing which is "appropriate for kids to give to relatives." To contact, send writing samples. Reports in 6 months. Material returned only if accompanied with SASE; materials filed. For greeting cards, pays flat fee. Pays on acceptance. Buys all rights. Credit line sometimes given. Writer's guidelines for SASE.

Illustration: Needs freelance illustration for children's greeting cards. Makes 10-25 illustration assignments/year. "Open to all mediums, all themes—use your creativity!" To contact, send published samples (up to 20 samples of any nature) and photocopies. Reports in 6 months. Returns materials with SASE; materials filed. For greeting cards, pays flat fee. Pays on acceptance. Buys all rights. Credit line sometimes given. Artist's guidelines for SASE.
Photography: Buys photography from freelancers. Buys stock. Buys 25-50 stock images/year. Wants florals, animals, seasonal (Christmas, Easter, valentines, etc.). Uses transparencies (any size). To contact, send slides. Reports in 6 months. Materials returned with SASE; materials filed. Pays on acceptance. Buys all rights. Credit line sometimes given. Photographer's guidelines for SASE.
Tips: Seasonal material should be submitted 6 months in advance. "We are open to all creative ideas—generally not fads, however. All mediums are considered equally. We have a great need for 'cute' Christmas subjects."

*PAINTED HEARTS & FRIENDS, 1222 N. Fair Oaks Ave., Los Angeles CA 91103. (818)798-3633. Fax: (818)793-7385. Chairman of the Board: David Mekelburg. Co-owner: Susan Kinney. Estab. 1988. Material produced includes greeting cards.
Illustration: Buys 5 freelance projects/year. Material returned with SASE. Reports in 1 week. Pays on publication.
Tips: Submit seasonal material 1 year in advance.

*PANDA INK, P.O. Box 5129, West Hills CA 91308-5129. (818)340-8061. Fax: (818)883-6193. Owner: Art/Creative Director: Ruth Ann Epstein. Estab. 1981. Greeting card company and producer of clocks, magnets, bookmarks. Produces Judaica—whimsical, metaphysical, general, everyday. Publishes greeting cards. 10% of products are made for kids or have kids' themes.
Writing: Needs freelance writing for children's greeting cards. Makes 10 writing assignments/month. For greeting cards, accepts both rhymed and unrhymed verse ideas. Looks for greeting card writing which is Judaica or metaphysical. To contact, send cover letter, ask for guidelines, send SASE. To query with specific ideas, write to request disclosure form first. Reports in 1 month. Materials returned with SASE; materials filed. For greeting cards, pays flat fee of $3-20. Pays on acceptance. Rights negotiable. Credit line sometimes given. Writer's guidelines available for SASE.
Illustration: Needs freelance illustration for children's greeting cards, magnets, bookmarks. Makes 2-3 illustration assignments/year. Needs Judaica (Hebrew wording), metaphysical themes. Uses color artwork only. To contact, send cover letter. To query with specific ideas, write to request disclosure form first. Reports in 1 month. Materials returned with SASE; materials filed. Payment is negotiable. Pays on acceptance. Rights negotiable. Credit line sometimes given. Artist's guidelines available for SASE.
Tips: Submit seasonal material 1 year in advance. "Follow our guidelines. No 'shoe box' art."

PEACEABLE KINGDOM PRESS, 707B Heinz Ave., Berkeley CA 94710. (510)644-9801. Fax: (510)644-9805. Website: http://www/pkpress.com. Art Director: Olivia Hurd. Estab. 1983. Produces posters, greeting cards, gift wrap and related products. Uses images from classic children's books. 50% of products are made for kids or have kids' themes.
Illustration: Needs freelance illustration for children's greeting cards and posters. Makes 120 illustration assignments/year. To contact, send cover letter and color photocopies. Contact Molly Gauld or Gail Peterson, creative directors. Reports in 4 weeks. Pays on publication with advance. Pays 5-10% of wholesale for greeting cards. Buys rights to distribution worldwide. Artist's guidelines available for SASE.
Tips: "We only choose from illustrations that are from published children's book illustrators, or commissioned art by established children's book illustrators. Submit seasonal and everyday greeting cards one year in advance."

*PLUM GRAPHICS INC., P.O. Box 136, Prince St. Station, New York NY 10012. Phone/fax: (212)337-0999. Owner: Yvette Cohen. Estab. 1983. Greeting card company. Produces die-cut greeting cards for ages 5-105. Publishes greeting cards and message boards.
Writing: Needs freelance writing for greeting cards. Makes 4 writing assignments/year. Looks for "greeting card writing which is fun. Tired of writing which is boring." To contact, send SASE for guidelines. Contact: Michelle Ingram. Reports in 2 months. Materials returned with SASE; materials filed. For greeting cards, pays flat fee of $40. Pays on publication. Buys all rights. Writer's guidelines available for SASE.

Illustration: Needs freelance illustration for greeting cards. Makes 10-15 freelance illustration assignments/year. Prefers very tight artwork, mostly realism. Uses color artwork only. To contact, send b&w photocopies. Contact: Yvette Cohen. Reports only if interested. Materials returned with SASE; materials filed. For greeting cards, pays flat fee of $350-450 "plus $50 each time we reprint." Pays on publication. Buys exclusive product rights. Credit line given.
Tips: Submit seasonal material 1 year in advance. "Go to a store and look at our cards and style before submitting work."

POCKETS OF LEARNING LTD., 31-G Union Ave., Sudbury MA 01776. (800)635-2994. Fax: (800)370-1580. Product Manager: Kyra Silva. Estab. 1989. Educational soft toy company. Specializes in design, import and distribution of high-quality educational cloth toys and gifts. Manufactures educational soft sculptures, wallhangings, travel bags. 100% of products are made for kids or have kids' themes.
Illustration: Needs freelance illustration for educational cloth toys. Makes 7 illustration assignments/year. "We introduce 20-30 new products per year, including cloth books, travel bags, soft sculpture and wallhangings." Uses both color and b&w artwork. To contact, send cover letter, slides, photocopies. To query with specific ideas, write to request disclosure form first. Reports in 3-4 weeks. Credit line sometimes given. Pays on acceptance. Buys all rights.
Tips: "We accept new product ideas year 'round."

PRATT & AUSTIN CO., P.O. Box 587, Holyoke MA 01041. (413)532-1491. Product Development: Lorilee Costello. Estab. 1934. Paper products company. Targets women ages 16-60: stationery, tablets, envelopes, calendars, children's craft items. Produces calendars, paper dolls, paper airplanes, mobiles, etc.
Illustration: Needs freelance illustration for paper airplanes, crafts, paper dolls, calendars, storage boxes. Makes 2-4 illustration assignments/month; 30-40/year.

*REFLECTIVE IMAGES, 42 Digital Dr. #10, Novato CA 94949. (415)883-5815. Fax: (415)883-8215. Owner: Kristin Greg. Estab. 1969. Screen-painted sportswear company. Produces T-shirts and sweats for zoos, animal parks, trains and ski resorts. 60% of products are made for kids or have kids' themes.
Illustration: Needs freelance illustration for children's T-shirts. Makes 10 illustration assignments/year. Prefers realistic and whimsical animals. Uses b&w artwork only. To contact, send cover letter, photocopies, promo pieces. "Call to discuss current needs." Reports back only if interested. Materials returned with SASE. Pays by the project (range: $50-200). Pays on acceptance. Buys all rights. Credit line sometimes given.
Tips: Submit seasonal material 6 months in advance.

*RESOURCE GAMES, 2704 185th Ave. NE, Redmond WA 98052. (206)883-3143. Fax: (206)883-3136. Owner: John Jaquet. Estab. 1987. Educational game manufacturer. Resource Games manufactures a line of high-quality geography theme board and card games for ages 6 and up. Publishes games. 100% of products made for kids or have kids' themes.
Tips: "We are always on the lookout for innovative educational games for the classroom and the home. If accepted, we enter into royalty agreements ranging from 5-10%."

SCANDECOR INC., 430 Pike Rd., Southampton PA 18966. (215)355-2410. Product Manager: Lauren H. Karp. Poster publisher. Publishes posters for the children's market. 90% of products are made for kids or have kids' themes.
Writing: Needs freelance writing for posters. Makes 20 writing assignments/year. For posters, prefers rhymed verse ideas. To contact, send writing samples. To query with specific ideas, send SASE. Reports in 1 month. Materials returned with SASE. Pays on publication. Rights negotiable. Credit line given. Writer's guidelines available for SASE.
Illustration: Needs freelance illustration for children's posters. Makes 15 illustration assignments/year. Prefers poster art in children's themes. Uses color artwork only. To contact, send color photocopies, color promo piece. To query with specific ideas, send SASE. Reports in 1 month. Materials returned with SASE; materials filed. Pays on publication. Rights negotiable. Credit line given. Artist's guidelines available for SASE.
Photography: Buys photography from freelancers. Buys stock and assigns work. Buys 100 stock images/year. Makes 10 assignments/year. Wants animals (in studio), children (model-released), cars, motorcycles, action sports. Uses color and b&w prints; 35mm, 2¼×2¼, 4×5, 8×10 transparencies. To contact, send stock photo list, promo piece, model-released duplicate

slides. Reports in 1 month. Materials returned; materials filed. Pays on usage. Rights negotiable. Credit line given. Guidelines available for SASE.
Tips: "We don't use seasonal material. Please look at the types/quality of photography/illustration being used for published products. We are working with more freelancers now than ever."

SMART ART, INC., P.O. Box 661, Chatham NJ 07928. (201)635-1690. President: Barb Hauck-Mah. Estab. 1992. Greeting card company. Publishes photo-insert cards for card, gift and photo shops. About 20% of products are made for kids or have kids' themes.
Illustration: Needs freelance illustration for photo-insert cards. Makes 12-14 illustration assignments/year. Uses color artwork only. To contact, send color photocopies. To query with specific ideas, write to request confidentiality form. Reports in 2-3 months. Materials returned with SASE; materials not filed. For greeting cards, pays annual royalties for life of card or 5 years. Pays on publication. Credit line given. Artist's guidelines available for SASE.
Tips: Submit seasonal material 6-8 months in advance. "Smart Art is looking for 'border design' artwork rendered in pen & ink with watercolors or in cut/torn paper. We are interested in artists who can create interesting abstract textures as well as representational designs."

TALICOR, INC., 190 Gentry St., Pomona CA 91767. (909)593-5877. President: Lew Herndon. Estab. 1971. Game manufacturer. Publishes games (adults' and children's). 80% of products are made for kids or have kids' themes.
Illustration: Needs freelance illustration for games. Makes 14 illustration assignments/year. To contact, send promo piece. Reports only if interested. Materials returned with SASE; materials filed. For artwork, pays by the hour or by the project or negotiable royalty. Pays on acceptance. Buys negotiable rights.
Photography: Buys stock and assigns work. Buys 6 stock images/year. Makes 6 assignments/year. Uses 4×5 transparencies. To contact, send color promo piece. Reports only if interested. Materials returned with SASE; materials filed. Pays per photo, by the hour, by the day or by the project (negotiable rates). Pays on acceptance. Buys negotiable rights.
Tips: Submit seasonal material 6 months in advance.

TEDCO, INC., 498 S. Washington St., Hagerstown IN 47346. (317)489-4527. Fax: (317)489-5752. Sales Director: Jane Shadle. Estab. 1982. Toy manufacturer. Produces educational toys: The Original Gyroscope, Gyros Gyroscope, prisms, magnet kits and science kits. Manufactures novelties, games, gyroscopes, prisms. 100% of products are made for kids or have kids' themes.
Writing: To contact, send cover letter, résumé, writing samples. Materials returned with SASE; materials filed. "We have never hired a freelance writer. We would be interested in learning more about available talent."

WARNER PRESS, P.O. Box 2499, Anderson IN 46018. Fax: (317)649-3664. Product Editor: Robin Fogle. Art Department Manager: Roger Hoffman. Photo Editor: Millie Corzine. Estab. 1880. Publishes children's greeting cards, coloring and activity books and posters, all religious-oriented. "Need fun, up-to-date stories for coloring books, with religious emphasis. Also considering activity books for Sunday school classroom use."
Writing: Needs freelance writing for children's greeting cards, coloring and activity books. To contact, request guidelines first. Contact: Robin Fogle, Production Editor. Reports in 4-6 weeks. For greeting cards, pays flat fee (range: $20-30). Pays on acceptance. Buys all rights. Credit line sometimes given. Writer's guidelines for SASE.
Illustration: Needs freelance illustration for children's greeting cards, coloring and activity books. Wants religious, cute illustrations. Makes 6 illustration assignments/month; 72/year. To contact, send published samples, photocopies and promo pieces (all nonreturnable). Contact: Roger Hoffman, creative manager. Reports in 2 weeks "if we are interested." For greeting cards, pays flat fee (range: $250-350). Pays on acceptance. Buys all rights. Credit line given. Guidelines available for SASE.
Photography: Buys photography from freelancers. Church bulletin covers, calendars and other products. Contact: Millie Corzine, photo editor. Guidelines available for SASE.
Tips: Write for guidelines before submitting. Send seasonal material 6 months in advance. Looking for "high-quality art in bright colors illustrated on flexible material for scanning. Meeting deadlines is very important for children's illustrations. We publish simple styles. Unsolicited material that does not follow guidelines will not be reviewed."

Play Publishers & Producers

You may notice a few changes in this section from past years. First, we've changed the name of the section from Scriptwriter's Markets to better describe what you'll find here. We've added subheadings in all the listings for Needs, How to Contact, and Terms to make the information you want easier to locate. You'll also find two Insider Reports this year. One is a question-and-answer interview with award-winning playwright and professor Joanna Kraus (page 258). The other is an interview with Janine Nina Trevens, creative director of TADA!, a New York City theater producing only original plays with child actors for family audiences (page 264).

Writing plays for children and family audiences is a special challenge. Whether creating an original work or adapting a classic, plays for children must hold the attention of audiences which often include children and adults. Using rhythm, repetition and dramatic action are effective ways of holding the attention of kids. Pick subjects children can relate to, and never talk down to them.

Theater companies often have limited budgets so plays with elaborate staging and costumes often can't be produced. Touring companies want simple sets that can be moved easily. Writers should keep in mind that they may have as few as three actors, so roles may have to be doubled up.

Many of the companies listed in this section produce plays with roles for adults and children, so check the percentage of plays written for adult and children's roles. Most importantly, study the types of plays a theater wants and doesn't want. Many name plays they've recently published or produced, and some may have additional guidelines or information available.

A.D. PLAYERS, 2710 W. Alabama, Houston TX 77098. (713)526-2721. Estab. 1967. Produces 4-5 children's plays/year in new Children's Theatre Series; 1-2 musical/year. Produces children's plays for professional productions.
- A.D. Players has received the Dove family approval stamp; an award from the Columbia International Film & Video Festival; and a Silver Angel Award.

Needs: 99-100% of plays/musicals written for adult roles; 0-1% for juvenile roles. "Cast must utilize no more than four actors. Need minimal, portable sets for proscenium or arena stage with no fly space and no wing space." Recently produced plays: *The Selfish Giant*, by Dr. Gillette Elvgren Jr. (a story of a child's sacrificial love, for ages 5-12); and *The Lion, the Witch and the Wardrobe*, dramatized by le Clanche du Rand, story by C.S. Lewis (Lewis's classic story of love, faith, courage and giving, for ages 5-14). Does not want to see large cast or set requirements or New Age themes.

How to Contact: Query with synopsis, character breakdown and set description; no tapes until requested. Will consider simultaneous submissions and previously performed work. Reports in 6-12 months.

Terms: Buys some residual rights. Pay negotiated. Submissions returned with SASE.

Tips: "Children's musicals tend to be large in casting requirements. For those theaters with smaller production capabilities, this can be a liability for a script. Try to keep it small and simple, especially if writing for theaters where adults are performing for children. We are interested in material that reflects family values, emphasizes the importance of responsibility in making choices, encourages faith in God and projects the joy and fun of telling a story."

AMERICAN STAGE, P.O. Box 1560, St. Petersburg FL 33731. (813)823-1600. Artistic Director: Lisa Powers. Estab. 1977. Produces 3 children's plays/year. Produces children's plays for professional children's theater program, mainstage, school tour, performing arts halls.

Needs: Limited by budget and performance venue. Subject matter: classics and original work for children (ages K-12) and families. Recently produced plays: *Beauty and the Beast*, by Philip Hall and Lee Ahlin (grades K-6); and *The Jungle Books*, adapted by Victorian Holloway, music by Lee Ahlin (Kipling's classic tale of Mowgli the Mancub, and his life being raised in the Jungle, for grades K-6). Does not want to see plays that look down on children. Approach must be that of the child or fictional beings or animals.

How to Contact: Query with synopsis, character breakdown and set description. Will consider simultaneous submissions, electronic submissions via disk or modem and previously performed work. Reports in 6 months.

Terms: Purchases "professional rights." Pays writers in royalties (6-8%); $25-35/performance. SASE for return of submission.

Tips: Sees a move in plays toward basic human values, relationships and multicultural communities.

*AMERICAN STAGE FESTIVAL, P.O. Box 225, Milford NH 03055. (603)889-2330. Fax: (603)889-2336. Artistic Director: Matthew Parent. Estab. 1972. Produces 5 children's plays and 4 children's musical plays/year.

Needs: American Stage Festival is a non-equity, educational aim of professional LORT theater—summer season. 75% of plays/musicals written for adult roles; 25% for juvenile roles. Requirements include limited cast size (under 10) and a minimal, tourable set. Musical needs: Piano orchestration. Recently produced plays: *Aladdin & the Wonderful Lamp*, by Jack Neary (traditional play for ages 5-12); and *Rapunzel*, by Jacque Lamanc (traditional play for ages 5-12).

How to Contact: Query with synopsis, character breakdown and set description. Include sample cassette if possible. Will consider simultaneous submissions and previously performed work. Reports back only if interested.

Terms: Buys subsidiary rights. Pays negotiable royalty/performance. Submissions returned with SASE.

*APPLE TREE THEATRE, 595 Elm Place, Suite 210, Highland Park IL 60035. (847)432-8223. Fax: (847)432-5214. Produces 3 children's plays/year.

Needs: Produces professional, daytime and educational outreach programs for grades 4-12. 98% of plays written for adult roles; 2% for juvenile roles. Uses a unit set and limited to 9 actors. No musicals. Straight plays only. Does not want to see: "children's theater," i.e. . . . Peter Rabbit, Snow White. Material *must* be based in social issues. Recently produced plays: *Number the Stars* (based on Lois Lowry's Newbery Medal-winning novel about the Holocaust experience in Denmark for grades 4-12); and *The Pearl*, by John Steinbeck (grades 4-12).

How to Contact: Query first. Query with synopsis, character breakdown and set description. Will consider simultaneous submissions and previously performed work. Reports in 2 months.

Terms: Pay negotiated per contract. Submissions returned with SASE.

Tips: "Never send an unsolicited manuscript. Include reply postcard for queries."

BAKER'S PLAYS, 100 Chauncy St., Boston MA 02111. (617)482-1280. Fax: (617)482-7613. Associate Editor: Raymond Pape. Estab. 1845. Publishes 10-20 children's plays/year; 2 musicals/year.

Needs: 80% of plays/musicals written for adult roles; 20% for juvenile roles. Subject matter: full lengths for family audience and full lengths and one act plays for teens."

How to Contact: Submit complete ms, score and tape of songs. Reports in 3-8 months.

Terms: Obtains worldwide rights. Pays writers in royalties (amount varies).

Tips: "Know the audience you're writing for before you submit your play anywhere. 90% of the plays we reject are not written for our market."

BIRMINGHAM CHILDREN'S THEATRE, P.O. Box 1362, Birmingham AL 35201. (205)458-8181. Executive Director: Charlotte Lane Dominick. Estab. 1947. Produces 8-10 children's plays/year; some children's musicals/year.

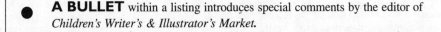

● **A BULLET** within a listing introduces special comments by the editor of *Children's Writer's & Illustrator's Market.*

Needs: "BCT is an adult professional theater performing for youth and family audiences September-May." 99% of plays/musicals written for adult roles; 1% for juvenile roles. "Our 'Wee Folks' Series is limited to four cast members and should be written with preschool-grade 1 in mind. We prefer interactive plays for this age group. We commission plays for our 'Wee Folks' Series (preschool-grade 1), our Children's Series (K-6) and our Young Adult Series (6-12)." Recently produced plays: *The Little Red Hen*, by Patricia Muse (classic story retold in interactive format for children in preschool through grade 1; 4 actors) and *Rapunzel*, by Randy Marsh (classic story told with a twist for children in grades K-6; 6 actors). Does not want plays which have references to witches, spells, incantations, evil magic or devils. No adult language. Will consider musicals, interactive theater for Wee Folks Series. Prefer mainstage limited to 4-7 cast members.
How to Contact: Query first, query with synopsis, character breakdown and set description. Reports in 4 months.
Terms: Buys negotiable rights. Submissions returned with SASE.
Tips: "We would like our commissioned scripts to teach as well as entertain. Keep in mind the age groups (defined by each series) that our audience is composed of. Send submissions to the attention of Charlotte Dominick, executive director."

BOARSHEAD: MICHIGAN PUBLIC THEATER, 425 S. Grand Ave., Lansing MI 48933. (517)484-7800. Fax: (517)484-2564. Artistic Director: John Peakes. Director of Education: Susan Townsend. Estab. 1966. Produces 3 children's plays/year.
Needs: Produces children's plays for professional production. Majority of plays written for young adult roles. Prefers 5 characters or less for touring productions, 5 characters for mainstage productions; one unit set, simple costumes. Recently produced plays: *The Lion, the Witch & the Wardrobe*, by Joseph Robinette (fantasy for ages 6-12); *1,000 Cranes*, by Katharine Schultz Miller; *Step on a Crack*, by Susan Zeder (family play for ages 6-12). Does not want to see musicals.
How to Contact: Query with synopsis, character breakdown and set description. Send "Attention: Educational Director." Include 10 pages of representative dialogue. Will consider previously performed work. Reports in 2 weeks on queries; 4 months "if we ask for submissions."
Terms: Pays writers $15-25/performance. Submissions returned with SASE. If no SASE, send self-addressed stamped post card for reply.

CALIFORNIA THEATRE CENTER, P.O. Box 2007, Sunnyvale CA 94087. (408)245-2979. Artistic Director: Gayle Cornelison. Estab. 1975. Produces 15 children's plays and 3 musicals for professional productions.
Needs: 75% of plays/musicals written for adult roles; 20% for juvenile roles. Prefers material suitable for professional tours and repertory performance; one-hour time limit, limited technical facilities. Recently produced *Jungle Book*, adapted by Will Huddleston (Kipling's classic for ages 4th grade-up); *Heidi*, by Gayle Cornelison (classic for ages K-up). Does not want to see arcane, artsy, cute material.
How to Contact: Query with synopsis, character breakdown and set description. Send to: Will Huddleston. Will consider previously performed work. Reports in 4 months.
Terms: Rights negotiable. Pays writers royalties; pays $35-50/performance. Submissions returned with SASE.
Tips: "We sell to schools, so the title and material must appeal to teachers who look for things familiar to them. We look for good themes, universality. Avoid the cute."

CHILDREN'S STORY SCRIPTS, Baymax Productions, Suite 130, 2219 W. Olive Ave., Burbank CA 91506. (818)563-6105. Fax: (818)563-2968. Editor: Deedra Bebout. Estab. 1990. Produces 1-10 children's scripts/year.
Needs: "Except for small movements and occasionally standing up, children remain seated in Readers Theatre fashion." Publishes scripts sold primarily to schools or wherever there's a program to teach or entertain children. "All roles read by children except K-2 scripts, where kids have easy lines, leader helps read the narration. Prefer multiple cast members, no props or sets." Subject matter: scripts on all subjects that dovetail with classroom subjects. Targeted age range—K-8th grade, 5-13 years old. Recently published stories: *Booga the Caveman Discovers Oil*, by Helen Ksypka (about Neanderthals and petroleum, grades 4, 5, 6); *Celebrate*, by M. Donnaleen Howett (10 holiday poems for grades 3-6). No stories that preach a point, no stories about catastrophic disease or other terribly heavy topics, no theatrical scripts without narrative prose to move the story along, no monologues of 1-character stories.

How to Contact: Submit complete ms. Will consider simultaneous submissions and previously performed work (if rights are available). Reports in 2 weeks.
Terms: Purchases all rights; authors retain copyrights. "We add support material and copyright the whole package." Pays writers in royalties (10-15% on sliding scale, based on number of copies sold). SASE for reply and return of submission.
Tips: "We're only looking for stories related to classsroom studies—educational topics with a freshness to them. Our scripts mix prose narration with character dialogue—we do not publish traditional, all-dialogue plays." Writer's guidelines packet available for business-sized SASE with 2 first-class stamps. Guidelines explain what Children's Story Scripts are, give 4-page examples from 2 different scripts, give list of suggested topics for scripts.

THE CHILDREN'S THEATRE COMPANY, 2400 Third Ave. S., Minneapolis MN 55404. (612)874-0500. Fax: (602)867-1414. Owner: Philip Lockard. Estab. 1965. Produces 7 children's plays/year; 1-3 children's musicals/year.
Needs: Produces children's plays for professional, not-for-profit productions. 60% of plays/musicals written for adult roles; 40% for juvenile roles in all productions. Recently produced plays: *The Story of Babar, The Little Elephant*; *Linnea in Monet's Garden*; and *Dr. Seuss' How The Grinch Stole Christmas*. Does not want to see plays written for child performers only.
How to Contact: Only interested in agented material. Submit complete ms and score (if a musical). Will consider simultaneous submissions and previously performed work. Reports in 2-6 months.
Terms: Rights negotiable. Pays writers in royalties (2%). Submissions returned with SASE.
Tips: "The Children's Theatre Company rarely (if ever) produces unsolicited manuscripts; we continue a long tradition of producing new works commissioned to meet the needs of our audience and catering to the artistic goals of a specific season. Though the odds of us producing submitted plays are very slim, we always enjoy the opportunity to become acquainted with the work of a variety of artists, particularly those who focus on young audiences."

CIRCA '21 DINNER THEATRE, P.O. Box 3784, Rock Island IL 61204-3784. (309)786-2667. Producer: Dennis Hitchcock. Estab. 1977. Produces 3 children's plays or musicals/year.
Needs: Produces children's plays for professional productions. 95% of plays/musicals written for adult roles; 5% written for juvenile roles. "Prefer a cast of 4-8—no larger than ten. Plays are produced on mainstage sets." Recently produced plays: *Pocahantas*, by Ted Morris (ages 6-10) and *Cinderella*, by Prince Street Players (ages 4-10).
How to Contact: Send complete script with audiotape of music. Reports in 3 months.
Terms: Payment negotiable.

I.E. CLARK PUBLICATIONS, (formerly I.E. Clark, Publisher), P.O. Box 246, Schulenburg TX 78956. (409)743-3232. Fax: (409)743-4765. General Manager: Donna Cozzaglio. Estab. 1956. Publishes 3 children's plays/year; 1 or 2 children's musicals/year.
Needs: Medium to large casts preferred. Publishes plays for all ages. Published plays: *Wind of a Thousand Tales*, by John Glore (story about a young girl who doesn't believe in fairy tales, for ages 5-12); *Rock'n'Roll Santa*, by R. Eugene Jackson (Santa's reindeer form a rock band, for ages 4-16). Does not want to see plays that have not been produced.
How to Contact: Submit complete ms and audio or video tape. Will consider simultaneous submissions and previously performed work. Reports in 2-4 months.
Terms: Pays writers in negotiable royalties. SASE for return of submission.
Tips: "We publish only high-quality literary works. Please send only on manuscript at a time."

CONTEMPORARY DRAMA SERVICE, Division of Meriwether Publishing Ltd., 885 Elkton Dr., Colorado Springs CO 80907. (719)594-4422. Fax: (719)594-9916. Executive Editor: Arthur Zapel. Estab. 1979. Publishes 50 children's plays/year; 6-8 children's musicals/year.
Needs: 15% of plays/musicals written for adult roles; 85% for juvenile roles. Recently published plays: *Children of the Holocaust*, by Robert Mauro; *And Then There Was One* (a short mystery play); *Westward Ho!* (comedy history play); *The Velveteen Rabbit* (a classic story about being loved for all ages). "We publish church plays for elementary level for Christmas and Easter. Most of our secular plays are for teens or college level." Does not want to see "full-length, 3-act plays unless they are adaptations of classic works or have unique comedy appeal."
How to Contact: Query with synopsis, character breakdown and set description; "query first if a musical." Will consider simultaneous submissions or previously performed work. Reports in 4-6 weeks.

Terms: Purchases first rights. Pays writers royalty (10%) or buys material outright for $200-1,000. SASE for return of submission.

Tips: "We prefer works with comedic or satirical overtones. Name recognition, full-length, play adaptations are important candidates for us now. Author must provide letters of clearance from copyright holders of adapted works. Inspirational plays are in demand provided that the author can present the message deftly without preaching. We like to publish 'prevention' plays about teenage problems in education, gangs and family."

THE COTERIE, 2450 Grand, Kansas City MO 64108. Phone/fax: (816)474-6785. Artistic Director: Jeff Church. Estab. 1979. Produces 7 children's plays/year; 1 children's musical/year.

Needs: "Prefer casts of between five-seven, no larger than 15." Produces children's plays for professional productions. 80% of plays/musicals written for adult roles; 20% for juvenile roles. "We produce original plays, musicals and literary adaptations for ages five through adult." Produced plays: *Amelia Lives*, by Laura Annawyn Shamas (one-woman show on Amelia Earhart, for 6th grade through adult); *Dinosaurus*, by Ed Mast and Lenore Bensinger (Mobil Oil workers discover cavern of dinosaurs, for ages 5 through adult). "We do *not* want to see 'camp' adaptations of fairytales."

How to Contact: Query with synopsis, sample scene, character breakdown and set description. Reports in 8-10 months.

Terms: Rights purchased "negotiable." Pays writers in royalties per play of approximately $1,000-1,500. SASE for return of submission.

Tips: "We're interested in adaptations of classic literature with small casts, simple staging requirements; also multicultural topics and biography plays of Latin and African-American figures. There is a need for non-condescending material for younger age groups (5-8) and for middle school (ages 9-13)."

CREEDE REPERTORY THEATRE, P.O. Box 269, Creede CO 81130. (719)658-2541. Fax: (719)658-2343. Artistic Director: Richard Baxter. Estab. 1966. Produces 1 children's play/year; 1 musical/year.

Needs: Limited to 4-6 cast members and must be able to tour. Produces children's plays for summer theater, school or professional productions. 100% of plays/musicals written for adult roles. Publishes plays for ages K-12. Recently produced plays: *Coyote Tales*, by Daniel Kramer and Company (Native American Coyote legend, for grades K-6); and *The Two of Us*, by Michael Frayn (contemporary relationship story, for ages 12-adult).

How to Contact: Query first, submit complete ms and score, or query with synopsis, character breakdown and set description. Will consider simultaneous submissions and previously performed work. Reports in 1 year.

Terms: Pays writers in royalties (5%); pays $15-30 per performance.

Tips: Sees trends in "non-sexist, non-traditional casting and Native American/Hispanic American interest. No fairy tales unless non-traditional."

EL CENTRO SU TEATRO, 4725 High, Denver CO 80216. (303)296-0219. Fax: (303)296-4614. Artistic Director: Anthony J. Garcia. Estab. 1971. Produces 6 children's plays/year.

Needs: "We are interested in plays by Chicanos or Latinos that speak to that experience. We do not produce standard musicals. We are a culturally specific company." Recently produced *Joaquim's Christmas*, by Anthony J. Garcia (children's Christmas play for ages 7-15); and *The Dragonslayer*, by Silviana Woods (young boy's relationship with grandfather for ages 7-15). Does not want to see "cutesy stuff."

How to Contact: Query with synopsis, character breakdown and set description. Will consider simultaneous submissions and previously performed work. Reports in 6 months. Buys regional rights.

Terms: Pays writers per performance: $35 1st night, $25 subsequent. Submissions returned with SASE.

✱ **THE ASTERISK** before a listing indicates the listing is new in this edition.

Tips: "People should write within their realm of experience but yet push their own boundaries. Writers should approach social issues within the human experience of their character."

ELDRIDGE PUBLISHING CO. INC., P.O. Box 1595, Venice FL 34284. (941)496-4679. Fax: (941)493-9680. Editor: Nancy Vorhis. Estab. 1906. Publishes approximately 30 children's plays/year (5 for elementary; 20 for junior and senior high); 2-3 high school musicals/year.
Needs: Prefers simple staging; flexible cast size. "We publish for junior and high school, community theater and children's theater (adults performing for children), all genres." Recently published plays: *Hollywood Hillbillies*, by Tim Kelly (comedy about country folks who strike it rich, for high school community theater audiences); and *Theatre for a Small Planet*, by Jules Tasca (3 plays for children from different countries, for elementary and up). Prefers work which has been performed or at least had a staged reading.
How to Contact: Submit complete ms, score and tape of songs (if a musical). Will consider simultaneous submissions ("please let us know, however"). Reports in 2 months.
Terms: Purchases all dramatic rights. Pays writers royalties of 50%; 10% copy sales; buys material outright for $200-500.
Tips: "We're always on the lookout for comedies which provide a lot of fun for our customers. But other more serious topics which concern teens, as well as intriguing mysteries, and children's theater programs are of interest to us as well. We know there are many new talented playwrights out there and we look forward to reading their fresh scripts."

ENCORE PERFORMANCE PUBLISHING, P.O. Box 692, Orem UT 84059. (801)225-0605. Estab. 1978. Publishes 10-20 children's plays/year; 8-15 children's musicals/year.
Needs: Prefers equal male/female ratio if possible. Adaptations for K-12 and older. 60% of plays written for adult roles; 40% for juvenile roles. Recently published plays: *Scars & Stripes*, by Thomas Cadwaleder Jones (about racial harmony for ages 11-20); *We've Got Something to Say (Algo Tenemos Que Decirles)*, by Sheila Revear (English/Hispanic monologues for teens 11-19). Looking for issue plays and unusual fairy tale adaptations.
How to Contact: Query first with synopsis, character breakdown, set description and production history. Will only consider previously performed work. Reports in 1 month.
Terms: Purchases all publication and production rights. Author retains copyright. Pays writers in royalties (50%). SASE for return of submission.
Tips: "Give us issue and substance, be controversial without offense. Use a laser printer! Don't send an old manuscript. Make yours look the most professional."

FLORIDA STUDIO THEATRE, 1241 N. Palm Ave., Sarasota FL 34236. (941)366-9017. Artistic Director: Richard Hopkins. Estab. 1980. Produces 3 children's plays/year; 1-3 children's musicals/year.
Needs: Produces children's plays for professional productions. 50% of plays/musicals written for adult roles; 50% for juvenile roles. "Prefer small cast plays that use imagination more than heavy scenery." Will consider simultaneous submissions and previously performed work.
How to Contact: Query with synopsis, character breakdown and set description. Reports in 3 months. Rights negotiable. Pay negotiable. Submissions returned with SASE.
Tips: "Children are a tremendously sophisticated audience. The material should respect this."

THE FOOTHILL THEATRE COMPANY, P.O. Box 1812, Nevada City CA 95959. (916)265-9320. Artistic Director: Philip Charles Sneed. Estab. 1977. Produces 0-2 children's plays/year; 0-2 children's musicals/year. Professional nonprofit theater.
Needs: 95% of plays/musicals written for adult roles; 5% for juvenile roles. "Small is better, but will consider anything." Produced *The Golden Grotto*, by Cleve Haubold/James Alfred Hitt (fantasy about a frog prince, comedy for all ages); *The Best Christmas Pageant Ever*, by Barbara Robinson (family Christmas comedy, for all ages). Does not want to see traditional fairy tales.
How to Contact: Query with synopsis, character breakdown and set description. Will consider simultaneous submissions and previously performed work. Reports in 6 months.
Terms: Buys negotiable rights. Payment method varies. Submissions returned with SASE.
Tips: "Trends in children's theater include cultural diversity, real life issues (drug use, AIDS, etc.), mythological themes with contemporary resonance. Don't talk down to or underestimate children."

THE FREELANCE PRESS, P.O. Box 548, Dover MA 02030. (508)785-8250. Managing Editor: Narcissa Campion. Estab. 1979. Produces 3 musicals and/or plays/year.

Needs: Casts are comprised of young people, ages 8-15, and number 25-30. "We publish original musicals on contemporary topics for children and adaptations of children's classics (e.g., Rip Van Winkle)." Published plays: *The Tortoise and the Hare* (based on story of same name, for ages 8-12); *Monopoly,* 3 (young people walk through board game, for ages 11-15). No plays for adult performers.

How to Contact: Submit complete ms and score with SASE. Will consider simultaneous submissions and previously performed work. Reports in 3 months.

Terms: Pays writers 10% royalties. SASE for return of submission.

*SAMUEL FRENCH, INC., 45 W. 25th St., New York NY 10010. (212)206-8990. Fax: (212)206-1429. Editor: Lawrence Harbison. Estab. 1830. Publishes 2 or 3 children's plays/year; "variable number of musicals."

Needs: Subject matter: "all genres, all ages. No puppet plays. No adaptations of any of those old 'fairy tales.' No 'Once upon a time, long ago and far away.' No kings, princesses, fairies, trolls, etc."

How to Contact: Submit complete ms and demo tape (if a musical). Reports in 2-8 months.

Terms: Purchases "publication rights, amateur and professional production rights, option to publish next 3 plays." Pays writers "book royalty of 10%; variable royalty for professional and amateur productions. SASE for return of submissions.

Tips: "Children's theater is a very tiny market, as most groups perform plays they have created themselves or have commissioned."

THE GROWING STAGE THEATRE, In Residence at the Palace, Rt. 183, Netcong NJ 07857. (201)347-4946. Executive Director: Stephen L. Fredericks. Estab. 1982. Produces 4 main-stage children's shows, a summer production for the whole family. Equity touring production to schools and other organizations. Professional actors work with community actors.

Needs: 60% of plays/musicals written for adult roles; 40% for juvenile roles. Produced: *Aladdin,* by Perry Arthur Kroeger, (adaptation from classic tale, for K-8th grade); and *The Pied Piper of Hamelin, AZ,* by Stephen L. Fredericks and Perry Arthur Kroeger (adaptation of classic poem, K-6th grades). Plays for young audiences only.

How to Contact: Query with synopsis, character breakdown and set description. Will consider previously performed work. Reports in 1 month.

Terms: "Contracts are developed individually." Pays $25-75/performance. Submissions returned with SASE.

Tips: "There's an overabundance on issue-oriented plays. Creativity, quality, the standards we place on theater aimed at adults should not be reduced in preparing a script for young people. We, together, are forming the audience of tomorrow. Don't repel young people by making the theater another resource for the infomercial—nurture, challenge and inspire them."

*HAYES SCHOOL PUBLISHING CO. INC., 321 Pennwood Ave., Wilkinsburg PA 15221. (412)371-2373. Fax: (412)371-6408. Estab. 1940. Produces plays.

Needs: Wants to see supplementary teaching aids for grades K-12. Interested in all subject areas.

How to Contact: Query first with synopsis, character breakdown and set description, or with complete ms and score. Will consider simultaneous and electronic submissions or previously performed work. Reports in 3-4 weeks.

Terms: Purchases all rights. Work purchased outright. SASE for return of submissions.

INDIANA REPERTORY THEATRE, 140 W. Washington, Indianapolis IN 46204. (317)635-5277. Artistic Director: Janet Allen. Estab. 1971. Produces 3 children's plays/year. Produces children's plays for professional productions.

Needs: 100% of plays written for adult roles. Limit 8 in cast, 75 minute running time. Recently produced plays: *Tales from the Arabian Nights,* by Michael Dixon; *Red Badge of Courage,* adaptation by Thomas Olson. Does not want to see preschool and K-4 material.

How to Contact: Query with synopsis, character breakdown and set description to Janet Allen, Association. Artistic Director. Will consider previously performed work. Reports in 6 months.

Terms: Pays writers negotiable royalty (6%) or commission fee. Submissions returned with SASE.

JEWISH ENSEMBLE THEATRE, 6600 W. Maple Rd., West Bloomfield MI 48322. (810)788-2900. Fax: (810)661-3680. Artistic Director: Evelyn Orbach. Estab. 1989. Produces children's plays for professional productions.

Needs: Is producing one children's play and is looking for additional scripts to create a repertoire. Prefers small casts and unit set. Recently produced play: *Shades of Grey*, by Eden Cooper Sage and Marshall Zweig (about inter-generational conflicts for middle and high school audience).
How to Contact: Send submission to Evelyn Orbach, artistic director. Reports on submissions in 6 months.
Tips: "Plays are toured to various schools and youth organizations. Our needs require a play as a teaching tool—usually values. No longer than 40-45 min. to be done by a small adult professional cast."

THE MUNY FIRST STAGE, (formerly The Muny Student Theatre), 634 N. Grand, Suite 1118, St. Louis MO 63103. (314)652-5213. Fax: (314)533-3345. Executive Artistic Director: Christopher Limber. Estab. 1979. Produces 5 children's plays/year; 1 or 2 children's musicals/year.
Needs: "We produce a touring and mainstage season September-May and offer extensive theater classes throughout the entire year." 100% of plays/musicals written for adult roles; 40% for juvenile roles. Prefers cast of 4 or 5 equity actors, for touring productions; no limit for mainstage productions. "Tour sets are limited in size." Produced plays: *Meet Willie*, adapted by Chris Limber (introduction to Shakespeare for 4th grade-adult); *On The Rays of The Sun* by Patton Hasegawa (about African heros and heroines for 1st grade-adult).
How to Contact: Query with synopsis, character breakdown and set description. Will consider simultaneous submissions and previously performed work. Reports in 3 months.
Terms: Rights negotiable.
Tips: "We emphasize diverse ethnic casting and multicultural material. Tour shows should fit into the school curriculum. The Muny First Stage's mission is to introduce theater to young people, to encourage creative learning and to develop future theater audiences. The company is now one of the most comprehensive theater education programs in Missouri. Each year the company reaches more than 100,000 students through its resident touring company, professional storytellers, mainstage productions and theater classes. As film and television become more sophisticated, we're seeing a focus on theatricality, imaginative use of the live theater medium; use of young actors in major roles; opera for young performers; strong adaptations of classics which highlight contemporary issues."

THE NEW CONSERVATORY THEATRE CENTER, 25 Van Ness Ave., San Francisco CA 94102. (415)861-4914. Fax: (415)861-6988. Executive Director: Ed Decker. Estab. 1981.
Needs: Limited budget and small casts only. Produces children's plays as part of "a professional theater arts training program for youths ages 4-19 during the school year and two summer sessions. The New Conservatory also produces educational plays for its touring company. We do not want to see any preachy or didactic material."
How to Contact: Query with synopsis, character breakdown and set description, or submit complete ms and score. Reports in 3 months.
Terms: Rights purchased negotiable. Pays writers in royalties. SASE for return of submission.
Tips: Sees trend in: "addressing socially relevant issues for young people and their families."

NEW PLAYS INCORPORATED, P.O. Box 5074, Charlottesville VA 22905. (804)979-2777. Publisher: Patricia Whitton. Estab. 1964. Publishes 4 plays/year; 1 or 2 children's musicals/year.
Needs: Publishes "generally material for kindergarten through junior high." Recently published: *Sitting in a Tree*, by Lou Furman (child's response to divorce for ages 7-12); and *3 Girls & Clorox*, by Belinda Acosta (relationships in middle school). Does not want to see "adaptations of titles I already have. No unproduced plays; no junior high improvisations."
How to Contact: Submit complete ms and score. Will consider simultaneous submissions and previously performed work. Reports in 2 months.
Terms: Purchases exclusive rights to sell acting scripts. Pays writers in royalties (50% of production royalties; 10% of script sales). SASE for return of submission.

ALWAYS INCLUDE a self-addressed, stamped envelope (SASE) with submissions within your own country. When sending material to other countries, include a self-addressed envelope (SAE) and International Reply Coupons (IRCs).

INSIDER REPORT

Observing human behavior is greatest resource for playwrights

Welcome to Playwriting 101 with Joanna H. Kraus. Kraus is Professor Emeritus of Theater and former Graduate Coordinator of the Interdisciplinary Arts for Children Program at the State University of New York College at Brockport.

She is also the author of 12 award-winning plays for children, including *Angel in the Night* (Dramatic Publishing) which received the Distinguished Play Award from the American Alliance for Theatre and Education, and *Remember My Name* (Samuel French) which won first prize in the IUPUI National Playwriting Competition.

Here she shares her advice on writing for young audiences, gives tips on submitting scripts and getting plays published and talks about common problems in playwriting. So open your notebooks—it's time for class.

Joanna H. Kraus

Were you always a playwright?

I began writing poetry when I was ten years old. Then when I was in high school, I wrote my first play, a sketch, for the Portland Children's Theater "end of season" banquet. At the time, Bette Davis was living up at Cape Elizabeth on the Maine coast. She was on the board of the theater, so she came to the banquet. Afterwards, she came up to me and in that gravelly voice of hers, said, "Darling, you've got talent. Keep writing."

How does a writer know if her play is for children?

For young people, you need a strong story line. They want the structure of a beginning, a middle, and an end. They don't want something amorphous and philosophical. You can't get away with sitting around and talking.

Are there certain subjects a playwright can't write about for children?

You can deal with child abuse. You can deal with divorce. But when you deal with these topics, it can't be hopeless. There has to be some feeling that if these people work hard enough and struggle long enough, they'll get out of their terrible predicaments. I don't mean it has to have a happy ending—it can be bittersweet—but a play for a young person should be life-affirming.

Do you think a playwright needs to work with actors?

When a play is in its embryonic stage, you need a group of decent actors to

INSIDER REPORT, *Kraus*

read it for you, or give a staged reading. You don't want them to tell you how to write, but you need to be aware of things like, "I have trouble with this line . . . this doesn't seem to follow . . . I've just said this and now I'm saying that." You need to know what actors pick up on because what is in your head may not have made it onto the page.

What's the best way to submit a script to a theater?

Sometimes I will call or write directors and say, "Look, I've got a new script. I'd like to get a workshop production of it. What's your schedule like?" These people often work a year or two in advance so it can take a while.

I enter contests. One of the big ones is held by Indiana University-Purdue University in Indianapolis. I've been a finalist once and I won first place once. The prize was money and a production.

But in the beginning I sent my scripts out. I don't recommend that. The best thing is to write a query letter. Introduce yourself: "I'm so-and-so. I've done such-and-such. Would you be interested in looking at it?" Mail it with a self-addressed, stamped envelope. Sometimes I send the play "Return Receipt Requested" to make sure they actually get it. After a few months, as anybody will tell you, you'll have to query again: "You have had my script for a few months. I haven't heard from you. I would like to know what the status is."

photo © John Weinstein

Joanna H. Kraus's "Angel in the Night" (Dramatic Publishing) premiered at National Louis University in 1991, and was a finalist in the Smokebrush Center for the Arts, New Plays Festival. In 1996, the Florida Jewish Theatre produced it with a grant from Steven Spielberg's Righteous Persons Foundation. The play is based on the true story of a young Jewish girl sheltered by Christians during the Holocaust.

INSIDER REPORT, *continued*

How does a playwright get a play published?

A play will not get published unless it's had productions. Most publishing houses will ask, "Where was it done? Send us its publicity and reviews." They want all of that. Many publishing houses will ask for three productions, none of which you directed yourself. This gives them a sense of whether there is a market.

What's your advice to an aspiring playwright?

Go to a great deal of theater, all kinds of theater. Go to new works. If you are serious about writing, you should hang around the theater. See what works, what doesn't work. Be familiar with different styles. Don't be closed-minded. See as much as you can—see Shakespeare; see things that were written centuries ago but are still being done; see different styles of the same production.

Young writers should have cameras in their heads and watch human behavior because that's their greatest resource. Look at ordinary people and the individual difference in the way they walk, the way they pick up a teacup. You don't have to go to India for enlightenment to become a writer. You just have to open your eyes in your own neighborhood. Look at what Jane Austin did. And read, read, read. The exercise of imagination is very important.

What are some of the problems you see with new plays?

Within a page-and-a-half somebody decides to commit suicide. Things happen too fast without development or depth or insight. The drama becomes melodrama.

And sometimes the dialogue is extraordinarily stiff. Go out and listen to real conversation. Listen to the way people talk and try to adapt that to a moment on stage. But stage speech isn't truly natural because if you listen to people, you hear redundancies. Stage speech is heightened naturally.

I also tell my students that their characters must sound different from one another. Sometimes new playwrights go to great lengths describing different characters who sound the same. Give yourself a test. Cover over the name of the character. Can you tell who's talking?

What's the hardest skill for a playwright to develop?

It's hard for new playwrights to dig deep down to what they care about. I ask my students to commit themselves, to identify a few topics that they take seriously, and to write about those.

And sometimes new playwrights don't appreciate how much hard work is involved. Writing is the first step, then there's rewriting . . . and rewriting. It may take a year or two, or longer, for a script to progress from inception to publication.

—Anna Olswanger

NEW YORK STATE THEATRE INSTITUTE, 155 River St., Troy NY 12180. (518)274-3200. Fax: (518)274-3815. Artistic Director: Patricia B. Snyder. Estab. 1976. Produces 5 children's plays/year; 1-2 children's musicals/year.
Needs: Produces family plays for professional theater. 90% of plays/musicals are written for adult roles; 10% for juvenile roles. Does not want to see plays for children only. Produced plays: *The Silver Skates*, by Robertson, Janis and Weiss (ages 10-100).
How to Contact: Query with synopsis, character breakdown and set description; submit complete ms and tape of songs (if a musical). Will consider simultaneous submissions and previously performed work. Reports in 3 months on submissions; 1 month for queries. SASE for return of submission.
Tips: Writers should be mindful of "audience *sophistication*. We do not wish to see material that is childish. Writers should submit work that is respectful of young people's intelligence and perception—work that is appropriate for families, but that is also challenging and provocative."

THE OPEN EYE THEATER, (formerly The Open Eye: New Stagings), P.O. Box 204, Denver NY 12421. Phone/fax: (607)326-4986. Fax: (607)326-4986. Artistic Director: Amie Brockway. Estab. 1972 (theater). Produces plays for a family audience. Most productions are with music, but are not musicals.
Needs: "Casts are usually limited to six performers. Technical requirements are kept to a minimum for touring purposes." Produces professional productions combining professional artists and artists-in-training. Most plays/musicals written for adult roles. Produced plays: *Across the Plains*, by Sandra Fenichel Asher (Reed family migrating to California-1846 for ages 8-adult); and *Selkie*, by Laurie Brooks Gollobin (based on The Selkie Legends for ages 8-adult).
How to Contact: "No videos or cassettes. Letter of inquiry only." Will consider previously performed work.
Terms: Rights agreement negotiated with author. Pays writers one time fee or royalty negotiated with publisher. SASE for return of submission.
Tips: "Send letter of inquiry only. We are interested in plays for a multigenerational audience (8-adult)."

PIONEER DRAMA SERVICE, P.O. Box 4267, Englewood CO 80155. (303)779-4035. Fax: (303)779-4315. Publisher: Steven Fendrich. Estab. 1960. Publishes 20 plays and musicals/year.
Needs: Subject matter: Publishes plays for ages preschool-high school. Recently published plays/musicals: *Coney Island of Dr. Moreau*, by Tim Kelly (musical comedy spoof for junior and senior high school on up); and *Fighting For My Self*, by Renee Clark (a series of scenes depicting young women's struggle for self-esteem in today's society for ages junior high on up). Wants to see "script, scores, tapes, pics and reviews."
How to Contact: Query with synopsis, character breakdown and set description. Submit complete ms and score (if a musical). Will consider simultaneous submissions, CAD electronic submissions via disk or modem, previously performed work. Contact: Lynne Zborowski, submissions editor. Reports in 3 months.
Terms: Purchases all rights. Pays writers in royalties (10% on sales, 50% royalties on productions).

PLAYERS PRESS, INC., P.O. Box 1132, Studio City CA 91614-0132. (818)789-4980. Vice President: R. W. Gordon. Estab. 1965. Publishes 5-50 children's plays/year; varying children's musicals/year.
Needs: Subject matter: "We publish for all age groups." Published plays: *The Crowning of Arthur*, by Nellie McCaslin (heroic young King Arthur for ages 6 and up) and *Buttonbush*, by Nancy E. Ryan (family musical about frogs for ages 5 and up).
How to Contact: Query with synopsis, character breakdown and set description; include #10 SASE with query. Considers previously performed work only. Reports on query in 2-4 weeks; submissions in 3-12 months.
Terms: Purchases stage, screen, TV rights. Payment varies; work purchased possibly outright upon written request. Submissions returned with SASE.
Tips: "Submit as requested—query first and send only previously produced material. Entertainment quality is on the upswing and needs to be directed at the world, no longer just the U.S. Please submit with two #10 SASEs plus ms-size SASE. Please do not call."

PLAYS FOR YOUNG AUDIENCES, P.O. Box 4267, Englewood CO 80155. (303)779-4035. Fax: (303)779-4315. Publisher: Steven Fendrich. Estab. 1989. Publishes 20 plays and musicals/year.

Needs: "We are looking for plays with simple sets up to 90 minutes long." Subject matter: Publishes plays for preschool-12th grade audience. Recently produced plays: *Bigger Than Life!*, by Cynthia Marcati (characters from American folklore show their stories for ages preschool-adult); and *A Little Princess*, by Vera Morris (adaptation of the classic tale for ages preschool-junior high). Wants to see "script, score, tape, pictures and reviews."
How to Contact: Query with synopsis, character breakdown and set description; submit complete ms and score (if a musical). Will consider simultaneous submissions, electronic submissions via disk or modem, previously performed work. Contact: Lynne Zborowski, submissions editor. Reports in 3 months.
Terms: Purchases all rights. Pays writers in royalties (10% in sales, 50% on productions).

PLAYS, The Drama Magazine for Young People, 120 Boylston St., Boston MA 02116-4615. (617)423-3157. Managing Editor: Elizabeth Preston. Estab. 1941. Publishes 70-75 children's plays/year.
Needs: "Props and staging should not be overly elaborate or costly. There is little call among our subscribers for plays with only a few characters; 10 or more (to allow all students in a class to participate, for instance) is preferred. Our plays are performed by children in school from lower elementary grades through junior-senior high." 100% of plays written for juvenile roles. Subject matter: Audience is lower grades through junior/senior high. Recently published plays: *Cinderella Hollywood*, by Claire Boiko (movie version of fairytale/spoof for middle grades); and *Minority of Millions*, by Mildred Hark and Noel McQueen (fighting prejudice for junior high ages). Send nothing downbeat—no plays about drugs, sex or other 'heavy' topics."
How to Contact: Query first on adaptations of folk tales and classics; otherwise submit complete ms. Reports in 2-3 weeks.
Terms: Purchases all rights. Pay rates vary. Guidelines available; send SASE. Sample copy $3.50.
Tips: "Get your play underway quickly. Above all, plays must be entertaining for young people with plenty of action, fast-paced dialogue and a satisfying conclusion. Any message imparted should be secondary to the entertainment value. No sex, drugs, violence, alcohol."

SEATTLE CHILDREN'S THEATRE, P.O. Box 9640, Seattle WA 98109. Literary Manager and Dramaturg: Deborah Frockt. Estab. 1975. Produces 6 full-length children's plays/year; 1 full-length children's musical/year. Produces children's plays for professional productions (September-June).
Needs: 95% of plays/musicals written for adult roles; 5% for juvenile roles. "We generally use adult actors even for juvenile roles." Prefers no turntable, no traps. Produced *The Rememberer*, adapted by Steven Dietz (Native American girl struggles to maintain her cultural legacy when she is forced to attend boarding school in 1912, for ages 8 and up); *Afternoon of the Elves*, adapted by Y. York, book by Janet Taylor Lisle (friendship, imagination, getting to know those you think are different, for 8 and up). Does not want to see anything that condescends to young people—anything overly broad in style.
How to Contact: Query with synopsis, maximum 10 sample pages of dialogue, résumé or bio. Will consider simultaneous submissions and previously performed work. Reports in 3-6 months on synopsis; 6-12 months on mss.
Terms: Rights vary. Payment method varies. Submissions returned with SASE.
Tips: "Please *do not* send unsolicited manuscripts. We welcome queries by all populations and encourage queries by women and minorities. We prefer sophisticated material (our weekend performances have an audience that is half adults). All shows SCT produces are multiracially cast."

STAGE ONE: THE LOUISVILLE CHILDREN'S THEATRE, 425 W. Market, Louisville KY 40202. (502)589-5946. Fax: (502)588-5910. E-mail: kystageone@aol.com. Producing Director: Moses Goldberg. Estab. 1946. Produces 6-8 children's plays/year; 1-4 children's musicals/year.
Needs: Stage One is an Equity company producing children's plays for professional productions. 100% of plays/musicals written for adult roles. "Sometimes we do use students in selected productions." Recently produced plays: *Young Black Beauty*, by Aurand Harris (about a colt growing up for ages 6-12); and *John Lennon & Me*, by Cherie Bennett (about cystic fibrosis; peer acceptance for ages 11-17). Does not want to see "camp or condescension."
How to Contact: Submit complete ms, score and tape of songs (if a musical); include the author's résumé if desired. Will consider simultaneous submissions, electronic submissions via

disk or modem and previously performed work. Reports in 3-4 months.

Terms: Pays writers in royalties (5-6%) or $25-75/performance.

Tips: Looking for "stageworthy and respectful dramatizations of the classic tales of childhood, both ancient and modern; plays relevant to the lives of young people and their families; and plays directly related to the school curriculum."

*STUDIO ARENA THEATRE SCHOOL, 710 Main St., Buffalo NY 14202. (716)856-8025, ext. 1770. Fax: (716)856-3415. Artistic Director: Ansley Valentine. Estab. 1927. Produces 2-6 children's plays/year; 1-2 children's musicals/year.

Needs: Studio Arena Theatre School is both a professional company and a school. 70% of plays/musicals written for adult roles; 30% for juvenile roles. "We like our touring productions to feature 4-5 actors and transport easily. Our student productions must feature a large cast (20) with many quality roles for young women. We are interested in musical adaptations of literature classics for student audiences 10 years old. We also produce musicals on our main stage during the summer, but we've tended to stick to known works with a wide audience appeal." Recently produced *Alice Saves Wonderland*, by Michael Roth (play about saving the environment for ages 8-12); *Christmas Carol for Two*, by Ansley Valentine (play about "Carol" produced with only 2 actors, ages 8-adult).

How to Contact: Plays: Query with synopsis, character breakdown and set description; submit complete ms. Musicals: Query with synopsis, character breakdown and set description; submit complete ms and score; tape with songs acceptable also. Will consider simultaneous submissions, electronic submissions via disk/modem and previously performed work. Reports only if interested.

Terms: Pays $25-50/performance. Submissions returned with SASE.

Tips: "Because we are both a school and a professional company, the material we seek cuts across a wide spectrum. We lean toward educational material that would be recognized by our audience with the occasional use of other work. We also have an Equity main stage that produces other work (non-children's theater)."

TADA!, 120 W. 28th St., New York NY 10001. (212)627-1732. Fax: (212)243-6736. Artistic Director: Janine Nina Trevens. Estab. 1984. Produces 3-4 staged readings of children's plays and musicals/year; 2-3 children's musicals/year.

Needs: "All actors are children, ages 8-17." Produces children's plays for professional, year-round theater. 100% of plays/musicals written for juvenile roles. Recently produced musicals: *Maggie and the Pirate*, book and lyrics by Winnie Holzman, composed by David Evans (based on the picture book of the same name by Ezra Jack Keats); and *The History Mystery*, book by Janine Nina Trevens and lyrics by Margaret Rose, music by Eric Rockwell (kids travel back in time and meet Martin Luther King, Jr., the Wright Brothers, and Ben Franklin when they were children. They also learn of the women's struggle to get the vote, Declaration of Independence and World War II, ages 4-adult). Does not want to see fairy tales or material that talks down to children.

How to Contact: Query with synopsis, character breakdown and set description; submit complete ms, score and tape of songs (if a musical). Reports in 6 months "or in March following the January deadline for our playwriting competition."

Terms: Rights purchased "depend on the piece." Pays writers in royalties of 1-6% and/or pays commissioning fee. SASE a must for return of submissions.

Tips: "For plays for our Staged Reading Contest, submit between September and January. We're looking for plays with current topics that specific age ranges can identify with, with a small cast of children and one or two adults. Our company is multi-racial and city-oriented. We are not interested in fairy tales. We like to produce material that kids relate to and that touches their lives today."

THEATRE FOR YOUNG AMERICA, 4881 Johnson Dr., Mission KS 66205. (913)831-2131. Artistic Director: Gene Mackey. Estab. 1974. Produces 9 children's plays/year; 3-5 children's musicals/year.

Needs: "We use a small cast (4-7), open thrust stage." Theatre for Young America is a professional equity company. 90% of plays/musicals written for adult roles; 10% for juvenile roles. Produced plays: *The Wizard of Oz*, by Jim Eiler and Jeanne Bargy (for ages 6 and up); *A Partridge in a Pear Tree*, by Lowell Swortzell (deals with the 12 days of Christmas, for ages 6 and up); *Three Billy Goats Gruff*, by Gene Mackey and Molly Jessup (Norwegian folk tales, for ages 6 and up).

Understanding kids is the key to writing for children's theater

TADA! is a great name for Janine Nina Trevens's New York City theater—what word better expresses the excitement and wonder of a children's theater featuring musical productions performed entirely by kids?

Trevens, artistic director of TADA!, began the theater in 1984 to bring together her two loves, musical theater and children. The full-scale musicals produced by TADA! are original and commissioned especially for the company, which is unusual in the world of children's theater. "I wanted to give writers a place to get their work seen, so they can have a long run with a big cast and a live band," Trevens says.

Janine Nina Trevens

When writing material for young performers, Trevens advises playwrights to keep their audience in mind. "You want them to have a good time and mix in humor that works for kids as well as for adults. You don't talk down to kids; it's not about that. It's about understanding what's going on with kids. And some adults just don't have that understanding."

Subject matter preferences for children's theater vary from company to company. Trevens is open to most anything. "I like subjects kids can relate to. A play doesn't have to have a heavy message. It can just be about working together, or about accepting people for who they are. It could have a general message of 'togetherness.' It should be entertaining and positive. It has to be something everyone can enjoy."

Small theaters like TADA! have small budgets, but artistic directors can often work closely with writers. "I get very involved with the writers who write for the mainstage productions and really help develop their pieces."

Trevens is interested in working with children's authors who have written books that can be adapted to the theater. TADA! has staged productions of Ezra Jack Keats's *Maggie and the Pirate*, and worked with author Irene Haas to bring *The Little Moon Theatre*, her picture book about a roaming troupe of actors, to the stage.

TADA! performs two or three mainstage musical productions a year, each running five to seven weeks for about 40 performances, with casts of about 20 multi-ethnic actors, ages 6-17, found through open auditions. The plays are written specifically for family audiences, "which means they have to have a wide range," Trevens says. "They need large ensemble casts in which children are playing children."

INSIDER REPORT, *Trevens*

What Trevens does not want are fairy tales or revised versions of something already done. She rejects preachy plays and work that condescends. "What I want are things that kids can relate to, plays in which kids are playing kids and dealing with stuff kids have to deal with."

If writers wanted to send something they thought wasn't really right for the company, but just a good example of their work, they could indicate that in the cover letter. "It's great to find writers who haven't written for kids yet but are interested in doing that."

Trevens finds a number of writers through TADA!'s annual Staged Reading Contest, for which she receives about 100 scripts for one-act plays with small casts, usually geared toward specific age groups. "I look at the contest entries and if there are writers I'm interested in pursuing, I talk to them. I like to get involved in the process, with the idea, and have writers bring ideas to me that we can develop together."

—*Alice P. Buening*

photo © Tal Hadani

New York City children's theater TADA!, under Artistic Director Janine Nina Trevens, produces original works specifically written for their company such as "Flies in the Soup," written by Jon Agee and Daniel Feigelson. The play, about two kids who escape from reform school and hide out in a school for brilliant and gifted students, features a multi-ethnic cast of child actors (left to right, Yooree Kim, Robin Atwell, Emmanuel Wilson and Marisol Rosa-Shapiro).

How to Contact: Query with synopsis, character breakdown and set description. Will consider simultaneous submissions and previously performed work. Reports in 2 months.
Terms: Purchases production rights, tour rights in local area. Pays writers in royalties or $10-50/performance.
Tips: Looking for "cross-cultural material that respects the intelligence, sensitivity and taste of the child audience."

THEATREWORKS/USA, 890 Broadway, New York NY 10003. (212)677-5959. Fax: (212)353-1632. Associate Artistic Director: Barbara Pasternack. Estab. 1960. Produces 3-4 new children's plays and musicals/year.
Needs: Cast of 5 or 6 actors. Play should be 1 hour long, tourable. Professional children's theatre comprised of adult equity actors. 100% of shows are written for adult roles. Produced plays: *Curious George*, book and lyrics by Thomas Toce, music by Tim Brown (adaptation, for grades K-3); *Little Women*, by Allan Knee, incidental music by Kim Oler and Alison Hubbard (adaptation, for grades 4-8). No fractured, typical "kiddy theater" fairy tales or shows written strictly to teach or illustrate.
How to Contact: Query first with synopsis, character breakdown and sample songs. Will consider previously performed work. Reports in 6 months.
Terms: Pays writers royalties of 6%. SASE for return of submission.
Tips: "Plays should be not only entertaining, but 'about something.' They should touch the heart and the mind. They should not condescend to children."

*THIS MONTH ON STAGE, P.O. Box 62, Hewlett NY 11557-0062. (800)536-0099. E-mail: tmonstage@aol.com or theatre @aol.com Publisher: David Lefkowitz. Estab. 1991. Publishes 1-2 children's plays/year; 0-1 children's musical/year.
Needs: Musical needs: Must work on the page. Prefers material for older audiences, or universally relevant material. Does not want to see: Patronizing, moralistic, Sunday School, etc.
How to Contact: Submit complete ms. Musicals: Submit complete ms and lyrics. Will consider simultaneous submissions and electronic submissions via disk/modem. Reports in months.
Terms: Buys one-time rights. Work purchased outright ($1-2); copies. Submissions returned with SASE (separate SASE for each ms please).
Tips: "Ask yourself: will adults enjoy it too?"

THE YOUNG COMPANY, P.O. Box 225, Milford NH 03055. (603)889-2330. Fax: (603)889-2336. Producing Director: Troy Siebels. Estab. 1984. Produces 3-4 children's plays/year; 2-3 children's musicals/year.
Needs: "Scripts should not be longer than an hour, small cast preferred; very small production budgets, so use imagination." The Young Company is a professional training program associated with American Stage Festival, a professional theater. Produced plays/musicals: *How To Eat Like A Child* (on being a kid and enjoying it a lot for ages 4-12); and *The Phantom Tollbooth* (for ages 7-14). Prefers adaptations with name recognition to young audiences. Does not want to see condescending material.
How to Contact: Query with synopsis, character breakdown and sample score.
Terms: Purchases first production credit rights on all future materials. Pays small fee and housing for rehearsals.
Tips: Looks for "concise and legible presentation, songs that further dramatic action. Develop material with strong marketing possibilities. See your work in front of an audience and be prepared to change it if your audience doesn't 'get it.' Don't condescend to your audience. Tell them a *story*."

There are seven **Writer's Digest School** courses to help you write better and sell more:

Novel Writing Workshop. A professional novelist helps you iron out your plot, develop your main characters, write the background for your novel, and complete the opening scene and a summary of your novel's complete story. You'll even identify potential publishers and write a query letter.

Marketing Your Nonfiction Book. You'll work with your mentor to create a book proposal that you can send directly to a publisher. You'll develop and refine your book idea, write a chapter-by-chapter outline of your subject, line up your sources of information, write sample chapters, and complete your query letter.

Writing & Selling Short Stories. Learn the basics of writing/selling short stories: plotting, characterization, dialogue, theme, conflict, and other elements of a marketable short story. Course includes writing assignments and one complete short story.

Writing & Selling Nonfiction Articles. Master the fundamentals of writing/selling nonfiction articles: finding article ideas, conducting interviews, writing effective query letters and attention-getting leads, targeting your articles to the right publication. Course includes writing assignments and one complete article manuscript (and its revision).

Writing Your Life Stories. With the help of a professional writer you'll chronicle your life or your family's. Learn the important steps to documenting your history including researching and organizing your material, continuity, pacing and more!

Writer's Digest Criticism Service. Have your work evaluated by a professional writer before you submit it for pay. Whether you write books, articles, short stories or poetry, you'll get an objective review plus the specific writing and marketing advice that only a professional can provide.

Secrets of Selling Your Manuscripts. Discover all the best-kept secrets for mailing out strategic, targeted manuscript submissions. Learn how to "slant" your writing so you can publish the same material over and over, which publishing houses are your best bet, and much more. Mail this card today for **FREE** information!

NO POSTAGE
NECESSARY
IF MAILED
IN THE
UNITED STATES

BUSINESS REPLY MAIL
FIRST-CLASS MAIL   PERMIT NO. 17   CINCINNATI, OHIO

POSTAGE WILL BE PAID BY ADDRESSEE

WRITER'S DIGEST SCHOOL
1507 DANA AVE
CINCINNATI OH 45207-9965

Young Writer's & Illustrator's Markets

The listings in this section are special because they publish work of young writers and artists (under age 18). Some of the magazines listed exclusively feature the work of young people. Others are adult magazines with special sections for the work of young writers. There are also a few book publishers listed which exclusively publish the work of young writers and illustrators.

You can read more about one such publisher in the Insider Report with Curt Jenkins of Raspberry Publications, a company which pays royalties and even has authors do book signings (page 278). Many of the other magazines and publishers pay only in copies, meaning authors and illustrators receive one or more free copies of the magazine or book to which they contributed.

As with adult markets, markets for children expect writers to be familiar with their editorial needs before submitting. Many of the markets listed will send guidelines to writers stating exactly what they need and how to submit it. You can usually get these by sending a request with a self-addressed, stamped envelope (SASE) to the magazine or publisher. In addition to sending for guidelines, read through a few copies of any magazines you'd like to submit to—this is the best way to determine if your work is right for them.

A number of kids' magazines are available on newsstands or in libraries. Others are only distributed through schools, churches or home subscriptions. If you can't find a magazine you'd like to see, most editors will send sample copies for a small fee. (You can write or call to find out.)

Before you submit your material to editors, take a few minutes to read Guide to Submitting Your Work on page 6 for more information on proper submission procedures. You may also want to check out the three sections that follow this one—Clubs & Organizations, Conferences & Workshops and Contests & Awards. Listings in these sections marked with a double dagger (‡) are open to students (some exclusively). Additional opportunities for writers can be found in *Market Guide for Young Writers* (Writer's Digest Books) and *A Teen's Guide to Getting Published: the only writer's guide written by teens for teens*, by Danielle Dunn and Jessica Dunn (Prufrock Press).

THE ACORN, 1530 Seventh St., Rock Island IL 61201. (309)788-3980. Newsletter. Estab. 1989. Audience consists of "kindergarten-12th grade students, parents, teachers and other adults. Purpose in publishing works for children: to expose children's manuscripts to others and provide a format for those who might not have one. We want to present wholesome writing, material that will entertain and educate—audience grades K-12." Children must be K-12 (put grade on manuscripts). Guidelines available for SASE.

Magazines: 100% of magazine written by children. Uses 6 fiction pieces (500 words), 20 pieces of poetry (32 lines). No payment; purchase of a copy isn't necessary to be printed. Sample copy $2. Subscription $10 for 4 issues. Submit mss to Betty Mowery, editor. Send complete ms. Will accept typewritten, legibly handwritten and/or computer printout. Include SASE. Reports in 1 week.

Artwork: Publishes artwork by children. Looks for "all types; size 4×5. Use black ink in artwork." No payment. Submit artwork either with ms or separately to Betty Mowery. Include SASE. Reports in 1 week.

Tips: "My biggest problem is not having names on the manuscripts. If the manuscript gets separated from the cover letter, there is no way to know whom to respond to. Always put name, age or grade and address on manuscripts, and if you want your material returned enclose a SASE. Don't send material with killing of humans or animals, or lost love poems or stories."

*AMELIA MAGAZINE, 329 "E" St., Bakersfield CA 93304-2031. (805)323-4064. Magazine. Published quarterly. Strives to offer the best of all genres. Purpose in publishing works for children: wants to offer first opportunities to budding writers. Also offers the annual Amelia Student Award for high school students. Submissions from young writers must be signed by parent, teacher or guardian verifying originality. Guidelines are not specifically for young writers; they cover the entire gamut of publication needs.

Magazines: 3% of magazine written by children. Uses primarily poetry, often generated by teachers in creative writing classes. Uses 1 story in any fiction genre (1,500 words), 4 pieces of poetry, usually haiku (3 lines). Would like to receive more general poetry from young writers. Pays in copies for haiku; $2-10 for general poetry. Regular $35 rate for fiction or nonfiction. Submit mss to Frederick A. Raborg, editor. Submit complete ms (teachers frequently submit student's work). Will accept typewritten ms. Include SASE. Reports in 3 weeks.

Artwork: Publishes artwork and photography by children, "have not yet, however." Looks for photos no smaller than 5 × 7; artwork in any method; also cartoons. Pays $5-20 on publication. Submit well-protected artwork with SASE. Submit artwork/photos to Frederick A. Raborg, Jr., editor. Include SASE. Reports in 3 weeks.

Tips: "Be neat and thorough. Photos should have captions. Cartoon gaglines ought to be funny; try them out on someone before submitting. We want to encourage young writers, because the seeds of literary creativity are sown quite young with strong desires to read and admiration for the authors of those early readings."

AMERICAN GIRL, 8400 Fairway Place, Middleton WI 53562. (608)836-4848. Fax: (608)831-7089. E-mail: ageditor@ag.pleasantco.com. Website: http://www.pleasantco.com. Bimonthly magazine. Audience consists of girls ages 8-12 who are joyful about being girls. Purpose in publishing works by young people: self-esteem boost and entertainment for readers. Young writers must be 8-12 years old. Writer's guidelines available with #10 SASE.

Magazines: 5% of magazine written by young people. "A few pages of each issue are set aside for children and feature articles that answer questions or requests that have appeared in a previous issue of *American Girl*." Pays in copies. Submit to Magazine Dept. Assistant. Will accept legibly handwritten ms. Include SASE. Reports in 8-12 weeks.

Tips: "Please, no stories, poems, etc. about American Girls Collection Characters (Felicity, Samantha, Molly, Kirsten, Addy)."

THE APPRENTICE WRITER, % Gary Fincke, Susquehanna University, Selinsgrove PA 17870. (717)372-4164. Fax: (717)372-4310. Magazine. Published annually. "Writing by high school students and for high school students." Purpose in publishing works by young people: to provide quality writing by students which can be read for pleasure and serve as a text for high school classrooms. Work is primarily from eastern and northeastern states, but will consider work from other areas of US. Students must be in grades 9-12. Writer's guidelines available for SASE.

Magazines: Uses 15 short stories (prefers under 5,000 words); 15 nonfiction personal essays (prefers under 5,000 words); 60 poems (no word limit) per issue. Pays in copies to writers and their schools. Submit mss to Gary Fincke, editor. Submit complete ms. Will accept typewritten mss. Include SASE. Submit ms by March 15. Responds by May of each year.

Artwork/Photography: Publishes artwork and photography by children. Looks for b&w. Pays in copies to artists and their schools. Submit originals or high quality copies. Submit art and photographs to Gary Fincke, editor. Include SASE. Submit artwork by March 15. Responds by May of each year.

✱ THE ASTERISK before a listing indicates the listing is new in this edition.

BEYOND WORDS PUBLISHING, INC., 4443 NE Airport Rd., Hillsboro OR 97124. (503)693-8700. Book publisher. Director of Children's Department: Michelle Roehm. Publishes 3-4 books by children per year. Looks for "books that encourage creativity and an appreciation of nature in children." Wants to "encourage children to write, create, dream and believe that it is possible to be published. The books must be unique, be of national interest and the child must be personable and promotable."
Books: Publishes stories and joke books.

*BLUE JEAN MAGAZINE: For Teen Girls Who Dare, P.O. Box 90856, Rochester NY 14609. (716)654-5070. E-mail: bluejeanmg@aol.com. Bimonthly magazine. "*Blue Jean Magazine* portrays real teen girls on the verge of changing the world. Our cover stories profile interesting and exciting teen girls in action. You will find no supermodels, tips on dieting or fashion spreads on our pages. We publish teen girl submissions of poetry, artwork, photography, fiction and much more!" Audience is girls ages 13-19. Purpose in publishing work by young people: "to stay true to our audience and our mission statement 'For Teen Girls, by Teen Girls.' " Writer's guidelines available for SASE.
Magazine: 75% of magazine written by young people. Uses 1 fiction story, 8-14 nonfiction stories (250-3,000 words); 1-3 poems. Pays $15 poetry, $50 feature story/article, $75 cover story. Payment will be sent with 2 complimentary issues within 30 days of publication. Submit mss to editors. Submit complete ms per submission guidelines. Will accept typewritten mss. Include SASE. Reports in 3-4 months at most. "Many times within two months."
Artwork: Publishes artwork and photography by teens. Will consider a variety of styles! Artwork must be submitted by a teen artist (ages 13-19). Submit art between 2 pieces of paperboard or cardboard. Submit artwork/photos to editors. Include SASE with enough postage for return. Reports in 3-4 months.
Tips: "Submissions may be sent via mail or e-mail. Do not inquire about your work by calling. Replies guaranteed when material sent through e-mail or mail with SASE."

BOODLE, P.O. Box 1049, Portland IN 47371. (219)726-8141. Magazine published quarterly. "Each quarterly issue offers children a special invitation to read stories and poems written by others. Children can learn from the ideas in these stories and the techniques of sharing ideas in pictures and written form. Audience is ages 6-12. We hope that publishing children's writing will enhance the self-esteem of the authors and motivate other children to try expressing themselves in this form." Submission requirements: "We ask that authors include grade when written, current grade, name of school, and a statement from parent or teacher that the work is original."
Magazines: 100% of magazine written by children. Uses 12 short stories (100-500 words), 1 nonfiction piece, usually animal (100-500 words), 30 poems (50-500 words), 2 puzzles and mazes (50-500 words) per issue. Pays 2 copies of issue. Submit mss to Mavis Catalfio, editor. Submit complete ms. Will accept typewritten and legibly handwritten mss. Include SASE.
Artwork: Wants "mazes, cartoons, drawings of animals or seasons or sports which will likely match a story or poem we publish." Pays 2 copies of issue. "Drawings should be done in black ink or marker." Submit artwork to Mavis Catalfio, editor. Reports in 2 months.
Tips: Submit seasonal materials at least a year in advance. "We love humor and offbeat stories. We seldom publish sad or depressing stories about death or serious illness."

BOYS' LIFE, 1325 W. Walnut Hill Lane, P.O. Box 152079, Irving TX 75015-2079. (214)580-2366. Magazine published monthly. Audience consists of children ages 7-17. *Boys' Life* is published by the Boy Scouts of America to make available to children the highest caliber of fiction and nonfiction, to stimulate an interest in good reading and to promote the principles of Scouting. Writer's guidelines available for SASE.
Magazines: Small percentage of magazine written by young people under 18. Uses hobby and collecting tips for "Hobby Hows" and "Collecting" columns. Pays $10/tip. Uses jokes for "Think & Grin" column. Pays choice of $2 or copy of *Scout Handbook* or *Scout Fieldbook*/joke accepted. Several times/year uses personal stories (500 words maximum) for "Readers' Page." Pays $25. Submit mss to column. Submit complete ms. Will accept typewritten and legibly handwritten mss for consideration. Reports in 6-8 weeks. For nonfiction mss, query first to Mike Goldman, articles editor. All fiction mss should be double-spaced and typed copy, 1,000-1,500 words. Pays $750 and up for accepted stories. Story categories: humor, mystery, science fiction, adventure. Send one copy of story plus cover letter. Submit to Shannon Lowry, associate editor. Include SASE.
Tips: "Study one year's worth of recent magazines before submitting."

✦CHICKADEE MAGAZINE, for Young Children from OWL, 179 John, Suite 500, Toronto, Ontario M5T 3G5 Canada. (416)971-5275. Magazine published 10 times/year. "*Chickadee* is for children ages 6-9. Its purpose is to entertain and educate children about science, nature and the world around them. We publish children's drawings to give readers the chance to express themselves. Drawings must relate to the topics that are given in the 'All Your Own' section of each issue."
Artwork: Publishes artwork by children. No payment given. Mail submissions with name, age and return address for thank you note. Submit to Mitch Butler, All Your Own Editor. Reports in 4 months.

CHILD LIFE, Children's Better Health Institute, 1100 Waterway Blvd., P.O. Box 567, Indianapolis IN 46206. (317)636-8881. Magazine. Published 8 times/year. Targeted toward kids ages 9-11. Focuses on health, sports, fitness, nutrition, safety and general interest.
Magazines: "Publishes jokes, riddles, poems and original stories (250 words maximum) by children." Kids should include name, address, phone number (for office use) and school photo. "No mass duplicated, multiple submissions." Submit complete mss for fiction and nonfiction written by adults.
Tips: "We use kids' submissions from our age range—9 to 11. Those older or younger should try one of our sister publications: *Children's Digest, Children's Playmate, Humpty Dumpty's Magazine, Jack And Jill, Turtle Magazine, U*S*Kids.*"

CHILDREN'S DIGEST, Children's Better Health Institute, 1100 Waterway Blvd., P.O. Box 567, Indianapolis IN 46206. (317)636-8881. Fax: (317)684-8094. Magazine. Published 8 times/year. Audience consists of preteens. Purpose in publishing works by children: to encourage children to express themselves through writing. Submissions must focus on health-related theme. Requires proof of originality before publishing stories. Writer's guidelines available on request.
Magazines: 10% of magazine written by children. Uses 1 fiction story (under 500 words), 6-10 poems, 10-15 jokes/riddles per issue. "There is no payment for manuscripts submitted by readers." Submit mss to *Children's Digest*, Layne Cameron, editor. Submit complete ms. Will accept typewritten, legibly handwritten and computer printout mss. "We don't respond unless the material will be published. Sorry, no materials can be returned."
Tips: "Submit jokes, poems and young author stories to me, Layne Cameron. I read every letter that comes to my magazine. We do not pay for children's submissions. We also don't encourage children to try to compete with professional writers. For best results, submit items to the columns listed above."

CHILDREN'S PLAYMATE, Children's Better Health Institute, P.O. Box 567, Indianapolis IN 46206. (317)636-8881. Magazine. Estab. 1929. Audience consists of children between 6 and 8 years of age. Emphasizes health, fitness, safety, good nutrition, and *good* humorous fiction for beginning readers. Writer's guidelines available on request with SASE.
Artwork: Publishes artwork by children. "Prefers black line drawings on white paper. No payment for children's artwork published." No material can be returned. Submit artwork to *Children's Playmate*, Chuck Horsman, art director.

✦THE CLAREMONT REVIEW, 4980 Wesley Rd., Victoria, British Columbia Canada V8Y 1Y9. (604)658-5221. E-mail: aurora@islandnet.com. Magazine. Publishes 2 books/year by young adults. Publishes poetry and fiction with literary value by students aged 13-19 anywhere in North America. Purpose in publishing by young people: to provide a literary venue.
Magazines: Uses 8-10 fiction stories (200-2,500 words), 25-35 poems. Pays in copies. Submit mss to editors. Submit complete ms. Will accept typewritten mss. SASE. Reports in 1 month (except during the summer).
Artwork: Publishes artwork by young adults. Looks for b&w copies of imaginative art. Pays in copies. Send picture for review. Negative may be requested. Submit art and photographs to editors. SASE. Reports in 1 month.

✦ THE MAPLE LEAF before a listing indicates that the market is Canadian.

CLUBHOUSE, P.O. Box 15, Berrien Springs MI 49103. (616)471-9009. Director of Publications: Elaine Trumbo. Magazine. Estab. 1949. Published monthly. Occasionally publishes items by kids. "Audience consists of kids ages 9-14; philosophy is God loves kids, kids are neat people." Purpose in publishing works by young people: to give encouragement and demonstration of talent. Children must be ages 9-14; must include parent's note verifying originality.

Magazines: Uses adventure, historical, everyday life experience (fiction/nonfiction-1,200 words); health-related short articles; poetry (4-24 lines of "mostly mood pieces and humor"). Pays in prizes for children, money for adult authors. Query. Will accept typewritten, legibly handwritten and computer printout mss. "Will not be returned without SASE." Reports in 6 weeks.

Artwork: Publishes artwork by children. Looks for all types of artwork—white paper, black pen. Pays in prizes for kids. Send b&w art to Christa Hainey, editor. "Won't be returned without SASE."

Tips: "All items submitted by kids are held in a file and used when possible. We normally suggest they do not ask for return of the item."

CREATIVE KIDS, P.O. Box 8813, Waco TX 76714. (800)998-2208. Fax: (817)756-3339. E-mail: creative_kids@prufrock.com. Website: http://www.prufrock.com. Editor: Libby Lindsey. Magazine published 4 times/year. Estab. 1979. "All material is by children, for children." Purpose in publishing works by children: "to create a product that provides children with an authentic experience and to offer an opportunity for children to see their work in print. *Creative Kids* contains the best stories, poetry, opinion, artwork, games and photography by kids ages 8-14." Writers ages 8-14 must have statement by teacher or parent verifying originality. Writer's guidelines available on request with SASE.

Magazines: Uses "about 6" fiction and nonfiction stories (800-900 words); poetry, plays, ideas to share (200-750 words) per issue. Pays in "free magazine." Submit mss to submissions editor. Will accept typewritten mss. Include SASE. Reports in 1 month.

Artwork/Photography: Publishes artwork and photos by children. Looks for "any kind of drawing, cartoon, or painting." Pays "free magazine." Send original or a photo of the work to submissions editor. No photocopies. Include SASE. Reports in 1 month.

Tips: "*Creative Kids* is a magazine by kids, for kids. The work represents children's ideas, questions, fears, concerns and pleasures. The material never contains racist, sexist or violent expression. The purpose is to provide children with an authentic experience. A person may submit one piece of work per envelope. Each piece must be labeled with the student's name, birth date, grade, school, home address and school address. Include a photograph, if possible. Recent school pictures are best. Material submitted to *Creative Kids* must not be under consideration by any other publication. Items should be carefully prepared, proofread and double checked (perhaps also by a parent or teacher). All activities requiring solutions must be accompanied by the correct answers. Young writers and artists should always write for guidelines and then follow them. It is very frustrating to receive submissions that are not complete."

CREATIVE WITH WORDS, Thematic anthologies, Creative with Words Publications, P.O. Box 223226, Carmel CA 93922. Fax: (408)655-8627. Editor: Brigitta Geltrich. Publishes 12 anthologies/year. Estab. 1975. "We publish the creative writing of children." Audience consists of children, schools, libraries, adults, reading programs. Purpose in publishing works by children: to offer them an opportunity to get started in publishing. "Work must be of quality, original, unedited, and not published before; age must be given (up to 19 years old)." SASE must be enclosed with all correspondence and mss. Writer's guidelines and theme list available on request with SASE.

Books: Considers all categories except those dealing with death, violence, pornography and overly religious. Uses fairy tales, folklore items (up to 1,200 words) and poetry (not to exceed 20 lines, 46 characters across). Published *Nature Series: Skies, Land, Forests, Seas*; also *Dinosaurs & Dragons*; and *Relationships* (all children and adults). Pays 20% discount on each copy of publication in which fiction or poetry by children appears. Submit mss to Brigitta Geltrich, editor. Query; child, teacher or parent can submit; teacher and/or parents must verify originality of writing. Will accept typewritten and/or legibly handwritten mss. SASE. Reports in 1-2 months after deadline of any theme.

Artwork/Photography: Publishes artwork, photos and computer artwork by children (language art work). Pays 20% discount on every copy of publication in which work by children appears. Submit artwork to Brigitta Geltrich, editor.

Tips: "Enjoy the English language, life and the world around you. Look at everything from a different perspective. Be less descriptive and use words wisely. Let the reader experience a story through a viewpoint character."

*ECLECTIC RAINBOWS, 1538 Tennessee Walker Dr., Roswell GA 30075-3152. (770)587-5711. E-mail: ltdennison@aol.com. Magazine. Published semi-annually. Purpose in publishing works by children: the satisfaction of giving a "born" writer a start and encouragement.
Magazines: 1 article/issue written by young people. Pays on publication $10-25; $10 reprints. Poetry pays in copies only. Submit mss to Linda T. Dennison, editor/publisher. If you query, be detailed in your outline. Submit complete ms if unpublished and don't have clips. Will accept typewritten mss only. Include SASE. Reports in 1-2 months.
Artwork/Photography: "No solo photos. With ms only." Submit photos only—no slides, no original art. "No payment for photos—they are used only to accompany your story—but they do mean I'll pay a bit more for the story."
Tips: "Keep trying—each nonsuccess teaches you more about what you need to do to succeed. Seek out *ruthless* criticism for maximum growth at fastest speed. Older teens have best chance. Writing and subject must be adult in nature and suitable for *E.R.* Nostalgia and what I did on summer break—no."

FREE SPIRIT PUBLISHING INC., 400 First Ave. North, Suite 616, Minneapolis MN 55401-1730. (612)338-2068. Fax: (612)337-5050. E-mail: help4kids@freespirit.com. Publishes 15-20 books/year. "We specialize in SELF-HELP FOR KIDS®. We aim to help kids help themselves. We were the *first* publisher of self-help materials for children, and today we are the *only* publisher of SELF-HELP FOR KIDS® materials. Our main audience is children and teens, but we also publish for parents, teachers, therapists, youth workers and other involved in caring for kids. Our main interests include the development of self-esteem, self-awareness, creative thinking and problem-solving abilities, assertiveness, and making a difference in the world. We do not publish fiction or poetry. We feel that children have important things to say. They have critical things to share and can reach and teach others the same age in a way that adults cannot. Most of our authors have degrees in education, psychology, social work, and/or counseling. We also accept submissions from young people ages 14 and older. Please send a letter from a parent/guardian/leader verifying originality." Request catalog, author guidelines, and "student guidelines" before submitting work.
Books: Publishes self-help for kids, how-to, classroom activities. Pays advance and royalties. Submit mss to Elizabeth Verdick, acquisitions editor. Send query and sample table of contents. Will accept typewritten mss. SASE required. Reports in 3-4 months.
Photography: Free Spirit accepts photography by children. Submit to Elizabeth Verdick, acquisitions editor.
Tips: "Free Spirit publishes very specific material, and it helps when writers request and study our catalog before submitting work to us. We also will send information on how to become a Free Spirit author. We do not accept general self-help books, autobiographies, or children's books that feature made-up stories. Our preference is books that help kids to gain self-esteem, succeed in school, stand up for themselves, resolve conflicts, and make a difference in the world. We do not publish books that have animals as the main characters."

THE FUDGE CAKE, P.O. Box 197, Citrus Heights CA 95611-0197. Magazine. Published bimonthly. Audience consists of children and young adults, grandparents, teachers, parents, etc. Purpose in publishing works by young people: to provide a showcase for young writers age 6-17. "We value the work of today's children. They have a lot to say and we feel they need an outlet to express themselves." To qualify for publication, children must be age 6-17; submit copies of original work; and include SASE. Writer's guidelines available on request. Sample copy for $3.
Magazines: Uses 2-3 pieces of fiction (all types—no erotica) (250-500 words), 15-20 poems (30 lines or less). Pays one copy of issue work appears in. Submit mss to Jancarl Campi, editor. Submit complete ms. Will accept typewritten form and legible handwritten mss. Include SASE. Reports in 1 month.
Tips: "Don't be afraid to use the pen—write and rewrite, then send it in. We often critique or comment on rejected ms."

FUTURIFIC, INC., Foundation for Optimism, Futurific, 305 Madison Ave., Suite 10B, New York NY 10165. Publisher: B. Szent-Miklosy. (212)297-0502. Magazine published monthly.

Audience consists of people interested in an accurate report of what is ahead. "We do not discriminate by age. We look for the visionary in all people. They must write what will be. No advice or 'maybe.' We've had 21 years of accurate forecasting." Sample copy for $5 postage and handling. Writer's guidelines available on request with SASE.

Magazines: Submit mss to B. Szent-Miklosy, publisher. Will accept typewritten, legibly hand-written, computer printout, 5.25 or 3.5 inch WordPerfect diskette mss.

Artwork: Publishes artwork by children. Looks for "what the future will look like." Pay is negotiable. Send b&w drawings or photos. Submit artwork to B. Szent-Miklosy, publisher.

THE GOLDFINCH, Iowa History for Young People, 402 Iowa Ave., Iowa City IA 52240. (319)335-3916. Fax: (319)335-3935. Magazine published quarterly. Audience is 4th-8th graders. "Magazine supports creative work by children: research, art, writing. *The Goldfinch* puts the fun back into history. We publish young Iowans' work to show them that they and their creative efforts are an important part of Iowa history." Submitted work must go with the historical theme of each issue.

Magazines: 10-20% written by children. Uses at least 1 nonfiction essay, poem, story/issue (500 words). Pays complimentary copies. Submit mss with SASE to Amy Ruth, editor. Submit complete ms. Will accept typewritten, legibly handwritten, computer disk (Apple) mss. Reports in 1 month.

Artwork/Photography: Publishes artwork/photographs by children. Art and photos must be b&w. Pays complimentary copies. Query first with SASE to Amy Ruth.

Tips: "We make the subject of Iowa history come alive through short features, games/puzzles/activities, fiction and cool historical photographs."

HIGH SCHOOL WRITER, P.O. Box 718, Grand Rapids MN 55744. (218)326-8025. Magazine published monthly during the school year. "The *High School Writer* is a magazine written *by* students *for* students. All submissions must exceed contemporary standards of decency." Purpose in publishing works by young people: "to provide a real audience for student writers—and text for study. Submissions by junior high and middle school students accepted for our junior edition. Senior high students' works are accepted for our senior high edition. Students attending schools that subscribe to our publication are eligible to submit their work." Writer's guidelines available on request.

Magazines: Uses fiction, nonfiction (2,000 words maximum) and poetry. Submit mss to Robert Lemen, editor. Submit complete ms (teacher must submit). Will accept typewritten, computer-generated (good quality) mss.

Tips: "Submissions should not be sent without first obtaining a copy of our guidelines. Also, submissions will not be considered unless student's school subscribes."

HIGHLIGHTS FOR CHILDREN, 803 Church St., Honesdale PA 18431. (717)253-1080. Magazine. Published monthly. "We strive to provide wholesome, stimulating, entertaining material that will encourage children to read. Our audience is children ages 2-12." Purpose in publishing works by young people: to encourage children's creative expression. Age limit to submit is 15.

Magazines: 15-20% of magazine written by children. Uses stories and poems. Also uses jokes, riddles, tongue twisters. Features which occur occasionally: "What Are Your Favorite Books?" (8-10/year), Recipes (8-10/year), "Science Letters" (15-20/year). Special features which invite children's submissions on a specific topic: "Tell the Story" (15-20/year), "You're the Reporter" (8-10/year), "Your Ideas, Please" (8-10/year), "Endings to Unfinished Stories" (8-10/year). Pays in copies. Submit complete ms to the editor. Will accept typewritten, legibly handwritten and computer printout mss. Reports in 3-6 weeks.

Artwork: Publishes artwork by children. Pays in copies. No cartoon or comic book characters. No commercial products. Submit b&w or color artwork for "Our Own Pages." Features include "Creatures Nobody Has Ever Seen" (5-8/year) and "Illustration Job" (18-20/year). Reports in 3-6 weeks.

HOW ON EARTH!, Youth supporting compassionate, ecologically sound living, P.O. Box 339, Oxford PA 19363-0339. (717)529-8638. Fax: (717)529-3000. E-mail: howonearth@aol.com. Magazine. Published quarterly. Youth audience. "Through providing a voice for youth, *How On Earth!* honors youth visions and expressions in creating and exploring options for compassionate, ecologically-sound living. *HOE!* acknowledges the interconnectedness of animal, environmental, human rights, peace and other social change issues and explores these relationships through the thoughts and feelings of youth." Must be ages 13-24 and work must be original. Articles well-referenced. "Please send SASE with 1 first-class stamp for submission guidelines." **Magazines:** 95% of magazine written by youth. Uses 1-2 creative writing stories, 2-5 research or informative articles, 4-5 poems per issue. Submit mss to Amina Chaudhri, editor. Query for articles. Will accept typewritten and legibly handwritten mss or 3.5 disk (Macintosh). Include SASE "only if they want it returned." Reports in 2 months.

Artwork/Photography: Publishes artwork and photographs taken by youth. "We accept material depicting nature, animals, ecology, social justice, activism, vegetarian food and anything concerning issues related to these topics. Full color art or photos accepted for cover. Cartoons welcome as well. Pen & ink or dark pencil only." No pay: "All volunteer at this point." Submit artwork and photos to Amina Chaudhri, editor. Include SASE "only if they want it returned." Reports in 2 months.

KIDS' WORLD, The Magazine That's All Kids!, 1300 Kicker Rd., Tuscaloosa AL 35404. (205)553-2284. Magazine. Published 4 times a year. Audience consists of young children up to age 10. "I'm creating a fun magazine for kids to read and a good place for young writers to get a start." Purpose in publishing works by young people: "So that my magazine will be unique— edited by a kid, for kids, by kids (all kids!). Authors must be under 17—no horror or romance." Writer's guidelines available on request.

Magazines: 100% of magazine written by young people. Uses 4-10 short stories; 1-2 essays about favorite things, etc.; 4-10 poems and art. Pays one free copy per ms or artwork. Submit mss to Morgan Kopaska-Merkel, editor. Submit complete mss. Will accept typewritten and legibly handwritten mss. Include SASE. Reports in 4-6 weeks.

Artwork/Photography: Publishes artwork and photography by children. Looks for "children/ babies and things of interest to them (food, toys, animals . . .)." Must be b&w in pen. Pays one free copy per artwork. Send the artwork, plus a note and SASE. Reports in 2-4 weeks.

Tips: "Have an adult check spelling, punctuation and grammar. I get a lot of submissions, so I can only publish the really good ones, within reason for a child's age."

*KIDSART, P.O. Box 274, Mt. Shasta CA 96067. (916)926-5076. E-mail: kidsart@macshasta.c om. Art education booklets published quarterly. Publishes "hands-on art projects, open-ended art lessons, art history, lots of child-made art to illustrate." Purpose in publishing works by children: "to provide achievable models for kids—give young artists a forum for their work. We always phone before publishing works to be sure it's OK with their folks, name is spelled correctly, etc."

Artwork/Photography: Publishes artwork/photographs by children. Any submissions by children welcomed. Pays free copies of published work. Submit artwork/photos to Kim Solga, editor. "Your originals will be returned to you in 4-6 weeks." SASE desired, but not required. Free catalog available describing KidsArt newsletter. Sample copy $3.

THE LOUISVILLE REVIEW—Children's Corner, Dept. of English, University of Louisville, 315 Bingham Humanities, Louisville KY 40292. (502)852-6801. Semiannual magazine. "We are a contemporary literary journal." Purpose in publishing works by young people: to encourage children to write with fresh images and striking metaphors. Not interested in the "cute" moral lesson on highly rhymed and metered verse. "We believe there are children writers who are as good as adult writers and therefore deserve to be published along with adult writers." Must supply SASE and permission slip from parent stating that work is original and giving permission to publish if accepted. Only accepts typewritten mss.

Magazines: 10-20% of magazine written by children. Uses poetry, any length. Pays in copies. Submit mss to Children's Corner. Submit complete ms. Will accept typewritten mss. Include SASE. Deadline December 31. Reads only January through March. Will reply by April.

ALWAYS INCLUDE a self-addressed, stamped envelope (SASE) with submissions within your own country. When sending material to other countries, include a self-addressed envelope (SAE) and International Reply Coupons (IRCs).

THE MCGUFFEY WRITER, 5128 Westgate Dr., Oxford OH 45056. Fax: (513)523-5565. E-mail: jchurch@hcnet.muohio.edu. Website: http://www.lac.net:80/~mcguffey/writer. Magazine published 3 times per year. "We publish poems and stories by children that compel the editors to read them to the end because of extraordinary originality of content or facility with language given the age of the child author." Purpose in publishing works by children: to reward by recognition those who strive to create in words and/or drawings and to motivate other children to try to meet a standard set in a sense by their peers. Requirements: be in grades K-12, originality must be attested to by adult parent or teacher. Writer's guidelines available on request.

Magazines: 100% of magazine written by young people. Uses 3-5 fiction short stories (600 or fewer words), 0-3 nonfiction stories (500 or fewer words), 5-10 poems (up to 30 lines). "We do not publish trite, violent, teen 'romance' or gloom and doom selections. We look for fresh, original writing on topics students know well." Pays 2 copies. Submit mss to Susan Kammeraad-Campbell, editor. Submit complete ms. "We make every effort to send a personal note to all children who submit work." Will accept typewritten form and legible handwriting. Include SASE. Responds in 3-6 months.

Artwork/Photography: Publishes b&w illustrations by children to fit $7\frac{1}{2} \times 8$ page—any theme. Pays 2 contributor copies. Submit art and photographs to Linda Sheppard, art editor. Responds in 3-6 months.

Tips: "Trust your own voice—know that what you think and feel is of value and worth sharing with others. Use all five senses in your writing. Don't just tell us how the rock looks or feels. Tell us how it smells, what it sounds like, what it tastes like. Be playful. And for goodness sake, use your imagination! Please tell us what inspired your submission. Tell us about your writing process. How did you get your idea? Did you discover/learn something while working on your writing?"

MAJESTIC BOOKS, P.O. Box 19097-CW, Johnston RI 02919. Book. Published 3 times/year. Majestic Books is a small press which was formed to give children an outlet for their work. "We publish softcover bound anthologies of fictional stories by children, for children and adults who enjoy the work of children." Purpose in publishing work by young people: "Our hope is that our publication will spark a child's interest in writing and give children talented in writing encouragement to continue." All children age 8 through 18 have a chance of being published as long as they state their age when submitting work. Writer's guidelines available on request. SASE required.

Books: Publishes short stories. Length: 2,000 words or less for fiction. Pays 10% commission on sales directly related to writer's inclusion. Submit mss to Cindy MacDonald, publisher. Submit complete mss for fiction or poetry. Will accept typewritten and legibly handwritten mss. Include SASE. Reports in 3 weeks (slightly longer in summer).

Tips: "Use your imagination to create the best fictional story you can and then send it to us. We need to know your age when you submit work so we can judge your talent accordingly. We love stories that leave the reader thinking long after they have read the last word."

MERLYN'S PEN: The National Magazines of Student Writing, P.O. Box 1058, East Greenwich RI 02818. (800)247-2027. Fax: (401)885-5222. Magazine. Published every 2 months during the school year, September-May. "By publishing student writing, *Merlyn's Pen* seeks to broaden and reward the young author's interest in writing. Strengthen the self-confidence of beginning writers, and promote among all students a positive attitude toward literature. We publish a Senior Edition (grades 9-12) and a Middle School Edition (grades 6-9) including 150 manuscripts annually by students in grades 6-12. The entire magazine is dedicated to young adults' writing. Our audience is classrooms, libraries and students from grades 6-12." Writers must be in grades 6-12 and must send a completed *Merlyn's Pen* cover sheet with each submission. When a student is accepted, he/she, a parent and a teacher must sign a statement of originality.

Magazines: Uses 25 short stories (less than 4,000 words), plays; 8 nonfiction essays (less than 3,000 words); 10 pieces of poetry; letters to the editor; editorials; reviews of previously published works; and reviews of books, music, movies per issue. Published authors receive 3 contributor's copies and payment. Also, a discount is offered for additional copies of the issue. Submit up to 3 titles at one time. Will only accept typewritten mss. "All rejected manuscripts receive an editor's constructive critical comment in the margin." Reports in 10 weeks.

Artwork/Photography: Publishes artwork and photography by young adults, grades 6-12. Looks for b&w line drawings, cartoons, color art for cover. Published artists receive 3 contributor's copies plus payment. A discount is offered for additional copies. Send unmatted original artwork. Reports in 10 weeks.

Tips: "All manuscripts and artwork must be accompanied by a completed copy of *Merlyn's Pen* official cover sheet for submissions. Call to request cover sheet.

NATIONAL GEOGRAPHIC WORLD, 17th and M St. NW, Washington DC 20036-4688. (202)857-7000. Magazine published monthly. Picture magazine for ages 8 and older. Purpose in publishing work by young people: to encourage in young readers a curiosity about the world around them.

• *National Geographic World* was not accepting unsolicited manuscripts at the time of publication.

Tips: Publishes art, letters, poems, games, riddles, jokes and craft ideas by children in mailbag section only. No payment given. Send by mail to: Submissions Committee. "Sorry, but *World* cannot acknowledge or return your contributions."

NEW MOON: The Magazine For Girls & Their Dreams, New Moon Publishing, Inc., P.O. Box 3620, Duluth MN 55803-3620. (218)728-5507. Fax: (218)728-0314. E-mail: newmoon @newmoon.duluth.mn.us. Website: http://newmoon.duluth.mn.us/~newmoon. Magazine. Published bimonthly. *New Moon*'s primary audience is girls ages 8-14. "We publish a magazine that listens to girls." More than 70% of *New Moon* is written by girls. Purpose in publishing work by children/teens: "We want girls' voices to be heard. *New Moon* wants girls to see that their opinions, dreams, thoughts and ideas counts." Writer's guidelines available for SASE. Reports in 2-4 months.

• To learn more about *New Moon*, see the Insider Report with Joe Kelly in the 1996 edition of *Children's Writer's & Illustrator's Market.*

Magazine: 75% of magazine written by young people. Uses 4 fiction mss (300-900 words); 12 nonfiction mss (300-900 words) per year. Submit to Tya Ward and Barbara Stretchberry, managing editors. Submit query, complete mss for fiction and nonfiction. Will accept typewritten, legibly handwritten mss and disk (IBM compatible). "We do not return unsolicited material." Please include SASE. Reports in 2-4 months.

Artwork/Photography: Publishes artwork and photography by children. Looks for cover and inside illustrations. Pay negotiated. Submit art and photographs to Tya Ward or Barbara Stretchberry, managing editors. "We do not return unsolicited material."

Tips: "Read *New Moon* to completely understand our needs."

RASPBERRY PUBLICATIONS INC., P.O. Box 925. Westerville OH 43086-6925. (800)759-7171. Fax: (614)899-6147. Book publisher. Publishes 6-10 books/year by children. "We believe what children write has value and children like to read what other children write." Purpose in publishing books by children: to provide opportunities for young authors to be published and motivate all children to write. Books must be written and illustrated by children from grades K-12. Writer's guidelines available for SASE.

Books: Publishes all genres of fiction; nonfiction should have educational value. Pays royalties, but no advances. Contact: Curt Jenkins, publisher. Submit complete ms for fiction and nonfiction. Will accept typewritten, legibly handwritten and computer-printed mss. Include SASE. Reports in 3 months.

Artwork/Photography: Publishes artwork and photography by children. Submit to Curt Jenkins, publisher.

Tips: "Be original and creative. Make sure you have solid beginning, middle and end. The 'conflict' should have a child as the main character, and should be resolved by the child without help from adults in the story. We are looking for good mysteries for our 'Raspberry Crime Files' series. Revise, revise, revise!"

*SHADOW MAGAZINE, P.O. Box 5464, Santa Rosa CA 95402. Phone/fax: (707)542-7114. E-mail: brianwts@aol.com. Quarterly magazine. "We publish quality fiction that will appeal to teens. We feel that young adults have the ability to write stories that will be the most interesting to their peers." Material must be presented in a professional manner.

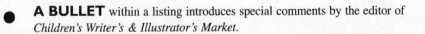

● **A BULLET** within a listing introduces special comments by the editor of *Children's Writer's & Illustrator's Market.*

Magazines: 10-20% of magazine written by young people. Uses 1-2 short fiction stories and various nonfiction articles/essays (1,000 words). Pays 2-3 sample copies. Submit mss to Brian P. Murphy, editor-in-chief. Submit complete ms. Will accept typewritten or disk mss and via e-mail. Include SASE. Reports in 1-2 months.

Tips: "Make sure the work you submit is polished and the best you can possibly do. We comment after and make a point to respond to work by students."

SHOFAR MAGAZINE, 43 Northcote Dr., Melville NY 11747. (516)643-4598. Fax: (516)643-4598. E-mail: graysonpsc@aol.com. Managing Editor: Gerald H. Grayson. Magazine published 6 times/school year. Audience consists of American Jewish children age 9-13. Purpose in publishing works by young people: to give them an opportunity to get their work printed.

Magazines: 10% of magazine written by young people. Uses fiction/nonfiction (750-1,000 words), Kids Page items (50-150 words). Submit mss to Gerald Grayson, publisher. Submit complete ms. Will accept typewritten, legibly handwritten mss and computer disk (Mac only). SASE. Reports in 2 months.

Artwork/Photography: Publishes artwork and photography by children. Pays "by the piece, depending on size and quantity." Submit original with SASE. Reports in 1-2 months.

SHOW AND TELL MAGAZINE, 2593 N. 140 W., Sunset UT 84015. Magazine. Published monthly. "*Show and Tell* was established to publish creative, classic fiction authored by writers ages 14-100. *Show and Tell's* audience is primarily readers/writers ages 18-70—well-read, open minded, creative readers." Purpose in publishing works by young people: "To show that children are just as creative and competent in writing fiction as adults. To give them a chance early in their lives and provide a fruitful outlet in a crazy, busy world. I am only interested in originality and proof that they had no help (significant) from an adult." Writer's guidelines available on request.

Magazines: 2% of magazine written by young people. (because of infrequent submissions only!) Uses 1 fiction story of any genre except horror (up to 2,000 words) per issue. Pays $5/story. Submit mss to Donna Clark, senior editor or Thomas Conger, associate editor (P.O. Box 11087, Salt Lake City, Utah 84147). Submit complete mss for fiction. Will accept typewritten and legibly handwritten mss. Include SASE. Reports in 1 month.

Artwork: Publishes artwork "if a child writer submits, with his or her submission, an illustration related to the story. I will do a simple photocopied paste-up of it near the story." Pays $5. Submit artwork as cleanly as possible, on a separate sheet of white paper, signed and labeled. Submit art to Donna Clark, senior editor. Include SASE. Reports in 1 month.

Tips: "Don't be afraid to express yourself, however, we are not interested in 'downer' fiction. Try hard for a positive ending."

SKIPPING STONES, Multicultural Children's Quarterly, P.O. Box 3939, Eugene OR 97403. (541)342-4956. Website: http://www.nonviolence.org/~nvweb/skipping/. Articles Editor: Arun N. Toké. Poetry/Fiction Editor: Rachel Johnson. Quarterly magazine. Estab. 1988. Circulation 3,000. "*Skipping Stones* is a multicultural, nonprofit, children's magazine to encourage cooperation, creativity and celebration of cultural and environmental richness. It offers itself as a creative forum for communication among children from different lands and backgrounds. We prefer work by children under 18 year olds. International, minorities and under represented populations receive priority, multilingual submissions are encouraged."

- *Skipping Stones* is winner of the 1995 Golden Shoestring Award of the Educational Press Association of America. Their theme for 1997 is "How I am making a difference . . ."

Magazines: 50% written by children. Uses 5-10 fiction short stories and plays (500-750 words); 5-10 nonfiction articles, interviews, letters, history, descriptions of celebrations (500-750 words); 15-20 poems, jokes, riddles, proverbs (250 words or less) per issue. Pays in contributor's copies. Submit mss to Arun Toké, editor. Submit complete ms for fiction or nonfiction work; teacher may submit; parents can also submit their contributions. Submissions should include "cover letter with name, age, address, school, cultural background, inspiration for piece, dreams for future . . . " Will accept typewritten, legibly handwritten and computer/word processor mss. Include SASE. Responds in 3 months. Accepts simultaneous submissions.

Artwork/Photography: Publishes artwork and photography for children. Will review all varieties of ms/illustration packages. Wants comics, cartoons, b&w photos, paintings, drawings (preferably, ink & pen or pencil), 8×10, color photos OK. Subjects include children, people, celebrations, nature, ecology, multicultural. Pays in contributor's copies.

Terms: "*Skipping Stones* is a labor of love. You'll receive complimentary contributor's (up to four) copies depending on the length of your contribution and illustrations." Reports back to

INSIDER REPORT

Publisher encourages good writing by children for children

"Raspberry fiction is more than feel-good fiction," says Curt Jenkins, whose company, Raspberry Publications, publishes books for children by children. Although many of his books include fantasy and humor, he says he's not afraid to tackle "the hard stuff, real life, nitty gritty" material. Children often deal with tough issues like disability, illness, violence and loss, and Jenkins feels these topics are suitable for children's books, especially if they are written by the children experiencing these things.

Curt Jenkins

Jenkins, a retired stockbroker, started his business three years ago. His partner, Susan Schmidt, who was then a director of photography, came across a book of ABCs written by a child for a younger cousin. It was a beautiful book and they were disappointed to learn there were few opportunities for publishing books by children. Determined to see *Hilary's Book of ABCs* in print, Jenkins and Schmidt decided to do it themselves.

"Maybe it would have been better if we had publishing experience when we started, but then we might not have taken the risk on that book. At first we had trouble finding new manuscripts. The first year we received 50 or 60, but now we get 400 to 500 to choose from. We don't publish a preset number of books each year. Last year we published six, but we do bring each book out in hardcover, softcover and audiotape, so each book we publish presents a triple expense," says Jenkins.

His business grew so rapidly that Jenkins hired two freelance editors to help with the manuscripts. His main markets are libraries and schools and he does all the marketing himself. "We're just getting to the point now where we are exploring co-publishing, licensing and distribution agreements with other publishers."

Raspberry books are sold all over the English-speaking world and one thing Jenkins discovered working with people in Australia, New Zealand and England is a difference in how children's work is valued. "While in this country we do value our children and what they want to do, adults here tend to place less value on what children produce and what they know."

At Raspberry, he says, they strongly value what children create and their ability to share their insight and experience with peers. Child authors are treated very much the same as adults. Children ages 6 to 16 can submit manuscripts all year long. They receive a contract, royalties (4 to 5 percent) and can go on promotional events (with their parents' permission).

In Raspberry Publications' *The Magic Pencil*, written and illustrated by Ariel J. Gonzalez at the age of 12, a boy finds a pencil in his school classroom which he discovers to be magic—whatever he draws with it comes to life. The boy "unconsciously doodles a black hole leading to another world," the land of Alibi, ruled by an evil viper. The boy is arrested and dragged to a dungeon by the viper and his soldiers. But with his magic pencil, he sketches "an army of giant yakkos" to save the day and free the Alibians from the viper. The book features a Parent's Guide and a Spanish translation in the back. Raspberry's books are published in hardcover, softcover and audio versions for consumers and libraries. Kids record audio books themselves.

INSIDER REPORT, *continued*

"When children do book signings, I think it's extremely motivational for them and for the other children coming to the event. The other kids say, 'Hey, I could do that too,' and they know someone out there is taking them seriously.

"I think contests like the National Written and Illustrated By contest offer excellent opportunities, but we provide a real-world experience. There aren't just one or two winners once a year. Some years we may publish up to 10 books."

When a young writer submits a story, Jenkins likes to see the entire manuscript along with a brief résumé, including the child's age, his school, the type of work he likes and how to contact him. Often, he says, children want to write and illustrate their books, but sometimes he'll pair a good illustrator with a writer. Illustrators should send examples of their work in black and white copies along with the same information as writers.

"No matter how many manuscripts we receive we return them with personal letters and often give ways the children can improve their writing. Teachers really welcome that. We don't try to overly encourage children, but we don't discourage anyone either."

Raspberry has a line of mysteries called Raspberry Crime Files. "We've been having trouble finding good manuscripts for our mystery line. These tend to be shorter stories and we put three or four in one paperback book. We don't want a lot of blood and gore, but there has to be a good mystery. A child must be the hero, must solve the mystery without the help of an adult, much the same as Nancy Drew used to do. And have it end on a good note."

For mysteries, as with all Raspberry books, Jenkins looks for a child's point of view. He doesn't want stories in which a child jumps in a car and drives to the scene of a crime. "Since children can't drive, I want the author to figure out exactly how the child will get around."

Jenkins has big plans for his company in the future. He is in the process of securing nonprofit status to start a magazine on writing for children and will soon be looking for pieces of artwork, poems and short articles and stories, all by children for children. He also hopes to award grants and scholarships in the future.

Jenkins says he's been encouraged by all the good writing and illustration he's received from children, as well as the popularity of his books with schools and libraries. For children, he gives the same advice publishers of adult books give: "Make sure your writing is good and you present a good story from beginning to middle to end. Ask yourself, 'Is this going to be interesting to somebody else?' Not just your dad or even the folks at your dad's office, but someone who doesn't know you. Good writing is good writing whether the writer is in elementary school or is an adult."

—Robin Gee

artists in 3 months. Sample copy for $5 and 8½ × 11 SAE with 4 first-class stamps.

Tips: "Let the 'inner child' within you speak out—naturally, uninhibited." Wants "material that gives insight on cultural celebrations, lifestyle, custom and tradition, glimpse of daily life in other countries and cultures. Please, no mystery for the sake of mystery! Photos, songs, artwork are most welcome if they illustrate/highlight the points. Upcoming features: How I am making a difference in the world, cooperative games and sports, religions and cultures from around the world, cycles of change: life and death, Native American cultures, street children, songs and recipes from around the world, resource conservation and sustainable lifestyles, indigenous architecture, living in the inner-city, grandparents and elders in your life, creative problem-solving approaches and substance abuse."

Sarah Roberts, an eighth grader at Rockford Middle School in Michigan, created this drawing with an international flavor for *Skipping Stones* magazine. It accompanied a poem called "Mother May I," written by Brooke Herron in the December '95 - January '96 issue. "We actively seek artwork by youth under 18 to illustrate the pages of *Skipping Stones*," says editor Arun Toké. He found Sarah's drawing to be "wonderfully done and visually attractive. We fell in love with it on first sight!"

SKYLARK, Purdue University Calumet, 2200 169th St., Hammond IN 46323. (219)989-2262. Editor: Pamela Hunter. Young Writers' Editor: Shirley Jo Moritz. Annual magazine. Circ. 650-1,000. 15% of material written by juvenile authors. Presently accepting material *by* children. "*Skylark* wishes to provide a vehicle for creative writing of all kinds, especially by writers ages five through eighteen, who live in the Illinois/Indiana area and who have not ordinarily been provided with such an outlet. Children need a place to see their work published alongside that of adults." Proof of originality is required from parents or teachers for all authors. Writer's guidelines available upon request.

Magazines: 15% of magazine written by young people. In previous issues, *Skylark* has published mysteries, fantasy, humor, good narrative fiction stories (400-1,000 words), personal essays, brief character sketches, nonfiction stories (400-650 words), poetry (no more than 16 lines). Does not want to see material that is obviously religious or sexual. Pays in contributor's copies. Submit ms to young writers' editor. Submit complete ms. Prefers typewritten ms. Must include SASE for response or return of material. Reports in 4 months. Byline given.

Artwork/Photography: Publishes artwork and photographs by children. Looks for "photos of animals, landscapes and sports, and for artwork to go along with text." Pays in contributor's copies. All artwork and photos must be b&w, 8½ × 11, unlined paper. Do not use pencil and no copyrighted characters. Markers are advised for best reproduction. Include name and address on the back of each piece. Package properly to avoid damage. Submit artwork/photos to Pamela Hunter, editor-in-chief. Include SASE. Reports in 5 months.

Tips: "Follow your feelings, be as original as you can and don't be afraid to be different. Some of our children or perhaps their teachers and parents don't understand that a SASE must accompany the submission in order to get a response or reply."

THE SOW'S EAR POETRY REVIEW, 19535 Pleasant View Dr., Abingdon VA 24211-6827. (703)628-2651. Magazine published quarterly. "Our editorial philosophy is to serve contemporary literature by publishing the best poetry we can find. Our audience includes serious poets throughout the U.S. We publish school-aged poets in most issues to encourage young writers and to show our older audience that able young poets are writing. We request young poets to furnish age, grade, school and list of any previous publication." Writer's guidelines available for SASE.

Magazines: 3% of magazine written by children. Uses 2-3 poems (1 page) per issue. Pays 1 copy. Submit complete ms to Larry K. Richman, managing editor. Will accept typewritten, legibly handwritten mss. SASE. Reports in 6 months.

STONE SOUP, The Magazine by Young Writers and Artists, Children's Art Foundation, P.O. Box 83, Santa Cruz CA 95063. (408)426-5557. Fax: (408)426-1161. E-mail: editor@stoneso up.com. Website: http://www.stonesoup.com. Articles/Fiction Editor, Art Director: Ms. Gerry Mandel. Magazine published 5 times/year. Circ. 20,000. "We publish fiction, poetry and artwork by children through age 13. Our preference is for work based on personal experiences and close observation of the world. Our audience is young people through age 13, as well as parents, teachers, librarians." Purpose in publishing works by young people: to encourage children to read and to express themselves through writing and art. Writer's guidelines available upon request.

Magazines: Uses animal, contemporary, fantasy, history, problem-solving, science fiction, sports, spy/mystery/adventure fiction stories. Uses 5-10 fiction stories (100-2,500 words), 5-10 nonfiction stories (100-2,500 words), 2-4 poems per issue. Does not want to see classroom assignments and formula writing. Buys 65 mss/year. Byline given. Pays on acceptance. Buys all rights. Pays $10 each for stories and poems, $15 for book reviews. Contributors also receive 2 copies. Sample copy $2. Free writer's guidelines. "We don't publish straight nonfiction, but we do publish stories based on real events and experiences." Send complete ms to Ms. Gerry Mandel, editor. Will accept typewritten and legibly handwritten mss. Include SASE. Reports in 1 month.

Artwork/Photography: Publishes any type, size or color artwork/photos by children. Pays $8 for b&w illustrations. Contributors receive 2 copies. Sample copy $2. Free illustrator's guidelines. Send originals if possible. Send submissions to Ms. Gerry Mandel, editor. Include SASE. Reports in 1 month. Original artwork returned at job's completion. All artwork must be by children through age 13.

Tips: "Be sure to enclose a SASE. Whether your work is about imaginary situations or real ones, use your own experiences and observations to give your work depth and a sense of reality."

STONEFLOWER LITERARY JOURNAL, 1824 Nacogdoches, Suite 191, San Antonio TX 78209. Magazine. Published annually. "We publish quality fiction and poetry with a section for children to age 16, which includes pen & ink drawings and b&w photography. Ours is a general reading audience with literary taste for good writing." Purpose in publishing works by young people: to encourage good writing and art among youth and to provide an outlet for their creative efforts. Submissions will be reviewed according to age group (i.e., work submitted by a child of 10 will only be compared to works by other children in his/her general age group and not to works by 16-year-olds). If possible, manuscripts should be typewritten. However, hand written or printed submissions will be considered if legibly written. We consider: poems to 25 lines; stories to 1,000 words; and pen & ink drawings. To teachers: if you organize a school project of submissions and want the mss or artwork returned, one SASE large enough to hold all mss or artwork is acceptable. All submissions should have the name, address, age, school attending, and grade clearly written on the top of all mss and on the back of art work. Submit a separate biographical page. The student's name should appear in the upper left corner of the "bio." Hobbies, participation in other school programs and activities, prior publications or honors, favorite pastimes, plans for the future, etc., should be included in the bio. Writer's guidelines available for SASE.

Magazine: 10% of magazine written by young people. Averages 2 fiction stories/issue (1,000 words), 5-10 poems/issue (25 lines). "Best of Issue" award given. Does not pay in copies. Submit mss to Brenda Davidson-Shaddox, editor. Submit complete fiction mss, poetry and art/photos, may submit as class project, fiction poetry and art/photo. Will accept typewritten and legibly handwritten mss. Include SASE. Reports in up to 3 months.

Artwork/Photography: Publishes pen & ink artwork and b&w photography. No color, please. Do not fold artwork. Looks for any subject except pornography. Pen & ink drawings (or top quality copies); 8½ × 11, no larger. Black & white photos. Pays $5/item. Submit to Brenda Davidson-Shaddox, editor. Include SASE. Reports in up to 3 months.

Tips: Submit quality work, clean and neat, shorter writing gets preference but only if of high standard. Keep copies of all submissions. We cannot be responsible for losses. Pay attention to guidelines and always include SASE. Submissions without SASE will be discarded. Send bio according to guidelines."

STRAIGHT MAGAZINE, Standard Publishing, 8121 Hamilton Ave., Cincinnati OH 45231. (513)931-4050. Fax: (513)931-0904. Magazine published weekly. Estab. 1951. Magazine includes fiction pieces and articles for Christian teens 13-19 years old to inform, encourage and uplift them. "*Straight* is a magazine for today's Christian teenagers. We use fiction and nonfiction to address modern-day problems from a Christian perspective." Purpose in publishing works by young people: to provide them with an opportunity to express themselves and communicate with their peers through poetry, fiction and nonfiction. Children must submit their birth dates and Social Security numbers. Writer's guidelines available on request, "included in regular guidelines."

Magazines: 15% of magazine written by children. Uses fiction (900-1,500 words), personal experience pieces (500-900 words), poetry (approximately 1 poem per issue). Pays flat fee for poetry; 5¢/word for stories/articles. Submit complete mss to Heather E. Wallace, editor. Will accept typewritten and computer printout mss. Reports in 1-2 months.

Artwork/Photography: Publishes artwork and photography by children. Send samples for review for consideration for assignment. Send samples for file to Heather Wallace, editor.

Tips: "Remember that we are a religious publication. Any submissions, including poetry should have a religious slant."

TEXAS YOUNG WRITERS' NEWSLETTER, P.O. Box 942, Adkins TX 78101-0942. E-mail: tywn1@aol.com. Newsletter. Published bimonthly during school year, monthly during summer. "Our audience is young writers 12-19, their teachers and their parents." Purpose in publishing works by young people: to give them an opportunity to publish their work in a reputable publication along with other talented young writers, and to show them that they can be published authors. Children must be 12-19 years old. "We do send a form for them to sign after their work is accepted that states that their work is original." Writer's guidelines available on request.

Magazines: 50% of magazine written by young people. Uses 1 fiction story (400-800 words) or 1 opinionated essay, personal experience, etc. (400-800 words), 2 poems (maximum 30 lines) per issue. "Very experienced young writers may submit articles discussing the art and business of writing; relate experience in cover letter." Pays 5 copies for stories, essays and articles; 2 copies for poetry. Submit mss to Susan Currie, editor. Submit fiction, nonfiction, poetry mss on disk, over e-mail. Will accept typewritten ms. Include SASE. Reports in 3 weeks.

Artwork: "Does not currently publish artwork by children, but we may in future! Write for current information."

Tips: "Be persistent and careful in your submissions! Keep trying until you've published. We also need articles on the art and business of writing from adults. Send SASE for guidelines. We appreciate cover letters!"

TURTLE MAGAZINE, Children's Better Health Institute, 1100 Waterway Blvd., P.O. Box 567, Indianapolis IN 46206. (317)636-8881. Magazine. "*Turtle* is a health-related magazine geared toward children from ages 2-5. *Turtle* seeks to entertain, educate and encourage children in healthy eating habits and fitness. Many of the features are interactive, providing a variety of resources for learning skills development." Purpose in publishing work by children/teens: "We want children to express their creativity and have an opportunity to share it with our audience."

Magazines: Submit ms to Nancy Axelrad, editor. Reports in 2-3 months.

Artwork: Publishes artwork by children in the "Our Own Pictures" regular features. Does not accept art with ms submissions. There is no payment for children's artwork. All artwork must have the child's name, age and complete address on it. Submit artwork to Bart Rivers, art director. "No artwork can be returned."

VIRGINIA WRITING, Longwood College, 201 High St., Farmville VA 23909. (804)395-2160. Magazine published twice yearly. "*Virginia Writing* publishes prose, poetry, fiction, nonfiction, art, photography, music and drama from Virginia high school students and teachers. The purpose of the journal is to publish 'promise,' giving the talented young people of Virginia an opportunity to have their works published. Our audience is mainly Virginia high schools, Virginia public libraries, Department of Education offices, and private citizens. It is also used as a supplementary text in many of Virginia's high school classrooms. The children must be attending a Virginia high school, preferably in no less than 9th grade (though some work has been accepted from 8th graders). Originality is strongly encouraged. The guidelines are in the front of our magazine or available with SASE." No profanity or racism accepted.

• *Virginia Writing* is the recipient of 12 national awards, including eight Distinguished Achievement Awards for Excellence in Educational Journalism and the Golden Lamp Honor Award as one of the top four educational magazines in the U.S. and Canada.

Magazines: 85% of magazine written by children. Uses approximately 5 fiction and nonfiction short stories, 56 poems and prose pieces per issue. Submit mss to Billy C. Clark, founder and editor. Submit complete ms. Will accept typewritten mss. Reports as soon as possible, "but must include SASE to receive a reply in the event manuscript is not accepted."

Artwork/Photography: Publishes artwork by children. Considers all types of artwork, including that done on computer. Color slides of artwork are acceptable. All original work is returned upon publication in a non-bendable, well protected package. Submit artwork to Billy C. Clark. Reports as soon as possible.

Tips: "All works should be submitted with a cover letter describing student's age, grade and high school currently attending. Submit as often as you like and in any quantity. We cannot accept a work if it features profanity or racism."

WHOLE NOTES, P.O. Box 1374, Las Cruces NM 88004. (505)382-7446. Magazine published twice yearly. "We look for original, fresh perceptions in poems that demonstrate skill in using language effectively, with carefully chosen images, clear ideas and fresh perceptions. Our audience (general) loves poetry. We try to recognize excellence in creative writing by children as a way to encourage and promote imaginative thinking." Writer's guidelines available for SASE.

Magazines: Every fourth issue is 100% by children. Writers should be 21 years old or younger. Uses 30 poems/issue (length open). Pays complimentary copy. Submit mss to Nancy Peters Hastings, editor. Submit complete ms. "No multiple submissions, please." Will accept typewritten and legibly handwritten mss. SASE. Reports in 3 weeks.

Artwork/Photography: Publishes artwork and photographs by children. Looks for b&w line drawings which can easily be reproduced; b&w photos. Pays complimentary copy. Send clear photocopies. Submit artwork to Nancy Peters Hastings, editor. SASE. Reports in 3 weeks.

Tips: Sample issue is $3. "We welcome translations."

WORD DANCE, Playful Productions, Inc., 59 Pavilions Dr., Manchester CT 06040. (203)648-2388. Magazine. Published quarterly. "We're a magazine of creative writing and art that is for *and* by children in kindergarten through grade 8."

Magazines: Uses adventure, fantasy, humorous, etc. (fiction); travel stories, poems and stories based on real life experiences (nonfiction). Publishes 250 total pieces of writing/year; maximum length: 3 pages. Submit mss to Stuart Ungar, articles editor. Sample copy $3. Free writer's guidelines and submissions form. SASE. Reports in 6-8 months.

Artwork: Illustrations accepted from young people in kindergarten through grade 8. Accepts illustrations of specific stories or poems and other general artwork. Must be high contrast. Query. Submit complete package with final art to Melissa Shapiro, art director. SASE. Reports in 6-8 months.

WRITERS' INTERNATIONAL FORUM, P.O. Box 516, Tracyton WA 98393. Magazine published bimonthly. Purpose in publishing works by young people: to promote an understanding of tight and clean traditional short story writing; this basis will serve young writers well as they and their writing mature. Our international readership offers a wide scope of opinions and helpful tips. Guidelines available with SASE; same as for adults, however. Please state age in cover letter.

Magazines: Publishes Special Juniors Edition twice a year, featuring stories which are all written either *by* children or *for* children. Also prints 1 or 2 stories in each standard issue written by children. Uses up to 12 fiction short stories, any genre (400-2,000 words) per issue. Pays $5 minimum on acceptance. Submit mss to Sandra E. Haven, editorial director. Submit complete ms with cover letter stating author's age. Will accept typewritten mss. Please send SASE for full guidelines *before* submitting. Reports in 2 months.

THE WRITERS' SLATE, (The Writing Conference, Inc.), P.O. Box 664, Ottawa KS 66067. (913)242-0407. Magazine. Publishes 3 issues/year. *The Writers' Slate* accepts original poetry and prose from students enrolled in kindergarten-12th grade. The audience is students, teachers and librarians. Purpose in publishing works by young people: to give students the opportunity to publish and to give students the opportunity *to read* quality literature written by other students. Writer's guidelines available on request.
Magazines: 90% of magazine written by young people. Uses 10-15 fiction, 1-2 nonfiction, 10-15 other mss per issue. Submit mss to Dr. F. Todd Goodson, editor, Dept. of English, East Carolina University, Greenville NC 27858-4353. Submit complete ms. Will accept typewritten mss. Reports in 1 month. Include SASE with ms if reply is desired.
Artwork: Publishes artwork by young people. Bold, b&w, student artwork may accompany a piece of writing. Submit to Dr. F. Todd Goodson, editor. Reports in 1 month.

WRITES OF PASSAGE, 817 Broadway, 6th Floor, New York NY 10003. Phone/fax: (212)473-7564. E-mail: wpusa@aol.com. Website: http://www.writes.org. Journal. Publishes 2 issues/year by children (spring/summer and fall/winter). "Our philosophy: 'It may make your parents cringe, your teacher blush, but your best friend will understand.' " Purpose in publishing works by young people: to give teenagers across the country a chance to express themselves through creative writing. Writers must be 12-18 years old, work must be original, short biography should be included. "We are also accepting columns of tips and advice for our young readers to be posted on the website."
 • To learn more about *Writes of Passage*, see the Insider Report with Wendy Mass in the 1996 edition of *Children's Writer's & Illustrator's Market*.
Magazines: Uses short stories (up to 4 double-spaced pages) and poetry. Pays in two copies. Submit to Laura Hoffman, president. Will accept typewritten and legibly handwritten mss. SASE. Reports in 2 months. Sample copies available for $6. Writer's guidelines for SASE.
Tips: "We began *Writes of Passage* to encourage teenage reading and writing as fun and desirable forms of expression and to establish an open dialogue between teenagers in every state. Our selection process does not censor topics and presents submissions according to the authors' intentions. It gives teens an opportunity to expand on what they have learned in reading and writing classes in school by opening up a world of writing in which they can be free. As a result, submissions often reveal a surprising candidness on the part of the authors, including topics such as love, fear, struggle and death and they expose the diverse backgrounds of contributors."

WRITING!, 900 Skokie Blvd., Suite 200, Northbrook IL 60062. (708)205-3000. Magazine published monthly September-May. Purpose in publishing work by young people: "to teach students to write and write well; grades 6-12. *Writing!* prints well-written, creative, and original writing by students to inspire other students. Should indicate age, address, school and teacher with submission. No formal guidelines; but letter is sent if request received."
Magazines: Small percentage of magazine written by children. Uses 1-10 mss/issue. No pay for student writing. Submit mss to Carol Elliott, editor. Submit complete ms; include student's age, address, school and teacher with submission; either child or child's teacher may submit. Prefers typewritten mss. Include SASE.

YOUNG VOICES MAGAZINE, P.O. Box 2321, Olympia WA 98507. (360)357-4683. E-mail: patcha@aol.com. Magazine published bimonthly. "*Young Voices* is by elementary and high school students for people interested in their work." Purpose in publishing work by young people: to provide a forum for their creative work. "Home schooled writers *definitely* welcome, too." Writer's guidelines available on request with SASE.
Magazines: Uses 20 fiction stories, 5 reviews, 5 essays and 5 poems per issue (lengths vary). Pays $3-5 on acceptance (more depending on the length and quality of the writing). Submit mss to Steve Charak. Query first. Will accept typewritten and legibly handwritten mss. SASE. Reports in 2 months.
Artwork/Photography: Publishes artwork and photography by children. "Prefer work that will show up in black and white." Pays $3-5 on acceptance. Submit artwork to Steve Charak. SASE. Reports in 2 months.

Resources

Clubs & Organizations

Contacts made through organizations such as the ones listed in this section can be quite beneficial for children's writers and illustrators. Professional organizations provide numerous educational, business and legal services in the form of newsletters, workshops or seminars. Organizations can provide tips about how to be better writers or artists, as well as what types of business records to keep, health and life insurance coverage to carry and competitions to consider.

An added benefit of belonging to an organization is the opportunity to network with those who have similar interests, creating a support system. As in any business, knowing the right people can often help your career, and important contacts can be made through your peers. Membership in a writer's or artist's group also shows publishers you're serious about your craft. This provides no guarantee your work will be published, but it gives you an added dimension of credibility and professionalism.

Some of the organizations listed here welcome anyone with an interest, while others are only open to published writers and professional artists. A few marked with a double dagger (‡) are open to student membership. Others, such as the Society of Children's Book Writers and Illustrators (SCBWI), have varying levels of membership. SCBWI offers associate membership to those with no publishing credits, and full membership to those who have had work for children published. Many national organizations such as SCBWI also have regional chapters throughout the country. Write or call for more information regarding any group that sounds interesting, or check the websites of the many organizations that list them. Be sure to get information about local chapters, membership qualifications, and services offered.

‡**AMERICAN ALLIANCE FOR THEATRE & EDUCATION**, Theatre Department, Arizona State University, Box 873411, Tempe AZ 85287-3411. (602)965-6064. Administrative Director: Katherine Krzys. Purpose of organization: to promote standards of excellence in theater and drama education by providing the artist and educator with a network of resources and support, a base for advocacy, and access to programs and projects that focus on the importance of drama in the human experience. Membership cost: $75 annually for individual in US and Canada, $100 annually for organization, $45 annually for students, $55 annually for retired people; add $20 outside Canada and US. Annual conference held jointly with the Educational Theatre Association in Charlotte, NC, August 1997. Newsletter published quarterly; must be member to subscribe. Contests held for unpublished play reading project and annual awards for best play for K-8 and 1 for secondary audience. Awards plaque and stickers for published playbooks. Publishes list of unpublished plays deemed worthy of performance in newsletter and press release, and staged readings at conference.

 THE DOUBLE DAGGER before a listing indicates the organization is open to students.

AMERICAN SOCIETY OF JOURNALISTS AND AUTHORS, 1501 Broadway, New York NY 10036. (212)997-0947. Fax: (212)768-7414. E-mail: 75227.1650@compuserve.com. Executive Director: Alexandra Owens. Qualifications for membership: "Need to be a professional nonfiction writer published 8-10 times in general circulation publications." Membership cost: Initiation fee—$100; annual dues—$165. Group sponsors national conferences; monthly workshops in New York City. Workshops/conferences open to nonmembers. Publishes a newsletter for members that provides confidential information for nonfiction writers.

‡ARIZONA AUTHORS ASSOCIATION, 3509 E. Shea Blvd., #117, Phoenix AZ 85028-3339. (602)867-9001. President: Iva Martin. Purpose of organization: to offer professional, educational and social opportunities to writers and authors and serve as a network. Qualifications for membership: 1) must be a writer or 2) an agent or publisher. Membership cost: $40/year professional and associate; $50/year affiliate; $25/year student. Different levels of membership include: Professional—published writers; Associate—writers working toward publication; Affiliate—professionals in publishing industry; Student—full-time students. Holds monthly educational workshops; contact office for current calendar. Publishes newsletter providing information useful to writers (markets, book reviews, calendar of meetings and events) and news about members. Nonmember subscription $25/year. Sponsors Annual Literary Contest. Awards include total of $1,000 in prizes in several categories. Contest open to non-members.

‡ASSITEJ/USA, % Jen Marlowe, P.O. Box 22365, Seattle WA 98122-0365. (206)392-2147. Fax: (206)443-0442. Editor, *TYA Today*: Cyndi Pock. Purpose of organization: to promote theater for children and young people by linking professional theaters and artists together; sponsoring national, international and regional conferences; and providing publications and information. Also serves as US Center for International Association of Theatre for Children and Young People. Membership cost: $100 for organizations with budgets below $250,000; $200 for organizations with budgets of $250,000-$999,000; $300 for organizatons with budgets over $1 million; $50 annually/individual; $30 libraries; $25 students and retirees; $65 for foreign organizations or individuals outside the US; $30 for library rate. Different levels of membership include: organizations, individuals, students, retirees, corresponding, libraries. *TYA Today* includes original articles, reviews and works of criticism and theory, all of interest to theater practitioners (included with membership). Sponsors workshops or conferences. Publishes journal that focuses on information on field in US and abroad.

♣CANADIAN SOCIETY OF CHILDREN'S AUTHORS, ILLUSTRATORS AND PERFORMERS, (CANSCAIP), 35 Spadina Rd., Toronto, Ontario M5R 2S9 Canada. (416)515-1559. Secretary: Nancy Prasad. Purpose of organization: development of Canadian children's culture and support for authors, illustrators and performers working in this field. Qualifications for membership: Members—professionals who have been published (not self-published) or have paid public performances/records/tapes to their credit. Friends—share interest in field of children's culture. Membership cost: $60 (members dues), $25 (friends dues), $30 (institution dues). Sponsors workshops/conferences. Publishes newsletter: includes profiles of members; news round-up of members' activities countrywide; market news; news on awards, grants, etc; columns related to professional concerns.

‡LEWIS CARROLL SOCIETY OF NORTH AMERICA, 18 5th Harding Place, Owensmill MD 21117. (410)356-5110. Secretary: Ellen Leuchinsky. "We are an organization of Carroll admirers of all ages and interests and a center for Carroll studies." Qualifications for membership: "An interest in Lewis Carroll and a simple love for Alice (or even the Snark)." Membership cost: $20/year. There is also a contributing membership of $50. Publishes a newsletter.

THE CHILDREN'S BOOK COUNCIL, INC., 568 Broadway, New York NY 10012. (212)966-1990. Website: http://www.cbcbooks.org/index.html. Purpose of organization: "A nonprofit trade association of children's and young adult publishers, CBC promotes the enjoyment of books for children and young adults, and works with national and international organizations

---

♣ **THE MAPLE LEAF** before a listing indicates that it is Canadian.

to that end. The CBC has sponsored National Children's Book Week since 1945." Qualifications for membership: US trade publishers of children's and young adult books are eligible for membership. Membership cost: "Individuals wishing to receive mailings from the CBC (our semi-annual newsletter, *CBC Features*, and our materials brochures) may be placed on our mailing list for a one-time-only fee of $60. Publishers wishing to join should contact the CBC for dues information." Sponsors workshops and seminars. Publishes a newsletter with articles about children's books and publishing, and listings of free or inexpensive materials available from member publishers. Sells reading encouragement graphics and informational materials suitable for libraries, teachers, booksellers, parents, and others working with children.

FLORIDA FREELANCE WRITERS ASSOCIATION, Cassell Network of Writers, P.O. Box A, North Stratford NH 03590. (603)922-8338. Fax: (603)922-8339. E-mail: fjwx43b@prodigy.com. Executive Director: Dana K. Cassell. Purpose of organization: To act as a link between Florida writers and buyers of the written word; to help writers run more effective communications businesses. Qualifications for membership: "None—we provide a variety of services and information, some for beginners and some for established pros." Membership cost: $90/year. Publishes a newsletter focusing on market news, business news, how-to tips for the serious writer. Nonmember subscription: $39—does not include Florida section—includes national edition only. Annual *Directory of Florida Markets* included in FFWA newsletter section. Publishes annual *Guide to CNW/Florida Writers*. Sponsors contest: annual deadline March 15. Guidelines available fall of year. Categories: juvenile, adult nonfiction, adult fiction. Awards include cash for top prizes, certificate for others. Contest open to non-members.

*GRAPHIC ARTISTS GUILD, 11 W. 20th St., New York NY 10011-3704. (212)463-7730. Fax: (212)463-8779. Website: http://www.gag.org/. Executive Director: Paul Basista, CAE. Purpose of organization: "to promote and protect the economic interests of member artists. It is committed to improving conditions for all creators of graphic arts and raising standards for the entire industry." Qualification for full membership: 51% of income derived from artwork. Associate members include those in allied fields, students and retirees. Initiation fee: $25. Full memberships $110, $150, $195, $245; student membership $55/year. Associate membership $105/year. Publishes *Graphic Artists Guild Handbook, Pricing and Ethical Guidelines* and quarterly *Guild News* (free to members, $15 to non-members). "The Guild is an egalitarian union that embraces all creators of graphics arts intended for presentation as originals or reproductions at all levels of skill and expertise. The long-range goals of the Guild are: to educate graphic artists and their clients about ethical and fair business practices; to educate graphic artists about emerging trends and technologies impacting the industry; to offer programs and services that anticipate and respond to the needs of our members, helping them prosper and enhancing their health and security; to advocate for the interests of our members in the legislative, judicial and regulatory arenas; to assure that our members are recognized financially and professionally for the value they provide; to be responsible stewards for our members by building an organization that works efficiently on their behalf."

THE INTERNATIONAL WOMEN'S WRITING GUILD, P.O. Box 810, Gracie Station, New York NY 10028. (212)737-7536. Executive Director and Founder: Hannelore Hahn. IWWG is "a network for the personal and professional empowerment of women through writing." Qualifications: open to any woman connected to the written word regardless of professional portfolio. Membership cost: $35 annually; $45 annually for foreign members. "IWWG sponsors 13 annual conferences a year in all areas of the US. The major conference is held in August of each year at Skidmore College in Saratoga Springs NY. It is a week-long conference attracting more than 400 women internationally." Also publishes a 32-page newsletter, *Network*, 6 times/year; offers health insurance at group rates, referrals to literary agents.

JEWISH PUBLICATION SOCIETY, 1930 Chestnut St., Philadelphia PA 19103-4599. (215)564-5925. Editor-in-Chief: Dr. Ellen Frankel. Children's Editor: Bruce Black. Purpose of organization: "To publish quality Jewish books and to promote Jewish culture and education. We are a non-denominational, nonprofit religious publisher. Our children's list specializes in fiction and nonfiction with substantial Jewish content for pre-school through young adult readers." Qualifications for membership: "One must purchase a membership of at least $25, which entitles the member to purchase a certain unit number of our books. Our membership is nondiscriminatory on the basis of religion, ethnic affiliation, race or any other criteria." Levels of membership include: JPS member, $25; Associate, $50; Friend, $100; Fellow, $125; Senior member, $200; Sustaining member, $500. "*The JPS Bookmark* reports on JPS Publications; activities of members, authors and trustees; JPS projects and goals; JPS history; children's books and activities." All members receive *The Bookmark* with their membership.

*‡LITERARY MANAGERS AND DRAMATURGS OF THE AMERICAS, Box 355, CASTA, CUNY Grad Center, 33 W. 42nd St., New York NY 10036. (212)642-2657. Fax: (212)642-1977. E-mail: ltimmel@email.gc.cuny.edu. LMDA is a not-for-profit service organization for the professions of literary management and dramaturgy. Student Membership: $20/year. Open to students in dramaturgy, performing arts and literature programs, or related disciplines. Proof of student status required. Includes national conference, New Dramaturg activities, local symposia, job phone and select membership meetings. Active Membership: $45/year. Open to full-time and part-time professionals working in the fields of literary management and dramaturgy. All privileges and services including voting rights and eligibility for office. Associate Membership: $35/year. Open to all performing arts professionals and academics, as well as others interested in the field. Includes national conference, local symposia and select membership meetings. Institutional Membership: $100/year. Open to theaters, universities, and other organizations. Includes all privileges and services except voting rights and eligibility for office. Publishes a newsletter featuring articles on literary management, dramaturgy, LMDA program updates and other articles of interest.

NATIONAL WRITERS ASSOCIATION, 1450 S. Havana, Suite 424, Aurora CO 80012. (303)751-7844. Executive Director: Sandy Whelchel. Purpose of organization: association for freelance writers. Qualifications for membership: associate membership—must be serious about writing; professional membership—must be published and paid writer (cite credentials). Membership cost: $50-associate; $60-professional. Sponsors workshops/conferences: TV/screenwriting workshops, NWA Annual Conferences, Literary Clearinghouse, editing and critiquing services, local chapters, National Writer's School. Open to non-members. Publishes industry news of interest to freelance writers; how-to articles; market information; member news and networking opportunities. Nonmember subscription $18. Sponsors poetry contest; short story contest; article contest; novel contest. Awards cash for top 3 winners; books and/or certificates for other winners; honorable mention certificate places 11-20. Contests open to nonmembers.

NATIONAL WRITERS UNION, 113 University Place, 6th Floor, New York NY 10003. (212)254-0279. Office Manager: Ron Johnson. Purpose of organization: Advocacy for freelance writers. Qualifications for membership: "Membership in the NWU is open to all qualified writers, and no one shall be barred or in any manner prejudiced within the Union on account of race, age, sex, sexual preference, disability, national origin, religion or ideology. You are eligible for membership if you have published a book, a play, three articles, five poems, one short story or an equivalent amount of newsletter, publicity, technical, commercial, government or institutional copy. You are also eligible for membership if you have written an equal amount of unpublished material and you are actively writing and attempting to publish your work." Membership cost: annual writing income under $5,000—$80/year; annual writing income $5,000-25,000—$132/year; annual writing income over $25,000—$180/year. National union newsletter quarterly, issues related to freelance writing and to union organization. Non-member subscription: $15.

PEN AMERICAN CENTER, 568 Broadway, New York NY 10012. (212)334-1660. Fax: (212)334-2181. Purpose of organization: "To foster understanding among men and women of letters in all countries. International PEN is the only worldwide organization of writers and the chief voice of the literary community. Members of PEN work for freedom of expression wherever it has been endangered." Qualifications for membership: "The standard qualification for a writer to join PEN is that he or she must have published, in the United States, two or more books of a literary character, or one book generally acclaimed to be of exceptional distinction. Editors who have demonstrated commitment to excellence in their profession (generally construed as five years' service in book editing), translators who have published at least two book-length literary

* THE ASTERISK before a listing indicates the listing is new in this edition.

translations, and playwrights whose works have been professionally produced, are eligible for membership." An application form is available upon request from PEN Headquarters in New York. Candidates for membership should be nominated by two current members of PEN. Inquiries about membership should be directed to the PEN Membership Committee. Friends of PEN is also open to writers who may not yet meet the general PEN membership requirements. PEN sponsors public events at PEN Headquarters in New York, and at the branch offices in Boston, Chicago, New Orleans, San Francisco and Portland, Oregon. They include tributes by contemporary writers to classic American writers, dialogues with visiting foreign writers, symposia that bring public attention to problems of censorship and that address current issues of writing in the United States, and readings that introduce beginning writers to the public. PEN's wide variety of literary programming reflects current literary interests and provides informal occasions for writers to meet each other and to welcome those with an interest in literature. Events are all open to the public and are usually free of charge. The Children's Book Authors' Committee sponsors biannual public events focusing on the art of writing for children and young adults and on the diversity of literature for juvenile readers. The PEN/Norma Klein Award was established in 1991 to honor an emerging children's book author. National union newsletter covers PEN activities, features interviews with international literary figures, transcripts of PEN literary symposia, reports on issues vital to the literary community. All PEN publications are available by mail order directly from PEN American Center. Individuals must enclose check or money order with their order. Subscription: $8 for 4 issues; sample issue $2. Pamphlets and brochures all free upon request. Sponsors several competitions per year. Monetary awards range from $700-7,500.

PLAYMARKET, P.O. Box 9767, Te Aro Wellington New Zealand. Phone/fax: 0064(4)3828461. Executive Officer: John McDavitt. Script Advisor: Susan Wilson. Purpose of organization: funded by the Arts Council of New Zealand, Playmarket serves as New Zealand's script advisory service and playwrights agency. Playmarket offers script assessment, development and agency services to help New Zealand playwrights secure professional production for their plays. Playmarket also assists with negotiations for film and television, radio and publishing. Holds workshops/conferences. Publishes *Playmarket Directory of New Zealand Plays and Playwrights*. Nonmember subscription $10/year. Assists with the Bruce Mason Award: "*Sunday Star Times* Bruce Mason Award for Playwright at Beginning of Career." Award includes $5,000 annually. Contest open to nonmembers.

PUPPETEERS OF AMERICA, INC., #5 Cricklewood Path, Pasadena CA 91107. (818)797-5748. Membership Officer: Gayle Schluter. Purpose of organization: to promote the art of puppetry. Qualifications for membership: interest in the art form. Membership cost: single adult, $35; junior member, $20; retiree, $35 ($25 after member for 5 years); group or family, $55; couple, $45. Membership includes a bimonthly newsletter. Sponsors workshops/conferences. Publishes newsletter. *The Puppetry Journal* provides news about puppeteers, puppet theaters, exhibitions, touring companies, technical tips, new products, new books, films, television, and events sponsored by the Chartered Guilds in each of the eight P of A regions. Subscription: $30.

SCIENCE-FICTION AND FANTASY WRITERS OF AMERICA, INC., 5 Winding Brook Dr., #1B, Guilderland NY 12084. (518)869-5361. Executive Secretary: Peter Dennis Pautz. Purpose of organization: to encourage public interest in science fiction literature and provide organization format for writers/editors/artists within the genre. Qualifications for membership: at least 1 professional sale or other professional involvement within the field. Membership cost: annual active dues—$50; affiliate—$35; one-time installation fee of $10; dues year begins July 1. Different levels of membership include: active—requires 3 professional short stories or 1 novel published; affiliate—requires 1 professional sale or professional involvement. Workshops/conferences: annual awards banquet, usually in April or May. Open to nonmembers. Publishes newsletter. Nonmember subscription: $15 in US. Sponsors SFWA Nebula® Awards for best published science fiction in the categories of novel, novella, novelette and short story. Awards trophy.

SOCIETY OF CHILDREN'S BOOK WRITERS AND ILLUSTRATORS, 22736 Vanowen St., Suite 106, West Hills CA 91307. (818)888-8760. Website: http://www.scbwi.org. Chairperson, Board of Directors: Sue Alexander. Purpose of organization: to assist writers and illustrators working or interested in the field. Qualifications for membership: an interest in children's literature and illustration. Membership cost: $50/year. Different levels of membership include: full membership—published authors/illustrators; associate membership—unpublished writers/

illustrators. Holds 30-40 events (workshops/conferences) around the country each year. Open to nonmembers. Publishes a newsletter focusing on writing and illustrating children's books. Sponsors grants for writers and illustrators who are members.

SOCIETY OF ILLUSTRATORS, 128 E. 63rd St., New York NY 10021. (212)838-2560. Director: Terrence Brown. Purpose of organization: to promote interest in the art of illustration for working professional illustrators and those in associated fields. Membership cost: Initiation fee—$250. Annual dues for Non-resident members (those living more than 125 air miles from SI's headquarters) are $240. Dues for Resident Artist Members are $416 per year; Resident Associate Members $480. Different levels of membership: *Artist Members* "shall include those who make illustration their profession" and through which they earn at least 60% of their income. *Associate Members* are "those who earn their living in the arts or who have made a substantial contribution to the art of illustration." This includes art directors, art buyers, creative supervisors, instructors, publishers and like categories. "All candidates for membership are admitted by the proposal of one active member and sponsorship of four additional members. The candidate must complete and sign the application form which requires a brief biography, a listing of schools attended, other training and a résumé of his or her professional career." Candidates for *Artist* membership, in addition to the above requirements, must submit examples of their work. Sponsors "The Annual of American Illustration." Awards include gold and silver medals. Open to nonmembers. Deadline: October 1. Sponsors "The Original Art: The Best of Children's Book Illustration." Deadline: mid-September. Call for details.

SOCIETY OF MIDLAND AUTHORS, % SMA, P.O. 10419, Chicago IL 60610-0419. Purpose of organization: create closer association among writers of the Middle West; stimulate creative literary effort; maintain collection of members' works; encourage interest in reading and literature by cooperating with other educational and cultural agencies. Qualifications for membership: author or co-author of a book demonstrating literary style and published by a recognized publisher or author of published or professionally produced play and be identified through residence with Illinois, Indiana, Iowa, Kansas, Michigan, Minnesota, Missouri, Nebraska, North Dakota, Ohio, South Dakota or Wisconsin. Membership cost: $25/year dues. Different levels of membership include: regular—published book authors; associate, nonvoting—not published as above but having some connection with literature, such as librarians, teachers, publishers, and editors. Program meetings at 410 Club, Chicago, held 5 times a year, featuring authors, publishers, editors or the like individually or on panels. Usually second Tuesday of October, November, February, March and April. Also holds annual awards dinner at 410 Club, Chicago, writers. Non-member subscription: $5. Sponsors contests. "Annual awards in six categories, given at annual dinner in May. Monetary awards for books published which premiered professionally in previous calendar year. Send SASE to contact person for details." Categories include adult fiction, adult nonfiction, biography, juvenile fiction, juvenile nonfiction, poetry, biography. No picture books. Contest open to non-members. Deadline for contest: January 1.

SOCIETY OF SOUTHWESTERN AUTHORS, P.O. Box 30355, Tucson AZ 85751-0355. Fax: (520)296-5562. President: Darrell Beach. Purpose of organization: to promote fellowship among members of the writing profession, to recognize members' achievements, to stimulate further achievement, and to assist persons seeking to become professional writers. Qualifications for membership: proof of publication of a book, articles, TV screenplay, etc. Membership cost: $25 initiation plus $20/year dues. The Society of Southwestern Authors has annual Writers' Conference, traditionally held the last Saturday of January (write for more information). Publishes a newsletter, *The Write Word*, about members' activities and news of interest to members. Each spring a short story contest is sponsored. Contest open to non-members. Applications are available in September. Send SASE to the P.O. Box, Attn: Contest.

VOLUNTEER LAWYERS FOR THE ARTS, 1 E. 53rd St., 6th Floor, New York NY 10022-4201. (212)319-2787 (administration); (212)319-2910 (Art Law Line) Fax: (212)752-6575. Acting Executive Director: Nancy Adelson. Purpose of organization: Volunteer Lawyers for the Arts is dedicated to providing free arts-related legal assistance to low-income artists and not-for-profit arts organizations in all creative fields. Over 800 attorneys in the New York area donate their time through VLA to artists and arts organizations unable to afford legal counsel. There is no membership required for our services. Everyone is welcome to use VLA's Art Law Line, a legal hotline for any artist or arts organization needing quick answers to arts-related questions. VLA also provides clinics, seminars and publications designed to educate artists on legal issues which affect their careers. Membership is through donations and is not required to use our services. Members receive discounts on publications and seminars as well as other benefits.

*WESTERN WRITERS OF AMERICA, INC., 1012 Fair St., Franklin TN 37064. (615)791-1444. Fax: (615)791-1444. Secretary/Treasurer: James A. Crutchfield. Purpose of organization: to further all types of literature that pertains to the American West. Membership requirements: must be a *published* author of Western material. Membership cost: $60/year ($80 foreign). Different levels of membership include: Active and Associate—the 2 vary upon number of books published. Holds annual convention. Publishes bimonthly magazine focusing on market trends, book reviews, news of members, etc. Non-members may subscribe for $30 ($40 foreign). Sponsors contests. Spur awards given annually for a variety of types of writing. Awards include plaque, certificate, publicity. Contest open to nonmembers.

THE WRITERS ALLIANCE, 12 Skylark Lane, Stony Brook NY 11790. (516)751-7080. Executive Director: Kiel Stuart. Purpose of organization: "a support/information group for all types of writers." Membership cost: $10/year, payable to Kiel Stuart. A corporate/group membership costs $15. Sponsors conference. Publishes newsletter for all writers who use (or want to learn about) computers; features reviews, how-tos, computer information, poetry, essays, and market information. Nonmember subscription $10—payable to Kiel Stuart.

‡WRITERS CONNECTION, P.O. Box 24770, San Jose CA 95154-4770. (408)445-3600. Fax: (408)445-3609. Editor: Jan Stiles. Vice President/Program Director: Meera Lester. Purpose of organization: to provide services and resources for writers. Qualifications for membership: interest in writing or publishing. Membership cost: $45/year. Conferences: Selling to Hollywood and various genre conferences, including writing for children. Publishes a newsletter focusing on writing and publishing (all fields except poetry), how-to, markets, contests, tips, etc., included with membership. Subscription $25.

✦‡WRITERS' FEDERATION OF NEW BRUNSWICK, Box 37, Station A, 404 Queen St., Fredericton, New Brunswick E3B 4Y2 Canada. (506)459-7228. Project Coordinator: Anna Mae Snider. Purpose of organization: "to promote the work of New Brunswick writers and to help them at all stages of their development." Qualifications for membership: interest in writing. Membership cost: $30, basic annual membership; $20, student/unemployed; $40, family membership; $50, institutional membership; $100, sustaining member; $250, patron; and $1,000, lifetime member. Holds workshops/conferences. Publishes a newsletter with articles concerning the craft of writing, member news, contests, markets, workshops and conference listings. Sponsors annual literary competition (for New Brunswick residents). Categories: fiction, nonfiction, poetry, children's literature—3 prizes per category of $200, $100, $30; Alfred Bailey Prize of $400 for poetry ms; The Richards Prize of $400 for short novel, collection of short stories or section of long novel; The Sheree Fitch Prize for writing by young people (14-18 years of age). Contest open to nonmembers (residents of New Brunswich only).

✦‡WRITERS GUILD OF ALBERTA, 11759 Groat Rd., 3rd Floor, Percy Page Centre, Edmonton, Alberta T5M 3K6 Canada. (403)422-8174. Fax: (403)422-2663. Executive Director: Mr. Miki Andrejevic. Purpose of organization: to provide meeting ground and collective voice for the writers in Alberta. Membership cost: $55/year; $20 for seniors/students. Holds workshops/conferences. Publishes a newsletter focusing on markets, competitions, contemporary issues related to the literary arts (writing, publishing, censorship, royalties etc.). Nonmembers may subscribe to newsletter. Subscription cost: $55/year. Sponsors annual literary awards program in 7 categories (novel, nonfiction, short fiction, children's literature, poetry, drama, best first book). Awards include $500, leather-bound book, promotion and publicity. Open to nonmembers.

‡WRITERS OF KERN, P.O. Box 6694, Bakersfield CA 93386-6694. (805)871-5834. Open to published writers and any person interested in writing. Dues: $35/year, $20 for students. Types of memberships: professional—writers with published work; associate—writers working toward publication, affiliate—beginners and students. Monthly meetings held on the third Saturday of every month, except September which is our conference month, with speakers who are authors, agents, etc., on topics pertaining to writing; critique groups for several fiction genres, nonfiction, journalism and screenwriting which meet weekly or biweekly. Members receive a monthly newsletter with marketing tips, conferences and contests; access to club library; discount to annual conference. Annual conference held the third Saturday in September; annual writing contest with winners announced at the conference. Send SASE for information.

Conferences & Workshops

Writers and illustrators eager to expand their knowledge of the children's industry should consider attending one of the many conferences and workshops held each year. Whether you're a novice or seasoned professional, conferences and workshops are great places to pick up information on a variety of topics and network with experts in the publishing industry, as well as your peers.

Many conferences and workshops included here focus on children's writing or illustrating and related business issues. Others appeal to a broader base of writers or artists, but still provide information that can be useful in creating material for children. Illustrators may be interested in painting and drawing workshops, for example, while writers can learn about techniques and meet editors and agents at general writing conferences. Workshops in this section which are open to student participants are marked with a double dagger (‡).

Listings in this section provide details about what conference and workshop courses are offered, where and when they are held, and the costs. Some of the national writing and art organizations also offer regional workshops throughout the year. Write or call them for information.

Artists can find a detailed directory of annual art workshops offered around the globe in the March issue of *The Artist's Magazine*. Writers should consult the May issue of *Writer's Digest*.

AMERICAN CHRISTIAN WRITERS CONFERENCE, P.O. Box 110390, Nashville TN 37222. 1(800)21-WRITE or (615)834-0450. Director: Reg Forder. Writer and illustrator workshops geared toward beginner, intermediate and advanced levels. Classes offered include: fiction, nonfiction, poetry, photography, music, etc. Workshops held in a two dozen US cities. Call or write for a complete schedule of conferences. 75 minutes. Maximum class size: 30 (approximate). Cost of conference: $99, 1-day session; $169, 2-day session; $229, 3-day session (discount given if paid 30 days advance).

AUTUMN AUTHORS' AFFAIR XIV, 1507 Burnham Ave., Calumet City IL 60409. (708)862-9797. President: Nancy McCann. Writer workshops geared toward beginner, intermediate, advanced levels. Emphasizes writing for children and young adults. Annual workshop. Workshops held generally the fourth weekend in October. Cost of workshop: $75 for 1 day, $120 for weekend, includes meals Friday night, Saturday morning and Saturday afternoon; dessert buffet Saturday night and breakfast/brunch Sunday morning. Write for more information.

BE THE WRITER YOU WANT TO BE—MANUSCRIPT CLINIC, Villa 30, 23350 Sereno Court, Cupertino CA 95014. (415)691-0300. Contact: Louise Purwin Zobel. Writer workshops geared toward beginner, intermediate, advanced levels. "Participants may turn in manuscripts at any stage of development to receive help with structure and style, as well as marketing advice. Manuscripts receive some written criticism and an oral critique from the instructor, as well as class discussion." Annual workshop. Usually held in the spring. Registration limited to 20-25. Cost of workshop: $45-65/day, depending on the campus; includes an extensive handout. SASE for more information.

*CELEBRATION OF CHILDREN'S LITERATURE, 51 Mannakee St., Office of Continuing Education, Room 220, Rockville MD 20850. (301)251-7914. Fax: (301)251-7937. Senior Program Director: Sandra Sonner. Writer and illustrator workshops geared toward all levels. Annual workshop. Registration limited to 200. Writing/art facilities available: performing arts center and continuing education classrooms. Cost of workshop: $60/Maryland residents; $84/

out-of-state; includes workshops, box lunch and coffee. Write for more information.

*‡CHARLESTON WRITERS' CONFERENCE, English Dept., College of Charleston, Charleston SC 29424. (803)953-5659. Fax: (803)953-3180. Contact: Director. Writer and illustrator workshops geared toward beginner, intermediate. Features sessions on craft and marketing. Annual conference. Conference held March 20-23, 1997. Cost of workshop: $150; includes tuition and all functions. For individual manuscript critiques, a separate fee is charged ($40). Write for more information. "This year we will have as keynote children's writer Eleanora Tate (*Thank You Dr. Martin Luther King, Jr.; The Secret of Gumbo Grove; A Blessing in Disguise*)."

CHILDREN'S LITERATURE CONFERENCE, 375 Hofstra University, U.C.C.E., Hempstead NY 11550. (516)463-5016. Fax: (516)463-4883. E-mail: dcelcs@hofstra.edu. Writers/Illustrators Contact: Lewis Shena, Assistant Dean, Liberal Arts Studies. Writer and illustrator workshops geared toward all levels. Emphasizes: fiction, nonfiction, poetry, submission procedures, picture books. Workshops held "usually in April." Length of each session: 1 hour. Registration limited to 35/class. Cost of workshop: approximately $60; includes 2 workshops, reception, lunch, 2 general sessions, and panel discussion with guest speakers and/or critiquing. Write for more information. Co-sponsored by Society of Children's Book Writers & Illustrators.

*CHRISTIAN WRITERS OF IDAHO WORKSHOP & CRITIQUE, sponsored by INC and the Arts Conference and Network for Christian Writers, Entertainers and Artists, P.O. Box 1754, Post Falls ID 83854. Phone/fax: (208)667-9730. Director: Sheri Stone. Writer workshops geared toward all levels. Illustrator workshops geared toward beginner, intermediate, advanced. "Topics covered include children's fiction and nonfiction; also poetry, songwriting, screenwriting and marketing. Annual conference and monthly workshops/critique (third Tuesday of each month). Writing/art facilities available: book and tape library. Conference planned for August 8-12, 1997. Submit up to 3 mss to Editor/Publisher for evaluation 2 weeks prior to conference. Write for more information. INC and The Arts also promotes a Young Writers Critique, 2 times a month, for 25 members. "They edit and write a two-page addition to our bimonthly newsletter. They also help with our annual conference."

*THE COLUMBUS WRITERS CONFERENCE, P.O. Box 20548, Columbus OH 43220. (614)451-3075. Fax: (614)451-0174. E-mail: angelapl28@aol.com. Director: Angela Palazzolo. Writer workshops geared toward all levels. "Since its inception in 1993, the conference has offered a wide variety of topics including writing in the following markets: children's, movie/television, humor, suspense, science fiction/fantasy, travel, educational and greeting card. Other topics have included writing the novel, the short story, the nonfiction book; playwriting, independent publishing, book reviewing, technical writing and time management for writers. Specific sessions that have pertained to children: children's writing, children's markets, writing and publishing children's poetry and stories. Annual conference. Workshop held in September. Cost of workshop: $75 (if registration is postmarked no later than two weeks prior to conference date, $89 if postmarked after that date); includes attendance at conference, continental breakfast, lunch and a networking/refreshments session. Write for more information.

CRAFT OF WRITING, University of Texas at Dallas, Center for Continuing Education, P.O. Box 830688, CN1.1, Richardson TX 75083-0688. (214)690-2204. Fax: (214)883-2995. E-mail: janeth@utdallas.edu. Director: Janet Harris. Writer workshops geared toward all levels. Sessions include Using the Internet to Research and Market Your Writing; The Novice Older Writer; An Insider's Look at Getting Published; Media Tie-ins: Writing the Lucrative Wave of the Future; and Writing for Children and Young Adults. Annual workshop. Workshop held every September. Two days. Cost of workshop: $195; includes choice of among 28 workshops, manuscript contest, valuable tips for marketing yourself, discussion sessions conducted by editors and agents, participation in one of the manuscript clinics held both days, 1 lunch, reception and banquet. Write for more information. "In addition to a manuscript contest, the conference also offers critiquing sessions as well as a chance to meet and mingle with professional writers, agents and editors."

*‡CREATING MAGIC IN THE REAL WORLD: PUBLISHING FOR CHILDREN TODAY, University of North Carolina, Friday Center, Chapel Hill NC 27514. Co-coordinator: Marnie Brooks. Regional Advisor: Frances Davis. Writer and illustrator workshops geared toward all levels. Sessions feature Editor Stephen Roxburg; Keynote address by James Cross Giblin; Author Bill Hooks; Illustrator Palmer-Preiss and workshops in illustration, writing. Annual conference. Conference held October 19. Writing/art facilities available: will hold illustrators' exhibition and writers' critiques. Cost of conference: $45 (SCBWI members); $50 NC writers network members; $55 others; includes sessions plus lunch buffet. August 30 deadline for writing critique sessions; $20 fee for critiques; 10 page limit. Write for more information.

PETER DAVIDSON'S WRITER'S SEMINAR; HOW TO WRITE A CHILDREN'S PICTURE BOOK SEMINAR, 982 S. Emerald Hills Dr., P.O. Box 497, Arnolds Park IA 51331. Seminar Presenter: Peter Davidson. "This seminar is for anyone interested in writing and/or illustrating children's picture books. Beginners and experienced writers alike are welcome. If participants have a manuscript in progress, or have an idea, they are welcome to bring it along to discuss with the seminar presenter." *Peter Davidson's Writer's Seminar* is a one-day seminar devoted to principles and techniques of writing and illustrating children's picture books. Topics include Definition of a Picture Book, Picture Book Sizes, Developing an Idea, Plotting the Book, Writing the Book, Illustrating the Book, Typing the Manuscript, Copyrighting Your Work, Marketing Your Manuscript and Contract Terms. Seminars are presented year round at community colleges. Even-numbered years, presents seminars in Minnesota, Iowa, Nebraska, Kansas, Colorado and Wyoming. Odd-numbered years, presents seminars in Illinois, Minnesota, Iowa, South Dakota, Missouri, Arkansas and Tennessee (write for a schedule). One day, 9 a.m.-4 p.m. Cost of workshop: varies from $39-59, depending on location; includes approximately 35 pages of handouts. Write for more information.

DEEP SOUTH WRITERS CONFERENCE, % English Dept. USL Box 44691, Lafayette LA 70504. (318)482-6910. E-mail: jlm8047@usl.edu. Professor, English: Sylvia Iskander. Writer workshops geared toward beginner and intermediate levels. Illustrator workshops geared toward beginner level. Topics offered include age-appropriateness, development of character and plot, and submission of mss (including query letter). Annual workshop. Workshop held third or fourth weekend in September. Registration limited to 10 people. Writing/art facilities available: special equipment can be made available if enough advanced notice is given. Cost of workshop: $40 and conference registration of $25-50, depending on status. Payment entitles workshop participants to workshop and all conference craft lectures and readings. Submit ms at least 3 weeks in advance (by end of August). Ms (not art) will be duplicated for all members of the workshop to critique. Write for more information.

*‡DO WRITE, WRITER'S GUILD OF ACADIANA, P.O. Box 51532, Lafayette LA 70505. Contact: Marilyn Conting (318)981-5153 or Ro Foley (318)234-8694. Writer conference geared toward beginner and intermediate levels. "We invite children's writers and agents, among other genres. The conference is not geared only to children's writings." Annual conference. Conference held March 14-15, 1997. Registration limited to 100. Cost of workshop: $85 member/$110 nonmember; includes 2 days of about 20 various sessions, some geared to children's writers; Friday night dinner, Saturday luncheon; a chance to have your ms looked at by agents. Also includes a year membership to Writer's Guild of Acadiana. Write for more information.

DOWN EAST MAINE WRITER'S WORKSHOPS, P.O. Box 446, Stockton Springs ME 04981. (207)567-4317. Fax: (207)567-3023. E-mail: 6249304@mcimail.com. Director: Janet J. Barron. Writing workshops geared towards beginning writers. We hold 1-, 2-, 3-, 5-, and 7-day "modular" workshops (writers can attend complete workshops, or for the specific days they find most valuable) during the summer and fall each year. 1997 workshops will include Writing for the Children's Market, Creative Writing (basics of Fiction & Nonfiction), How to Get Your Writing Published, and a Sampler (a half day gourmet taste of Fiction, Nonfiction, Writing for the Children's Market, Poetry, Scriptwriting, and How to Get Published). Tuition (includes lunch): by-the-day, $115; 3-day, $295; 5-day, $495; 7-day, $675 (we accept Visa and MC). Reasonable local accommodations additional. Expert, individual, personal, practical instruction on the fundamentals of writing for publication. We also offer a writer's clinic for writing feedback if partici-

---

‡ **THE DOUBLE DAGGER** before a listing indicates the conference is open to students.

pants seeks this type of guidance. No requirements prior to registration. For more information, contact DEMWW at any of the numbers listed.

FISHTRAP, INC., P.O. Box 38, Enterprise OR 97828. (541)426-3623. Fax: (541)426-3281. Director: Rich Wandschneider. Writer workshops geared toward beginner, intermediate, advanced and professional levels. Not specifically writing for children, although we have offered occasional workshops such as "The Children's Picture Book." A series of eight writing workshops (enrollment 12/workshop) and a writers' gathering is held each July; a winter gathering concerning writing and issues of public policy (e.g. "Violence," "Fire") is held in February. During the school year Fishtrap brings writers into local schools and offers occasional workshops for teachers and writers of children's and young adult books. Cost of workshop: $40-210 for 1-4 days; includes workshop only. Food and lodging can be arranged. College credit is available for $35/hour. Please contact for more information.

FLORIDA CHRISTIAN WRITERS CONFERENCE, 2600 Park Ave., Titusville FL 32780. (407)269-6702, ext. 202. Conference Director: Billie Wilson. Writer and illustrator workshops geared toward all levels. "We offer 48 one-hour workshops and 5 five-hour classes. Many of these are for the children's genre: Seeing Through the Eyes of an Artist; Characters . . . Inside and Out; Seeing Through the Eyes of a Child; Picture Book Toolbox; and CD-Rom & Interactive Books for Children. Annual workshop held in late January. We have 30 publishers and publications represented by editors teaching workshops and reading manuscripts from the conferees. The conference is limited to 200 people. Usually workshops are limited to 25-30. Advanced or professional workshops are by invitation only via submitted application." Cost of workshop: $375; includes food, lodging, tuition and manuscript critiques and editor review of your manuscript. Write for more information.

FLORIDA SUNCOAST WRITERS' CONFERENCE, Department of English, University of South Florida, Tampa FL 33620. (813)974-1711. Fax: (813)974-2270. Directors: Ed Hirshberg and Steve Rubin. Writer workshops geared toward beginner through advanced levels. Emphasizes writing for children and young adults (including craft, marketing, etc.). Workshops held first weekend in February. Class sizes range from 30-100. Cost of workshop: $100; $85 for students/teachers; includes all sessions, receptions, panels. Conference is held on St. Petersburg campus of USF. Call for information.

GREAT LAKES WRITER'S WORKSHOP, Alverno College, 3401 S. 39th St., P.O. Box 343922, Milwaukee WI 53234-3922. (414)382-6176. Fax: (414)382-6354. Director: Debra Pass. Writing workshops geared toward beginner and intermediate levels; subjects include writing techniques/focuses such as character development, scene development, etc.; techniques for getting over writer's block; marketing strategies; and publishing strategies. Annual workshop. Workshop usually held second full week in July. Average length of each session: 2 hours. Cost of workshop: $99 (in 1996); includes entrance into 6 sessions. Write for more information.

GREEN LAKE WRITERS CONFERENCE, Green Lakes Conference Center, Green Lake WI 54941-9300. (800)558-8898. Writer workshops geared toward beginner, intermediate and advanced levels. Emphasizes poetry, nonfiction, writing for children, fiction. Classes/courses offered include: same as above plus total group session and 1 all-day seminar. Conference held July 13-20, 1997. Length of conference: Saturday dinner through the following Saturday breakfast. Registration limited to 20/class. Writing and/or art facilities available: housing, conference rooms, etc. "No special equipment for writing." Cost of workshop: $80; includes all instruction. Room and meals extra. Write for more information. "The conference focuses on helping writers to refine their writing skills in a caring atmosphere utilizing competent, caring faculty. This annual conference has been held every year since 1948."

THE HEIGHTS WRITER'S CONFERENCE, Sponsored by Writer's World Press, P.O. Box 24684, Cleveland OH 44124-0684. (216)481-1974. Fax: (216)481-2057. Conference Director: Lavern Hall. Writer workshops geared toward beginner, intermediate, advanced and professional levels. Our workshop topics vary yearly. We *always* have children's literature. Annual workshop held first Saturday in May. Registration is open for seminars. The two teaching workshops are limited to 25 and pre-registration is a must. Cost of workshop: $70; includes continental breakfast, registration packet, lunch, seminars and/or workshops, general session and networking reception at the end of the day. SASE for brochure.

HIGHLAND SUMMER CONFERENCE, Box 7014 Radford University, Radford VA 24142. (703)831-5366. Fax: (540)831-5004. E-mail: gedwards@runet.edu. Director: Grace Toney Edwards. Assistant to the Director: Jo Ann Asbury. Writer workshops geared toward beginner, intermediate and advanced levels. Emphasizes Appalachian literature. Annual workshop. Workshop held June 17-28, 1996 (last 2 weeks in June annually). Registration limited to 20. Writing facilities available: computer center. Cost of workshop: Regular tuition (housing/meals extra). Must be registered student or special status student. Write for more information. Past visiting authors include: Wilma Dykeman, Sue Ellen Bridgers, George Ella Lyons Lou Kassem.

HIGHLIGHTS FOUNDATION WRITERS WORKSHOP AT CHAUTAUQUA, Dept. CWL, 814 Court St., Honesdale PA 18431. (717)253-1192. Fax: (717)253-0179. Conference Director: Jan Keen. Writer workshops geared toward those interested in writing for children; beginner, intermediate and advanced levels. Classes offered include: "Children's Interests," "Writing Dialogue," "Beginnings and Endings," "Rights, Contracts, Copyrights," "Science Writing." Annual workshop. Workshops held July 13-20, 1996, at Chautauqua Institution, Chautauqua, NY. Registration limited to 100/class. Cost of workshop: $1,285; includes tuition, meals, conference supplies. Cost does not include housing. Call for availability and pricing. Grants are available for first-time attendees. Write for more information.

HOFSTRA UNIVERSITY SUMMER WRITERS' CONFERENCE, 375 Hofstra University, UCCE, Hempstead NY 11550-1009. (516)463-5016. Assistant Director of Liberal Arts Studies: Lewis Shena. Writer workshops geared toward all levels. Classes offered include fiction, nonfiction, poetry, children's literature, stage/screenwriting and other genres. Children's writing faculty has included Pam Conrad, Johanna Hurwitz, Tor Seidler and Jane Zalben, with Maurice Sendak once appearing as guest speaker. Annual workshop. Workshops held for 2 weeks in July commencing the first Monday after July 4. Each workshop meets for 2½ hours daily for a total of 25 hours. Students can register for two workshops, schedule an individual conference with the writer/instructor and submit a short ms (less than 10 pages) for critique. Enrollees may register as certificate students or credit students. Cost of workshop: certificate students enrollment fee is approximately $350 plus $26 registration fee; 2-credit student enrollment fee is approximately $900 undergraduate and $1,682 graduate; 4-credit student enrollment fee is approximately $1,682 undergraduate and $1,762 graduate. On-campus accommodations for the sessions are available for approximately $400/person. Students may attend any of the ancillary activities, a private conference, special programs and social events.

INTERNATIONAL WOMEN'S WRITING GUILD, P.O. Box 810, Gracie Station, New York NY 10028. (212)737-7536. Executive Director: Hannelore Hahn. Writer and illustrator workshops geared toward all levels. Offers 60 different workshops—some are for children's book writers and illustrators. Also sponsors 13 other events throughout the US. Annual workshops. Workshops held in August. Length of each session: 1 hour-15 minutes; sessions take place for an entire week. Registration limited to 400. Cost of workshop: $300 (plus $300 room and board). Write for more information. "This workshop always takes place at Skidmore College in Saratoga Springs NY."

THE IUPUI NATIONAL YOUTH THEATRE PLAYWRITING SYMPOSIUM, 425 N. University Blvd., Indianapolis IN 46202-5140. (317)274-0566. Literary Manager: W. Mark McCreary. "The purpose of the Symposium is to provide a forum in which we can examine and discuss those principles which characterize good dramatic literature for young people and to explore ways to help playwrights and the promotion of quality drama. Publishers, playwrights, directors, producers, librarians and educators join together to examine issues central to playwriting." Holds playwriting competition. Send SASE for guidelines and entry form. Deadline: September 1, 1997.

I'VE ALWAYS WANTED TO WRITE BUT—BEGINNERS' CLASS, Villa 30, 23350 Sereno Ct., Cupertino CA 95014. (415)691-0300. Contact: Louise Purwin Zobel. Writer workshops geared toward beginner, intermediate levels. "This seminar/workshop starts at the beginning, although the intermediate writer will benefit, too. There is discussion of children's magazine and book literature today, how to write it and how to market it. Also, there is discussion of other types of writing and the basics of writing for publication." Annual workshops. "Usually held several times a year; fall, winter and spring." Sessions last 1-2 days. Cost of workshop: $45-65/day, depending on the campus; includes extensive handout. Write with SASE for more information.

JACK LONDON WRITERS' CONFERENCE, 135 Clark Dr., San Mateo CA 94402-1002. (415)342-9123. Fax: (415)342-9155. Coordinator: Marlo Faulkner. Writer workshops geared toward beginner, intermediate, advanced and professional levels. Sample workshop subjects include queries, self editing and poetry. Annual workshop. Workshop held the second weekend in March. The conference is a program of speakers, panels and workshops—writing depends on the workshop leader. Cost of workshop: $95; includes continental breakfast, lunch, all programs and Ask a Pro sessions. Write for more information.

MAKING WAVES WITH WRITERS, Northern Arizona University, P.O. Box 6024, Flagstaff AZ 86011-6024. Workshop Directors: Ray Newton, Carol O'Hara and Nancy Elliot. "While experiencing the elegance of MS Ryndam (commissioned in 1994) and the majesty that is Alaska, you'll have the unparalleled opportunity to enhance your ability in all facets of the writing and speaking profession. Among the noted editors and instructors eager to guide you to success are Thomas Clark, Editor-in-Chief, *Writer's Digest*; Caroll Shreeve, *Gibbs/Smith Publishing*; Carol O'Hara, *Cat-Tails Press*; and Robert Early, *Arizona Highways*." Workshop held September 22-29, 1996. Cost of workshop: $995-2,515; includes Alaskan cruise from Anchorage to Vancouver and workshop. Low-cost round-trip air fare from home city available. For more information, contact Carol O'Hara at (916)987-9489 or 1(800)979-3548, or Sue Cagle at (916)723-3355.

MANHATTANVILLE WRITERS' WEEK, Manhattanville College, 2900 Purchase St., Purchase NY 10577. (914)694-3425. Fax: (914)694-3488. Dean, Adult and Special Programs: Ruth Dowd. Writer workshops geared toward beginner, intermediate and advanced levels. Writers' week offers a special workshop for writers interested in children's/young adult writing. We have featured such workshop leaders as: Patricia Gauch, Patricia Horner, Elizabeth Winthrop and Lore Segal. Annual workshop held last week in June. Length of each session: one week. Cost of workshop: $560 (non-credit); includes a full week of writing activities, 5-day workshop on children's literature, lectures, readings, sessions with editors and agents, etc. Workshop may be taken for 2 graduate credits. Write for more information.

MAPLE WOODS COMMUNITY COLLEGE WRITERS' CONFERENCE, 2601 NE Barry Rd., Kansas City MO 64156. (816)437-3010. Coordinator, Continuing Education: Paula Schumacher. Writer workshops geared toward beginner, intermediate levels. Various writing topics and genres covered. Conference held September 7. Length of each session: 1 hour. Registration limited to 150/class. Cost of workshop: $59; includes lunch.

✦MARITIME WRITERS' WORKSHOP, Department Extension & Summer School, P.O. Box 4400, University of New Brunswick, Fredericton, New Brunswick E3B 5A3 Canada. (506)453-4646. Fax: (506)453-3572. Coordinator: Glenda Turner. Week-long workshop on writing for children, general approach, dealing with submitted material, geared to all levels and held in July. Annual workshop. 3 hours/day. Group workshop plus individual conferences, public readings, etc. Registration limited to 10/class. Cost of workshop: $300 tuition; includes tuition only. Meals and accommodations extra. 10-20 ms pages due before conference (deadline announced). Scholarships available.

*METROPOLITAN WRITERS CONFERENCE, Continuing Education-Seton Hall University, South Orange NJ 07079. (201)761-9783. Fax: (201)761-9794. E-mail: degnaja@lanmal.shu. edu. Website: http://www.shu.edu./academic/univcoll/index.html. Director of Continuing Education: Jane Degnan. Writer conference geared toward beginner and intermediate levels. Conference includes workshop entitled "Everything You Wanted to Know about Writing a Children's Book." Annual conference. Conference usually held in October. Cost of conference $55; includes all workshops, lectures, coffee and Danish in a.m. Write for more information.

MIDLAND WRITERS CONFERENCE, Grace A. Dow Memorial Library, 1710 W. St. Andrews, Midland MI 48640. (517)835-7151. Fax: (517)835-9791. E-mail: kred@vlc.lib.mi.us. Conference Chair: Katherine Redwine. Writer and illustrator workshops geared toward all levels. "We always have one session each on children's, poetry and basics." Classes offered include: how to write poetry, writing for youth, your literary agent/what to expect. Workshops held usually second Saturday in June. Length of each session: concurrently, 4 1-hour and 2-hour sessions. Maximum class size: 40. "We are a public library." Cost of workshop: $55; $45 seniors and students; includes choice of workshops and the keynote speech given by a prominent author (last year Pat Conroy). Write for more information.

Join Writer's Digest Book Club and take

2 BOOKS FREE

SAVE up to $60.00 or more!

with a third book for only $9⁹⁵
plus postage & handling costs

Your Satisfaction Guaranteed 100%

When you receive your books, take a full 15 days to look them over. If you're not completely satisfied, just return them all. We'll cancel your membership and refund your money. No questions asked!

HOW THE CLUB WORKS

Every 4 weeks (14 times a year), you'll receive a *Bulletin* describing the Main Selection and up to 100 more writing books. If you want the Main Selection, do nothing and it will be sent automatically. If you want a different book, or want nothing that month, you'll always have at least 10 days to decide and return your selection card. If late mail delivery should ever cause you to receive a book you don't want, you may return it at club expense.

As a new member, you agree to buy one book from the *Bulletin* in the next 6 months. After that, you may cancel at any time. Every time you buy a book from the *Bulletin*, your membership will be renewed for 6 months from the purchase date.

*MIDWEST RADIO THEATRE WORKSHOP, 915 E. Broadway, Columbia MO 65201. (314)874-5676. Fax: (314)499-1662. E-mail: mrtw@mrtw.org. Director: Debbie Karwoski. Send SASE for more information. Also sponsors annual radio play contest.

MIDWEST WRITERS' CONFERENCE, 6000 Frank Ave. NW, Canton OH 44720. (330)499-9600. Fax: (330)494-6121. Assistant Director: Debbie Ruhe. Writer workshops geared toward beginner, intermediate and advanced levels. Topics include: Fiction, Nonfiction, Juvenile Literature, Poetry and a rotating category. Titles for Juvenile Literature have included Writing as Power, Writing for Children, and Lifting Them Up To Our Windows: Writing for Kids. Annual conference. Conference held early October. Length of each session: 1 hour. Registration limited to 400 total people. Cost of workshop: $65; includes Friday afternoon workshops, keynote address, Saturday workshops, box lunch, up to 2-ms entries in contest. Write for more information.

MISSISSIPPI VALLEY WRITERS CONFERENCE, 3403 45th St., Moline IL 61265. Conference Director: David R. Collins. Writer workshops geared toward all levels. Classes offered include Juvenile Writing—1 of 9 workshops offered. Annual workshop. Workshops held June 8-13, 1997; usually it is the second week in June each year. Length of each session: Monday-Friday, 1 hour each day. Registration limited to 20 participants/workshop. Writing facilities available: college library. Cost of workshop: $25 registration; $50 to participate in 1 workshop, $90 in 2, $30 for each additional; $25 to audit a workshop. Write for more information.

MONTROSE CHRISTIAN WRITER'S CONFERENCE, 5 Locust St., Montrose PA 18801-1112. (717)278-1001. Fax: (717)278-3061. E-mail: jfahring@epix.net Director: Jim Fahringer. Writer workshops geared toward beginner, intermediate and advanced levels. Annual workshop. Cost of workshop: $70-85; includes tuition. Write for more information.

MOUNT HERMON CHRISTIAN WRITERS CONFERENCE, Mount Hermon Christian Conference Center, P.O. Box 413, Mount Hermon CA 95041. (408)335-4466. Fax: (408)335-9218. Director of Specialized Programs: David R. Talbott. Writer workshops geared toward all levels. Emphasizes religious writing for children via books, articles; Sunday school curriculum; marketing. Classes offered include: "Suitable Style for Children"; "Everything You Need to Know to Write and Market Your Children's Book"; "Take-Home Papers for Children." Workshops held annually over Palm Sunday weekend: March 21-25, 1997. Length of each session: 5-day residential conferences held annually. Registration limited 45/class, but most are 10-15. Conference center with hotel-style accommodations. Cost of workshop: $450-675 variable; includes tuition, resource notebook, refreshment breaks, full room and board for 13 meals and 4 nights. Write for more information.

THE NATIONAL WRITERS ASSOCIATION CONFERENCE, Suite 424, 1450 S. Havana, Aurora CO 80012. (303)751-7844. Executive Director: Sandy Whelchel. Writer workshops geared toward all levels. Classes offered include marketing, agenting, "What's Hot in the Market." Annual workshop. "In 1997 the workshop will be held in Denver, Colorado, June 13-15. Write for more information.

NORTH CAROLINA WRITERS' NETWORK FALL CONFERENCE, P.O. Box 954, Carrboro NC 27510. (919)967-9540. Fax: (919)929-0535. Writer workshops geared toward beginner, intermediate, advanced and professional levels. "We offer workshops and critique sessions in a variety of genres: fiction, poetry, children's. Past young adult and children's writing classes include: 'Writing for Kids' with Bill Brittain, 'Young Adult Fiction: Discovering the Charm' with Suzanne Newton." Annual conference. Conference held November 14-16, 1997 (Wilmington, NC). Cost of workshop: approximately $110-125, includes workshops, panel discussions, 3 meals.

NORTHWEST OKLAHOMA WRITERS WORKSHOP, P.O. Box 1308, Enid OK 73702. (405)234-4562. Workshop Chairman: Dr. Earl Mabry. Writer workshops geared toward beginner, intermediate, advanced and professional levels. Annual workshop. Workshop held in spring (usually March). Cost of workshop: $40; includes registration, handouts. Write for more information. "Our workshops are not geared, per se, to children's writers. We generally have one speaker for the day. Past speakers were Mike McQuay (now deceased), Norma Jean Lutz, Deborah Bouziden, Anna Meyers (the only time we've had a Children's Writer), Sandra Soli and Marcia Preston. The speaker for the 1997 workshop has not yet been determined.

*‡OHIO KENTUCKY INDIANA CHILDREN'S LITERATURE CONFERENCE, % Greater Cincinnati Library Consortium, 3333 Vine St., Suite 605, Cincinnati OH 45220. (513)751-4422. Fax: (513)751-0463. E-mail: gclc@uc.edu. Website: http://www.libraries.uc.edu/gclc. Staff Development Coordinator: Ronald Frommeyer. Writer and illustrator conference geared toward all levels. 1996 conference featured keynote speakers Will Hillenbrand and J. Patrick Lewis; Tristate Authors & Illustrators Showcase; workshops by children's literature specialists/authors/illustrators; Anita Haller—Storytelling. Annual conference. Conference held November 8, 1997. Registration limited to 250. Cost of conference: $25 (1996 cost); includes registration/attendance at all workshop sessions, coffee break, lunch, author/illustrator signings. Write for more information.

OKLAHOMA FALL ARTS INSTITUTES, P.O. Box 18154, Oklahoma City OK 73154. (405)842-0890. Director of Programs: Mary Gordon Taft. Writer and illustrator workshops geared toward intermediate, advanced and professional levels. Writing topics include writing for children, poetry, fiction, nonfiction, screenwriting; art topics include drawing, painting, illustrating children's books, sculpture, printmaking. Annual workshop. Workshop held each year in October. Registration is limited to 20 participants per workshop; 5 workshops each weekend. Cost of workshop: $450; includes tuition, double-occupancy room and board. Write for more information. "Catalogues are available. Each workshop is taught by a professional artist of national reputation. Workshops held at Quartz Mountain Lodge, a beautiful, secluded location."

OUTDOOR WRITERS ASSOCIATION OF AMERICA ANNUAL CONFERENCE, 2017 Cato Ave., Suite 101, State College PA 16801-2768. (814)234-1011. Fax: (814)234-9692. E-mail: 76711,1725@compuserve.com. Meeting Planner: Eileen King. Writer workshops geared toward all levels. Annual workshop. Workshop held in June. Cost of workshop: $130; includes attendance at all workshops and most meals. Attendees must have prior approval from Executive Director before attendance is permitted. Write for more information.

OZARK CREATIVE WRITERS, INC. CONFERENCE, 6817 Gingerbread Lane, Little Rock AR 72204. (501)565-8889. Counselor: Peggy Vining. Writer's workshops geared to all levels. "All forms of the creative process dealing with the literary arts. We have expanded to songwriting. We invite excellent speakers who are selling authors. We also promote writing by providing competitions in all genres." Always the second weekend in October at Inn of the Ozarks in Eureka Springs AR (a resort town). Morning sessions are given to main attraction author . . . 6 1-hour satellite speakers during each of the 2 afternoons. Two banquets. "Approximately 125-150 attend the conference yearly . . . many others enter the creative writing competition." Cost of registration/contest entry fee approximately $40-50. Includes entrance to all sessions, contest entry fees. "This does not include meals or lodging. We do block off 60 rooms prior to September 1 for OCW guests." Send #10 SASE for brochure. "Reserve early."

PENNWRITERS ANNUAL CONFERENCE, P.O. Box 339, Edinboro PA 16412. (814)734-5189. Fax: (814)734-7162. E-mail: tims@trumbull.com. Conference Coordinator: Jamie Saloff. Writer workshops geared to all levels. Annual workshop. Workshop usually held third weekend in May. Cost of workshop: $90; includes Saturday workshops, lunch, book signing tea. Additional fee for networking dinner Friday and Saturday nights and breakfast Sunday. Write for more information. Other workshops and 1-day seminars on writing for children as well as other category genre are held by Pennwriters throughout the year. For more information contact Pennwriter Secretary Joy Hopkins, 108 Jasper Way, Cannonsburg PA 15317. "Pennwriters is dedicated to helping beginners—getting valuable information into their hands, helping them with the basics. We also do a lot for our members who have become published by sponsoring book signings, sending out newsletters and providing other help."

*PHOTOGRAPHY: A DIVERSE FOCUS, 610 W. Poplar St., Zionsville IN 46077-1220. Phone/fax: (317)873-0738. Director: Charlene Faris. Writer and illustrator workshops geared to beginners. "Conferences focus primarily on children's photography; also literature and illustration. Annual conferences are held very often throughout year." Registration is not limited, but "sessions are generally small." Cost of conference: $150 (2 days), $75 (1 day). "Inquiries with an SASE only will receive information on seminars."

PORT TOWNSEND WRITER'S CONFERENCE, Centrum, P.O. Box 1158, Port Townsend WA 98368. (206)385-3102. Director: Carol Jane Bangs. Writer workshops geared toward intermediate, advanced and professional levels. Emphasizes writing for children and young adults. Classes offered include: Jane Yolen master class; intermediate/advanced writing for children. Workshops held 10 days in mid-July. Registration limited to 16/class. Writing facilities available: classrooms. Cost of workshop: $425; includes tuition. Publication list for master class. Write for more information. $100 deposit necessary. Applications accepted after December 1 for following July; workshops fill by February.

ROBERT QUACKENBUSH'S CHILDREN'S BOOK WRITING AND ILLUSTRATING WORKSHOP, 460 E. 79th St., New York NY 10021. Phone/fax: (212)744-3822. E-mail: naap95@aol.com. Website: http://www.dgandf.com/naap. Contact: Robert Quackenbush. Writer and illustrator workshops geared toward all levels. Emphasizes picture books from start to finish. Also covered is writing fiction and nonfiction for middle grades and young adults, if that is the attendees' interest. Current trends in illustration are also covered. Workshops held fall, winter and summer. Courses offered fall and winter include 10 weeks each—1½ hour/week; July workshop is a full five day (9 a.m.-4 p.m) extensive course. Registration limited to 10/class. Writing and/or art facilities available; work on the premises; art supply store nearby. Cost of workshop: $650 for instruction. Cost of workshop includes instruction in preparation of a ms and/or book dummy ready to submit to publishers. Attendees are responsible for arranging their own hotel and meals, although suggestions are given on request for places to stay and eat. "This unique five-day workshop, held annually since 1982, provides the opportunity to work with Robert Quackenbush, a prolific author and illustrator of children's books with more than 160 fiction and nonfiction books for young readers to his credit, including mysteries, biographies and song-books."

READER'S DIGEST WRITER'S WORKSHOP, Northern Arizona University, P.O. Box 6024, Flagstaff AZ 86011-6024. (602)523-3559. Workshop Director: Ray Newton. Writer workshops geared toward all levels. Classes offered include major emphasis on nonfiction magazine articles for major popular publications. Annual workshops in various locations in western US. Time of year varies, depending on location. Registration limited to 250. Cost of workshop: $150 registration fee; includes three meals. Does not include travel or lodging. "Participants will have opportunity for one-on-one sessions with major editors, writers representing national magazines, including the *Reader's Digest*." Write for more information.

SAN DIEGO STATE UNIVERSITY WRITERS' CONFERENCE, The College of Extended Studies, San Diego CA 92182-1920. (619)594-2517. Fax: (619)594-8566. E-mail: ealcara z@mail.sdsu.edu. Website: http://rohan.sdsu.edu/dept/extstd/writers.html. Conference Facilitator: Erin Grady Alcaraz. Writer workshops geared toward beginner, intermediate and advanced levels. Emphasizes nonfiction, fiction, screenwriting, advanced novel writing; includes sessions specific to writing and illustrating for children. Workshops held third weekend in January each year. Registration limited. Cost of workshop: $214 if preregistered before January 10; includes Saturday reception, 2 lunches and all sessions and one read and critique appointment with an editor or agent. Write for more information or see our home page at the above website.

*SEATTLE CHRISTIAN WRITERS CONFERENCE, P.O. Box 11337, Bainbridge Island WA 98110. (206)842-9103. Fax: (206)842-0536. Director: Elaine Colvin. Writer workshops geared toward all levels. Past conferences have featured subjects such as 'Making It to the Top as a Children's Book Author,' featuring Debbie Trafton O'Neal. Quarterly workshop (4 times/year). Workshop held September, January, March, June. Cost of workshop: $25. Write for more information.

*‡SNAKE RIVER INSTITUTE, P.O. Box 128, Wilson WY 83014. (307)733-2214. Fax: (307)739-1710. E-mail: snakeriverinst@wyoming.com. Website: http://www.wyoming.com/jack sonhole/sri/. Adult Programs Director: Samantha Strawbridge. Writer and illustrator workshops geared toward all levels. "Our workshops are not geared specifically to children's writing and illustrating. However, we do offer a variety of writing and painting classes. They change every year." Workshop held summers—May-September; 3-5 day seminars. Registration limited to 15. Cost of workshop: $195-950; depends on the class—may include food, lodging. "We are a nonprofit organization. We offer arts and humanities classes based on the history and culture of the West. Classes are a variety of painting, photography, writing and history." Write for more information.

SOCIETY OF CHILDREN'S BOOK WRITERS AND ILLUSTRATORS—FLORIDA REGION, 2158 Portland Ave., Wellington FL 33414. (407)798-4824. Florida Regional Advisor:

Barbara Casey. Writer and illustrator workshops geared toward beginner, intermediate, advanced and professional levels. Subjects to be announced. Annual workshop. Workshop held second Saturday of September in the meeting rooms of the Palm Springs Public Library, 217 Cypress Lane, Palm Springs FL. Registration limited to 100/class. Cost of workshop: $50 for members, $55 for non-members. Special rates are offered through the West Palm Beach Airport Hilton Hotel for those attending the conference who wish to spend the night. Write for more information.

SOCIETY OF CHILDREN'S BOOK WRITERS AND ILLUSTRATORS—HAWAII, 2355 Alawai Blvd. #502, Honolulu HI 96815. (808)926-0115. E-mail: omasters@sprynet.com. Regional Advisor: Elaine Masters. Writer and illustrator conferences geared toward all levels. Conferences feature general topics—writing, illustrating, publishing and marketing; also specific skills workshops are offered such as "writing plays for children." Conferences are held in fall; workshops in winter and spring. Cost varies. Reduced rate for SCBWI members. Open to non-members. SASE for more information.

SOCIETY OF CHILDREN'S BOOK WRITERS AND ILLUSTRATORS—INDIANA SPRING WRITERS' CONFERENCE, P.O Box 36, Garrett IN 46738. E-mail: 70334.1145@c ompuserve.com. Conference Director: Lola M. Schaefer. Writer and illustrator workshops geared toward all levels. Workshop sessions include "Nuts and Bolts for Beginners," "Plotting the Middle-Grade Novel," "Lasting Themes in Picture Books" "Researching the Biography," and "Nonfiction for Children." All are geared toward children's writers and illustrators. Conference held annually in June. 1996 conference: June 29. Length of each session: 45 minutes to 1½ hours. Cost of workshop: approximately $60-90; includes meal and workshops. Write for more information. "Manuscript and portfolio critiques by published writers and illustrators will be offered at additional charge."

*SOCIETY OF CHILDREN'S BOOK WRITERS AND ILLUSTRATORS—MICHIGAN (SCBWI-MI) WORKING WRITERS AND ILLUSTRATORS RETREAT, 2011 Waite Ave., Kalamazoo MI 49008. (616)345-6906. Retreat Chair: Ellen Howard. Writer and illustrator workshops geared toward intermediate, advanced and professional levels. Topics include craft lecture for writers; ms/dummy workshopping group sessions (peer critique facilitated by an experienced writer and/or illustrator); nonfiction workshop; educational market workshop; and editors' workshops on marketing (workshop subjects vary from year to year). Annual workshop. Workshop held October. Registration limited to approximately 40. Cost of workshop $130 (to members); includes meals, lodging, registration. Those wishing an individual ms critique by a member of the faculty should send a copy of their ms, neatly typed and double-spaced, with a check for $35 to Ellen Howard before October 1. (Limit: complete picture book text, or 1 chapter of a novel or nonfiction work, or a complete magazine story.) Write for more information.

SOCIETY OF CHILDREN'S BOOK WRITERS AND ILLUSTRATORS—MINNESOTA, 7080 Coachwood Rd., Woodbury MN 55125. (612)739-0119. E-mail: kidlit@juno.com. Minnesota Regional Advisor: Peg Helminski. Writer and illustrator workshops geared toward beginner, intermediate, advanced and professional levels. All of our workshops and conferences focus on the needs of children's writers and illustrators. Critique sessions and portfolio reviews are also available. We try to have one full day conference and one evening event per year. Twice a year workshop. Workshop held late April and early October. Cost of workshop: varies $20-85. Full day conferences usually include luncheon, coffee breaks and snack. Evening workshops usually include snack. SASE for more information 6 weeks prior to each event.

SOCIETY OF CHILDREN'S BOOK WRITERS AND ILLUSTRATORS—NORCAL RETREAT AT ASILOMAR, 1316 Rebecca Dr., Suisun CA 94585. (707)426-6776. Fax: (707)427-2885. Regional Advisor: Bobi Martin. Writer and illustrator workshops geared toward beginner, intermediate, advanced and professional levels. Emphasizes various topics from writing or illustrating picture books to young adult novels. Past speakers include agents, publishers, editors, published authors and illustrators. Annual workshop. Workshop generally held last weekend in February; Friday evening through Sunday lunch. Registration limited to 65. Rooms are shared with one other person. Desks available in most rooms. All rooms have private baths. Cost of workshop: $225 SCBWI members; $250 nonmembers; includes shared room, 6 meals, ice breaker party and conference. A full scholarship is available to SCBWI members. Call Bobi Martin for application procedure. Registration opens October 1st and usually is full by October 31st. A waiting list is formed. SASE for more information. "This is a small retreat with a relaxed pace."

SOCIETY OF CHILDREN'S BOOK WRITERS AND ILLUSTRATORS—POCONO MOUNTAINS WRITERS' RETREAT, 708 Pine St., Moscow PA 18444. Conference Director: Susan Campbell Bartoletti. Workshop held third weekend in April, depending upon Easter and Passover. Registration limited to 75. Cost of workshop: tuition about $350; includes tuition, room and board. Send SASE for more information.

SOCIETY OF CHILDREN'S BOOK WRITERS AND ILLUSTRATORS—SAN DIEGO CHAPTER, Writing for Children, the Words and the Pictures, Society of Children's Book Writers and Illustrators/San Diego Chapter, 1238 Valencia Dr., Escondido CA 92025. (619)738-1629. E-mail: lpflueger@ucsd.edu. Conference Chairman: Lynda Pflueger. Writer and illustrator workshops geared toward all levels. Topics vary every year but emphasize writing and illustrating for children. Annual workshop. Workshop held on the second or third Saturday in March. Length: all day workshop with 6 1-hour sessions. Cost of workshop: $55-65; includes all day workshop and luncheon. Write for more information. "Meeting other writers, networking and marketing information is stressed during workshop."

SOCIETY OF CHILDREN'S BOOK WRITERS AND ILLUSTRATORS—SOUTHERN BREEZE (ALABAMA/GEORGIA/MISSISSIPPI REGION), 1616 Kestwick Dr., Birmingham AL 35226. Fax: (205)979-0274. E-mail: joanbroer@aol.com. Regional Advisor: Joan Broerman. "The fall conference, 'Writing and Illustrating for Kids,' is always the third Saturday in October in Birmingham, and offers entry level and professional track workshops (i.e. 'Foundations of Writing and Submitting,' 'CD-ROM—Will It Change My Life?') as well as numerous talks on craft from early picture books through young adult novels." Cost of workshop: $50-60 for SCBWI members; $65-70 for nonmembers; ms critiques and portfolio review available for additional cost. Write for more information (include SASE). "Our spring conference, Springmingle!, is in different parts of the three-state region. Springmingle '97! will be held in Columbus, GA, March 14-16, 1997." Preregistration important for both conferences.

SOCIETY OF CHILDREN'S BOOK WRITERS AND ILLUSTRATORS—SOUTHERN CALIFORNIA; ILLUSTRATORS DAY, 1937 Pelham Ave., #2, Los Angeles CA 90025. (310)446-4799. Co-regional Advisor: Judith Ross Enderle. Illustrator sessions geared toward all levels. Emphasizes illustration and illustration markets. Conference includes: presentations by art director, children's book editor and panel of artists/author-illustrators. Conference held annually in the fall. Length of session: full day. "Editors and art directors will view portfolios. We want to know if each conferee is bringing a portfolio or not." This is a chance for illustrators to meet editors/art directors and each other. Writers Day held in the spring. National conference for authors *and* illustrators held every August." Cost of workshop: $70; includes entire day of speakers and open marketplace ($10 extra for private portfolio review).

SOCIETY OF CHILDREN'S BOOK WRITERS AND ILLUSTRATORS—TENNESSEE/KENTUCKY SPRING CONFERENCE, Box 3342, Clarksville TN 37043-3342. (615)358-9849. E-mail: czauthor@aol.com. Regional Advisor: Cheryl Zach. Writer workshop geared toward all levels. Illustrator workshops geared toward beginner, intermediate levels. Previous workshop topics have included Writing the Picture Book, Editors Look at First Pages, Historical Fiction and Nonfiction, Writing Poetry and Songs, Writing for Magazines, Illustrators' Workshops and more. Workshop held in the spring (April 26, 1997). 1 day. Cost of workshop: $60 SCBWI members, $65 nonmembers; includes all day of workshops and lunch. Registration limited to 100. "SCBWI-Tennessee's 1997 conference is scheduled for April 26 in Nashville." Send SASE for flier.

SOCIETY OF CHILDREN'S BOOK WRITERS AND ILLUSTRATORS—VENTURA/ SANTA BARBARA FALL CONFERENCE, 101 Hillveil Lane, Simi Valley CA 93065. (805)581-1906. Regional Advisor: Alexis O'Neill. Writers conference geared toward all levels. "We invite editors, authors and author/illustrators and agents. We have had speakers on the picture book, middle grade, YA, magazine and photo essay books. Both fiction and nonfiction are covered." Conference held in October from 9:00 a.m.-4 p.m. on Saturdays. Cost of conference $55; includes all sessions and lunch. Write for more information.

SOCIETY OF CHILDREN'S BOOK WRITERS & ILLUSTRATORS—WISCONSIN ANNUAL FALL RETREAT, Rt. 1, Box 137, Gays Mills WI 54631. (608)735-4707. Fax: (608)735-4700. E-mail: pfitsch@mwt.net. Regional Advisor: Patricia Pfitsch. Writer workshops geared toward working writers. Group critique sessions with faculty and participant participation—each full time participant receives critique from well-known editors, writers and or agents as well as other participants. Also talks by faculty on various aspects of writing and selling your work. "The entire retreat is geared *only* to children's book writing." Annual workshop. Retreat held in Oct. or Nov., from Friday evening to Sunday afternoon. Registration limited to approximately 60. Cost of workshop: about $250 for SCBWI members, higher for nonmembers; includes room, board and program. "We strive to offer an informal weekend with an award-winning children's writer, an agent or illustrator and an editor from a trade house in New York in attendance." There's usually a waiting list by mid-July. Send SASE for flier.

SOUTHEASTERN WRITER'S CONFERENCE, Rt. 1, Box 102, Cuthbert GA 31740. Phone/fax: (912)679-5445. Secretary: Pat Laye. Writer workshops geared toward beginner and intermediate levels. We offer a 5-session juvenile writing class. Annual conference held on St. Simon's Island, CA. Registration limited to 100. Cost of workshops: $250; includes tuition only. "Attendees may submit one chapter of three different manuscripts for free professional critiques."

SOUTHWEST WRITERS WORKSHOP, Suite B, 1338 Wyoming Blvd. NE, Albuquerque NM 87112. (505)293-0303. Fax: (505)237-2665. Website: http://www.US1net/sww/. Contact: Conference Director. Writer workshops geared toward all genres at all levels of writing. Various aspects of writing covered. Examples from conferences: Preconference workshops on the juvenile/young adult/novel taught by Penny Durant; on picture books by April Halprin Wayland; on Writing a Juvenile Novel in 6 weeks by Shirley Raye Redmond; on writing for children's magazines by C. Walskel (of Cricket). Annual conference. Conference held August 14-17, 1997 at Hilton Hotel. Length of each session: Friday-Sunday. Cost of workshop: $240 (approximately); includes all workshops and meals. Also offers ongoing writers' groups (for $35/year, offers 2 monthly meetings and occasional workshops). Write for more information.

SPACE COAST WRITERS GUILD 16TH CONFERENCE, Box 804, Melbourne FL 32902. (407)727-0051. President: Dr. Edwin J. Kirschner. Writer conference geared toward beginner through professional levels. Annual writers conference. Held 1st Friday and Saturday in November. Registration limited. Cost of workshop: SCWG members and teachers, $50 both days; nonmembers, $65; students, $25. Price includes 2 days of workshops. Write for program/registration after September 1.

STATE OF MAINE WRITERS' CONFERENCE, 47 Winona Ave., P.O. Box 7146, Ocean Park ME 04063. (207)934-9806 (summer). (413)596-6734 (winter). E-mail: rburns@kraken.mvn et.wnec.edu. Chairman: Richard F. Burns. Writers' workshops geared toward beginner, intermediate, advanced levels. Emphasizes poetry, prose, mysteries, editors, publishers, etc. 1996 theme: Writing Community and Local History. Annual conference held August 19-22, 1997. Cost of workshop: $80 ($45 for students 22 and under); includes all sessions and banquet, snacks, poetry booklet. Send SASE for more information.

*STEAMBOAT SPRINGS WRITERS CONFERENCE, P.O. Box 774284, Steamboat Springs CO 80477. (970)879-8079. Conference Director: Harriet Freiberger. Writers' workshops geared toward intermediate levels. Annual workshop. Workshops held usually third weekend in July. Registration limited to 25-30. Cost of workshop: $45; includes 2 seminars and luncheon. Write for more information.

TRENTON STATE COLLEGE WRITERS' CONFERENCE, English Dept, Trenton State College, Hillwood Lakes CN 4700, Trenton NJ 08650-4700. (609)771-3254. Director: Jean Hollander. Writer workshops geared toward all levels. Workshops held in April of every year. Length of each session: 2 hours. Registration limited to 50. Cost of workshop: $60 (reduced rates for students); includes conference, workshop and ms critique. Write for more information.

MARK TWAIN WRITERS CONFERENCE, 921 Center St., Hannibal MO 63401. (314)221-2462 or (800)747-0738. Conference coordinator: Cyndi Allison. Three week-long workshops offered. Conference 1 (June 16-20, 1997) covers fiction and nonfiction writing, magazine and short story. Conference 2 (June 30-July 4, 1997) covers writing for children and storytelling. Conference 3 (Sept. 29-Oct. 3, 1997) covers books and humor. Registration limited. Cost of workshop: $465; includes four nights lodging, meals from Monday supper through Friday lunch and all tuition costs. Write for more information.

✤‡**VANCOUVER INTERNATIONAL WRITERS FESTIVAL**, 1243 Cartwright St., Vancouver, British Columbia V6H 4B7 Canada. Phone/fax: (604)681-6330. Producer: Alma Lee. "The mission of the Vancouver International Writers Festival is to encourage an appreciation of literature and to promote literacy by providing a forum where writers and readers can interact. This is accomplished by the production of special events and an annual Festival which feature writers from a variety of countries, whose work is compelling and diverse. The Festival attracts over 8,000 people and presents approximately 40 events in four venues during 5 days on Granville Island, located in the heart of Vancouver. The first 3 days of the festival are programmed for elementary and secondary school students." Annual festival. Held third week in October (5-day festival). All writers who participate are invited by the producer. The events are open to anyone who wishes to purchase tickets. Cost of events ranges from $10-15.

***VASSAR INSTITUTE OF PUBLISHING AND WRITING: CHILDREN'S BOOKS IN THE MARKETPLACE**, Box 300, Vassar College, Poughkeepsie NY 12601. (914)437-5903. Fax: (914)437-7209. E-mail: mabruno@vassar.edu. Program Coordinator: Maryann Bruno. Director: Barbara Lucas. Writer and illustrator conference geared toward all levels. Emphasizes "the editorial, production, marketing and reviewing processes, on writing fiction and nonfiction for all ages, creating the picture book, understanding the markets and selling your work." Workshop usually held in summer. Length of each session: 3½-hour morning critique sessions, afternoon and evening lectures. Registration limited to 30/class (with 2 instructors). Cost of conference: approximately $800, includes room, board and tuition for all critique sessions, lectures and social activities. "Proposals are pre-prepared and discussed at morning critique sessions. Art portfolio review given on pre-prepared works." Write for more information. "This conference gives a comprehensive look at the publishing industry as well as offering critiques of creative writing and portfolio review."

*✤**THE VICTORIA SCHOOL OF WRITING**, 607 Linden Ave., Victoria, British Columbia V8V 4G6 Canada. (604)385-8982. Fax: (604)995-9391. E-mail: writeawy@islandnet.com. Website: http://www.islandnet.com/~writeawy. Director: Margaret Dyment. Writer conference geared toward intermediate level. In the 1997 conference there will be one workshop on writing for children and young adults. Annual conference. Workshop held July 15-19, 1997. Registration limited to 100. Conference includes close mentoring from established writers. Cost of conference: $395 (Canada); $290 (U.S.); includes tuition and 1 brunch. To attend, submit 3-10 pages of writing samples. Write for more information.

*‡**VIRGINIA CHRISTIAN WRITERS CONFERENCE**, P.O. Box 12624, Roanoke VA 24027. Phone/fax: (540)342-7511. E-mail: cccbbr@worldnet.att.net. Director: Betty Robertson. Writer conference geared toward all levels. Annual conference. Conference held April 12, 1997. Cost of conference: $24.95 (early); $29.95; includes free magazine samples, refreshments, choice of workshops. Write for more information.

WELLS WRITERS' WORKSHOP, 69 Broadway, Concord NH 03301. (603)225-3774. Fax: (603)225-9162. E-mail: forbine@tiac.net. Coordinator: Vic Levine. Writer workshops geared toward beginner, intermediate levels. "Sessions focus on careful plot preparation, economical text and artwork relationship, as well as on effective writing (characterization, dialogue and exposition), with lots of time for writing." Workshops which meet on Maine seacoast, are offered twice a year—May 18-23 and September 7-12. Registration limited to 6/class. Writing facilities available: space, electrical outlets, resident Mac computer. Cost of workshop: $1,050; includes tuition, room and board; some scholarship money available. Write for more information. "I invite interested writers to call or write. I'd be happy to meet with them if they're reasonably close by. Workshop stresses the importance of getting the structure right when writing stories for children."

WESLEYAN WRITERS CONFERENCE, Wesleyan University, Middletown CT 06459. (860)685-3604. Fax: (860)685-2441. E-mail: agreene@wesleyan.edu. Director: Anne Greene. Writer workshops geared toward all levels. "This conference is useful for writers interested in

---

✤ **THE MAPLE LEAF** before a listing indicates that it is Canadian.

how to structure a story, poem or nonfiction piece. Although we don't always offer classes in writing for children, the advice about structuring a piece is useful for writers of any sort, no matter who their audience is." Classes in the novel, short story, fiction techniques, poetry, journalism and literary nonfiction. Guest speakers and panels offer discussion of fiction, poetry, reviewing, editing and publishing. Individual ms consultations available. Conference held annually the last week in June. Length of each session: 6 days. "Usually, there are 100 participants at the Conference." Classrooms, meals, lodging and word processing facilities available on campus. Cost of workshop: tuition—$450, room—$105, meals (required of all participants)—$185. "Anyone may register; people who want financial aid must submit their work and be selected by scholarship judges." Call for a brochure.

WILLAMETTE WRITERS ANNUAL WRITERS CONFERENCE, Suite 5A, 9045 SW Barbur Blvd., Portland OR 97219. (503)452-1592. Fax: (503)452-0372. E-mail: wilwrite@telepo rt.com. Writer workshops geared toward all levels. Emphasizes all areas of writing, including children's and young adult. Opportunities to meet one-on-one with leading literary agents and editors. Workshops held in August.

*WRITE FOR SUCCESS WORKSHOP: CHILDREN'S BOOKS, 3748 Harbor Heights Dr., Largo FL 34644. (813)581-2484. Workshop Leader: Theo Carroll. Writer and illustrator workshops geared toward intermediate levels. Program covers: writing and defining the picture book; finding and developing ideas; creating characters; plotting; writing dialogue; trends in publishing; developing conflict; revising. Annual workshop. Registration limited to 50-110. Cost of workshop: $85; includes hand outs and writers magazines. Write for more information.

WRITE ON THE SOUND WRITERS CONFERENCE, 700 Main St., Edmonds WA 98020. (206)771-0228. Fax: (206)771-0253. Website: http://ourworld.compuserve.com/homepa ges/city_of_Edmonds_WA/Edmonds.htm. Contact: Edmonds Arts Commission. Writer workshops geared toward beginner, intermediate, advanced and professional levels. "We offer fiction and nonfiction writing for children." Workshop held "usually the first weekend in October with 2 full days of a variety of lectures and workshops." Registration limited to 200. Cost of workshop: approximately $40/day, or $75 for the weekend, includes 4 workshops daily plus one ticket to keynote lecture. Optional boxed lunches available. Write for more information. "Brochures are mailed in August. Attendees must preregister. Write or call for brochure."

*WRITERS RETREAT WORKSHOP, % Write It/Sell It, South Lancaster MA 01561. (800)642-2494 (for brochure). Writer workshops geared toward beginner, intermediate, advanced levels. Workshops are appropriate for writers of full length novels for children/YA. Also, for writers of all novels or narrative nonfiction. Annual workshop. Workshops held in May and October. Registration limited to small groups: beginners and advanced. Writing/art facilities available: private rooms with desks. Cost of workshop: $1,595; includes tuition, food and lodging for nine nights, daily classes, writing space, time and assignments, consultation and instruction. Requirements: short synopsis required to determine appropriateness of novel for our nuts and bolts approach to getting the work in shape for publication. Write for more information. For complete details, call 800 number.

WRITERS STUDIO SPRING WRITERS CONFERENCE, 3403 45th St., Moline IL 61265. (309)762-8985. Coordinator, Pro Tem: David R. Collins. Writer workshops geared toward intermediate level. Emphasizes all aspects of writing for children, including basic writing and mechanics. Workshops held annually in March or April. Workshop is free. Write for more information.

*‡"WRITING FOR THE LOCAL CHURCH . . . AND BEYOND", P.O. Box 12624, Roanoke VA 24027. Phone/fax: (540)342-7511. E-mail: ccmbbr@worldnet.att.net. Director: Betty Robertson. Writer and illustrator workshops geared toward beginner, intermediate and advanced levels. Includes sessions on stories for children, puppet scripts, puzzles, curriculum. Workshops held in fall (one in Virginia, one in South Carolina). Cost of workshop: $24.95-34.95; includes comprehensive handbook, refreshments, free magazine samples. Write for more information.

Contests & Awards

Publication is not the only way to get your work recognized. Contests can also be viable vehicles to gain recognition in the industry. Placing in a contest or winning an award validates the time spent writing and illustrating. Even for those who don't place, many competitions offer the chance to obtain valuable feedback from judges and other established writers or artists.

Not all of the contests here are strictly for professionals. Many are designed for those who have not yet been published. Several of the contests in this section are open to students (some exclusively). Young writers and illustrators will find all contests open to students marked with a double dagger (‡). Young writers can find additional contests in *Market Guide for Young Writers*, by Kathy Henderson (Writer's Digest Books).

When considering contests, be sure to study guidelines and requirements. Regard entry deadlines as gospel and note whether manuscripts and artwork should be previously published or unpublished. Also, be aware that awards vary. While one contest may award a significant amount of money, another may award a certificate or medal instead.

Note that some contests require nominations. For published authors and illustrators, competitions provide an excellent way to promote your work. If your book is eligible for a contest or award, have the appropriate person at your publishing company nominate or enter your work for consideration.

To select potential contests for your work, read through the listings that interest you, then send for more information about the types of written or illustrated material considered and other important details, such as who retains the rights to prize-winning material. A number of contests offer such information through websites given in their listings. If you are interested in knowing who has received certain awards in the past, check your local library or bookstores or consult *Children's Books: Awards & Prizes*, compiled and edited by the Children's Book Council. Many bookstores have special sections for books which are Caldecott and Newbery Medal winners.

‡AIM Magazine Short Story Contest, P.O. Box 20554, Chicago IL 60620. (312)874-6184. Contest Directors: Ruth Apilado, Mark Boone. Annual contest. Estab. 1983. Purpose of contest: "We solicit stories with social significance. Youngsters can be made aware of social problems through the written word and hopefully they will try solving them." Unpublished submissions only. Deadline for entries: August 15. SASE for contest rules and entry forms. SASE for return of work. No entry fee. Awards $100. Judging by editors. Contest open to everyone. Winning entry published in fall issue of *AIM*. Subscription rate $10/year. Single copy $4.

♣ALCUIN CITATION AWARD, The Alcuin Society, P.O. Box 3216, Vancouver, British Columbia V6B 3X8 Canada. Phone/fax: (604)888-9049. Secretary: Doreen E. Eddy. Annual award. Estab. 1983. Purpose of contest: Alcuin Citations are awarded annually for excellence in Canadian book design. Previously published submissions only, "in the year prior to the Awards Invitation to enter; i.e., 1996 awards went to books published in 1995." Submissions made by the author, publishers and designers. Deadline for entries: March 15. SASE. Entry fee is $10. Awards certificate. Judging by professionals and those experienced in the field of book design. Requirements for entrants: Winners are selected from books designed and published in Canada. Awards are presented annually at the Annual General Meeting of the Alcuin Society held in late May or early June each year.

‡AMERICA & ME ESSAY CONTEST, Farm Bureau Insurance, Box 30400, 7373 W. Saginaw, Lansing MI 48909. (517)323-7000. Fax: (517)323-6615. Contest Coordinator: Lisa Fedewa.

Annual contest. Estab. 1968. Purpose of the contest: to give Michigan 8th graders the opportunity to express their thoughts/feelings on America and their roles in America. Unpublished submissions only. Deadline for entries: mid-November. SASE for contest rules and entry forms. "We have a school mailing list. Any school located in Michigan is eligible to participate." Entries not returned. No entry fee. Awards savings bonds and plaques for state top ten ($500-1,000), certificates and plaques for top 3 winners from each school. Each school may submit up to 10 essays for judging. Judging by home office employee volunteers. Requirements for entrants: "Participants must work through their schools or our agents' sponsoring schools. No individual submissions will be accepted. Top ten essays and excerpts from other essays are published in booklet form following the contest. State capitol/schools receive copies."

AMERICAS AWARD, Consortium of Latin American Studies Programs (CLASP), CLASP Committee on Teaching and Outreach, % Center for Latin America, University of Wisconsin-Milwaukee, P.O. Box 413, Milwaukee WI 53201. (414)229-5986. Fax: (414)229-2879. E-mail address: cla@csd.uwm.edu. Website: http://www.uwm.edu/Dept/CLA. Coordinator: Julie Kline. Annual award. Estab. 1993. Purpose of contest: "The award is given each spring in recognition of a U.S. published work (from the previous year) of fiction, poetry or folklore (from picture books to works for young adults) in English or Spanish which authentically and engagingly presents the experience of individuals in Latin America or the Caribbean, or of Latinos in the United States. By combining both and linking the "Americas," our intent is to go beyond geographic borders, as well as multicultural-international boundaries, focusing instead upon cultural heritages within the hemisphere." Previously published submissions only. Submissions open to anyone with an interest in the theme of the award. Deadline for entries: January 15. SASE for contest rules. Awards $200 cash prize, plaque and a formal presentation at the Library of Congress, Washington DC. Judging by a review committee consisting of individuals in teaching, library work, outreach and children's literature specialists.

‡AMHA LITERARY CONTEST, American Morgan Horse Association Youth, P.O. Box 960, Shelburne VT 05482. (802)985-4944. Contest Director: Erica Richard. Annual contest. The contest includes categories for both poetry and essays. The 1994 theme was "Olympic Size Morgan Dreams." Entrants should write to receive the 1995 entry form and theme. Unpublished submissions only. Submissions made by author. Deadline for entries: December 1. SASE for contest rules and entry forms. No entry fee. Awards $50 cash and ribbons to up to 5th place. "Winning entry will be published in *AMHA News and Morgan Sales Network*, a monthly publication."

‡AMHA MORGAN ART CONTEST, American Morgan Horse Association, Box 960, Shelburne VT 05482. (802)985-4944. Fax: (802)985-8897. E-mail: amha@together.net. Promotional Recognition Coordinator: Susan Bell. Annual contest. The art contest consists of three categories: Morgan art (pencil sketches, oils, water colors, paintbrush), Morgan cartoons, Morgan specialty pieces (sculptures, carvings). Unpublished submissions only. Deadline for entries: December 1. Contest rules and entry forms available for SASE. Entries not returned. Entry fee is $2. Awards $50 first prize in 3 divisions (for adults) and AMHA gift certificates to top 5 places (for children). Judging by *The Morgan Horse* magazine staff. "All work submitted becomes property of The American Morgan Horse Association. Selected works may be used for promotional purposes by the AMHA." Requirements for entrants: "We consider all work submitted." Works displayed at the annual convention and the AMHA headquarters; published in *AMAHA News* and *Morgan Sales Network*. The contest divisions consist of Junior (to age 17), Senior (18 and over) and Professional (commercial artists). Each art piece must have its own application form and its own entry fee. Matting is optional.

HANS CHRISTIAN ANDERSEN AWARD, IBBY International Board on Books for Young People, Nonnenweg 12, Postfach, CH-4003 Basel Switzerland. (004161)272 29 17. Fax: (004161)272 27 57. Award offered every two years. Purpose of award: A Hans Christian Ander-

---

‡   **THE DOUBLE DAGGER** before a listing indicates the contest is open to students.

sen Medal shall be awarded every two years by the International Board on Books for Young People (IBBY) to an author and to an illustrator, living at the time of the nomination, who by the outstanding value of their work are judged to have made a lasting contribution to literature for children and young people. The complete works of the author and of the illustrator will be taken into consideration in awarding the medal, which will be accompanied by a diploma. Previously published submissions only. Submissions are nominated by national sections of IBBY in good standing. The National Sections select the candidates. The Hans Christian Andersen Award, named after Denmark's famous storyteller, is the highest international recognition given to an author and an illustrator of children's books. The Author's Award has been given since 1956, the Illustrator's Award since 1966. The Andersen Award is often called the "Little Nobel Prize." Her Majesty Queen Margrethe of Denmark is the Patron of the Hans Christian Andersen Awards. At the discretion of the jury the distinction "Highly Commended" may also be awarded. The Hans Christian Andersen Jury judges the books submitted for medals according to literary and artistic criteria.

‡ARTS RECOGNITION AND TALENT SEARCH (ARTS), National Foundation for Advancement in the Arts, 800 Brickell Ave., Suite 500, Miami FL 33131. (305)377-1140. Fax: (305)377-1149. Contact: Sherry Thompson. Open to students/high school seniors or 17 and 18-year-olds. Annual award. Estab. 1981. "Created to recognize and reward outstanding accomplishment in dance, music, jazz, theater, photography, visual arts and/or writing. Arts Recognition and Talent Search (ARTS) is an innovative national program of the National Foundation for Advancement in the Arts (NFAA). Established in 1981, ARTS touches the lives of gifted young people across the country, providing financial support, scholarships and goal-oriented artistic, educational and career opportunities. Each year, from a pool of approximately 7,000 applicants, an average of 400 ARTS awardees are chosen for NFAA support by panels of distinguished artists and educators. Deadline for entries: June 1 and October 1. SASE for award rules and entry forms. Entry fee is $25/35. Fee waivers available based on need. Awards $100-3,000—unrestricted cash grants. Judging by a panel of authors and educators recognized in the field. Rights to submitted/winning material: NFAA/ARTS retains the right to duplicate work in an anthology or in Foundation literature unless otherwise specified by the artist. Requirements for entrants: Artists must be high school seniors or, if not enrolled in high school, must be 17 or 18 years old. Applicants must be US citizens or residents, unless applying in jazz. Works will be published in an anthology distributed during ARTS Week, the final adjudication phase which takes place in Miami.

‡BAKER'S PLAYS HIGH SCHOOL PLAYWRITING CONTEST, Baker's Plays, 100 Chauncy St., Boston MA 02111. (617)482-1280. Contest Director: Raymond Pape. Annual contest. Estab. 1990. Purpose of the contest: to acknowledge playwrights at the high school level and to insure the future of American theater. Unpublished submissions only. Deadline for entries: January 31 each year. Notification: May. SASE for contest rules and entry forms. No entry fee. Awards $500 to the first place playwright and Baker's Plays will publish the play; $250 to the second place playwright with an honorable mention; and $100 to the third place playwright with an honorable mention in the series. Judged anonymously. Open to any high school student. Teachers must not submit student's work. The first place playwright will have his/her play published in an acting edition the September following the contest. The work will be described in the Baker's Plays Catalogue, which is distributed to 50,000 prospective producing organizations. Plays must be accompanied by the signature of a sponsoring high school drama or English teacher, and it is recommended that the play receive a production or a public reading prior to the submission. "Please include a SASE."

MARGARET BARTLE ANNUAL PLAYWRITING AWARD, Community Children's Theatre of Kansas City, 8021 E. 129th Terrace, Grandview MO 64030. (816)761-5775. Chairperson: Blanche Sellens. Annual contest. Estab. 1947. "Community Children's Theatre of Kansas City, Inc. was organized in 1947 to provide live theater for elementary aged children. We are now recognized as being one of the country's largest organizations providing this type of service." Unpublished submissions only. Deadline for entries: end of January. SASE for award rules. SASE for return of entries. No entry fee. Awards $500. Judging by a committee of 5. "CCT reserves the right for one of the units to produce the prize winning play for two years. The plays are performed before students in elementary schools. Although our 5- to 12-year-old audiences are sophisticated, gratuitous violence, mature love stories, or slang are not appropriate—cursing is *not acceptable*. In addition to original ideas, subjects that usually provide good plays are legends, folklore, historical incidents, biographies and adaptations of children's classics."

BAY AREA BOOK REVIEWER'S ASSOCIATION (BABRA), %Chandler & Sharp, 11A Commercial Blvd., Novato CA 94949. (415)883-2353. Fax: (415)883-4280. Contact: Jonathan Sharp. Annual award for outstanding book in children's literature, open to Bay Area authors, northern California from Fresno north. Annual award. Estab. 1981. "BABRA presents annual awards to Bay Area (northern California) authors annually in fiction, nonfiction, poetry and children's literature. Purpose is to encourage Bay Area writers and stimulate interest in books and reading." Previously published submissions only. Must be published the calendar year prior to spring awards ceremony. Submissions nominated by publishers; author or agent could also nominate published work. Deadline for entries: December. No entry forms. Send 3 copies of the book to Jonathan Sharp. No entry fee. Awards $100 honorarium and award certificate. Judging by voting members of the Bay Area Book Reviewer's Association. Books that reach the "finals" (usually 3-5 per category) displayed at annual award ceremonies (spring). Nominated books are displayed and sold at BABRA's annual awards ceremonies, in the spring of each year.

JOHN AND PATRICIA BEATTY AWARD, California Library Association, 717 K. Street Suite 300, Sacramento CA 95814. (916)447-8541. Executive Director: Mary Sue Ferrell. Annual award. Estab. 1987. Purpose of award: "The purpose of the John and Patricia Beatty Award is to encourage the writing of quality children's books highlighting California, its culture, heritage and/or future." Previously published submissions only. Submissions made by the author, author's agent or review copies sent by publisher. The award is given to the author of a children's book published the preceding year. Deadline for entries: Submissions may be made January-December. Contact CLA Executive Director who will liaison with Beatty Award Committee. Awards cash prize of $500 and an engraved plaque. Judging by a 5-member selection committee appointed by the president of the California Library Association. Requirements for entrants: "Any children's or young adult book set in California and published in the U.S. during the calendar year preceding the presentation of the award is eligible for consideration. This includes works of fiction as well as nonfiction for children and young people of all ages. Reprints and compilations are not eligible. The California setting must be depicted authentically and must serve as an integral focus for the book." Winning selection is announced through press release during National Library Week in April. Author is presented with award at annual California Library Association Conference in November.

*❧THE GEOFFREY BILSON AWARD FOR HISTORICAL FICTION, The Canadian Children's Book Centre, 35 Spadina Rd., Toronto, Ontario M5R 2S9 Canada. (416)975-0010. Fax: (416)975-1839. E-mail: ccbc@lglobal.com. Website: http://www.lglobal.com/~ccbc. Program Coordinator: Jeffrey Canton. Annual award. Estab. 1988. Purpose of contest: To reward excellence in the writing of an outstanding work of historical fiction. Previously published submissions only. Submissions picked by the Children's Book Centre "based on our *Our Choice* catalogue." Must be published the previous calendar year. Writers should *not* contact the centre. No entry fee. Awards $1,000 (Canadian). Judging by a jury made up of a writer, bookseller, children's book specialist, historian, librarian. Requirements for entrants: "All books written by Canadians and selected for inclusion in *Our Choice*, will be eligible for consideration. A Canadian shall, for the purposes of the Committee, be deemed a citizen of Canada or a permanent resident who has lived in Canada for at least two years. Historical fiction is fiction in which history informs the work in a significant way and is historically authentic. An historical setting alone does not constitute a work of historical fiction."

THE IRMA S. AND JAMES H. BLACK BOOK AWARD, Bank Street College of Education, 610 W. 112th St., New York NY 10025. (212)222-6700. Fax: (212)875-4752. E-mail: lindag @bnk1.bnkst.edu. Website: http://www.bnkst.edu/library/clib/isb.html. Contact: Linda Greengrass. Annual award. Estab. 1972. Purpose of award: "The award is given each spring for a book for young children, published in the previous year, for excellence of both text and illustrations." Entries must have been published during the previous calendar year (between January '96 and December '96 for 1996 award). Deadline for entries: January 1. "Publishers submit books to us by sending them here to me at the Bank Street library. Authors may ask their publishers to submit their books. Out of these, three to five books are chosen by a committee of older children and children's literature professionals. These books are then presented to children in selected second, third and fourth grade classes here and at a few other cooperating schools on the East Coast. These children are the final judges who pick the actual award. A scroll (one each for the author and illustrator, if they're different) with the recipient's name and a gold seal designed by Maurice Sendak are awarded in May."

❦BOOK OF THE YEAR FOR CHILDREN, Canadian Library Association, 200 Elgin St., Suite 206, Ottawa, Ontario K2P 1L5 Canada. (613)232-9625. Fax: (613)563-9895. Contact: Chairperson, Canadian Association of Children's Librarians. Annual award. Estab. 1947. "The main purpose of the award is to encourage writing and publishing in Canada of good books for children up to and including age 14. If, in any year, no book is deemed to be of award calibre, the award shall not be made that year. To merit consideration, the book must have been published in Canada and its author must be a Canadian citizen or a permanent resident of Canada." Previously published submissions only; must be published between January 1 and December 1 of the previous year. Deadline for entries: January 1. SASE for award rules. Entries not returned. No entry fee. Awards a medal. Judging by committee of members of the Canadian Association of Children's Librarians. Requirements for entrants: Contest open only to Canadian authors or residents of Canada. Winning books are on display at CLA headquarters.

BOOK PUBLISHERS OF TEXAS, Children's/Young People's Award, The Texas Institute of Letters, %TCU Press, P.O. Box 298300, Ft. Worth TX 76129. (817)921-7822. Fax: (817)921-7822. E-mail: jalter@gamma.is.tcu.edu. Contact: Judy Alter. Send to above address for list of judges to whom entries should be submitted. Annual award. Purpose of the award: "to recognize notable achievement by a Texas writer of books for children or young people or by a writer whose work deals with a Texas subject. The award goes to the author of the winning book, a work published during the calendar year before the award is given. Judges list available each October. Submissions go directly to judges, so current list of judges is necessary. Write to above address. Deadline is first postally operative day of January." Previously published submissions only. SASE for award rules and entry forms. No entry fee. Awards $250. Judging by a panel of 3 judges selected by the TIL Council. Requirements for entrants: The writer must have lived in Texas for 2 consecutive years at some time, or the work must have a Texas theme.

THE BOSTON GLOBE-HORN BOOK AWARDS, The Boston Globe & The Horn Book, Inc., The Horn Book, 11 Beacon St., Suite 1000, Boston MA 02108. (617)227-1555. Award Directors: Stephanie Loer and Roger Sutton. Writing Contact: Stephanie Loer, children's book editor for *The Boston Globe*, 298 North St., Medfield MA 02052. Annual award. Estab. 1967. "Awards are for picture books, nonfiction and fiction. Up to two honor books may be chosen for each category." Books must be published between June 1, 1996 and May 30, 1997. Deadline for entries: May 15. "Publishers usually submit books. Award winners receive $500 and silver engraved bowl, honor book winners receive a silver plate." Judging by 3 judges involved in children's book field who are chosen by Roger Sutton, editor-in-chief for The Horn Book, Inc. (*The Horn Book Magazine* and the *Horn Book Guide*) and Stephanie Loer, children's book editor for *The Boston Globe*. "*The Horn Book Magazine* publishes speeches given at awards ceremonies. The book must have been published in the U.S. The awards are given at the fall conference of the New England Library Association."

‡ANN ARLYS BOWLER POETRY CONTEST, *Read* Magazine, 245 Long Hill Rd., Middletown CT 06457. (203)638-2406. Fax: (860)346-5826. E-mail: kdavis@weeklyreader.com. Website: http://www.weeklyreader.com/read.html. Contest Director: Kate Davis. Annual contest. Estab. 1988. Purpose of the contest: to reward young-adult poets (grades 6-12). Unpublished submissions only. Submissions made by the author or nominated by a person or group of people. Entry form must include signature of teacher, parent or guardian, and student verifying originality. Deadline for entries: December 20. SASE for contest rules and entry forms. No entry fee. Awards 6 winners $100 each, medal of honor and publication in *Read*. Semifinalists receive $50 each. Judging by *Read* and *Weekly Reader* editors and teachers. "Entrant understands that prize will include publication, but sometimes pieces are published in other issues." Requirements for entrants: the material must be original. Winning entries will be published in the May 2 issue of *Read* (all-student issue).

*❦ANN CONNOR BRIMER AWARD, Nova Scotia Library Association, P.O. Box 36036, Halifax, Nova Scotia B3J 3S9 Canada. (902)490-5875. Fax: (902)490-5893. Award Director:

Linda Hodgins. Annual award. Estab. 1991. Purpose of the contest: to recognize excellence in writing. Given to an author of a children's book who resides in Atlantic Canada. Previously published submissions only. Submissions made by the author's agent or nominated by a person or group of people. Must be published May 1-April 30. Deadline for entries: April 30. SASE for contest rules and entry forms. No entry fee. Awards $1,000. Judging by a selection committee. Requirements for entrants: Book must be intended for children up to age 15; in print and readily available; fiction or nonfiction except textbooks.

BUCKEYE CHILDREN'S BOOK AWARD, State Library of Ohio, 65 S. Front St., Columbus OH 43215-4163. (614)644-7061. Fax: (614)466-3584. E-mail: rmetcalf@slonet.ohio.gov. Nancy Short, Chairperson. Correspondence should be sent to Floyd C. Dickman at the above address. Award every two years. Estab. 1981. Purpose of the award: "The Buckeye Children's Book Award Program was designed to encourage children to read literature critically, to promote teacher and librarian involvement in children's literature programs, and to commend authors of such literature, as well as to promote the use of libraries. Awards are presented in the following three categories: grades K-2, grades 3-5 and grades 6-8." Previously published submissions only. Deadline for entries: February 1. "The nominees are submitted by this date during the even year and the votes are submitted by this date during the odd year. This award is nominated and voted upon by children in Ohio. It is based upon criteria established in our bylaws. The winning authors are awarded a special plaque honoring them at a banquet given by one of the sponsoring organizations. The BCBA Board oversees the tallying of the votes and announces the winners in March of the voting year in a special news release and in a number of national journals. The book must have been written by an author, a citizen of the United States and originally copyrighted in the U.S. within the last three years preceding the nomination year. The award-winning books are displayed in a historical display housed at the Columbus Metropolitan Library in Columbus, Ohio."

BYLINE MAGAZINE CONTESTS, P.O. Box 130596, Edmond OK 73013. E-mail: bylinemp @aol.com. Website: http://www.bylinemag.com. Contest Director: Marcia Preston. Purpose of contest: *ByLine* runs 4 contests a month on many topics to encourage and motivate writers. Past topics include first chapter of a novel, children's fiction, children's poem, nonfiction for children, personal essay, greeting card verse, valentine or love poem, etc. Send SASE for contest flier with topic list. Unpublished submissions only. Submissions made by the author. "We do not publish the contests' winning entries, just the names of the winners." SASE for contest rules and entry forms. Entry fee is $3-4. Awards cash prizes for first, second and third place. Amounts vary. Judging by qualified writers or editors. List of winners will appear in magazine.

‡**BYLINE MAGAZINE STUDENT PAGE**, P.O. Box 130596, Edmond OK 73013. (405)348-5591. E-mail: bylinemp@aol.com. Website: http://www.bylinemag.com. Contest Director: Marcia Preston, publisher. Estab. 1981. "We offer student writing contests on a monthly basis, September through June, with cash prizes and publication of top entries." Previously unpublished submissions only. "This is not a market for illustration." Deadline for entries varies. "Entry fee usually $1." Awards cash and publication. Judging by qualified editors and writers. "We publish top entries in student contests. Winners' list published in magazine dated 3 months past deadline." Send SASE for details.

RANDOLPH CALDECOTT MEDAL, Association for Library Service to Children, Division of the American Library Association, 50 E. Huron, Chicago IL 60611. (312)280-2163. Executive Director ALSC: Susan Roman. Annual award. Estab. 1938. Purpose of the award: to honor the artist of the most distinguished picture book for children published in the US (Illustrator must be US citizen or resident.) Must be published year preceding award. Deadline for entries: December. SASE for award rules. Entries not returned. No entry fee. "Medal given at ALA Annual Conference during the Newbery/Caldecott Banquet."

CALIFORNIA WRITERS' CONFERENCE AWARDS, California Writers' Club, 2214 Derby St., Berkeley CA 94705. (510)841-1217. "Ask for award rules before submitting entries." Award offered every 2 years. Next conference, June 23-25, 1995. Purpose of the award: "To encourage writers." Categories: adult short stories, adult novels, adult nonfiction, juvenile fiction or nonfiction, picture books, poetry and scripts. Unpublished submissions only. SASE for award rules and entry forms. SASE for return of entries. Entry fee is $10 for each submission. Awards are $150 first prize; $100, second; $75, third; honorable mention certificates at judges' discretion.

Judging by "published writer-members of California Writers' Club. Open to all."

‡**CALIFORNIA YOUNG PLAYWRIGHTS CONTEST**, Playwrights Project, Suite 215, 1450 Frazee Rd., San Diego CA 92108. (619)298-9242. Director: Deborah Salzer. Open to Californians under age 19. Annual contest. Estab. 1985. "Our organization, and the contest, is designed to nurture promising young writers. We hope to develop playwrights and audiences for live theater. We also teach playwriting." Submissions required to be unpublished and not produced professionally. Submissions made by the author. Deadline for entries: April 1. SASE for contest rules and entry form. No entry fee. Award is professional productions of 3-5 short plays each year, participation of the writers in the entire production process, with a royalty award of $100 per play. Judging by professionals in the theater community, a committee of 5-7; changes somewhat each year. Works performed "in San Diego at the Cassius Carter Centre Stage of the Old Globe Theatre. Writers submitting scripts of 10 or more pages receive a detailed script evaluation letter."

*❦**CANADA COUNCIL GOVERNOR GENERAL'S LITERARY AWARDS**, 350 Albert St., P.O. Box 1047, Ottawa, Ontario K1P 5V8 Canada. (613)566-4376. Officer, Writing and Publishing Section: Josiane Polidori. Annual award. Estab. 1937. Purpose of award: to encourage Canadian authors and illustrators of books for young people as well as to recognize the importance of their contribution to literary activity. Award categories include children's text and children's illustration. Must be published between August 1 and July 31 of award year. Eligible books in French or English are submitted by publishers (4 copies must be sent to Canada Council). All books must be received by August 15. Submission forms available on request. Entries not returned. No entry fee. Awards $10,000 (Canadian). Judging by practicing writers and illustrators. Contest open to Canadian writers and illustrators only.

❦‡**CANADIAN AUTHORS ASSOCIATION STUDENTS' CREATIVE WRITING CONTEST**, Box 119, Campbellford, Ontario K0L 1L0 Canada. (705)653-0323. Fax: (705)653-0593. E-mail: canauth@redden.on.ca. Contact: Bernice Lever-Farrar. Entrants must be enrolled in secondary schools, colleges or universities and must be Canadian residents or Canadian citizens living abroad. Entries to be typed on one side of letter-sized white paper, and not published previously except in a student class anthology, student newspaper or student yearbook. Entries will not be returned. Entry fees: $5 per short story of 2,000 words or less; $5 per article of 2,000 words or less; $5 for 2 to 3 poems of not more than 30 lines each. Awards: $500 for best story; $500 for best article; $500 for best poem. Four Honourable Mentions in each category. All 15 winners will receive *Canadian Author* magazine for 1 year. Entry forms will be in the Winter and Spring issues of *Canadian Author*; deadline March 1997.

REBECCA CAUDILL YOUNG READERS' BOOK AWARD, Illinois Reading Council, Illinois School Library Media Association, Illinois Association of Teachers of English, P.O. Box 871, Arlington Heights IL 60006-0871. (708)420-6406. Fax: (708)420-3242. Award Director Jackie Plourde. Annual award. Estab. 1988. Purpose of contest: to award the Children's Choice Award for grades 4-8 in Illinois. Submissions nominated by students. Must be published within the last 5 years. Awards honorarium, plaque. Judging by children, grades 4-8.

❦‡**CHICKADEE COVER CONTEST**, Chickadee Magazine, Owl Communications, Suite 500, 179 John St., Toronto, Ontario M5T 3G5 Canada. (416)971-5275. Contest Director: Mitch Butler, Chirp Editor. Annual contest. There is a different theme published each year. Announcement published each October issue. No entry fee. Winning drawing published on cover of February issue. Judging by staff of *Chickadee*. Requirements for entrants: Must be 3- to 9-year-old readers.

❦‡**CHICKADEE'S GARDEN EVENT**, Chickadee Magazine, Owl Communications, Suite 500, 179 John St., Toronto, Ontario M5T 3G5 Canada. (416)971-5275. Contest Director: Mitch

---

❋ **THE ASTERISK** before a listing indicates the listing is new in this edition.

Butler, Chirp Editor. Annual. *Chickadee* readers are asked "to grow a favorite fruit or vegetable (anything as long as you can eat it) and submit a photo or drawing of you and your plant, and tell us why you chose the plant you did, and who helped you to care for it. Include experiences and humorous adventures along the way." Unpublished submissions only. Contest is announced in May issue. Deadline for entries: September. Results published in January issue. Judging by staff of *Chickadee*. Requirements for entrants: Must be 3-9 year-old readers.

CHILDREN'S BOOK AWARD, Federation of Children's Book Groups. 30 Senneleys Park Rd., Northfield Birmingham B31 1AL England. (0121)427-4860. Fax: (0121)643-3152. Coordinator: Jenny Blanch. Purpose of the award: "The C.B.A. is an annual prize for the best children's book of the year judged by the children themselves." Categories: (I) picture books, (II) short novels, (III) longer novels. Estab. 1980. Previously unpublished submissions only. Deadline for entries: December 31. SASE for rules and entry forms. Entries not returned. Awards "a magnificent silver and oak trophy worth over $6,000 and a portfolio of children's work." Silver dishes to each category winner. Judging by children. Requirements for entrants: Work must be fiction and published during the current year (poetry is ineligible). Work will be published in current "Pick of the Year" publication.

CHILDREN'S WRITER WRITING CONTESTS, 95 Long Ridge Rd., West Redding CT 06896. (203)792-8600. Contest offered every 4 months by *Children's Writer*, the monthly newsletter of writing and publishing trends. Purpose of the award: To promote higher quality children's literature. "Each contest has its own theme. Our last three were: (1) A how-to article for ages 8 to 12; to 850 words. (2) Young adult fiction for ages 13 to 16; to 1,000 words. (3) A humorous story for ages 8 to 12; to 900 words. Any original unpublished piece, not accepted by any publisher at the time of submission, is eligible." Submissions made by the author. Deadline for entries: Last Friday in February, June and October. "We charge a $10 entry fee for nonsubscribers only, which is applicable against a subscription to *Children's Writer*." Awards 1st place—$100 or $1,000, a certificate and publication in *Children's Writer*; 2nd place—$50 or $500, and certificate; 3rd-5th places—$25 or $250 and certificates. One or two contests each year with the higher cash prizes also include $100 prizes plus certificates for 6th-12th places. To obtain the rules and theme for the current contest send a SASE to *Children's Writer* at the above address. Put "Contest Request" in the lower left of your envelope. Judging by a panel of 5 selected from the staff of the Institute of Children's Literature. "We acquire First North American Serial Rights (to print the winner in *Children's Writer*), after which all rights revert to author." Open to any writer. Entries are judged on age targeting, originality, quality of writing and, for nonfiction, how well the information is conveyed and accuracy. "Submit clear photocopies only, not originals; submission will *not* be returned. Manuscripts should be typed double-spaced. No pieces containing violence or derogatory, racist or sexist language or situations will be accepted, at the sole discretion of the judges."

*‡CHILDREN'S WRITERS FICTION CONTEST, Goodin Williams Goodwin Literary Associates, P.O. Box 8863, Springfield MO 65801. (417)863-7670 or (417)833-5724. Coordinator: V.R. Williams. Annual contest. Estab. 1994. Purpose of contest: To promote writing for children, by giving children's writers an opportunity to submit work in competition. Unpublished submissions only. Submissions made by the author. Deadline for entries: July 31st. SASE for contest rules and entry forms. Entry fee is $3. Awards cash prize and publication in *Hodgepodge* chap book in fall; certificates for Honorable Mention. Judging by Goodin, Williams and Goodwin. First rights to winning material acquired or purchased. Requirements for entrants: Work must be suitable for children and no longer than 800 words. "Send SASE for list of winners."

MR. CHRISTIE'S BOOK AWARD® PROGRAM, Christie Brown & Co., Division of Nabisco Ltd., 2150 Lakeshore Blvd., Toronto, Ontario M8V 1A3 Canada. (416)503-6050. Fax: (416)503-6288. Coordinator: Marlene Yustin. Competition is open to Canadian citizens, landed imigrants or books published in Canada in 1996. Annual award. Estab. 1990. Purpose of award: to honor Canadian authors and illustrators of good English/French Canadian published children's books. Contest includes three categories: Best Book for 7 and under; 8-11; and 12 and up. Submissions are made by the author, made by the author's agent, publishers. Deadline for entries: January 31. SASE for contest rules and entry forms. No entry fee. Awards a total of $45,000. Judging by a panel consisting of people in the literary/teaching community across Canada. Requirements for entrants: must be published children's literature in English or French.

THE CHRISTOPHER AWARD, The Christophers, 12 E. 48th St., New York NY 10017. (212)759-4050. Christopher Awards Coordinators: Peggy Flanagan and Virginia Armstrong. Annual award. Estab. 1969 (for young people; books for adults honored since 1949). "The award is given to works, published in the calendar year for which the award is given, that 'have achieved artistic excellence, affirming the highest values of the human spirit.' They must also enjoy a reasonable degree of popular acceptance." Previously published submissions only; must be published between January 1 and December 31. "Books should be submitted all year. Two copies should be sent to Peggy Flanagan, 12 E. 48th St., New York NY 10017 and two copies to Virginia Armstrong, 22 Forest Ave., Old Tappan NJ 07675." Entries not returned. No entry fee. Awards a bronze medallion. Books are judged by both reading specialists and young people. Requirements for entrants: "only published works are eligible and must be submitted during the calendar year in which they are first published."

CHRISTOPHER COLUMBUS SCREENPLAY DISCOVERY AWARDS, Christopher Columbus Society of the Creative Arts, #600, 433 N. Camden Dr., Beverly Hills CA 90210. (310)288-1988. Fax: (310)288-0257. E-mail: awards@screenwriters.com. Website: http://screen writers.com. Award Director: Mr. Carlos Abreu. Annual and monthly awards. Estab. 1990. Purpose of award: to discover new screenplay writers. Unpublished submissions only. Submissions are made by the author or author's agent. Deadline for entries: December 1st and monthly (last day of month). Entry fee is $45. Awards: (1) Feedback—development process with industry experts. (2) Financial rewards—option moneys up to $10,000. (3) Access to key decision makers. Judging by entertainment industry experts, producers and executives.

‡**CRICKET LEAGUE**, *Cricket Magazine*, 315 Fifth St., Peru IL 61354. (815)224-6643. Address entries to: Cricket League. Monthly. Estab. 1973. "The purpose of Cricket League contests is to encourage creativity and give young people an opportunity to express themselves in writing, drawing, painting or photography. There is a contest each month. Possible categories include story, poetry, art or photography. Each contest relates to a *specific theme* described on each *Cricket* issue's Cricket League page. Signature verifying originality, age and address of entrant required. Entries which do not relate to the current month's theme cannot be considered." Unpublished submissions only. Deadline for entries: the 25th of each month. Cricket League rules, contest theme, and submission deadline information can be found in the current issue of *Cricket*. "We prefer that children who enter the contests subscribe to the magazine, or that they read *Cricket* in their school or library." No entry fee. Awards certificate suitable for framing and children's books or art/writing supplies. Judging by *Cricket* editors. Obtains right to print prize-winning entries in magazine. Refer to contest rules in current *Cricket* issue. Winning entries are published on the Cricket League pages in the *Cricket* magazine 3 months subsequent to the issue in which the contest was announced.

MARGUERITE DE ANGELI PRIZE, Bantam Doubleday Dell Books for Young Readers, 1540 Broadway, New York NY 10036. Estab. 1992. Fax: (212)782-9452 (note re: Marguerite De Angeli Prize). Annual award. Purpose of the award: to encourage the writing of fiction for children aged 7-10, either contemporary or historical; to encourage unpublished writers in the field of middle grade fiction. Unpublished submissions only. Length: between 40-144 pages. Submissions made by author or author's agent. Entries should be postmarked between April 1st and June 30th. SASE for award rules. No entry fee. Awards a $1,500 cash prize plus a hardcover and paperback book contract with a $3,500 advance against a royalty to be negotiated. Judging by Bantam Doubleday Dell Books for Young Readers editorial staff. Open to US and Canadian writers who have not previously published a novel for middle-grade readers (ages 7-10). Works published in an upcoming Bantam Doubleday Dell Books for Young Readers list.

DELACORTE PRESS PRIZE FOR A FIRST YOUNG ADULT NOVEL, Delacorte Press, Books for Young Readers Department, 1540 Broadway, New York NY 10036. (212)354-6500. Fax: (212)782-9452. Annual award. Estab. 1982. Purpose of award: to encourage the writing of contemporary young adult fiction. Previously unpublished submissions only. Mss sent to Delacorte Press may not be submitted to other publishers while under consideration for the prize. "Entries must be submitted between October 1 and New Year's Day. The real deadline is a December 31 postmark. Early entries are appreciated." SASE for award rules. No entry fee. Awards a $1,500 cash prize and a $6,000 advance against royalties on a hardcover and paperback book contract. Works published in an upcoming Bantam Doubleday Dell Books for Young Readers list. Judged by the editors of the Books for Young Readers Department of Bantam Doubleday

Dell. Requirements for entrants: The writer must be American or Canadian and must *not* have previously published a young adult novel but may have published anything else.

MARGARET A. EDWARDS AWARDS, American Library Association, 50 East Huron St., Chicago IL 60611-2795. (312)944-6780 or (800)545-2433. Fax: (312)440-9374. Annual award administered by the Young Adult Library Services Association (YALSA) of the American Library Association (ALA) and sponsored by *School Library Journal* magazine. Purpose of award: "ALA's Young Adult Library Services Association (YALSA), on behalf of librarians who work with young adults in all types of libraries, will give recognition to those authors whose book or books have provided young adults with a window through which they can view their world and which will help them to grow and to understand themselves and their role in relationships, society and the world." Previously published submissions only. Submissions are nominated by young adult librarians and teenagers. Must be published five years before date of award. SASE for award rules and entry forms. No entry fee. Judging by members of the Young Adult Library Services Association. "The award will be given annually to an author whose book or books, over a period of time, have been accepted by young adults as an authentic voice that continues to illuminate their experiences and emotions, giving insight into their lives. The book or books should enable them to understand themselves, the world in which they live, and their relationship with others and with society. The book or books must be in print at the time of the nomination."

‡JOAN FASSLER MEMORIAL BOOK AWARD, Association for the Care of Children's Health, 7910 Woodmont Ave., Suite 300, Bethesda MD 20814. (301)654-6549. Fax: (301)986-4553. Membership Manager: Trish McClean. Competition open to adults and children. Annual award. Estab. 1989. Previously published submissions only. Submissions made by the author, author's agent. Must be published between 1995 and 1996. SASE for award rules and entry forms. No entry fee. Award $1,000 honorarium, plaque. Judging by multidisciplinary committee of ACCH members. Requirements for entrants: open to any writer. Display and book signing opportunities at annual conference.

DOROTHY CANFIELD FISHER CHILDREN'S BOOK AWARD, Vermont Department of Libraries, Vermont State PTA and Vermont Congress of Parents and Teachers, % Southwest Regional Library, Pierpoint Ave., Rutland VT 05701. (802)773-5879. Chairman: Sandra S. Roy. Annual award. Estab. 1957. Purpose of the award: to encourage Vermont children to become enthusiastic and discriminating readers by providing them with books of good quality by living American authors published in the current year. Deadline for entries: "January of the following year." SASE for award rules and entry forms. No entry fee. Awards a scroll presented to the winning author at an award ceremony. Judging is by the children grades 4-8. They vote for their favorite book. Requirements for entrants: "Titles must be original work, published in the United States, and be appropriate to children in grades 4 through 8. The book must be copyrighted in the current year. It must be written by an American author living in the U.S."

FLICKER TALE CHILDREN'S BOOK AWARD, North Dakota Library Association, 515 N. Fifth St., Bismarck ND 58501. (701)222-6410. Fax: (701)221-6854. Award Director: Verna LaBounty, P.O. Box 145, Kindred ND 58051. Estab. 1979. Purpose of award: to give children across the state of North Dakota a chance to vote for their book of choice from a nominated list of 10: 5 in the picture book category; 5 in the juvenile category. Also, to promote awareness of quality literature for children. Previously published submissions only. Submissions nominated by a person or group of people. Awards a plaque from North Dakota Library Association and banquet dinner. Judging by children in North Dakota.

FLORIDA STATE WRITING COMPETITION, Florida Freelance Writers Assocociation, P.O. Box A, North Stratford NH 03590. (603)922-8338. Fax: (603)922-8339. E-mail: fjwx43b@p rodigy.com. Executive Director: Dana K. Cassell. Annual contest. Estab. 1984. Categories include children's short story and children's nonfiction article or book chapter (length appropriate to age category). Entry fee is $5 (members), $10 (nonmembers). Awards $75 first prize, membership second prize, book third prize, certificates for honorable mentions. Judging by teachers, editors and published authors. Judging criteria: interest and readability within age group, writing style and mechanics, originality, salability. Deadline: March 15. For copy of official entry form, send #10 SASE.

‡4-H ESSAY CONTEST, American Beekeeping Federation, Inc., P.O. Box 1038, Jesup GA 31545. (912)427-8447. Contest Director: Troy H. Fore. Annual contest. Purpose of contest: to educate youth about the beekeeping industry. 1997 essay topic: a "news event" in the bee colony. Some examples are "Queen and Loyalists Flee Anarchists" (swarm leaves to set up new colony); "New Queen Takes the Throne" (bees replace failing or dead queen bee). Unpublished submissions only. Deadline for entries: before March 1. No entry fee. Awards 1st place: $250; 2nd place: $100; 3rd place: $50. Judging by American Beekeeping Federation's Essay Committee. "All national entries become the property of the American Beekeeping Federation, Inc., and may be published or used as it sees fit. No essay will be returned. Essayists *should not* forward essays directly to the American Beekeeping Federation office. Each state 4-H office is responsible for selecting the state's winner and should set its deadline so state judging can be completed at the state level in time for the winning state essay to be mailed to the ABF office before March 1, 1997. Each state winner receives a book on honey bees, beekeeping or honey. The National Winner will announced by May 1, 1997." Requirements for entrants: Contest is open to active 4-H Club members only.

DON FREEMAN MEMORIAL GRANT-IN-AID, Society of Children's Book Writers and Illustrators, 22736 Vanowen St., Suite 106, West Hills CA 91307. (818)888-8760. Website: http://www.scbwi.com. Estab. 1974. Purpose of award: to "enable picture book artists to further their understanding, training and work in the picture book genre." Applications and prepared materials will be accepted between January 15 and February 15. Grant awarded and announced on June 15. SASE for award rules and entry forms. SASE for return of entries. No entry fee. Annually awards one grant of $1,000 and one runner-up grant of $500. "The grant-in-aid is available to both full and associate members of the SCBWI who, as artists, seriously intend to make picture books their chief contribution to the field of children's literature."

❀**AMELIA FRANCES HOWARD GIBBON AWARD FOR ILLUSTRATION**, Canadian Library Association, Suite 602, 200 Elgin St., Ottawa, Ontario K2P 1L5 Canada. (613)232-9625. Contact: Chairperson, Canadian Association of Children's Librarians. Annual award. Estab. 1971. Purpose of the award: "to honor excellence in the illustration of children's book(s) in Canada. To merit consideration the book must have been published in Canada and its illustrator must be a Canadian citizen or a permanent resident of Canada." Previously published submissions only; must be published between January 1 and December 31 of the previous year. Deadline for entries: January 1. SASE for award rules. Entries not returned. No entry fee. Awards a medal. Judging by selection committee of members of Canadian Association of Children's Librarians. Requirements for entrants: illustrator must be Canadian or Canadian resident. Winning books are on display at CLA Headquarters.

GOLD MEDALLION BOOK AWARDS, Evangelical Christian Publishers Association, 1969 East Broadway Rd., Suite Two, Tempe AZ 85282. (602)966-3998. Fax: (602)966-1944. President: Doug Ross. Annual award. Estab. 1978. Categories include Preschool Children's Books, Elementary Children's Books, Youth Books. "All entries must be evangelical in nature and cannot be contrary to ECPA's Statement of Faith (stated in official rules)." Deadlines for entries: December 1. SASE for award rules and entry form. "The work must be submitted by the publisher." Entry fee is $250 for nonmembers. Awards a Gold Medallion plaque.

GOLDEN KITE AWARDS, Society of Children's Book Writers and Illustrators, 22736 Vanowen St., Suite 106, West Hills CA 91307. (818)888-8760. Website: http://www.scbwi.org. Coordinator: Sue Alexander. Annual award. Estab. 1973. "The works chosen will be those that the judges feel exhibit excellence in writing, and in the case of the picture-illustrated books—in illustration, and genuinely appeal to the interests and concerns of children. For the fiction and nonfiction awards, original works and single-author collections of stories or poems of which at least half are new and never before published in book form are eligible—anthologies and translations are not. For the picture-illustration awards, the art or photographs must be original works (the texts—which may be fiction or nonfiction—may be original, public domain or previously published). Deadline for entries: December 15. SASE for award rules. Self-addressed mailing label for return of entries. No entry fee. Awards statuettes and plaques. The panel of judges will consist of two children's book authors, a children's book artist or photographer (who may or may not be an author), a children's book editor and a librarian." Requirements for entrants: "must be a member of SCBWI." Winning books will be displayed at national conference in August. Books to be entered, as well as further inquiries, should be submitted to: The Society of Children's Book Writers and Illustrators, above address.

HIGHLIGHTS FOR CHILDREN FICTION CONTEST, 803 Church St., Honesdale PA 18431. (717)253-1080. Mss should be addressed to Fiction Contest. Editor: Kent L. Brown Jr. Annual contest. Estab. 1980. Purpose of the contest: to stimulate interest in writing for children and reward and recognize excellence. Unpublished submissions only. Deadline for entries: February 28; entries accepted after January 1 only. SASE for contest rules and return of entries. No entry fee. Awards 3 prizes of $1,000 each in cash and a pewter bowl (or, at the winner's election, attendance at the Highlights Foundation Writers Workshop at Chautauqua). Judging by *Highlights* editors. Winning pieces are purchased for the cash prize of $1,000 and published in *Highlights*; semifinalists go to out-of-house judges (educators, editors, writers, etc.). Requirements for entrants: open to any writer; student writers must be 16 or older. Winners announced in June. "The 1997 contest is for mystery stories for children. Length up to 900 words. Stories for beginning readers should not exceed 500 words. Stories should be consistent with *Highlights* editorial requirements. No violence, crime or derogatory humor."

*HRC'S ANNUAL PLAYWRITING CONTEST, Hudson River Classics, Inc., P.O. Box 940, Hudson NY 12534. (518)828-1329. President: W. Keith Hedrick. Annual contest. Estab. 1992. Hudson River Classics is a not-for-profit professional theater company dedicated to the advancement of performing in the Hudson River Valley area through reading of plays and providing opportunities for new playwrights. Unpublished submissions only. Submissions made by author and by the author's agent. Deadlines for entries: June 1st. SASE for contest rules and entry forms. Entry fee is $5. Awards $500 cash plus concert reading by professional actors. Judging by panel selected by Board of Directors. Requirements for entrants: Entrants must live in the northeastern US.

IBBY HONOUR LIST, International Board on Books for Young People, Nonnerweg 12, Postfach CH-4003 Basel, Switzerland. (004161)272-2917. Fax: (004161)272-2757. Biennial award. The IBBY Honour List is a selection of outstanding recently published books honoring writers, illustrators, and translators from IBBY member countries. Important considerations in selecting the Honour List titles are that the books chosen be representative of the best in children's literature from each country, and that the books are recommended as suitable for publication throughout the world, thus furthering the IBBY objective of encouraging international understanding through children's literature. The selection of IBBY Honour List books has resulted in greater international awareness and recognition of these titles by book publishers and has considerably increased the number of translations and foreign editions of quality children's books. Previously published submissions only. Submissions are by IBBY National sections in good standing. The books are shown in five parallel travelling exhibitions before they are kept as permanent deposits in some of the world's leading children's book institutions. The accompanying catalogue presenting the Honour List books, their authors, illustrators and translators, is distributed throughout the world. The Honour List diplomas are presented to the recipients at the IBBY Congresses.

INDIAN PAINTBRUSH BOOK AWARD, Wyoming Library Association, P.O. Box 1387, Cheyenne WY 82003. (307)632-7622. Award Director: Laura Grott. Annual award. Estab. 1986. Purpose of award: to encourage the children of Wyoming to read good books. Previously published submissions only. Deadline for entries: April 1. Books can only be submitted for the nominations list by the children of Wyoming. No entry fee. Awards a watercolor painting. Judging by the children of Wyoming (grades 4-6) voting from a nominations list of 20. Requirements for entrants: only Wyoming children may nominate; books must be published in last 5 years, be fiction, have good reviews; final list chosen by a committee of librarians.

*‡INSPIRATIONAL WRITERS ALIVE! OPEN WRITERS COMPETITION, IWA, Rt. 4 Box 81-H, Rusk TX 75785-9410. (903)795-3986. Contest Director: Maxine E. Holder. Annual contest. Estab. 1990. Purpose of contest: to help aspiring writers to inspire through the inspirational/religion markets. Unpublished submissions only. Submissions made by author. Deadline for entries: April 1st. SASE for contest rules. Entry fee is $4 (devotional short story or article); $2 (3 poems). Awards certificate of merit and cash for 1st, 2nd and 3rd place. Anthology of winning entry entitled *Timbrels of God* published every other year. Judging by well-known, published authors. Requirements for entrants: Cannot enter published material. "We want to aid especially new and aspiring writers." Contest has 6 categories—one for children and teens only.

‡IOWA TEEN AWARD, Iowa Educational Media Association, 306 E. H Ave., Grundy Center IA 50638. (319)824-6788. Contest Director: Don Osterhaus. Annual award. Estab. 1983. Previously published submissions only. Purpose of award: to allow students to read high quality literature and to have the opportunity to select their favorite from this list. Must have been published "in last 3-4 years." Deadline for entries: April 1995 for '96-'97 competition. SASE for award rules/entry forms. No entry fee. "Media specialists, teachers and students nominate possible entries." Awards an inscribed brass apple. Judging by Iowa students in grades 6-9. Requirements: Work must be of recent publication, so copies can be ordered for media center collections. Reviews of submitted books must be available for the nominating committee. Works displayed "at participating classrooms, media centers, public libraries and local bookstores in Iowa."

‡**IYC ETHICS WRITING CONTEST**, *It's Your Choice Magazine*, P.O. Box 7135, Richmond VA 23221. Contact: Editor. Annual contest. Estab. 1993. Purpose of contest: to arouse interest in ethics and encourage discussion of ethical ideas. "All articles/stories must be related to ethics/ morality issues in an essential way. Tacking on a couple of statements abouts ethics/morality to a story you have already written will not do. We regard ethics as the scientific study of the rightness or wrongness of human behavior in any context, which opens the field to a wide variety of articles. You might write about the larger social issues such as abortion, murder, capital punishment, war, greed; or about personal actions such as your son's hiding his report card because he got an F." Unpublished submissions only. Submissions made by the author. Deadline monthly. School districts may submit at any time (elementary, junior and senior high in separate batches) but only once in any calendar year. Monthly prizes: elementary, $25; junior high, $50; high school, $100. Winning entries are automatically entered in regional and national contests for larger prizes and awards ceremonies. Submissions from school age children should be sent by school officials batched by grade level, with a fee of $1 per manuscript submitted: vastly greater prize opportunities. SASE for contest rules and entry forms. Entry fee is $2 for purchase of mss registration form. Judging by editor. Right to publish entry in a collection of winning mss without further pay is required.

THE EZRA JACK KEATS NEW WRITER AWARD, Ezra Jack Keats Foundation/Admin-istered by the New York Public Library Early Childhood Resource and Information Center, 66 Leroy St., New York NY 10014. (212)929-0815. Program Coordinator: Hannah Nuba. Biennial award. Purpose of the award: "The award will be given to a promising new writer of picture books for children. Selection criteria include books for children (ages nine and under) that reflect the tradition of Ezra Jack Keats. These books portray: the universal qualities of childhood, strong and supportive family and adult relationships, the multicultural nature of our world." Submissions made by the author, by the author's agent or nominated by a person or group of people. Must be published in the 2-year period preceding the award. SASE for contest rules and entry forms. No entry fee. Awards $1,000 coupled with Ezra Jack Keats Silver Medal. Judging by a panel of experts. "The author should have published no more than six books. Entries are judged on the outstanding features of the text, complemented by illustrations. Candidates need not be both author and illustrator. Entries should carry a 1995 or 1996 copyright (for the 1996 award)." Winning book and author to be at a reception at The New York Public Library. Book should be for ages 9 and under.

EZRA JACK KEATS/KERLAN COLLECTION MEMORIAL FELLOWSHIP, University of Minnesota, 109 Walter Library, 117 Pleasant St. SE, Minneapolis MN 55455. (612)624-4576. Fax: (612)625-5525. Competition open to adults. Offered annually. Deadline for entries: first Monday in May. Send request with SASE, including 52¢ postage. The Ezra Jack Keats/Kerlan Collection Memorial Fellowship from the Ezra Jack Keats Foundation will provide $1,500 to a "talented writer and/or illustrator of children's books who wishes to use the Kerlan Collection for the furtherance of his or her artistic development. Special consideration will be given to someone who would find it difficult to finance the visit to the Kerlan Collection." The fellowship winner will receive transnportation and per diem. Judging by the Kerlan Award Committee—3 representatives from the University of Minnesota faculty, one representative from the Kerlan Collection, one from the Kerlan Friends, and one from the Minnesota Library Association.

‡   **THE DOUBLE DAGGER** before a listing indicates the contest is open to students.

‡**KENTUCKY STATE POETRY SOCIETY ANNUAL CONTEST**, Kentucky State Poetry Society, % *Pegasus* editor Miriam L. Woolfolk, 3289 Hunting Hills Dr., Lexington KY 40515. (606)271-4662. Annual contest. Estab. 1966. Purpose of award: To encourage the creative mind and the continuing appreciation of poetry. Unpublished poems only. Deadline for entries: June 30. SASE for contest rules and entry forms. Student categories are free; Grand Prix, $5; all others $1. Offers more than 30 categories and awards certificates of merit and cash prizes from $3 to $200. Sponsors pick judges. Contest open to all. "One-time printing rights acquired for publication of first prize winner in the Prize Poems Issue of *Pegasus*, our annual journal (late fall/ early winter issue). All other winners will be displayed at our October annual awards banquet."

KERLAN AWARD, University of Minnesota, 109 Walter Library, 117 Pleasant St. SE, Minneapolis MN 55455. (612)624-4576. Curator: Karen Nelson Hoyle. Annual award. Estab. 1975. "Given in recognition of singular attainments in the creation of children's literature and in appreciation for generous donation of unique resources to the Kerlan Collection." Previously published submissions only. Deadline for entries: November 1. Anyone can send nominations for the award, directed to the Kerlan Collection. No materials are submitted other than the person's name. Requirements for entrants: open to all who are nominated. "For serious consideration, entrant must be a published author and/or illustrator of children's books (including young adult fiction) and have donated original materials to the Kerlan Collection."

·**CORETTA SCOTT KING AWARD**, Coretta Scott King Task Force, Social Responsibility Round Table, American Library Association, 50 E. Huron St., Chicago IL 60611. "The Coretta Scott King Award is an annual award for a book (1 for text and 1 for illustration) that conveys the spirit of brotherhood espoused by M.L. King, Jr.—and also speaks to the Black experience— for young people. There is an award jury that judges the books—reviewing over the year—and making a decision in January. A copy of an entry must be sent to each juror. Acquire jury list from SRRT office in Chicago."

‡**LONGMEADOW JOURNAL LITERARY COMPETITION**, % Rita and Robert Morton, 6750 N. Longmeadow, Lincolnwood IL 60646. (312)726-9789. Fax: (312)726-9772. Contest Director: Rita and Robert Morton. Competition open to students (anyone age 10-19). Held annually and published every year. Estab. 1986. Purpose of contest: to encourage the young to write. Submissions are made by the author, made by the author's agent, nominated by a person or group of people, by teachers, librarians or parents. Deadline for entries: Dec. 31. SASE. No entry fee. Awards first place, $175; second place, $100; and five prizes of $50. Judging by Rita Morton, Robert Morton and Laurie Levy. Works are published every year and are distributed to teachers and librarians and interested parties at no charge.

LOUISE LOUIS/EMILY F. BOURNE STUDENT POETRY AWARD, Poetry Society of America, 15 Gramercy Park, New York NY 10003. (212)254-9628. Fax: (212)673-2352. Website: http://www.poetrysociety.com. Award Director: Timothy Donnelly. Annual award. Purpose of the award: Award is for the best unpublished poem by a high or preparatory school student (grades 9-12) from the US and its territories. Unpublished submissions only. Deadline for entries: Oct. 1 to Dec. 21. SASE for award rules and entry forms. Entries not returned. "High schools can send an unlimited number of submissions with one entry per individual student for a flat fee of $10." Award: $100. Judging by a professional poet. Requirements for entrants: Award open to all high school and preparatory students from the US and its territories. School attended, as well as name and address, should be noted. PSA submission guidelines must be followed. These are printed in our fall calendar, and are readily available if those interested send us a SASE. Line limit: none. "The award-winning poem will be included in a sheaf of poems that will be part of the program at the award ceremony and sent to all PSA members."

MAGAZINE MERIT AWARDS, Society of Children's Book Writers and Illustrators, 22736 Vanowen St., #106, West Hills CA 91307. (818)888-8760. Website: http://www.scbwi.org. Award Coordinator: Dorothy Leon. Annual award. Estab. 1988. Purpose of the award: "to recognize outstanding original magazine work for young people published during that year and having been written or illustrated by members of SCBWI." Previously published submissions only. Entries must be submitted between January 31 and December 15 of the year of publication. For brochure (rules) write Award Coordinator. No entry fee. Must be a SCBWI member. Awards plaques and honor certificates for each of the 3 categories (fiction, nonfiction, illustration). Judging by a magazine editor and two "full" SCBWI members. "All magazine work for young people by an SCBWI member—writer, artist or photographer—is eligible during the year of original publication. In the case of co-authored work, both authors must be SCBWI members. Members must submit their own work." Requirements for entrants: 4 copies each of the published work and proof of publication (may be contents page) showing the name of the magazine and the date of issue. The SCBWI is a professional organization of writers and illustrators and others interested in children's literature. Membership is open to the general public at large.

‡THE MAGIC-REALISM-MAGAZINE SHORT-FICTION AWARD, Pyx Press, P.O. Box 922648, Syllmar CA 91392-2648. Award Director: C. Darren Butler. Annual award. Estab. 1994. Previously published submissions only. Submissions made by the author, made by the author's agent, nominated by a person or group of people. Must be published between January 1, 1997 and December 31, 1997. Deadline for entries: February 15, 1998. SASE for award rules and entry forms. Awards publication in chapbook form and $50 cash to author and original publisher. Judging by Pyx Press for 1997.

‡MAJESTIC BOOKS WRITING CONTEST, Majestic Books, P.O. Box 19097, Johnston RI 02919-0097. Contest Director: Cindy MacDonald. Open to students. Annual contest. Estab. 1992. Purpose of contest: to encourage students to write to the best of their ability and to be proud of their work. Unpublished submissions only. Submissions made by the author or teacher. Deadline for entries: second Friday in October. No entry fee, however, we do ask for a large self-addressed envelope (9×12) for our reply and certificate. Winners are published in an anthology. All entrants receive a certificate acknowledging their efforts. Judging by a panel of published writers and an English teacher. One-time publishing rights to submitted material required or purchased. Our contest is open to all students, age 6-17 in Rhode Island. *Anthology* comes off the press in December and a presentation ceremony is held for all winning students. Students must include their age, grade, school and statement of authenticity signed by the writer and a parent or teacher. Entries must be neat and will not be returned. In order to encourage all children, every entrant receives a personalized award acknowledging their efforts.

‡MICHIGAN STUDENT FILM & VIDEO FESTIVAL, Detroit Area Film and Television, Harrison High School, 29995 W. 12 Mile Rd., Farmington Hills MI 48334. (810)489-3491. Fax: (810)489-3512. Contest Director: Margaret Culver. Open to students in grades K-12; *entrants must be Michigan residents or attend Michigan schools.* Annual contest. Estab. 1968. Purpose of contest: to support student involvement in film and video production. Film entries must be VHS video or film that has been transferred to video; categories for video entries are teleplay, commercials, music, documentary, series, artistic, general entertainment, sports, news, editing, unedited, drug awareness (public service announcement), instructional and animation. Submissions may be made by the student or teacher. Deadline for entries is February 17, 1997. Contest rules and entry form available with SASE. Entry fee is $10. Prizes include certificates and medals for all entries; prizes for Best of Show award range from cameras to scholarships. Judging is done by professionals in media, education and production of film and video. The festival reserves the right to use the material for educational or promotional purposes. Work will be shown at the Detroit Film Theater, Detroit Institute of Arts at the May 3, 1997 Michigan Student Film and Video Festival Awards Ceremony. An hour long television program, *Young Media Makers*, is produced and broadcast by WTUS Detroit Public Television. This program highlights student work from each year's Michigan Student Film and Video Festival.

MILKWEED PRIZE FOR CHILDREN'S LITERATURE, Milkweed Editions, 430 First Ave. N., Suite 400, Minneapolis MN 55401-1473. (612)332-3192. Award Director: Emilie Buchwald, publisher/editor. Annual award. Estab. 1993. Purpose of the award: to encourage writers to turn their attention to readers in the 8-12 age group. Unpublished submissions only "in book form." Must send SASE for award guidelines. The prize is awarded to the best work for children ages 8-12 that Milkweed agrees to publish in a calendar year by a writer not published by Milkweed before. The Prize consists of $2,000 cash over and above any advance or royalties agreed to at the time of acceptance. Submissions must follow our usual children's guidelines. Must send SASE with submission form.

THE MARY MOLLOY FELLOWSHIP FOR JUVENILE NOVEL IN PROGRESS, The Heekin Group Foundation/Children's Literature Division, P.O. Box 209, Middlebury VT 05753. (802)388-8651. E-mail: hgfh3@sover.net. Children's Literature Division Director: Deirdre M.

Heekin. Annual award. Estab. 1994. (The Heekin Group Foundation was established in 1992.) In order to foster the development of the literary arts, The Mary Molloy Fellowship for Juvenile Novel in Progress is awarded each year to the beginning career writer whose work exhibits literary merit, perception, and is rich in imagination. Unpublished submissions only. Submissions made by the author. Deadline for entries: December 1. SASE for award rules and entry forms. Entry fee is $25. Submission requires the first 35-50 pages of a ms. Manuscripts should be a children's novel in progress and geared toward the 9-14 age group. Awards $2,000. Judging by a children's literature publisher (1997 award to be judged by HarperCollins). The competition is open to all beginning career writers who have not yet been published in children's fiction for middle readers (9-14 years old). "For further information regarding our other fiction and nonfiction fellowships, please contact our headquarters: The Heekin Group, 68860 Goodrich Rd., Foundation Sisters, OR 97759."

*✦ELIZABETH MRAZIK-CLEAVER CANADIAN PICTURE BOOK AWARD, IBBY-Canada, 35 Spadina Rd., Toronto, Ontario M5R 2S9 Canada. (416)975-0010. Fax: (416)975-1839. Award Director: Molly Walsh. Annual contest. Estab. 1986. Award is given for outstanding illustrations in a Canadian children's book in either French or English and all genres. Previously published submissions only. Submissions made by author or publisher. Must be published the previous calendar year. Deadline for entries: end of year. Awards £1,000 Canadian and a certificate. Judging by a committee of professionals of children's literature. Requirements for entrants: Canadian citizenship.

✦THE NATIONAL CHAPTER OF CANADA IODE VIOLET DOWNEY BOOK AWARD, Suite 254, 40 Orchard View Blvd., Toronto, Ontario M5R 1B9 Canada. (416)487-4416. Award Director: Marty Dalton. Annual award. Estab. 1985. Purpose of the award: to honor the best children's English language book, by a Canadian, published in Canada for ages 5-13, over 500 words. Fairy tales, anthologies and books adapted from another source are not eligible. Previously published submissions only. Books must have been published in Canada between February 1 and January 31. Submissions made by author, author's agent; anyone may submit. Three copies of each entry are required. Must have been published during previous calendar year. Deadline for entries: January 31, 1997. SASE for award rules and entry forms. No entry fee. Awards $3,000 for the year 1997 for books published in 1996. Judging by a panel of 6, 4 IODE members and 2 professionals.

NATIONAL JEWISH BOOK AWARD FOR CHILDREN'S LITERATURE, Jewish Book Council Inc., 15 E. 26th St., New York NY 10010. (212)532-4949. Awards Coordinator: Carolyn Starman Hessel. Annual award. Estab. 1950. Previously published submissions only; must be published in 1996 for 1997 award. Deadline for entries: September 15, 1997. SASE for award rules and entry forms. Entries not returned. Entry fee is $36/title; $72 if listed in 2 categories. Awards $500. Judging by 3 authorities in the field. Requirements for entrants: Jewish children's books, published only for ages 2-16. Books will be displayed at the awards ceremony in NYC during Jewish Book Month, November 6—December 16, 1997.

‡NATIONAL PEACE ESSAY CONTEST, United States Institute of Peace, Suite 700, 1550 M St. NW, Washington DC 20005-1708. (202)429-3854. Fax: (202)429-6063. E-mail: usip_reque sts@usip.org. Website: http://www.usip.org. Contest Director: Heather Kerr-Stewart. Annual contest. Estab. 1987. "The contest gives students the opportunity to do valuable research, writing and thinking on a topic of importance to international peace and conflict resolution. Submissions, instead of being published, can be a classroom assignment"; previously published entries must have appeared between September 1 and January 23 previous to the contest deadline. Deadline for entries: varies. "Interested students, teachers and others may write or call to receive free contest kits. Please do not include SASE." No entry fee. State Level Awards are college scholarships in the following amounts: first place $750. National winners are selected from among the 1st place state winners. National winners receive scholarships in the following amounts: first place $5,000; second $2,500; third $1,000. Judging is conducted by education professionals from across the country and by the Board of Directors of the United States Institute of Peace. "All submissions become property of the U.S. Institute of Peace to use at its discretion and without royalty or any limitation, any winning essay. Students grades 9-12 in the U.S., its territories and overseas schools may submit essays for review by completing the application process. U.S. citizenship required for students attending overseas schools. National winning essays for each competition will be published by the U.S. Institute of Peace for public consumption."

NATIONAL WRITERS ASSOCIATION NONFICTION CONTEST, 1450 S. Havana, Suite 424, Aurora CO 80012. (303)751-7844. Executive Director: Sandy Whelchel. Annual contest. Estab. 1971. Purpose of contest: "to encourage writers in this creative form and to recognize those who excel in nonfiction writing." Submissions made by author. Deadline for entries: December 31. SASE for contest rules and entry forms. Entry fee is $15. Awards three cash prizes; choice of books; Honorable Mention Certificate. "Two people read each entry; third party picks three top winners from top five." Top 3 winners are published in an anthology published by National Writers Association, if winners agree to this. Judging sheets sent if entry accompanied by SASE.

NATIONAL WRITERS ASSOCIATION NOVEL WRITING CONTEST, 1450 S. Havana, Suite 424, Aurora CO 80012. (303)751-7844. Executive Director: Sandy Whelchel. Annual contest. Estab. 1971. Purpose of contest: "to encourage writers in this creative form and to recognize those who excel in novel writing." Submissions made by the author. Deadline for entries: April 1. SASE for contest rules and entry forms. Entry fee is $35. Awards top 3, cash prizes; 4 to 10, choice of books; 10 to 20, Honorable Mention Certificates. Judging: "two people read the manuscripts; a third party picks the three top winners from the top 5. We display our members' published books in our offices." Judging sheets available for SASE.

NATIONAL WRITERS ASSOCIATION SHORT STORY CONTEST, 1450 Havana St., Suite 424, Aurora CO 80012. (303)751-7844. Executive Director: Sandy Whelchel. Annual contest. Estab. 1971. Purpose of contest: "To encourage writers in this creative form and to recognize those who excel in fiction writing." Submissions made by the author. Deadline for entries: July 1. SASE for contest rules and entry forms. Entry fee is $15. Awards 3 cash prizes, choice of books and certificates for Honorable Mentions. Judging by "two people read each entry; third person picks top three winners." Judging sheet copies available for SASE. Top three winners are published in an anthology published by National Writers Association, if winners agree to this.

‡THE NATIONAL WRITTEN & ILLUSTRATED BY . . . AWARDS CONTEST FOR STUDENTS, Landmark Editions, Inc., P.O. Box 270169, Kansas City MO 64127-0169. (816)241-4919. Fax: (816)483-3755. Contest Director: Teresa Melton. Annual awards contest with 3 published winners. Estab. 1986. Purpose of the contest: to encourage and celebrate the creative efforts of students. There are 3 age categories (ages 6-9, 10-13 and 14-19). Unpublished submissions only. Deadline for entries: May 1. For a free copy of the contest rules, send a self-addressed, business-sized envelope, stamped with 64¢ postage. "Need to send a self-addressed, sufficiently stamped (at least $3 postage) book mailer with book entry for its return. All entries which do not win are mailed back in November or December of each contest year." Entry fee is $1. Awards publication of book. Judging by national panel of educators, editors, illustrators, authors and school librarians. "Each student winner receives a publishing contract allowing Landmark to publish the book. Copyright is in student's name and student receives royalties on sale of book. Books must be in proper contest format and submitted with entry form signed by a teacher or librarian. Students may develop their illustrations in any medium of their choice, as long as the illustrations remain two-dimensional and flat to the surface of the paper." Winners are notified by phone by October 15 of each contest year. During November/December all other book entries are returned, accompanied by a list of winners and finalists. By September of the following year, all winners' books are published—after several months of pre-production work on the books by the students and the editorial and artistic staff of Landmark editions. Works are published in Kansas City, Missouri for distribution nationally and internationally.

*‡N.C. WRITERS' NETWORK INTERNATIONAL LITERARY PRIZES, N.C. Writers' Network, P.O. Box 954, Carrboro NC 27510. (919)967-9540. Fax: (919)929-0535. E-mail: nc_wr iters@unc.edu. Annual contest. *Thomas Wolfe Fiction Prize* (TWFP), est. 1994, awards $500 prize for best piece of fiction (short story or novel excerpt not to exceed 12 pp.); *Paul Green Playwrights Prize* (PGPP), est. 1995, awards $500 prize for best play, any length, no musicals; *Randall Jarrell Poetry Prize* (RJPP), est. 1990, awards $500 prize, publication and reading/ reception for best poem. Unpublished submissions only. Submissions made by the author. Deadline for entries: TWFP—Aug. 31; PGPP—Sept. 30; RJPP—Nov. 1. SASE for award rules and entry forms. Entry fee is $5-TWFP; $5-RJPP; $10-PGPP ($7.50 for NCWN members). Judging by published writers or editors. Previous judges have included: Anne Tyler, Barbara Kingsolver, Donald Hall, Lucille Clifton, Romulus Linney.

THE NENE AWARD, Hawaii State Library, 478 S. King St., Honolulu HI 96813. (808)586-3510. Estab. 1964. "The Nene Award was designed to help the children of Hawaii become acquainted with the best contemporary writers of fiction, become aware of the qualities that make a good book and choose the best rather than the mediocre." Previously published submissions only. Books must have been copyrighted not more than 6 years prior to presentation of award. Work is nominated. Awards Koa plaque. Judging by the children of Hawaii in grades 4-6. Requirements for entrants: books must be fiction, written by a living author, copyrighted not more than 6 years ago and suitable for children in grades 4, 5 and 6. Current and past winners are displayed in all participating school and public libraries. The award winner is announced in April by the author of the previous year's winning title.

*NEW ENGLAND BOOK AWARDS, New England Booksellers Association, 847 Massachusetts Ave., Cambridge MA 02139. (617)576-3070. Fax: (617)576-3091. Award Director: Nan Sorensen. Annual award. Estab. 1990. Previously published submissions only. Submissions made by New England booksellers; publishers. Entries must be still in print and available. Deadline for entries: October 31. SASE for contest rules and entry forms. No entry fee. Judging by NEBA membership. Requirements for entrants: Author/illustrator must live in New England or write about New England. Submit written nominations only; actual books should not be sent. Member bookstores receive materials to display winners' books.

‡NEW ERA WRITING ART, PHOTOGRAPHY & MUSIC CONTEST, The Church of Jesus Christ of Latter-day Saints, 50 E. North Temple, Salt Lake City UT 84150. (801)240-2951. Fax: (801)240-5997. Managing Editor: Richard M. Romney. Annual contest. Estab. 1971. Purpose of the contest: to feature the creative abilities of young Latter-day Saints. Unpublished submissions only. Submissions made by the author. Deadline for entries: January 6. SASE for contest rules and entry forms. No entry fee. Awards partial scholarships to LDS colleges, cash prizes. Judging by *New Era* magazine editorial and design staffs. All rights acquired; reassigned to author upon written request. Requirements for entrants: must be an active member of the LDS Church, ages 12-23. Winning entries published in each August's issue.

JOHN NEWBERY MEDAL AWARD, Association for Library Service to Children, Division of the American Library Association, 50 E. Huron, Chicago IL 60611. (312)280-2163. Executive Director, ALSC: Susan Roman. Annual award. Estab. 1922. Purpose of award: to recognize the most distinguished contribution to American children's literature published in the US. Previously published submissions only; must be published prior to year award is given. Deadline for entries: December. SASE for award rules. Entries not returned. No entry fee. Medal awarded at Caldecott/Newbery banquet during annual conference. Judging by Newbery Committee.

‡NORTH AMERICAN INTERNATIONAL AUTO SHOW SHORT STORY HIGH SCHOOL POSTER CONTEST, Detroit Auto Dealers Association, 1800 W. Big Beaver Rd., Troy MI 48084-3531. (810)643-0250. Public Relations/Writing: Lisa Barkey. Public Relations/Art: Mary Kay McGovern. Annual contest. Submissions made by the author and illustrator. Deadline to be determined for 1997. Contact DADA. SASE for contest rules and entry forms. No entry fee. five winners of the short story contest will each receive $500. Entries will be judged by an independent panel comprised of knowledgeable persons engaged in the literary field in some capacity. Entrants must be Michigan residents, including high school students enrolled in grades 9-12. Junior high school students in 9th grade are also eligible. Winners of the High School Poster Contest will receive $1,000, first place; $500, second; $250, third. Entries will be judged by an independent panel of recognized representatives of the art community. Entrants must be Michigan high school students enrolled in grades 9-12. Junior high students in 9th grade are also eligible. Winners will be announced during the North American International Auto Show in January and may be published in the *Auto Show Program* at the sole discretion of the DADA.

*‡THE SCOTT O'DELL AWARD FOR HISTORICAL FICTION, 1700 E. 56th St., Suite 3907, Chicago IL 60637-1936. Award Director: Mrs. Zena Sutherland. Annual award. Estab. 1981. Purpose of the award: "To promote the writing of historical fiction of good quality for children and young adults." Previously published submissions only; must be published between January 1 and December 31 previous to deadline. Deadline for entries: December 31. "Publishers send books, although occasionally a writer sends a note or a book." SASE for award rules. No entry fee. Awards $5,000. Judging by a committee of 3. Requirements for entrants: "Must be published by a U.S. publisher in the preceding year; must be by an American citizen; must be set in North or South America; must be historical fiction."

OHIOANA AWARD FOR CHILDREN'S LITERATURE, Ohioana Library Association, 65 S. Front St., Room 1105, Columbus OH 43215. (614)466-3831. Fax: (614)728-6974. Award Director: Linda R. Hengst. Open to adults. Annual award. Purpose of award: "to provide recognition for an Ohio author of children's literature." Submissions are made by the author, made by the author's agent, nominated by a person or group of people. Deadline for entries: December 31, 1997. SASE for award rules and entry forms. No entry fee. Awards approximately $1,000. Judging by a committee of three to five individuals familiar with children's literature, teachers, librarians, etc. "The recipient must have been born in Ohio, or lived in Ohio for a minimum of five years; the recipient must have established a distinguished publishing record of books for children and young people; the author's body of work has made, and continues to make, a significant contribution to the literature for young people; through the recipient's work as a writer, teacher, administrator, or through community service, interest in children's literature has been encouraged and children have become involved with reading. Also, it is desirable for the recipient to be present at Ohioana Day to receive the award. Only authors are considered at this time, for this award—illustrators are elegible for other Ohioana Awards."

OKLAHOMA BOOK AWARDS, Oklahoma Center for the Book, 200 NE 18th, Oklahoma City OK 73105. (405)521-2502. Fax: (405)525-7804. Annual award. Estab. 1989. Purpose of award: "to honor Oklahoma writers and books about our state." Previously published submissions only. Submissions made by the author, author's agent, or entered by a person or group of people, including the publisher. Must be published during the calendar year preceding the award. Deadline for entries: January. SASE for award rules and entry forms. No entry fee. Awards a medal—no cash prize. Judging by a panel of 5 people for each category—a librarian, a working writer in the genre, editors, etc. Requirements for entrants: author must be an Oklahoma native, resident, former resident or have written a book with Oklahoma theme. Book will be displayed at banquet at the Cowboy Hall of Fame in Oklahoma City.

ORBIS PICTUS AWARD FOR OUTSTANDING NONFICTION FOR CHILDREN, National Council of Teachers of English, 1111 W. Kenyon Rd., Urbana IL 61801-1096. (217)328-3870, ext. 268. Chair, NCTE Committee on the Orbis Pictus Award for Outstanding Nonfiction for Children: Myra Zarnowski, The Ohio State University at Newark, Newark Ohio. Annual award. Estab. 1989. Purpose of award: to honor outstanding nonfiction works for children. Previously published submissions only. Submissions made by author, author's agent, by a person or group of people. Must be published January 1-December 31 of contest year. Deadline for entries: December 31. Call for award information. No entry fee. Awards a plaque given at the NCTE Elementary Section Luncheon at the NCTE Annual Convention in November. Judging by a committee.

THE ORIGINAL ART, Society of Illustrators, 128 E. 63rd St., New York NY 10021. (212)838-2560. Fax: (212)838-2561. Annual contest. Estab. 1981. Purpose of contest: to celebrate the fine art of children's book illustration. Previously published submissions only. Deadline for entries: Sept. 8th. SASE for contest rules and entry forms. Entry fee is $15/book. Judging by seven professional artists and editors. Works will be displayed at the Society of Illustrators Museum of American Illustration in New York City October-November annually. Medals awarded.

HELEN KEATING OTT AWARD FOR OUTSTANDING CONTRIBUTION TO CHILDREN'S LITERATURE, Church and Synagogue Library Association, P.O. Box 19357, Portland OR 97280. (503)244-6919. Fax: (503)977-3734. Chair of Committee: Lillian Koppin. Annual award. Estab. 1980. "This award is given to a person or organization that has made a significant contribution to promoting high moral and ethical values through children's literature." Deadline for entries: March 30. "Recipient is honored in July during the conference." Awards certificate of recognition and a conference package consisting of registration, all meals day of awards banquet, two nights' housing and a complementary 1 year membership. "A nomination for an award may be made by anyone. It should include the name, address and telephone number of the nominee plus the church or synagogue relationship where appropriate. Nominations of an organization should include the name of a contact person. A detailed description of the reasons for the nomination should be given, accompanied by documentary evidence of accomplishment. The person(s) making the nomination should give his/her name, address and telephone number and a brief explanation of his/her knowledge of the nominee's accomplishments. Elements of creativity and innovation will be given high priority by the judges."

‡✹OWL MAGAZINE CONTESTS, Writing Contest, Photo Contest, Poetry Contest, Cover Contest, *OWL Magazine*, 179 John St., Suite 500, Toronto, Ontario M5T 3G5 Canada. (416)971-5275. Annual contest. Purpose of contest: "to encourage children to contribute and participate in the magazine. *Owl* also recognizes excellence in an individual or group effort to help the environment. Unpublished submissions only. Deadlines change yearly. Prizes/awards "change every year. Often we give books as prizes." Winning entries published in the magazine. Judging by art and editorial staff. Entries become the property of Owl Communications. "The contests and awards are open to children up to 14 years of age."

PEN/NORMA KLEIN AWARD FOR CHILDREN'S FICTION, PEN American Center, 568 Broadway, New York NY 10012. (212)334-1660. Awarded in odd-numbered years. Estab. 1990. "In memory of the late PEN member and distinguished children's book author Norma Klein, the award honors new authors whose books demonstrate the adventuresome and innovative spirit that characterizes the best children's literature and Norma Klein's own work." Previously published submissions only. "Candidates may not nominate themselves. We welcome all nominations from authors and editors of children's books." Deadline for entries: December. Awards $3,000 which will be given in May. Judging by a panel of 3 distinguished children's book authors. Nominations open to authors of books for elementary school to young adult readers. "It is strongly recommended that the nominator describe in some detail the literary character of the candidate's work and how it promises to enrich American literature for children."

‡PLEASE TOUCH MUSEUM BOOK AWARD, Please Touch Museum, 210 N. 21st St., Philadelphia PA 19103. (215)963-0667. Fax: (215)963-0424. E-mail: pleastch@libertynet.org. Website: http://www.libertynet.pleastch. Director of Education and Research: Marzy Sykes, Ph.D. Annual award. Estab. 1985. Purpose of the award: "to recognize and encourage the publication of books for young children by American authors that are of the highest quality and will aid them in enjoying the process of learning through books. Awarded to two picture books that are particularly imaginative and effective in exploring a concept or concepts, one for children age three and younger, and one for children ages four-seven." Previously published submissions only. "To be eligible for consideration a book must: (1) Explore and clarify an idea for young children. This could include the concept of numbers, colors, shapes, sizes, senses, feelings, etc. There is no limitation as to format. (2) Be distinguished in both text and illustration. (3) Be published within the last year by an American publisher. (4) Be the first book by an American author and/or illustrator." Deadline for entries: April 30 (submissions may be made throughout the year). SASE for award rules and entry forms. No entry fee. Judging by selected jury of children's literature experts, librarians and early childhood educators. Education store purchases books for selling at Book Award Celebration Day and throughout the year. Receptions and autographing sessions held in bookstores, Please Touch Museum, and throughout the city.

POCKETS MAGAZINE FICTION CONTEST, The Upper Room, P.O. Box 189, Nashville TN 37202-0189. (615)340-7333. Fax: (615)340-7006. Associate Editor: Lynn Gilliam. Annual contest. Estab. 1990. Purpose of contest: "to discover new freelance writers for our magazine and to encourage freelance writers to become familiar with the needs of our magazine." Unpublished submissions only. Submissions made by the author. Deadline for entries: August 15. SASE for contest rules and entry forms. No entry fee. Awards $1,000 and publication. Judging by *Pocket*'s editors and 3 other editors of other Upper Room publications. Winner published in the magazine.

EDGAR ALLAN POE AWARD, Mystery Writers of America, Inc., 6th Floor, 17 E. 47th St., New York NY 10017. (212)888-8171. Fax: (212)888-8107. Executive Director: Priscilla Ridgway. Annual award. Estab. 1945. Purpose of the award: to honor authors of distinguished works in the mystery field. Previously published submissions only. Submissions made by the author, author's agent; "normally by the publisher." Work must be published/produced the year of the contest. Deadline for entries: December 1 "except for works only available in the month of December." SASE for award rules and entry forms. No entry fee. Awards ceramic bust of "Edgar" for winner; scrolls for all nominees. Judging by professional members of Mystery Writers of America (writers). Nominee press release sent after first Wednesday in February. Winner announced at the Edgar Banquet, held in late April.

‡**QUILL AND SCROLL INTERNATIONAL WRITING/PHOTO CONTEST**, *Quill and Scroll*, School of Journalism, University of Iowa, Iowa City IA 52242. (319)335-5795. Contest Director: Richard Johns. Annual contest. Previously published submissions only. Submissions made by the author or school newspaper adviser. Must be published February 6, 1995 to February 4, 1996. Deadline for entries: February 5. SASE for contest rules and entry forms. Entry fee is $2/entry. Awards engraved plaque to junior high level sweepstakes winners. Each high school sweepstakes winner receives electric typewriter. Judging by various judges. *Quill and Scroll* acquires the right to publish submitted material in the magazine if it is chosen as a winning entry. Requirements for entrants: must be students in grades 6-9 for junior high school division; 9-12 for high school division.

‡**READ WRITING & ART AWARDS**, *Read* Magazine, 245 Long Hill Rd., Middletown CT 06457. (203)638-2406. Fax: (860)346-5826. E-mail: kdavis@weeklyreader.com. Website: http://www.weeklyreader.com/read.html. Contest Director: Kate Davis. Annual award. Estab. 1978. Purpose of the award: to reward excellence in writing and art in the categories of fiction, essay and art. Unpublished submissions only. Submissions made by the author or nominated by a person or group of people. Students in grades 6-12 are eligible to enter. Must include entry coupon and signature of teacher, parent or guardian and student. Deadline for entries: December 13. SASE for contest/award rules and entry forms. No entry fee. Awards first prize ($100), second prize ($75), third prize ($50). Prizes are given in each category, plus publication of first place winners. Judging by *Read* editorial staff. "Entrant understands that prize will include publication, but sometimes pieces are published in other issues. A story may be bought later." Work must be original. Prefer art entries in color, but b&w may be submitted. Artwork should be original in composition and execution, not *copied* from another artist's work. Prefers original artwork, although color photocopies are accepted. Art will be returned only if proper SASE is included. No tubes, boxes, loose stamps, or money—prefers artwork to be submitted flat, with chipboard or bubblewrap packaging. Published in May 2 issue of *Read* (all-student issue).

‡**ANNA DAVIDSON ROSENBERG AWARD FOR POEMS ON THE JEWISH EXPERIENCE**, Judah L. Magnes Museum, 2911 Russell St., Berkeley CA 94705. (510)849-2710. Poetry Award Director: Paula Friedman. Annual award. Estab. 1986-87. Purpose of the award: to encourage poetry in English on the Jewish experience (writer does not need to be Jewish). Previously unpublished submissions only. Deadline for entries: August 31. SASE for award rules and entry forms by July 31. Entry forms must be included with submissions. SASE for list of winners. Awards $100-first prize, $50-second prize, $25-third prize; honorable mention certificates; *$25* Youth Commendation (poets under 19); Emerging Poet Award. Judging by committee of 3 well-published poets with editing/teaching experience. There will be a reading of top award winners in December at Magnes Museum. Prospective anthology of selected winning entries. "We request permission to use in potential anthologies." Write for entry form and guidelines *first*; entries must follow guidelines and be accompanied by entry form. *Please do not phone.*

CARL SANDBURG LITERARY ARTS AWARDS, Friends of the Chicago Public Library, Harold Washington Library Center, 400 S. State St., Chicago IL 60605. (312)747-4907. Fax: (312)747-4077. Annual award. Categories: fiction, nonfiction, poetry, children's literature. Published submissions only; must be published between June 1 and May 31 (the following year). Deadline for entries: August 1. SASE for award rules. Entries not returned. No entry fee. Awards medal and $1,000 prize. Judging by authors, reviewers, book buyers, librarians from Chicago literary community. Requirements for entrants: native born Chicagoan or presently residing in the 6 county metropolitan area. Two copies must be submitted by August 1. All entries become the property of the Friends.

‡**SEVENTEEN FICTION CONTEST**, 850 Third Ave., 9th Floor, New York NY 10022. Fiction Editor: Ben Schrank. Annual contest. Estab. 1945. Fax: (212)407-9899. E-mail: seventeen m@aol.com. Unpublished submissions only. Deadline for entries: April 30. SASE for contest rules and entry forms; contest rules also published in November issue of *Seventeen*. Entries not returned. No entry fee. Awards cash prize and possible publication in *Seventeen*. Judging by "inhouse panel of editors, external readers." If first prize, acquires first North American rights for piece to be published. Requirements for entrants: "Our annual fiction contest is open to anyone between the ages of 13 and 21 who submit on or before April 30 (check November issue of *Seventeen* for details). Submit only original fiction that has not been published in any form other than in school publications. Stories should be between 1,500 and 3,000 words in length

(6-12 pages). All manuscripts must be typed double-spaced on a single side of paper. Submit as many original stories as you like, but each story must include your full name, address, birth date and signature in the top right-hand corner of the first page. Your signature on submission will constitute your acceptance of the contest rules."

‡SHUBERT FENDRICH MEMORIAL PLAYWRIGHTING CONTEST, Pioneer Drama Service, Inc., P.O. Box 4267, Englewood CO 80155-4267. Fax: (303)779-4315. E-mail: piodrama @aol.com. Director: Steven Fendrich. Annual contest. Estab. 1990. Purpose of the contest: "to encourage the development of quality theatrical material for educational and family theater." Previously unpublished submissions only. Deadline for entries: March 1. SASE for contest rules and entry forms. No entry fee. Application must accompany all submissions. Awards $1,000 royalty advance and publication. Upon receipt of signed contracts, plays will be published and made available in our next catalog. Judging by editors. All rights acquired with acceptance of contract for publication. Restrictions for entrants: Any writers currently published by Pioneer Drama Service are not eligible.

CHARLIE MAY SIMON BOOK AWARD, Arkansas Elementary School Council, Arkansas Department of Education, Room 302B, #4 Capitol Mall, Little Rock AR 72201. (501)682-4371. Fax: (501)682-5013. E-mail: hesterj@loki-k12.ar.us. Award Director: James A. Hester. Annual contest. Estab. 1970. Purpose of award: to promote reading—to encourage reading of quality literature and book discussion among children in grades 4-6. Previously published submissions only; must be published between January 1 and December 31 of calendar year preceding award; all books must have recommendations from 3 published sources. "Books are selected based on being published in previous calendar year from time of committee work; *Horn Book* is used as selection guide." Students in grades 4-6 vote on their favorite book on a reading list; the book with the most votes receives the Charlie May Simon Medallion and runner-up receives a plaque as honor book winner; reading list prepared by committee of 25 people representing cooperating organizations. No entry fee. Contest open to any book for children in grades 4-6 provided book is printed in year being considered.

‡SKIPPING STONES YOUTH HONOR AWARDS, *Skipping Stones*, P.O. Box 3939, Eugene OR 97403. (541)342-4956. Website: http://www.nonviolence.org/~nvweb/skipping/. Annual award. Purpose of contest: "to recognize youth, 16 and under, for their contributions to multicultural awareness, nature and ecology, social issues, peace and nonviolence. Also to promote creativity, self-esteem and writing skills, and to recognize important work being done by youth organizations." Submissions made by the author. For 1997, the theme is "How I am Making a Difference. . ." Deadline for entries: June 20, 1997. SASE for contest rules. Entries must include certificate of originality by parents and/or teachers, and background information on the author written by the author. Entry fee is $3. Judging by *Skipping Stones*' staff. "Ten awards are given in three categories: (1) Compositions—(essays, poems, short stories, songs, travelogues, etc.) should be typed (double-spaced) or neatly handwritten. Fiction or nonfiction should be limited to 750 words; poems to 30 lines. Non-English writings are also welcome. (2) Artwork—(drawings, cartoons, paintings or photo essays with captions) should have the artist's name, age and address on the back of each page. Send the originals with SASE. Black & white photos are especially welcome. Limit: 8 plates. (3) Youth Organizations—Tell us how your club or group works to: (a) preserve the nature and ecology in your area, (b) enhance the quality of life for low-income, minority or disabled, or (c) improve racial or cultural harmony in your school or community. Use the same format as for compositions." The 1997 winners will be published in Vol. 9, #4 (September-October 1997) issue of *Skipping Stones*.

KAY SNOW WRITERS' CONTEST, Williamette Writers, 9045 SW Barbur Blvd. #5A, Portland OR 97219. (503)452-1592. Fax: (503)452-0372. E-mail: wilwrite@teleport.com. Contest Director: Bruce Babb. Annual contest. Purpose of contest: "to encourage beginning and established writers to continue the craft." Unpublished, original submissions only. Submissions made by the author or author's agent. Deadline for entries: May 15. SASE for contest rules and entry forms. Entry fee is $10, Williamette Writers' members;, $15, nonmembers; $5, student writer. Awards cash prize of $200 per category (fiction, nonfiction, juvenile, poetry, script writing). "Judges are anonymous."

SOCIETY OF MIDLAND AUTHORS AWARDS, Society of Midland Authors, P.O. Box 10419, Chicago IL 60610-0419. Annual award. Estab. 1915. Purpose of award: "to stimulate creative literary effort, one of the goals of the Society. There are six categories, including children's fiction, children's nonfiction, adult fiction and nonfiction, biography and poetry." Previously published submissions only. Submissions made by the author or publisher. Must be published during calendar year previous to deadline. Deadline for entries: January 15. SASE for award rules and entry forms. No entry fee. Awards plaque given at annual dinner, cash (minimum $300). Judging by panel (reviewers, university faculty, writers, librarians) of 3 per category. "Award is for book published in the awards year." Author to be currently residing in the Midlands, i.e., Illinois, Indiana, Iowa, Kansas, Michigan, Minnesota, Missouri, Nebraska, North Dakota, South Dakota, Ohio or Wisconsin.

GEORGE G. STONE CENTER FOR CHILDREN'S BOOKS RECOGNITION OF MERIT AWARD, George G. Stone Center for Children's Books, The Claremont Graduate School, 131 E. 10th St., Claremont CA 91711-6188. (909)607-3670. Fax: (909)621-8390. Award Director: Doty Hale. Annual award. Estab. 1965. Purpose of the award: to recognize an author or illustrator of a children's book or a body of work exhibiting the "power to please and expand the awareness of children and teachers as they have shared the book in their classrooms." Previously published submissions only. SASE for award rules and entry forms. Entries not returned. No entry fee. Awards a scroll. Judging by a committee of teachers, professors of children's literature and librarians. Requirements for entrants: "Nominations are made by students, teachers, professors and librarians. Award made at annual Claremont Reading Conference in spring (March)."

JOAN G. SUGARMAN CHILDREN'S BOOK AWARD, Washington Independent Writers Legal and Educational Fund, Inc., #220, 733 15th St. NW, Washington DC 20005. (202)347-4973. Director: Isolde Chapin. Open to residents of D.C., Maryland, Virginia. Award offered every 2 years. Next awards presented in 1998 for publications done in 1996-1997. Estab. 1987. Purpose of award: to recognize excellence in children's literature, ages 1-15. Previously published submissions only. Submissions made by the author or author's agent or by publishers. Must be published in the 2 years preceeding award year. Deadline for entries: January 31, 1998. SASE for award rules and entry forms. No entry fee. Awards $1,000. Judging by selected experts in children's books. Requirements for entrants: publication of material; residence in DC, Maryland or Virginia. No picture-only books. Works displayed at reception for award winners and become part of the Sugarman Collection at The George Washington University.

SUGARMAN FAMILY AWARD FOR JEWISH CHILDREN'S LITERATURE, District of Columbia Jewish Community Center, 1836 Jefferson Place NW, Washington DC 20036. (202)775-1765. Fax: (202)331-7667. Award director: Marcia F. Goldberg. Open to adults. Biannual award. Estab. 1994. Purpose of contest: to enrich all children's appreciation of Jewish culture and to inspire writers and illustrators for children. Newly published submissions only. Submissions made by the author, made by the author's agent. Must be published January-December of year previous to award year. SASE for entry deadlines, award rules and entry forms. Entry fee is $25. Award at least $750. Judging by a panel of three judges—a librarian, a children's bookstore owner and a reviewer of books. Requirements for entrants: must live in the United States. Work displayed at the D.C. Jewish Community Center Library after March.

SYDNEY TAYLOR MANUSCRIPT COMPETITION, Association of Jewish Libraries, 1327 Wyntercreek Lane, Dunwoody GA 30338. (770)394-2060. Fax: (770)671-8380. E-mail: m-psand@mindspring.com. Coordinator: Paula Sandfelder. Annual contest. Estab. 1985. Purpose of the contest: "This competition is for unpublished writers of fiction. Material should be for readers ages 8-11, with universal appeal that will serve to deepen the understanding of Judaism for all children, revealing positive aspects of Jewish life." Unpublished submissions only. Deadline for entries: January 15. SASE for contest rules and entry forms. No entry fee. Awards $1,000. Winning entries will be displayed at the Association of Jewish Libraries annual convention. Judging by qualified judges from within the Association of Jewish Libraries. Requirements for entrants: must be an unpublished fiction writer; also, books must range from 64 to 200 pages in length. "AJL assumes no responsibility for publication, but hopes this cash incentive will serve to encourage new writers of children's stories with Jewish themes for all children."

*TREASURE STATE AWARD, Missoula Public Library, Missoula County Schools, Montana Library Assoc., 301 E. Main, Missoula MT 59802. (406)721-2005. Fax: (406)728-5900. E-mail: bammon@mtlib.org. Website: http://www.ism.net/~mslaplib. Award Directors: Bette Ammon and Carole Monlux. Annual award. Estab. 1990. Purpose of the award: Children in grades K-3 read or listen to a ballot of 5 picture books and vote on their favorite. Previously published submissions only. Submissions made by author, nominated by a person or group of people—children, librarians, teachers. Must be published in previous 5 years to voting year. Deadline for entries: April 15. SASE for contest rules and entry forms. No entry fee. Awards a plaque or sculpture. Judging by popular vote by Montana children grades K-3.

*UTAH PLAYFEST, Utah State University, Theatre Arts Department, Logan UT 84322-4025. (801)797-3021. Fax: (801)797-0086. Contest Director: Roger Held. Competition open to adults only. Annual contest. Estab. 1994. Purpose of award: to promote work of playwrights on the edge of acknowledgement as new voices in the American Theater. Unpublished submissions only. Submissions nominated by artistic director of a theatre who knows the work of the playwright. No entry fee. Awards $5,000 and production. Judging by professional artistic directors, playwrights and faculty. Playwrights should send names and addresses of theaters which support their work to the Playfest Director.

‡VEGETARIAN ESSAY CONTEST, The Vegetarian Resource Group, P.O. Box 1463, Baltimore MD 21203. (410)366-VEGE. Fax: (410)366-8804. E-mail: thevrg@aol.com. Website: http://envirolink.org/arrs/VRG/home.html. Address to Vegetarian Essay Contest. Annual contest. Estab. 1985. Purpose of contest: to promote vegetarianism in young people. Unpublished submissions only. Deadline for entries: May 1 of each year. SASE for contest rules and entry forms. No entry fee. Awards $50 savings bond. Judging by awards committee. Acquires right for The Vegetarian Resource Group to reprint essays. Requirements for entrants: age 18 and under. Winning works may be published in *Vegetarian Journal*, instructional materials for students. "Submit 2-3 page essay on any aspect of vegetarianism, which is the abstinence of meat, fish and fowl. Entrants can base paper on interviewing, research or personal opinion. Need not be vegetarian to enter."

‡VERY SPECIAL ARTS YOUNG PLAYWRIGHTS PROGRAM, Very Special Arts, Education Office, The John F. Kennedy Center for the Performing Arts, Washington DC 20566. (202)628-2800 or 1-800-933-8721. National Programs Coordinator: Elena Widder. Annual contest. Estab. 1984. "All scripts must address or incorporate some aspect of disability." Unpublished submissions only. Deadline for entries: April 14. Write to Young Playwrights Coordinator for contest rules and entry forms. No entries returned. No entry fee. Judging by Artists Selection Committee. Entrants must be students age 25 and under, with a disability. "Script will be selected for production at The John F. Kennedy Center for the Performing Arts, Washington DC. The winning play is presented each October."

‡VFW VOICE OF DEMOCRACY, Veterans of Foreign Wars of the U.S., 406 W. 34th St., Kansas City MO 64111. (816)968-1117. Fax: (816)968-1157. Annual contest. Estab. 1960. Purpose of contest: to give high school students the opportunity to voice their opinions about their responsibility to our country and to convey those opinions via the broadcast media to all of America. Deadline for entries: November 1st. No entry fee. Winners receive awards ranging from $1,000-20,000. Requirements for entrants: "Tenth-twelfth grade students in public, parochial and private schools in the United States and overseas are eligible to compete. Former national and/or first place state winners are not eligible to compete again. Contact your high school counselor or your local VFW Post to enter."

‡VIDEO VOYAGES CONTEST, Weekly Reader Corporation, 245 Long Hill Rd., P.O. Box 2791, Middletown CT 06457-9291. (860)638-2400. Co-sponsor: Panasonic Company. Contest Director: Lois Lewis. Annual contest. Estab. 1991. Purpose of contest: to reward original videos made by elementary and upper grade students. Unpublished original student videos only. Submissions made by teams or classes of students. Deadline for entry: March 17. Write or call contest director for rules and entry forms. No entry fee. Prizes: Panasonic video equipment, including televisions, VCRs and camcorders. Additional prizes include t-shirts, books on video production and certificates. "All video equipment prizes are courtesy of Panasonic Company. All prizes are awarded to the winners' schools." Judging by staff members from Weekly Reader Corp. and Panasonic Company. All entries become the property of Weekly Reader Corp. and none will be returned. Requirements for entrants: open to students in grades 4-12. Each entry form must be signed by the supervising teacher(s).

TARGET THE MARKETS.

Order Form

☐ YES! Start my subscription to *Writer's Digest*, the magazine thousands of successful writers rely on to hit their target markets. I pay just $19.97 for 12 monthly issues...a savings of more than $15 off the newsstand price.

☐ I'm enclosing payment (or paying by credit card). Add an extra issue to my subscription FREE — 13 in all!

Charge my ☐ Visa ☐ MC

Exp. _____

Signature _____

☐ I prefer to be billed later for 12 issues.

NAME _____

ADDRESS _____

CITY_____ STATE _____ ZIP _____

Outside U.S. add $10 (includes GST in Canada) and remit in U.S. funds.
Annual newsstand rate $35.88. Allow 4-6 weeks for first issue delivery.

YOUR MONTHLY GUIDE TO GETTING PUBLISHED

SAVE MORE THAN $15!

TVCM5

VIRGINIA LIBRARY ASSOCIATION/JEFFERSON CUP, Virginia Library Association, 669 S. Washington St., Alexandria VA 22314. Award Director changes year to year. Annual award. Estab. 1983. Purpose of award: to honor a distinguished biography, historical fiction, or American history book for young people, thereby promoting reading about America's past, and encouraging writing of U.S. history, biography and historical fiction. Previously published submissions only. Must be published in the year prior to selection. SASE for contest rules and entry forms. Judging by committee. The book must be about U.S. history or an American person, 1492 to present, or fiction that highlights the U.S. past; author must reside in the U.S. The book must be published especially for young people.

*VOLUNTEER STATE BOOK AWARD, Tennessee Library Association, P.O. Box 158417, Nashville TN 37215-8417. (615)297-8316. Award Director: Dr. Beverly N. Youree. Competition open to adults only. Annual award. Estab. 1978. Purpose of award: to promote awareness, interest, and enjoyment of good new children's and young adult literature and to promote literacy and life-long reading habits by encouraging students to read quality contemporary literature which broadens understanding of the human experience and provides accurate, factual information. Previously published submissions only. Submissions made by author, by the author's agent and nominated by a person or group of people. Must be published in 5 years prior to year of voting. SASE for contest rules and entry forms. No entry fee. Awards plaque. Judging by children. Any public or private school in Tennessee is eligible to participate. It is not required that the entire school be involved. Each participating school must have a minimum of twelve of the twenty titles per division available.

‡THE STELLA WADE CHILDREN'S STORY AWARD, *Amelia* Magazine, 329 E St., Bakersfield CA 93304. (805)323-4064. Editor: Frederick A. Raborg, Jr. Annual award. Estab. 1988. Purpose of award: "With decrease in the number of religious and secular magazines for young people, the juvenile story and poetry must be preserved and enhanced." Unpublished submissions only. Deadline for entries: August 15. SASE for award rules. Entry fee is $5 per adult entry; there is no fee for entries submitted by young people under the age of 17, but such entry must be signed by parent, guardian or teacher to verify originality. Awards $125 plus publication. Judging by editorial staff. Previous winners include Maxine Kumin and Sharon E. Martin. "We use First North American serial rights only for the winning manuscript." Contest is open to all interested. If illustrator wishes to enter only an illustration without a story, the entry fee remains the same. Illustrations will also be considered for cover publication. Restrictions of mediums for illustrators: Submitted photos should be no smaller than 5×7; illustrations (drawn) may be in any medium. "Winning entry will be published in the most appropriate issue of either *Amelia*, *Cicada* or *SPSM&H*—subject matter would determine such. Submit clean, accurate copy."

‡WE ARE WRITERS, TOO!, Creative With Words Publications, P.O. Box 223226, Carmel CA 93922. Fax: (408)655-8627. Contest Director: Brigitta Geltrich. Annual contest. Estab. 1975. Purpose of award: to further creative writing in children. Unpublished submissions only. Deadline for entries: June 30. SASE for contest rules and entry forms. SASE for return of entries "if not winning poem." No entry fee. Awards publication in an anthology. Judging by selected guest editors and educators. Contest open to children only (up to and including 19 years old). Writer should request contest rules. SASE with all correspondence. Age of child must be stated and manuscript must be verified of its authenticity. Each story or poem must have a title. Creative with Words Publications publishes the top 100 manuscripts submitted to the contest, and also publishes anthologies on various themes throughout the year to which young writers may also submit. Request theme list, include SASE.

‡WESTERN HERITAGE AWARDS, National Cowboy Hall of Fame, 1700 NE 63rd St., Oklahoma City OK 73111. (405)478-2250. Fax: (405)478-4714. E-mail: nchf@aol.com. Website: http://www.horseworld.com. Director of Public Relations: Lynda Haller. Annual award. Estab. 1961. Purpose of award: The WHA are presented annually to encourage the accurate and artistic telling of great stories of the West through 15 categories of western literature, television and film, including fiction, nonfiction, children's books and poetry. Previously published submissions only; must be published the calendar year before the awards are presented. Deadline for literary entries: November 30. Deadline for film, music and television entries: December 31. SASE for award rules and entry forms. Entries not returned. No entry fee. Awards a Wrangler award. Judging by a panel of judges selected each year with distinction in various fields of western art and heritage. Requirements for entrants: The material must pertain to the development or preservation of the West, either from a historical or contemporary viewpoint. Historical accuracy is vital. Literary entries must have been published Dec. 1 and Nov. 30 of calendar year. Film, music or television entries must have been released or aired between January 1 and December 31 of calendar year of entry. Works recognized during special awards ceremonies held annually third weekend in March at the museum. There is an autograph party preceding the awards. Film clips are shown during the awards presentation. Awards ceremonies are broadcast.

*‡JACKIE WHITE MEMORIAL NATIONAL CHILDREN'S PLAYWRITING CONTEST, Columbia Entertainment Company, 309 Parkade Blvd., Columbia MO 65202. (573)874-5628. Contest Director: Betsy Phillips. Annual contest. Estab. 1988. Purpose of contest: to find good plays for 30-45 theater school students, 6-9 grade, to perform in CEC's theater school. Previously unpublished submissions only. Submissions made by author. Deadline for entries: June 1. SASE for contest rules and entry forms. Entry fee is $10. Awards $250, production of play, travel expenses to come see production. Judging by board members of CEC and at least 1 theater school parent. Play is performed during the following season, i.e. 1997 winner to be presented during CEC's 1997-98 season.

‡PAUL A. WITTY OUTSTANDING LITERATURE AWARD, International Reading Association, Special Interest Group, Reading for Gifted and Creative Learning, School of Education, P.O. Box 32925, Fort Worth TX 76129. (817)921-7660. Award Director: Dr. Cathy Collins Block. Annual award. Estab. 1979. Categories of entries: poetry/prose at elementary, junior high and senior high levels. Unpublished submissions only. Deadline for entries: February 1. SASE for award rules and entry forms. SASE for return of entries. No entry fee. Awards $25 and plaque, also certificates of merit. Judging by 2 committees for screening and awarding. Works will be published in International Reading Association publications. "The elementary students' entries must be legible and may not exceed 1,000 words. Secondary students' prose entries should be typed and may exceed 1,000 words if necessary. At both elementary and secondary levels, if poetry is entered, a set of five poems must be submitted. All entries and requests for applications must include a self-addressed, stamped envelope."

PAUL A. WITTY SHORT STORY AWARD, International Reading Association, P.O. Box 8139, 800 Barksdale Rd., Newark DE 19714-8139. (302)731-1600. The entry must be an original short story appearing in a young children's periodical for the first time during 1997. The short story should serve as a literary standard that encourages young readers to read periodicals. Deadline for entries: The entry must have been published for the first time in the eligibility year; the short story must be submitted during the calendar year of publication. Anyone wishing to nominate a short story should send it to the designated Paul A. Witty Short Award Subcommittee Chair by December 1. Guidelines are available from Debra Gail Herrera, 111 E. Conner, Eastland TX 76448. Award is $1,000 and recognition at the annual IRA Convention.

ALICE LOUISE WOOD OHIOANA AWARD FOR CHILDREN'S LITERATURE, Ohioana Library Association, 65 S. Front St., Suite 1105, Columbus OH 43215. (614)466-3831. Fax: (614)728-6974. Director: Linda R. Hengst. Annual award. Estab. 1991. Purpose of award: "to recognize an Ohio author whose body of work has made, and continues to make, a significant contribution to literature for children or young adults." SASE for award rules and entry forms. Gives monetary award (amount may vary). Requirements for entrants: "must have been born in Ohio, or lived in Ohio for a minimum of five years; established a distinguished publishing record of books for children and young people; body of work has made, and continues to make, a significant contribution to the literature for young people; through whose work as a writer, teacher, administrator, or through community service, interest in children's literature has been encouraged and children have become involved with reading."

CARTER G. WOODSON BOOK AWARD, National Council for the Social Studies, 3501 Newark St. NW, Washington DC 20016. (202)966-7840. Fax: (202)966-2061. E-mail: information@ncss.org Staff Competition Coordinator: Rose-Kathryn Young Chaisson. Annual award. Purpose of contest: to recognize books relating to ethnic minorities and authors of such books. NCSS established the Carter G. Woodson Book Awards for the most distinguished social science books appropriate for young readers which depict ethnicity in the United States. This award is intended to "encourage the writing, publishing, and dissemination of outstanding social studies books for young readers which treat topics related to ethnic minorities and race relations sensitively and accurately." Submissions must be previously published. Submissions generally made by publishers "because copies of the book must be supplied to each member of the committee and copies of winning books must be provided to NCSS headquarters." Eligible books must be published in the year preceding the year in which award is given, i.e., 1996 for 1997 award. Books must be received by members of the committee by February 1. Rules, criteria and requirements are available for SASE. No entry fee. Award consists of: an announcement published in NCSS periodicals and forwarded to national and Council affiliated media. The publisher and author receive written notification of the committee decision. Reviews of award recipients and outstanding merit book are published in the NCSS official journal, *Social Education*. The award is presented at the NCSS Annual Conference in November. Judging by committee of social studies educators (teachers, curriculum supervisors and specialists, college/university professors, teacher educators—with a specific interest in multicultural education and the use of literature in social studies instruction) appointed from the NCSS membership at large.

WORK-IN-PROGRESS GRANTS, Society of Children's Book Writers and Illustrators, #106, 22736 Vanowen St., West Hills CA 91307. (818)888-8760. Annual award. "The SCBWI Work-in-Progress Grants have been established to assist children's book writers in the completion of a specific project." Five categories: (1) General Work-in-Progress Grant. (2) Grant for a Contemporary Novel for Young People. (3) Nonfiction Research Grant. (4) Grant for a work whose author has never had a book published. (5) Grant for a picture book writer. Requests for applications may be made beginning October 1. Completed applications accepted February 1-May 1 of each year. SASE for applications for grants. In any year, an applicant may apply for any of the grants except the one awarded for a work whose author has never had a book published. (The recipient of this grant will be chosen from entries in all categories.) Five grants of $1,000 will be awarded annually. Runner-up grants of $500 (one in each category) will also be awarded. "The grants are available to both full and associate members of the SCBWI. They are not available for projects on which there are already contracts." Previous recipients not eligible to apply.

‡**WRITER'S EXCHANGE POETRY CONTEST**, R.S.V.P. Press, Box 394, Society Hill SC 29593. (803)378-4556. Contest Director: Gene Boone. Quarterly contest. Estab. 1985. Purpose of the contest: to promote friendly competition among poets of all ages and backgrounds, giving these poets a chance to be published and win an award. Submissions are made by the author. Continuous deadline; entries are placed in the contest closest to date received. SASE for contest rules and entry forms. Entry fee is $1 per poem. Awards 50% of contest proceeds, usually $35-100 varying slightly in each quarterly contest due to changes in response. Judging by Gene Boone or a guest judge such as a widely published poet or another small press editor. "From the entries received, we reserve the right to publish the winning poems in an issue of *Writer's Exchange*, a literary newsletter. The contest is open to any poet. Poems on any subject/theme, any style, to 24 lines, may be entered. Poems should be typed, single-spaced, with the poet's name in the upper left corner."

‡**WRITER'S INTERNATIONAL FORUM CONTESTS**, *Writer's International Forum*, P.O. Box 516, Tracyton WA 98393. Contest Director: Sandra E. Haven. Estab. 1991. Purpose of contest: to inspire excellence in the traditional short story format. "We like identifiable characters, strong storylines, and crisp, fresh endings. We particularly like helping new writers, writers changing genres and young writers." Unpublished submissions only. Submissions made by the author. Deadlines, fees, and cash award prizes vary per contest. SASE for dates of each upcoming contest, contest rules and entry forms. Entry fee waived for subscribers. Judging by *Writer's International Forum* staff. "We reserve the right to publish cash award winners." Please state genre of story and age of intended audience (as "ages 9-11") in cover letter. Contest winners announced and first place and grand prize winners published in issue following each contest. Word count restrictions vary with each contest. Some contests require following a theme or other stipulation. Please request guidelines for contest you want to enter.

‡**WRITING CONFERENCE WRITING CONTESTS**, The Writing Conference, Inc., P.O. Box 664, Ottawa KS 66067. (913)242-0407. Contest Director: John H. Bushman. Annual contest. Estab. 1988. Purpose of contest: to further writing by students with awards for narration, exposition and poetry at the elementary, middle school and high school levels. Unpublished submissions only. Submissions made by the author or teacher. Deadline for entries: January 6. SASE for contest rules and entry form. No entry fee. Awards plaque and publication of winning entry in

The Writers' Slate, March issue. Judging by a panel of teachers. Requirements for entrants: must be enrolled in school—K-12th grade.

‡**YEARBOOK EXCELLENCE CONTEST**, *Quill and Scroll*, School of Journalism, University of Iowa, Iowa City IA 52242. (319)335-5795. Executive Director: Richard Johns. Annual contest. Estab. 1987. Previously published submissions only. Submissions made by the author or school yearbook adviser. Must be published between November 1, 1995 and November 1, 1996. Deadline for entries: November 1. SASE for contest rules and entry form. Entry fee is $2 per entry. Awards National Gold Key; sweepstakes winners receive plaque; seniors eligible for scholarships. Judging by various judges. Winning entries may be published in *Quill and Scroll* magazine.

✦**YOUNG ADULT CANADIAN BOOK AWARD**, The Canadian Library Association, Suite 602, 200 Elgin St., Ottawa, Ontario K2P 1L5 Canada. (613)232-9625. Fax: (613)563-9895. Contact: Committee Chair. Annual award. Estab. 1981. Purpose of award: "to recognize the author of an outstanding English-language Canadian book which appeals to young adults between the ages of 13 and 18 that was published the preceding calendar year. Information is available for anyone requesting. We approach publishers, also send news releases to various journals, i.e. *Quill & Quire*." Entries are not returned. No entry fee. Awards a leather-bound book. Requirement for entrants: must be a work of fiction (novel or short stories), the title must be a Canadian publication in either hardcover or paperback, and the author must be a Canadian citizen or landed immigrant. Award given at the Canadian Library Association Conference.

YOUNG READER'S CHOICE AWARD, Pacific Northwest Library Association, Box 352930, University of Washington, Graduate School of Library and Information Science, Seattle WA 98195-2930. (206)543-1897. Secretary: Carol Doll. Award Director: named annually. Annual award for published authors. Estab. 1940. Purpose of award: "to promote reading as an enjoyable activity and to provide children an opportunity to endorse a book they consider an excellent story." Previously published submissions only; must be published 3 years before award year. Deadline for entries: February 1. SASE for award rules and entry forms. No entry fee. Awards a silver medal, struck in Idaho silver. "Children vote for their favorite (books) from a list of titles nominated by librarians, teachers, students and other interested persons."

Helpful Resources

The editor of *Children's Writer's & Illustrator's Market* suggests the following books, periodicals and websites to keep you informed on writing and illustrating techniques, trends in the field, business issues, industry news and changes, and additional markets.

BOOKS

CHILDREN'S WRITER GUIDE TO 1997, (annual), The Institute of Children's Literature, 95 Long Ridge Rd., West Redding CT 55104. (800)443-6078.

CHILDREN'S WRITER'S WORD BOOK, by Alijandra Mogilner, Writer's Digest Books, 1507 Dana Ave., Cincinnati OH 45207. (800)289-0963.

GETTING STARTED AS A FREELANCE ILLUSTRATOR OR DESIGNER, by Michael Fleischman, North Light Books, 1507 Dana Ave., Cincinnati OH 45207, (800)289-0963.

GUIDE TO LITERARY AGENTS, (annual) edited by Don Prues, Writer's Digest Books, 1507 Dana Ave., Cincinnati OH 45207. (800)289-0963.

HOW TO SELL YOUR PHOTOGRAPHS & ILLUSTRATIONS, by Elliot & Barbara Gordon, North Light Books, 1507 Dana Ave., Cincinnati OH 45207. (800)289-0963.

HOW TO WRITE A CHILDREN'S BOOK & GET IT PUBLISHED, by Barbara Seuling, Charles Schribner's Sons, 1230 Avenue of the Americas, New York NY 10020. (212)702-2000.

HOW TO WRITE AND ILLUSTRATE CHILDREN'S BOOKS AND GET THEM PUBLISHED, edited by Treld Pelkey Bicknell and Felicity Trottman, Writer's Digest Books, 1507 Dana Ave., Cincinnati OH 45207. (800)289-0963.

HOW TO WRITE AND SELL CHILDREN'S PICTURE BOOKS, by Jean E. Karl, Writer's Digest Books, 1507 Dana Ave., Cincinnati OH 45207. (800)289-0963.

HOW TO WRITE, ILLUSTRATE, AND DESIGN CHILDREN'S BOOKS, by Frieda Gates, Lloyd-Simone Publishing Company, distributed by Library Research Associates, Inc., Dunderberg Rd. RD 6, Box 41, Monroe NY 10950. (914)783-1144.

LEGAL GUIDE FOR THE VISUAL ARTIST, by Tad Crawford, North Light Books, 1507 Dana Ave., Cincinnati OH 45207. (800)289-0963.

MARKET GUIDE FOR YOUNG WRITERS, Fifth Edition, by Kathy Henderson, Writer's Digest Books, 1507 Dana Ave., Cincinnati OH 45207. (800)289-0963.

A TEEN'S GUIDE TO GETTING PUBLISHED, by Danielle Dunn & Jessica Dunn, Prufrock Press, P.O. Box 8813, Waco TX 76714-8813. (800)998-2208.

THE ULTIMATE PORTFOLIO, by Martha Metzdorf, North Light Books, 1507 Dana Ave., Cincinnati OH 45207. (800)289-0963.

THE WRITER'S DIGEST GUIDE TO MANUSCRIPT FORMATS, by Dian Dincin Buchman & Seli Groves, Writer's Digest Books, 1507 Dana Ave., Cincinnati OH 45207. (800)289-0963.

THE WRITER'S ESSENTIAL DESK REFERENCE, Second Edition, Writer's Digest Books, 1507 Dana Ave., Cincinnati OH 45207. (800)289-0963.

WRITING AND ILLUSTRATING CHILDREN'S BOOKS FOR PUBLICATION: TWO PERSPECTIVES, by Berthe Amoss and Eric Suben, Writer's Digest Books, 1507 Dana Ave., Cincinnati OH 45207. (800)289-0963.

WRITING & PUBLISHING BOOKS FOR CHILDREN IN THE 1990s: THE INSIDE STORY FROM THE EDITOR'S DESK, by Olga Litowinsky, Walker & Co., 435 Hudson St., New York NY 10014. (212)727-8300.

WRITING BOOKS FOR YOUNG PEOPLE, Second Edition, by James Cross Giblin, The Writer, Inc., 120 Boylston St., Boston MA 02116-4615. (617)423-3157.

WRITING FOR CHILDREN & TEENAGERS, Third edition, by Lee Wyndham and Arnold Madison, Writer's Digest Books, 1507 Dana Ave., Cincinnati OH 45207. (800)289-0963.

WRITING WITH PICTURES: HOW TO WRITE AND ILLUSTRATE CHILDREN'S BOOKS, by Uri Shulevitz, Watson-Guptill Publications, 1515 Broadway, New York NY 10036. (212)764-7300.

PUBLICATIONS

BOOK LINKS, editor Judith O'Malley, American Library Association, 50 E. Huron St., Chicago IL 60611. (800)545-2433.

CHILDREN'S BOOK INSIDER, editor Laura Backes, P.O. Box 1030, Fairplay CO 80440-1030. (800)807-1916. E-mail: cbi@rmi.net. Web site: http://www.mindspring.com/~cbi. *Official Update Source for* Children's Writer's & Illustrator's Market, *featuring quarterly lists of changes and updates to listings in* CWIM.

CHILDREN'S WRITER, editor Susan Tierney, The Institute of Children's Literature, 95 Long Ridge Rd., West Redding CT 55104. (800)443-6078.

THE FIVE OWLS, editor Susan Stan, Hamline University Crossroads Center, MS-C1924, 1536 Hewitt Ave., St. Paul MN 55104. (612)644-7377. Fax: (612)641-2956.

THE HORN BOOK MAGAZINE, editor-in-chief Robert Sutton, The Horn Book Inc., 11 Beacon St., Suite 1000, Boston MA 02108. (617)227-1555. E-mail: magazine@hbook.com.

THE LION AND THE UNICORN: A CRITICAL JOURNAL OF CHILDREN'S LITERATURE, editors Jack Zipes and Louisa Smith, The Johns Hopkins University Press—Journals Publishing Division, 2175 N. Charles St., Baltimore MD 21218-4319. (410)516-6987.

ONCE UPON A TIME . . ., editor Audrey Baird, 553 Winston Court, St. Paul MN 55118. (612)457-6233.

PUBLISHERS WEEKLY, editor-in-chief Nora Rawlinson, Bowker Magazine Group, Cahners Publishing Co., 249 W. 17th St., New York NY 10011. (800)278-2991.

SOCIETY OF CHILDREN'S BOOK WRITERS AND ILLUSTRATORS BULLETIN, editors Stephen Mooser and Lin Oliver, SCBWI, 22736 Vanowen St., Suite 106, West Hills CA 91307. (818)888-8760.

WEBSITES

CBCONLINE, THE WEBSITE OF THE CHILDREN'S BOOK COUNCIL: http://www.cbcbooks.-org/index.html
This site includes a complete list of CBC members with addresses, names and descriptions of what each publishes; previews of upcoming titles from members; articles from CBC Features, *the Council's newsletter; and their catalog.*

CHILDREN'S LITERATURE WEB GUIDE: http://www.ucalgary.ca/~dkbrown/index.html
This site includes stories, poetry, resource lists, lists of conferences, links to book reviews, lists of awards (international), and information on books from classic to contemporary.

CHILDREN'S MUSIC WEB GUIDE: http://www.childrensmusic.org
This site includes an index of children's music sites on the web, a database of children's music events in the U.S. and worldwide, an e-mail forum for children's music professionals and enthusiasts, a music magazine with activities for kids, and links to other sites.

CHILDREN'S WRITERS RESOURCE CENTER: http://www.mindspring.com/~cbi
This site includes highlights from the newsletter Children's Book Insider; *definitions of publishing terms; answers to frequently asked questions; information on trends; information on small presses; a research center for web information; and a catalog of material available from* CBI.

KIDS 'N STUFF WRITING FOR CHILDREN HOMEPAGE: http://www.pages.prodigy.com/childrens_writers/index.html
Site coordinator Jody Blosser includes articles for writers, lists of resources, lists of clubs and organizations, and links to other sites including companion site A World of Pictures. Blosser is looking for articles from writers to include on the page.

SOCIETY OF CHILDREN'S BOOK WRITERS AND ILLUSTRATORS: http://www.scbwi.org
Site coordinator Bruce Balan includes information on awards and grants available to SCBWI members, a calender of events listed by date and region, a list of publications available to members, and a site map for easy navigation. Balan welcomes suggestions for the site from visitors.

A WORLD OF PICTURES WEBSITE FOR CHILDREN'S ILLUSTRATORS:
http://www.pages.prodigy.com/picbooks/
Site coordinator Kimberly Dahl includes a wealth of articles on marketing and self-promotion and articles for beginners; a detailed list of resources; an illustrators' forum and message board; and links to a number of other sites with descriptions including companion site Kids 'n Stuff.

WRITES OF PASSAGE: http://www.writes.org
Run by Writes of Passage *magazine (a literary magazine for teens), this site includes features from the magazine; links to a list of teen resources on the web, including high school and college newspapers and online dictionaries; and a database of high school websites.*

Glossary

Advance. A sum of money a publisher pays a writer or illustrator prior to the publication of a book. It is usually paid in installments, such as one half on signing the contract; one half on delivery of a complete and satisfactory manuscript. The advance is paid against the royalty money that will be earned by the book.

All rights. The rights contracted to a publisher permitting the use of material anywhere and in any form, including movie and book club sales, without additional payment to the creator. (See Know Your Rights.)

Anthology. A collection of selected writings by various authors or gatherings of works by one author.

Anthropomorphization. The act of attributing human form and personality to things not human (such as animals).

ASAP. As soon as possible.

ASCAP. American Society of Composers, Authors and Publishers. A performing rights organization.

Assignment. An editor or art director asks a writer, illustrator or photographer to produce a specific piece for an agreed-upon fee.

B&W. Black & white.

Backlist. A publisher's list of books not published during the current season but still in print.

Biennially. Occurring once every two years.

Bimonthly. Occurring once every two months.

Biweekly. Occurring once every two weeks.

BMI. Broadcast Music, Inc. A performing rights organization.

Book packager. A company which draws all elements of a book together, from the initial concept to writing and marketing strategies, then sells the book package to a book publisher and/or movie producer. Also known as book producer or book developer.

Book proposal. Package submitted to a publisher for consideration usually consisting of a synopsis, outline and sample chapters. (See Guide to Submitting Your Work.)

Business-size envelope. Also known as a #10 envelope. The standard size used in sending business correspondence.

Camera-ready. Refers to art that is completely prepared for copy camera platemaking.

Caption. A description of the subject matter of an illustration or photograph; photo captions include persons' names where appropriate. Also called cutline.

CD-ROM. Compact disc read-only memory. Non-erasable electronic medium used for digitalized image and document storage capable of holding enormous amounts of information. A computer user must have a CD-ROM drive to access a CD-ROM.

Clean-copy. A manuscript free of errors and needing no editing; it is ready for typesetting.

Clips. Samples, usually from newspapers or magazines of a writer's published work.

Concept books. Books that deal with ideas, concepts and large-scale problems, promoting an understanding of what's happening in a child's world. Most prevalent are alphabet and counting books, but also includes books dealing with specific concerns facing young people (such as divorce, birth of a sibling, friendship or moving).

Contract. A written agreement stating the rights to be purchased by an editor, art director or producer and the amount of payment the writer, illustrator or photographer will receive for that sale. (See Tips on Contracts & Negotiation.)

Contributor's copies. The magazine issues sent to an author, illustrator or photographer in which her work appears.

Co-op publisher. A publisher that shares production costs with an author, but, unlike subsidy publishers, handles all marketing and distribution. An author receives a high percentage of royalties until her initial investment is recouped, then standard royalties.

Copy. The actual written material of a manuscript.

Copyediting. Editing a manuscript for grammar usage, spelling, punctuation and general style.

Copyright. A means to legally protect an author's/illustrator's/photographer's work. This can be shown by writing ©, the creator's name, and year of work's creation. (See Know Your Rights.)

Cover letter. A brief letter, accompanying a complete manuscript, especially useful if responding to an editor's request for a manuscript. May also accompany a book proposal. (See Guide to Submitting Your Work.)

Cutline. See caption.

Disk. A round, flat magnetic plate on which computer data may be stored.

Division. An unincorporated branch of a company.

Dummy. Handmade mock-up of a book.

Electronic submission. A submission of material by modem or on computer disk.

E-mail. Electronic mail. Messages sent from one computer to another via a modem or computer network.

Final draft. The last version of a polished manuscript ready for submission to an editor.

First North American serial rights. The right to publish material in a periodical before it appears in book form, for the first time, in the United States or Canada. (See Know Your Rights.)

Flat fee. A one-time payment.

Galleys. The first typeset version of a manuscript that has not yet been divided into pages.

Genre. A formulaic type of fiction, such as horror, mystery, romance, science fiction or western.

Glossy. A photograph with a shiny surface as opposed to one with a non-shiny matte finish.

Gouache. Opaque watercolor with an appreciable film thickness and an actual paint layer.

Halftone. Reproduction of a continuous tone illustration with the image formed by dots produced by a camera lens screen.

Hard copy. The printed copy of a computer's output.

Hardware. All the mechanically-integrated components of a computer that are not software—circuit boards, transistors and the machines that are the actual computer.

Hi-Lo. High interest, low reading level. Pertains mostly to books for beginning adult readers.

Home page. The first page of a World Wide Web document.

Imprint. Name applied to a publisher's specific line of books.

Interactive. A type of computer interface that takes user input, such as answers to computer-generated questions, and then acts upon them.

Internet. A worldwide network of computers that offers access to a wide variety of electronic resources.

IRC. International Reply Coupon. Sold at the post office to enclose with text or artwork sent to a foreign buyer to cover postage costs when replying or returning work.

Keyline. Identification, through signs and symbols, of the positions of illustrations and copy for the printer.

Layout. Arrangement of illustrations, photographs, text and headlines for printed material.

Line drawing. Illustration done with pencil or ink using no wash or other shading.

Mechanicals. Paste-up or preparation of work for printing.

Middle reader. The general classification of books written for readers ages 9-11.

Modem. A small electrical box that plugs into the serial card of a computer, used to transmit data from one computer to another, usually via telephone lines.

Ms (mss). Manuscript(s).

One-time rights. Permission to publish a story in periodical or book form one time only. (See Know Your Rights.)

Outline. A summary of a book's contents in 5-15 double-spaced pages; often in the form of chapter headings with a descriptive sentence or two under each heading to show the scope of the book.

Package sale. The sale of a manuscript and illustrations/photos as a "package" paid for with one check.

Payment on acceptance. The writer, artist or photographer is paid for her work at the time the editor or art director decides to buy it.

Payment on publication. The writer, artist or photographer is paid for her work when it is published.

Photostat. Black & white copies produced by an inexpensive photographic process using paper negatives; only line values are held with accuracy. Also called stat.

Picture book. A type of book aimed at preschoolers to 8-year-olds that tells a story primarily or entirely with artwork.

Print. An impression pulled from an original plate, stone, block, screen or negative; also a positive made from a photographic negative.

Production house. A film company which creates video material including animation, special effects, graphics, filmstrips, slides, live action and documentaries.

Proofreading. Reading a manuscript to correct typographical errors.

Query. A letter to an editor designed to capture her interest in an article or book you propose to write. (See Guide to Submitting Your Work.)

Reading fee. An arbitrary amount of money charged by some agents and publishers to read a submitted manuscript.

Reprint rights. Permission to print an already published work whose first rights have been sold to another magazine or book publisher. (See Know Your Rights.)

Response time. The average length of time it takes an editor or art director to accept or reject a query or submission and inform the creator of the decision.

Rights. What are offered to an editor or art director in exchange for printing a manuscript, artwork or photographs. (See Know Your Rights.)

Rough draft. A manuscript which has been written but not checked for errors in grammar, punctuation, spelling or content.

Roughs. Preliminary sketches or drawings.

Royalty. An agreed percentage paid by a publisher to a writer, illustrator or photographer for each copy of her work sold.

SAE. Self-addressed envelope.

SASE. Self-addressed, stamped envelope.

SCBWI. The Society of Children's Book Writers and Illustrators. (See listing in Clubs & Organizations section.)

Second serial rights. Permission for the reprinting of a work in another periodical after its first publication in book or magazine form. (See Know Your Rights.)

Semiannual. Occurring once every six months.

Semimonthly. Occurring twice a month.

Semiweekly. Occurring twice a week.

Serial rights. The rights given by an author to a publisher to print a piece in one or more periodicals. (See Know Your Rights.)

Simultaneous submissions. Material sent to several publishers at the same time. (See Guide to Submitting Your Work.)

Slant. The approach to a story or piece of artwork that will appeal to readers of a particular publication.

Slush pile. Editors' term for their collections of unsolicited manuscripts.

SOCAN. Society of Composers, Authors and Music Publishers of Canada. A performing rights organization.

Software. Programs and related documentation for use with a particular computer system.

Solicited manuscript. Material which an editor has asked for or agreed to consider before being sent by a writer.

Speculation (Spec). Creating a piece with no assurance from an editor or art director that it will be purchased or any reimbursements for material or labor paid.

Stat. See photostat.

Subsidiary rights. All rights other than book publishing rights included in a book contract, such as paperback, book club and movie rights. (See Know Your Rights.)

Subsidy publisher. A book publisher that charges the author for the cost of typesetting, printing and promoting a book. Also called a vanity publisher.

Synopsis. A brief summary of a story or novel. Usually a page to a page and a half, single-spaced, if part of a book proposal.

Tabloid. Publication printed on an ordinary newspaper page turned sideways and folded in half.

Tearsheet. Page from a magazine or newspaper containing your printed art, story, article, poem or photo.

Thumbnail. A rough layout in miniature.

Transparencies. Positive color slides; not color prints.

Unsolicited manuscript. Material sent without an editor's or art director's request.

Vanity publisher. See subsidy publisher.

Word processor. A computer that produces typewritten copy via automated typing, text-editing, and storage and transmission capabilities.

World Wide Web. An Internet resource that utilizes hypertext to access information. It also supports formatted text, illustrations and sounds, depending on the user's computer capabilities.

Work-for-hire. An arrangement between a writer, illustrator or photographer and a company under which the company retains complete control of the work's copyright. (See Know Your Rights.)

Young adult. The general classification of books written for readers ages 12-18.

Young reader. The general classification of books written for readers ages 5-8.

Age-Level Index

This index lists book and magazine publishers by the age-groups for which they publish. Use it to locate appropriate markets for your work, then carefully read the listings and follow the guidelines of each publisher. Use this index in conjunction with the Subject Index to further narrow your list of markets. Listings new to this edition are marked with an asterisk (*).

BOOK PUBLISHERS

Picture books (preschoolers to 8-year-olds): ABC, All Books for Children; *Abingdon; Advocacy; Africa World; African American Images; *After Midnight; Aladdin; Alyson, Inc.; American Bible Society; American Education Publishing; *Arroyo Projects Studio; Atheneum; Augsburg Fortress, Publishers; A/V Concepts Corp.; Bantam; Barrons Educational; Behrman House; Bess Press; Blackbirch; Blizzard; Boingo Books, Inc.; Boyds Mills; Broadman & Holman; *Callaway Editions; Archway/Minstrel; *Capstone Inc.; Carolina Wren; Carolrhoda Books; Chariot; Charlesbridge; Children's Book Press; Childrens Press; Christian Ed. Publishers; *Christian Publications; Chronicle; Cobblehill; *Colonial Williamsburg Foundation; Concordia Publishing House; Crosspoint International; Crossway; Crown; CSS Publishing; Dawn; Dial; *Dove Kids; Down East; Down East; Dutton; E.M. Press; Eerdmans, Wm. B.; Evan-Moor Educational Publishers; Farrar, Straus & Giroux; Fitzhenry & Whiteside Ltd.; Free Spirit Publishing; Geringer Books, Laura; Gibbs Smith, Publisher; Godine, Publisher, David R.; Golden Books; Grapevine Publications, Inc.; *Greene Bark Press; Greenwillow Books; Grosset & Dunlap, Inc.; HaChai Publishing; Harcourt Brace & Co.; HarperCollins; Hendrick-Long; Herald; Highsmith; Hodder Children's Books; Holiday House; Holt, Henry; Houghton Mifflin; Humanics Children's House; Huntington House; Hyperion; Hyperion Press Limited; Ideals; Jalmar; Jewish Publication Society; Kar-Ben Copies, Inc.; Knopf; Laredo; Little, Brown; Lodestar; Lothrop Lee & Shepard Books; *Lowell House Juvenile; Lucas/Evans; McClanahan; Macelderry Books, Margaret K.; Mage; Magination; Meadowbrook; Millbrook; Millbrook; Mondo; Morehouse; Morris, Joshua; Northland; NorthWord; Open Hand; Orca; Orchard; Our Child Press; Owen, Richard C.; Pacific Educational; Parenting Press; Peachtree; Pelican; Perspectives; Philomel; *Phoenix Learning Resources; Pieper; Polychrome; *Prep; Price Stern Sloan; Putnam; Questar; *Raintree Steck-Vaughn; Random House; Sasquatch; Silver Moon; Simon & Schuster; Soundprints; Speech Bin, Inc., The; Standard; Stemmer House; *Stoddart; Sunbelt Media/Eakin; *Synchronicity; *Transworld; Treasure Chest; *Treasure; Tricycle; Troll; Tyndale House; University Classics; *Volcano; Walker And Co.; Whispering Coyote; Whitebird; Willowisp; *World Book; Zino

Young readers (5- to 8-year olds): ABC, All Books for Children; Advocacy; Africa World; African American Images; *After Midnight; Aladdin; Alyson, Inc.; American Bible Society; American Education Publishing; *Arroyo Projects Studio; Atheneum; A/V Concepts Corp.; Bantam; Barrons Educational; Behrman House; Bess Press; Bethany House; Bethel; Blackbirch; Blizzard; Blue Sky; Boingo Books, Inc.; Boyds Mills; Bright Ring; Broadman & Holman; *Callaway Editions; Archway/Minstrel; *Capstone Inc.; Carolina Wren; Carolrhoda Books; Chariot; Chicago Review; Childrens Press; Christian Ed. Publishers; *Christian Publications; Chronicle; Cobblehill; *Colonial Williamsburg Foundation; Concordia Publishing House; Coteau; Crossway; Crown; CSS Publishing; Davenport, Publishers, May; Denison, T.S.; Dial; Dutton; E.M. Press; Eerdmans, Wm. B.; Enslow Publishers Inc.; Evan-Moor Educational Publishers; Farrar, Straus & Giroux; Feminist Press at The City University of New York, The; Fitzhenry & Whiteside Ltd.; Franklin Watts; Free Spirit Publishing; Friends United Press; Geringer Books, Laura; Godine, Publisher, David R.; Golden Books; Grapevine Publications, Inc.; *Greene Bark Press; Greenwillow Books; Grosset & Dunlap, Inc.; HaChai Publishing; Harcourt Brace & Co.; HarperCollins; Hendrick-Long; Herald; Highsmith; Hodder Children's Books; Holiday House; Houghton Mifflin; Humanics Children's House; Huntington House; Hyperion; Hyperion Press Limited; Ideals; Incentive; Jalmar; Jewish Publication Society; Jones University, Bob; Just Us Books; Kar-Ben Copies, Inc.; Knopf; Laredo; *Learning Works; Little, Brown; Lodestar; Lothrop Lee & Shepard Books; *Lowell House Juvenile; Lucas/Evans; Macelderry Books, Margaret K.; Magination; Meadowbrook; Millbrook; Morehouse; Morgan Reynolds; Morris, Joshua; Northland; NorthWord; Open Hand; Orca; Orchard; Our Child Press; Owen, Richard C.; Pacific Educational; Parenting Press; Peachtree; Pelican; Perspectives; Philomel; *Phoenix Learning Resources; Pieper; Planet Dexter; Players; *Pleasant Company; Polychrome; *Prep; Price Stern Sloan; Putnam; Questar; *Raintree Steck-Vaughn; Random House;

Reidmore; Sasquatch; Seedling; Silver Moon; Simon & Schuster; Speech Bin, Inc., The; Sri Rama Publishing; Standard; *Stoddart; *Storey Communications; Sunbelt Media/Eakin; *Synchronicity; *Transworld; *Treasure; Troll; Tyndale House; University Classics; *Volcano; Walker And Co.; Weigl Educational; Weiss, Daniel; *Whitecap; Williamson; Willowisp; *World Book; Zino

Middle readers (9- to 11-year-olds): ABC, All Books for Children; Advocacy; Africa World; African American Images; *After Midnight; Aladdin; Alyson, Inc.; American Bible Society; Archway/Minstrel; *Arroyo Projects Studio; Atheneum; A/V Concepts Corp.; Avon Books; B&B; Bantam; Barrons Educational; Behrman House; Bess Press; Bethany House; Bethel; Blackbirch; Blizzard; Boingo Books, Inc.; Boyds Mills; Bright Ring; *Callaway Editions; Archway/Minstrel; *Capstone Inc.; Carolrhoda Books; Chariot; Chicago Review; Children's Book Press; Childrens Press; Christian Ed. Publishers; *Christian Publications; Chronicle; Clear Light; Cobblehill; *Colonial Williamsburg Foundation; Concordia Publishing House; Coteau; Crossway; Crown; CSS Publishing; Davis Pubilcations, Inc.; Denison, T.S.; Dial; Down East; Down East; Dutton; E.M. Press; Eerdmans, Wm. B.; Enslow Publishers Inc.; Evan-Moor Educational Publishers; *Facts on File; Farrar, Straus & Giroux; Fawcett Juniper; Feminist Press at The City University of New York, The; Fitzhenry & Whiteside Ltd.; Franklin Watts; Free Spirit Publishing; Friends United Press; Geringer Books, Laura; Gibbs Smith, Publisher; Godine, Publisher, David R.; Golden Books; Grapevine Publications, Inc.; Greenhaven Press; Greenwillow Books; Grosset & Dunlap, Inc.; HaChai Publishing; Harcourt Brace & Co.; HarperCollins; Hendrick-Long; Herald; Highsmith; Hodder Children's Books; Holiday House; Holt, Henry; Houghton Mifflin; Huntington House; Hyperion; Hyperion Press Limited; Incentive; Jalmar; Jewish Publication Society; Jones University, Bob; Kar-Ben Copies, Inc.; Knopf; Laredo; *Learning Works; Lerner; Little, Brown; Lodestar; Lorimer, James; Lothrop Lee & Shepard Books; *Lowell House Juvenile; Lucas/Evans; Lucent; Macelderry Books, Margaret K.; Meadowbrook; Meriwether; Milkweed Editions; Millbrook; Millbrook; *Mitchell Lane; Mondo; Morehouse; Morgan Reynolds; Morris, Joshua; Muir Publications, Inc, John; Oliver; Open Hand; Orca; Orchard; Our Child Press; Pacific Educational; Pacific-Rim; Pando; *Paper-Star; Parenting Press; Peachtree; Pelican; Philomel; *Phoenix Learning Resources; Planet Dexter; Players; *Pleasant Company; Polychrome; *Prep; Price Stern Sloan; Putnam; Questar; *Raintree Steck-Vaughn; Random House; Reidmore; St. Anthony Messenger; Seedling; Silver Moon; Simon & Schuster; *Southwest Parks & Monuments; Speech Bin, Inc., The; Standard; Stemmer House; Sterling; *Storey Communications; Sunbelt Media/Eakin; *Synchronicity; Thistledown; *Transworld; Troll; Tyndale House; University Classics; *Volcano; Walker And Co.; Weigl Educational; Weiss, Daniel; *Whitecap; Wiley, John; Willowisp; *World Book; Zino

Young adults (ages 12 and up): Africa World; African American Images; *After Midnight; Aladdin; Alyson, Inc.; American Bible Society; Archway/Minstrel; *Arroyo Projects Studio; Atheneum; A/V Concepts Corp.; Avon Books; B&B; Bantam; Barrons Educational; Behrman House; Berkley Publishing Group; Bethany House; Bethel; Blackbirch; Blizzard; Blue Sky; Boyds Mills; Broadman & Holman; Archway/Minstrel; *Capstone Inc.; Chariot; Chicago Review; Children's Book Press; Childrens Press; *Christian Publications; Chronicle; Clear Light; Cobblehill; *Colonial Williamsburg Foundation; Concordia Publishing House; Crossway; CSS Publishing; Davenport, Publishers, May; Davis Pubilcations, Inc.; Dial; Dutton; E.M. Press; Enslow Publishers Inc.; *Facts on File; Farrar, Straus & Giroux; Fawcett Juniper; Feminist Press at The City University of New York, The; Fitzhenry & Whiteside Ltd.; Franklin Watts; Free Spirit Publishing; Friends United Press; Geringer Books, Laura; Godine, Publisher, David R.; Golden Books; Grapevine Publications, Inc.; Greenhaven Press; Greenwillow Books; Grosset & Dunlap, Inc.; Harcourt Brace & Co.; HarperCollins; Hendrick-Long; Herald; Highsmith; Hodder Children's Books; Holiday House; Holt, Henry; Houghton Mifflin; Huntington House; Hyperion; Incentive; Jalmar; Jewish Publication Society; Jones University, Bob; Knopf; Laredo; *Learning Works; Lerner; Lion; Little, Brown; Lodestar; Lorimer, James; Lothrop Lee & Shepard Books; *Lowell House Juvenile; Lucas/Evans; Lucent; McElderry Books , Margaret K.; Meriwether; Milkweed Editions; Millbrook; Millbrook; *Mitchell Lane; Mondo; Morehouse; Oliver; Open Hand; Orca; Orchard; Our Child Press; Pacific Educational; Pacific-Rim; Pando; Peachtree; Pelican; Philomel; *Phoenix Learning Resources; Players; Polychrome; *Prep; Price Stern Sloan; Putnam; Questar; *Raintree Steck-Vaughn; Reidmore; Rosen; St. Anthony Messenger; Silver Moon; Simon & Schuster; Speech Bin, Inc., The; Standard; *Stoddart; Sunbelt Media/Eakin; *Synchronicity; Thistledown; *Transworld; Tricycle; Troll; University Classics; *Volcano; Walker And Co.; Weigl Educational; Weiss, Daniel; Wiley, John; Willowisp; *World Book

MAGAZINES

Picture-oriented material (preschoolers to 8-year-olds): Babybug; Bread for God's Children; Chickadee Magazine; Focus on the Family Clubhouse; Focus on the Family Clubhouse Jr.; Friend Magazine, The; Highlights for Children; Hopscotch; Humpty Dumpty's Magazine; Ladybug, the Magazine for Young Children; Nature Friend Magazine; Science Weekly; Scienceland; Skipping Stones; Story Friends; Totally Fox Kids Magazine; Turtle Magazine; Wonder Time; *Your Big Backyard

Young readers (5- to 8-year-olds): ASPCA Animal Watch; Bread for God's Children; Chickadee Magazine; Children's Playmate; *Cogniz; DynaMath; Focus on the Family Clubhouse; Focus on the

Family Clubhouse Jr.; Friend Magazine, The; Highlights for Children; Hopscotch; Jack And Jill; Lighthouse; My Friend; *National Geographic World; Nature Friend Magazine; Pockets; Primary Days; School Mates; Science Weekly; Scienceland; Skipping Stones; Soccer Jr.; Spider; Straight; Totally Fox Kids Magazine; U*S* Kids; *Your Big Backyard

Middle readers (9- to 11-year-olds): Advocate, PKA's Publication; ASPCA Animal Watch; Boys' Life; Bread for God's Children; Calliope; *Cat Fancy; Child Life; Children's Digest; Cobblestone; Counselor; Cricket Magazine; Crusader; Current Health 1; Discovery; Dolphin Log; DynaMath; *Explorer; Faces; Falcon For Kids; Field & Stream; Focus on the Family Clubhouse; Focus on the Family Clubhouse Jr.; Friend Magazine, The; Goldfinch, The; Guide Magazine; Guideposts for Kids; Highlights for Children; Hopscotch; Jack And Jill ; Junior Scholastic; Kids World Magazine; Lighthouse; Magic Realism; My Friend; *National Geographic World; Nature Friend Magazine; Odyssey; On The Line; OWL Magazine; Pockets; Power and Light; R-A-D-A-R; Ranger Rick; Ranger Rick; School Mates; Science Weekly; *Science World; Shofar; Skipping Stones; Soccer Jr.; 3-2-1 Contact; Totally Fox Kids Magazine; Touch; U*S* Kids; Writers' International Forum; *Young Judaean

Young adults (ages 12 and up): Advocate, PKA's Publication; AIM Magazine; American Cheerleader; Bread for God's Children; Calliope; *Cat Fancy; Challenge; Cobblestone; Cricket Magazine; Crusader; Current Health 2; Dolphin Log; DynaMath; Exploring; Faces; For Seniors Only; Guide Magazine; Hobson's Choice; Hype Hair; Junior Scholastic; Lighthouse; Magic Realism; *National Geographic World; Nature Friend Magazine; New Era Magazine; Odyssey; On Course; On The Line; react magazine; Scholastic Math Magazine; School Mates; Science Weekly; *Science World; Seventeen Magazine; Skipping Stones; Soccer Jr.; Street Times; Student Leadership Journal; Teen Life; Teen Power; 3-2-1 Contact; Touch; *What! A Magazine; With; Writers' International Forum; Young Salvationist; Youth Update; Zelos

Subject Index

This index lists book and magazine publishers by the fiction and nonfiction subject area in which they publish. Use it to locate appropriate markets for your work, then carefully read the listings and follow the guidelines of each publisher. Use this index in conjunction with the Age-Level Index to further narrow your list of markets. Listings new to this edition are marked with an (*).

BOOK PUBLISHERS: FICTION

Adventure: ABC All Books for Children; Advocacy; Africa World; American Education Publishing; Archway/Minstrel; Arroyo Projects Studio; Avon Books; Bantam; Barrons Educational; Bess Press; Bethany House; Bethel; Blue Sky; Boyds Mills; Broadman & Holman; *Callaway Editions; Childrens Press; Christian Ed. Publishers; Cobblehill; *Colonial Williamsburg Foundation; Concordia Publishing House; Coteau; Crosspoint International; Crossway; Dial; *Dove Kids; Down East; Dutton; Farrar, Straus & Giroux; Feminist Press; Fitzhenry & Whiteside Ltd.; Geringer Books, Laura; Gibbs Smith; Godine, David R.; Golden Books; Grapevine Publications; *Greene Bark; Grosset & Dunlap; HaChai Publishing; HarperCollins; Hodder Children's Books; Holiday House; Holt, Henry; Houghton Mifflin; Hyperion; Ideals; Jewish Publication Society; Jones University, Bob; Just Us Books; Knopf; Laredo; Lerner; Little, Brown; Lodestar; Lorimer, James; *Lowell House Juvenile; McElderry Books, Margaret K.; Milkweed Editions; Mondo; Morehouse; Morris, Joshua; Northland; Orca; *PaperStar; *Paws IV; Peachtree; Perfection Learning; Philomel; *Piñata; Place In The Woods; Polychrome; *Prep; Putnam; Ragweed; Random House; *Roussan; Sasquatch; Seedling; Standard; *Stoddart; *Synchronicity; Thistledown; Time-Life for Children; TOR; *Transworld; Tyndale House; Whispering Coyote; Whitman, Albert; Willowisp; Zino

Animal: ABC All Books for Children; Advocacy; Alyson, Inc.; American Education Publishing; Archway/Minstrel; Arroyo Projects Studio; Atheneum; Bantam; Barrons Educational; Bess Press; Bethel; Blue Sky; Boyds Mills; *Callaway Editions; Archway/Minstrel; Childrens Press; Chronicle; Cobblehill; *Colonial Williamsburg Foundation; Crosspoint International; Crown; Dawn; Dial; *Dove Kids; Down East; Down East; Dutton; Eerdmans, Wm. B.; Farrar, Straus & Giroux; Geringer Books, Laura; Godine, David R.; Golden Books; Grapevine Publications; Grosset & Dunlap; Harcourt Brace; HarperCollins; Hodder Children's Books; Holiday House; Holt, Henry; Houghton Mifflin; Humanics Children's House; Hyperion; Ideals; *Ivory Tower; Jones University, Bob; Knopf; Little, Brown; Lodestar; McClanahan; Milkweed Editions; Mondo; Morris, Joshua; Northland; NorthWord; Orchard; *Owl; Pando; *Paws IV; Peachtree; Philomel; Pieper; Place

In The Woods; Random House; Sasquatch; Seedling; Simon & Schuster; Soundprints; Speech Bin, Inc., The; Standard; *Stoddart; Sunbelt Media/Eakin; *Synchronicity; Time-Life for Children; *Transworld; Treasure Chest; Troll; University Classics; Walker And Co.; Whispering Coyote; Whitman, Albert; Willowisp; Zino

Anthology: Bess Press; Blue Sky; Archway/Minstrel; Crosspoint International; Farrar, Straus & Giroux; HarperCollins; Houghton Mifflin; Hyperion; Knopf; Lee & Low Books; *Lowell House Juvenile; Meriwether; Orchard; Pieper; *Piñata; Polychrome; Ragweed; Simon & Schuster; *Synchronicity; Thistledown; *Transworld; Troll; Willowisp

Concept: ABC All Books for Children; Advocacy; Africa World; American Education Publishing; Arroyo Projects Studio; Barrons Educational; Bess Press; Blue Sky; Broadman & Holman; *Callaway Editions; Archway/Minstrel; Childrens Press; *Colonial Williamsburg Foundation; Crosspoint International; Dial; Farrar, Straus & Giroux; Feminist Press; Geringer Books, Laura; Grapevine Publications; Grosset & Dunlap; Hodder Children's Books; Holt, Henry; Houghton Mifflin; Humanics Children's House; Ideals; Jalmar; Jones University, Bob; Knopf; Lee & Low Books; Magination; Meriwether; Morris, Joshua; *Owl; Pando; *Paws IV; Peachtree; Pieper; Putnam; Simon & Schuster; *Synchronicity; Time-Life for Children; Tricycle; University Classics; Whitman, Albert

Contemporary: ABC All Books for Children; Advocacy; Africa World; American Education Publishing; Archway/Minstrel; Arroyo Projects Studio; Atheneum; Avon Books; Bantam; *Beach Holme; Bess Press; Blizzard; Blue Sky; Boyds Mills; Broadman & Holman; Archway/Minstrel; Children's Book Press; Childrens Press; Christian Ed. Publishers; Cobblehill; Concordia Publishing House; Coteau; Crosspoint International; Crossway; Davenport, Publishers, May; *Dove Kids; Dutton; E.M. Press; *Fairview; Farrar, Straus & Giroux; Fawcett Juniper; Feminist Press; Fitzhenry & Whiteside Ltd.; Gibbs Smith; Godine, David R.; Golden Books; Grapevine Publications; HaChai Publishing; Harcourt Brace; HarperCollins; Herald; Hodder Children's Books; Holiday House; Holt, Henry; Houghton Mifflin; Humanics Children's House; Hyperion; Ideals; Jewish Publication Society; Jones University, Bob; Just Us Books; Knopf; Lee & Low Books; Lerner; Little, Brown; Lodestar; Lorimer, James; *Lowell House Juvenile; McClanahan; McElderry Books, Margaret K.; Mage; Milkweed Editions; Mondo; Morehouse; Orca; Orchard; Owen, Richard C.; Pacific Educational; *PaperStar; *Paws IV; Pieper; *Piñata; Polychrome; Ragweed; *Roussan; Simon & Schuster; Standard; *Stoddart; *Synchronicity; Thistledown; TOR; *Transworld; Treasure Chest; Troll; Walker And Co.; Whispering Coyote; Whitman, Albert; Willowisp; Zino

Fantasy: Advocacy; Alyson, Inc.; American Education Publishing; Archway/Minstrel; Arroyo Projects Studio; Atheneum; Bantam; Blizzard; Blue Sky; *Callaway Editions; Archway/Minstrel; Coteau; Crosspoint International; Crossway; Dial; Dutton; Farrar, Straus & Giroux; Fawcett Juniper; Feminist Press; Grapevine Publications; *Greene Bark; Harcourt Brace; *Harkey Multimedia; HarperCollins; Hodder Children's Books; Holiday House; Houghton Mifflin; Humanics Children's House; Hyperion; Ideals; *Ivory Tower; Knopf; Little, Brown; *Lowell House Juvenile; Macelderry Books, Margaret K.; Milkweed Editions; Mondo; Orchard; Philomel; Pieper; Place In The Woods; *Roussan; Seedling; Simon & Schuster; Speech Bin, Inc., The; Thistledown; *Transworld; Treasure Chest; Whispering Coyote; Willowisp

Folktales: Advocacy; Africa World; American Education Publishing; Arroyo Projects Studio; Bess Press; Blizzard; *Callaway Editions; Carolrhoda Books; Children's Book Press; Childrens Press; Chronicle; Crosspoint International; Dial; *Dove Kids; Eerdmans, Wm. B.; Farrar, Straus & Giroux; Feminist Press; Fitzhenry & Whiteside Ltd.; Geringer Books, Laura; Godine, David R.; Golden Books; Grapevine Publications; *Harkey Multimedia; HarperCollins; Holt, Henry; Houghton Mifflin; Humanics Children's House; Hyperion; Hyperion Press Limited; Ideals; Jewish Publication Society; Kar-Ben Copies, Inc.; Knopf; Little, Brown; Lodestar; McElderry Books, Margaret K.; Mage; Mondo; Morehouse; Northland; Orca; Owen, Richard C.; Pacific Educational; Pacific-Rim; Pando; Peachtree; Pelican; Perfection Learning; Philomel; Pieper; *Piñata; Place In The Woods; Sasquatch; Seedling; *Stoddart; *Synchronicity; *Transworld; Treasure Chest; Troll; Whitebird; Whitman, Albert; Williamson; Willowisp

Health: *After Midnight; Crosspoint International; Dial; *Fairview; Farrar, Straus & Giroux; Fitzhenry & Whiteside Ltd.; Houghton Mifflin; Ideals; Knopf; Lerner; Little, Brown; Magination; Pieper; Speech Bin, Inc., The; Time-Life for Children; Tricycle; Troll; University Classics; Whitman, Albert

Hi-Lo: A/V Concepts Corp.; Bess Press; Childrens Press; Crosspoint International; Farrar, Straus & Giroux; Fitzhenry & Whiteside Ltd.; Geringer Books, Laura; Grapevine Publications; HarperCollins; Knopf; Lerner; Lorimer, James; Pieper; Place In The Woods; Seedling; Whispering Coyote

History: Africa World; *After Midnight; Alyson, Inc.; *Beach Holme; Bess Press; Blue Sky; Boyds Mills; *Callaway Editions; Archway/Minstrel; Carolrhoda Books; Chronicle; *Colonial Williamsburg Foundation; Coteau; Crosspoint International; Crossway; Crown; Dial; *Dove Kids; Down East; Dutton; Farrar, Straus & Giroux; Feminist Press; Fitzhenry & Whiteside Ltd.; Friends United; Geringer Books, Laura; Godine, David R.; Golden Books; Grapevine Publications; Grosset & Dunlap; HaChai Publishing; Harcourt Brace; *Harkey Multimedia; HarperCollins; Hendrick-Long; Herald; Holiday House; Holt, Henry; Houghton Mifflin; Hyperion; Ideals; Jewish Publication Society; Jones University, Bob; Just Us Books; Knopf; Lee & Low

Books; Little, Brown; Lodestar; Milkweed Editions; Mondo; Morehouse; Northland; Open Hand; Orca; Orchard; Pacific Educational; *Pacific View; Pando; Peachtree; Pelican; Perfection Learning; Philomel; Pieper; *Pleasant Company; Polychrome; Putnam; Random House; *Roussan; Simon & Schuster; Soundprints; Stemmer House; *Stoddart; Sunbelt Media/Eakin; *Synchronicity; Time-Life for Children; TOR; Treasure Chest; Troll; Walker And Co.; Whispering Coyote; Whitman, Albert; Willowisp

Humor: Alyson, Inc.; American Education Publishing; Archway/Minstrel; Arroyo Projects Studio; Avon Books; Bantam; Bess Press; Blizzard; Blue Sky; Boyds Mills; Broadman & Holman; *Callaway Editions; Archway/Minstrel; Children's Book Press; Childrens Press; Concordia Publishing House; Coteau; Crosspoint International; Crossway; Crown; Davenport, Publishers, May; *Dove Kids; Farrar, Straus & Giroux; Feminist Press; Fitzhenry & Whiteside Ltd.; Geringer Books, Laura; Gibbs Smith; Golden Books; Grapevine Publications; Grosset & Dunlap; Hodder Children's Books; Holiday House; Holt, Henry; Houghton Mifflin; Hyperion; Ideals; Knopf; Little, Brown; Lodestar; *Lowell House Juvenile; Meriwether; Milkweed Editions; Mondo; Morehouse; Northland; Orca; Owen, Richard C.; *Owl; *PaperStar; Peachtree; Pieper; Place In The Woods; Putnam; Simon & Schuster; *Stoddart; *Synchronicity; Thistledown; Time-Life for Children; TOR; *Transworld; Whispering Coyote; Whitman, Albert; Willowisp

Multicultural: ABC All Books for Children; Advocacy; Africa World; African American Images; *After Midnight; A/V Concepts Corp.; Barrons Educational; *Beach Holme; Bess Press; Blue Sky; Archway/Minstrel; Carolina Wren; Carolrhoda Books; Children's Book Press; Childrens Press; Chronicle; *Colonial Williamsburg Foundation; Coteau; Crosspoint International; Dutton; Farrar, Straus & Giroux; Feminist Press; Fitzhenry & Whiteside Ltd.; Geringer Books, Laura; Gibbs Smith; Golden Books; *Harkey Multimedia; HarperCollins; Holiday House; Holt, Henry; Houghton Mifflin; Humanics Children's House; Hyperion; Ideals; Jones University, Bob; Just Us Books; Kar-Ben Copies, Inc.; Knopf; Laredo; Lee & Low Books; Lerner; Little, Brown; Lodestar; Lorimer, James; Mage; Magination; Milkweed Editions; Mondo; Morehouse; Northland; Open Hand; Orca; Orchard; Our Child Press; Owen, Richard C.; Pacific Educational; *Pacific View; *PaperStar; Perfection Learning; Philomel; Pieper; *Piñata; Place In The Woods; Polychrome; Ragweed; Sasquatch; Seedling; Stemmer House; *Stoddart; *Synchronicity; TOR; *Transworld; Treasure Chest; Tricycle; Walker And Co.; Whitman, Albert; Williamson; Willowisp; Zino

Nature/Environment: ABC All Books for Children; Advocacy; Alyson, Inc.; Arroyo Projects Studio; Barrons Educational; *Beach Holme; Bess Press; Blizzard; Blue Sky; *Callaway Editions; Archway/Minstrel; Carolrhoda Books; Chronicle; *Colonial Williamsburg Foundation; Coteau; Crosspoint International; Crown; Dawn; Dial; Down East; Dutton; E.M. Press; Farrar, Straus & Giroux; Fitzhenry & Whiteside Ltd.; Gibbs Smith; Godine, David R.; Golden Books; Grapevine Publications; Grosset & Dunlap; HarperCollins; Hodder Children's Books; Houghton Mifflin; Humanics Children's House; Ideals; Jones University, Bob; Knopf; Lerner; Little, Brown; Lodestar; *Lowell House Juvenile; Milkweed Editions; Mondo; Morris, Joshua; Northland; NorthWord; Orca; Orchard; Owen, Richard C.; *Owl; Pando; Peachtree; Perfection Learning; Philomel; Pieper; Sasquatch; Seedling; Soundprints; Stemmer House; *Synchronicity; Time-Life for Children; TOR; *Transworld; Treasure Chest; Tricycle; Troll; University Classics; Whitman, Albert; Willowisp

Poetry: Advocacy; *Beach Holme; Blue Sky; Boyds Mills; Archway/Minstrel; Chronicle; Crosspoint International; Dial; Dutton; Eerdmans, Wm. B.; Farrar, Straus & Giroux; Geringer Books, Laura; Godine, David R.; Grapevine Publications; HarperCollins; Hyperion; Knopf; Lee & Low Books; Macelderry Books, Margaret K.; Meadowbrook; Orchard; Peachtree; Philomel; Pieper; *Piñata; Simon & Schuster; *Synchronicity; Thistledown; *Transworld; *Transworld; Troll; Whispering Coyote; Willowisp

Problem Novels: *After Midnight; Avon Books; Barrons Educational; Berkley Publishing Group; Bethany House; Boyds Mills; Broadman & Holman; *Callaway Editions; Chronicle; Cobblehill; Dial; E.M. Press; Farrar, Straus & Giroux; HaChai Publishing; Harcourt Brace; Herald; Holt, Henry; Houghton Mifflin; Hyperion; Jewish Publication Society; Knopf; Lerner; Lorimer, James; Magination; Orca; Philomel; *Piñata; Place In The Woods; Polychrome; Putnam; *Roussan; *Synchronicity; TOR; *Transworld; Troll; University Classics; Whitman, Albert; Willowisp

Religious: Augsburg Fortress, Publishers; Bethel; Broadman & Holman; *Christian Publications; Concordia Publishing House; Crosspoint International; Crossway; CSS Publishing; Dial; E.M. Press; Eerdmans, Wm. B.; Farrar, Straus & Giroux; Forward Movement; Friends United; Golden Books; HaChai Publishing; *Harkey Multimedia; HarperCollins; Herald; Holt, Henry; Huntington House; Jewish Publication Society; Kar-Ben Copies, Inc.; Knopf; Meriwether; Morehouse; Morris, Joshua; Our Sunday Visitor; Pelican; Questar; Standard; Time-Life for Children; Tyndale House

Romance: Archway/Minstrel; Avon Books; Berkley Publishing Group; Bethany House; Concordia Publishing House; Crosspoint International; Farrar, Straus & Giroux; Fawcett Juniper; Harcourt Brace; Houghton Mifflin; Hyperion; Jewish Publication Society; Just Us Books; Knopf; Pieper; Thistledown; *Transworld; Troll; Willowisp

Science Fiction: Alyson, Inc.; Arroyo Projects Studio; *Callaway Editions; Archway/Minstrel; Coteau;

Crosspoint International; Dial; Dutton; Farrar, Straus & Giroux; Fawcett Juniper; Harcourt Brace; *Harkey Multimedia; HarperCollins; Houghton Mifflin; Hyperion; Ideals; Knopf; Little, Brown; *Lowell House Juvenile; Orchard; Pieper; *Roussan; Simon & Schuster; *Synchronicity; Thistledown; *Transworld; Walker And Co.

Special Needs: *After Midnight; Alyson, Inc.; Arroyo Projects Studio; A/V Concepts Corp.; Carolrhoda Books; Crosspoint International; *Fairview; Farrar, Straus & Giroux; *Harkey Multimedia; Houghton Mifflin; Jalmar; Kar-Ben Copies, Inc.; Knopf; Magination; Orca; Our Child Press; Philomel; Pieper; Putnam; Sasquatch; Seedling; Speech Bin, Inc., The; University Classics; Whitman, Albert

Sports: Archway/Minstrel; Arroyo Projects Studio; Avon Books; Bantam; Bess Press; Broadman & Holman; Archway/Minstrel; Cobblehill; Crosspoint International; Dial; Farrar, Straus & Giroux; Feminist Press; Fitzhenry & Whiteside Ltd.; Geringer Books, Laura; Grosset & Dunlap; Harcourt Brace; Holt, Henry; Houghton Mifflin; Hyperion; Ideals; Jewish Publication Society; Jones University, Bob; Knopf; Lerner; *Lowell House Juvenile; Mondo; Orchard; Owen, Richard C.; *PaperStar; Peachtree; Perfection Learning; Pieper; Place In The Woods; *Prep; Putnam; Random House; *Roussan; Seedling; Standard; Sunbelt Media/Eakin; Time-Life for Children; *Transworld; Troll; Willowisp; Lorimer, James

Suspense/Mystery: Lorimer, James; Alyson, Inc.; Archway/Minstrel; Arroyo Projects Studio; Avon Books; Bantam; Barrons Educational; Berkley Publishing Group; Bess Press; Bethany House; Broadman & Holman; *Callaway Editions; Archway/Minstrel; Christian Ed. Publishers; Cobblehill; *Colonial Williamsburg Foundation; Concordia Publishing House; Coteau; Crosspoint International; Crossway; Dial; Dutton; Farrar, Straus & Giroux; Feminist Press; Fitzhenry & Whiteside Ltd.; Geringer Books, Laura; Gibbs Smith; Godine, David R.; Golden Books; Grapevine Publications; Harcourt Brace; *Harkey Multimedia; HarperCollins; Hodder Children's Books; Holiday House; Holt, Henry; Houghton Mifflin; Hyperion; Jewish Publication Society; Jones University, Bob; Just Us Books; Knopf; Laredo; Lerner; Little, Brown; Lodestar; *Lowell House Juvenile; McElderry Books, Margaret K.; Morehouse; Northland; Orca; Orchard; *PaperStar; Pieper; Place In The Woods; Polychrome; *Prep; Putnam; Random House; *Roussan; Simon & Schuster; Standard; *Stoddart; *Synchronicity; Thistledown; Time-Life for Children; TOR; *Transworld; Troll; Tyndale House; Whitman, Albert; Willowisp

BOOK PUBLISHERS: NONFICTION

Activity Books: American Bible Society; American Education Publishing; Arroyo Projects Studio; A/V Concepts Corp.; Bess Press; Bright Ring; Broadman & Holman; Archway/Minstrel; *Capstone Inc.; Chicago Review; *Colonial Williamsburg Foundation; Concordia Publishing House; Crosspoint International; Crown; Davenport, Publishers, May; Davis Pubilcations, Inc.; Denison, T.S.; Dial; Enslow; Evan-Moor; *Fairview; Farrar, Straus & Giroux; Franklin Watts; Gibbs Smith; Godine, David R.; Grosset & Dunlap; Gryphon House; *Harkey Multimedia; HarperCollins; Highsmith; Hodder Children's Books; Humanics Children's House; Ideals; Jalmar; *Learning Works; Lion; Little, Brown; Lodestar; *Lowell House Juvenile; McClanahan; Meadowbrook; Meriwether; Millbrook; Morris, Joshua; NorthWord; Pacific-Rim; Pando; *Paws IV; Pieper; Place In The Woods; *Pleasant Company; Rhache; Sasquatch; Speech Bin, Inc., The; Sterling; Tricycle; Troll; Tyndale House; University Classics; Wiley, John; Williamson; Willowisp; *World Book

Animal: American Education Publishing; Arroyo Projects Studio; Atheneum; Blackbirch; Blue Sky; Boyds Mills; Archway/Minstrel; *Capstone Inc.; Carolrhoda Books; Childrens Press; Chronicle; Cobblehill; *Colonial Williamsburg Foundation; *Copper Beech Books; Crosspoint International; Crown; Dawn; Denison, T.S.; Dial; *Dove Kids; Down East; Dutton; Enslow; Evan-Moor; *Facts on File; Farrar, Straus & Giroux; Franklin Watts; Godine, David R.; Golden Books; Grosset & Dunlap; Harcourt Brace; HarperCollins; Hodder Children's Books; Holiday House; Humanics Children's House; Ideals; *Ivory Tower; Jones University, Bob; Knopf; *Learning Works; Lerner; Little, Brown; Lodestar; McClanahan; Millbrook; Mondo; Morris, Joshua; Muir Publications, Inc, John; Northland; NorthWord; Orca; Orchard; Owen, Richard C.; *Owl; Pando; Peachtree; Pieper; Place In The Woods; *Raintree Steck-Vaughn; Random House; Rhache; Sasquatch; Seedling; Soundprints; *Southwest Parks & Monuments; Stemmer House; Sterling; *Storey Communications; Sunbelt Media/Eakin; Time-Life for Children; Treasure Chest; Troll; University Classics; Walker And Co.; *Whitecap; Whitman, Albert; Wiley, John; Williamson; Willowisp; *World Book

Arts/Crafts: Arroyo Projects Studio; Bright Ring; *Capstone Inc.; Chicago Review; Childrens Press; Chronicle; Concordia Publishing House; *Copper Beech Books; Crosspoint International; Davis Pubilcations, Inc.; Farrar, Straus & Giroux; Fitzhenry & Whiteside Ltd.; Franklin Watts; Gibbs Smith; Golden Books; Grosset & Dunlap; Humanics Children's House; Ideals; Knopf; *Learning Works; Lerner; Lion; Little, Brown; *Lowell House Juvenile; Millbrook; Millbrook; Mondo; Muir Publications, Inc, John; *Owl; Pando; *Paws IV; Philomel; Pieper; *Pleasant Company; Rhache; Sasquatch; Sterling; *Storey Communications; Tricycle; University Classics; Wiley, John; Williamson; Willowisp; *World Book

Biography: Arroyo Projects Studio; Atheneum; B&B; Blackbirch; Blizzard; Blue Sky; Boyds Mills;

Broadman & Holman; Archway/Minstrel; *Capstone Inc.; Carolrhoda Books; Childrens Press; Chronicle; *Colonial Williamsburg Foundation; *Copper Beech Books; Coteau; Crown; Dial; *Dove Kids; Dutton; Eerdmans, Wm. B.; Enslow; Evan-Moor; *Facts on File; Farrar, Straus & Giroux; Fitzhenry & Whiteside Ltd.; Franklin Watts; Godine, David R.; Greenhaven; Grosset & Dunlap; Harcourt Brace; *Harkey Multimedia; HarperCollins; Hendrick-Long; Holiday House; Jewish Publication Society; Jones University, Bob; Just Us Books; Knopf; *Learning Works; Lee & Low Books; Lerner; Lion; Little, Brown; Lodestar; McElderry Books, Margaret K.; Millbrook; *Mitchell Lane; Mondo; Morehouse; Morgan Reynolds; Muir Publications, Inc, John; Oliver; Pacific Educational; Pando; *Paws IV; Peachtree; Pelican; Perfection Learning; Philomel; Pieper; *Piñata; *Pleasant Company; *Prep; Putnam; *Raintree Steck-Vaughn; Random House; Simon & Schuster; Stemmer House; Troll; Walker And Co.; Whitman, Albert; Wiley, John; Willowisp

Careers: Advocacy; Arroyo Projects Studio; B&B; *Capstone Inc.; Childrens Press; Crosspoint International; Crown; Dial; Enslow; *Facts on File; Farrar, Straus & Giroux; Fitzhenry & Whiteside Ltd.; Franklin Watts; Hodder Children's Books; Laredo; *Learning Works; Lerner; Lodestar; Millbrook; Owen, Richard C.; Pieper; *Prep; Raintree Steck-Vaughn; Rhache; Rosen; Troll; Walker And Co.; Weigl Educational; Whitman, Albert; Williamson; Willowisp; *World Book

Concepts: ABC All Books for Children; Africa World; Alyson, Inc.; American Education Publishing; Arroyo Projects Studio; B&B; Barrons Educational; Bess Press; Blackbirch; Blue Sky; Archway/Minstrel; *Capstone Inc.; Childrens Press; *Colonial Williamsburg Foundation; Concordia Publishing House; *Copper Beech Books; Crosspoint International; Farrar, Straus & Giroux; Franklin Watts; Golden Books; Grosset & Dunlap; *Harkey Multimedia; Holiday House; Ideals; Jones University, Bob; *Learning Works; Lerner; Little, Brown; Lodestar; *Lowell House Juvenile; McClanahan; Magination; Millbrook; Muir Publications, Inc, John; *Owl; Pando; Pieper; Putnam; Rhache; Seedling; Simon & Schuster; Standard; Time-Life for Children; Tricycle; University Classics; Whitman, Albert; Wiley, John; Williamson; Willowisp; *World Book

Cooking: Arroyo Projects Studio; Bright Ring; *Capstone Inc.; Chronicle; *Copper Beech Books; Crosspoint International; Farrar, Straus & Giroux; Franklin Watts; Golden Books; Ideals; *Learning Works; Lerner; Little, Brown; *Lowell House Juvenile; Pando; Pelican; Pieper; *Pleasant Company; Rhache; Sasquatch

Geography: Arroyo Projects Studio; B&B; Blackbirch; Boyds Mills; Archway/Minstrel; *Capstone Inc.; Charlesbridge; Childrens Press; Chronicle; *Copper Beech Books; Crosspoint International; Denison, T.S.; Down East; Down East; Evan-Moor; *Facts on File; Farrar, Straus & Giroux; Fitzhenry & Whiteside Ltd.; Franklin Watts; Golden Books; HarperCollins; Holiday House; Jones University, Bob; *Learning Works; Lerner; Little, Brown; Lodestar; *Lowell House Juvenile; Millbrook; Mondo; Oliver; Pando; Perfection Learning; Pieper; *Pleasant Company; *Raintree Steck-Vaughn; Reidmore; Sasquatch; *Southwest Parks & Monuments; Sterling; Time-Life for Children; TOR; Tricycle; Whitman, Albert; Wiley, John; Williamson; Willowisp; *World Book

Health: Arroyo Projects Studio; Broadman & Holman; *Capstone Inc.; Childrens Press; *Copper Beech Books; Crosspoint International; Crown; Denison, T.S.; Dial; Enslow; *Facts on File; *Fairview; Farrar, Straus & Giroux; Fitzhenry & Whiteside Ltd.; Franklin Watts; Hodder Children's Books; Ideals; Laredo; *Learning Works; Lerner; *Lowell House Juvenile; Lucent; Magination; Millbrook; Parenting Press; Pelican; Pieper; *Pleasant Company; *Raintree Steck-Vaughn; Rhache; Speech Bin, Inc., The; Time-Life for Children; Tricycle; Troll; University Classics; *Volcano; Walker And Co.; Whitman, Albert; John Wiley & Sons, Inc.; Williamson; *World Book

Hi-Lo: Arroyo Projects Studio; A/V Concepts Corp.; Barrons Educational; *Capstone Inc.; Childrens Press; Crosspoint International; *Facts on File; Farrar, Straus & Giroux; Fitzhenry & Whiteside Ltd.; Franklin Watts; *Learning Works; Lerner; Pieper; Place In The Woods; Rosen; Seedling

History: Africa World; Arroyo Projects Studio; Atheneum; B&B; Blackbirch; Blizzard; Blue Sky; Boyds Mills; Archway/Minstrel; *Capstone Inc.; Carolrhoda Books; Childrens Press; Chronicle; *Colonial Williamsburg Foundation; *Copper Beech Books; Coteau; Crosspoint International; Crown; Denison, T.S.; Dial; *Dove Kids; Dutton; Eerdmans, Wm. B.; Enslow; Evan-Moor; Farrar, Straus & Giroux; Feminist Press; Fitzhenry & Whiteside Ltd.; Franklin Watts; Friends United; Godine, David R.; Greenhaven; Grosset & Dunlap; Harcourt Brace; Hendrick-Long; Ideals; Jewish Publication Society; Jones University, Bob; Knopf; *Learning Works, TLee & Low Books; Lerner; Lion; Little, Brown; Lodestar; *Lowell House Juvenile; Lucent; Macelderry Books, Margaret K.; Millbrook; Mondo; Morgan Reynolds; Northland; Oliver; Open Hand; Orchard; Pacific Educational; Pando; Peachtree; Pelican; Philomel; Pieper; Place In The Woods; Planet Dexter; *Pleasant Company; Putnam; *Raintree Steck-Vaughn; Random House; Reidmore; Rhache; Soundprints; *Southwest Parks & Monuments; Sunbelt Media/Eakin; Time-Life for Children; TOR; Troll; *Volcano; Walker And Co.; Whitman, Albert; Williamson; Willowisp; *World Book; Zino

Hobbies: American Education Publishing; Arroyo Projects Studio; Avon Books; Bright Ring; *Capstone Inc.; Carolrhoda Books; Chicago Review; Childrens Press; Crosspoint International; Crown; Enslow; Farrar, Straus & Giroux; Fitzhenry & Whiteside Ltd.; Harcourt Brace; Lerner; Lion; *Lowell House Juvenile;

Millbrook; Muir Publications, Inc, John; *Owl; Pando; Pieper; Place In The Woods; Planet Dexter; *Pleasant Company; Random House; Rhache; Sterling; *Storey Communications; Troll; Walker And Co.; Whitman, Albert; Wiley, John; Williamson; Willowisp; *World Book

How-to: *After Midnight; Arroyo Projects Studio; Barrons Educational; Broadman & Holman; *Capstone Inc.; Childrens Press; *Colonial Williamsburg Foundation; *Copper Beech Books; Crosspoint International; Farrar, Straus & Giroux; Gibbs Smith; Grapevine Publications; HarperCollins; Herald; Knopf; *Learning Works; Lerner; Lion; Magination; Meriwether; Mondo; *Owl; Pando; Pieper; Place In The Woods; Planet Dexter; *Pleasant Company; Rhache; Sasquatch; Sterling; *Storey Communications; TOR; Tricycle; Wiley, John; Williamson; Willowisp; *World Book

Multicultural: Advocacy; Africa World; African American Images; American Bible Society; Arroyo Projects Studio; A/V Concepts Corp.; B&B; Bess Press; Blackbirch; Blue Sky; Boyds Mills; *Capstone Inc.; Carolrhoda Books; Childrens Press; Chronicle; Clear Light; *Colonial Williamsburg Foundation; Coteau; Crosspoint International; Davis Pubilcations, Inc.; Dutton; *Facts on File; *Fairview; Farrar, Straus & Giroux; Feminist Press; Fitzhenry & Whiteside Ltd.; Franklin Watts; Godine, David R.; *Harkey Multimedia; Harper-Collins; Hendrick-Long; Highsmith; Humanics Children's House; Ideals; Jones University, Bob; Knopf; *Learning Works; Lee & Low Books; Lerner; Lion; Little, Brown; Lodestar; Lucent; Mage; Magination; Millbrook; *Mitchell Lane; Mondo; Morgan Reynolds; Muir Publications, Inc, John; Northland; Oliver; Open Hand; Orchard; Our Child Press; Owen, Richard C.; Pacific Educational; *Pacific View; Pacific-Rim; Pando; Pelican; Philomel; Pieper; *Piñata; Place In The Woods; Polychrome; Putnam; *Raintree Steck-Vaughn; Reidmore; Rosen; Sasquatch; Seedling; Stemmer House; Sterling; Tilbury House; TOR; Treasure Chest; *Volcano; Walker And Co.; Weigl Educational; Whitman, Albert; Williamson; Willowisp; Zino

Music/Dance: Arroyo Projects Studio; Avon Books; Bright Ring; *Capstone Inc.; *Colonial Williamsburg Foundation; *Copper Beech Books; Crosspoint International; Crown; Denison, T.S.; Dial; Farrar, Straus & Giroux; Fitzhenry & Whiteside Ltd.; Franklin Watts; Harcourt Brace; Humanics Children's House; Knopf; Lerner; Lodestar; Millbrook; Pacific Educational; Pacific-Rim; Pelican; Philomel; Pieper; Players; Rhache; Sasquatch; Seedling; Sterling; Troll; Walker And Co.; Whitman, Albert; Williamson

Nature/Environment: ABC All Books for Children; American Bible Society; Archway/Minstrel; Arroyo Projects Studio; B&B; Blizzard; Blue Sky; Boyds Mills; Bright Ring; Archway/Minstrel; *Capstone Inc.; Carolrhoda Books; Childrens Press; Chronicle; Cobblehill; *Colonial Williamsburg Foundation; *Copper Beech Books; Coteau; Crosspoint International; Crown; Dawn; Denison, T.S.; Dial; Down East; Dutton; Eerdmans, Wm. B.; Enslow; Evan-Moor; *Facts on File; Farrar, Straus & Giroux; Fitzhenry & Whiteside Ltd.; Franklin Watts; Gibbs Smith; Godine, David R.; Golden Books; Greenhaven; Grosset & Dunlap; Harcourt Brace; HarperCollins; Holiday House; Humanics Children's House; Ideals; Jones University, Bob; Knopf; *Learning Triangle; *Learning Works; Lerner; Little, Brown; Lodestar; Lucent; Millbrook; Mondo; Morehouse; Morris, Joshua; Muir Publications, Inc, John; NorthWord; Orca; Orchard; *Owl; Pacific Educational; Pando; *Paws IV; Peachtree; Pelican; Perfection Learning; Pieper; Planet Dexter; Raintree Steck-Vaughn; Reidmore; Rhache; Sasquatch; Simon & Schuster; *Southwest Parks & Monuments; Standard; Stemmer House; Sterling; *Storey Communications; Time-Life for Children; TOR; Treasure Chest; Tricycle; Troll; University Classics; *Volcano; Walker And Co.; *Whitecap; Whitman, Albert; Wiley, John; Williamson; Willowisp; *World Book

Reference: American Bible Society; Arroyo Projects Studio; B&B; Barrons Educational; Behrman House; Bess Press; Blackbirch; Broadman & Holman; *Capstone Inc.; Childrens Press; *Copper Beech Books; Crosspoint International; Denison, T.S.; *Facts on File; Farrar, Straus & Giroux; Fitzhenry & Whiteside Ltd.; Franklin Watts; Highsmith; *Learning Works; *Lowell House Juvenile; McClanahan; Millbrook; Pando; Pieper; Rhache; Simon & Schuster; Sterling; Time-Life for Children; Wiley, John; Willowisp; *World Book

Religious: *Abingdon; American Bible Society; Arroyo Projects Studio; Augsburg Fortress, Publishers; Bethany House; Bethel; Broadman & Holman; Christian Ed. Publishers; *Christian Publications; Concordia Publishing House; Crosspoint International; Crown; CSS Publishing; Dial; *Dove Kids; Eerdmans, Wm. B.; *Facts on File; Farrar, Straus & Giroux; Forward Movement; Franklin Watts; Friends United; Harcourt Brace; *Harkey Multimedia; Herald; Holiday House; Huntington House; Jewish Publication Society; Kar-Ben Copies, Inc.; Meriwether; Morehouse; Morris, Joshua; Pelican; Questar; *Rainbow; St. Anthony Messenger; Standard; Time-Life for Children; *Treasure; Tyndale House; Walker And Co.; Reidmore

Science: American Education Publishing; Arroyo Projects Studio; A/V Concepts Corp.; B&B; Blackbirch; Bright Ring; *Capstone Inc.; Carolrhoda Books; Charlesbridge; Childrens Press; Chronicle; *Copper Beech Books; Crosspoint International; Crown; Evan-Moor; *Facts on File; Farrar, Straus & Giroux; Feminist Press; Franklin Watts; Gibbs Smith; Golden Books; Grapevine Publications; Grosset & Dunlap; Holiday House; Ideals; Knopf; *Learning Triangle; *Learning Works; Lerner; Lodestar; *Lowell House Juvenile; Millbrook; Mondo; Muir Publications, Inc, John; *Owl; Pacific Educational; Pando; Pieper; Planet Dexter; *Raintree Steck-Vaughn; Rhache; Seedling; Sterling; Time-Life for Children; TOR; Tricycle; Walker And Co.; Whitman, Albert; Wiley, John; Williamson; Willowisp; *World Book

Self Help: Advocacy; American Bible Society; Arroyo Projects Studio; A/V Concepts Corp.; Avon Books; Barrons Educational; Bethany House; Broadman & Holman; *Capstone Inc.; Crosspoint International; *Fairview; Farrar, Straus & Giroux; Free Spirit; Grapevine Publications; Herald; Hodder Children's Books; Humanics Children's House; Jalmar; Knopf; Leadership; Lerner; Little, Brown; *Lowell House Juvenile; Parenting Press; Pieper; Place In The Woods; Rhache; Rosen; TOR; University Classics; *Volcano; Wiley, John; Williamson

Social Issues: Advocacy; Alyson, Inc.; American Bible Society; Arroyo Projects Studio; B&B; Barrons Educational; Bethany House; Broadman & Holman; *Capstone Inc.; Carolrhoda Books; Childrens Press; Chronicle; Coteau; Crosspoint International; Denison, T.S.; Dutton; *Facts on File; *Fairview; Farrar, Straus & Giroux; Fitzhenry & Whiteside Ltd.; Franklin Watts; Greenhaven; Herald; Hodder Children's Books; Jalmar; Knopf; *Learning Works; Lerner; Little, Brown; Lodestar; Lucent; Millbrook; Morehouse; Morgan Reynolds; Muir Publications, Inc, John; Pacific Educational; Pando; Parenting Press; Perspectives; Pieper; Place In The Woods; Putnam; Tricycle; *Volcano; Walker And Co.; Whitman, Albert; Willowisp

Special Needs: American Bible Society; Arroyo Projects Studio; Blackbirch; Carolrhoda Books; Childrens Press; Crosspoint International; Davenport, Publishers, May; *Fairview; Farrar, Straus & Giroux; Franklin Watts; *Harkey Multimedia; *Learning Works; Lerner; Magination; Our Child Press; Pando; Pieper; Place In The Woods; Rhache; Rosen; Sasquatch; Speech Bin, Inc., The; University Classics; *Volcano; Whitman, Albert; Zino

Sports: Archway/Minstrel; Arroyo Projects Studio; Avon Books; Broadman & Holman; *Capstone Inc.; Childrens Press; Cobblehill; *Copper Beech Books; Crosspoint International; Crown; Dial; *Dove Kids; Enslow; *Facts on File; Farrar, Straus & Giroux; Fitzhenry & Whiteside Ltd.; Franklin Watts; Grosset & Dunlap; Harcourt Brace; Holiday House; Ideals; Jewish Publication Society; Knopf; Lerner; Lodestar; *Lowell House Juvenile; Lucent; Millbrook; Mondo; Owen, Richard C.; Pando; Pelican; Perfection Learning; Pieper; Place In The Woods; *Pleasant Company; *Raintree Steck-Vaughn; Random House; Seedling; Standard; Sterling; Sunbelt Media/Eakin; Time-Life for Children; Troll; Walker And Co.; Willowisp

Textbooks: Advocacy; *After Midnight; A/V Concepts Corp.; Bess Press; Crosspoint International; Davis Pubilcations, Inc.; Denison, T.S.; Farrar, Straus & Giroux; Grapevine Publications; Gryphon House; Jalmar; Laredo; *Phoenix Learning Resources; Pieper; Reidmore; Speech Bin, Inc., The; University Classics; Weigl Educational

MAGAZINES: FICTION

Adventure: Advocate, PKA's Publication; Boys' Life; *Boys' Quest; Bread for God's Children; Calliope; Challenge; Children's Digest; *Cogniz; Counselor; Cricket Magazine; Cricket Magazine; Crusader; Discovery; *Explorer; Flicker Magazine, The; Focus on the Family Clubhouse; Focus on the Family Clubhouse Jr.; Friend Magazine, The; Guideposts for Kids; Highlights for Children; Hopscotch; Humpty Dumpty's Magazine; Jack And Jill ; *Kids at Home; Kids World Magazine; Ladybug, the Magazine for Young Children; Lighthouse; My Friend; Odyssey; On Course; Power and Light; Primary Days; R-A-D-A-R; Seventeen Magazine; Spider; Street Times; Teen Life; Teen Power; Touch; Turtle Magazine; U*S* Kids; Wonder Time; Writers' International Forum; *Your Big Backyard

Animal: Boys' Life; *Boys' Quest; *Cat Fancy; Challenge; Chickadee Magazine; Children's Digest; Children's Playmate; Cricket Magazine; Crusader; Flicker Magazine, The; Focus on the Family Clubhouse Jr.; Friend Magazine, The; Guideposts for Kids; Highlights for Children; Hopscotch; Humpty Dumpty's Magazine; *Kids at Home; Ladybug, the Magazine for Young Children; My Friend; R-A-D-A-R; Ranger Rick; Scholastic Math Magazine; Seventeen Magazine; Skipping Stones; Spider; Touch; Turtle Magazine; U*S* Kids; Writers' International Forum; *Your Big Backyard

Contemporary: Advocate, PKA's Publication; Boys' Life; Bread for God's Children; Challenge; Children's Digest; Children's Playmate; *Cogniz; Cricket Magazine; Crusader; Discovery; *Explorer; Faces; Friend Magazine, The; Guideposts for Kids; Highlights for Children; Humpty Dumpty's Magazine; Jack And Jill ; *Kids at Home; Kids World Magazine; My Friend; New Era Magazine; On Course; On The Line; Pockets; Power and Light; R-A-D-A-R; Seventeen Magazine; Shofar; Skipping Stones; Spider; Story Friends; Straight; Street Times; Teen Life; Teen Power; Turtle Magazine; U*S* Kids; With; Wonder Time; Writers' International Forum; Young Salvationist

Fantasy: Advocate, PKA's Publication; *Beckett Publications; Boys' Life; Children's Digest; Children's Playmate; Cricket Magazine; Crusader; Discovery; Highlights for Children; Hobson's Choice; Humpty Dumpty's Magazine; Jack And Jill ; Ladybug, the Magazine for Young Children; Magic Realism; Ranger Rick; Seventeen Magazine; Spider; Street Times; Turtle Magazine; With; Writers' International Forum; *Your Big Backyard

Folktales: Advocate, PKA's Publication; Calliope; Children's Digest; Children's Playmate; Cricket Magazine; Crusader; *Explorer; Faces; Flicker Magazine, The; Focus on the Family Clubhouse; Focus on the

Family Clubhouse Jr.; Friend Magazine, The; Guideposts for Kids; Highlights for Children; Humpty Dumpty's Magazine; *Kids at Home; Kids World Magazine; Ladybug, the Magazine for Young Children; Magic Realism; Odyssey; Pockets; Seventeen Magazine; Spider; Street Times; Touch; Turtle Magazine; With; Writers' International Forum

Health: Advocate, PKA's Publication; Challenge; Children's Digest; Crusader; Flicker Magazine, The; Focus on the Family Clubhouse; Focus on the Family Clubhouse Jr.; For Seniors Only; Guideposts for Kids; Holidays & Seasonal Celebrations; Humpty Dumpty's Magazine; Seventeen Magazine; Straight; Touch; Turtle Magazine; U*S* Kids

History: AIM Magazine; *Beckett Publications; Boys' Life; *Boys' Quest; Bread for God's Children; Calliope; Challenge; Children's Digest; Children's Playmate; Cobblestone; Counselor; Cricket Magazine; Crusader; *Explorer; Faces; Flicker Magazine, The; Focus on the Family Clubhouse; Focus on the Family Clubhouse Jr.; Friend Magazine, The; Goldfinch, The; Guideposts for Kids; Highlights for Children; Hopscotch; Humpty Dumpty's Magazine; Jack And Jill ; *Kids at Home; Lighthouse; Odyssey; On Course; On The Line; R-A-D-A-R; Seventeen Magazine; Spider; Street Times; Teen Life; Turtle Magazine; U*S* Kids

Humorous: Advocate, PKA's Publication; *Beckett Publications; Boys' Life; *Boys' Quest; Bread for God's Children; Chickadee Magazine; Children's Digest; Children's Playmate; *Cogniz; Cricket Magazine; Crusader; Discovery; *Explorer; Flicker Magazine, The; For Seniors Only; Friend Magazine, The; Guideposts for Kids; Highlights for Children; Hopscotch; Humpty Dumpty's Magazine; Jack And Jill ; Kids World Magazine; Ladybug, the Magazine for Young Children; My Friend; New Era Magazine; On Course; On The Line; R-A-D-A-R; Ranger Rick; School Mates; Seventeen Magazine; Shofar; Skipping Stones; Spider; Story Friends; Straight; Street Times; Teen Life; Teen Power; Touch; Turtle Magazine; U*S* Kids; With; Writers' International Forum; *Your Big Backyard; Zelos

Multicultural: AIM Magazine; *Cogniz; Counselor; Cricket Magazine; Crusader; *Explorer; Faces; Flicker Magazine, The; Focus on the Family Clubhouse; Focus on the Family Clubhouse Jr.; Friend Magazine, The; Guideposts for Kids; Highlights for Children; Holidays & Seasonal Celebrations; Humpty Dumpty's Magazine; *Kids at Home; Kids World Magazine; Ladybug, the Magazine for Young Children; Pockets; Power and Light; Primary Days; Skipping Stones; Spider; Story Friends; Street Times; Student Leadership Journal; Teen Power; Touch; Turtle Magazine; U*S* Kids; With; Wonder Time; Young Salvationist; *Your Big Backyard

Nature/Environment: Advocate, PKA's Publication; *Boys' Quest; Bread for God's Children; Challenge; Chickadee Magazine; Children's Digest; Counselor; Cricket Magazine; Crusader; Flicker Magazine, The; Focus on the Family Clubhouse; Focus on the Family Clubhouse Jr.; Guideposts for Kids; Highlights for Children; Holidays & Seasonal Celebrations; Hopscotch; Humpty Dumpty's Magazine; *Kids at Home; Kids World Magazine; Ladybug, the Magazine for Young Children; Lighthouse; My Friend; Pockets; Power and Light; Primary Days; R-A-D-A-R; Skipping Stones; Spider; Story Friends; Turtle Magazine; U*S* Kids; Wonder Time; Writers' International Forum; *Your Big Backyard

Problem-Solving: Advocate, PKA's Publication; Boys' Life; *Boys' Quest; Bread for God's Children; Challenge; Children's Digest; Counselor; Crusader; Flicker Magazine, The; Friend Magazine, The; Guideposts for Kids; Humpty Dumpty's Magazine; Jack And Jill ; Kids World Magazine; Ladybug, the Magazine for Young Children; Lighthouse; On The Line; Pockets; Power and Light; Primary Days; R-A-D-A-R; Spider; Story Friends; Straight; Street Times; Teen Power; Touch; Turtle Magazine; U*S* Kids; With

Religious: Challenge; Counselor; Crusader; Faces; Flicker Magazine, The; Friend Magazine, The; Guideposts for Kids; My Friend; New Era Magazine; On Course; On The Line; Pockets; Power and Light; Primary Days; R-A-D-A-R; Seventeen Magazine; Shofar; Story Friends; Straight; Student Leadership Journal; Teen Life; Teen Power; Touch; With; Wonder Time; *Young Judaean; Young Salvationist; Zelos

Romance: Advocate, PKA's Publication; Guideposts for Kids; Lighthouse; New Era Magazine; Seventeen Magazine; Touch; Writers' International Forum

Science/Fiction: Advocate, PKA's Publication; Boys' Life; Children's Digest; Children's Playmate; *Cogniz; Discovery; *Explorer; Focus on the Family Clubhouse; Focus on the Family Clubhouse Jr.; Guideposts for Kids; Highlights for Children; Hobson's Choice; Hopscotch; Kids World Magazine; Ladybug, the Magazine for Young Children; My Friend; New Era Magazine; Ranger Rick; Ranger Rick; *Science World; Seventeen Magazine; Spider; With

Suspense/Mystery: Advocate, PKA's Publication; Boys' Life; Children's Digest; Children's Playmate; *Cogniz; Cricket Magazine; Crusader; Discovery; *Explorer; Friend Magazine, The; Guideposts for Kids; Hopscotch; Humpty Dumpty's Magazine; *Kids at Home; Kids World Magazine; Ladybug, the Magazine for Young Children; Lighthouse; On The Line; R-A-D-A-R; Seventeen Magazine; Spider; Turtle Magazine; U*S* Kids; Writers' International Forum

MAGAZINES: NONFICTION

Animal: Advocate, PKA's Publication; ASPCA Animal Watch; Boys' Life; *Boys' Quest; *Cat Fancy; Challenge; Chickadee Magazine; Child Life; Children's Digest; Children's Playmate; Cricket Magazine; Crusader; Discovery; Dolphin Log; DynaMath; *Explorer; Falcon For Kids; Field & Stream; Flicker Magazine, The; Focus on the Family Clubhouse Jr.; Friend Magazine, The; Girls' Life; Guide Magazine; Guideposts for Kids; Highlights for Children; Holidays & Seasonal Celebrations; Hopscotch; Humpty Dumpty's Magazine; Jack And Jill ; *Kids at Home; Kids World Magazine; Ladybug, the Magazine for Young Children; *National Geographic World; Nature Friend Magazine; New Moon: The Magazine for Girls & Their Dreams; On The Line; OWL Magazine; R-A-D-A-R; Ranger Rick; Ranger Rick; react magazine; Scholastic Math Magazine; *Science World; Scienceland; Seventeen Magazine; Skipping Stones; Spider; Story Friends; 3-2-1 Contact; Touch; Turtle Magazine; U*S* Kids; *Your Big Backyard

Arts/Crafts: Advocate, PKA's Publication; *Boys' Quest; Calliope; *Cat Fancy; Challenge; Chickadee Magazine; Child Life; Children's Digest; Children's Playmate; Counselor; *Crayola Kids; Cricket Magazine; Crusader; DynaMath; Faces; Flicker Magazine, The; Focus on the Family Clubhouse Jr.; Friend Magazine, The; Girls' Life; Goldfinch, The; Highlights for Children; Holidays & Seasonal Celebrations; Hopscotch; Humpty Dumpty's Magazine; *Kids at Home; Ladybug, the Magazine for Young Children; My Friend; *National Geographic World; New Moon: The Magazine for Girls & Their Dreams; Odyssey; On The Line; OWL Magazine; Primary Days; R-A-D-A-R; Scholastic Math Magazine; Scienceland; Spider; Street Times; Turtle Magazine; U*S* Kids; *Your Big Backyard; *Zillions

Biography: Advocate, PKA's Publication; Calliope; Children's Digest; Children's Playmate; Cobblestone; *Cogniz; Counselor; Cricket Magazine; Crusader; Discovery; *Explorer; Friend Magazine, The; Girls' Life; Goldfinch, The; Guide Magazine; Guideposts for Kids; Highlights for Children; Holidays & Seasonal Celebrations; Hopscotch; Kids World Magazine; *National Geographic World; New Era Magazine; Odyssey; On The Line; Primary Days; R-A-D-A-R; *Science World; Scienceland; Skipping Stones; Teen Life; Teen Power; *What! A Magazine

Careers: Advocate, PKA's Publication; American Cheerleader; Challenge; Child Life; Crusader; Flicker Magazine, The; Florida Leader; For Seniors Only; Girls' Life; Guideposts for Kids; Highlights for Children; Hopscotch; Hype Hair; Keynoter; *Kids at Home; Kids World Magazine; New Moon: The Magazine for Girls & Their Dreams; On Course; Scholastic Math Magazine; *Science World; Scienceland; Seventeen Magazine; Street Times; Teen Life; Touch; *What! A Magazine; *Zillions

Concept: Advocate, PKA's Publication; *Cogniz; Crusader; *Explorer; Field & Stream; Flicker Magazine, The; Girls' Life; Guideposts for Kids; Holidays & Seasonal Celebrations; Humpty Dumpty's Magazine; Kids World Magazine; Ladybug, the Magazine for Young Children; New Moon: The Magazine for Girls & Their Dreams; Street Times; *What! A Magazine

Cooking: Advocate, PKA's Publication; *Boys' Quest; Calliope; Child Life; Children's Digest; Children's Playmate; Crusader; DynaMath; Flicker Magazine, The; Focus on the Family Clubhouse; Focus on the Family Clubhouse Jr.; Friend Magazine, The; Girls' Life; Guideposts for Kids; Holidays & Seasonal Celebrations; Hopscotch; Humpty Dumpty's Magazine; Ladybug, the Magazine for Young Children; *National Geographic World; Odyssey; On The Line; Pockets; R-A-D-A-R; Spider; Turtle Magazine; U*S* Kids

Fashion: Advocate, PKA's Publication; American Cheerleader; DynaMath; Girls' Life; Guideposts for Kids; Hype Hair; Seventeen Magazine; Touch

Games/Puzzles: Advocate, PKA's Publication; *Boys' Quest; Calliope; Challenge; Chickadee Magazine; Child Life; Children's Digest; Children's Playmate; Class Act; Cobblestone; Counselor; *Crayola Kids; Cricket Magazine; Crusader; Discovery; Dolphin Log; DynaMath; *Explorer; Faces; Field & Stream; Flicker Magazine, The; Focus on the Family Clubhouse; Focus on the Family Clubhouse Jr.; For Seniors Only; Friend Magazine, The; Girls' Life; Goldfinch, The; Guide Magazine; Guideposts for Kids; Highlights for Children; Holidays & Seasonal Celebrations; Hopscotch; Humpty Dumpty's Magazine; Hype Hair; Kids World Magazine; My Friend; *National Geographic World; New Era Magazine; New Moon: The Magazine for Girls & Their Dreams; Odyssey; On The Line; OWL Magazine; Pockets; Primary Days; R-A-D-A-R; react magazine; Scholastic Math Magazine; School Mates; Scienceland; Shofar; Skipping Stones; Soccer Jr.; Spider; Teen Power; Touch; Turtle Magazine; U*S* Kids; *Your Big Backyard; *Zillions

Geography: Advocate, PKA's Publication; Challenge; Children's Digest; *Cogniz; Cricket Magazine; Crusader; Dolphin Log; *Explorer; Flicker Magazine, The; Girls' Life; Guideposts for Kids; Highlights for Children; Holidays & Seasonal Celebrations; Hopscotch; Junior Scholastic; *Kids at Home; *National Geographic World; R-A-D-A-R; Spider; Turtle Magazine

Health: American Cheerleader; *Black Belt For Kids; Boys' Life; Challenge; Child Life; Children's Digest; Children's Playmate; *Cogniz; Crusader; Current Health 1; Current Health 2; DynaMath; Flicker Magazine, The; Focus on the Family Clubhouse; Focus on the Family Clubhouse Jr.; For Seniors Only;

Girls' Life; Guideposts for Kids; Highlights for Children; Holidays & Seasonal Celebrations; Hopscotch; Humpty Dumpty's Magazine; Hype Hair; Keynoter; My Friend; *National Geographic World; New Moon: The Magazine for Girls & Their Dreams; On The Line; react magazine; Scholastic Math Magazine; *Science World; Scienceland; Seventeen Magazine; Straight; 3-2-1 Contact; Turtle Magazine; U*S* Kids; *What! A Magazine; Young Salvationist; *Zillions;

History: Advocate, PKA's Publication; *Beckett Publications; *Black Belt For Kids; Boys' Life; *Boys' Quest; Bread for God's Children; Calliope; Challenge; Children's Digest; Children's Playmate; Cobblestone; *Cogniz; Counselor; Cricket Magazine; Crusader; DynaMath; *Explorer; Faces; Flicker Magazine, The; Focus on the Family Clubhouse Jr.; Friend Magazine, The; Girls' Life; Goldfinch, The; Guideposts for Kids; Highlights for Children; Holidays & Seasonal Celebrations; Hopscotch; Jack And Jill ; Junior Scholastic; *Kids at Home; Kids World Magazine; My Friend; *National Geographic World; New Era Magazine; New Moon: The Magazine for Girls & Their Dreams; On The Line; Primary Days; R-A-D-A-R; Scholastic Math Magazine; Scienceland; Skipping Stones; Spider; Street Times; Student Leadership Journal; Teen Life; U*S* Kids; *Young Judaean

Hobbies: Advocate, PKA's Publication; *Beckett Publications; Challenge; Children's Digest; Cricket Magazine; Crusader; DynaMath; Flicker Magazine, The; Focus on the Family Clubhouse Jr.; Girls' Life; Hopscotch; Humpty Dumpty's Magazine; Hype Hair; Keynoter; *Kids at Home; Kids World Magazine; My Friend; *National Geographic World; New Moon: The Magazine for Girls & Their Dreams; On Course; On The Line; Primary Days; R-A-D-A-R; react magazine; Scholastic Math Magazine; Seventeen Magazine; Straight; Touch; U*S* Kids; *What! A Magazine; *Zillions

How-to: Advocate, PKA's Publication; American Cheerleader; *Black Belt For Kids; *Boys' Quest; Challenge; Children's Digest; Children's Playmate; Class Act; *Crayola Kids; Cricket Magazine; Crusader; DynaMath; Field & Stream; Flicker Magazine, The; For Seniors Only; Friend Magazine, The; Girls' Life; Guideposts for Kids; Hobson's Choice; Hopscotch; Humpty Dumpty's Magazine; Hype Hair; Jack And Jill; Keynoter; Kids World Magazine; My Friend; On The Line; Primary Days; R-A-D-A-R; Scholastic Math Magazine; *Science World; Scienceland; Seventeen Magazine; Teen Power; 3-2-1 Contact; Touch; U*S* Kids; With; *Zillions

Humorous: Advocate, PKA's Publication; *Beckett Publications; *Boys' Quest; Challenge; Chickadee Magazine; Child Life; Children's Digest; Children's Playmate; *Cogniz; *Crayola Kids; Cricket Magazine; Crusader; DynaMath; *Explorer; Flicker Magazine, The; Focus on the Family Clubhouse Jr.; For Seniors Only; Friend Magazine, The; Girls' Life; Guide Magazine; Guideposts for Kids; Highlights for Children; Hopscotch; Humpty Dumpty's Magazine; Jack And Jill ; Ladybug, the Magazine for Young Children; My Friend; New Moon: The Magazine for Girls & Their Dreams; On Course; On The Line; OWL Magazine; R-A-D-A-R; Ranger Rick; Scholastic Math Magazine; *Science World; Seventeen Magazine; Shofar; Skipping Stones; Story Friends; Straight; Teen Life; Teen Power; Touch; U*S* Kids; *What! A Magazine; With; Zelos; *Zillions

Interview/Profile: Advocate, PKA's Publication; AIM Magazine; *Black Belt For Kids; Challenge; Child Life; Children's Digest; Cobblestone; *Cogniz; Counselor; Cricket Magazine; Crusader; Discovery; Dolphin Log; *Explorer; Exploring; Faces; Field & Stream; Flicker Magazine, The; Focus on the Family Clubhouse; Focus on the Family Clubhouse Jr.; For Seniors Only; Girls' Life; Goldfinch, The; Guideposts for Kids; Highlights for Children; Hobson's Choice; Hype Hair; Jack And Jill ; Junior Scholastic; Kids World Magazine; My Friend; *National Geographic World; New Moon: The Magazine for Girls & Their Dreams; On Course; OwOWL Magazine; Pockets; Primary Days; R-A-D-A-R; react magazine; Scholastic Math Magazine; School Mates; *Science World; Seventeen Magazine; Shofar; Skipping Stones; Story Friends; Straight; Street Times; Student Leadership Journal; Teen Life; Teen Power; 3-2-1 Contact; Touch; U*S* Kids; *What! A Magazine; Young Salvationist; Zelos

Math: *Boys' Quest; *Cogniz; Crusader; DynaMath; *Explorer; Girls' Life; Guideposts for Kids; Holidays & Seasonal Celebrations; Hopscotch; Ladybug, the Magazine for Young Children; New Moon: The Magazine for Girls & Their Dreams; R-A-D-A-R; Scholastic Math Magazine; Spider

Multicultural: AIM Magazine; ASPCA Animal Watch; Challenge; *Cogniz; Cricket Magazine; Crusader; Dolphin Log; DynaMath; *Explorer; Flicker Magazine, The; Girls' Life; Guideposts for Kids; Highlights for Children; Holidays & Seasonal Celebrations; Junior Scholastic; *Kids at Home; *National Geographic World; New Moon: The Magazine for Girls & Their Dreams; Pockets; Primary Days; Scholastic Math Magazine; *Science World; Skipping Stones; Spider; Story Friends; Street Times; Student Leadership Journal; Teen Life; Teen Power; 3-2-1 Contact; Touch; Turtle Magazine; U*S* Kids; With; Young Salvationist

Nature/Environment: Advocate, PKA's Publication; ASPCA Animal Watch; Boys' Life; Challenge; Chickadee Magazine; Children's Digest; *Cogniz; Counselor; Cricket Magazine; Crusader; Current Health 1; Current Health 2; Discovery; Dolphin Log; DynaMath; *Explorer; Falcon For Kids; Field & Stream; Flicker Magazine, The; Focus on the Family Clubhouse Jr.; Girls' Life; Guide Magazine; Guideposts for Kids; Holidays & Seasonal Celebrations; Humpty Dumpty's Magazine; Junior Scholastic; *Kids at Home;

Kids World Magazine; Ladybug, the Magazine for Young Children; My Friend; *National Geographic World; Nature Friend Magazine; New Moon: The Magazine for Girls & Their Dreams; On The Line; OWL Magazine; Pockets; Primary Days; R-A-D-A-R; react magazine; Scholastic Math Magazine; *Science World; Scienceland; Skipping Stones; Spider; Story Friends; Student Leadership Journal; 3-2-1 Contact; Turtle Magazine; U*S* Kids; *What! A Magazine; *Your Big Backyard; *Zillions

Problem-Solving: Advocate, PKA's Publication; American Cheerleader; *Boys' Quest; Bread for God's Children; Challenge; *Cogniz; Counselor; Crusader; Current Health 2; DynaMath; *Explorer; Exploring; Flicker Magazine, The; Friend Magazine, The; Girls' Life; Guide Magazine; Guideposts for Kids; Highlights for Children; Hype Hair; Jack And Jill ; Keynoter; Kids World Magazine; Ladybug, the Magazine for Young Children; My Friend; New Moon: The Magazine for Girls & Their Dreams; On The Line; Pockets; Primary Days; R-A-D-A-R; *Science World; Skipping Stones; Spider; Straight; Street Times; Teen Power; Touch; With; Wonder Time; Young Salvationist; *Zillions

Religious: Bread for God's Children; Challenge; Counselor; Crusader; Faces; Flicker Magazine, The; Friend Magazine, The; Guide Magazine; Guideposts for Kids; Highlights for Children; My Friend; New Era Magazine; On Course; Power and Light; Primary Days; Seventeen Magazine; Shofar; Skipping Stones; Straight; Student Leadership Journal; Teen Power; Touch; With; Wonder Time; *Young Judaean; Young Salvationist; Youth Update; Zelos

Science: Advocate, PKA's Publication; Boys' Life; *Boys' Quest; Challenge; Chickadee Magazine; Children's Digest; *Cogniz; Counselor; Cricket Magazine; Crusader; Dolphin Log; DynaMath; *Explorer; Flicker Magazine, The; Focus on the Family Clubhouse Jr.; Girls' Life; Guideposts for Kids; Highlights for Children; Hobson's Choice; Holidays & Seasonal Celebrations; Humpty Dumpty's Magazine; *Kids at Home; Kids World Magazine; Ladybug, the Magazine for Young Children; My Friend; *National Geographic World; New Moon: The Magazine for Girls & Their Dreams; Odyssey; OWL Magazine; R-A-D-A-R; react magazine; Scholastic Math Magazine; Science Weekly; *Science World; Spider; 3-2-1 Contact; Turtle Magazine; U*S* Kids; *What! A Magazine

Social Issues: Advocate, PKA's Publication; Bread for God's Children; Challenge; *Cogniz; Counselor; Crusader; DynaMath; Flicker Magazine, The; Florida Leader; Focus on the Family Clubhouse Jr.; For Seniors Only; Girls' Life; Guide Magazine; Guideposts for Kids; Highlights for Children; Junior Scholastic; Keynoter; Kids World Magazine; *National Geographic World; New Era Magazine; New Moon: The Magazine for Girls & Their Dreams; On Course; OWL Magazine; R-A-D-A-R; react magazine; Seventeen Magazine; Straight; Street Times; Student Leadership Journal; Teen Life; Teen Power; Touch; U*S* Kids; *What! A Magazine; With; Wonder Time; *Young Judaean; Young Salvationist; *Zillions

Sports: Advocate, PKA's Publication; American Cheerleader; *Beckett Publications; *Black Belt For Kids; Boys' Life; Bread for God's Children; Challenge; Child Life; Children's Digest; Children's Playmate; Counselor; Cricket Magazine; Crusader; Discovery; DynaMath; *Explorer; Falcon For Kids; Field & Stream; Flicker Magazine, The; Florida Leader; Focus on the Family Clubhouse Jr.; For Seniors Only; Friend Magazine, The; Girls' Life; Guide Magazine; Guideposts for Kids; Highlights for Children; Humpty Dumpty's Magazine; *Junior League Baseball; *Kids at Home; Kids World Magazine; My Friend; *National Geographic World; New Era Magazine; New Moon: The Magazine for Girls & Their Dreams; On Course; OWL Magazine; Primary Days; R-A-D-A-R; react magazine; Scholastic Math Magazine; *Science World; Seventeen Magazine; Skipping Stones; Soccer Jr.; Straight; Teen Life; Teen Power; Touch; Turtle Magazine; U*S* Kids; *What! A Magazine; *Zillions

Travel: Advocate, PKA's Publication; *Black Belt For Kids; Challenge; Chickadee Magazine; Children's Digest; Children's Playmate; Cobblestone; *Cogniz; Cricket Magazine; Crusader; *Explorer; Exploring; Faces; Flicker Magazine, The; Florida Leader; For Seniors Only; Girls' Life; Guideposts for Kids; Highlights for Children; Jack And Jill ; Keynoter; *Kids at Home; *National Geographic World; New Era Magazine; New Moon: The Magazine for Girls & Their Dreams; OWL Magazine; R-A-D-A-R; Skipping Stones; Touch; U*S* Kids; Advocate, PKA's Publication; AIM Magazine; American Cheerleader; ASPCA Animal Watch; *Beckett Publications; *Boys' Quest; Calliope; *Cat Fancy; Challenge; Chickadee Magazine; Children's Digest; Children's Playmate; Cobblestone; *Cogniz; Counselor; Crusader; Discovery; Dolphin Log; *Explorer; Faces; Field & Stream; Flicker Magazine, The; Florida Leader; Focus on the Family Clubhouse Jr.; For Seniors Only; Girls' Life; Goldfinch, The; Guideposts for Kids; Hobson's Choice; Holidays & Seasonal Celebrations; Hopscotch; Hype Hair; *Junior League Baseball; Junior Scholastic; Magic Realism; My Friend; *National Geographic World; New Moon: The Magazine for Girls & Their Dreams; Odyssey; On Course; On The Line; OWL Magazine; Pockets; Power and Light; Primary Days; react magazine; School Mates; Scienceland; Skipping Stones; Spider; Story Friends; Straight; Student Leadership Journal; Teen Life; Teen Power; 3-2-1 Contact; Totally Fox Kids Magazine; Turtle Magazine; U*S* Kids; With; Young Salvationist; *Your Big Backyard; Youth Update; Zelos

Photography Index

This index lists markets which buy photos from freelancers. It's divided into book publishers, magazines and greeting cards. It's important to carefully read the listings and follow the guidelines of each publisher to which you submit. Listings new to this edition are marked with an asterisk (*).

BOOKS

*Abingdon; *After Midnight; American Bible Society; Arroyo Projects Studio; A/V Concepts Corp.; B&B; Behrman House; Bethel; Blackbirch; Blue Sky; Boingo Books, Inc.; Boyds Mills; *Capstone Inc.; Carolrhoda Books; Chicago Review; Childrens Press; Chronicle; Coteau; Davis Publications; Dial; *Dove Kids; Dutton; Fitzhenry & Whiteside Ltd.; Franklin Watts; Free Spirit; Grosset & Dunlap; Gryphon House; *Harkey Multimedia; Herald; Hodder Children's Books; Huntington House; Just Us Books; *Learning Works; Lerner; Little, Brown; Lodestar; Lorimer, James; *Lowell House Juvenile; Millbrook; Mondo; Morehouse; Muir Publications, Inc, John; NorthWord; Oliver; Our Sunday Visitor; Owen, Richard C.; *Owl; Pacific Educational; *Phoenix Learning Resources; Pieper; Place In The Woods; *Pleasant Company; Price Stern Sloan; Questar; *Rainbow; *Raintree Steck-Vaughn; Reidmore; Rhache; Rosen; St. Anthony Messenger; Sasquatch; Seedling; Silver Burdett; Silver Moon; *Sourcebooks; *Southwest Parks & Monuments; Speech Bin, Inc., The; *Storey Communications; *Synchronicity; Time-Life for Children; *Transworld; Treasure Chest; Troll; Tyndale House; Weigl Educational; *Whitecap; Whitman, Albert; Williamson; Willowisp; *World Book

MAGAZINES

Advocate, PKA's Publication; AIM Magazine; American Cheerleader; ASPCA Animal Watch; *Beckett Publications; *Boys' Quest; Calliope; *Cat Fancy; Challenge; Chickadee Magazine; Children's Digest; Children's Playmate; Cobblestone; *Cogniz; Counselor; Crusader; Discovery; Dolphin Log; *Explorer; Faces; Field & Stream; Flicker Magazine, The; Florida Leader; Focus on the Family Clubhouse; Focus on the Family Clubhouse Jr.; For Seniors Only; Girls' Life; Goldfinch, The; Guideposts for Kids; Hobson's Choice; Holidays & Seasonal Celebrations; Hopscotch; Hype Hair; *Junior League Baseball; Junior Scholastic; Magic Realism; My Friend; *National Geographic World; New Moon: The Magazine for Girls & Their Dreams; Odyssey; On Course; On The Line; OWL Magazine; Pockets; Power and Light; Primary Days; react magazine; School Mates; Scienceland; Skipping Stones; Spider; Story Friends; Straight; Student Leadership Journal; Teen Life; Teen Power; 3-2-1 Contact; Totally Fox Kids Magazine; Turtle Magazine; U*S* Kids; With; Young Salvationist; *Your Big Backyard; Youth Update

GREETING CARDS

Aristoplay, Ltd.; Beistle Company, The; Berrie & Company, Inc., Russ; Design Design Inc.; EPI Group Limited; Everything Gonzo!; Fotofolio/Artpost; Galison Books; *Innova; Love Greeting Card Co. Inc.; Marcel Schurman Company; P.S. Greetings/Fantus Paper Products; Scandecor Inc.; Talicor, Inc.; Warner Press; Zelos

General Index

An asterisk (*) appears before listings that are new to this edition. Companies that appeared in the 1996 edition of *Children's Writer's & Illustrator's Market* but do not appear in this edition are identified with a two-letter code explaining why the market was omitted: (**ED**)—Editorial Decision; (**NS**)—Not Accepting Submissions; (**NR**)—No (or late) Response to Listing Request; (**OB**)—Out of Business; (**RR**)—Removed by Request; (**UC**)—Unable to Contact; (**RP**)—Business Restructured or Purchased; (**SR**)—Subsidy/Royalty Publisher; (**UF**)—Uncertain Future.

1997 Insider Reports

Portrait Artist: Ann Barrow

Judith Caseley
Illustrator/Author
Page 82

Joanna Kraus
Playwright
Page 258

Curt Jenkins
Publisher
Page 278